The *BORZOI* *COLLEGE* fourth edition *READER*

The
BORZOI
COLLEGE
fourth *READER*
edition

Charles Muscatine
University of California, Berkeley

Marlene Griffith
Laney College

Alfred A. Knopf   New York

Fourth Edition
98765432
Copyright © 1966, 1971, 1976, 1980 by Charles Muscatine and Marlene Griffith

Cover design: Gene Krackehl

Library of Congress Cataloging in Publication Data

Muscatine, Charles, ed.
The Borzoi college reader.
Includes index.
1. College readers. I. Griffith, Marlene.
II. Title.
PE1122.M8 1980   808'.042   79-24555
ISBN: 0-394-32419-6

Manufactured in the United States of America

Acknowledgments

HANNAH ARENDT, "Anton Schmidt," from *Eichmann in Jerusalem*, by Hannah Arendt. Copyright © 1963 by Hannah Arendt. Reprinted by permission of Viking Penguin, Inc.

ISAAC ASIMOV, "The Nightmare Life Without Fuel," from *TIME*. Copyright © 1977 by Time Inc. Reprinted by permission of *TIME*, The Weekly Newsmagazine.

MARGARET ATWOOD, "First Neighbours," from *The Journals of Susanna Moodie*, by Margaret Atwood. Copyright © 1970 by Oxford University Press. Reprinted by permission of the publisher.

JAMES BALDWIN, "Notes of a Native Son," from *Notes of a Native Son*, by James Baldwin. Copyright © 1955 by James Baldwin. Reprinted by permission of Beacon Press.

IMAMU AMIRI BARAKA (LEROI JONES), "Young Soul," from *Black Magic: Poetry 1961-1967*, by LeRoi Jones. Copyright © 1969 by LeRoi Jones. Reprinted by permission of the Sterling Lord Agency.

PETER BERGER, "A Tale of Two Moralities," from *Pyramids of Sacrifice: Political Ethics and Social Change*, by Peter Berger. Copyright © 1974 by Peter Berger. Reprinted by permission of Basic Books, Inc., Publishers (New York).

COLIN BLAKEMORE, from *Mechanics of the Mind*, pp. 155-173. Copyright © 1977 by Cambridge University Press. Reprinted by permission of Cambridge University Press.

DANIEL BOORSTIN, "The Rhetoric of Democracy," from *Democracy and Its Discontents*, by Daniel Boorstin. Copyright © 1971, 1972, 1973, 1974 by Daniel J. Boorstin. Reprinted by permission of Random House, Inc.

HAIG BOSMAJIAN, from *The Language of Oppression*, pp. 1-9. Reprinted by permission of Public Affairs Press.

JAMES BRITTON, "Language and Experience," from *Language and Learning*, by James Britton. Copyright © 1970 by James Britton. Reprinted by permission of Penguin Books, Ltd.

BRIGID BROPHY, "Women Are Prisoners of Their Sex," from *The Saturday Evening Post* (November 2, 1963), pp. 10-11. Copyright © 1963 by The Curtis Publishing Company. Reprinted by permission of *The Saturday Evening Post*.

ROBERT COLES, "Boston and the South," from *Harvard Magazine* (September 1975). Copyright © 1975 by Harvard Magazine, Inc. Reprinted by permission of the publisher.

HENRY STEELE COMMAGER, "A Declaration of Interdependence," from *Today's Education* (March/April 1976), pp. 86-87. Copyright © 1976 by Henry Steele Commager. Reprinted by permission of the author and publisher.

NORMAN COUSINS, "The Computer and the Poet," from *Saturday Review* (July 23, 1976), p. 42. Copyright © 1966 by *Saturday Review*. Reprinted by permission of the author and publisher.

e. e. cummings, "since feeling is first," from *IS 5*, by e. e. cummings. Copyright 1926 by Boni and Liveright, copyright renewed 1953 by e. e. cummings. Reprinted by permission of Liveright Publishing Corporation.

CLARENCE DARROW, "Why I Am An Agnostic," from *Verdicts Out of Court*, edited by Arthur and Lila Weinberg, Chicago, Quadrangle Books, 1963. Reprinted by permission.

JOAN DIDION, "On Morality" and "Some Dreamers of the Golden Dream," from *Slouching Towards Bethlehem*, by Joan Didion. Copyright © 1961, 1964, 1965, 1966, 1967, 1968 by Joan Didion. Reprinted by permission of Farrar, Straus & Giroux, Inc.

J. P. DONLEAVY, "Meet My Maker," excerpted from *Meet My Maker the Mad Molecule*, by J. P. Donleavy. Copyright © 1955, 1956, 1959, 1960, 1961, 1963, 1964 by J. P. Donleavy. Copyright © 1960 by the Curtis Publishing Company. Reprinted by permission of Delacorte Press/Seymour Lawrence.

HUBERT L. DREYFUS, "Introduction," adapted by Hubert L. Dreyfus from *What Computers Can't Do*, revised edition by Hubert L. Dreyfus (Harper & Row Publishers, Harper Colophon Books 1979). Reprinted by permission of the publisher.

BOB DYLAN, "It's All Over Now, Baby Blue." Copyright © 1965 by Warner Bros. Inc. All rights reserved. Reprinted by permission.

MURRAY EDELMAN, "The Political Language of the Helping Professions," from *Political Language: Words that Succeed and Policies that Fail*, by Murray Edelman. Copyright © 1977 by the Board of Regents of the University of Wisconsin System. Reprinted by permission of the author and Academic Press, Inc.

HENRY FAIRLIE, "Can You Believe Your Eyes?" from *Horizon*, Vol. IX, No. 2 (Spring 1967). Copyright © 1967 by American Heritage Publishing Company. Reprinted by permission of the publisher.

MARC FEIGEN FASTEAU, from *The Male Machine*, pp. 6–19. Copyright © 1974 by Marc Feigen Fasteau. Reprinted by permission of McGraw-Hill Book Company.

ERICH FROMM, "Work in an Alienated Society," from *The Sane Society*, by Erich Fromm. Copyright © 1955 by Erich Fromm. Reprinted by permission of Holt, Rinehart and Winston, Publishers.

MARTIN GANSBERG, "37 Who Saw Murder Didn't Call Police," from *The New York Times* (March 27, 1964). Copyright © 1964 by The New York Times Company. Reprinted by permission of the publisher.

WILLIAM GOLDING, "Thinking as a Hobby," from *Holiday* (August 1961). Reprinted by permission of Travel Magazine, Inc. Floral Park, New York 11001.

DICK GREGORY, "Shame," from *Nigger: An Autobiography*, by Dick Gregory with Robert Lipsyte. Copyright © 1964 by Dick Gregory Enterprises, Inc. Reprinted by permission of E. P. Dutton & Co., Inc.

ANDREW GRIFFIN, "Sympathy for the Werewolf," from *University Publishing* (Winter 1979). Reprinted by permission of the author.

GARRETT HARDIN, "Lifeboat Ethics: The Case Against Helping the Poor," from *Psychology Today* (September 1974), pp. 38–43, 123–126. Copyright © 1974 by Ziff-Davis Publishing Company. Reprinted by permission of the publisher.

ROBERT HAYDEN, "Aunt Jemima of the Ocean Waves," from *Words in the Mourning Time*, by Robert Hayden. Copyright © 1970 by Robert Hayden. Reprinted by permission of October House, Stonington, Connecticut.

MERLE HODGE, "The Shadow of the Whip," excerpted from *Is Massa Dead?*, edited by Orde Coombs. Copyright © 1974, by Doubleday & Company, Inc. Reprinted by permission of the publisher.

MATINA HORNER, "Fail: Bright Women," from *Psychology Today* (November 1969), pp.

37-38, 62. Copyright © 1969 by Ziff-Davis Publishing Company. Reprinted by permission of the publisher.

JEANNE WAKATSUKI HOUSTON and JAMES D. HOUSTON, from *Farewell to Manzanar*, pp. 81-88. Copyright © 1973 by James D. Houston. Reprinted by permission of Houghton Mifflin Company.

ALDOUS HUXLEY, "Propaganda Under a Dictatorship" and "The Arts of Selling," from *Brave New World Revisited*, by Aldous Huxley. Copyright © 1958 by Aldous Huxley. Reprinted by permission of Harper & Row, Publishers, Inc., Mrs. Laura Huxley, and Chatto and Windus Ltd.

THOMAS H. HUXLEY, "The Method of Scientific Investigation," from *Darwinia: Essays by Thomas H. Huxley*, originally published in 1896. Reprinted by permission of AMS Press, Inc.

IVAN ILLICH, "Two Watersheds," from *Tools for Conviviality*, by Ivan Illich. Volume Forty-seven of *World Perspective Series*, Planned and Edited by Ruth Nanda Anshen. Copyright © 1973 by Ivan Illich. Reprinted by permission of Harper & Row, Publishers, Inc.

PAUL JACOBS, "The Most Cheerful Graveyard in the World," from *The Reporter* (September 18, 1958), pp. 26-30. Reprinted by permission.

MARTIN LUTHER KING, JR., "Letter from Birmingham Jail - April 16, 1963," from *Why We Can't Wait*, by Martin Luther King, Jr. Copyright © 1963 by Martin Luther King, Jr. Reprinted by permission of Harper & Row, Publishers, Inc.

MAXINE HONG KINGSTON, "How Are You?" "I Am Fine, Thank You, And You?" from *The State of the Language*, edited by Leonard Michaels and Christopher Ricks. Reprinted by permission of the University of California Press.

JOSEPH WOOD KRUTCH, "A Commencement Address," from *A Krutch Omnibus*, by Joseph Wood Krutch. Copyright © 1967 by Joseph Wood Krutch. Reprinted by permission of William Morrow and Company.

ELISABETH KÜBLER-ROSS, "On the Fear of Death," from *On Death and Dying*, by Elisabeth Kübler-Ross. Copyright © 1969 by Elisabeth Kübler-Ross. Reprinted by permission of Macmillan Publishing Co., Inc.

ROBIN LAKOFF, "You Are What You Say," from *Ms Magazine* (July 1974). Reprinted by permission of the author.

LAWRENCE LANGER, "The Human Use of Language," from *The Chronicle of Higher Education* (Vol. XIII, No. 19), p. 32. Copyright © 1977 by Editorial Projects for Education, Inc. Reprinted by permission.

SUSANNE K. LANGER, "The Prince of Creation," from *Fortune* (January 1944), pp. 127-128, 130, 132, 134, 136, 139-140, 142, 144, 146, 148, 150, 152, 154. Reprinted by permission of the author. Originally entitled "The Lord of Creation."

URSULA Le GUIN, "The Ones Who Walk Away from Omelas," from *The Hugo Winners, Vol. III*, edited by Isaac Asimov. Copyright © 1973, 1975 by Ursula Le Guin. Reprinted by permission of the author and her agent, Virginia Kidd.

WALTER LIPPMANN, "The Indispensable Opposition," from *The Atlantic Monthly* (August 1939). Copyright 1939, 1967, The Atlantic Monthly Company, Boston, Mass. Reprinted by permission of the author and publisher.

PHYLLIS McGINLEY, "Suburbia, of Thee I Sing," from *The Province of the Heart*, by Phyllis McGinley. Copyright 1949 by Phyllis McGinley; copyright © renewed 1977 by Phyllis McGinley. Reprinted by permission of Viking Penguin, Inc.

JAMES ALAN McPHERSON, "On Becoming an American Writer," from *Atlantic Monthly*. Copyright © 1978 by James Alan McPherson. Reprinted by permission of Brandt and Brandt Literary Agents, Inc.

NICCOLÒ MACHIAVELLI, from *The Prince*, pp. 63–66, translated by Luigi Ricci, revised by E. R. P. Vincent. Reprinted by permission of Oxford University Press. This selection is taken from The Modern Library edition.

JERRY MANDER, "TV's Capture of the Mind," from *Mother Jones* (January 1978), pp. 51–61. Adapted from *Four Arguments for the Elimination of Television*, published by William Morrow and Company. Copyright © 1978 by Jerry Mander. Reprinted by permission of the author.

JERRE MANGIONE, "When I Grow Up . . ." from *Mount Allegro* by Jerre Mangione. Copyright 1942, 1952, 1972 by Jerre Mangione. All rights reserved. Reprinted by permission of the author.

PETER MARIN, "The New Narcissism," from *Harper's Magazine* (October 1975). Copyright © 1975 by Peter Marin. Reprinted by permission of International Creative Management, Inc. "Spiritual Disobedience," from *Harper's Magazine* (February 1979). Copyright © 1979 by Peter Marin. Reprinted by permission of International Creative Management, Inc.

MARGARET MEAD, "The Egalitarian Error" and "Race and Intelligence," from *A Way of Seeing*, by Margaret Mead and Rhoda Metraux. Copyright © 1963, 1969 by Margaret Mead and Rhoda Metraux. Reprinted by permission of William Morrow and Company.

JOSEPHINE MILES, "Essay in Reason," from *Educational Leadership*, Vol. 19, No. 5 (February 1962), pp. 311–313. Copyright © 1962 by the Association for Supervision and Curriculum Development. All rights reserved. Reprinted by permission of the author and publisher.

WILLIAM LEE MILLER, "Television Power and American Values," from *Working Papers: The Search for a Value Consensus*, Proceedings of a Rockefeller Foundation Conference (March 28–29, 1978). Reprinted by permission of the author and the Rockefeller Foundation.

N. SCOTT MOMADAY, from *The Way to Rainy Mountain*, pp. 5–12. Copyright © 1969 by the University of New Mexico Press. Reprinted by permission of the publisher. Originally appeared in *The Reporter* (January 26, 1967).

THE NEW YORKER, "The Wisdom of the Worm," from "The Talk of the Town," *The New Yorker* (August 29, 1970), pp. 17–18. Copyright © 1970 The New Yorker Magazine, Inc. Reprinted by permission of the publisher.

WILLIAM NICHOLS, "The Burden of Imagination: Stanley Milgram's *Obedience to Authority*," from *Writing from Experience*, edited by William Nichols. Copyright © 1975 by Harcourt Brace Jovanovich, Inc. Reprinted by permission of Harcourt Brace Jovanovich, Inc.

JOYCE CAROL OATES, "Where Are You Going, Where Have You Been?" from *The Wheel of Love*, by Joyce Carol Oates. Copyright © 1965, 1966, 1967, 1968, 1969, 1970, by Joyce Carol Oates. Reprinted by permission of the publisher, Vanguard Press, Inc.

GEORGE ORWELL, "Politics and the English Language" and "Shooting an Elephant," from *Shooting an Elephant and Other Essays*, by George Orwell. Copyright, 1945, 1946, 1949, 1950, by Sonia Brownell Orwell; copyright, 1973, 1974, by Sonia Orwell. "Marrakech" and "Why I Write," from *Such, Such Were the Joys*, by George Orwell. Copyright, 1945, 1952, 1953, by Sonia Brownell Orwell. Reprinted by permission of Harcourt Brace Jovanovich, Inc., Mrs. Sonia Brownell Orwell, and Secker & Warburg Ltd.

J. H. PLUMB, "De Mortuis," from *In the Light of History*, by J. H. Plumb. Copyright © 1972 by J. H. Plumb. Reprinted by permission of Houghton Mifflin Company and Allen Lane, Literary Agent.

COLE PORTER, "Don't Fence Me In." Copyright 1944 by Warner Bros., Inc., Copyright renewed. All rights reserved. Reprinted by permission.

KATHERINE ANNE PORTER, "The Future is Now," from *The Collected Essays and Occasional Writings of Katherine Anne Porter*. Copyright 1950, renewed 1978 by Katherine Anne Porter. Reprinted by permission of Delacorte Press/Seymour Lawrence.

MARCEL PROUST, "Prologue," from *By Way of Sainte-Beuve*, by Marcel Proust, translated by Sylvia Townsend Warner. Reprinted by permission of Sylvia Townsend Warner, Chatto and Windus Ltd. and George Borchardt, Inc.

MARY CAROLINE RICHARDS, "Centering as Dialogue," from *Centering*, by Mary Caroline Richards. Copyright © 1964 by M. C. Richards. Reprinted by permission of Wesleyan University Press.

MICHAEL ROBERTS, "The Vicarious Heroism of the Sports Spectator," from *The New Republic* (November 24, 1974), pp. 17-20. Copyright © 1974 by The New Republic, Inc. Reprinted by permission of the publisher.

JAMES HARVEY ROBINSON, "On Various Kinds of Thinking," from *The Mind in the Making*, by James Harvey Robinson. Copyright 1921 by Harper & Row, Publishers, Inc.; renewed 1949 by Bankers Trust Company. Reprinted by permission of Harper & Row, Publishers, Inc.

APPLETREE RODDEN, "Why Small Refrigerators Can Preserve the Human Race," from *Harper's Magazine* (January 1975). Copyright © 1974 by *Harper's Magazine*. All rights reserved. Reprinted by permission of the publisher.

RICHARD RODRIGUEZ, "Going Home Again," from *American Scholar* (Winter 1974/ 1975), pp. 15-28. Copyright © 1975 by Richard Rodriguez. Reprinted by permission of Brandt and Brandt Literary Agents, Inc. "None of This is Fair," from *Politicks and Other Human Interests*. Copyright © 1977 by Richard Rodriguez. Reprinted by permission of Brandt and Brandt Literary Agents, Inc.

HAROLD ROSENBERG, "Masculinity: Real and Put On," from *Vogue* (November 15, 1967), p. 150. Reprinted by permission of *Vogue*.

CARL SAGAN, "In Defense of Robots," excerpted from pp. 239-240; "A Sunday Sermon," excerpted from pp. 281-291 of *Broca's Brain*, by Carl Sagan. Copyright © 1974, 1975, 1976, 1977, 1978, 1979 by Carl Sagan. Reprinted by permission of Random House, Inc.

E. F. SCHUMACHER, "A Culture of Poverty," from *Voices for Life: Reflections on the Human Condition*, edited by Dom Moraes. Copyright © 1975 by United Nations Fund for Population Activities. Reprinted by permission of Holt, Rinehart and Winston.

RICHARD SELZER, "The Exact Location of the Soul," from *Mortal Lessons*, by Richard Selzer. Copyright © 1974, 1975, 1976 by Richard Selzer. Reprinted by permission of Simon & Schuster, a Division of Gulf and Western Corporation.

JOHN SIMON, "In Defense of Elitism," from *Atlantic Monthly* (December 1978). Copyright © 1978 by John Simon. Reprinted by permission of Wallace and Sheil Agency, Inc.

ISAAC BASHEVIS SINGER, "The Son from America," from *A Crown of Feathers*, by Isaac Bashevis Singer. Copyright © 1970, 1971, 1972, 1973 by Isaac Bashevis Singer. Reprinted by permission of Farrar, Straus & Giroux, Inc. "The Son from America" originally appeared in *The New Yorker*.

PHILIP SLATER, "Community and Competition: Getting Together," excerpted from pp. 9-18 of *The Pursuit of Loneliness: American Culture at the Breaking Point*, by Philip Slater. Copyright © 1970, 1976 by Philip Slater. Reprinted by permission of Beacon Press.

WILLIAM STAFFORD, "A Way of Writing," from *Writing the Australian Crawl: Views on the Writer's Vocation*, by William Stafford. Copyright © 1978 by the University of Michigan Press. Reprinted by permission of the publisher.

GLORIA STEINEM, "Erotica and Pornography: A Clear and Present Difference," from *Ms Magazine* (November 1978). Copyright © 1978 by Ms. Foundation for Education and Communications, Inc.

JUDY SYFERS, "I Want a Wife," from *Ms Magazine* (December 1971). Copyright © 1971 by Judy Syfers. Reprinted by permission of the author.

RATHINDRANATH TAGOR, "Fruit Gathering," from *Collected Poems and Plays*, by Rathindranath Tagore. Copyright 1916 by Macmillan Publishing Co., Inc., renewed 1944 by Rathindranath Tagore. Reprinted by permission of the Trustees of the Tagore Estate, Macmillan Publishing Co., Inc. and Macmillan Administration (Basingstoke) Ltd.

STUDS TERKEL, "Carl Murray Bates-Mason," "Nora Watson-Editor" and "Mike LeFevre-Steelworker," from *Working: People Talk About What They Do All Day and How They Feel About What They Do*, by Studs Terkel. Copyright © 1972, 1974 by Studs Terkel. Reprinted by permission of Pantheon Books, a Division of Random House, Inc.

PAUL TILLICH, "The Lost Dimension in Religion," from *The Saturday Evening Post* (June 14, 1958). Copyright © 1958 by The Curtis Publishing Company. Reprinted by permission of *The Saturday Evening Post*.

ALEXIS de TOCQUEVILLE, "On Individualism in Democratic Countries" and "In What Spirit the Americans Cultivate the Arts," from *Democracy in America, Vol. II*, translated by Henry Reeves, revised by Francis Bowan, edited by Phillips Bradley. Copyright 1945 and renewed 1973, by Alfred A. Knopf, Inc. Reprinted by permission of the publisher.

ESTHER VILAR, "What Is Woman?" from *The Manipulated Man*, by Esther Vilar, Copyright © 1972 by Farrar, Straus & Giroux, Inc. Reprinted by permission of Farrar, Straus & Giroux, Inc.

KURT VONNEGUT, Jr., "Harrison Bergeron," from *Welcome to the Monkey House*, by Kurt Vonnegut, Jr. Copyright © 1961 by Kurt Vonnegut, Jr. Reprinted by permission of Delacorte Press/Seymour Lawrence. Originally published in *Fantasy and Science Fiction*.

JAMES D. WATSON, "Moving Toward the Clonal Man," from *Atlantic Monthly* (May 1971). Copyright © 1971 by James D. Watson. Reprinted by permission of the author.

JOSEPH WEIZENBAUM, from *Computer Power and Human Reason*, pp. 1-16. Copyright © 1976 by W. H. Freeman and Company. Reprinted by permission of the publisher.

JUDITH WELLS, "Daddy's Girl," from *Libra #1* (Winter 1972), pp. 43-45. Reprinted by permission of the author.

E. B. WHITE, "The Morning of the Day They Did It (February 25, 1950)," from *The Second Tree from the Corner*, by E. B. White. Copyright 1950 by E. B. White. Reprinted by permission of Harper & Row, Publishers, Inc. Originally appeared in *The New Yorker*.

VIRGINIA WOOLF, "Shakespeare's Sister," from *A Room of One's Own*, by Virginia Woolf. Copyright, 1929, by Harcourt Brace Jovanovich, Inc.; copyright, 1957, by Leonard Woolf. Reprinted by permission of Harcourt Brace Jovanovich, Inc., the Author's Literary Estate, and The Hogarth Press.

PEREGRINE WORSTHORNE, "The New Inequality," from the *Sunday Telegraph*. Copyright © 1972 by the *Sunday Telegraph* (London). Reprinted by permission of the publisher.

WILLIAM BUTLER YEATS, "Leda and the Swan," from *Collected Poems*, by William Butler Yeats. Copyright © 1928 by Macmillan Publishing Co., Inc., renewed 1956 by Georgie Yeats. Reprinted by permission of Macmillan Publishing Co., Inc., M. B. Yeats, Miss Anne Yeats, and Macmillan of London & Basingstoke.

WILLIAM K. ZINSSER, from *On Writing Well*, pp. 6-17. Copyright © 1976 by William K. Zinsser. Reprinted by permission of the author.

Preface

Most of the pieces in this book were written by the kind of person who thinks, feels, and cares. We present it in the hope that it will help readers to discover their own thoughts and feelings, to test them actively among the thoughts and feelings of others, and to develop attitudes based on rational insight and human sympathy. We can think of few better means to this end than honest reading and honest writing, and no better time and place than a beginning college course.

This fourth edition of our book has profited much from the generous advice of those who used the previous edition. We have become particularly aware of the desire of teachers for a text more responsive to the wide range of student preparation and interests now encountered in college courses. The book thus contains five new sections: On Writing, The Individual and Community, Culture and Race, Mass Culture and Mass Media, and On Death and Dying. Each of the continuing sections, furthermore, has new pieces in it. The book contains a greater proportion of short pieces, and four new short stories by Kurt Vonnegut, J. P. Donleavy, Ursula Le Guin, and Joyce Carol Oates. As was inevitable, additions have entailed the regretted omission of some pieces that teachers will miss. But the collection as a whole, we think, has even greater accessibility for students than before, and its main theme—human values— has, if anything, been strengthened.

For users new to the book we should add that its basic organization is the same. We have collected under each topic pieces representing a variety of attitudes, sometimes in direct conflict with each other. The readings present, then, a wide range of ideas and assumptions, and at the same time a continuous dialogue or debate among them. We hope that in raising issues this book will help readers to see that they have something to think about. Suggesting comparison at every point, giving ready occasion to take sides and to criticize, the book is directly suited to generating discussion and writing.

While expository prose has remained our main concern, we regard exposition as a wide-ranging term that covers everything from autobiographical writing to the research paper. The book is thus rich in styles and genres. We have included many pieces that describe personal experience, that work experience into ideas or that speak about ideas in strong personal voices and out of personal contexts, as well as pieces that offer more intellectual arguments.

The book can be studied for the ways in which the major rhetorical **xi** categories—description, narration, definition, comparison, and the like—can be used to express or support ideas; the opening piece in the book offers some assistance in this regard. Since all but a few of the essays are English originals, they can serve as authentic examples of English style. Most of the pieces are either complete works in themselves or coherent sections (usually chapters) of longer works that can be studied as compositional wholes. In any case, we have done no silent editing. A rhetorical index will be found at the end.

A Teacher's Guide is available on request from the publisher.

Berkeley, California   C.M.
1980   M.G.

Many friends and colleagues have helped us with criticisms and suggestions for this edition. We wish to thank particularly VeVe Clark, John Dekema, David Follmer, Francine Foltz, Richard Garretson, Robert J. Griffin, Christine Hilary, Don Lazere, Monique de Lebesgues, Mary Luckey, James B. Smith and Smokey Wilson. We are much indebted, too, to colleagues from other colleges and universities who took the trouble to give us in writing the benefit of their experience with the third edition. We are most happy to have been able to carry out practical suggestions made by Elizabeth Anderson of Cameron University; Owen E. Brady and David Craig of Clarkson College; Dr. James A. Brenneman of the University of Evansville; Lynda W. Brown of Auburn University; William Campbell, Toni Buzzeo Cyll, John Reidy and Carol Sontag of Wayne County Community College; Ronald L. Dotterer of Susquehanna University; Alice Fox and Dr. Fred Keefer of Miami University; Carol Freeman of the University of California, Santa Cruz; John Gage of Arizona State University; William R. Hersey of the University of Lowell; Elaine J. Jones of Gettysburg College; Brenda M. Larkin of Louisiana State University; Judith Martyn of the University of Iowa; Dr. Leo F. O'Connor of Fairfield University; Lois Rew of San Jose State University; Ted Schaefer of the College of Lake County, Illinois; and Dr. William P. Taylor of Southern University.

Eva Fuchs and Donna Kerr provided expert bibliographical assistance; Susan Broadhead, Susan McCallister and Marie Wilson helped prepare manuscript and proof under difficult conditions. Lois Pryor's editorial assistance and support was of a quality far beyond what we had a right to expect; and June Smith saw the book through the press with her usual but no less remarkable combination of calmness and expertise.

Contents

xiii

Advice to the Student: On Reading an Essay

In offering here some practical advice on how to read an essay, we do not mean to imply that there is just one way to go at it. Essays differ, and readers differ even more, and how a given reader comes to an understanding of an author's message may be a very individual process indeed. But for our present purpose—which is to offer some initial guidance to the comparatively inexperienced reader of essays—it will be safe to assume that if you have no settled way of starting out on your own, a good way to learn is to use standard moves that have worked well for others. The method we will offer, indeed, corresponds closely to what many college teachers do when an essay is being discussed in class. Thus students who follow our suggestions in the order given will often find that they have not only read an essay critically, but have prepared themselves for active class discussion and for writing about it.

First of all, you must be prepared—and leave time—to read the essay more than once. The first reading, which may be comparatively rapid, is to get a preliminary overview. This overview—a sense of how the essay goes from beginning to end—is essential to getting a good general sense of the essay's purpose and point. That is, the two main questions one asks oneself on first reading are: What is this essay trying to do? and What is its "main idea"?

What is the essay trying to do? Why is the writer telling us what he or she is telling us? A preliminary answer is essential to appreciating the essay, to coming to a secure conclusion about what it means. Most essays are prose statements that make some kind of a point, but within that rough definition they vary as much as the motives behind any human communication can vary. The writer may be trying, as one human being to another, to share an experience; or helpfully to explain something that might be interesting or puzzling to the reader; or to persuade the reader to an opinion about something, to move him or her to action, perhaps political. Some writers may even have selfish or questionable motives: to promote themselves or to deceive the reader. In any case, you need some general idea of what the writer is up to in order to ask the right questions and to come to secure conclusions about the meaning and value of the essay in all its details. In the present volume, the essays are marshaled around a number of important issues in our culture, and most of them will be found to be expository—that is, writ- **xix** ten to set out, explain, or prove to the reader the truth of an idea. Yet the essay "Shame" by Dick Gregory, the piece entitled "Manzanar, USA" by Jeanne Wakatsuki Houston, or the writings of St. Teresa and St. Augustine in the section on religion, however they may involve ideas, are principally narratives. They tell us—share with us—some important experiences in the authors' lives. Other essays in the volume seem to move, as we read them, from narrative of this kind to an explicit idea that is drawn, finally, from the events narrated. Such, for instance, are Hannah Arendt's "Anton Schmidt," George Orwell's "Shooting an Elephant"and Richard Rodriguez's "None of This Is Fair." Many others announce right off that they are about ideas. Alexis de Tocqueville tells us this in the first sentence of "Of Individualism in Democratic Countries." Still others let us know, earlier or later, that they want us to take sides in an ongoing controversy; Martin Luther King, Jr., on the activities of the civil rights movement; Brigid Brophy on the status of women; Hubert Dreyfus on the possibility of computer intelligence; Clarence Darrow on belief in God.

While we are coming to a rough idea of what the essay is for, we will already be working on the second question, What is the essay's main idea? The two questions are related, but they are not the same. It is important to have read an essay right to the end before deciding what the main idea is, for quite often the idea with which an essay begins is not the principal idea of an essay. The opening sections of the essay may be introducing the topic, laying the groundwork, perhaps getting the reader into a frame of mind for accepting the main idea, which may itself be reserved for the end. Thus Orwell's "Politics and the English Language" starts out with the idea that "the English language is in a bad way" (p. 99), and in the second paragraph, that the badness of our language "makes it easier for us to have foolish thoughts" and that clear thinking may have something to do with our "political regeneration." He then spends some nine pages beautifully elaborating these preliminary ideas, not coming again to a full expression of what turns out to be his main idea—each aspect of which he has already argued in some detail—until his last paragraph: "The present political chaos is connected with the decay of language, and . . . one can probably bring about some improvement by starting at the verbal end." In "The Indispensable Opposition," Walter Lippmann gives us his main idea at the end of the fourth paragraph: "We must protect the right of our opponents to speak because we must hear what they have to say." We know that this *is* the main idea because by the end of the essay nothing else tops it; the rest of the essay is devoted to expounding and defending it. Of course, many essays will announce their main idea quite early, as does Brigid Brophy's, at the end of the first paragraph: "The barriers which keep them [women] in now are invisible"; or Marc Fasteau's, at the end of the second: "Despite the time men spend together, their contact rarely goes beyond the external, a limitation which tends to make their friendships shallow and unsatisfactory." And many, like Brophy's and Fasteau's (and even Orwell's "Politics"), by ending on an upbeat or corrective note, seem to have not one but two main ideas—the one that occupies the body of the essay and the one that follows it at the end. Be that as it may, you will have done your reading well if the first time through you can put your finger on a statement that all or most of the essay seems to be supporting. Notice that a main idea *is* an idea: It says something *about* something. You can test whether you are identifying an *idea* as opposed, merely, to a *topic* like "sex roles" or "politics and language" by whether you can express it in a sentence.

Sometimes the main idea is not stated anywhere by the author in so many words, and sometimes, as in poetry or fiction, it is not reducible to simple terms; in these cases the reader can supply only an approximation of it. The "main idea" of Dick Gregory's narrative, a narrative that freely mingles ideas and feelings, is something about the way shame can get in the way of human sympathy. Martin Gansberg's account of the murder of Kitty Genovese, designed to make us feel as much as think, is mainly not just a news story about a murder but a statement about how terribly deep apathy goes in a certain neighborhood in New York City—and perhaps more widely. Its main idea was expressed only approximately by the editor who wrote its headline.

The reason that it is useful to start with a notion of the purpose and the main idea of an essay is that most good essays are *organized* or *unified* around their purpose and main idea, and so can be understood most handily in those terms. Much of an appreciative, critical reading comes from being able to explain the various parts or features of the essay and relate them to the essay's purpose and main idea. The main features that a good reader will be on the alert for by the second reading will be organization or argument, the kinds of evidence presented, and any elements of technique, tone or style that contribute to its full meaning. By this time the reader should be well past the "receptive" stage of just sitting there and letting the words come. Try to take an active role, working along with the writer step by step, or standing behind the writer and watching and appreciating how it is done.

There are many ways to organize an essay; but in general, in the essay that tries to establish an idea, the main parts will be the steps used to get the reader to accept the idea. As we have said, the author's strategy may lead to announcing the idea at the beginning or withholding it until the end, but the body of the essay will have to consist, in one way or another, of some organized combination of argument and evidence.

One of the simplest and best ways for a writer to make a point is to mention one by one all the things in personal experience or reading that make one feel the idea is true, organizing them by groups and subgroups in order to avoid diffuseness. Thus Marc Fasteau, after stating his main idea about the quality of friendships among men, starts in paragraph 3 with a group of observations about uncommunicativeness among men. He talks first about the general quality of male conversations, then in the next paragraph about the use of games as a substitute for conversation; in the next paragraph comes some evidence from his experience with a college friend and with his father; in the next comes an example from popular literature; then, after dealing with some exceptions, he lets us know, with the adverb *finally*, that his last piece of evidence for uncommunicativeness "is the way men depend on women to facilitate certain conversations" (p. 441). The next paragraph sees him summarizing for us the meaning of this subsection of his essay and announcing that he is now going to turn to "the reasons why men hide from each other," which "lie in the taboos and imperatives of the masculine stereotype" (p. 441). The alert reader will expect then, in the ensuing paragraphs, a list of cultural prohibitions or commands that make men behave the way they do, with some discussion of each. And sure enough, that is what he gives us, with due attention to some exceptions, and with a brief, constructive conclusion. Notice that a writer will often use adverbs and transitional phrases—*first of all, finally, however, furthermore,* and the like—to let the reader know continuously what is going on.

Your acceptance of the main idea of this kind of essay depends on your acceptance of the evidence presented. Is it true to your experience? Or, if it is not within your experience, do you believe it? What is the author's reliability? Is the author the kind of person who should be believed on this subject?

Sometimes the author will try to persuade by using some form of logic, a chain of argument. Thus Garrett Hardin (p. 232) argues that since the poor multiply many times faster than the rich, simply feeding the poor creates that much more of a surplus of poor people, and makes the problem of world poverty ultimately greater, not less. In dealing with arguments based on logic, the experienced reader will want to test (perhaps with the aid of further research or wider reading) whether all the parts of the argument are true, whether the conclusions really do follow from the facts given, and whether anywhere in the argument the reader is being asked to accept a hidden assumption—something that is quietly assumed by the writer and intended to stand without proof. The essay by Thomas H. Huxley (p. 20) will give you a good idea of two major forms of logic.

Writers use many other means to help them make their meanings clear. Sometimes they offer contrasting comparisons or definitions, which help clarify each other, as both William Golding and James Harvey Robinson do with kinds of thinking, Gloria Steinem does with erotica and pornography (p. 447), and as de Tocqueville does with egoism and individualism (p. 241). Sometimes they use analogy, that is, a comparison with something similar that the reader may be more familiar with. Thus James Britton (p. 74) starts out with the idea of the successive additions to a map in order to introduce the reader to the mechanism of learning; Walter Lippmann (p. 177) uses our tolerance of our doctor's diagnosis as an analogy to what he means by political tolerance. Sometimes the writer relies heavily on a simple incident or anecdote, which seems to sum up or symbolize the whole meaning all at once. Marcel Proust (p. 66) uses the remembered taste of a piece of toast in this way; and Katherine Anne Porter (p. 648) depends on the simple image of a young man polishing a table top to support much of what she wants us to feel about our future as humans. Sometimes, as with James Baldwin, the writer seems to take us through the actual network of experiences that led him to his final conclusions. As you encounter these various devices, your appreciation of them will deepen if you continually ask yourself how and why they work to support or embody the author's main purpose and idea.

Of course, much that a writer does in an essay will go beyond the requirements of simply making ideas clear. The writer will, quite legitimately, want to appeal to the reader's feelings, to share feelings, or to suggest a proper emotional response to the topic. You should be sensitively aware of this aspect of the essay, not only to be on guard against improper manipulation of feelings—as, for instance, in appeals to sentimentality or prejudice—but also to enhance your understanding and enjoyment of the feelings themselves.

Feelings are powerfully generated by the techniques that the essay writer shares with the poet and novelist—the choice of particular words, sounds, and rhythms, the setting of scenes, telling of stories, creation of atmosphere—and by the particular tone of voice that the writer seems to adopt. An adequate account of all these would require many volumes. Here we must be content to point briefly to some easily noticed effects of literary style in the essays of the present collection.

Some writers—often professors and scientists—write in an impersonal style that seems calculated to keep feelings neutral or at a distance. The kind of words they use seems to be saying: Let the ideas or facts speak for themselves. James Harvey Robinson writes like this, and so do James Watson and Matina Horner. Other writers have more personal styles, as if they had found their own unique voices, and seem to be addressing us personally. This is the way Mary Caroline Richards sounds, and James Baldwin, and Henry David Thoreau. The personal relationship and directness implied by the way they write may have an important effect on the reader, often suggesting that the reader return the confidence and relative intimacy offered by the writer.

Some writers—Orwell is the greatest among them—try for a plain style, in which the writing, like a pane of glass, rarely calls attention to itself, rarely interposes itself between the reader and what there is to be seen and felt. This style is much admired nowadays; it has an economy that harmonizes with the pace of modern life, and it suggests an attractive modesty on the part of the writer. Other authors seem almost intoxicated with words; they write a highly colored prose, with heavily distinctive word choice and rhythms—the most notable example in this volume is that of the surgeon Richard Selzer—the effect of which can be very moving indeed, or conversely, give the effect of excessiveness or self-display.

Some of the writers in this volume clearly use techniques characteristic of fiction. Thus the descriptions in Joan Didion's "Some Dreamers of the Golden Dream" are used less to give us the facts than to create artistically a certain atmosphere or tone. For instance, her opening description (p. 277), the choice and sequencing of details in the description of the funeral (p. 278), the vivid characterization she gives to even the minor actors in her story, all suggest the talents of a fiction writer and all contribute to what she wants to say about the culture she is describing. The same can be said of the way N. Scott Momaday creates atmosphere through description in his "Introduction" to *The Way to Rainy Mountain*. Indeed most good essay writers have some sensitivity to scene, atmosphere, character, word choice, and tone, and you should try to appreciate how any of these aspects adds to the meaning of the piece you are reading. Finally, you should be alert to the great devices of irony and humor, which often convey their meanings indirectly, through some implied reversal of what they seem to say, often for the sake of satire. The classic example of this is Jonathan Swift's "A Modest Proposal"; other, lighter examples are Paul Jacobs' "The Most Cheerful Graveyard in the World" (p. 636) and E. B. White's "The Morning of the Day They Did It."

Because you are in a college classroom situation, you may well have started out to read an essay because of compulsion or on faith—on someone else's say so. It is wise to start out with a certain humility or faith or optimism that an essay someone wrote, and that was published and perhaps republished and then recommended or assigned—that such an essay must have a message of value. It is well to have started out with some receptiveness and some respect for the writer; but in the end, reading is for yourself, and once a couple of careful readings have given you an idea of the essay's meaning for the author, the final question to ask is: What does it mean for me? The words on the page will not take on their deepest meaning until you have come to terms with the essay, as if you had just had (what deep reading really is) a personal encounter with the writer. How does the message fit with what you already knew, wanted to know, or needed to know? How does the essay relate to others you have read; to ideas and experiences you have already had? If it challenges or disturbs you, where are the points of conflict? If it confirms your ideas, does it merely tell you what you already knew, or make you feel surer of yourself? Is it true to your experience, or false? If new to you, does it enlarge your experience or fail to find a place there; and if it fails, why so? What has it changed in your ideas or feelings? How, in fact, does it make you feel? Even your response to the writer's tone, or to the writer's own degree of involvement with the subject, is a legitimate part of the meaning of the essay for you.

The answers to any of these questions, besides capping your sense of the essay's meaning, will begin to move you from the role of reader to that of thinker, discussant, and writer. Even before you have clearly formulated ideas about the essay, your first emotional response to it will be useful; but you must try to follow out the line of that response, staying on its trail. It may lead you to finding its source in a significant complex of ideas about the essay, about the world, or about yourself. That experience is just what William Nichols describes in his essay, "The Burden of Imagination" (p. 148). He talks of having read a book, experiencing "raging disappointment" as he read it. Tracing this feeling, Nichols found that it was not only a reaction to the book's ideas but to its assumptions, some of which remained hidden. He read the book critically, trying to uncover these hidden assumptions, analyze them, and understand them. In the course of this process, he not only found out why he was angry, but came up with his own main idea, the thought-provoking one with which his essay ends.

The BORZOI COLLEGE READER

fourth edition

On Writing

VERY few of us would feel offended if a friend or teacher returned our math problem marked "wrong." Yet almost all of us would feel at least hurt if something we had written were returned to us marked "wrong." Words are more intimately connected than numbers to our sense of self. We may be wrong about facts, but when we try to express an idea or a feeling, we risk not being understood. And writing is riskier than talking, for we cannot follow our listeners' responses by watching their faces, by interjecting "What I mean is . . . ." or simply changing direction or even the subject. Not knowing how our reader will read (as partner or judge? as critic or editor?) can cramp our sense of how to begin.

The four writers in this section present us with different perspectives on writing and, by implication, on what to ask or hope from our readers. William Stafford sees writing as a way to help create what we want to say. A writer, he says, "is not so much someone who has something to say as he is someone who has found a process that will bring about new things he would not have thought of if he had not started to say them." Clearly there is no "wrong" here, and clearly the writer must simply have the courage to begin. Lawrence Langer thinks the fear of being judged keeps many students from saying anything that means very much to them and thus to others. They avoid language that could break down barriers between reader and writer and lead to genuine understanding. Instead they build barriers of "abstract diction and technical jargon" to protect themselves from their readers. Langer also reminds us of the responsibility of the reader, citing a poignant example of a student who risked a very personal essay and an instructor who responded only by correcting. Risk-taking, of course, does not need to mean giving up privacy. Just to think honestly is to take great risks. These first two essays, so eloquent on the need to take risks with language, do not, however, imply that everything that we write has equal finish. "Most of what I write, like most of what I say in casual conversation, will not amount to much," says Stafford, and Langer knows quite well that the essay he refers to is not yet "finished."

In the article that follows, William Zinsser gives excellent advice on fighting clutter, echoing the great William Strunk's admonition to "omit needless words." Yet his main idea in this essay seems to contradict what the first two writers recommend. "Clear thinking becomes clear writing," he says. "It is impossible for a muddy thinker to write good English." Josephine Miles supports that view, drawing our attention to how the thesis statement's predication embodies the idea and structures the argument. Both seem to say that we need to know what we think in order to know what to say and how to say it. What does this do to Stafford's advice to write, and so discover what we think?

What seems to be a contradiction here may not be. Different people do, of course, compose differently. There have always been those who work themselves through several drafts before they get a good handle on their idea, and others who have a clear idea in mind, perhaps even an outline, before they begin putting words on paper. Readers will want to discover their own best ways of getting started.

It may also be that, whatever the individual style or emphasis, the ways described above are different parts of one process. Writers who simply begin to write as Stafford recommends may newly discover their ideas, but with the discovery may also come the need to start again, to ensure that they can communicate those ideas clearly to someone else.

WILLIAM STAFFORD

William Stafford is a poet who now lives in Washington, D.C., where he works as a Consultant in Poetry to the Library of Congress. He was born and raised in Kansas. During his school years, he writes, "we moved from one little town to another. . . . Our lives were quiet and the land was very steady. Our teachers were good. Not till I finished my BA degree at the University of Kansas and went on to graduate school in another state did I see an adult drunk or enraged or seriously menacing. Higher education and the coming of World War II supplied a new aspect of experience." A pacifist, he spent the war years in camps for conscientious objectors, fighting forest fires, building trails, and terracing eroding land. After the war he taught at Lewis and Clark College in Oregon, left to study in the creative writing program at the State University of Iowa (where he received his Ph.D. in 1954), and then returned to Lewis and Clark until he moved to Washington.

Stafford has published widely. His four main collections are Traveling Through the Dark *(1962), for which he won the 1963 National Book Award in Poetry;* The Rescued Year *(1966), which includes an autobiographical account of his Kansas childhood;* Allegiances *(1970); and* Someday, Maybe *(1973). His work also includes criticism and a collection of personal and autobiographical pieces on writing, published in 1978 as* Writing the Australian Crawl. *From this we take the chapter printed below.*

A Way of Writing

A writer is not so much someone who has something to say as he is someone who has found a process that will bring about new things he would not have thought of if he had not started to say them. That is, he does not draw on a reservoir; instead, he engages in an activity that brings to him a whole succession of unforeseen stories, poems, essays, plays, laws, philosophies, religions, or—but wait!

Back in school, from the first when I began to try to write things, I felt this richness. One thing would lead to another; the world would give and give. Now, after twenty years or so of trying, I live by that certain richness, an idea hard to pin, difficult to say, and perhaps offensive to some. For there are strange implications in it.

One implication is the importance of just plain receptivity. When I write, I like to have an interval before me when I am not likely to be interrupted. For me, this means usually the early morning, before others are awake. I get pen and paper, take a glance out of the window (often it is dark out there), and wait. It is like fishing. But I do not wait very long, for there is always a nibble—and this is where receptivity comes in. To get started I will accept anything that occurs to me. Something always occurs, of course, to any of us. We can't keep from thinking. Maybe I have to settle for an immediate impression: it's cold, or hot, or dark, or bright, or in between! Or—well, the possibilities are endless. If I put down something, that thing will help the next thing come, and I'm off. If I let the process go on, things will occur to me that were not at all in my mind when I started. These things, odd or trivial as they may be, are somehow connected. And if I let them string out, surprising things will happen.

If I let them string out. . . . Along with initial receptivity, then, there is another readiness: I must be willing to fail. If I am to keep on writing, I cannot bother to insist on high standards. I must get into action and not let anything stop me, or even slow me much. By "standards" I do not mean "correctness"—spelling, punctuation, and so on. These details become mechanical for anyone who writes for a while. I am thinking about such matters as social significance, positive values, consistency, etc. I resolutely disregard these. Something better, greater, is happening! I am following a process that leads so wildly and originally into new territory that no judgment can at the moment be made about values, significance, and so on. I am making something new, something that has not been judged before. Later others—and maybe I myself—will make judgments. Now, I am headlong to discover. Any distraction may harm the creating.

So, receptive, careless of failure, I spin out things on the page. And a wonderful freedom comes. If something occurs to me, it is all right to accept it. It has one justification: it occurs to me. No one else can guide me. I must follow my own weak, wandering, diffident impulses.

A strange bonus happens. At times, without my insisting on it, my writings become coherent; the successive elements that occur to me are clearly related. They lead by themselves to new connections. Sometimes the language, even the syllables that happen along, may start a trend. Sometimes the materials alert me to something waiting in my mind, ready for sustained attention. At such times, I allow myself to be eloquent, or intentional, or for great swoops (Treacherous! Not to be trusted!) reasonable. But I do not insist on any of that; for I know that back of my activity there will be the coherence of my self, and that indulgence of my impulses will bring recurrent patterns and meanings again.

This attitude toward the process of writing creatively suggests a problem for me, in terms of what others say. They talk about "skills" in writing. Without denying that I do have experience, wide reading, automatic orthodoxies and maneuvers of various kinds, I still must insist that I am often baffled about what "skill" has to do with the precious little area of confusion when I do not know what I am going to say and then I find out what I am going to say. That precious interval I am unable to bridge by skill. What can I witness about it? It remains mysterious, just as all of us must feel puzzled about how we are so inventive as to be able to talk along through complexities with our friends, not needing to plan what we are going to say, but never stalled for long in our confident forward progress. Skill? If so, it is the skill we all have, something we must have learned before the age of three or four.

A writer is one who has become accustomed to trusting that grace, or luck, or—skill.

Yet another attitude I find necessary: most of what I write, like most of what I say in casual conversation, will not amount to much. Even I will realize, and even at the time, that it is not negotiable. It will be like practice. In conversation I allow myself random remarks—in fact, as I recall, that is the way I learned to talk—so in writing I launch many expendable efforts. A result of this free way of writing is that I am not writing for others, mostly; they will not see the product at all unless the activity eventuates in something that later appears to be worthy. My guide is the self, and its adventuring in the language brings about communication.

This process-rather-than-substance view of writing invites a final, dual reflection:

1. Writers may not be special—sensitive or talented in any usual sense. They are simply engaged in sustained use of a language skill we all have. Their "creations" come about through confident reliance on stray impulses that will, with trust, find occasional patterns that are satisfying.

2. But writing itself is one of the great, free human activities. There is scope for individuality, and elation, and discovery, in writing. For the person who follows with trust and forgiveness what occurs to him, the world remains always ready and deep, an inexhaustible environment, with the combined vividness of an actuality and flexibility of a dream. Working back

and forth between experience and thought, writers have more than space and time can offer. They have the whole unexplored realm of human vision.

LAWRENCE LANGER

Lawrence Langer is a professor of English at Simmons College in Boston. Born in New York City in 1929, he graduated from City College in 1951 and then did graduate work at Harvard University (M.A., 1952; Ph.D., 1961). His considerable research in the literature of the Holocaust has led to several books and articles, including The Holocaust and the Literary Imagination *(1975),* The Age of Atrocity: Death in Modern Literature *(1978), and "Time, Space and Dreams in the Holocaust Universe," in the* Journal of Interdisciplinary Studies *(1977). The article reprinted below first appeared in* The Chronicle of Higher Education, *January 1977.*

The Human Use of Language

A friend of mine recently turned in a paper to a course on behavior modification. She had tried to express in simple English some of her reservations about this increasingly popular approach to education. She received it back with the comment: "Please rewrite this in behavioral terms."

It is little wonder that human beings have so much trouble saying what they feel, when they are told that there is a specialized vocabulary for saying what they think. The language of simplicity and spontaneity is forced to retreat behind the barricades of an official prose developed by a few experts who believe that jargon is the most precise means of communication. The results would be comic, if they were not so poisonous; unfortunately, there is an attitude toward the use of language that is impervious to human need and drives some people back into silence when they realize the folly of risking human words on insensitive ears.

The comedy is easy to come by. Glancing through my friend's textbook on behavior modification, I happened on a chapter beginning with the following challenging statement: "Many of the problems encountered by teachers in the daily management of their classes could be resolved if. . . ." Although I was a little wary of the phrase "daily management," I was encouraged to plunge ahead, because as an educator I have always been interested in ideas for improving learning. So I plunged. The entire sentence reads: "Many of the problems encountered by teachers in the daily management of their classes could be resolved if the emission of desirable student behaviors was increased."

Emission? At first I thought it was a misprint for "omission," but the omission of desirable student behaviors (note the plural) hardly seemed an appropriate goal for educators. Then I considered the possibility of metaphor, both erotic and automotive, but these didn't seem to fit, either. A footnote clarified the matter: " 'Emission' is a technical term used in behavioral analysis. The verb, 'to emit,' is used specifically with a certain category of behavior called 'operant behavior.' Operant behaviors are modified by their consequences. Operant behaviors correspond closely to the behavior colloquially referred to as voluntary." Voluntary? Is jargon then an attack on freedom of the will?

Of course, this kind of abuse of language goes on all the time—within the academic world, one regrets to say, as well as outside it. Why couldn't the author of this text simply say that we need to motivate students to learn willingly? The more I read such non-human prose, and try to avoid writing it myself, the more I am convinced that we must be in touch with ourselves before we can use words to touch others.

Using language meaningfully requires risk; the sentence I have just quoted takes no risks at all. Much of the discourse that poses as communication in our society is really a decoy to divert our audience (and often ourselves) from that shadowy plateau where our real life hovers on the precipice of expression. How many people, for example, have the courage to walk up to someone they like and actually *say* to them: "I'm very fond of you, you know"?

Such honesty reflects the use of language as revelation, and that sort of revelation, brimming with human possibilities, is risky precisely because it invites judgment and rebuff. Perhaps this is one reason why, especially in academe, we are confronted daily with so much neutral prose: Our students are not yet in touch with themselves; not especially encouraged by us, their instructors, to move in that direction; they are encouraged indeed to expect judgment and hence perhaps rebuff, too, in our evaluation of them. Thus they instinctively retreat behind the anonymity of abstract diction and technical jargon to protect themselves against us—but also, as I have suggested, against themselves.

This problem was crystallized for me recently by an encounter only peripherally related to the issue. As part of my current research, I have been interviewing children of concentration-camp survivors. One girl I have been meeting with says that her mother does not like to talk about the experience, *except with other survivors.* Risk is diminished when we know in advance that our audience shares with us a sympathy for our theme. The nakedness of pain *and* the nakedness of love require gentle responses. So this survivor is reticent, except with fellow victims.

But one day a situation arose which tempted her to the human use of language although she could not be sure, in advance, of the reception her words would receive. We all recognize it. This particular woman, at the age of 40, decided to return to school to get a college degree. Her first assignment in freshman composition was to write a paper on something that was of great importance to her personally. The challenge was immense; the risk was even greater. For the first time in 20 years, she resolved to confront a silence in her life that she obviously needed to rouse to speech.

She was 14 when the Germans invaded Poland. When the roundup of the

Jews began a year later, some Christian friends sent their young daughter to "call for her" one day, so that they might hide her. A half hour later, the friends went themselves to pick up her parents, but during that interval, a truck had arrived, loaded aboard the Jewish mother and father—and the daughter never saw them or heard from them again. Their fate we can imagine. The girl herself was eventually arrested, survived several camps, and after the war came to America. She married, had children of her own, and except for occasional reminiscences with fellow survivors, managed to live adequately without diving into her buried personal past. Until one day her instructor in English composition touched a well-insulated nerve, and it began to throb with a painful impulse to express. I present verbatim the result of that impulse, a paper called "People I Have Forgotten":

"Can you forget your own Father and Mother? If so—how or why?

"I thought I did. To mention their names, for me is a great emotional struggle. The brutal force of this reality shakes my whole body and mind, wrecking me into ugly splinters; each crying to be mended anew. So the silence I maintain about their memory is only physical and valid as such but not true. I could never forget my parents, nor do I want to do it. True, I seldom talk about them with my husband or my children. How they looked, who they were, why they perished during the war. The love and sacrifices they have made for me during their lifetime, never get told.

"The cultural heritage to which each generation is entitled to have access seems to be nonexistant [sic], since I dare not talk about anything relating to my past, my parents.

"This awful, awesome power of not-remembering, this heart-breaking sensation of the conspiracy of silence is my dilemma.

"Often, I have tried to break through my imprisoning wall of irrational silence, but failed: now I hope to be able to do it.

"Until now, I was not able to face up to the loss of my parents, much less talk about them. The smallest reminder of them would set off a chain reaction of results that I could anticipate but never direct. The destructive force of sadness, horror, fright would then become my master. And it was this subconscious knowledge that kept me paralyzed with silence, not a conscious desire to forget my parents.

"My silent wall, my locked shell existed only of real necessity; I needed time.

"I needed time to forget the tragic loss of my loved ones, time to heal my emotional wound so that there shall come a time when I can again remember the people I have forgotten."

The essay is not a confrontation, only a prelude, yet it reveals qualities which are necessary for the human use of language: In trying to reach her audience, the author must touch the deepest part of herself. She risks self-exposure—when we see the instructor's comment, we will realize how great was her risk—and she is prepared for judgment and perhaps even rebuff, although I doubt whether she was prepared for the form they took. This kind of prose, for all its hesitant phraseology, throws down a gauntlet to the reader, a challenge asking him to understand that life is pain as well as plenty, chaos as well as form. Its imagery of locked shells and imprisoning walls hints at a silent world of horror and sadness far less enchanting than the more familiar landscape of love where most of us dwell. Language is a two-edged tool, to pierce the wall which hides that world, or build high abstract barriers to protect us from its threats.

The instructor who graded the paper I have just read preferred walls to honest words. At the bottom of the last page she scrawled a large "D-minus," emphatically surrounded by a circle. Her only comment was: "Your theme is not clear—you should have developed your 1st paragraph. You talk around your subject." At this moment, two realms collide: a universe of unarticulated feeling seeking expression (and the courage and encouragement to express) and a nature made so immune to feeling by heaven-knows-what that she hides behind the tired, tired language of the professional theme-corrector.

Suddenly we realize that reading as well as writing requires risks, and that the metaphor of insulation, so central to the efforts of the Polish woman survivor to re-establish contact with her past, is a metaphor governing the response of readers, too. Some writing, like "the emission of desirable student behaviors," thickens the insulation that already separates the reader from the words that throw darts at his armor of indifference. But even when language unashamedly reveals the feeling that is hidden behind the words, it must contend with a different kind of barrier, the one behind which our instructor lies concealed, unwilling or unable to hear a human voice and return a human echo of her own.

Ironically, the victor in this melancholy failure at communication is the villain of the piece, behavior modification. For the Polish survivor wrote her next theme on an innocuous topic, received a satisfactory grade, and never returned to the subject of her parents. The instructor, who had encountered a problem in the daily management of her class in the form of an essay which she could not respond to in a human way, altered the attitude of her student by responding in a non-human way, thus resolving her problem by increasing the emission of desirable student behavior. The student now knows how vital it is to develop her first paragraph, and how futile it is to reveal her first grief.

Even more, she has learned the danger of talking around her subject: She not only refuses to talk *around* it now, she refuses to talk *about* it. Thus the human use of language leads back to silence—where perhaps it should have remained in the first place.

WILLIAM ZINSSER

William Zinsser has been a writer for most of his life. He was born in New York in 1922. Graduating from Princeton in 1944, he served in the army for two years. He then joined the New York Herald Tribune, *where he stayed until 1959, first as feature writer, then as drama editor and film critic, and finally as editorial writer. For the next ten years he worked as a free-lance writer, contributed to many magazines including* Look *and* Life, *and published two books of nonfiction (*Pop Goes America, *1966;* The Lunacy Boom, *1970) and one novel (*The Paradise Bit, *1967). In 1970 he became a member of the English faculty of Yale University. A course he teaches there in writing nonfiction led to a book* On Writing Well *(1976), from which we reprint the second chapter. In the first chapter he says that there isn't any "right" way to write, but all good writing, he adds, "has an aliveness that keeps the reader reading from one paragraph to the next, and it's not a question of gimmicks to 'personalize' the author. It's a question of using the English language in a way that will achieve the greatest strength and the least clutter." Such principles can be learned, he concludes, although perhaps they cannot be taught.*

Simplicity

Clutter is the disease of American writing. We are a society strangling in unnecessary words, circular constructions, pompous frills and meaningless jargon.

Who really knows what the average businessman is trying to say in the average business letter? What member of an insurance or medical plan can decipher the brochure that tells him what his costs and benefits are? What father or mother can put together a child's toy—on Christmas Eve or any other eve—from the instructions on the box? Our national tendency is to inflate and thereby sound important. The airline pilot who wakes us to announce that he is presently anticipating experiencing considerable weather wouldn't dream of saying that there's a storm ahead and it may get bumpy. The sentence is too simple—there must be something wrong with it.

But the secret of good writing is to strip every sentence to its cleanest components. Every word that serves no function, every long word that could be a short word, every adverb that carries the same meaning that is already in the verb, every passive construction that leaves the reader unsure of who is doing what—these are the thousand and one adulterants that weaken the strength of a sentence. And they usually occur, ironically, in proportion to education and rank.

During the late 1960's the president of Princeton University wrote a letter to mollify the alumni after a spell of campus unrest. "You are probably aware," he began, "that we have been experiencing very considerable potentially explosive expressions of dissatisfaction on issues only partially related." He meant that the students had been hassling them about different things. As an alumnus I was far more upset by the president's syntax than by the students' potentially explosive expressions of dissatisfaction. I would have preferred the presidential approach taken by Franklin D. Roosevelt when he tried to convert into English his own government's memos, such as this blackout order of 1942:

> Such preparations shall be made as will completely obscure all Federal buildings and non-Federal buildings occupied by the Federal government during an air raid for any period of time from visibility by reason of internal or external illumination.

"Tell them," Roosevelt said, "that in buildings where they have to keep the work going to put something across the windows."

Simplify, simplify. Thoreau said it, as we are so often reminded, and no American writer more consistently practiced what he preached. Open *Walden* to any page and you will find a man saying in a plain and orderly way what is on his mind:

> I love to be alone. I never found the companion that was so companionable as solitude. We are for the most part more lonely when we go abroad among men than when we stay in our chambers. A man thinking or working is always alone, let him be where he will. Solitude is not measured by the miles of space that intervene between a man and his fellows. The really diligent student in one of the crowded hives of Cambridge College is as solitary as a dervish in the desert.

How can the rest of us achieve such enviable freedom from clutter? The answer is to clear our heads of clutter. Clear thinking becomes clear writing: one can't exist without the other. It is impossible for a muddy thinker to write good English. He may get away with it for a paragraph or two, but soon the reader will be lost, and there is no sin so grave, for he will not easily be lured back.

Who is this elusive creature, the reader? He is a person with an attention span of about twenty seconds. He is assailed on every side by forces competing for his time: by newspapers and magazines, by television and radio and stereo, by his wife and children and pets, by his house and his yard and all the gadgets that he has bought to keep them spruce, and by that most potent of competitors, sleep. The man snoozing in his chair with an unfinished magazine open on his lap is a man who was being given too much unnecessary trouble by the writer.

It won't do to say that the snoozing reader is too dumb or too lazy to keep pace with the train of thought. My sympathies are with him. If a reader is lost, it is generally because the writer has not been careful enough to keep him on the path.

This carelessness can take any number of forms. Perhaps a sentence is so excessively cluttered that the reader, hacking his way through the verbiage, simply doesn't know what it means. Perhaps a sentence has been so shoddily constructed that the reader could read it in any of several ways. Perhaps the writer has switched pronouns in mid-sentence, or has switched tenses, so the reader loses track of who is talking or when the action took place. Perhaps Sentence B is not a logical sequel to Sentence A—the writer, in whose head the connection is clear, has not bothered to provide the missing link. Perhaps the writer has used an important word incorrectly by not taking the trouble to look it up. He may think that "sanguine" and "sanguinary" mean the same thing, but the difference is a bloody big one. The reader can only infer (speaking of big differences) what the writer is trying to imply.

Faced with these obstacles, the reader is at first a remarkably tenacious bird. He blames himself—he obviously missed something, and he goes back over the mystifying sentence, or over the whole paragraph, piecing it out like an ancient rune, making guesses and moving on. But he won't do this for long. The writer is making him work too hard, and the reader will look for one who is better at his craft.

The writer must therefore constantly ask himself: What am I trying to say? Surprisingly often, he doesn't know. Then he must look at what he has written and ask: Have I said it? Is it clear to someone encountering the subject for the first time? If it's not, it is because some fuzz has worked its way into the machinery. The clear writer is a person clear-headed enough to see this stuff for what it is: fuzz.

I don't mean that some people are born clear-headed and are therefore natural writers, whereas others are naturally fuzzy and will never write well. Thinking clearly is a conscious act that the writer must force upon himself, just as if he were embarking on any other project that requires logic: adding up a laundry list or doing an algebra problem. Good writing doesn't come naturally, though most people obviously think it does. The professional writer is forever being bearded by strangers who say that they'd like to "try a little writing some time" when they retire from their real profession. Good writing takes self-discipline and, very often, self-knowledge.

Many writers, for instance, can't stand to throw anything away. Their sentences are littered with words that mean essentially the same thing and with phrases which make a point that is implicit in what they have already said. When students give me these littered sentences I beg them to select from the surfeit of words the few that most precisely fit what they want to say. Choose one, I plead, from among the three almost identical adjectives. Get rid of the unnecessary adverbs. Eliminate "in a funny sort of way" and other such qualifiers—they do no useful work.

The students look stricken—I am taking all their wonderful words away. I am only taking their superfluous words away, leaving what is organic and strong.

"But," one of my worst offenders confessed, "I never can get rid of anything—you should see my room." (I didn't take him up on the offer.) "I have two lamps where I only need one, but I can't decide which one I like better, so I keep them both." He went on to enumerate his duplicated or unnecessary objects, and over the weeks ahead I went on throwing away his duplicated and unnecessary words. By the end of the term—a term that he found acutely painful—his sentences were clean.

"I've had to change my whole approach to writing," he told me. "Now I have to *think* before I start every sentence and I have to *think* about every word." The very idea amazed him. Whether his room also looked better I never found out. I suspect that it did.

JOSEPHINE MILES

Josephine Miles is a teacher, a scholar, and a poet. Born in Chicago in 1911, she was educated at the University of California at Los Angeles (B.A., 1932) and at Berkeley (M.A., 1934; Ph.D., 1938). In 1940 she began teaching in the English Department at Berkeley, became a full professor in 1952, was honored as one of seven University Professors in 1973, and is now Professor Emeritus. She has published widely and won prizes both for her poetry and scholarship. Among her books are several collections of poems, including Poems 1930–1960 *(1960),* Kinds of Affection *(1967),* To All Appearances: New and Selected Poems *(1974), and* Coming to Terms *(1979).* Poetry and Change: Donne, Milton, Wordsworth and the Equilibrium of the Present *(1974) won the Modern Language Association Lowell Award for literary scholarship. Throughout her teaching career her interest in style, structure, and language has been demonstrated not only in print but also in many talks to teachers' groups and in a commitment to the teaching of freshman English. The essay that follows first appeared in* Educational Leadership *in February 1962; it has been edited by the author for inclusion in this book.*

Essay in Reason

Prose essay like prose narrative or prose drama is an art of prose, and as an art it works in basic patterns. Rather than a sequence of events, it is a sequence of ideas, and it shapes up in certain ways, depending upon its main idea, its attempt or "essay." It makes a leading statement, that is, predicates its subject, and then unfolds, develops, substantiates both subject and predicate in the specific relation it has proposed for them.

Students in California have usually read widely and well in books of essays in ideas. The first week of the Fall term of 1961, 30 freshmen, my teaching assistant, and I talked about ideas we had met with during the past year. We were able to range from Thoreau to Jung and Freud, from Milton to Edith Hamilton, from Plato to Riesman. There were enough ideas for months of talking and writing.

Then I asked the students each to make a statement of one idea which particularly interested him, to suggest two or three different ways in which it might be developed into an essay. Blockade. Few associated the concept of an *idea* with the concept of a *statement* or a *sentence*. For many, ideas were at best abstract words or phrases; at worst, as one student suggested, "opinions or untrue facts." Inasmuch as a fact or topic assumes no responsibility for predication, no pattern of organization is obvious for it, and the student is at a loss to know what development may mean for it. Therefore the most typical response to the assignment is something like: "The importance of music: (a) development by examples, (b) general development." Or "The necessity for world government: (a) subjective, (b) objective." Not many aids to reason here!

First need then is to talk about ideas as sentences, that is, predicating the subjects, saying something about something, establishing relations. The student hopefully proposes, "Music is important" or "World government is necessary," and then goes on: "First I'll write a paragraph saying what I mean by *music* or *world government*. Then I'll develop my point in the predicate about important or necessary." But can importance or necessity be shown without showing possible alternatives? "Sure," says the student triumphantly. "Here's where I switch from objective to subjective!"

After some time discussing these terms as well as *general* and *particular*, demonstrating the need for both pairs and for the clarity of their relations, we come back to develop the useful structural implications of a good leading sentence. Here is one of the few really organizable ones achieved in the first week. Please ignore the horrors of its wordiness. These problems are secondary to sheer understanding of the point, and will mostly clear up when the writer's thought clears up. And he is on the right track: "A prevalent disease, mental retardation has received a minimum of public attention and this neglect has hampered any progress toward alleviating the problems of the disease."

What is the main point here? "Well, that lack of public interest in the disease has hampered progress in understanding it." Cheers. The subject is *lack*; the predicate, *has hampered*; so what will the basic organization be? "Chronological—stages of hampering, development of the verb. But now I see I don't want that kind of organization. I want to talk about ways of studying retardation and how they need public support." So? So: "Most ways of studying and improving mental retardation depend on public understanding and support." Then you'll have to demonstrate the predicate *depend*, and talk about *how* and *why*. "That's what I want to talk about— three *hows* and one *why*." Now we are beginning to work out the development of an idea.

Chronology, spatial description, sequences work mainly with additive connectives: *and-and-and*; *then-then-then*; *also*; *moreover*—"Here are the main states in the study of retardation: such and such and such." Alternatives strive to separate, sometimes to compare: *either-or*; *on the one hand-on the other*; *not this, but that*—"Either we get public interest, or we give up." Conditional shows interdependent causal relations: *if-then*; *because-therefore*—"If public interest improves, our study of retardation will be aided in the following ways." This is the structure which, it turned out, our student intended to establish. Each of these procedures has its negatives. For example, *but* is a negative for *and*; *nor* for *or*; and concessional *though* for *if*.

The first help we can give the student writer then is to make him see whether the predication he has chosen to make, the verb he has chosen to apply to the subject, is really supportable by what he knows or can discover: and then, second, to see whether he has arranged the elements of support in the order and connection best for his purposes. A syllogism, the classic unit of reasoning, is in itself a small paragraph of substantiation. "I want to say something about Socrates, and what I want to say about him is that despite his great wisdom he is still mortal. Why is he mortal? Because all men are mortal, and Socrates is a man, as I can show in a paragraph of characteristics." Most of our thought concerns *some*, rather than the *all* referred to in this syllogism, but the pattern may be adapted to *some* by using recognition of negative as well as positive evidence: "Though two specific authorities deny it, public interest in retardation does help, and by public interest I mean not press-publicity, but active individual concern."

Reasoning means giving reasons: that is, it deals with the relations between statements, and these relations as we have said are of a few basic kinds: of cause or purpose—*if* this, therefore this, or this is so *because*; or of choice—this *or* this—both are impossible at once; or of association—this *and* this go along with this. Once a student recognizes that his own thought moves in these basic relations, he will be apt to enjoy both the art and the social force of the simple reasoning process of the paragraph. His planning or outlining will show first what main point or predication he is planning to make about his subject; then the main blocks of material he will use to support it, guided by such *pro* connections as *and, or, if* (and such *con* connections as *but, nor, though*); and finally a new main point, revised from the first hypothesis in the light of the evidence as it has developed. It is the predicate, not the subject, which is planned to be thus supported and modified. There is no such thing as too large or unwieldy a subject; what the student wants to say about the subject is what needs estimation. A student who tries to outline his material rather than his idea is trying, as one student has put it, to eat sardines without opening the can.

Man does not receive raw materials through the senses and then try to make meanings of them through the mind. Rather, the meanings that he makes, tentative and provisional as they may be at every stage, lead him to look for materials of experience which will test his meanings. So the writer does not need to stuff his mind with so-called "facts" before he can be responsible for a tentative statement; and so, on the other hand, for *any* statement he makes he can be held responsible. If we do not teach the student writer how to make responsible statements, we give in to the myths of "raw fact" or of individual autonomy, and make him the victim either of the outer world or of the inner. Thus we see the dangers on the one hand of the so-called "report" in composition-writing, which leads to an inert sort of copying, and on the other hand the dangers of journal writing or of so-called "creative" writing in which anything goes because there seems to be no valid outer check.

Why should we allow ourselves to be pulled between two extremes, when what we share is that very human power which philosophers have always spoken of, the power to agree on basic issues and to subordinate minor issues to major? For the Renaissance humanist, such reasonable powers served to mediate between man's sense and his spirit: so today it may mediate between man's psyche and his society. Robert Nisbet's *The Quest for Community* warns that so-called individual autonomy at one extreme and totalitarianism at the other tend to create a vacuum in between, where men actually live; and that men, to prevent this vacuum, need to strengthen the working categories of their own activities—their church, their club, their voting precinct, their job, to build a solid structure of human community between the forces of the personal and impersonal. So, I think, we need also to compose our thoughts: to learn to get from where we have been, to where we are, to where we want to go.

Thinking
and Feeling

ALMOST all the pieces in this book are records of men and women deliberately using their capacities to think and to feel in an effort to comprehend experience—either their own experience or that of other people and other times. It is fitting, then, that we present here a group of essays about thinking and feeling, activities that, however unavoidably and characteristically human, seem to have taken on a more problematic character than ever in recent times.

Many persons, notably the scientists, have been saying that in the post-atomic age thinking has become a matter of survival. The eminent biochemist Albert Szent-Gyorgyi, with the possibility of atomic war in mind, has put it plainly: "If it is our intelligence which led us into trouble it may be our intelligence which can lead us out of it." Though we cannot yet be certain what intelligence is (see the Dreyfus essay below), there has been general agreement since Plato and Aristotle's time that logical thought is one (though only one) of its components. Logical thought, a mastering of the processes of clear thinking, would seem, then, to be essential to us. The piece by Thomas H. Huxley which begins the section is the clearest exposition we know of two of the most common processes of logical thinking: induction and deduction.

But simply knowing the rules of logical thinking is not enough. What we accept rationally we often find hard to put into practice. Thinking is a discipline and an art, and often it is subverted rather than energized by feeling. Within us, what we think we think may be unsettling and sometimes in unconscious conflict with what we really feel. Recognition of this gives persuasiveness to the next three essays. William Golding's essay arises out of his awareness of the need to distinguish thought and feeling and is developed by a witty account of three different kinds of thinking. James Harvey Robinson's fuller and more philosophical treatment of kinds of   19 thinking rests similarly on his recognition of the unconscious and his wish to distinguish real thinking from emotional prejudice. Aldous Huxley, contrasting the intellectual's taste for rationality with the crowd's incapacity for moral choice, shows how "exploiting the secret fears and hopes, the cravings, anxieties and frustrations" of people can lead to their political enslavement. (The reader may wish to ponder whether "intellectuals" and "masses" are really different groups, as Huxley seems to imply, or whether the difference comes about in our own minds from one occasion to another.)

But even for trained thinkers, thinking is not enough. Threatened as we seem to be today by an impersonal, bureaucratic world, by a mechanized, standardized, alienating environment, we need more and more to be concerned with preserving our capacity to feel: to love, to sympathize, to imagine, to appreciate. For expressing feeling in words, of course, poetry is best; and so we print next three poems written largely in appreciation of feeling. (William Butler Yeats' poem, the most passionate and difficult of the three, uses the Greek myth of the god Zeus, who, in the form of a swan, made love to Queen Leda, engendering the beautiful Helen; Helen's abduction started the legendary Trojan War.)

Each of the four concluding essays takes up the relationship of feeling and thought. Norman Cousins, using the "computer" and the "poet" broadly as symbols of logical intelligence and creative imagination, points out the dangers of being satisfied with just the former. Colin Blakemore comments on some misinterpretations of recent split-brain research—misinterpretations which hold that the two sides of our brains, the one more verbal and ordered, and the other more nonverbal and intuitive, are somehow independent. He recommends that we strive in education for "the marriage and harmony of the two." Similarly, Mary Caroline Richards argues for wholeness, for the self coming together in equilibrium, the integration of thought and feeling in total experience. Marcel Proust, finally, takes up an instance in which thinking is properly dominated by feeling: Instinct comes before intellect at the moment when the artist tries to reach back to the impressions that are "the only material of art."

ON KINDS OF THINKING

THOMAS H. HUXLEY

Thomas Huxley (1825-1895)—British anatomist, embryologist, essayist, and lecturer— is one of the most memorable figures in nineteenth-century science. He was educated in medicine at the University of London. His extensive researches on marine animals, made in the course of serving as assistant surgeon on a naval vessel in the waters off Australia, gave him an early reputation as a first-class scientific investigator. He continued to publish technical scientific papers all his life, but he became engrossed early in advocating the

scientific method and its findings to a wide audience. The publication of Charles Dar-
win's Origin of Species *in 1859, and the controversy that it aroused, brought Huxley to*
Darwin's defense. His lectures and writings on evolution, and on the place of humans in
the universe, did much to establish a new freedom of debate and expression about matters
of religion.

A tireless person, Huxley also made notable contributions to elementary, technical, and
medical education, and was a strong advocate for higher education for women. He was
one of the first members of the London School Board. A great believer in liberal education
and in literature and the arts, he maintained that "a perfect culture . . . could not be
acquired without training in the methods of physical science."

Although Huxley spent much of his career as a college teacher and administrator, his
educational fervor embraced all types of people. In 1855 he began giving lectures specifi-
cally addressed to laborers. Many of his audience posed as workers in order to hear them.
Six of the lectures given in 1862, "On Our Knowledge of the Causes of the Phenomena
of Organic Nature," were devoted to Darwin's theories. The passage excerpted below is
from the third lecture in the series. It is found in the second volume of Huxley's Collected Essays *(9 vols., 1893–1894). For Huxley "the method of scientific investigation"*
was by no means limited to science. He confidently recommended its application "to all the
problems of life . . . in the conviction . . . that there is no alleviation for the sufferings of
mankind except veracity of thought and action, and the resolute facing of the world as it
is." The "missing links" referred to on page 24 are creatures of an imagined stage in
evolution between apes and humans.

The Method of Scientific Investigation

The method of scientific investigation is nothing but the expression of the
necessary mode of working of the human mind. It is simply the mode at
which all phenomena are reasoned about, rendered precise and exact.
There is no more difference, but there is just the same kind of difference,
between the mental operations of a man of science and those of an ordinary
person, as there is between the operations and methods of a baker or of a
butcher weighing out his goods in common scales, and the operations of a
chemist in performing a difficult and complex analysis by means of his
balance and finely-graduated weights. It is not that the action of the scales
in the one case, and the balance in the other, differ in the principles of their
construction or manner of working; but the beam of one is set on an infinitely finer axis than the other, and of course turns by the addition of a
much smaller weight.

You will understand this better, perhaps, if I give you some familiar
example. You have all heard it repeated, I dare say, that men of science
work by means of induction and deduction, and that by the help of these
operations, they, in a sort of sense, wring from Nature certain other things,
which are called natural laws, and causes, and that out of these, by some
cunning skill of their own, they build up hypotheses and theories. And it is
imagined by many, that the operations of the common mind can be by no

means compared with these processes, and that they have to be acquired by a sort of special apprenticeship to the craft. To hear all these large words, you would think that the mind of a man of science must be constituted differently from that of his fellow men; but if you will not be frightened by terms, you will discover that you are quite wrong, and that all these terrible apparatus are being used by yourselves every day and every hour of your lives.

There is a well-known incident in one of Molière's plays, where the author makes the hero express unbounded delight on being told that he had been talking prose during the whole of his life. In the same way, I trust, that you will take comfort, and be delighted with yourselves, on the discovery that you have been acting on the principles of inductive and deductive philosophy during the same period. Probably there is not one here who has not in the course of the day had occasion to set in motion a complex train of reasoning, of the very same kind, though differing of course in degree, as that which a scientific man goes through in tracing the causes of natural phenomena.

A very trivial circumstance will serve to exemplify this. Suppose you go into a fruiterer's shop, wanting an apple,—you take up one, and, on biting it, you find it is sour; you look at it, and see that it is hard and green. You take up another one, and that too is hard, green, and sour. The shopman offers you a third; but, before biting it, you examine it, and find that it is hard and green, and you immediately say that you will not have it, as it must be sour, like those that you have already tried.

Nothing can be more simple than that, you think; but if you will take the trouble to analyse and trace out into its logical elements what has been done by the mind, you will be greatly surprised. In the first place, you have performed the operation of induction. You found that, in two experiences, hardness and greenness in apples went together with sourness. It was so in the first case, and it was confirmed by the second. True, it is a very small basis, but still it is enough to make an induction from; you generalise the facts, and you expect to find sourness in apples where you get hardness and greenness. You found upon that a general law, that all hard and green apples are sour; and that, so far as it goes, is a perfect induction. Well, having got your natural law in this way, when you are offered another apple which you find is hard and green, you say, "All hard and green apples are sour; this apple is hard and green, therefore this apple is sour." That train of reasoning is what logicians call a syllogism, and has all its various parts and terms,—its major premiss, its minor premiss, and its conclusion. And, by the help of further reasoning, which, if drawn out, would have to be exhibited in two or three other syllogisms, you arrive at your final determination, "I will not have that apple." So that, you see, you have, in the first place, established a law by induction, and upon that you have founded a deduction, and reasoned out the special conclusion of the particular case. Well now, suppose, having got your law, that at some time afterwards, you are discussing the qualities of apples with a friend: you will say to him, "It is a very curious thing,—but I find that all hard and green apples are sour!" Your friend says to you, "But how do you know that?" You at once reply, "Oh, because I have tried them over and over again, and have always found them to be so." Well, if we were talking science instead of common sense, we should call that an experimental verification. And, if still opposed, you go further, and say, "I have heard from the people in Somersetshire and Devonshire, where a large number of apples are grown, that they have observed the same thing. It is also found to be the case in Normandy, and in North America. In short, I find it to be the universal experience of mankind wherever attention has been directed to the subject." Whereupon, your friend, unless he is a very unreasonable man, agrees with you, and is convinced that you are quite right in the conclusion you have drawn. He believes, although perhaps he does not know he believes it, that the more extensive verifications are,—that the more frequently experiments have been made, and results of the same kind arrived at,—that the more varied the conditions under which the same results are attained, the more certain is the ultimate conclusion, and he disputes the question no further. He sees that the experiment has been tried under all sorts of conditions, as to time, place, and people, with the same result; and he says with you, therefore, that the law you have laid down must be a good one, and he must believe it.

In science we do the same thing;—the philosopher exercises precisely the same faculties, though in a much more delicate manner. In scientific inquiry it becomes a matter of duty to expose a supposed law to every possible kind of verification, and to take care, moreover, that this is done intentionally, and not left to a mere accident, as in the case of the apples. And in science, as in common life, our confidence in a law is in exact proportion to the absence of variation in the result of our experimental verifications. For instance, if you let go your grasp of an article you may have in your hand, it will immediately fall to the ground. That is a very common verification of one of the best established laws of nature—that of gravitation. The method by which men of science establish the existence of that law is exactly the same as that by which we have established the trivial proposition about the sourness of hard and green apples. But we believe it in such an extensive, thorough, and unhesitating manner because the universal experience of mankind verifies it, and we can verify it ourselves at any time; and that is the strongest possible foundation on which any natural law can rest.

So much, then, by way of proof that the method of establishing laws in science is exactly the same as that pursued in common life. Let us now turn to another matter (though really it is but another phase of the same question), and that is, the method by which, from the relations of certain phenomena, we prove that some stand in the position of causes towards the others.

I want to put the case clearly before you, and I will therefore show you what I mean by another familiar example. I will suppose that one of you, on coming down in the morning to the parlour of your house, finds that a teapot and some spoons which had been left in the room on the previous evening are gone,—the window is open, and you observe the mark of a dirty hand on the window-frame, and perhaps, in addition to that, you notice the impress of a hob-nailed shoe on the gravel outside. All these phenomena have struck your attention instantly, and before two seconds have passed you say, "Oh somebody has broken open the window, entered the room, and run off with the spoons and the tea-pot!" That speech is out of your mouth in a moment. And you will probably add, "I know there has; I am quite sure of it!" You mean to say exactly what you know; but in reality you are giving expression to what is, in all essential particulars, an hypothesis. You do not *know* it at all; it is nothing but an hypothesis rapidly framed in your own mind. And it is an hypothesis founded on a long train of inductions and deductions.

What are those inductions and deductions, and how have you got at this hypothesis? You have observed, in the first place, that the window is open; but by a train of reasoning involving many inductions and deductions, you have probably arrived long before at the general law—and a very good one it is—that windows do not open of themselves; and you therefore conclude that something has opened the window. A second general law that you have arrived at in the same way is, that tea-pots and spoons do not go out of a window spontaneously, and you are satisfied that, as they are not now where you left them, they have been removed. In the third place, you look at the marks on the window-sill, and the shoe-marks outside, and you say that in all previous experience the former kind of mark has never been produced by anything else but the hand of a human being; and the same experience shows that no other animal but man at present wears shoes with hob-nails in them such as would produce the marks in the gravel. I do not know, even if we could discover any of those "missing links" that are talked about, that they would help us to any other conclusion! At any rate the law which states our present experience is strong enough for my present purpose. You next reach the conclusion, that as these kinds of marks have not been left by any other animals than men, or are liable to be formed in any other way than by a man's hand and shoe, the marks in question have been formed by a man in that way. You have, further, a general law, founded on observation and experience, and that, too, is, I am sorry to say, a very universal and unimpeachable one,—that some men are thieves; and you assume at once from all these premises—and that is what constitutes your hypothesis—that the man who made the marks outside and on the window-sill, opened the window, got into the room, and stole your tea-pot and spoons. You have now arrived at a *vera causa*;—you have assumed a cause which, it is plain, is competent to produce all the phenomena you have observed. You can explain all these phenomena only by the hypothesis of a thief. But that is a hypothetical conclusion, of the justice of which you have no absolute proof at all; it is only rendered highly probable by a series of inductive and deductive reasonings.

I suppose your first action, assuming that you are a man of ordinary common sense, and that you have established this hypothesis to your own satisfaction, will very likely be to go off for the police, and set them on the track of the burglar, with the view to the recovery of your property. But just as you are starting with this object, some person comes in, and on learning what you are about, says, "My good friend, you are going on a great deal too fast. How do you know that the man who really made the marks took the spoons? It might have been a monkey that took them, and the man may have merely looked in afterwards." You would probably reply, "Well, that is all very well, but you see it is contrary to all experience of the way tea-pots and spoons are abstracted; so that, at any rate, your hypothesis is less probable than mine." While you are talking the thing over in this way, another friend arrives, one of that good kind of people that I was talking of a little while ago. And he might say, "Oh, my dear sir, you are certainly going on a great deal too fast. You are most presumptuous. You admit that all these occurrences took place when you were fast asleep, at a time when you could not possibly have known anything about what was taking place. How do you know that the laws of Nature are not suspended during the night? It may be that there has been some kind of supernatural interference in this case." In point of fact, he declares that your hypothesis is one of which you cannot at all demonstrate the truth, and that you are by no means sure that the laws of Nature are the same when you are asleep as when you are awake.

Well, now, you cannot at the moment answer that kind of reasoning. You feel that your worthy friend has you somewhat at a disadvantage. You will feel perfectly convinced in your own mind, however, that you are quite right, and you say to him, "My good friend, I can only be guided by the natural probabilities of the case, and if you will be kind enough to stand aside and permit me to pass, I will go and fetch the police." Well, we will suppose that your journey is successful, and that by good luck you meet with a policeman; that eventually the burglar is found with your property on his person, and the marks correspond to his hand and to his boots. Probably any jury would consider those facts a very good experimental verification of your hypothesis, touching the cause of the abnormal phenomena observed in your parlour, and would act accordingly.

Now, in this suppositious case, I have taken phenomena of a very common kind, in order that you might see what are the different steps in an ordinary process of reasoning, if you will only take the trouble to analyse it carefully. All the operations I have described, you will see, are involved in the mind of any man of sense in leading him to a conclusion as to the course he should take in order to make good a robbery and punish the offender. I say that you are led, in that case, to your conclusion by exactly the same train of reasoning as that which a man of science pursues when he is endeav-ouring to discover the origin and laws of the most occult phenomena. The process is, and always must be, the same; and precisely the same mode of reasoning was employed by Newton and Laplace in their endeavours to discover and define the causes of the movements of the heavenly bodies, as you, with your own common sense, would employ to detect a burglar. The only difference is, that the nature of the inquiry being more abstruse, every step has to be most carefully watched, so that there may not be a single crack or flaw in your hypothesis. A flaw or crack in many of the hypotheses of daily life may be of little or no moment as affecting the general correctness of the conclusions at which we may arrive; but, in a scientific inquiry, a fallacy, great or small, is always of importance, and is sure to be in the long run constantly productive of mischievous, if not fatal results.

Do not allow yourselves to be misled by the common notion that an hypothesis is untrustworthy simply because it is an hypothesis. It is often urged, in respect to some scientific conclusion, that, after all, it is only an hypothesis. But what more have we to guide us in nine-tenths of the most important affairs of daily life than hypotheses, and often very ill-based ones? So that in science, where the evidence of an hypothesis is subjected to the most rigid examination, we may rightly pursue the same course. You may have hypotheses and hypotheses. A man may say, if he likes, that the moon is made of green cheese: that is an hypothesis. But another man, who has devoted a great deal of time and attention to the subject, and availed himself of the most powerful telescopes and the results of the observations of others, declares that in his opinion it is probably composed of materials very similar to those of which our own earth is made up: and that is also only an hypothesis. But I need not tell you that there is an enormous difference in the value of the two hypotheses. That one which is based on sound scientific knowledge is sure to have a corresponding value; and that which is a mere hasty random guess is likely to have but little value. Every great step in our progress in discovering causes has been made in exactly the same way as that which I have detailed to you. A person observing the occurrence of certain facts and phenomena asks, naturally enough, what process, what kind of operation known to occur in Nature applied to the particular case, will unravel and explain the mystery? Hence you have the scientific hypothesis; and its value will be proportionate to the care and completeness with which its basis had been tested and verified. It is in these matters as in the commonest affairs of practical life: the guess of the fool will be folly, while the guess of the wise man will contain wisdom. In all cases, you see that the value of the result depends on the patience and faithfulness with which the investigator applies to his hypothesis every possible kind of verification.

WILLIAM GOLDING

William Gerald Golding, a British author, was born in 1911 and educated at Marlborough grammar school and at Oxford. At first destined for a scientific career, he shifted his attention to literature after two years in the university and published a volume of poems. During World War II he served in the Royal Navy, rising to the command of a rocket-launching ship. Since the war he has devoted himself to teaching and writing, and to his hobbies, which he once described as "thinking, classical Greek, sailing, and archaeology." He is widely known for his strikingly original novels, especially Pincher Martin *(1956), describing the feelings of a shipwrecked sailor on an isolated rock in mid-ocean, and* Lord of the Flies *(1954), a symbolic account of a group of schoolboys who revert to savagery when marooned on an island. His more recent fiction includes three novellas entitled* The Scorpion God *(1971), and* Darkness Visible *(1979), a "magical fable" set in contemporary England. The present essay first appeared in the August 1961 issue of* Holiday.

Thinking as a Hobby

While I was still a boy, I came to the conclusion that there were three grades of thinking; and since I was later to claim thinking as my hobby, I came to an even stranger conclusion—namely, that I myself could not think at all.

I must have been an unsatisfactory child for grownups to deal with. I remember how incomprehensible they appeared to me at first, but not, of course, how I appeared to them. It was the headmaster of my grammar school who first brought the subject of thinking before me—though neither in the way, nor with the result he intended. He had some statuettes in his study. They stood on a high cupboard behind his desk. One was a lady wearing nothing but a bath towel. She seemed frozen in an eternal panic lest the bath towel slip down any farther; and since she had no arms, she was in an unfortunate position to pull the towel up again. Next to her, crouched the statuette of a leopard, ready to spring down at the top drawer of a filing cabinet labeled A–AH. My innocence interpreted this as the victim's last, despairing cry. Beyond the leopard was a naked, muscular gentleman, who sat, looking down, with his chin on his fist and his elbow on his knee. He seemed utterly miserable.

Some time later, I learned about these statuettes. The headmaster had placed them where they would face delinquent children, because they symbolized to him the whole of life. The naked lady was the Venus of Milo. She was Love. She was not worried about the towel. She was just busy being beautiful. The leopard was Nature, and he was being natural. The naked, muscular gentleman was not miserable. He was Rodin's Thinker, an image of pure thought. It is easy to buy small plaster models of what you think life is like.

I had better explain that I was a frequent visitor to the headmaster's study, because of the latest thing I had done or left undone. As we now say, I was not integrated. I was, if anything, disintegrated; and I was puzzled. Grownups never made sense. Whenever I found myself in a penal position before the headmaster's desk, with the statuettes glimmering whitely above him, I would sink my head, clasp my hands behind my back and writhe one shoe over the other.

The headmaster would look opaquely at me through flashing spectacles.

"What are we going to do with you?"

Well, what *were* they going to do with me? I would writhe my shoe some more and stare down at the worn rug.

"Look up, boy! Can't you look up?"

Then I would look up at the cupboard, where the naked lady was frozen in her panic and the muscular gentleman contemplated the hindquarters of the leopard in endless gloom. I had nothing to say to the headmaster. His spectacles caught the light so that you could see nothing human behind them. There was no possibility of communication.

"Don't you ever think at all?"

No, I didn't think, wasn't thinking, couldn't think—I was simply waiting in anguish for the interview to stop.

"Then you'd better learn—hadn't you?"

On one occasion the headmaster leaped to his feet, reached up and plonked Rodin's masterpiece on the desk before me.

"That's what a man looks like when he's really thinking."

I surveyed the gentleman without interest or comprehension.

"Go back to your class."

Clearly there was something missing in me. Nature had endowed the rest of the human race with a sixth sense and left me out. This must be so, I mused, on my way back to the class, since whether I had broken a window, or failed to remember Boyle's Law, or been late for school, my teachers produced me one, adult answer: "Why can't you think?"

As I saw the case, I had broken the window because I had tried to hit Jack Arney with a cricket ball and missed him; I could not remember Boyle's Law because I had never bothered to learn it; and I was late for school because I preferred looking over the bridge into the river. In fact, I was wicked. Were my teachers, perhaps, so good that they could not understand the depths of my depravity? Were they clear, untormented people who could direct their every action by this mysterious business of thinking? The whole thing was incomprehensible. In my earlier years, I found even the statuette of the Thinker confusing. I did not believe any of my teachers were naked, ever. Like someone born deaf, but bitterly determined to find out about sound, I watched my teachers to find out about thought.

There was Mr. Houghton. He was always telling me to think. With a modest satisfaction, he would tell me that he had thought a bit himself. Then why did he spend so much time drinking? Or was there more sense in drinking than there appeared to be? But if not, and if drinking were in fact ruinous to health—and Mr. Houghton was ruined, there was no doubt about that—why was he always talking about the clean life and the virtues of fresh air? He would spread his arms wide with the action of a man who habitually spent his time striding along mountain ridges.

"Open air does me good, boys—I know it!"

Sometimes, exalted by his own oratory, he would leap from his desk and hustle us outside into a hideous wind.

"Now, boys! Deep breaths! Feel it right down inside you—huge draughts of God's good air!"

He would stand before us, rejoicing in his perfect health, an open-air man. He would put his hands on his waist and take a tremendous breath. You could hear the wind, trapped in the cavern of his chest and struggling with all the unnatural impediments. His body would reel with shock and his ruined face go white at the unaccustomed visitation. He would stagger back to his desk and collapse there, useless for the rest of the morning.

Mr. Houghton was given to high-minded monologues about the good life, sexless and full of duty. Yet in the middle of one of these monologues, if a girl passed the window, tapping along on her neat little feet, he would interrupt his discourse, his neck would turn of itself and he would watch her out of sight. In this instance, he seemed to me ruled not by thought but by an invisible and irresistible spring in his nape.

His neck was an object of great interest to me. Normally it bulged a bit over his collar. But Mr. Houghton had fought in the First World War alongside both Americans and French, and had come—by who knows what illogic?—to a settled detestation of both countries. If either country happened to be prominent in current affairs, no argument could make Mr. Houghton think well of it. He would bang the desk, his neck would bulge still further and go red. "You can say what you like," he would cry, "but I've thought about this—and I know what I think!"

Mr. Houghton thought with his neck.

There was Miss Parsons. She assured us that her dearest wish was our welfare, but I knew even then, with the mysterious clairvoyance of childhood, that what she wanted most was the husband she never got. There was Mr. Hands—and so on.

I have dealt at length with my teachers because this was my introduction to the nature of what is commonly called thought. Through them I discovered that thought is often full of unconscious prejudice, ignorance and hypocrisy. It will lecture on disinterested purity while its neck is being remorselessly twisted toward a skirt. Technically, it is about as proficient as most businessmen's golf, as honest as most politicians' intentions, or—to come near my own preoccupation—as coherent as most books that get written. It is what I came to call grade-three thinking, though more properly, it is feeling, rather than thought.

True, often there is a kind of innocence in prejudices, but in those days I viewed grade-three thinking with an intolerant contempt and an incautious mockery. I delighted to confront a pious lady who hated the Germans with the proposition that we should love our enemies. She taught me a great truth in dealing with grade-three thinkers; because of her, I no longer dismiss lightly a mental process which for nine-tenths of the population is the nearest they will ever get to thought. They have immense solidarity. We had better respect them, for we are outnumbered and surrounded. A crowd of grade-three thinkers, all shouting the same thing, all warming their hands at the fire of their own prejudices, will not thank you for pointing out the contradictions in their beliefs. Man is a gregarious animal, and enjoys agreement as cows will graze all the same way on the side of a hill.

Grade-two thinking is the detection of contradictions. I reached grade two when I trapped the poor, pious lady. Grade-two thinkers do not stampede easily, though often they fall into the other fault and lag behind. Grade-two thinking is a withdrawal, with eyes and ears open. It became my hobby and brought satisfaction and loneliness in either hand. For grade-two thinking destroys without having the power to create. It set me watching the crowds cheering His Majesty the King and asking myself what all the fuss was about, without giving me anything positive to put in the place of that heady patriotism. But there were compensations. To hear people justify their habit of hunting foxes and tearing them to pieces by claiming that the foxes liked it. To hear our Prime Minister talk about the great benefit we conferred on India by jailing people like Pandit Nehru and Gandhi. To hear American politicians talk about peace in one sentence and refuse to join the League of Nations in the next. Yes, there were moments of delight.

But I was growing toward adolescence and had to admit that Mr. Houghton was not the only one with an irresistible spring in his neck. I, too, felt the compulsive hand of nature and began to find that pointing out contradiction could be costly as well as fun. There was Ruth, for example, a serious and attractive girl. I was an atheist at the time. Grade-two thinking is a menace to religion and knocks down sects like skittles. I put myself in a position to be converted by her with an hypocrisy worthy of grade three. She was a Methodist—or at least, her parents were, and Ruth had to follow suit. But, alas, instead of relying on the Holy Spirit to convert me, Ruth was foolish enough to open her pretty mouth in argument. She claimed that the Bible (King James Version) was literally inspired. I countered by saying that the Catholics believed in the literal inspiration of Saint Jerome's *Vulgate*, and the two books were different. Argument flagged.

At last she remarked that there were an awful lot of Methodists, and they couldn't be wrong, could they—not all those millions? That was too easy, said I restively (for the nearer you were to Ruth, the nicer she was to be near to) since there were more Roman Catholics than Methodists anyway; and they couldn't be wrong, could they—not all those hundreds of millions? An awful flicker of doubt appeared in her eyes. I slid my arm round her waist and murmured breathlessly that if we were counting heads, the Buddhists were the boys for my money. But Ruth had *really* wanted to do me good, because I was so nice. She fled. The combination of my arm and those countless Buddhists was too much for her.

That night her father visited my father and left, red-cheeked and indignant. I was given the third degree to find out what had happened. It was lucky we were both of us only fourteen. I lost Ruth and gained an undeserved reputation as a potential libertine.

So grade-two thinking could be dangerous. It was in this knowledge, at the age of fifteen, that I remember making a comment from the heights of grade two, on the limitations of grade three. One evening I found myself alone in the schoolhall, preparing it for a party. The door of the headmaster's study was open. I went in. The headmaster had ceased to thump Rodin's Thinker down on the desk as an example to the young. Perhaps he had not found any more candidates, but the statuettes were still there, glimmering and gathering dust on top of the cupboard. I stood on a chair and rearranged them. I stood Venus in her bath towel on the filing cabinet, so that now the top drawer caught its breath in a gasp of sexy excitement. "A-ah!" The portentous Thinker I placed on the edge of the cupboard so that he looked down at the bath towel and waited for it to slip.

Grade-two thinking, though it filled life with fun and excitement, did not make for content. To find out the deficiencies of our elders bolsters the young ego but does not make for personal security. I found that grade two was not only the power to point out contradictions. It took the swimmer some distance from the shore and left him there, out of his depth. I decided that Pontius Pilate was a typical grade-two thinker. "What is truth?" he said, a very common grade-two thought, but one that is used always as the end of an argument instead of the beginning. There is a still higher grade of thought which says, "What is truth?" and sets out to find it.

But these grade-one thinkers were few and far between. They did not visit my grammar school in the flesh though they were there in books. I aspired to them, partly because I was ambitious and partly because I now saw my hobby as an unsatisfactory thing if it went no further. If you set out to climb a mountain, however high you climb, you have failed if you cannot reach the top.

I *did* meet an undeniably grade-one thinker in my first year at Oxford. I was looking over a small bridge in Magdalen Deer Park, and a tiny mustached and hatted figure came and stood by my side. He was a German who had just fled from the Nazis to Oxford as a temporary refuge. His name was Einstein.

But Professor Einstein knew no English at that time and I knew only two words of German. I beamed at him, trying wordlessly to convey by my bearing all the affection and respect that the English felt for him. It is possible—and I have to make the admission—that I felt here were two grade-one thinkers standing side by side; yet I doubt if my face conveyed more than a formless awe. I would have given my Greek and Latin and French and a good slice of my English for enough German to communicate. But we were divided; he was as inscrutable as my headmaster. For perhaps five minutes we stood together on the bridge, undeniable grade-one thinker and breathless aspirant. With true greatness, Professor Einstein realized that any contact was better than none. He pointed to a trout wavering in midstream.

He spoke: *"Fisch."*

My brain reeled. Here I was, mingling with the great, and yet helpless as the veriest grade-three thinker. Desperately I sought for some sign by which I might convey that I, too, revered pure reason. I nodded vehemently. In a brilliant flash I used up half of my German vocabulary. *"Fisch. Ja. Ja."*

For perhaps another five minutes we stood side by side. Then Professor Einstein, his whole figure still conveying good will and amiability, drifted away out of sight.

I, too, would be a grade-one thinker. I was irreverent at the best of times. Political and religious systems, social customs, loyalties and traditions, they all came tumbling down like so many rotten apples off a tree. This was a fine hobby and a sensible substitute for cricket, since you could play it all the year round. I came up in the end with what must always remain the justification for grade-one thinking, its sign, seal and charter. I devised a coherent system for living. It was a moral system, which was wholly logical. Of course, as I readily admitted, conversion of the world to my way of thinking might be difficult, since my system did away with a number of trifles, such as big business, centralized government, armies, marriage. . . .

It was Ruth all over again. I had some very good friends who stood by me, and still do. But my acquaintances vanished, taking the girls with them. Young women seemed oddly contented with the world as it was. They valued the meaningless ceremony with a ring. Young men, while willing to concede the chaining sordidness of marriage, were hesitant about abandoning the organizations which they hoped would give them a career. A young man on the first rung of the Royal Navy, while perfectly agreeable to doing away with big business and marriage, got as red-necked as Mr. Houghton when I proposed a world without any battleships in it.

Had the game gone too far? Was it a game any longer? In those prewar days, I stood to lose a great deal, for the sake of a hobby.

Now you are expecting me to describe how I saw the folly of my ways and came back to the warm nest, where prejudices are so often called loyalties, where pointless actions are hallowed into custom by repetition, where we are content to say we think when all we do is feel.

But you would be wrong. I dropped my hobby and turned professional.

If I were to go back to the headmaster's study and find the dusty statuettes still there, I would arrange them differently. I would dust Venus and put her aside, for I have come to love her and know her for the fair thing she is. But I would put the Thinker, sunk in his desperate thought, where there were shadows before him—and at his back, I would put the leopard, crouched and ready to spring.

JAMES HARVEY ROBINSON

James Harvey Robinson (1863–1936), American historian and university professor, was educated at Harvard and Freiburg. He taught history at the University of Pennsylvania and from 1895 to 1919 at Columbia. Resigning in 1919 in protest against the expulsion of a group of professors for their opposition to World War I, he attacked Columbia president Nicholas Murray Butler for his alleged attempts to suppress freedom of expression at the University. Robinson then helped to found the New School for Social Research in New York City, and he taught there until 1921, when he retired to devote the rest of his life to writing. Among his dozen volumes of historical and philosophical writing, perhaps the best known to the general public is The Mind in the Making *(1921), subtitled* The Relation of Intelligence to Social Reform. *Chapter 2 of this book has been excerpted and reprinted so often that it has itself been the subject of an amusing article by Professor David Novarr ("OVKOT," AAUP Bulletin, vol. 37, 1951). But familiarity has not reduced its value. We reprint the chapter here in full, using the heading of the first section as title for the whole.*

On Various Kinds of Thinking

Good sense is, of all things among men, the most equally distributed; for everyone thinks himself so abundantly provided with it that those even who are the most difficult to satisfy in everything else do not usually desire a larger measure of this quality than they already possess.

—DESCARTES

We see man to-day, instead of the frank and courageous recognition of his status, the docile attention to his biological history, the determination to let nothing stand in the way of the security and permanence of his future, which alone can establish the safety and happiness of the race, substituting blind confidence in his destiny, unclouded faith in the essentially respectful attitude of the universe toward his moral code, and a belief no less firm that his traditions and laws and institutions necessarily contain permanent qualities of reality.

—WILLIAM TROTTER

1. On Various Kinds of Thinking

The truest and most profound observations on Intelligence have in the past been made by the poets and, in recent times, by story-writers. They have been keen observers and recorders and reckoned freely with the emotions and sentiments. Most philosophers, on the other hand, have exhibited a grotesque ignorance of man's life and have built up systems that are elaborate and imposing, but quite unrelated to actual human affairs. They have almost consistently neglected the actual process of thought and have set the mind off as something apart to be studied by itself. *But no such mind, exempt from bodily processes, animal impulses, savage traditions, infantile impressions, conventional reactions, and traditional knowledge, ever existed,* even in the case of the most abstract of metaphysicians. Kant entitled his great work *A Critique of Pure Reason.* But to the modern student of mind pure reason seems as mythical as the pure gold, transparent as glass, with which the celestial city is paved.

Formerly philosophers thought of mind as having to do exclusively with conscious thought. It was that within man which perceived, remembered, judged, reasoned, understood, believed, willed. But of late it has been shown that we are unaware of a great part of what we perceive, remember, will, and infer; and that a great part of the thinking of which we are aware is determined by that of which we are not conscious. It has indeed been demonstrated that our unconscious psychic life far outruns our conscious. This seems perfectly natural to anyone who considers the following facts:

The sharp distinction between the mind and the body is, as we shall find, a very ancient and spontaneous uncritical savage prepossession. What we think of as "mind" is so intimately associated with what we call "body" that we are coming to realize that the one cannot be understood without the other. Every thought reverberates through the body, and, on the other hand, alterations in our physical condition affect our whole attitude of mind. The insufficient elimination of the foul and decaying products of digestion may plunge us into deep melancholy, whereas a few whiffs of nitrous monoxide may exalt us to the seventh heaven of supernal knowledge and godlike complacency. And *vice versa*, a sudden word or thought may cause our heart to jump, check our breathing, or make our knees as water. There is a whole new literature growing up which studies the effects of our bodily secretions and our muscular tensions and their relation to our emotions and our thinking.

Then there are hidden impulses and desires and secret longings of which we can only with the greatest difficulty take account. They influence our conscious thought in the most bewildering fashion. Many of these unconscious influences appear to originate in our very early years. The older philosophers seem to have forgotten that even they were infants and children at their most impressionable age and never could by any possibility get over it.

The term "unconscious," now so familiar to all readers of modern works on psychology, gives offense to some adherents of the past. There should, however, be no special mystery about it. It is not a new animistic abstraction, but simply a collective word to include all the physiological changes which escape our notice, all the forgotten experiences and impressions of the past which continue to influence our desires and reflections and conduct, even if we cannot remember them. What we can remember at any time is indeed an infinitesimal part of what has happened to us. We could not remember anything unless we forgot almost everything. As Bergson says, the brain is the organ of forgetfulness as well as of memory. Moreover, we tend, of course, to become oblivious to things to which we are thoroughly accustomed, for habit blinds us to their existence. So the forgotten and the habitual make up a great part of the so-called "unconscious."

If we are ever to understand man, his conduct and reasoning, and if we aspire to learn to guide his life and his relations with his fellows more happily than heretofore, we cannot neglect the great discoveries briefly noted above. We must reconcile ourselves to novel and revolutionary conceptions of the mind, for it is clear that the older philosophers, whose works still determine our current views, had a very superficial notion of the subject with which they dealt. But for our purposes, with due regard to what has just been said and to much that has necessarily been left unsaid (and with the indulgence of those who will at first be inclined to dissent), *we shall consider mind chiefly as conscious knowledge and intelligence, as what we know and our attitude toward it—our disposition to increase our information, classify it, and apply it.*

We do not think enough about thinking, and much of our confusion is the result of current illusions in regard to it. Let us forget for the moment any impressions we may have derived from the philosophers, and see what seems to happen in ourselves. The first thing that we notice is that our thought moves with such incredible rapidity that it is almost impossible to arrest any specimen of it long enough to have a look at it. When we are offered a penny for our thoughts we always find that we have recently had so many things in mind that we can easily make a selection which will not compromise us too nakedly. On inspection we shall find that even if we are not downright ashamed of a great part of our spontaneous thinking it is far too intimate, personal, ignoble or trivial to permit us to reveal more than a small part of it. I believe this must be true of everyone. We do not, of course, know what goes on in other people's heads. They tell us very little and we tell them very little. The spigot of speech, rarely fully opened, could never emit more than driblets of the ever renewed hogshead of thought—*noch grösser wie's Heidelberger Fass*. We find it hard to believe that other people's thoughts are as silly as our own, but they probably are.

We all appear to ourselves to be thinking all the time during our waking hours, and most of us are aware that we go on thinking while we are asleep, even more foolishly than when awake. When uninterrupted by some practical issue we are engaged in what is now known as a *reverie*. This is our spontaneous and favorite kind of thinking. We allow our ideas to take their own course and this course is determined by our hopes and fears, our spontaneous desires, their fulfillment or frustration; by our likes and dislikes, our loves and hates and resentments. There is nothing else anything like so interesting to ourselves as ourselves. All thought that is not more or less laboriously controlled and directed will inevitably circle about the beloved Ego. It is amusing and pathetic to observe this tendency in ourselves and in others. We learn politely and generously to overlook this truth, but if we dare to think of it, it blazes forth like the noontide sun.

The reverie or "free association of ideas" has of late become the subject of scientific research. While investigators are not yet agreed on the results, or at least on the proper interpretation to be given to them, there can be no doubt that our reveries form the chief index to our fundamental character. They are a reflection of our nature as modified by often hidden and forgotten experiences. We need not go into the matter further here, for it is only necessary to observe that the reverie is at all times a potent and in many cases an omnipotent rival to every other kind of thinking. It doubtless influences all our speculations in its persistent tendency to self-magnification and self-justification, which are its chief preoccupations, but it is the last thing to make directly or indirectly for honest increase of knowledge.[1] Philosophers usually talk as if such thinking did not exist or were in some way negligible. This is what makes their speculations so unreal and often worthless.

The reverie, as any of us can see for himself, is frequently broken and interrupted by the necessity of a second kind of thinking. We have to make practical decisions. Shall we write a letter or no? Shall we take the subway or a bus? Shall we have dinner at seven or half past? Shall we buy U.S. Rubber or a Liberty Bond? Decisions are easily distinguishable from the free

---

[1] The poet-clergyman, John Donne, who lived in the time of James I, has given a beautifully honest picture of the doings of a saint's mind: "I throw myself down in my chamber and call in and invite God and His angels thither, and when they are there I neglect God and His angels for the noise of a fly, for the rattling of a coach, for the whining of a door. I talk on in the same posture of praying, eyes lifted up, knees bowed down, as though I prayed to God, and if God or His angels should ask me when I thought last of God in that prayer I cannot tell. Sometimes I find that I had forgot what I was about, but when I began to forget it I cannot tell. A memory of yesterday's pleasures, a fear of to-morrow's dangers, a straw under my knee, a noise in mine ear, a light in mine eye, an anything, a nothing, a fancy, a chimera in my brain troubles me in my prayer."—Quoted by Robert Lynd, *The Art of Letters*, pp. 46–47.

flow of the reverie. Sometimes they demand a good deal of careful pondering and the recollection of pertinent facts; often, however, they are made impulsively. They are a more difficult and laborious thing than the reverie, and we resent having to "make up our mind" when we are tired, or absorbed in a congenial reverie. Weighing a decision, it should be noted, does not necessarily add anything to our knowledge, although we may, of course, seek further information before making it.

2. Rationalizing

A third kind of thinking is stimulated when anyone questions our belief and opinions. We sometimes find ourselves changing our minds without any resistance or heavy emotion, but if we are told that we are wrong we resent the imputation and harden our hearts. We are incredibly heedless in the formation of our beliefs, but find ourselves filled with an illicit passion for them when anyone proposes to rob us of their companionship. It is obviously not the ideas themselves that are dear to us, but our self-esteem, which is threatened. We are by nature stubbornly pledged to defend our own from attack, whether it be our person, our family, our property, or our opinion. A United States Senator once remarked to a friend of mine that God Almighty could not make him change his mind on our Latin-America policy. We may surrender, but rarely confess ourselves vanquished. In the intellectual world at least peace is without victory.

Few of us take the pains to study the origin of our cherished convictions; indeed, we have a natural repugnance to so doing. We like to continue to believe what we have been accustomed to accept as true, and the resentment aroused when doubt is cast upon any of our assumptions leads us to seek every manner of excuse for clinging to them. *The result is that most of our so-called reasoning consists in finding arguments for going on believing as we already do.*

I remember years ago attending a public dinner to which the Governor of the state was bidden. The chairman explained that His Excellency could not be present for certain "good" reasons; what the "real" reasons were the presiding officer said he would leave us to conjecture. This distinction between "good" and "real" reasons is one of the most clarifying and essential in the whole realm of thought. We can readily give what seem to us "good" reasons for being a Catholic or a Mason, a Republican or a Democrat, an adherent or opponent of the League of Nations. But the "real" reasons are usually on quite a different plane. Of course the importance of this distinction is popularly, if somewhat obscurely, recognized. The Baptist missionary is ready enough to see that the Buddhist is not such because his doctrines would bear careful inspection, but because he happened to be born in a Buddhist family in Tokio. But it would be treason to his faith to acknowledge that his own partiality for certain doctrines is due to the fact that his mother was a member of the First Baptist church of Oak Ridge. A savage can give all sorts of reasons for his belief that it is dangerous to step on a man's shadow, and a newspaper editor can advance plenty of arguments against the Bolsheviki. But neither of them may realize why he happens to be defending his particular opinion.

The "real" reasons for our beliefs are concealed from ourselves as well as from others. As we grow up we simply adopt the ideas presented to us in regard to such matters as religion, family relations, property, business, our country, and the state. We unconsciously absorb them from our environment. They are persistently whispered in our ear by the group in which we happen to live. Moreover, as Mr. Trotter has pointed out, these judgments, being the product of suggestion and not of reasoning, have the quality of perfect obviousness, so that to question them

> . . . is to the believer to carry skepticism to an insane degree, and will be met by contempt, disapproval, or condemnation, according to the nature of the belief in question. When, therefore, we find ourselves entertaining an opinion about the basis of which there is a quality of feeling which tells us that to inquire into it would be absurd, obviously unnecessary, unprofitable, undesirable, bad form, or wicked, we may know that that opinion is a nonrational one, and probably, therefore, founded upon inadequate evidence.[2]

Opinions, on the other hand, which are the result of experience or of honest reasoning do not have this quality of "primary certitude." I remember when as a youth I heard a group of business men discussing the question of the immortality of the soul, I was outraged by the sentiment of doubt expressed by one of the party. As I look back now I see that I had at the time no interest in the matter, and certainly no least argument to urge in favor of the belief in which I had been reared. But neither my personal indifference to the issue, nor the fact that I had previously given it no attention, served to prevent an angry resentment when I heard *my* ideas questioned.

This spontaneous and loyal support of our preconceptions—this process of finding "good" reasons to justify our routine beliefs—is known to modern psychologists as "rationalizing"—clearly only a new name for a very ancient thing. Our "good" reasons ordinarily have no value in promoting honest enlightenment, because, no matter how solemnly they may be marshaled, they are at bottom the result of personal preference or prejudice, and not of an honest desire to seek or accept new knowledge.

In our reveries we are frequently engaged in self-justification, for we cannot bear to think ourselves wrong, and yet have constant illustrations of our weaknesses and mistakes. So we spend much time finding fault with circumstances and the conduct of others, and shifting on to them with great ingenuity the onus of our own failures and disappointments. *Rationalizing is the self-exculpation which occurs when we feel ourselves, or our group, accused of misapprehension or error.*

The little word *my* is the most important one in all human affairs, and properly to reckon with it is the beginning of wisdom. It has the same force whether it is *my* dinner, *my* dog, and *my* house, or *my* faith, *my* country, and *my* God. We not only resent the imputation that our watch is wrong, or our car shabby, but that our conception of the canals of Mars, of the pronunci-

---

[2] *Instincts of the Herd*, p. 44.

ation of "Epictetus," of the medicinal value of salicine, or the date of Sargon I, are subject to revision.

Philosophers, scholars, and men of science exhibit a common sensitiveness in all decisions in which their *amour propre* is involved. Thousands of argumentative works have been written to vent a grudge. However stately their reasoning, it may be nothing but rationalizing, stimulated by the most commonplace of all motives. A history of philosophy and theology could be written in terms of grouches, wounded pride, and aversions, and it would be far more instructive than the usual treatments of these themes. Sometimes, under Providence, the lowly impulse of resentment leads to great achievements. Milton wrote his treatise on divorce as a result of his troubles with his seventeen-year-old wife, and when he was accused of being the leading spirit in a new sect, the Divorcers, he wrote his noble *Areopagitica* to prove his right to say what he thought fit, and incidentally to establish the advantage of a free press in the promotion of Truth.

All mankind, high and low, thinks in all the ways which have been described. The reverie goes on all the time not only in the mind of the mill hand and the Broadway flapper, but equally in weighty judges and godly bishops. It has gone on in all the philosophers, scientists, poets, and theologians that have ever lived. Aristotle's most abstruse speculations were doubtless tempered by highly irrelevant reflections. He is reported to have had very thin legs and small eyes, for which he doubtless had to find excuses, and he was wont to indulge in very conspicuous dress and rings and was accustomed to arrange his hair carefully.[3] Diogenes the Cynic exhibited the impudence of a touchy soul. His tub was his distinction. Tennyson in beginning his "Maud" could not forget his chagrin over losing his patrimony years before as the result of an unhappy investment in the Patent Decorative Carving Company. These facts are not recalled here as a gratuitous disparagement of the truly great, but to insure a full realization of the tremendous competition which all really exacting thought has to face, even in the minds of the most highly endowed mortals.

And now the astonishing and perturbing suspicion emerges that perhaps almost all that had passed for social science, political economy, politics, and ethics in the past may be brushed aside by future generations as mainly rationalizing. John Dewey has already reached this conclusion in regard to philosophy.[4] Veblen[5] and other writers have revealed the various unperceived presuppositions of the traditional political economy, and now comes an Italian sociologist, Vilfredo Pareto, who, in his huge treatise on general sociology, devotes hundreds of pages to substantiating a similar thesis affecting all the social sciences.[6] This conclusion may be ranked by students of a

---

[3] Diogenes Laertius, book v.

[4] *Reconstruction in Philosophy.*

[5] *The Place of Science in Modern Civilization.*

[6] *Traité de Sociologie Générale, passim.* The author's term *"dérivations"* seems to be his precise way of expressing what we have called the "good" reasons, and his *"résidus"* correspond to the "real" reasons. He well says, *"L'homme éprouve le besoin de raisonner, et en outre d'étendre un voile sur ses instincts et sur ses sentiments"*—hence, rationalization. (P. 788.) His aim is to reduce sociology to the "real" reasons. (P. 791.)

hundred years hence as one of the several great discoveries of our age. It is by no means fully worked out, and it is so opposed to nature that it will be very slowly accepted by the great mass of those who consider themselves thoughtful. As a historical student I am personally fully reconciled to this newer view. Indeed, it seems to me inevitable that just as the various sciences of nature were, before the opening of the seventeenth century, largely masses of rationalizations to suit the religious sentiments of the period, so the social sciences have continued even to our own day to be rationalizations of uncritically accepted beliefs and customs.

It will become apparent as we proceed that the fact that an idea is ancient and that it has been widely received is no argument in its favor, but should immediately suggest the necessity of carefully testing it as a probable instance of rationalization.

3. How Creative Thought Transforms the World

This brings us to another kind of thought which can fairly easily be distinguished from the three kinds described above. It has not the usual qualities of the reverie, for it does not hover about our personal complacencies and humiliations. It is not made up of the homely decisions forced upon us by everyday needs, when we review our little stock of existing information, consult our conventional preferences and obligations, and make a choice of action. It is not the defense of our own cherished beliefs and prejudices just because they are our own—mere plausible excuses for remaining of the same mind. On the contrary, it is that peculiar species of thought which leads us to *change* our mind.

It is this kind of thought that has raised man from his pristine, subsavage ignorance and squalor to the degree of knowledge and comfort which he now possesses. On his capacity to continue and greatly extend this kind of thinking depends his chance of groping his way out of the plight in which the most highly civilized peoples of the world now find themselves. In the past this type of thinking has been called Reason. But so many misapprehensions have grown up around the word that some of us have become very suspicious of it. I suggest, therefore, that we substitute a recent name and speak of "creative thought" rather than of Reason. *For this kind of meditation begets knowledge, and knowledge is really creative in as much as it makes things look different from what they seemed before and may indeed work for their reconstruction.*

In certain moods some of us realize that we are observing things or making reflections with a seeming disregard of our personal preoccupations. We are not preening or defending ourselves; we are not faced by the necessity of any practical decision, nor are we apologizing for believing this or that. We are just wondering and looking and mayhap seeing what we never perceived before.

Curiosity is as clear and definite as any of our urges. We wonder what is in a sealed telegram or in a letter in which some one else is absorbed, or what is being said in the telephone booth or in low conversation. This inquisitiveness is vastly stimulated by jealousy, suspicion, or any hint that we ourselves are directly or indirectly involved. But there appears to be a fair amount of personal interest in other people's affairs even when they do not concern us except as a mystery to be unraveled or a tale to be told. The reports of a divorce suit will have "news value" for many weeks. They constitute a story, like a novel or play or moving picture. This is not an example of pure curiosity, however, since we readily identify ourselves with others, and their joys and despair then become our own.

We also take note of, or "observe," as Sherlock Holmes says, things which have nothing to do with our personal interests and make no personal appeal either direct or by way of sympathy. This is what Veblen so well calls "idle curiosity." And it is usually idle enough. Some of us when we face the line of people opposite us in a subway train impulsively consider them in detail and engage in rapid inferences and form theories in regard to them. On entering a room there are those who will perceive at a glance the degree of preciousness of the rugs, the character of the pictures, and the personality revealed by the books. But there are many, it would seem, who are so absorbed in their personal reverie or in some definite purpose that they have no bright-eyed energy for idle curiosity. The tendency to miscellaneous observation we come by honestly enough, for we note it in many of our animal relatives.

Veblen, however, uses the term "idle curiosity" somewhat ironically, as is his wont. It is idle only to those who fail to realize that it may be a very rare and indispensable thing from which almost all distinguished human achievement proceeds, since it may lead to systematic examination and seeking for things hitherto undiscovered. For research is but diligent search which enjoys the high flavor of primitive hunting. Occasionally and fitfully idle curiosity thus leads to creative thought, which alters and broadens our own views and aspirations and may in turn, under highly favorable circumstances, affect the views and lives of others, even for generations to follow. An example or two will make this unique human process clear.

Galileo was a thoughtful youth and doubtless carried on a rich and varied reverie. He had artistic ability and might have turned out to be a musician or painter. When he had dwelt among the monks at Valambrosa he had been tempted to lead the life of a religious. As a boy he busied himself with toy machines and he inherited a fondness for mathematics. All these facts are of record. We may safely assume also that, along with many other subjects of contemplation, the Pisan maidens found a vivid place in his thoughts.

One day when seventeen years old he wandered into the cathedral of his native town. In the midst of his reverie he looked up at the lamps hanging by long chains from the high ceiling of the church. Then something very difficult to explain occurred. He found himself no longer thinking of the building, worshipers, or the services; of his artistic or religious interests; of his reluctance to become a physician as his father wished. He forgot the question of a career and even the *graziosissime donne*. As he watched the swinging lamps he was suddenly wondering if mayhap their oscillations, whether long or short, did not occupy the same time. Then he tested his hypothesis by counting his pulse, for that was the only timepiece he had with him.

This observation, however remarkable in itself, was not enough to produce a really creative thought. Others may have noticed the same thing and yet nothing came of it. Most of our observations have no assignable results. Galileo may have seen that the warts on a peasant's face formed a perfect isosceles triangle, or he may have noticed with boyish glee that just as the officiating priest was uttering the solemn words, *ecce agnus Dei*, a fly lit on the end of his nose. To be really creative, ideas have to be worked up and then "put over," so that they become a part of man's social heritage. The highly accurate pendulum clock was one of the later results of Galileo's discovery. He himself was led to reconsider and successfully to refute the old notions of falling bodies. It remained for Newton to prove that the moon was falling, and presumably all the heavenly bodies. This quite upset all the consecrated views of the heavens as managed by angelic engineers. The universality of the laws of gravitation stimulated the attempt to seek other and equally important natural laws and cast grave doubts on the miracles in which mankind had hitherto believed. In short, those who dared to include in their thought the discoveries of Galileo and his successors found themselves in a new earth surrounded by new heavens.

On the 28th of October, 1831, two hundred and fifty years after Galileo had noticed the isochronous vibrations of the lamps, creative thought and its currency had so far increased that Faraday was wondering what would happen if he mounted a disk of copper between the poles of a horseshoe magnet. As the disk revolved an electric current was produced. This would doubtless have seemed the idlest kind of an experiment to the staunch business men of the time, who, it happened, were just then denouncing the child-labor bills in their anxiety to avail themselves to the full of the results of earlier idle curiosity. But should the dynamos and motors which have come into being as the outcome of Faraday's experiment be stopped this evening, the business man of to-day, agitated over labor troubles, might, as he trudged home past lines of "dead" cars, through dark streets to an unlighted house, engage in a little creative thought of his own and perceive that he and his laborers would have no modern factories and mines to quarrel about had it not been for the strange practical effects of the idle curiosity of scientists, inventors, and engineers.

The examples of creative intelligence given above belong to the realm of modern scientific achievement, which furnishes the most striking instances of the effects of scrupulous, objective thinking. But there are, of course, other great realms in which the recording and embodiment of acute observation and insight have wrought themselves into the higher life of man. The great poets and dramatists and our modern story-tellers have found themselves engaged in productive reveries, noting and artistically presenting their discoveries for the delight and instruction of those who have the ability to appreciate them.

The process by which a fresh and original poem or drama comes into being is doubtless analogous to that which originates and elaborates so-called scientific discoveries; but there is clearly a temperamental difference. The genesis and advance of painting, sculpture, and music offer still other problems. We really as yet know shockingly little about these matters, and indeed very few people have the least curiosity about them.[7] Nevertheless, creative intelligence in its various forms and activities is what makes man. Were it not for its slow, painful, and constantly discouraged operations through the ages man would be no more than a species of primate living on seeds, fruit, roots, and uncooked flesh, and wandering naked through the woods and over the plains like a chimpanzee.

The origin and progress and future promotion of civilization are ill understood and misconceived. These should be made the chief theme of education, but much hard work is necessary before we can reconstruct our ideas of man and his capacities and free ourselves from innumerable persistent misapprehensions. There have been obstructionists in all times, not merely the lethargic masses, but the moralists, the rationalizing theologians, and most of the philosophers, all busily if unconsciously engaged in ratifying existing ignorance and mistakes and discouraging creative thought. Naturally, those who reassure us seem worthy of honor and respect. Equally naturally those who puzzle us with disturbing criticisms and invite us to change our ways are objects of suspicion and readily discredited. Our personal discontent does not ordinarily extend to any critical questioning of the general situation in which we find ourselves. In every age the prevailing conditions of civilization have appeared quite natural and inevitable to those who grew up in them. The cow asks no questions as to how it happens to have a dry stall and a supply of hay. The kitten laps its warm milk from a china saucer, without knowing anything about porcelain; the dog nestles in the corner of a divan with no sense of obligation to the inventors of upholstery and the manufacturers of down pillows. So we humans accept our breakfasts, our trains and telephones and orchestras and movies, our national Constitution, our moral code and standards of manners, with the simplicity and innocence of a pet rabbit. We have absolutely inexhaustible capacities for appropriating what others do for us with no thought of a "thank you." We do not feel called upon to make any least contribution to the merry game ourselves. Indeed, we are usually quite unaware that a game is being played at all.

We have now examined the various classes of thinking which we can readily observe in ourselves and which we have plenty of reasons to believe go on, and always have been going on, in our fellow-men. We can sometimes get quite pure and sparkling examples of all four kinds, but commonly they are so confused and intermingled in our reverie as not to be readily distinguishable. The reverie is a reflection of our longings, exultations, and complacencies, our fears, suspicions, and disappointments. We are chiefly engaged in struggling to maintain our self-respect and in asserting that supremacy which we all crave and which seems to us our natural preroga-

---

[7] Recently a re-examination of creative thought has begun as a result of new knowledge which discredits many of the notions formerly held about "reason." See, for example, *Creative Intelligence*, by a group of American philosophic thinkers; John Dewey, *Essays in Experimental Logic* (both pretty hard books); and Veblen, *The Place of Science in Modern Civilization*. Easier than these and very stimulating are Dewey, *Reconstruction in Philosophy*, and Woodworth, *Dynamic Psychology*.

tive. It is not strange, but rather quite inevitable, that our beliefs about what is true and false, good and bad, right and wrong, should be mixed up with the reverie and be influenced by the same considerations which determine its character and course. We resent criticisms of our views exactly as we do of anything else connected with ourselves. Our notions of life and its ideals seem to us to be *our own* and as such necessarily true and right, to be defended at all costs.

We very rarely consider, however, the process by which we gained our convictions. If we did so, we could hardly fail to see that there was usually little ground for our confidence in them. Here and there, in this department of knowledge or that, some one of us might make a fair claim to have taken some trouble to get correct ideas of, let us say, the situation in Russia, the sources of our food supply, the origin of the Constitution, the revision of the tariff, the policy of the Holy Roman Apostolic Church, modern business organization, trade unions, birth control, socialism, the League of Nations, the excess-profits tax, preparedness, advertising in its social bearings; but only a very exceptional person would be entitled to opinions on all of even these few matters. And yet most of us have opinions on all these, and on many other questions of equal importance, of which we may know even less. We feel compelled, as self-respecting persons, to take sides when they come up for discussion. We even surprise ourselves by our omniscience. Without taking thought we see in a flash that it is most righteous and expedient to discourage birth control by legislative enactment, or that one who decries intervention in Mexico is clearly wrong, or that big advertising is essential to big business and that big business is the pride of the land. As godlike beings why should we not rejoice in our omniscience?

It is clear, in any case, that our convictions on important matters are not the result of knowledge or critical thought, nor, it may be added, are they often dictated by supposed self-interest. Most of them are *pure prejudices* in the proper sense of that word. We do not form them ourselves. They are the whisperings of "the voice of the herd." We have in the last analysis no responsibility for them and need assume none. They are not really our own ideas, but those of others no more well informed or inspired than ourselves, who have got them in the same careless and humiliating manner as we. It should be our pride to revise our ideas and not to adhere to what passes for respectable opinion, for such opinion can frequently be shown to be not respectable at all. We should, in view of the considerations that have been mentioned, resent our supine credulity. As an English writer has remarked:

"If we feared the entertaining of an unverifiable opinion with the warmth with which we fear using the wrong implement at the dinner table, if the thought of holding a prejudice disgusted us as does a foul disease, then the dangers of man's suggestibility would be turned into advantages."[8]

The purpose of this essay is to set forth briefly the way in which the notions of the herd have been accumulated. This seems to me the best, easiest, and least invidious educational device for cultivating a proper dis-

---

[8]Trotter, *op. cit.*, p. 45. The first part of this little volume is excellent.

trust for the older notions on which we still continue to rely.

The "real" reasons, which explain how it is we happen to hold a particular belief, are chiefly historical. Our most important opinions—those, for example, having to do with traditional, religious, and moral convictions, property rights, patriotism, national honor, the state, and indeed all the assumed foundations of society—are, as I have already suggested, rarely the result of reasoned consideration, but of unthinking absorption from the social environment in which we live. Consequently, they have about them a quality of "elemental certitude," and we especially resent doubt or criticism cast upon them. So long, however, as we revere the whisperings of the herd, we are obviously unable to examine them dispassionately and to consider to what extent they are suited to the novel conditions and social exigencies in which we find ourselves to-day.

The "real" reasons for our beliefs, by making clear their origins and history, can do much to dissipate this emotional blockade and rid us of our prejudices and preconceptions. Once this is done and we come critically to examine our traditional beliefs, we may well find some of them sustained by experience and honest reasoning, while others must be revised to meet new conditions and our more extended knowledge. But only after we have undertaken such a critical examination in the light of experience and modern knowledge, freed from any feeling of "primary certitude," can we claim that the "good" are also the "real" reasons for our opinions.

I do not flatter myself that this general show-up of man's thought through the ages will cure myself or others of carelessness in adopting ideas, or of unseemly heat in defending them just because we have adopted them. But if the considerations which I propose to recall are really incorporated into our thinking and are permitted to establish our general outlook on human affairs, they will do much to relieve the imaginary obligation we feel in regard to traditional sentiments and ideals. Few of us are capable of engaging in creative thought, but some of us can at least come to distinguish it from other and inferior kinds of thought and accord to it the esteem that it merits as the greatest treasure of the past and the only hope of the future.

ALDOUS HUXLEY

Aldous Leonard Huxley (1894–1963), one of the most well known of modern English novelists and essayists, came from a family celebrated for intellectual achievement. He was the son of Leonard Huxley, author and editor; grandson of the naturalist Thomas Huxley (see above, p. 20); and grandnephew of Matthew Arnold. His brother Sir Julian is a distinguished biologist and his half-brother David won the 1963 Nobel Prize in physiology. Huxley studied at Eton and Oxford, despite a serious eye disease that made him almost totally blind for three years. Reading with the aid of a magnifying glass, he graduated from Oxford in 1915 with honors in English literature. In 1919 he joined the staff of Athenaeum, a London literary magazine, and then followed a steady production of writings in all genres.

The success of his early novels allowed Huxley to move to Italy in 1923 and thence to France; in 1934 he traveled in the United States and finally settled in southern California, near Los Angeles. Here he continued to write books, articles, and an occasional movie scenario. He studied Vedanta and other Eastern religions and became interested in the effect of drugs on the mind.

Huxley wrote eleven novels, the best known being Antic Hay *(1923),* Point Counter Point *(1928),* Brave New World *(1932), and* After Many a Summer Dies the Swan *(1939). Huxley's reputation rests equally on his over twenty volumes of essays and belles-lettres, including* On the Margin *(1923),* Jesting Pilate *(1926),* Vulgarity in Literature *(1930),* Ends and Means *(1937),* The Perennial Philosophy *(1945),* Science, Liberty, and Peace *(1946),* The Doors of Perception *(1954), and* Literature and Science *(1963).*

Huxley's Brave New World *(1932) has turned out to be devastatingly accurate both as a piece of futuristic science fiction and as a satire on modern technological mass-produced civilization. It became so widely known that in 1958 Huxley could safely give the title* Brave New World Revisited *to a study of the progress of dehumanization and mental tyranny in the intervening quarter century. Both Huxley essays in the present volume are taken from* Brave New World Revisited. *The following is Chapter 5.*

Propaganda Under a Dictatorship

At his trial after the Second World War, Hitler's Minister for Armaments, Albert Speer, delivered a long speech in which, with remarkable acuteness, he described the Nazi tyranny and analyzed its methods. "Hitler's dictatorship," he said, "differed in one fundamental point from all its predecessors in history. It was the first dictatorship in the present period of modern technical development, a dictatorship which made complete use of all technical means for the domination of its own country. Through technical devices like the radio and the loud-speaker, eighty million people were deprived of independent thought. It was thereby possible to subject them to the will of one man. . . . Earlier dictators needed highly qualified assistants even at the lowest level—men who could think and act independently. The totalitarian system in the period of modern technical development can dispense with such men; thanks to modern methods of communication, it is possible to mechanize the lower leadership. As a result of this there has arisen the new type of the uncritical recipient of orders."

In the Brave New World of my prophetic fable technology had advanced far beyond the point it had reached in Hitler's day; consequently the recipients of orders were far less critical than their Nazi counterparts, far more obedient to the order-giving elite. Moreover, they had been genetically standardized and postnatally conditioned to perform their subordinate functions, and could therefore be depended upon to behave almost as predictably as machines. As we shall see in a later chapter, this conditioning of "the lower leadership" is already going on under the Communist dictatorships. The Chinese and the Russians are not relying merely on the indirect effects of advancing technology; they are working directly on the psychophysical organisms of their lower leaders, subjecting minds and bodies to a system of ruthless and, from all accounts, highly effective conditioning. "Many a man," said Speer, "has been haunted by the nightmare that one day nations might be dominated by technical means. That nightmare was almost realized in Hitler's totalitarian system." Almost, but not quite. The Nazis did not have time—and perhaps did not have the intelligence and the necessary knowledge—to brainwash and condition their lower leadership. This, it may be, is one of the reasons why they failed.

Since Hitler's day the armory of technical devices at the disposal of the would-be dictator has been considerably enlarged. As well as the radio, the loud-speaker, the moving picture camera and the rotary press, the contemporary propagandist can make use of television to broadcast the image as well as the voice of his client, and can record both image and voice on spools of magnetic tape. Thanks to technological progress, Big Brother can now be almost as omnipresent as God. Nor is it only on the technical front that the hand of the would-be dictator has been strengthened. Since Hitler's day a great deal of work has been carried out in those fields of applied psychology and neurology which are the special province of the propagandist, the indoctrinator and the brainwasher. In the past these specialists in the art of changing people's minds were empiricists. By a method of trial and error they had worked out a number of techniques and procedures, which they used very effectively without, however, knowing precisely why they were effective. Today the art of mind-control is in process of becoming a science. The practitioners of this science know what they are doing and why. They are guided in their work by theories and hypotheses solidly established on a massive foundation of experimental evidence. Thanks to the new insights and the new techniques made possible by these insights, the nightmare that was "all but realized in Hitler's totalitarian system" may soon be completely realizable.

But before we discuss these new insights and techniques let us take a look at the nightmare that so nearly came true in Nazi Germany. What were the methods used by Hitler and Goebbels for "depriving eighty million people of independent thought and subjecting them to the will of one man"? And what was the theory of human nature upon which those terrifyingly successful methods were based? These questions can be answered, for the most part, in Hitler's own words. And what remarkably clear and astute words they are! When he writes about such vast abstractions as Race and History and Providence, Hitler is strictly unreadable. But when he writes about the

German masses and the methods he used for dominating and directing them, his style changes. Nonsense gives place to sense, bombast to a hard-boiled and cynical lucidity. In his philosophical lucubrations Hitler was either cloudily daydreaming or reproducing other people's half-baked notions. In his comments on crowds and propaganda he was writing of things he knew by firsthand experience. In the words of his ablest biographer, Mr. Alan Bullock, "Hitler was the greatest demagogue in history." Those who add, "only a demagogue," fail to appreciate the nature of political power in an age of mass politics. As he himself said, "To be a leader means to be able to move the masses." Hitler's aim was first to move the masses and then, having pried them loose from their traditional loyalties and moralities, to impose upon them (with the hypnotized consent of the majority) a new authoritarian order of his own devising. "Hitler," wrote Hermann Rausch-ning in 1939, "has a deep respect for the Catholic church and the Jesuit order; not because of their Christian doctrine, but because of the 'machin-ery' they have elaborated and controlled, their hierarchical system, their extremely clever tactics, their knowledge of human nature and their wise use of human weaknesses in ruling over believers." Ecclesiasticism without Christianity, the discipline of a monastic rule, not for God's sake or in order to achieve personal salvation, but for the sake of the State and for the greater glory and power of the demagogue turned Leader—this was the goal toward which the systematic moving of the masses was to lead.

Let us see what Hitler thought of the masses he moved and how he did the moving. The first principle from which he started was a value judgment: the masses are utterly contemptible. They are incapable of abstract thinking and uninterested in any fact outside the circle of their immediate experience. Their behavior is determined, not by knowledge and reason, but by feelings and unconscious drives. It is in these drives and feelings that "the roots of their positive as well as their negative attitudes are implanted." To be successful a propagandist must learn how to manipulate these instincts and emotions. "The driving force which has brought about the most tremendous revolutions on this earth has never been a body of scientific teaching which has gained power over the masses, but always a devotion which has inspired them, and often a kind of hysteria which has urged them into action. Whoever wishes to win over the masses must know the key that will open the door of their hearts." . . . In post-Freudian jargon, of their unconscious.

Hitler made his strongest appeal to those members of the lower middle classes who had been ruined by the inflation of 1923, and then ruined all over again by the depression of 1929 and the following years. "The masses" of whom he speaks were these bewildered, frustrated and chronically anxious millions. To make them more masslike, more homogeneously subhuman, he assembled them, by the thousands and the tens of thousands, in vast halls and arenas, where individuals could lose their personal identity, even their elementary humanity, and be merged with the crowd. A man or woman makes direct contact with society in two ways: as a member of some familial, professional or religious group, or as a member of a crowd. Groups are capable of being as moral and intelligent as the individuals who form them; a crowd is chaotic, has no purpose of its own and is capable of anything except intelligent action and realistic thinking. Assembled in a crowd, people lose their powers of reasoning and their capacity for moral choice. Their suggestibility is increased to the point where they cease to have any judgment or will of their own. They become very excitable, they lose all sense of individual or collective responsibility, they are subject to sudden accesses of rage, enthusiasm and panic. In a word, a man in a crowd behaves as though he had swallowed a large dose of some powerful intoxicant. He is a victim of what I have called "herd-poisoning." Like alcohol, herd-poison is an active, extraverted drug. The crowd-intoxicated individual escapes from responsibility, intelligence and morality into a kind of frantic, animal mindlessness.

During his long career as an agitator, Hitler had studied the effects of herd-poison and had learned how to exploit them for his own purposes. He had discovered that the orator can appeal to those "hidden forces" which motivate men's actions, much more effectively than can the writer. Reading is a private, not a collective activity. The writer speaks only to individuals, sitting by themselves in a state of normal sobriety. The orator speaks to masses of individuals, already well primed with herd-poison. They are at his mercy and, if he knows his business, he can do what he likes with them. As an orator, Hitler knew his business supremely well. He was able, in his own words, "to follow the lead of the great mass in such a way that from the living emotion of his hearers the apt word which he needed would be suggested to him and in its turn this would go straight to the heart of his hearers." Otto Strasser called him a "loud-speaker, proclaiming the most secret desires, the least admissible instincts, the sufferings and personal revolts of a whole nation." Twenty years before Madison Avenue embarked upon "Motivational Research," Hitler was systematically exploring and exploiting the secret fears and hopes, the cravings, anxieties and frustrations of the German masses. It is by manipulating "hidden forces" that the advertising experts induce us to buy their wares—a toothpaste, a brand of cigarettes, a political candidate. And it is by appealing to the same hidden forces—and to others too dangerous for Madison Avenue to meddle with—that Hitler induced the German masses to buy themselves a Fuehrer, an insane philosophy and the Second World War.

Unlike the masses, intellectuals have a taste for rationality and an interest in facts. Their critical habit of mind makes them resistant to the kind of propaganda that works so well on the majority. Among the masses "instinct is supreme, and from instinct comes faith. . . .While the healthy common folk instinctively close their ranks to form a community of the people" (under a Leader, it goes without saying) "intellectuals run this way and that, like hens in a poultry yard. With them one cannot make history; they cannot be used as elements composing a community." Intellectuals are the kind of people who demand evidence and are shocked by logical inconsistencies and fallacies. They regard over-simplification as the original sin of the mind and have no use for the slogans, the unqualified assertions and sweeping generalizations which are the propagandist's stock in trade. "All effective propaganda," Hitler wrote, "must be confined to a few bare necessities and then must be expressed in a few stereotyped formulas." These stereotyped formulas must be constantly repeated, for "only constant repetition will finally succeed in imprinting an idea upon the memory of a crowd." Philosophy teaches us to feel uncertain about the things that seem to us self-evident. Propaganda, on the other hand, teaches us to accept as self-evident matters about which it would be reasonable to suspend our judgment or to feel doubt. The aim of the demagogue is to create social coherence under his own leadership. But, as Bertrand Russell has pointed out, "systems of dogma without empirical foundations, such as scholasticism, Marxism and fascism, have the advantage of producing a great deal of social coherence among their disciples." The demagogic propagandist must therefore be consistently dogmatic. All his statements are made without qualification. There are no grays in his picture of the world; everything is either diabolically black or celestially white. In Hitler's words, the propagandist should adopt "a systematically one-sided attitude towards every problem that has to be dealt with." He must never admit that he might be wrong or that people with a different point of view might be even partially right. Opponents should not be argued with; they should be attacked, shouted down, or, if they become too much of a nuisance, liquidated. The morally squeamish intellectual may be shocked by this kind of thing. But the masses are always convinced that "right is on the side of the active aggressor."

Such, then, was Hitler's opinion of humanity in the mass. It was a very low opinion. Was it also an incorrect opinion? The tree is known by its fruits, and a theory of human nature which inspired the kind of techniques that proved so horribly effective must contain at least an element of truth. Virtue and intelligence belong to human beings as individuals freely associating with other individuals in small groups. So do sin and stupidity. But the subhuman mindlessness to which the demagogue makes his appeal, the moral imbecility on which he relies when he goads his victims into action, are characteristic not of men and women as individuals, but of men and women in masses. Mindlessness and moral idiocy are not characteristically human attributes; they are symptoms of herd-poisoning. In all the world's higher religions, salvation and enlightenment are for individuals. The kingdom of heaven is within the mind of a person, not within the collective mindlessness of a crowd. Christ promised to be present where two or three are gathered together. He did not say anything about being present where thousands are intoxicating one another with herd-poison. Under the Nazis enormous numbers of people were compelled to spend an enormous amount of time marching in serried ranks from point A to point B and back again to point A. "This keeping of the whole population on the march seemed to be a senseless waste of time and energy. Only much later," adds Hermann Rauschning, "was there revealed in it a subtle intention based on a well-judged adjustment of ends and means. Marching diverts men's thoughts. Marching kills thought. Marching makes an end of individuality. Marching is the indispensable magic stroke performed in order to accustom the people to a mechanical, quasi-ritualistic activity until it becomes second nature."

From his point of view and at the level where he had chosen to do his dreadful work, Hitler was perfectly correct in his estimate of human nature. To those of us who look at men and women as individuals rather than as members of crowds, or of regimented collectives, he seems hideously wrong. In an age of accelerating over-population, of accelerating over-organization and ever more efficient means of mass communication, how can we preserve the integrity and reassert the value of the human individual? This is a question that can still be asked and perhaps effectively answered. A generation from now it may be too late to find an answer and perhaps impossible, in the stifling collective climate of that future time, even to ask the question.

ON KINDS OF FEELING

e. e. cummings
(1894–1962)

since feeling is first

since feeling is first
who pays any attention
to the syntax of things
will never wholly kiss you;

wholly to be a fool
while Spring is in the world

my blood approves,
and kisses are a better fate
than wisdom
lady i swear by all flowers. Don't cry
—the best gesture of my brain is less than
your eyelids' flutter which says

we are for each other: then
laugh, leaning back in my arms
for life's not a paragraph

And death i think is no parenthesis

(1926)

WILLIAM BUTLER YEATS
(1865–1939)

Leda and the Swan

A sudden blow: the great wings beating still
Above the staggering girl, her thighs caressed
By the dark webs, her nape caught in his bill,
He holds her helpless breast upon his breast.
How can those terrified vague fingers push
The feathered glory from her loosening thighs?
And how can body, laid in that white rush,
But feel the strange heart beating where it lies?

A shudder in the loins engenders there
The broken wall, the burning roof and tower
And Agamemnon dead.

                  Being so caught up,
So mastered by the brute blood of the air,
Did she put on his knowledge with his power
Before the indifferent beak could let her drop?

                               (1923)

IMAMU AMIRI BARAKA
(LeROI JONES)
(1934–)

Young Soul

First, feel, then feel, then
read, or read, then feel, then
fall, or stand, where you
already are. Think
of your self, and the other
selves . . . think
of your parents, your mothers
and sisters, your bentslick
father, then feel, or
fall, on your knees
if nothing else will move you,

then read
and look deeply
into all matters
come close to you
city boys—
country men

Make some muscle
in your head, but
use the muscle
in yr heart

NORMAN COUSINS

Norman Cousins (born 1912) is a prominent American editor and essayist. He graduated from Columbia Teachers College in 1933, then turned to a career in journalism. His name is most closely associated with the Saturday Review, *which, as executive editor, he brought to prominence in the 1940s, and which he still serves as Chairman of the Editorial Board. In the intervening decades Cousins has written steadily and fearlessly on most of the major issues of his time. Perhaps his best-known work is* Modern Man Is Obsolete *(1945), written in response to the dropping of the atomic bomb on Hiroshima. He also has written memorably on American democracy and on world federation. Cousins' writing, it has been said, is characterized by "a passionate concern for mankind." He has received many awards for both journalism and citizenship. The present essay was an editorial in the* Saturday Review *for July 23, 1966, at a time when computer technology was just beginning to gain full public attention.*

The Computer and the Poet

The essential problem of man in a computerized age remains the same as it has always been. That problem is not solely how to be more productive, more comfortable, more content, but how to be more sensitive, more sensible, more proportionate, more alive. The computer makes possible a phenomenal leap in human proficiency; it demolishes the fences around the practical and even the theoretical intelligence. But the question persists and indeed grows whether the computer will make it easier or harder for human beings to know who they really are, to identify their real problems, to respond more fully to beauty, to place adequate value on life, and to make their world safer than it now is.

Electronic brains can reduce the profusion of dead ends involved in vital research. But they can't eliminate the foolishness and decay that come from the unexamined life. Nor do they connect a man to the things he has to be connected to—the reality of pain in others; the possibilities of creative growth in himself; the memory of the race; and the rights of the next generation.

The reason these matters are important in a computerized age is that there may be a tendency to mistake data for wisdom, just as there has always been a tendency to confuse logic with values, and intelligence with insight. Unobstructed access to facts can produce unlimited good only if it is matched by the desire and ability to find out what they mean and where they would lead.

Facts are terrible things if left sprawling and unattended. They are too easily regarded as evaluated certainties rather than as the rawest of raw materials crying to be processed into the texture of logic. It requires a very unusual mind, Whitehead said, to undertake the analysis of a fact. The computer can provide a correct number, but it may be an irrelevant number until judgment is pronounced.

To the extent, then, that man fails to make the distinction between the intermediate operations of electronic intelligence and the ultimate responsibilities of human decision and conscience, the computer could prove a digression. It could obscure man's awareness of the need to come to terms with himself. It may foster the illusion that he is asking fundamental questions when actually he is asking only functional ones. It may be regarded as a substitute for intelligence instead of an extension of it. It may promote undue confidence in concrete answers. "If we begin with certainties," Bacon said, "we shall end in doubts; but if we begin with doubts, and we are patient with them, we shall end in certainties."

The computer knows how to vanquish error, but before we lose ourselves in celebration of the victory, we might reflect on the great advances in the human situation that have come about because men were challenged by error and would not stop thinking and probing until they found better approaches for dealing with it. "Give me a good fruitful error, full of seeds, bursting with its own corrections," Ferris Greenslet wrote. "You can keep your sterile truth for yourself."

The biggest single need in computer technology is not for improved circuitry, or enlarged capacity, or prolonged memory, or miniaturized containers, but for better questions and better use of the answers. Without taking anything away from the technicians, we think it might be fruitful to effect some sort of junction between the computer technologist and the poet. A genuine purpose may be served by turning loose the wonders of the creative imagination on the kinds of problems being put to electronic tubes and transistors. The company of poets may enable the men who tend the machines to see a larger panorama of possibilities than technology alone may inspire.

A poet, said Aristotle, has the advantage of expressing the universal; the specialist expresses only the particular. The poet, moreover, can remind us that man's greatest energy comes not from his dynamos but from his dreams. The notion of where a man ought to be instead of where he is; the liberation from cramped prospects; the intimations of immortality through art—all these proceed naturally out of dreams. But the quality of a man's dreams can only be a reflection of his subconscious. What he puts into his subconscious, therefore, is quite literally the most important nourishment in the world.

Nothing really happens to a man except as it is registered in the subconscious. This is where event and feeling become memory and where the proof of life is stored. The poet—and we use the term to include all those who have respect for and speak to the human spirit—can help to supply the subconscious with material to enhance its sensitivity, thus safeguarding it. The poet, too, can help to keep man from making himself over in the image of his electronic marvels. For the danger is not so much that man will be controlled by the computer as that he may imitate it.

The poet reminds men of their uniqueness. It is not necessary to possess the ultimate definition of this uniqueness. Even to speculate on it is a gain.

COLIN BLAKEMORE

Colin Blakemore is a British neurobiologist. He was born in 1944, and attended Cambridge University (B.A., 1965; M.A., 1966) and the University of California, Berkeley (Ph.D., 1968). He does outstanding research in neurology and in the behavioral sciences, and in 1975 was awarded the Bing Prize of the Swiss Academy of Medical Sciences. The next year he gave the prestigious Reith Lectures for the British Broadcasting Corporation. They were published in 1977 as a book, Mechanics of the Mind, *from which we take the opening section of Chapter 6, on split-brain research and some of its implications. Dr. Blakemore is presently a fellow of Downing College, Cambridge. He serves on the editorial boards of such journals as* Perception *and* Behavioral and Brain Sciences, *and is coauthor of* Handbook of Psychobiology *(1975).*

From Mechanics of the Mind

I was walking along the road with two friends.
The sun set. I felt a tinge of melancholy.
Suddenly the sky became a bloody red.

I stopped and leaned against the railing, dead
tired, and looked at the flaming clouds that
hung like blood and a sword over the blue-black
fjord and the city.

My friends walked on. I stood there, trembling
with fright. And I felt a loud, unending scream
piercing nature.

Edvard Munch (1863-1944)

Gustav Fechner was the founder of a new and objective approach to the
measurement of mental events, a concept that he crystallized in the name
that he coined for his science—psychophysics. Fechner hoped that the kind
of strict experiments that had beaten the forces of Nature into the laws of
physics could work for the mind of man as well. Yet despite the orderly,
reductionist nature of his ideas, Fechner, in 1860, permitted himself an
extraordinary speculation about personal consciousness. The brain, he
knew, is bilaterally symmetrical; it has two sides, which are virtually mirror-
images of each other. Nowhere is this clearer than in the cerebral hemispheres; there is a deep cleft between the two halves, which are linked by an
enormous strap, containing millions of nerve fibres—the *corpus callosum*. If
consciousness is a property of the brain (which Fechner certainly believed),
what would happen if the cerebral hemispheres were literally split apart
completely? As the psychologist William McDougall reported in 1911,
Fechner asserted 'that if a man's brain could be mechanically divided into
two parts (as by the transection of the *corpus callosum*) without arresting the
life of the parts, the nervous activities of each part would be accompanied by
its own stream of consciousness'. In other words, Fechner believed that one
mind would become two if the brain that kept it caged were cut in half.
McDougall himself, however, was convinced that no mere split in the brain
could divide the mind.

Fechner, of course, thought that this experiment would never and could
never be done. And McDougall surely believed the same, though he
taunted the eminent Oxford physiologist Sir Charles Sherrington with a
request that if he, McDougall, were ever struck by an incurable disease,
Sherrington himself should operate on him and cut his *corpus callosum*. 'If I
am right,' he said, 'my consciousness will remain a unitary consciousness.'

The hypothetical, inconceivable experiment of Fechner and McDougall
has actually been performed; and its results are, quite simply, some of the
most fascinating produced during research on the brain. The rationale behind this unlikely story is that an epileptic seizure originating at a focus of
damage on one side of the brain can spread to the other hemisphere through
the nerve fibres of the *corpus callosum*. The attack then takes on the terrible
proportions of a *grand mal* convulsion, involving the whole body. Nowadays
the treatment of epilepsy with palliative drugs is quite successful, but in a
few cases the fits become worse and worse, until the regular occurrence of
seizures, sometimes many each day, makes normal life impossible. Now in
California, in the 1950s, experiments with animals had demonstrated that
cutting the *corpus callosum* did not interfere in a gross way with movement or
any vital function. So a bold (some would say reckless) surgeon decided to
split the *corpus callosum* in a few patients who had intractable epilepsy, hoping that it would moderate their fits. It did—to an unexpected extent. Not

only did the convulsions no longer involve both sides of the body, but they were reduced in frequency too, though the reason for this therapeutic bonus is still unknown. But what of the other consequences of this unlikely invasion of the mind; who was right, Fechner or McDougall?

Roger Sperry and his collaborators, at the California Institute of Technology, who had already done much of the preliminary work with animals, had the chance to examine these people whose brains had been split. At first, apart from the usual after-effects of any neurosurgical operation, the patients seemed remarkably normal; indeed that had always been the conclusion in previous studies of people who had suffered damage to the *corpus callosum*. However, careful and often ingenious testing revealed a bizarre mental syndrome. It is surely significant that Sperry made one of the first reports of his studies at a conference entitled 'Brain and Conscious Experience', at the Pontifical Academy of Sciences—a meeting that was addressed by Pope Paul VI. In Sperry's own words, in his report to that conference: 'Everything we have seen so far indicates that the surgery has left these people with two separate minds, that is two separate spheres of consciousness. What is experienced in the right hemisphere seems to be entirely outside the realm of awareness of the left.'

Roger Sperry took advantage of the fact that the connections to and from one hemisphere are principally concerned with the opposite side of the body. If a split-brain patient is blindfolded, and some familiar object, like a comb or a coin, is put into one hand, he can use that same hand to retrieve the object from a collection of similar things by touch alone. But ask the other hand to do it and the result is pure guesswork. Imagine the patient looking fixedly at a point when a picture of an object is flashed momentarily just to the left of that point (so that it is seen only by the right hemisphere, because of the distribution of nerve fibres from the eyes to the brain). Now, the patient can select the object portrayed by sight, or even by touch alone, when he uses his left hand, but not his right, to choose from an array of objects.

Each hemisphere, then, seems whole in itself, but with only half a body to serve it. Judged by any simple criterion, like seeing, feeling, remembering or moving, there is not much to choose between the skills of the two hemispheres. To that extent Fechner was correct. Indeed, Sperry's descriptions convey an eerie impression that the split-brain patient is no longer one person, but two; both hands do indeed have minds of their own.

But 'mind-left' and 'mind-right' are not equal in every respect. The biggest difference between them (or at least the most immediate) is that one hemisphere—the left in all of Sperry's patients—does the talking. Put an object in the right hand or flash a picture on the right of the visual field, and the patient, or rather his left hemisphere, can tell you what it is. But show it on the left side, so that only the right hemisphere knows about it, and the articulate left is lost for words. So the mind that makes its presence felt, because it can speak, is that of the so-called major hemisphere, usually the left. To that extent, McDougall was correct. The speechlessness of the right hemisphere has been seized upon by some as evidence that the consciousness of man cannot be truly divided. But such an argument seems to me quite specious—rather like saying that a brain-damaged patient who simply cannot speak, but understands speech perfectly well, is not conscious and is therefore not human.

The minor, right hemisphere is not even totally illiterate; it can read. When the word 'comb' is flashed on the left of a screen, so that only the right hemisphere can see it, the patient cannot *say* what was written but can reach with his left hand and select the correct object from a choice. If a picture of a steaming cup of coffee is shown to the right hemisphere, the left hand can point out, amongst an array of cards, the one with the word 'hot' written on it. So adjectives as well as nouns are understood by 'mind-right'. But all the time the left hemisphere, speaking through the mouth of the patient, has no idea what is going on. By all accounts the right hemisphere is not very good with verbs, but it does have the vocabulary and the syntactical ability of a young child.

And what is more, in certain respects the subordinate right *excels* over the 'dominant' left. It is much *better* at any job that involves recognizing patterns and shapes, and particularly complicated solid objects. The right hemisphere can draw quite well with its left hand but the left hemisphere even has problems in copying simple diagrams of houses and cubes—it is much more at home writing than drawing. Recognizing faces, surely an immensely important part of human social behaviour, is also apparently a speciality of the so-called 'minor' hemisphere.

Fascinating though these observations on split-brain people are, I believe that they have been misinterpreted in their relevance to the functions of the normal human brain. Protagonists of different factions have all nurtured the idea that you and I have virtually independent sides to our brains and therefore to our intellects. The dominant side, usually the left, talks, writes, does mathematics, and thinks in a logical, serial way; the minor right side recognizes shapes and faces, appreciates music, puts on its owner's clothes, and works in a global, intuitive fashion. The verbal ordered culture of the Western world, dominated by scientific and technological progress, is, we are told, managed by the left hemispheres of its populations; the mystical, artistic and religious cultures of the East must be driven by their right hemispheres.

There is a growing, vocal movement that calls (presumably with its left hemisphere) for the liberation of its right. Some psychologists, most vociferously Robert Ornstein, want a revolution in Western education with more emphasis on non-verbal skills and the special attributes of the minor hemisphere, which are supposed to rule the cultures of the East. One cannot help feeling that some Oriental Robert Ornstein, contemplating the material progress that those attributes of the left hemisphere have given to the Western world, might make just the opposite recommendation.

In fact, Hugh Sykes Davies, the scholar of English, recently attacked the 'rightist' movement, and complained that verbal skills are degenerating, not dominating, in our society. All this fiery rhetoric seems to me to be based on a curious assumption that the two hemispheres of a normal man are as divided as those of Sperry's patients. Under exceptional circumstances, in unusual people, the separate characteristics of the two halves of the brain might come into conflict. The author J. M. Barrie, for instance, was ambidextrous; he even wrote his plays with either hand, and his desk is worn smooth on both sides to prove it. He was sure that his two hands had different characters and that he was inhabited by two different people. But in most of us there is a constant traffic of information between the two hemispheres, a tying-together of separate experiences, a sharing of special talents.

Even in split-brain people, the ability of the two sides of the brain to whisper to each other in the subtlest of ways is quite remarkable. Take the case of one experiment in which a spot of light, either red or green, was flashed to the right hemisphere and the split-brain patient was asked to say what colour he had seen. Both hemispheres understood the question but, of course, only the left could reply, so it simply guessed the answer, and therefore got it wrong half the time. But to Sperry's surprise, if allowed a second chance to correct himself, the patient always got the answer right. What seemed to be happening was this: the mute right hemisphere heard the guess of its verbose leftist colleague and if the answer was wrong, the right hemisphere triggered an intense emotional reaction. The patient frowned, blushed and shook his head immediately after making the faulty guess; and the left hemisphere, detecting the dissatisfaction of the knowledgeable right, quickly changed its mind and corrected itself. If the cerebral hemispheres are capable of this kind of collaboration with no overt connections at all between them, how much more certain should they be to share their skills when they have millions of fibres in the *corpus callosum* to bind them together!

What we should be striving to achieve for ourselves and our brains is not the pampering of one hemisphere to the neglect of the other (whether right or left), or their independent development, but the marriage and harmony of the two. It so happens that the special mental territories of the minor, right hemisphere—spatial perception, pictorial recognition and intuitive thought—are not easily amenable to conventional education, nor is it clear that they would benefit from years of formal instruction. Systems of education, especially higher education (and this applies to every culture) seem designed to develop and exploit the powers of the hemisphere that is dominant for speech, for those powers depend most on factual knowledge and prolonged training.

The ripening of cerebral dominance is one of the most important processes in the maturation of the brain. Unitary control of delicate motor skills, like speech and the fine movements of the dominant hand, requires the firm planting of the special apparatus for their control in one side of the brain. To ignore the special role and the particular educational needs of the dominant hemisphere, and to encourage the minor side to take charge may produce deleterious consequences in behaviour. It could cause problems as profound as the disorders of emotion and speech, especially stuttering, that are attributed to another cultural interference with cerebral dominance—the forced use of the right hand in naturally left-handed children. This form of social brain control was common in Europe and the United States, and was virtually mandatory in the Soviet Union, until quite recently.

The debate about liberating the minor hemisphere is only a fashionable twist to an ancient and inextinguishable aspiration of man—to control his brain; or, more often, to control someone else's. The brain is the organ of behaviour, and the dream of every leader, whether a tyrannical despot or a benign prophet, is to regulate the behaviour of his people. There is a growing fear that a considerable fraction of brain research is aimed at making such control a reality.

It is true that animals will work ceaselessly to receive electrical stimulation through electrodes implanted in so-called 'pleasure centres' in their brains. The most effective areas lie in the hypothalamus (which is involved in the regulation of motivated behaviour, like eating, drinking and sex) and in the nearby limbic system (which is thought to control emotions like rage, fear and joy). It is also true that electrical stimulation at certain sites or local damage at others can calm the fiercest beast or turn a placid animal into a savage killer. The physiologist J. F. Fulton wrote that a certain tiny injury to a monkey's brain 'yields an animal that is formidably ferocious . . . I finally had to decree that no one should ever examine [such a] monkey alone, for . . . they attack to kill, and they single out the examiner's neck as their initial objective. The aggressive behaviour comes in waves and is accompanied by salivation . . . baring of the teeth, and a kind of guttural vocalization that one seldom hears in a normal monkey.'

There is, naturally, widespread apprehension, nurtured by popular publications and not always discouraged by over-enthusiastic experimenters, that such techniques will soon be part and parcel of everyday life. Such fears are, in the main, quite unfounded; fortunately, the sheer paraphernalia of experimental brain manipulation, the implanted electrodes, the cables and electronics, the tedious surgical techniques, make that kind of brain control beyond the reach of any modern-day Alexander or Genghis Khan who wishes to motivate an army or subjugate the world at the push of a button. And in any case, are our brains not already more totally disciplined, our opinions more firmly moulded, and our minds more sharply directed by the political and social environment, than by any electrode that could be put in our heads? The stentorian voices of the mass media are more universally powerful than the indiscriminate persuasions of any mind-altering drug. . . .

MARY CAROLINE RICHARDS

Mary Caroline Richards was educated at Reed College and the University of California at Berkeley, where she received a Ph.D. in English in 1942. It was only then that "instead of taking up a college professorship," she turned to the art of pottery. She has been potter, poet, and teacher, and in Centering: In Pottery, Poetry and the Person *(1964), a provocative spiritual autobiography, she chronicles her need to think, to feel, and to make in order to be. "As we come into touch with other beings," she concludes, "we discover ourselves. This is precise. As I experience the presence of a tree or a field or a stream or another person or a tremor that runs through me with a force of its own, I know myself through that experience"; and at the same time "It is important to let the reins hang loose . . . to be well enough seated not to fall in the energetic release . . . to have a good balance, on center." The excerpts below are from Chapter 2 of the book. Ms. Richards is a regular contributor to* Craft Horizons *and the author of* Crossing Point: Selected Talks and Writings *(1973).*

Centering as Dialogue

Centering: that act which precedes all others on the potter's wheel. The bringing of the clay into a spinning, unwobbling pivot, which will then be free to take innumerable shapes as potter and clay press against each other. The firm, tender, sensitive pressure which yields as much as it asserts. It is like a handclasp between two living hands, receiving the greeting at the very moment that they give it. It is this speech between the hand and the clay that makes me think of dialogue. And it is a language far more interesting than the spoken vocabulary which tries to describe it, for it is spoken not by the tongue and lips but by the whole body, by the whole person, speaking and listening. And with listening too, it seems to me, it is not the ear that hears, it is not the physical organ that performs that act of inner receptivity. It is the total person who hears. Sometimes the skin seems to be the best listener, as it prickles and thrills, say to a sound or a silence; or the fantasy, the imagination: how it bursts into inner pictures as it listens and then responds by pressing its language, its forms, into the listening clay. To be open to what we hear, to be open in what we say . . .

   I am a question-asker and a truth-seeker. I do not have much in the way of status in my life, nor security. I have been on quest, as it were, from the beginning. For a long time I thought there was something wrong with me: no ambition, no interest in tenure, always on the march, changing every seven years, from landscape to landscape. Certain elements were constant: the poetry, the desire for relationship, the sense of voyage. But lately I have developed also a sense of destination, or destiny. And a sense that if I am to be on quest, I must expect to live like a pilgrim; I must keep to the inner path. I must be able to be whoever I am.

   For example, it seemed strange to me, as to others, that, having taken my Ph.D. in English, I should then in the middle of my life, instead of taking up a college professorship, turn to the art of pottery. During one period, when people asked me what I did, I was uncertain what to answer; I guessed I could say I taught English, wrote poetry, and made pottery. What was my occupation? I finally gave up and said "Person."

   Having been imbued with the ordinary superstitions of American higher education, among which is the belief that something known as the life of the mind is more apt to take you where you want to go than any other kind of life, I busied myself with learning to practice logic, grammar, analysis, summary, generalization; I learned to make distinctions, to speculate, to purvey information. I was educated to be an intellectual of the verbal type. I might have been a philosophy major, a literature major, a language major. I was always a kind of oddball even in undergraduate circles, as I played kick-goal on the Reed College campus with President Dexter Keezer. And in graduate school, even more so. Examinations tended to make me merry, often seeming to me to be some kind of private game, some secret ritual compulsively played by the professors and the institution. I invariably became facetious in all the critical hours. All that solemnity for a few facts! I couldn't believe they were serious. But they were. I never quite understood it. But I loved the dream and the reality that lay behind those texts and in the souls of my teachers. I often felt like a kind of fraud, because I suspected that the knowledge I was acquiring and being rewarded for by academic diploma was wide wide of the truth I sensed to live somewhere, somewhere. I felt that I knew little of real importance; and when would the day come that others would realize it too, and I would be exposed? I have had dream after dream in which it turns out that I have not really completed my examinations for the doctorate and have them still to pass. And I sweat with anxiety. A sense of occupying a certain position without possessing the real thing: the deeper qualifications of wisdom and prophecy. But of course it was not the world who exposed me, it was my dreams. I do not know if I am a philosopher, but if philosophy is the love of wisdom, then I am a philosopher, because I love wisdom and that is why I love the crafts, because they are wise.

I became a teacher quite by chance. Liked it, found in education an image through which I could examine the possibilities of growth, of nourishment, of the experiences that led to knowledge of nature and of self. It was a good trade to be in if you were a question-asker.

But the trouble was that though the work absorbed my mind, it used very little else. And I am by now convinced that wisdom is not the product of mental effort. Wisdom is a state of the total being, in which capacities for knowledge and for love, for survival and for death, for imagination, inspiration, intuition, for all the fabulous functioning of this human being who we are, come into a center with their forces, come into an experience of meaning that can voice itself as wise action. It is not enough to belong to a Society of Friends who believe in non-violence if, when frustrated, your body spontaneously contracts and shoots out its fist to knock another man down. It is in our bodies that redemption takes place. It is the physicality of the crafts that pleases me: I learn through my hands and my eyes and my skin what I could never learn through my brain. I develop a sense of life, of the world of earth, air, fire, and water—and wood, to add the fifth element according to Oriental alchemy—which could be developed in no other way. And if it is life I am fostering, I must maintain a kind of dialogue with the clay, listening, serving, interpreting as well as mastering. The union of our wills, like a marriage, it is a beautiful act, the act of centering and turning a pot on the potter's wheel; and the sexual images implicit in the forming of the cone and opening of the vessel are archetypal; likewise the give-and-take in the forming of a pot out of slabs, out of raw shards, out of coils; the union of natural intelligences: the intelligence of the clay, my intelligence, the intelligence of the tools, the intelligence of the fire.

You don't need me to tell you what education is. Everybody really knows that education goes on all the time everywhere all through our lives, and that it is the process of waking up to life. Jean Henri Fabre said something just about like that, I think. He said that to be educated was not to be taught but to wake up. It takes a heap of resolve to keep from going to sleep in the middle of the show. It's not that we want to sleep our lives away. It's that it requires certain kinds of energy, certain capacities for taking the world into our consciousness, certain real powers of body and soul to be a match for reality. That's why knowledge and consciousness are two quite different things. Knowledge is like a product we consume and store. All we need are good closets. By consciousness I mean a state of being "awake" to the world throughout our organism. This kind of consciousness requires not closets but an organism attuned to the finest perceptions and responses. It allows experience to breathe through it as light enters and changes a room. When knowledge is transformed into consciousness and into will, ah then we are on the high road indeed . . .

That which we consume, with a certain passivity, accepting it for the most part from our teachers, who in turn have accepted it from theirs, is like the food we eat. And food, in order to become energy, or will, is transformed entirely by the processes of metabolism. We do not become the food we eat. Rather the food turns into us. Similarly with knowledge, at best. Hopefully, we do not turn into encyclopedias or propaganda machines or electric brains. Our knowledge, if we allow it to be transformed within us, turns into capacity for life-serving human deeds. If knowledge does not turn into life, it makes cripples and madmen and dunces. It poisons just as food would if it stayed in the stomach and was never digested, and the waste products never thrown off.

It is dangerous to seek to possess knowledge, as if it could be stored. For one thing, it tends to make one impatient with ignorance, as people busy with money-seeking tend to be impatient with idlers. Though ignorance is the prime prerequisite for education, many teachers appear offended by it— or worse, contemptuous. Perhaps it is partly for this reason that many prefer to give advanced courses to select or "gifted" groups.

The possession of knowledge may create a materialism of its own. Knowledge becomes property. Teachers compete with each other for status, wealth, influence. A professor of education was speaking to friends of education in the county where I live, and she was urging pay raises as bait for hiring good teachers, "for after all, the standard of success is the salary check." Naturally in this climate professional educators are apt to quarrel over tactics and to engage in pressure politics, motivated by a desire to protect their security and to establish their views as ruling policy. In other words, education may be sacrificed to knowledge-as-commodity. Just as life is sometimes sacrificed to art-as-arrangement. The quest is abandoned. Instead, property is bought at the site of the last dragon killed, and a ruling class is formed out of the heroes. The knights grow fat and lazy and conceited and petulant. They parade in their armor on special occasions to bedazzle the populace. But in their hearts are terror and duplicity. And when difficult times come, they fall upon each other with their rusty axes and try to divide the world into those who know and those who don't. There is nothing to equal in bitterness and gall, childishness and spite, the intramural warfare of the academic community. Where is honor? Where is devotion? Where is responsibility of soul?

Such an atmosphere brought me gradually to imagine possible shortcomings in the educational system I had docilely trusted. Initiative and imagination seemed sorely lacking. Teachers seemed to apply to their students the same pressures that had crippled them. Most of us have been brainwashed to think that knowledge and security make the world go round. And if the world seems to be going round very poorly, we do not think of questioning deeply its education. The need for creative imagination in the intellectually trained person is drastic. Also the need for spontaneous human feeling.

Fashionable thinking may dominate the scientist and artist and scholar alike. For them, knowledge is the body of facts currently in fashion. Art is the image and compositional practice now in fashion. Since it is difficult to test the truth of most facts, faculty and students alike settle for "interesting," "original," and "self-consistent" theories. An ability to marshal and interpret "evidence" is highly esteemed, though evidence is often no more than opinions strongly held or secondary research. Very little stress is placed on developing powers of observation or on intuition. Thus, with primary experience held so at a distance, sensory life in particular, I find that my principal task in teaching adults is to win their trust. They tend to be overwhelmingly oriented to manipulation and to effect. It rarely occurs to them to work in a direct way with what they know and are. Their primary motivations are to please, to make a strong impression, to do either what is expected (if they are docile) or what is unexpected (if they are hostile). They assume that pretense and falsity are virtues. The whole thing sometimes seems like a massive confidence game.

Like other men, teachers tend to withhold themselves from naked personal contact. They tend to pin their hopes on jargon and style. And this, I have observed, is what many students learn from them: afraid to reveal themselves, burdened with shame and dismay and hopelessness, or expertise and cunning.

A theory much in vogue is that Western man is sick with sexual repression and pleasure anxiety. I believe that the squelching of the "person" and his spontaneous intuitive response to experience is as much at the root of our timidity, our falseness. Teachers and students who in the great school markets barter their learning for salaries and grades are hungry for respect, for personal relationship, for warmth. Unfortunately, they have the impression that these are extracurricular (like Newton's secondary qualities of color and so on)—and their capacity for balance between the life within and the world without shrinks or falters, or their desperation turns rank.

It is a sensitive matter, of course. I am not going to all these words merely to insult the spirit of true research. But my life as a teacher and as a member of the human community advises me that education may estrange us from life-commitment as well as bind us firmly within it. There are all kinds of things to learn, and we had best learn them all. One of the reasons formal education is in danger today is that a sense of work is split off from human earnestness. How may this split be healed? Working with our materials as artist-craftsmen may help to engender a new health here.

An act of the self, that's what one must make. An act of the self, from me to you. From center to center. We must mean what we say, from our inner-most heart to the outermost galaxy. Otherwise we are lost and dizzy in a maze of reflections. We carry light within us. There is no need merely to reflect. Others carry light within them. These lights must wake to each other. My face is real. Yours is. Let us find our way to our initiative.

For must we not show ourselves to each other, and will we not know then who are the teachers and who are the students? Do we not all learn from one another? My students at City College are worldly-wise and naïve as lambs. I am sophisticated and uninformed. We make a good combination. They have never heard of e. e. cummings, who lived in their city, nor of the New York painters. They do not know that there are free art galleries where they may see the latest works of modern artists. They do not know very much about contemporary "culture." But they know well the life of the subway, the office, the factory, the union hall, the hassle for employment; they know what they did in the war or in their escape from Hungary or Germany, or in occupied France, or Israel. They know what it is like to be black in America. They are patient with my obtuseness, they check my too quick judgments, my sarcasm which is unperceptive. I help them to un-mask, to be openly as tender and hopeful and generous as they inwardly are. I help them to open themselves to knowledge. They help me to open myself to life. We are equal in courage.

Must weakness be concealed in order that respect be won? Must love and fervor be concealed? Must we pretend to fearlessness? and certainty? Surely education should equip us to know what to fear and what to be uncertain of. Surely it should equip us in personal honor.

Must. Should. Convenient words! Exhortations meant to loosen the grip of congealed behavior . . . Perhaps these perceptions are not the proper work of intellect, but of some other faculty deeply neglected in our education. In any case, at a critical moment in life my hunger for nakedness and realism and nobility turned to the clay of earth itself, and to water and fire.

I took up pottery also, in a sense, by chance. Unforeseen opportunity joined with interest and readiness. Like teaching, not a consciously sought but surely a destined union. For the materials and processes of pottery spoke to me of cosmic presences and transformations quite as surely as the pots themselves enchanted me. Experiences of the plastic clay and the firing of the ware carried more than commonplace values. Joy resonated deep within me, and it has stirred these thoughts only slowly to the surface. I have come to feel that we live in a universe of spirit, which materializes and de-materializes grandly; all things seem to me to live, and all acts to contain meaning deeper than matter-of-fact; and the things we do with deepest love and interest compel us by the spiritual forces which dwell in them. This seems to me to be a dialogue of the visible and the invisible to which our ears are attuned.

There was, first of all, something in the nature of the clay itself. You can do very many things with it, push this way and pull that, squeeze and roll and attach and pinch and hollow and pile. But you can't do everything with it. You can go only so far, and then the clay resists. To know ourselves by our resistances—this is a thought first expressed to me by the poet Charles Olson.

And so it is with persons. You can do very many things with us: push us together and pull us apart and squeeze us and roll us flat, empty us out and fill us up.You can surround us with influences, but there comes a point when you can do no more. The person resists, in one way or another (if it is only by collapsing, like the clay). His own will becomes active.

This is a wonderful moment, when one feels his will become active, come as a force into the total assemblage and dynamic intercourse and interpenetration of will impulses. When one stands like a natural substance, plastic but with one's own character written into the formula, ah then one feels oneself part of the world, taking one's shape with its help—but a shape only one's own freedom can create.

And the centering of the clay, of which I have spoken. The opening of the form. And the firing of the pot. This experience has deep psychic reverberations: how the pot, which was originally plastic, sets into dry clay, brittle and fragile, and then by being heated to a certain temperature hardens into stone. By natural law as it were, it takes its final form. Ordeal by fire. Then, the form once taken, the pot may not last, the body may perish; but the inner form has been taken, and it cannot break in the same sense.

I, like everyone I know, am instinctively motivated toward symbols of wholeness. What is a simpler, more natural one than the pot fired? Wholeness may be thought of as a kind of inner equilibrium, in which all our capacities have been brought into functioning as an organism. The potencies of the whole organism flow into the gestures of any part. And the sensation in any part reverberates throughout the soul. The unconscious and conscious levels of being can work together at the tasks of life, conveying messages to each other, assimilating one another. In wholeness I sense an integration of those characteristics which are uniquely ME and those interests which I share with the rest of mankind. As for example any bowl is symbolic of an archetypal circular form, which I share with all, but which *I* make and which therefore contains those very qualities of myself which are active in the making. I believe that pots have the smell of the person who makes them: a smell of tenderness, of vanity or ambition, of ease and naturalness, of petulance, uncertainty, callousness, fussiness, playfulness, solemnity, exuberance, absent-mindedness. The pot gives off something. It gives off its innerness, that which it holds but which cannot be seen.

In pottery, by developing sensitivity in manipulating natural materials by hand, I found a wisdom which had died out of the concepts I learned in the university: abstractions, mineralized and dead; while the minerals themselves were alive with energy and meaning. The life I found in the craft helped to bring to a new birth my ideals in education. Some secret center became vitalized in those hours of silent practice in the arts of transformation.

The experience of centering was one I particularly sought because I thought of myself as dispersed, interested in too many things. I envied people who were "single-minded," who had one powerful talent and who knew when they got up in the morning what it was they had to do. Whereas I, wherever I turned, felt the enchantment: to the window for the sweetness of the air; to the door for the passing figures; to the teapot, the typewriter, the knitting needles, the pets, the pottery, the newspaper, the telephone. Wherever I looked, I could have lived.

It took me half my life to come to believe I was OK even if I did love experience in a loose and undiscriminating way and did not know for sure the difference between good and bad. My struggles to accept my nature were the struggles of centering. I found myself at odds with the propaganda of our times. One is supposed to be either an artist or a homemaker, by one popular superstition. Either a teacher or a poet, by a theory which says that poetry must not sermonize. Either a craftsman or an intellectual, by a snobbism which claims either hand or head as the seat of true power. One is supposed to concentrate and not to spread oneself thin, as the jargon goes. And this is a jargon spoken by a cultural leadership from which it takes time to win one's freedom, if one is not lucky enough to have been born free. Finally, I hit upon an image: a seed-sower. Not to worry about which seeds sprout. But to give them as my gift in good faith.

But in spite of my self-acceptance, I still clung to a concept of purity which was chaste and aloof from the fellowship of man, and had yet to center the image of a pure heart in whose bright warm streams the world is invited to bathe. A heart who can be touched and who stirs in response, bringing the whole body into an act of greeting.

Well then, I became a potter.

MARCEL PROUST

Marcel Proust's literary fame comes from his long novel À la Recherche du temps perdu (Remembrance of Things Past). *He published the first volume in 1913 and was dictating passages of the eighth the night before he died in 1922. Although the novel is not autobiographical, it does record the life of a Paris dilettante, wealthy and purposeless until one day when he realizes that the memories of his own life, relived and reshaped into art, will provide the subject for a great novel.*

Proust, asthmatic and nervous from earliest childhood, lived in his family home in Paris from his birth in 1871 until his mother's death in 1905. While in school he wrote essays and poems that show his early interest in the Decadent movement—a school of French writers who stressed the abnormal and artificial in their works. At the Sorbonne he enrolled as a student of law and political science, but his only academic interest was in philosophy. He spent most of his time widening his circle of acquaintances in the literary and artistic society of Paris and sporadically composing novels and shorter works. Though only a few were printed, he later worked parts of them into his major novel.

His mother's death grieved Proust excessively, for she had given his life a continuity and a portion of her own strict discipline. Her death did enable Proust to stop hiding his homosexuality—though none of his series of affairs lasted long, and the most intense ended tragically when his lover died in a plane crash in 1914.

In 1907 Proust moved to a flat, which he had made soundproof and from which, in later years, he almost never stirred. By 1909 he had begun steady work on Remembrance of Things Past. *He saw less and less of aristocratic Paris society; because of his asthma he often worked on his novel all night and slept during the day. He became progressively weaker and more nervous, took large amounts of drugs for his asthma, and died of pneumonia in 1922.*

Contre Sainte-Beuve (By Way of Sainte-Beuve), *written between 1908 and 1910, was the only major interruption to the work on his novel. It began as a critical study but soon turned into an account of Proust's own processes of memory, thought, and feeling. The present essay, which opens the book, is celebrated as a description of how his masterpiece may have originated. The translation is by Sylvia Townsend Warner (1958). "Sainte-Beuve's Method," referred to in the final paragraph, is described elsewhere by Proust as "not separating the man and his work," "to surround oneself with every possible piece of information about a writer" before making a judgment on his writings. Proust did not admire this method.*

Prologue

Every day I set less store on intellect. Every day I see more clearly that if the writer is to repossess himself of some part of his impressions, reach something personal, that is, and the only material of art, he must put it aside. What intellect restores to us under the name of the past, is not the past. In reality, as soon as each hour of one's life has died, it embodies itself in some material object, as do the souls of the dead in certain folk-stories, and hides there. There it remains captive, captive forever, unless we should happen on the object, recognise what lies within, call it by its name, and so set it free. Very likely we may never happen on the object (or the sensation, since we apprehend every object as sensation) that it hides in; and thus there are hours of our life that will never be resuscitated: for this object is so tiny, so lost in the world, and there is so little likelihood that we shall come across it.

Several summers of my life were spent in a house in the country. I thought of those summers from time to time, but they were not themselves.

They were dead, and in all probability they would always remain so. Their resurrection, like all these resurrections, hung on a mere chance. One snowy evening, not long ago, I came in half frozen, and had sat down in my room to read by lamplight, and as I could not get warm my old cook offered to make me a cup of tea, a thing I never drink. And as chance would have it, she brought me some slices of dry toast. I dipped the toast in the cup of tea and as soon as I put it in my mouth, and felt its softened texture, all flavoured with tea, against my palate, something came over me—the smell of geraniums and orange-blossom, a sensation of extraordinary radiance and happiness. I sat quite still, afraid that the slightest movement might cut short this incomprehensible process which was taking place in me, and concentrated on the bit of sopped toast which seemed responsible for all these marvels; then suddenly the shaken partitions in my memory gave way, and into my conscious mind there rushed the summers I had spent in the aforesaid house in the country, with their early mornings, and the succession, the ceaseless onset, of happy hours in their train. And then I remembered. Every morning, when I was dressed, I went down to my grandfather in his bedroom, where he had just woken up and was drinking his tea. He soaked a rusk in it, and gave me the rusk to eat. And when those summers were past and gone, the taste of a rusk soaked in tea was one of the shelters where the dead hours—dead as far as intellect knew—hid themselves away, and where I should certainly never have found them again if, on that winter's evening when I came in frozen from the snow, my cook had not offered me the potion to which, by virtue of a magic past I knew nothing about, their resurrection was plighted.

But as soon as I had tasted the rusk, a whole garden, up till then vague and dim, mirrored itself, with its forgotten walks and all their urns with all their flowers, in the little cup of tea, like those Japanese flowers which do not reopen as flowers until one drops them into water. In the same way, many days in Venice, which intellect had not been able to give back, were dead for me until last year, when crossing a courtyard I came to a standstill among the glittering uneven paving-stones. The friends I was with were afraid that I might have slipped, but I waved to them to go on, and that I would catch up with them. Something of greater importance engaged me, I still did not know what it was, but in the depth of my being I felt the flutter of a past that I did not recognise; it was just as I set foot on a certain paving-stone that this feeling of perplexity came over me. I felt an invading happiness, I knew that I was going to be enriched by that purely personal thing, a past impression, a fragment of life in unsullied preservation (something we can only know in preservation, for while we live in it, it is not present in the memory, since other sensations accompany and smother it) which asked only that it might be set free, that it might come and augment my stores of life and poetry. But I did not feel that I had the power to free it. No, intellect could have done nothing for me at such a moment! Trying to put myself back into the same state, I retraced my steps a little so that I might come afresh to those uneven shining paving-stones. It was the same sensation underfoot that I had felt on the smooth, slightly uneven pavement of the baptistry of Saint Mark's. The shadow which had lain that day on the canal, where a gondola waited for me, and all the happiness, all the wealth of those hours—this recognised sensation brought them hurrying after it, and that very day came alive for me.

It is not merely that intellect can lend no hand in these resurrections; these past hours will only hide themselves away in objects where intellect has not tried to embody them. The objects which you have consciously tried to connect with certain hours of your life, these they can never take shelter in. What is more, if something else should resuscitate those hours, the objects called back with them will be stripped of their poetry.

I remember how once when I was travelling by train I strove to draw impressions from the passing landscape. I wrote about the little country churchyard while it was still passing before my eyes, I noted down the bright bars of sunlight on the trees, the wayside flowers like those in *Le Lys dans la Vallée*. Since then, calling to mind those trees streaked with light and that little churchyard, I have often tried to conjure up that day, that day *itself*, I mean, not its pallid ghost. I could never manage it, and I had lost all hope of doing so, when at lunch, not long ago, I let my spoon fall on my plate. And then it made the same noise as the hammers of the linesmen did that day, tapping on the wheels when the train halted at stations. The burning blinded hour when that noise rang out instantly came back to me, and all that day in its poetry—except for the country churchyard, the trees streaked with light, and the Balzacian flowers, gained by deliberate observation and lost from the poetic resurrection.

Now and again, alas, we happen on the object, and the lost sensation thrills in us, but the time is too remote, we cannot give a name to the sensation, or call on it, and it does not come alive. As I was walking through a pantry the other day, a piece of green canvas plugging a broken window-pane made me stop dead and listen inwardly. A gleam of summer crossed my mind. Why? I tried to remember. I saw wasps in a shaft of sunlight, a smell of cherries came from the table—I could not remember. For a moment I was like those sleepers who wake up in the dark and do not know where they are, who ask their bodies to give them a bearing as to their where-abouts, not knowing what bed, what house, what part of the world, which year of their life they are in. For a moment I hesitated like this, groping round the square of green canvas to discover the time and the place where my scarcely awakened memory would find itself at home. All the sensations of my life, confused, or known, or forgotten, I was hesitating among all of them at once. This only lasted a minute. Soon I saw nothing more; my memory had fallen asleep again forever.

How often during our walks have not my friends known me halt like this at the turning-off of an avenue, or beside a clump of trees, and ask them to leave me alone for a minute. Nothing came of it. I shut my eyes and made my mind a blank to recruit fresh energies for my pursuit of the past, then suddenly reopened them, all in an attempt to see those same trees as if for the first time. I could not tell where I had seen them. I could recognise their shapes and their grouping, their outline seemed to have been traced from some beloved drawing that trembled in my heart. But I could tell no more of them, and they themselves seemed by their artless passionate attitude to say how sorry they felt not to be able to make themselves clear, not to be able to tell me the secret that they well knew I could not unriddle. Ghosts of a dear past, so dear that my heart beat to bursting, they held out powerless arms to me, like the ghosts that Aeneas met in the underworld. Was it in the walks near the town of my happy childhood, was it only in that imagined country where, later on, I dreamed that Mamma was so ill, close to a lake and in a forest where it was light all night long, a dream country only but almost as real as the country of my childhood which was already no more than a dream? I should never know more of it. And I had to rejoin my friends who were waiting for me at the turn of the road, with the anguish of turning my back forever on a past I might see no more, of disowning the dead who held out their powerless fond arms to me, and seemed to say, Recall us to life. And before I fell into step and into conversation with my friends, I again turned round for a moment to cast a less and less discerning glance towards the crooked, receding line of mutely expressive trees still undulating before my eyes.

Compared with this past, this private essence of ourselves, the truths of intellect seem scarcely real at all. So, and above all from the time when our vitality begins to dwindle, it is to whatever may help us to recover this past that we resort, even though this should entail being very ill-understood by intellectual people who do not know that the artist lives to himself, that the absolute value of what he sees means nothing to him and that his scale of values is wholly subjective. A nauseating musical show put on by a provincial company, or a ball that people of taste would laugh at, may be far more quickening to his memories, far more relevant to the nature of what he dreams of and dwells on, than a brilliant performance at the Opera House or an ultra-elegant evening party in the Faubourg Saint-Germain. A railway time-table with its names of stations where he loves to fancy himself getting out of the train on an autumn evening when the trees are already stripped of their leaves and the bracing air is full of their rough scent, or a book that means nothing to people of discrimination but is full of names he has not heard since he was a child, can be worth incommensurably more to him than admirable philosophical treatises, so that people of discrimination will remark that for a man of talent he has very stupid likings.

Perhaps it will cause surprise that I, who make light of the intellect, should have devoted the following few pages precisely to some of these considerations that intellect, in contradiction to the platitudes that we hear said or read in books, suggests to us. At a time when my days may be numbered (and besides, are we not all in the same case?) it is perhaps very frivolous of me to undertake an intellectual exercise. But if the truths of intellect are less precious than those secrets of feeling that I was talking about just now, yet in one way they too have their interest. A writer is not only a poet; in our imperfect world where masterpieces are no more than the shipwrecked flotsam of great minds, even the greatest writers of our century have spun a web of intellect round jewels of feeling which only here or there show through it. And if one believes that on this important point one hears the best among one's contemporaries making mistakes, there comes a time when one shakes off one's indolence and feels the need to speak out. Sainte-Beuve's Method is not, at first sight, such an important affair. But perhaps in the course of these pages we may be led to realise that it touches on very important intellectual problems, and on what is perhaps for an artist the greatest of all: this relative inferiority of the intellect which I spoke of at the beginning. Yet all the same, it is intellect we must call on to establish this inferiority. Because if intellect does not deserve the crown of crowns, only intellect is able to award it. And if intellect ranks only second in the hierarchy of virtues, intellect alone is able to proclaim that the first place must be given to instinct.

The Right Use of Language

T HE subject we propose in this section is an ancient one, going back at least to the first rhetoricians and philosophers—Plato and Aristotle among them—who were deeply concerned with the distinction between eloquence devoted to good ends and eloquence devoted to bad. This distinction was crucial in a culture in which direct speech was the main mode of communication, and a capacity to speak, argue, and answer well was the sole protection of a person's rights.

In the intervening centuries the ethics of rhetoric has lost none of its importance. If anything, readers, writers, listeners, and viewers in an age of mass communication—of public relations, advertising, and image manufacturing—need to be especially aware of the difference between honest language and deceit. Beneath "the right use of language" lie the profoundest matters of our political and moral welfare.

The section begins with two different but closely related accounts of how language means. Both deal with language as symbolism and with the use of symbolism as the activity most typical of humans. James Britton's essay emphasizes the function of symbolism and of language in representing—making sense of—experience. Susanne K. Langer's essay stresses our unique capacity to *manipulate* symbols (with its paradoxical gifts of both reason and lunacy) and so opens the political and moral question in the broadest terms: "The envisagements of good and evil, which make man a moral agent, make him also a conscript, a prisoner, and a slave. His constant problem is to escape the tyrannies he has created." She notes, too, "We control our inferiors by setting up symbols of our power, and the mere idea that words or images convey stands there to hold our fellows in subjection even when we cannot lay our hands on them."

Each of the remaining essays follows out some of the implications of the idea   73 of language as power. George Orwell's essay shows how bad thinking and bad writing propagate each other and how they are related to badness in political life. Haig Bosmajian dwells on the importance of names and labels in the language of oppression: "The power which comes from names and naming is related directly to the power to define others—individuals, races, sexes, ethnic groups." Robin Lakoff illustrates this point precisely as regards the language used by women and the language used to describe them. Murray Edelman investigates the network of status, power, and authority propagated by the professional language of doctors, nurses, social workers, prison authorities, teachers, and other members of the "helping professions."

HOW LANGUAGE MEANS

JAMES N. BRITTON

James N. Britton (born 1908) is a leading British thinker and writer on the writing and teaching of English. He was educated at the University of London and for many years taught English in various state schools. In 1970 he became head of the English Department of the University of London's Institute of Education, where he was involved in a major research project, published in 1975 as The Development of Writing Abilities *(11–18). Since the early 1960s his ideas have caused him to be widely sought as a speaker to teachers' groups, and he has taught as visitor and lecturer in all the principal English-speaking countries in the world. He has written books for children as well as scholarly studies on writing and English. He is coauthor of* Language, the Learner and the School *(1969) and author of* Language and Learning *(1970), from which we take the first two sections of the opening chapter.*

Language and Experience

[I]

From a childhood in city suburbs, I went at the age of fourteen to live on the outskirts of a town. I could walk into the country. On Saturdays we did, my brother and I. As we explored the area we drew a map of this precious bit of countryside, and I can recall one name on it—there was a long winding lane called Hobbleythick Lane. With the name comes a picture of a tall, ragged hawthorn hedge: one only, though I suppose there may have been a hedge on the other side also.

The map was a record of our wanderings, and each time we returned we added to it or corrected it. It was, though a crude one, a representation of the area; we valued it as a cumulative record of our activities there. Furthermore, looking forward instead of back, the map set forth our *expectations* concerning this area as we approached it afresh each time. By means of it we might hope to move around more purposefully, more intelligently: and this would be particularly true if we had returned to the place after a long absence, or if a stranger had gone to it and used our expectations to guide his movements.

There were other representations made of the area, too—not I think on my part, but my brother certainly used to stop occasionally and make a drawing of something he had seen. Neither the drawing nor the map *was* Hobbleythick Lane: each was a representation, and each representation was differently related to the thing itself. Each was in a different way a record of experience and each was capable, in a different way, of setting up or reviving expectations about the area. The map, we might say, was a more general representation, the drawing more particular.

In the summer, when we went there often, we carried, of course, our own expectations, 'in our heads'. The place was 'familiar' to us—which is another way of saying that the general outline of our expectations regarding it was appropriate. Indeed, the picture I can still see of a tall ragged hedge is 'an expectation' that has survived in me from that time.

I have arrived at this general point, then (*via* Hobbleythick Lane, which may have seemed to you as circuitous a route as I remember it to have been): that we construct a representation of the world as we experience it, and from this representation, this cumulative record of our own past, we generate expectations concerning the future; expectations which, as moment by moment the future becomes the present, enable us to interpret the present.

If I suddenly catch sight of a familiar face in a crowd, what I have just seen must somehow chime with something I already 'possess', something I carry with me: that something is an example of one kind of representation, a visual image. We shall see later that there are many kinds, many ways of representing the world to ourselves. The matter is complicated enough if for the moment we limit ourselves to visual images. As I sit here I can visualize with greater or less distinctness the faces of scores of my friends and acquaintances. But my storehouse, my representation of the world, in terms of the visual images of faces alone, is far, far richer than that, since faces I cannot recall would be familiar to me if I saw them again. Further, from past looking I would find a great deal that was familiar about faces I had *never* seen before—that they were human faces, that they were male or female (though not always), that they were old or young, perhaps, or Red Indian or Eskimo or Chinese.

In suggesting that a visual image of this sort *represents* a face I know, or a kind of face I know; that the drawing *represented* something in the landscape, and that the map *represented* an area of the countryside; further, that we habitually create representations of one kind or another of the things we meet in the actual world in order to use them in making sense of fresh encounters—in suggesting all this I am putting forward a view of human behaviour, or *one way of representing* what goes on in man's transactions with his environment. The view or the theory is, in fact, an example of itself. When the theory is put forward in its most general terms, and avoiding what are no doubt over-simplifications in the way I have put it, the word 'symbol' is usually used where I have used 'representation', and 'symbolizes' for 'represents'. It is a theory that attempts to explain what is characteristically human about human behaviour, what essentially distinguishes man from the other animals.

There have been other ways of explaining this distinction. Man has been called 'the talking animal' and that might have seemed an appropriate starting point for this book on language. But language, as we shall see, is only one way of symbolizing what is in the universe, and we cannot explain the particular workings of language unless we see their relations with other ways of symbolizing and with the nature of the symbolizing process itself (or with what is common to all ways). Philosophers have frequently taken *reason* to be the essentially human characteristic. Ernst Cassirer, the German philosopher, disposes of that claim:

> Reason is a very inadequate term with which to comprehend the forms of man's cultural life in all their richness and variety. But all these forms are symbolic forms. Hence, instead of defining man as an *animal rationale*, we should define him as an *animal symbolicum*. By so doing we can designate his specific difference, and we can understand the new way open to man—the way to civilisation. . . . That symbolic thought and symbolic behaviour are among the most characteristic features of human life, and that the whole progress of human culture is based on these conditions, is undeniable.[1]

The ability to speak and to reason are, of course, highly characteristic features of human life, distinguishing man from the other animals, but the point is that we have to dig beneath them to get to the root of the matter since both are dependent upon the ability to generate and use symbols, the ability to create representations of actuality. The world we respond to, in fact, the world towards which our behaviour is directed, is the world as we symbolize it, or represent it to ourselves. Changes in the actual world must be followed by changes in our representation of it if they are to affect our expectations and, hence, our subsequent behaviour.

Your representation of the world differs from mine, and this is not only in so far as the world has used us differently—that is to say we have had differing experiences of it. It is also because your *way of representing* is not the same as mine. We are neither of us cameras. A part of what we do at any moment can in fact be explained in terms of the camera, for just as the screen of the camera bears a picture of what is there outside, so our representation of the world is a partial likeness. It is a partial likeness because, at any moment, at the same time as we are drawing in from the outside world (to put it very crudely) we are also projecting our own wishes, our hopes and fears and expectations about the world. Our representation of that situation is the resultant of the two processes, that of *internalizing* and that of *externalizing*: and because what you project is a function of your personality (your

---

[1] Ernst Cassirer, *An Essay on Man* (New Haven, 1944), pp. 26 and 27.

mood of the moment as well as your habitual ways of feeling and thinking about things), and what I project is a function of my personality, our representations of the shared situation will be different. Moreover, the way I represent similar situations on different occasions will be different. Thor Heyerdahl, in the story of Kon Tiki, records how the party had a frightening experience with snakes one afternoon in the garden of a place they were visiting. Later that evening, we are told, they were sitting indoors by the light of oil lamps and they mistook the giant shadow of a perfectly ordinary scorpion for the shadow of a *giant scorpion*. Their representation, in other words, was strongly influenced by the feelings set up by the previous experience.

My representation of the present moment, then, reflects both the mood I happen to be in and also more enduring features of my personality. My way of representing encounters with the actual builds up, over a period of time, to produce my 'world representation': which, as we said at the beginning, is different from yours.

I look at the world in the light of what I have learned to expect from past experience of the world. That is to say, there is on the one hand my world representation—the accumulated record of my past experience—and there is on the other hand the process of representing to myself whatever of the world confronts me at any given moment. It is as though, in confrontation, my world representation were a body of expectations from which I select and match: the selecting and matching being in response to whatever cues the situation offers (but influenced also by my mood of the moment). What takes place in the confrontation may contradict or modify or confirm my expectations. My expectations are hypotheses which I submit to the test of encounter with the actual. The outcome affects not only my representation of the present moment, but, if necessary, my whole accumulated representation of the world. *Every encounter with the actual is an experimental committal of all I have learned from experience.* If what takes place lies entirely outside my expectations, so that nothing in my past experience provides the basis-for-modification, then I shall be able to make nothing of it: it might constitute 'an experience' for somebody else, but for me it cannot. (What does the infant who gazes in fascination at the bright light of the screen make of the television drama that his mother will call 'a gripping experience'? It is the flickering light that fascinates him and constitutes this 'experience' for him: the 'experience' for his mother—a slice of life in photo-images—is one the infant can 'make nothing of'.)

George Kelly, an American psychologist who died recently, has put forward a general theory of human behaviour which is consistent with what I have been saying, and with much that is yet to be said about the workings of language. Kelly suggests that all men behave in what is essentially the way a scientist behaves. He tells us how he arrived at this view:

> One of my tasks in the 1930s was to direct graduate studies leading to the Master's Degree. A typical afternoon might find me talking to a graduate student, doing all those familiar things that thesis directors have to do—

encouraging the student to pinpoint the issues, to observe, to become intimate with the problem, to form hypotheses either inductively or deductively, to make some preliminary test runs, to relate his data to his predictions, to control his experiments so that he will know what led to what, to generalize cautiously and to revise his thinking in the light of experience.

At two o'clock I might have an appointment with a client. During this interview I would not be taking the role of scientist but rather helping the distressed person work out some solutions to his life's problems. So what would I do? Why, I would try to get him to pinpoint the issues, to observe, to become intimate with the problem, to form hypotheses, to make test runs, to relate outcomes to anticipations, to control his ventures so that he will know what led to what, to generalize cautiously and to revise his dogma in the light of experience.[2]

The scientist's method of inquiry is to formulate hypotheses, or make predictions about the way things are, and then to put these to the test of what actually happens, and reframe his hypotheses in the light of what does happen. Kelly suggests that we look upon this as typical of human behaviour in general. This is a very different view from that of the popular legend about Newton—that truth hit him on the head with the apple. It stresses the *active* nature of man's approach to experience. To enlarge on it in Kelly's own words:

> Man looks at his world through transparent patterns or templates which he creates and then attempts to fit over the realities of which the world is composed. The fit is not always very good. Yet without such patterns the world appears to be such an undifferentiated homogeneity that man is unable to make any sense out of it. Even a poor fit is more helpful to him than nothing at all.[3]

Thus, the television drama that was a notable experience for the mother I referred to above, remained for the infant 'an undifferentiated homogeneity' of flickering lights and persistent noises. The template Kelly refers to is the equivalent of the 'representation' of the present moment actively produced by selecting and matching and modifying expectations drawn from the 'body of expectations' that constitutes an individual's representation of the world.

The 'template' and the 'representation' are crude analogies, crutches on which to lean until we can do without them. What Kelly first calls 'fitting a template' he goes on to describe as 'construing' or 'placing a construction upon' experience. And he has this to say about the cumulative nature of the process:

[2]George A. Kelly, "*The Strategy of Psychological Research*," in *Clinical Psychology and Personality*, ed. Brendan Maher (New York, 1969), pp. 60-61.
[3]George A. Kelly, *A Theory of Personality* (New York, 1963), pp. 8-9.

> Experience is made up of the successive construing of events. It is not consti-
> tuted merely by the succession of events themselves. . . . It is not what happens
> around him that makes a man's experiences; it is the successive construing
> and reconstruing of what happens, as it happens, that enriches the experience
> of life.

The outcome of this process, and the equivalent in Kelly's theory of what we
have called the 'world representation', is a person's 'construction system'.

The constructions one places upon events are working hypotheses which
are about to be put to the test of experience. As one's anticipations or
hypotheses are successively revised in the light of the unfolding sequence of
events, a construction system undergoes a progressive evolution.[4]

Kelly's conception of man as essentially concerned to anticipate events
and to extend and improve his predictive apparatus is important to the
purposes of this book. It is a view of human behaviour that makes living very
like learning; that equates learning with learning from experience; and that
underlines therefore the importance of our present inquiry into the means
by which a man brings his past to bear upon his present.

Events take place and are gone: it is the representation that lasts and
accumulates and undergoes successive modification. It is from the representation we make that we gain a sense of a continuing existence in a world
that has a past and a future, a world that remains in existence whether we
are there to prove it or not. Cassirer calls the world of space and time a
human world. 'Only symbolic expression', he says, 'can yield the possibility
of prospect and retrospect, because it is only by symbols that distinctions are
not merely *made*, but *fixed* in consciousness.'[5]

What is fixed in consciousness is there to go back to: a prediction, an
expectation, is formulated by reference back. Our representation of past
experience constitutes a frame of reference by means of which we recognize
familiar aspects of the present (the face of a friend in the crowd or the
strange face recognizably a child's or an old man's or Chinese). Moreover
what remains in consciousness is there to go back to and *modify* in the light of
the fresh encounter: it is a continuing sense of the world that is continually
brought up to date.

We can discuss representation no further without making specific reference to language. Language is one way of representing experience, but it is,
as we shall find when we examine the matter more fully, a key way. It is for
most of us the means by which all ways of representing combine to work
efficiently together.

The modification, the 'bringing up to date', of our representations of
experience is something that we habitually accomplish by means of talk. We

---

[4] Kelly, *Theory of Personality*, pp. 72 and 73. We have suggested that there are many ways of representing
experience, varying in the relationship between the representation and what is represented. It seems
appropriate to suggest that Kelly's 'construction system' does not cover all forms of representation, but is
in fact more like the map than the drawing or the visual image.

[5] Ernst Cassirer, *Language and Myth* (New York, 1946), p. 38.

have spoken so far as though the 'successive reconstruing', the modification of our representation, took place only as our expectations were put to the test in moment-by-moment encounters with the actual. But we habitually use talk to go back over events and interpret them, make sense of them in a way that we were unable to while they were taking place. This is to work upon our representation of the particular experience and our world representation in order to incorporate the one into the other more fully. We may of course achieve a similar end without talking: we may simply meditate in silence upon past events. In doing so we should, in my view, be using processes which we had acquired as a direct result of our past uses of language.

We habitually use talk also as a means of modifying each other's representations of experience. Martin Buber, the Jewish philosopher, came to London many years ago and gave a series of lectures that I have never forgotten. One of the things he said was, 'Experience comes to man "as I" but it is by experience "as we" that he builds the common world in which he lives.' We each build our own representation of the world, but we greatly affect each other's representation, so that much of what we build is built in common. We must suppose that primitive man's struggle to represent the world to himself with the help of language went on side by side with his attempts to bring his experiences of it into the area of communication with others. At no stage, therefore, could his representation be unaffected by the representations made by other men. This human characteristic is central to the distinction between man's social nature and the gregariousness of animals.

What has been said so far about language as a symbolic system, one of the means of representing the world, may be summed up in the words of Edward Sapir, the great American linguist. Sapir notes that 'the primary function of language is generally said to be communication' but goes on to offer an alternative view:

> It is best to admit that language is primarily a vocal actualisation of the tendency to see realities symbolically . . . an actualisation in terms of vocal expression of the tendency to master reality not by direct and *ad hoc* handling of this element but by the reduction of experience to familiar form.[6]

The primary task for speech is to symbolize reality: we symbolize reality in order to handle it.

We have been considering how man represents the actual world to himself in order to operate in it. It would be a mistake, however, to limit our idea of man's symbol-making to such activities. Indeed, it is clear that once we see man as creating a representation of his world so that he may operate in it, another order of activity is also open to him: he may operate *directly upon the representation itself.* He may opt out of the handling of reality for a time and improvise to his own satisfaction upon his represented world. In gossip, in our dreams and our daydreams, and in much of our reading, we improvise freely, wildly, light-heartedly upon our representation of past ex-

---

[6]Edward Sapir, *Culture, Language and Personality* (Berkeley, 1961), pp. 14–15.

periences with little concern for what those experiences have shown the world to be really like. Perhaps even the wildest fantasies may be found in the long run to be related to our need to extend and enrich our predictive capacity, to build up so vast a store of hypotheses that no conceivable possibility of experience could find us unprepared; but certainly our improvisations vary very widely in the degree to which we regard them as hypothetically related to actuality, the degree to which we regard them as of practical use.

Susanne Langer sees man as a proliferator of symbols, and speaks of 'the stream of symbols which constitutes the human mind'. Our participation in the world's affairs does not account for the whole of this activity.

> The material furnished by the senses [to quote Susanne Langer], is constantly wrought into symbols, which are our elementary ideas. Some of these ideas can be combined and manipulated in the manner we call 'reasoning', others do not lend themselves to this use, but are naturally telescoped into dreams, or vapour off in conscious fantasy; and a vast number of them build the most typical and fundamental edifice of the human mind—religion.

She goes on to suggest that the expression of these elementary ideas, these symbolizations, is 'the typically human form of overt activity'. 'How else shall we account for man's love of talk? From the first dawning recognition that words *express* something, talk is a dominant interest, an irresistible desire.' [7]

[II]

In what ways does language differ from other means of representing the world to ourselves, what claim has it to be called a 'key system', and in what ways is it related to the other systems or means of representation? What has to be explained may be put briefly: language is a highly organized, systematic means of representing experience, and as such it assists us to organize all other ways of representing.

We can most of us recall having had experiences in which so much was happening at the same time around us that we were in utter confusion. We could make nothing of it all. (A backwoodsman coming to a cinema for the first time and seeing Fellini's *8½* or some such film might be similarly at a loss.) Robert Graves in 'Welsh Incident' makes his eye-witness describe the strange creatures he saw on the beach in these words:

> But at last
> The most odd, indescribable thing of all
> Which hardly one man there could see for wonder
> Did something recognizably a something.

In a struggle to convey what he saw, he seems to have a method of working but not much to work it on!

---

[7] Susanne Langer, *Philosophy in a New Key*, 3d ed. (Cambridge, Mass., 1960), pp. 42-43.

But to speak of 'an experience', 'an event', 'an incident' is already to have moved some distance out from confusion. What the senses encounter moment by moment is a stream, an unbroken continuum: 'an incident'—thinking of the smallest item that might refer to—is a segment of that continuum. Before we can make something of what the senses deliver us we have therefore to extract from the stream some segment that is, from some aspect, a repetition of previous segments. (Or rather, of what may now be recognized as segments of the past continuum, for the recognition must be made on the basis of the similarity.) George Kelly refers to the process as 'construing the replications of events' and describes it thus:

> The substance that a person construes is itself a process. . . . It presents itself from the beginning as an unending and undifferentiated process. Only when man attunes his ear to recurrent themes in the monotonous flow does his universe begin to make sense to him. Like a musician, he must phrase his experience in order to make sense of it. The phrases are distinguished events. The separation of events is what man produces for himself when he decides to chop time up into manageable lengths. Within these limited segments, which are based on recurrent themes, man begins to discover the bases for likenesses and differences.[8]

Bruner[9] has pointed out that it is of no value to a man to know that in a sequence of his past experiences Event A was followed by Event B. It is of no value, because Event A will never happen again. But it is a different matter altogether to recognize that an event of *Type A* was followed by an event of *Type B*: that is to learn from experience, for when next an event of Type A occurs we shall be in a position to anticipate an event of Type B. To recognize segments of experience that are, from certain aspects, repetitions of previous segments is to begin grouping or classifying events, to begin labelling events as Type A, Type B, Type C and so on.

It is clear from their behaviour that animals are able to link together similar events and form what are, operationally speaking, categories. Most dogs—in suburban homes at all events—get excited when somebody in the family picks up the lead. They have learnt from past experience to expect that an event of type A—reaching for the lead—tends to be followed by an event of type B—going for a walk. The training of animals relies upon the setting up of linked categories of behaviour and experience: the creature must connect categories of its own actions with categories of subsequent reward or punishment. But because man uses language he is able to handle an infinitely greater number of categories than any other creature can. Language is our principal means of classifying, and it is this classifying function that goes furthest towards accounting for the role of language as an organizer of our representations of experience.

The objects of the world do not present themselves to us ready classified.

---

[8] Kelly, *Theory of Personality*, p. 52.
[9] Jerome S. Bruner, J. Goodnow and G. A. Austin, *A Study of Thinking* (New York, 1956).

The categories into which they are divided are categories into which *we divide them*. And the fact that we use language as a means of doing so may be inferred in a number of ways. From a child's own experiences of the world he comes to divide objects in very much the same way as his parents do, though the way he labels things shows that this is not true of his early experiences. The fact that as an infant he may call a whole variety of creatures 'ba' indicates that he is grouping together many objects that his parents would distinguish. It is as he learns to use language that he takes over, for the most part, the class divisions embodied in the language. But another child, growing up in another part of the world will divide experiences in a somewhat different way: he too is taking over, in general, the divisions embodied in his language, but it is a different language. Languages differ from each other in the way they divide objects into categories.

Malinowski, the British anthropologist,[10] suggested that societies classify their surroundings in accordance with their own particular needs and purposes. Thus, in one island community, he found there was a name for the kind of tree from which the natives made their canoes, a name for the kind of tree whose fruit they ate, and one general term (equivalent to 'the green thing', perhaps) for all other trees irrespective of any differences between them. And the same was true of fish: the fish they ate and the fish that if they were not watching out would eat them—these each had a name: all other fish were lumped together so that any one of them would be called 'the swimming thing'. An observer who did not know their language could have produced a simple classification of trees and fish (and so on) in terms of the islanders' behaviour with regard to them: and the trees and fish with which there were no particular dealings would have been left in the mass, unclassified. Going on to study their language he would have then found that it was by means of language that the behaviourally required categories had been set up and maintained. The categories into which the world is divided are the categories into which we have divided it to suit our particular purposes, and language is the means by which we mark the distinctions and pass them on.

One of the first things that anybody does who discovers a new feature on the earth's surface, or produces a new kind of rose, or invents a new game, or even a new system of analysis, is to give it a name. He may also plot it, register it, give it a serial number, or patent it—but it is the name that marks its existence in his society or in the world of human affairs. We take over in childhood the classification of experience embodied in our mother tongue: but we find no difficulty when the need arises in re-classifying by adding new items to the language.

The way we classify colours is one of the best (and most widely used) examples of the fact that categories are *made* and not *given*, the fact that different languages make them differently, and the fact, above all, that we could not handle experience at all if we did not first divide sense data into

---

[10]B. Malinowski, Supplement (i) to *The Meaning of Meaning* by C. K. Ogden and A. A. Richards (London, 1923), p. 331.

categories. The colour spectrum is a continuum: any colour we perceive must lie at some point in the infinity of points of that continuum. Bruner[11] records the fact that according to the estimates of physicists the human eye can distinguish one shade of colour from another seven million times over throughout the spectrum. That is to say, using the word colour in a rather special sense, there are seven million distinguishable 'colours'. But this is a statement about the discriminating power of the human eye rather than a statement about human purposes. For most of our ordinary human purposes we use a word that refers not to a 'colour' in this refined sense, but to a whole area or band of the spectrum. The point to be made is that we have to use broad categories if we are ever to get through the business of the day in terms of colour alone. If any one of the minimally distinguishable colours—the seven million—be regarded as a unique colour experience, then we usually handle this experience by referring to it with a word which represents a grouping of thousands of such unique experiences: the word 'red', for example. I say 'usually' because if our purpose requires us to be more specific we can be: we may say 'a particularly vivid scarlet', or 'a dull cherry'. But it would be *un*usual f⌐ ⌐us to say, 'Pass me the particularly vivid scarlet ink, please'.

Anthropologists have found languages in existence which do not divide the spectrum into the same bands as are found in the languages familiar to us. Bruner quotes two examples, one a language in which blue and green form a single group, and another in which brown and grey do so. Other examples could be used to show that languages divide phenomena differently. (The Eskimo language is said to have seven words for our one word 'snow'. Snow, which they see more of and which enters more into their purposes, for good or ill, has been divided into seven classes where we make one of it.) Our interest in such examples is the evidence they offer that classifying relies upon language.

The point to underline, however, is the degree to which we rely upon the process of classification. Experience is kaleidoscopic: the experience of every moment is unique and unrepeatable. Until we can group items in it on the basis of their similarity we can set up no expectations, make no predictions: lacking these we can make nothing of the present moment. Without categories of experience, therefore, we should remain imprisoned in the uniqueness of the here and now. What Piaget has called 'the manifold and irreducible present' is in fact conquered by what Sapir described as 'the reduction of experience to familiar form'.

The cutting into segments of the stream of sense experience and the recognition of similarities between segments enables us to build up a representation, let us say, of an object such as a cup. From the overlap of many experiences, focused upon as the word 'cup' is used by other people or ourselves, the basis of similarity and disimilarity becomes more clearly defined and more objects, different from the original cup in what does not matter but alike in what does—what defines the category—are admitted to

[11]Bruner et al., *A Study of Thinking*.

the category. The word, then, unlike the visual image I have of a cup I have seen and can recall, is a generalized representation, classifying as it represents.

Taking a leap from there, it is difficult to imagine how some experiences could be classified at all were it not for the agency of language. Four-year-old children will cheerfully and confidently talk about their *holidays*—about who is on holiday and where they have gone, and about what they are going to do on their own holidays. The definition of the category, criteria by which to decide what is properly called 'a holiday' and what is not, would be a complicated task for us and certainly the four-year-old could not attempt it. And there is nothing to point to, as he might point to a cup to show he knew the meaning. The ability to operate the category has grown from the overlap of experiences of the *word in use* as applied to his own familiar experiences.

It is not simply in the number of categories they possess that men are superior to dogs, but also in the inter-relatedness of the categories. Language, because of its own highly complex internal organization, provides us with systematically related categories of many kinds. There are categories of meaning, one of which, 'synonymity', is essentially the relationship we have been considering in speaking of the process by which the word 'cup' or the word 'holiday' comes to apply to a class of items instead of a single item of our experience. *Oppositeness* is another relationship that is built into language. In referring to the 'width' of a thing, for example we have a set of three words at our disposal—'wide', 'narrow' and 'width'. A child may discover that what seems wide to him on one occasion, in one context, seems narrow to him on another, and then he comes to learn that even the narrowest thing is said to have 'width'; and similarly even the lightest thing is said to have 'weight'. He can ask 'How heavy is your bag?' when obviously it is not heavy at all and 'How old is the kitten?' when it is obviously very young. In other words there is built into the English language a way of helping him to deal with the complicated nature of bi-polar oppositeness. Perhaps the most powerfully useful relationship in language is that of *hierarchy*. We have seen that all words are generalized representations; there are among them, however, different *levels of generality*. Since all buttercups are flowers but all flowers are not buttercups, it is clear that 'buttercup' represents a class of objects that is a sub-class of that represented by 'flower'; and that in turn is a sub-class of the class of objects represented by 'plant'. It is the existence of classes at different levels of generality that finally makes possible the higher forms of thought process, including what we call 'reasoning'. To be able to group objects in accordance with words existing in the language at different levels of generality is a mere beginning, but it is the essential foundation for the higher thought processes, as we shall see later when we come to look at the development of language and of learning in children. There is no need to add here that man's representation of the world owes more to the mental processes achieved in this way than to any other agency.

Grammatical relationships constitute another kind of organization to be found in language, and as such affect the way we represent experience in speech and thought. Aspects of our experience are habitually represented as nouns while others are represented as verbs: their further relations are governed by rules of syntax. But we shall postpone to a later chapter (Chapter 5) a fuller consideration of some of the complicated ways in which these factors affect what we make of our experiences.

Our world representation is a storehouse of the data of our experience: it is of predictive value to us in so far as the data are retrievable. And this calls for complex and efficient organization. Language, we are told, is 'rule-governed behaviour': as we represent experience in words we submit it to the rules, we bring to bear upon it the highly complex relationships systematically embodied in language itself. The process begins—though, as we shall see, it does not end—in talk.

SUSANNE K. LANGER

Susanne K. Langer, born in 1895, was educated at Radcliffe College, where she received a doctorate in 1926. She has taught philosophy at Radcliffe, Wellesley, Smith, and Columbia, and in 1954 became head of the Philosophy Department at Connecticut College. She is now Professor Emeritus and research scholar, pursuing investigations in the philosophy of art, expression, and meaning. One of the few notable women in a field traditionally dominated by men, Professor Langer has reached a large audience and has had great influence on recent thinking, especially about the arts. Her best-known book is Philosophy in a New Key *(1942), in which, taking her cue from the researches of philosopher Ernst Cassirer, she investigates "the symbolism of reason, rite, and art." She has also written* An Introduction to Symbolic Logic *(1937),* Feeling and Form *(1953),* The Problem of Art *(1957), and* Mind: An Essay on Human Feeling *(2 vols., 1967, 1972). The present essay, clearly deriving from her interest in symbolism, appeared in* Fortune *in January 1944, at the height of World War II.*

The Prince of Creation

The world is aflame with man-made public disasters, artificial rains of brimstone and fire, planned earthquakes, cleverly staged famines and floods. The Prince of Creation is destroying himself. He is throwing down the cities he has built, the works of his own hand, the wealth of many thousand years in his frenzy of destruction, as a child knocks down its own handiwork, the whole day's achievement, in a tantrum of tears and rage.

What has displeased the royal child? What has incurred his world-shattering tantrum?

The bafflement of the magnificent game he is playing. Its rules and its symbols, his divine toys, have taken possession of the player. For this global war is not the old, hard, personal fight for the means of life, *bellum omnium contra omnes*, which animals perpetually wage; this is a war of monsters. Not mere men but great superpersonal giants, the national states, are met in combat. They do not hate and attack and wrestle as injured physical creatures do; they move heavily, inexorably, by strategy and necessity, to each other's destruction. The game of national states has come to this pass, and the desperate players ride their careening animated toys to a furious suicide.

These moloch gods, these monstrous states, are not natural beings; they are man's own work, products of the power that makes him lord over all other living things—his mind. They are not of the earth, earthy, as families and herds, hives and colonies are, whose members move and fight as one by instinct and habit until a physical disturbance splits them and the severed parts reconstitute themselves as new organized groups. The national states are not physical groups; they are social symbols, profound and terrible.

They are symbols of the new way of life, which the past two centuries have given us. For thousands of years, the pattern of daily life—working, praying, building, fighting, and raising new generations—repeated itself with only slow or unessential changes. The social symbols expressive of this life were ancient and familiar. Tribal gods or local saints, patriarchs, squires, or feudal lords, princes and bishops, raised to the highest power in the persons of emperors and popes—they were all expressions of needs and duties and opinions grounded in an immemorial way of life. The average man's horizon was not much greater than his valley, his town, or whatever geographical ramparts bounded his community. Economic areas were small, and economic problems essentially local. Naturally in his conception the powers governing the world were local, patriarchal, and reverently familiar.

Then suddenly, within some two hundred years, and for many places far less than that, the whole world has been transformed. Communities of different tongues and faiths and physiognomies have mingled; not as of old in wars of conquest, invading lords and conquered population gradually mixing their two stocks, but by a new process of foot-loose travel and trade, dominated by great centers of activity that bring individuals from near and far promiscuously together as a magnet draws filings from many heaps into close but quite accidental contact. Technology has made old horizons meaningless and localities indefinite. For goods and their destinies determine the structure of human societies. This is a new world, a world of persons, not of families and clans, or parishes and manors. The proletarian order is not founded on a hearth and its history. It does not express itself in a dialect, a local costume, a rite, a patron saint. All such traditions by mingling have canceled each other, and disappeared.

Most of us feel that since the old controlling ideas of faith and custom are gone, mankind is left without anchorage of any sort. None of the old social symbols fit this modern reality, this shrunken and undifferentiated world in which we lead a purely economic, secular, essentially homeless life.

But mankind is never without its social symbols; when old ones die, new ones are already in process of birth; and the new gods that have superseded all faiths are the great national states. The conception of them is mystical and moral, personal and devotional; they conjure with names and emblems, and demand our constant profession and practice of the new orthodoxy called "Patriotism."

Of all born creatures, man is the only one that cannot live by bread alone. He lives as much by symbols as by sense report, in a realm compounded of tangible things and virtual images, of actual events and ominous portents, always between fact and fiction. For he sees not only actualities but meanings. He has, indeed, all the impulses and interests of animal nature; he eats, sleeps, mates, seeks comfort and safety, flees pain, falls sick and dies, just as cats and bears and fishes and butterflies do. But he has something more in his repertoire, too—he has laws and religions, theories and dogmas, because he lives not only through sense but through symbols. That is the special asset of his mind, which makes him the master of earth and all its progeny.

By the agency of symbols—marks, words, mental images, and icons of all sorts—he can hold his ideas for contemplation long after their original causes have passed away. Therefore, he can think of things that are not presented or even suggested by his actual environment. By associating symbols in his mind, he combines things and events that were never together in the real world. This gives him the power we call imagination. Further, he can symbolize only part of an idea and let the rest go out of consciousness; this gives him the faculty that has been his pride throughout the ages—the power of abstraction. The combined effect of these two powers is inestimable. They are the roots of his supreme talent, the gift of reason.

In the war of each against all, which is the course of nature, man has an unfair advantage over his animal brethren; for he can see what is not yet there to be seen, know events that happened before his birth, and take possession of more than he actually eats; he can kill at a distance; and by rational design he can enslave other creatures to live and act for him instead of for themselves.

Yet this mastermind has strange aberrations. For in the whole animal kingdom there is no such unreason, no such folly and impracticality as man displays. He alone is hounded by imaginary fears, beset by ghosts and devils, frightened by mere images of things. No other creature wastes time in unprofitable ritual or builds nests for dead specimens of its race. Animals are always realists. They have intelligence in varying degrees—chickens are stupid, elephants are said to be very clever—but, bright or foolish, animals react only to reality. They may be fooled by appearance, by pictures or reflections, but once they know them as such, they promptly lose interest. Distance and darkness and silence are not fearful to them, filled with voices or forms, or invisible presences. Sheep in the pasture do not seem to fear phantom sheep beyond the fence, mice don't look for mouse goblins in the clock, birds do not worship a divine thunderbird.

But oddly enough, men do. They think of all these things and guard against them, worshiping animals and monsters even before they conceive of divinities in their own image. Men are essentially unrealistic. With all their extraordinary intelligence, they alone go in for patently impractical actions—magic and exorcism and holocausts—rites that have no connection with common-sense methods of self-preservation, such as a highly intelligent animal might use. In fact, the rites and sacrifices by which primitive man claims to control nature are sometimes fatal to the performers. Indian puberty rites are almost always intensely painful, and African natives have sometimes died during initiations into honorary societies.

We usually assume that very primitive tribes of men are closer to animal estate than highly civilized races; but in respect of practical attitudes, this is not true. The more primitive man's mind, the more fantastic it seems to be; only with high intellectual discipline do we gradually approach the realistic outlook of intelligent animals.

Yet this human mind, so beclouded by phantoms and superstitions, is probably the only mind on earth that can reach out to an awareness of things beyond its practical environment and can also conceive of such notions as truth, beauty, justice, majesty, space and time and creation.

There is another paradox in man's relationship with other creatures: namely, that those very qualities he calls animalian—"brutal," "bestial," "inhuman"—are peculiarly his own. No other animal is so deliberately cruel as man. No other creature intentionally imprisons its own kind, or invents special instruments of torture such as racks and thumbscrews for the sole purpose of punishment. No other animal keeps its own brethren in slavery; so far as we know, the lower animals do not commit anything like the acts of pure sadism that figure rather largely in our newspapers. There is no torment, spite, or cruelty for its own sake among beasts, as there is among men. A cat plays with its prey, but does not conquer and torture smaller cats. But man, who knows good and evil, is cruel for cruelty's sake; he who has a moral law is more brutal than the brutes, who have none; he alone inflicts suffering on his fellows with malice aforethought.

If man's mind is really a higher form of the animal mind, his morality a specialized form of herd instinct, then where in the course of evolution did he lose the realism of a clever animal and fall prey to subjective fears? And why should he take pleasure in torturing helpless members of his own race?

The answer is, I think, that man's mind is *not* a direct evolution from the beast's mind, but is a unique variant and therefore has had a meteoric and startling career very different from any other animal history. The trait that sets human mentality apart from every other is its preoccupation with symbols, with images and names that *mean* things, rather than with things themselves. This trait may have been a mere sport of nature once upon a time. Certain creatures do develop tricks and interests that seem biologically unimportant. Pack rats, for instance, and some birds of the crow family take a capricious pleasure in bright objects and carry away such things for which they have, presumably, no earthly use. Perhaps man's tendency to see certain forms as *images*, to hear certain sounds not only as signals but as expressive tones, and to be excited by sunset colors or starlight, was originally just a peculiar sensitivity in a rather highly developed brain. But whatever its cause, the ultimate destiny of this trait was momentous; for all human activity is based on the appreciation and use of symbols. Language, religion, mathematics, all learning, all science and superstition, even right and wrong, are products of symbolic expression rather than direct experience. Our commonest words, such as "house" and "red" and "walking," are symbols; the pyramids of Egypt and the mysterious circles of Stonehenge are symbols; so are dominions and empires and astronomical universes. We live in a mind-made world, where the things of prime importance are images or words that embody ideas and feelings and attitudes.

The animal mind is like a telephone exchange; it receives stimuli from outside through the sense organs and sends out appropriate responses through the nerves that govern muscles, glands, and other parts of the body. The organism is constantly interacting with its surroundings, receiving messages and acting on the new state of affairs that the messages signify.

But the human mind is not a simple transmitter like a telephone exchange. It is more like a great projector; for instead of merely mediating between an event in the outer world and a creature's responsive action, it transforms or, if you will, distorts the event into an image to be looked at, retained, and contemplated. For the images of things that we remember are not exact and faithful transcriptions even of our actual sense impressions. They are made as much by what we think as by what we see. It is a well-known fact that if you ask several people the size of the moon's disk as they look at it, their estimates will vary from the area of a dime to that of a barrel top. Like a magic lantern, the mind projects its ideas of things on the screen of what we call "memory"; but like all projections, these ideas are transformations of actual things. They are, in fact, *symbols* of reality, not pieces of it.

A symbol is not the same thing as a sign; that is a fact that psychologists and philosophers often overlook. All intelligent animals use signs; as do we. To them as well as to us sounds and smells and motions are signs of food, danger, the presence of other beings, or of rain or storm. Furthermore, some animals not only attend to signs but produce them for the benefit of others. Dogs bark at the door to be let in; rabbits thump to call each other; the cooing of doves and the growl of a wolf defending his kill are unequivocal signs of feelings and intentions to be reckoned with by other creatures.

We use signs just as animals do, though with considerably more elaboration. We stop at red lights and go on green; we answer calls and bells, watch the sky for coming storms, read trouble or promise or anger in each other's eyes. That is animal intelligence raised to the human level. Those of us who are dog lovers can probably all tell wonderful stories of how high our dogs have sometimes risen in the scale of clever sign interpretation and sign using.

A sign is anything that announces the existence or the imminence of some event, the presence of a thing or a person, or a change in a state of affairs. There are signs of the weather, signs of danger, signs of future good or evil, signs of what the past has been. In every case a sign is closely bound up with something to be noted or expected in experience. It is always a part of the situation to which it refers, though the reference may be remote in space and time. In so far as we are led to note or expect the signified event we are making correct use of a sign. This is the essence of rational behavior, which animals show in varying degrees. It is entirely realistic, being closely bound up with the actual objective course of history—learned by experience, and cashed in or voided by further experience.

If man had kept to the straight and narrow path of sign using, he would be like the other animals, though perhaps a little brighter. He would not talk, but grunt and gesticulate and point. He would make his wishes known, give warnings, perhaps develop a social system like that of bees and ants, with such a wonderful efficiency of communal enterprise that all men would have plenty to eat, warm apartments—all exactly alike and perfectly convenient—to live in, and everybody could and would sit in the sun or by the fire, as the climate demanded, not talking but just basking, with every want satisfied, most of his life. The young would romp and make love, the old would sleep, the middle-aged would do the routine work almost unconsciously and eat a great deal. But that would be the life of a social, superintelligent, purely sign-using animal.

To us who are human, it does not sound very glorious. We want to go places and do things, own all sorts of gadgets that we do not absolutely need, and when we sit down to take it easy we want to talk. Rights and property, social position, special talents and virtues, and above all our ideas, are what we live for. We have gone off on a tangent that takes us far away from the mere biological cycle that animal generations accomplish; and that is because we can use not only signs but symbols.

A symbol differs from a sign in that it does not announce the presence of the object, the being, condition, or whatnot, which is its meaning, but merely *brings this thing to mind*. It is not a mere "substitute sign" to which we react as though it were the object itself. The fact is that our reaction to hearing a person's name is quite different from our reaction to the person himself. There are certain rare cases where a symbol stands directly for its meaning: in religious experience, for instance, the Host is not only a symbol but a Presence. But symbols in the ordinary sense are not mystic. They are the same sort of thing that ordinary signs are; only they do not call our attention to something necessarily present or to be physically dealt with— they call up merely a conception of the thing they "mean."

The difference between a sign and a symbol is, in brief, that a sign causes us to think or act *in face of* the thing signified, whereas a symbol causes us to think *about* the thing symbolized. Therein lies the great importance of symbolism for human life, its power to make this life so different from any other animal biography that generations of men have found it incredible to suppose that they were of purely zoological origin. A sign is always embedded in reality, in a present that emerges from the actual past and stretches to the future; but a symbol may be divorced from reality altogether. It serves, therefore, to liberate thought from the immediate stimuli of a physically present world; and that liberation marks the essential difference between human and nonhuman mentality. Animals think, but they think *of* and *at* things; men think primarily *about* things. Words, pictures, and memory images are symbols that may be combined and varied in a thousand ways. The result is a symbolic structure whose meaning is a complex of all their respective meanings, and this kaleidoscope of *ideas* is the typical product of the human brain that we call the "stream of thought."

The process of transforming all direct experience into imagery or into that supreme mode of symbolic expression, language, has so completely taken possession of the human mind that it is not only a special talent but a dominant, organic need. All our sense impressions leave their traces in our memory not only as signs disposing our practical reactions in the future but also as symbols, images representing our *ideas* of things; and the tendency to manipulate ideas, to combine and abstract, mix and extend them by playing with symbols, is man's outstanding characteristic. It seems to be what his brain most naturally and spontaneously does. Therefore his primitive mental function is not judging reality, but *dreaming his desires.*

Dreaming is apparently a basic function of human brains, for it is free and unexhausting like our metabolism, heartbeat, and breath. It is easier to dream than not to dream, as it is easier to breathe than to refrain from breathing. The symbolic character of dreams is fairly well established. Symbol mongering, on this ineffectual, uncritical level, seems to be instinctive, the fulfillment of an elementary need rather than the purposeful exercise of a high and difficult talent.

The special power of man's mind rests on the evolution of this special activity, not on any transcendently high development of animal intelligence. We are not immeasurably higher than other animals; we are different. We have a biological need and with it a biological gift that they do not share.

Because man has not only the ability but the constant need of *conceiving* what has happened to him, what surrounds him, what is demanded of him—in short, of symbolizing nature, himself, and his hopes and fears—he has a constant and crying need of *expression.* What he cannot express, he cannot conceive; what he cannot conceive is chaos, and fills him with terror.

If we bear in mind this all-important craving for expression we get a new picture of man's behavior; for from this trait spring his powers and his weaknesses. The process of symbolic transformation that all our experiences undergo is nothing more nor less than the process of *conception*, which underlies the human faculties of abstraction and imagination.

When we are faced with a strange or difficult situation, we cannot react directly, as other creatures do, with flight, aggression, or any such simple instinctive pattern. Our whole reaction depends on how we manage to conceive the situation—whether we cast it in a definite dramatic form, whether we see it as a disaster, a challenge, a fulfillment of doom, or a fiat of the Divine Will. In words or dreamlike images, in artistic or religious or even in cynical form, we must *construe* the events of life. There is great virtue in the figure of speech, "I can *make* nothing of it," to express a failure to understand something. Thought and memory are processes of *making* the thought content and the memory image; the pattern of our ideas is given by the symbols through which we express them. And in the course of manipulating those symbols we inevitably distort the original experience, as we abstract certain features of it, embroider and reinforce those features with other ideas, until the conception we project on the screen of memory is quite different from anything in our real history.

Conception is a necessary and elementary process; what we do with our conceptions is another story. That is the entire history of human culture—of intelligence and morality, folly and superstition, ritual, language, and the arts—all the phenomena that set man apart from, and above, the rest of the animal kingdom. As the religious mind has to make all human history a drama of sin and salvation in order to define its own moral attitudes, so a scientist wrestles with the mere presentation of "the facts" before he can reason about them. The process of *envisaging* facts, values, hopes, and fears underlies our whole behavior pattern; and this process is reflected in the evolution of an extraordinary phenomenon found always, and only, in human societies—the phenomenon of language.

Language is the highest and most amazing achievement of the symbolistic human mind. The power it bestows is almost inestimable, for without it anything properly called "thought" is impossible. The birth of language is the dawn of humanity. The line between man and beast—between the highest ape and the lowest savage—is the language line. Whether the primitive Neanderthal man was anthropoid or human depends less on his cranial capacity, his upright posture, or even his use of tools and fire, than on one issue we shall probably never be able to settle—whether or not he spoke.

In all physical traits and practical responses, such as skills and visual judgments, we can find a certain continuity between animal and human mentality. Sign using is an ever evolving, ever improving function throughout the whole animal kingdom, from the lowly worm that shrinks into his hole at the sound of an approaching foot, to the dog obeying his master's command, and even to the learned scientist who watches the movements of an index needle.

This continuity of the sign-using talent has led psychologists to the belief that language is evolved from the vocal expressions, grunts and coos and cries, whereby animals vent their feelings or signal their fellows; that man has elaborated this sort of communion to the point where it makes a perfect exchange of ideas possible.

I do not believe that this doctrine of the origin of language is correct. The essence of language is symbolic, not signific; we use it first and most vitally to formulate and hold ideas in our own minds. Conception, not social control, is its first and foremost benefit.

Watch a young child that is just learning to speak play with a toy; he says the name of the object, e.g.: "Horsey! horsey! horsey!" over and over again, looks at the object, moves it, always saying the name to himself or to the world at large. It is quite a time before he talks to anyone in particular; he talks first of all to himself. This is his way of forming and fixing the *conception* of the object in his mind, and around this conception all his knowledge of it grows. *Names* are the essence of language; for the *name* is what abstracts the conception of the horse from the horse itself, and lets the mere idea recur at the speaking of the name. This permits the conception gathered from one horse experience to be exemplified again by another instance of a horse, so that the notion embodied in the name is a general notion.

To this end, the baby uses a word long before he *asks for* the object; when he wants his horsey he is likely to cry and fret, because he is reacting to an actual environment, not forming ideas. He uses the animal language of *signs* for his wants; talking is still a purely symbolic process—its practical value has not really impressed him yet.

Language need not be vocal; it may be purely visual, like written language, or even tactual, like the deaf-mute system of speech; but it *must be denotative.* The sounds, intended or unintended, whereby animals communicate do not constitute a language, because they are signs, not names. They never fall into an organic pattern, a meaningful syntax of even the most rudimentary sort, as all language seems to do with a sort of driving necessity. That is because signs refer to actual situations, in which things have obvious relations to each other that require only to be noted; but symbols refer to ideas, which are not physically there for inspection, so their connections and features have to be represented. This gives all true language a natural tendency toward growth and development, which seems almost like a life of its own. Languages are not invented; they grow with our need for expression.

In contrast, animal "speech" never has a structure. It is merely an emotional response. Apes may greet their ration of yams with a shout of "Nga!" But they do not say "Nga" between meals. If they could *talk about* their yams instead of just saluting them, they would be the most primitive men instead of the most anthropoid of beasts. They would have ideas, and tell each other things true or false, rational or irrational; they would make plans and invent laws and sing their own praises, as men do.

The history of speech is the history of our human descent. Yet the habit of transforming reality into symbols, of contemplating and combining and distorting symbols, goes beyond the confines of language. All *images* are symbols, which make us think about the things they mean.

This is the source of man's great interest in "graven images," and in *mere appearances* like the face of the moon or the human profiles he sees in rocks and trees. There is no limit to the meanings he can read into natural phenomena. As long as this power is undisciplined, the sheer enjoyment of finding meanings in everything, the elaboration of concepts without any regard to truth and usefulness, seems to run riot; superstition and ritual in their pristine strength go through what some anthropologists have called a "vegetative" stage, when dreamlike symbols, gods and ghouls and rites, multiply like the overgrown masses of life in a jungle. From this welter of symbolic forms emerge the images that finally govern a civilization; the great symbols of religion, society, and selfhood.

What does an image "mean"? Anything it is thought to resemble. It is only because we can abstract quite unobvious forms from the actual appearance of things that we see line drawings in two dimensions as images of colored, three-dimensional objects, find the likeness of a dipper in a constellation of seven stars, or see a face on a pansy. Any circle may represent the sun or moon; an upright monolith may be a man.

Wherever we can fancy a similarity we tend to see something represented. The first thing we do, upon seeing a new shape, is to assimilate it to our own idea of something that it resembles, something that is known and important to us. Our most elementary concepts are of our own actions, and the limbs or organs that perform them; other things are named by comparison with them. The opening of a cave is its mouth, the divisions of a river its arms. Language, and with it all articulate thought, grows by this process of unconscious metaphor. Every new idea urgently demands a word; if we lack a name for it, we call it after the first namable thing seen to bear even a remote analogy to it. Thus all the subtle and variegated vocabulary of a living language grows up from a few roots of very general application; words as various in meaning as "gentle" and "ingenious" and "general" spring from the one root "ge" meaning "to give life."

Yet there are conceptions that language is constitutionally unfit to express. The reason for this limitation of our verbal powers is a subject for logicians and need not concern us here. The point of interest to us is that, just as rational, discursive thought is bound up with language, so the life of feeling, of direct personal and social consciousness, the emotional stability of man and his sense of orientation in the world are bound up with images directly given to his senses: fire and water, noise and silence, high mountains and deep caverns, the brief beauty of flowers, the persistent grin of a skull. There seem to be irresistible parallels between the expressive forms we find in nature and the forms of our inner life; thus the use of light to represent all things good, joyful, comforting, and of darkness to express all sorts of sorrow, despair, or horror, is so primitive as to be well-nigh unconscious.

A flame is a soul; a star is a hope; the silence of winter is death. All such images, which serve the purpose of metaphorical thinking, are *natural symbols*. They have not conventionally assigned meanings, like words, but recommend themselves even to a perfectly untutored mind, a child's or a savage's, because they are definitely articulated *forms*, and to see something expressed in such forms is a universal human talent. We do not have to learn to use natural symbols; it is one of our primitive activities.

The fact that sensuous forms of natural processes have a significance beyond themselves makes the range of our symbolism, and with it the horizon of our consciousness, much wider and deeper than language. This is the source of ritual, mythology, and art. Ritual is a symbolic rendering of certain emotional *attitudes*, which have become articulate and fixed by being constantly expressed. Mythology is man's image of his world, and of himself in the world. Art is the exposition of his own subjective history, the life of feeling, the human spirit in all its adventures.

Yet this power of envisagement, which natural symbolism bestows, is a dangerous one; for human beings can envisage things that do not exist, and create horrible worlds, insupportable duties, monstrous gods and ancestors. The mind that can see past and future, the poles and the antipodes, and guess at obscure mechanisms of nature, is ever in danger of seeing what is not there, imagining false and fantastic causes, and courting death instead of life. Because man can play with ideas, he is unrealistic; he is inclined to neglect the all-important interpretation of signs for a rapt contemplation of symbols.

Some twenty years ago, Ernst Cassirer set forth a theory of human mentality that goes far toward explaining the vagaries of savage religions and the ineradicable presence of superstition even in civilized societies: a symbol, he observed, is the embodiment of an idea; it is at once an abstract and a physical fact. Now its great emotive value lies in the concept it conveys; this inspires our reverent attitude, the attention and awe with which we view it. But man's untutored thought always tends to lose its way between the symbol and the fact. A skull represents death; but to a primitive mind the skull *is* death. To have it in the house is not unpleasant but dangerous. Even in civilized societies, symbolic objects—figures of saints, relics, crucifixes—are revered for their supposed efficacy. Their actual power is a power of *expression*, of embodying and thus revealing the greatest concepts humanity has reached; these concepts are the commanding forces that change our estate from a brute existence to the transcendent life of the spirit. But the symbol-loving mind of man reveres the meaning not *through* the articulating form but *in* the form so that the image appears to be the actual object of love and fear, supplication and praise.

Because of this constant identification of concepts with their expressions, our world is crowded with unreal beings. Some societies have actually realized that these beings do not belong to nature, and have postulated a so-called "other world" where they have their normal existence and from which they are said to descend, or arise, into our physical realm. For savages it is chiefly a nether world that sends up spooks; for more advanced cults it is from the heavens that supernatural beings, the embodiments of human ideas—of virtue, triumph, immortality—descend to the mundane realm. But from this source emanates also a terrible world government, with heavy commands and sanctions. Strange worship and terrible sacrifices may be the tithes exacted by the beings that embody our knowledge of nonanimalian human nature.

So the gift of symbolism, which is the gift of reason, is at the same time the seat of man's peculiar weakness—the danger of lunacy. Animals go mad with hydrophobia or head injuries, but purely mental aberrations are rare; beasts are not generally subject to insanity except through a confusion of signs, such as the experimentally produced "nervous breakdown" in rats. It is man who hears voices and sees ghosts in the dark, feels irrational compulsions and holds fixed ideas. All these phantasms are symbolic forms that have acquired a false factual status. It has been truly said that everybody has some streak of insanity; i.e., the threat of madness is the price of reason.

Because we can think of things potential as well as actual, we can be held in nonphysical bondage by laws and prohibitions and commands and by images of a governing power. This makes men tyrants over their own kind. Animals control each other's actions by immediate threats, growls and snarls and passes; but when the bully is roving elsewhere, his former domain is free of him. We control our inferiors by setting up symbols of our power, and the mere idea that words or images convey stands there to hold our fellows in subjection even when we cannot lay our hands on them. There is no flag over the country where a wolf is king; he is king where he happens to prowl, so long as he is there. But men, who can embody ideas and set them up to view, oppress each other by symbols of might.

The envisagements of good and evil, which make man a moral agent, make him also a conscript, a prisoner, and a slave. His constant problem is to escape the tyrannies he has created. Primitive societies are almost entirely tyrannical, symbol-bound, coercive organizations; civilized governments are so many conscious schemes to justify or else to disguise man's inevitable bondage to law and conscience.

Slowly, through ages and centuries, we have evolved a picture of the world we live in; we have made a drama of the earth's history and enhanced it with a backdrop of divinely ordered, star-filled space. And all this structure of infinity and eternity against which we watch the pageant of life and death, and all the moral melodrama itself, we have wrought by a gradual articulation of such vast ideas in symbols—symbols of good and evil, triumph and failure, birth and maturity and death. Long before the beginning of any known history, people saw in the heavenly bodies, in the changes of day and night or of the seasons, and in great beasts, symbolic forms to express those ultimate concepts that are the very frame of human existence. So gods, fates, the cohorts of good and evil were conceived. Their myths were the first formulations of cosmic ideas. Gradually the figures and traditions of religion emerged; ritual, the overt expression of our mental attitudes, became more and more intimately bound to definite and elaborate concepts of the creative and destructive powers that seem to control our lives.

Such beings and stories and rites are sacred because they are the great symbols by which the human mind orients itself in the world. To a creature that lives by reason, nothing is more terrible than what is formless and meaningless; one of our primary fears is fear of chaos. And it is the fight against chaos that has produced our most profound and indispensable images—the myths of light and darkness, of creation and passion, the symbols of the altar flame, the daystar, and the cross.

For thousands of years people lived by the symbols that nature presented to them. Close contact with earth and its seasons, intimate knowledge of stars and tides, made them feel the significance of natural phenomena and gave them a poetic, unquestioning sense of orientation. Generations of erudite and pious men elaborated the picture of the temporal and spiritual realms in which each individual was a pilgrim soul.

Then came the unprecedented change, the almost instantaneous leap of history from the immemorial tradition of the plow and the anvil to the new age of the machine, the factory, and the ticker tape. Often in no more than the length of a life-time the shift from handwork to mass production, and with it from poetry to science and from faith to nihilism, has taken place. The old nature symbols have become remote and have lost their meanings; in the clatter of gears and the confusion of gadgets that fill the new world, there will not be any obvious and rich and sacred meanings for centuries to come. All the accumulated creeds and rites of men are suddenly in the melting pot. There is no fixed community, no dynasty, no family inheritance—only the one huge world of men, vast millions of men, still looking on each other in hostile amazement.

A sane, intelligent animal should have invented, in the course of ten thousand years or more, some sure and obvious way of accommodating indefinite numbers of its own kind on the face of a fairly spacious earth. Modern civilization has achieved the highest triumphs of knowledge, skill, ingenuity, theory; yet all around its citadels, engulfing and demolishing them, rages the maddest war and confusion, inspired by symbols and slogans as riotous and irrational as anything the "vegetative" stage of savage phantasy could provide. How shall we reconcile this primitive nightmare excitement with the achievements of our high, rational, scientific culture?

The answer is, I think, that we are no longer in possession of a definite, established culture; we live in a period between an exhausted age—the European civilization of the white race—and an age still unborn, of which we can say nothing as yet. We do not know what races shall inherit the earth. We do not know what even the next few centuries may bring. But it is quite evident, I think, that we live in an age of transition, and that before many more generations have passed, mankind will make a new beginning and build itself a different world. Whether it will be a "brave, new world," or whether it will start all over with an unchronicled "state of nature" such as Thomas Hobbes described, wherein the individual's life is "nasty, brutish, and short," we simply cannot tell. All we know is that every tradition, every institution, every tribe is gradually becoming uprooted and upset, and we are waiting in a sort of theatrical darkness between the acts.

Because we are at a new beginning, our imaginations tend to a wild, "vegetative" overgrowth. The political upheavals of our time are marked, therefore, by a veritable devil dance of mystical ideologies, vaguely conceived, passionately declared, holding out fanatic hopes of mass redemption and mass beatitudes. Governments vie with each other in proclaiming social plans, social aims, social enterprises, and demanding bloody sacrifices in the name of social achievements.

New conceptions are always clothed in an extravagant metaphorical form, for there is no language to express genuinely new ideas. And in their pristine strength they imbue the symbols that express them with their own mystery and power and holiness. It is impossible to disengage the welter of ideas embodied in a swastika, a secret sign, or a conjuring word from the physical presence of the symbol itself; hence the apparently nonsensical symbol worship and mysticism that go with new movements and visions. This identification of symbolic form and half-articulate meaning is the essence of all mythmaking. Of course the emotive value is incomprehensible to anyone who does not see such figments as expressive forms. So an age of vigorous new conception and incomplete formulation always has a certain air of madness about it. But it is really a fecund and exciting period in the life of reason. Such is our present age. Its apparent unreason is a tremendous unbalance and headiness of the human spirit, a conflict not only of selfish wills but of vast ideas in the metaphorical state of emergence.

The change from fixed community life and ancient local custom to the mass of unpedigreed human specimens that actually constitutes the world in our industrial and commercial age has been too sudden for the mind of man to negotiate. Some transitional form of life had to mediate between those extremes. And so the idol of nationality arose from the wreckage of tribal organization. The concept of the national state is really the old tribe concept applied to millions of persons, unrelated and different creatures gathered under the banner of a government. Neither birth nor language nor even religion holds such masses together, but a mystic bond is postulated even where no actual bond of race, creed, or color may ever have existed.

At first glance it seems odd that the concept of nationality should reach its highest development just as all actual marks of national origins—language, dress, physiognomy, and religion—are becoming mixed and obliterated by our new mobility and cosmopolitan traffic. But it is just the loss of these things that inspires this hungry seeking for something like the old egocentric pattern in the vast and formless brotherhood of the whole earth. While mass production and universal communication clearly portend a culture of world citizenship, we cling desperately to our nationalism, a more and more attenuated version of the old clan civilization. We fight passionate and horrible wars for the symbols of our nations, we make a virtue of self-glorification and exclusiveness and invent strange anthropologies to keep us at least theoretically set apart from other men.

Nationalism is a transition between an old and a new human order. But even now we are not really fighting a war of nations; we are fighting a war of fictions, from which a new vision of the order of nature will someday emerge. The future, just now, lies wide open—open and dark, like interstellar space; but in that emptiness there is room for new gods, new cultures, mysterious now and nameless as an unborn child.

LANGUAGE AND POLITICS

GEORGE ORWELL

George Orwell's reputation as a writer has shown no sign of decline since his death at forty-six in 1950. He is likely to be ranked permanently among the great English essayists. On presenting him an award in 1949, the editors of Partisan Review *commented that his writing "has been marked by a singular directness and honesty, a scrupulous fidelity to his experience that has placed him in that valuable class of the writer who is a witness to his time."*

His real name was Eric Arthur Blair, and he was born in 1903 in Bengal, a province of British India. His first school experience is described in the essay "Such, Such Were the Joys." He attended Eton on a King's Scholarship from 1917 to 1921, then served for five years in the Imperial Police in Burma. These early years are the subject of a biography by Peter Stansky and William Abraham entitled The Unknown Orwell *(1972). Returning to Europe, he spent several poverty-stricken years doing odd jobs, from teaching to dishwashing, while he wrote novels and short stories that did not sell. His* Down and Out in Paris and London *(1933) is a vivid record of those years. In 1936 Orwell went to Spain to take part in the civil war and reported his experiences in* Homage to Catalonia *(1938). Among his other books are the celebrated* Nineteen Eighty-Four *(1949), a terrifying novel picturing the complete victory of totalitarianism;* Animal Farm: A Fairy Story *(1945); and the essay collections* Shooting an Elephant and Other Essays *(1950),* Such, Such Were the Joys *(1953), and* Collected Essays *(1966). The present essay first appeared in the London monthly* Horizon *in 1946 and was reprinted in the 1950 collection. It was written with the horrors of World War II vividly in mind; unfortunately, it has not lost a bit of its relevance since.*

Politics and the English Language

Most people who bother with the matter at all would admit that the English language is in a bad way, but it is generally assumed that we cannot by conscious action do anything about it. Our civilization is decadent and our language—so the argument runs—must inevitably share in the general collapse. It follows that any struggle against the abuse of language is a sentimental archaism, like preferring candles to electric light or hansom cabs to aeroplanes. Underneath this lies the half-conscious belief that language is a natural growth and not an instrument which we shape for our own purposes.

Now, it is clear that the decline of a language must ultimately have political and economic causes: it is not due simply to the bad influence of this or that individual writer. But an effect can become a cause, reinforcing the original cause and producing the same effect in an intensified form, and so on indefinitely. A man may take to drink because he feels himself to be a failure, and then fail all the more completely because he drinks. It is rather the same thing that is happening to the English language. It becomes ugly and inaccurate because our thoughts are foolish, but the slovenliness of our language makes it easier for us to have foolish thoughts. The point is that the process is reversible. Modern English, especially written English, is full of bad habits which spread by imitation and which can be avoided if one is willing to take the necessary trouble. If one gets rid of these habits one can think more clearly, and to think clearly is a necessary first step towards political regeneration: so that the fight against bad English is not frivolous and is not the exclusive concern of professional writers. I will come back to this presently, and I hope that by that time the meaning of what I have said here will have become clearer. Meanwhile, here are five specimens of the English language as it is now habitually written.

These five passages have not been picked out because they are especially bad—I could have quoted far worse if I had chosen—but because they illustrate various of the mental vices from which we now suffer. They are a little below the average, but are fairly representative samples. I number them so that I can refer back to them when necessary:

(1) I am not, indeed, sure whether it is not true to say that the Milton who once seemed not unlike a seventeenth-century Shelley had not become, out of an experience ever more bitter in each year, more alien [*sic*] to the founder of that Jesuit sect which nothing could induce him to tolerate.

PROFESSOR HAROLD LASKI
(ESSAY IN *Freedom of Expression*).

(2) Above all, we cannot play ducks and drakes with a native battery of idioms which prescribes such egregious collocations of vocables as the Basic *put up with* for *tolerate* or *put at a loss* for *bewilder*.

PROFESSOR LANCELOT HOGBEN
(*Interglossa*).

(3) On the one side we have the free personality: by definition it is not neurotic, for it has neither conflict nor dream. Its desires, such as they are, are transparent, for they are just what institutional approval keeps in the forefront of consciousness; another institutional pattern would alter their number and intensity; there is little in them that is natural, irreducible, or culturally dangerous. But *on the other side*, the social bond itself is nothing but the mutual reflection of these self-secure integrities. Recall the definition of love. Is not this the very picture of a small academic? Where is there a place in this hall of mirrors for either personality or fraternity?

ESSAY ON PSYCHOLOGY IN *Politics*
(NEW YORK).

(4) All the "best people" from the gentlemen's clubs, and all the frantic fascist captains, united in common hatred of Socialism and bestial horror of the rising tide of the mass revolutionary movement, have turned to acts of provocation, to foul incendiarism, to medieval legends of poisoned wells, to legalize their own destruction of proletarian organizations, and rouse the agitated petty-bourgeoisie to chauvinistic fervor on behalf of the fight against the revolutionary way out of the crisis.

COMMUNIST PAMPHLET.

(5) If a new spirit *is* to be infused into this old country, there is one thorny and contentious reform which must be tackled, and that is the humanization and galvanization of the B.B.C. Timidity here will bespeak canker and atrophy of the soul. The heart of Britain may be sound and of strong beat, for instance, but the British lion's roar at present is like that of Bottom in

Shakespeare's *Midsummer Night's Dream*—as gentle as any sucking dove. A virile new Britain cannot continue indefinitely to be traduced in the eyes or rather ears, of the world by the effete languors of Langham Place, brazenly masquerading as "standard English." When the voice of Britain is heard at nine o'clock, better far and infinitely less ludicrous to hear aitches honestly dropped than the present priggish, inflated, inhibited, school-ma'amish arch braying of blameless bashful mewing maidens!

LETTER IN *Tribune.*

Each of these passages has faults of its own, but, quite apart from avoidable ugliness, two qualities are common to all of them. The first is staleness of imagery; the other is lack of precision. The writer either has a meaning and cannot express it, or he inadvertently says something else, or he is almost indifferent as to whether his words mean anything or not. This mixture of vagueness and sheer incompetence is the most marked characteristic of modern English prose, and especially of any kind of political writing. As soon as certain topics are raised, the concrete melts into the abstract and no one seems able to think of turns of speech that are not hackneyed: prose consists less and less of *words* chosen for the sake of their meaning, and more and more of *phrases* tacked together like the sections of a prefabricated henhouse. I list below, with notes and examples, various of the tricks by means of which the work of prose-construction is habitually dodged:

Dying metaphors. A newly invented metaphor assists thought by evoking a visual image, while on the other hand a metaphor which is technically "dead" (e.g. *iron resolution*) has in effect reverted to being an ordinary word and can generally be used without loss of vividness. But in between these two classes there is a huge dump of worn-out metaphors which have lost all evocative power and are merely used because they save people the trouble of inventing phrases for themselves. Examples are: *Ring the changes on, take up the cudgels for, toe the line, ride roughshod over, stand shoulder to shoulder with, play into the hands of, no axe to grind, grist to the mill, fishing in troubled waters, on the order of the day, Achilles' heel, swan song, hotbed.* Many of these are used without knowledge of their meaning (what is a "rift," for instance?), and incompatible metaphors are frequently mixed, a sure sign that the writer is not interested in what he is saying. Some metaphors now current have been twisted out of their original meaning without those who use them even being aware of the fact. For example, *toe the line* is sometimes written *tow the line.* Another example is *the hammer and the anvil,* now always used with the implication that the anvil gets the worst of it. In real life it is always the anvil that breaks the hammer, never the other way about: a writer who stopped to think what he was saying would be aware of this, and would avoid perverting the original phrase.

Operators or *verbal false limbs.* These save the trouble of picking out appropriate verbs and nouns, and at the same time pad each sentence with extra syllables which give it an appearance of symmetry. Characteristic phrases are *render inoperative, militate against, make contact with, be subjected to, give rise to, give grounds for, have the effect of, play a leading part (role) in, make itself felt, take effect, exhibit a tendency to, serve the purpose of, etc., etc.* The keynote is the elimination of simple verbs. Instead of being a single word, such as *break, stop, spoil, mend, kill,* a verb becomes a *phrase,* made up of a noun or adjective tacked on to some general-purpose verb such as *prove, serve, form, play, render.* In addition, the passive voice is wherever possible used in preference to the active, and noun constructions are used instead of gerunds (*by examination of* instead of *by examining*). The range of verbs is further cut down by means of the *-ize* and *de-* formations, and the banal statements are given an appearance of profundity by means of the *not un-* formation. Simple conjunctions and prepositions are replaced by such phrases as *with respect to, having regard to, the fact that, by dint of, in view of, in the interests of, on the hypothesis that*; and the ends of sentences are saved from anticlimax by such resounding common-places as *greatly to be desired, cannot be left out of account, a development to be expected in the near future, deserving of serious consideration, brought to a satisfactory conclusion,* and so on and so forth.

Pretentious diction. Words like *phenomenon, element, individual* (as noun), *objective, categorical, effective, virtual, basic, primary, promote, constitute, exhibit, exploit, utilize, eliminate, liquidate,* are used to dress up simple statements and given an air of scientific impartiality to biased judgments. Adjectives like *epoch-making, epic, historic, unforgettable, triumphant, age-old, inevitable, inexorable, veritable,* are used to dignify the sordid processes of international politics, while writing that aims at glorifying war usually takes on an archaic color, its characteristic words being: *realm, throne, chariot, mailed fist, trident, sword, shield, buckler, banner, jackboot, clarion.* Foreign words and expressions such as *cul de sac, ancien régime, deus ex machina, mutatis mutandis, status quo, gleichschaltung, weltanschauung,* are used to give an air of culture and elegance. Except for the useful abbreviations *i.e., e.g.,* and *etc.,* there is no real need for any of the hundreds of foreign phrases now current in English. Bad writers, and especially scientific, political and sociological writers, are nearly always haunted by the notion that Latin or Greek words are grander than Saxon ones, and unnecessary words like *expedite, ameliorate, predict, extraneous, deracinated, clandestine, subaqueous* and hundreds of others constantly gain ground from their Anglo-Saxon opposite numbers.[1] The jargon peculiar to Marxist writing (*hyena, hangman, cannibal, petty bourgeois, these gentry, lacquey, flunkey, mad dog, White Guard,* etc.) consists largely of words and phrases translated from Russian, German or French; but the normal way of coining a new word is to use a Latin or Greek root with the appropriate affix and, where necessary, the *-ize* formation. It is often easier to make up words of this kind (*deregionalize, impermissible, extramarital, non-fragmentary* and so forth) than to think up the English words that will cover one's meaning. The result, in general, is an increase in slovenliness and vagueness.

---

[1] An interesting illustration of this is the way in which the English flower names which were in use till very recently are being ousted by Greek ones, *snapdragon* becoming *antirrhinum, forget-me-not* becoming *myosotis,* etc. It is hard to see any practical reason for this change of fashion: it is probably due to an instinctive turning-away from the more homely word and a vague feeling that the Greek word is scientific.

Meaningless words. In certain kinds of writing, particularly in art criticism and literary criticism, it is normal to come across long passages which are almost completely lacking in meaning.[2] Words like *romantic, plastic, values, human, dead, sentimental, natural, vitality*, as used in art criticism, are strictly meaningless, in the sense that they not only do not point to any discoverable object, but are hardly ever expected to do so by the reader. When one critic writes, "The outstanding feature of Mr. X's work is its living quality," while another writes, "The immediately striking thing about Mr. X's work is its peculiar deadness," the reader accepts this as a simple difference of opinion. If words like *black* and *white* were involved, instead of the jargon words *dead* and *living*, he would see at once that language was being used in an improper way. Many political words are similarly abused. The word *Fascism* has now no meaning except in so far as it signifies "something not desirable." The words *democracy, socialism, freedom, patriotic, realistic, justice*, have each of them several different meanings which cannot be reconciled with one another. In the case of a word like *democracy*, not only is there no agreed definition, but the attempt to make one is resisted from all sides. It is almost universally felt that when we call a country democratic we are praising it: consequently the defenders of every kind of régime claim that it is a democracy, and fear that they might have to stop using the word if it were tied down to any one meaning. Words of this kind are often used in a consciously dishonest way. That is, the person who uses them has his own private definition, but allows his hearer to think he means something quite different. Statements like *Marshal Pétain was a true patriot, The Soviet Press is the freest in the world, The Catholic Church is opposed to persecution*, are almost always made with intent to deceive. Other words used in variable meanings, in most cases more or less dishonestly, are: *class, totalitarian, science, progressive, reactionary, bourgeois, equality*.

Now that I have made this catalogue of swindles and perversions, let me give another example of the kind of writing that they lead to. This time it must of its nature be an imaginary one. I am going to translate a passage of good English into modern English of the worst sort. Here is a well-known verse from *Ecclesiastes*:

"I returned and saw under the sun, that the race is not to the swift, nor the battle to the strong, neither yet bread to the wise, nor yet riches to men of understanding, nor yet favour to men of skill; but time and chance happeneth to them all."

Here it is in modern English:

"Objective consideration of contemporary phenomena compels the conclusion that success or failure in competitive activities exhibits no tendency to be commensurate with innate capacity, but that a considerable element of the unpredictable must invariably be taken into account."

[2]Example: "Comfort's catholicity of perception and image, strangely Whitmanesque in range, almost the exact opposite in aesthetic compulsion, continues to evoke that trembling atmospheric accumulative hinting at a cruel, an inexorably serene timelessness. . . . Wrey Gardiner scores by aiming at simple bull's-eyes with precision. Only they are not so simple, and through this contented sadness runs more than the surface bittersweet of resignation." (*Poetry Quarterly*.)

This is a parody, but not a very gross one. Exhibit (3), above, for instance, contains several patches of the same kind of English. It will be seen that I have not made a full translation. The beginning and ending of the sentence follow the original meaning fairly closely, but in the middle the concrete illustrations—race, battle, bread—dissolve into the vague phrase "success or failure in competitive activities." This had to be so, because no modern writer of the kind I am discussing—no one capable of using phrases like "objective consideration of contemporary phenomena"—would ever tabulate his thoughts in that precise and detailed way. The whole tendency of modern prose is away from concreteness. Now analyse these two sentences a little more closely. The first contains forty-nine words but only sixty syllables, and all its words are those of everyday life. The second contains thirty-eight words of ninety syllables: eighteen of its words are from Latin roots, and one from Greek. The first sentence contains six vivid images, and only one phrase ("time and chance") that could be called vague. The second contains not a single fresh, arresting phrase, and in spite of its ninety syllables it gives only a shortened version of the meaning contained in the first. Yet without a doubt it is the second kind of sentence that is gaining ground in modern English. I do not want to exaggerate. This kind of writing is not yet universal, and outcrops of simplicity will occur here and there in the worst-written page. Still, if you or I were told to write a few lines on the uncertainty of human fortunes, we should probably come much nearer to my imaginary sentence than to the one from *Ecclesiastes*.

As I have tried to show, modern writing at its worst does not consist in picking out words for the sake of their meaning and inventing images in order to make the meaning clearer. It consists in gumming together long strips of words which have already been set in order by someone else, and making the results presentable by sheer humbug. The attraction of this way of writing is that it is easy. It is easier—even quicker, once you have the habit—to say *In my opinion it is not an unjustifiable assumption that* than to say *I think*. If you use ready-made phrases, you not only don't have to hunt about for words; you also don't have to bother with the rhythms of your sentences since these phrases are generally so arranged as to be more or less euphonious. When you are composing in a hurry—when you are dictating to a stenographer, for instance, or making a public speech—it is natural to fall into a pretentious, Latinized style. Tags like *a consideration which we should do well to bear in mind* or *a conclusion to which all of us would readily assent* will save many a sentence from coming down with a bump. By using stale metaphors, similes and idioms, you save much mental effort, at the cost of leaving your meaning vague, not only for your reader but for yourself. This is the significance of mixed metaphors. The sole aim of a metaphor is to call up a visual image. When these images clash—as in *The Fascist octopus has sung its swan song, the jackboot is thrown into the melting pot*—it can be taken as certain that the writer is not seeing a mental image of the objects he is naming; in other words he is not really thinking. Look again at the examples I gave at the beginning of this essay. Professor Laski (1) uses five negatives in fifty-three words. One of these is superfluous, making nonsense of the whole passage, and in addition there is the slip *alien* for *akin*, making further nonsense, and several avoidable pieces of clumsiness which increase the general vagueness. Professor Hogben (2) plays ducks and drakes with a battery which is able to write prescriptions, and, while disapproving of the everyday phrase *put up with*, is unwilling to look *egregious* up in the dictionary and see what it means; (3), if one takes an uncharitable attitude towards it, is simply meaningless: probably one could work out its intended meaning by reading the whole of the article in which it occurs. In (4), the writer knows more or less what he wants to say, but an accumulation of stale phrases chokes him like tea leaves blocking a sink. In (5), words and meaning have almost parted company. People who write in this manner usually have a general emotional meaning—they dislike one thing and want to express solidarity with another—but they are not interested in the detail of what they are saying. A scrupulous writer, in every sentence that he writes, will ask himself at least four questions, thus: What am I trying to say? What words will express it? What image or idiom will make it clearer? Is this image fresh enough to have an effect? And he will probably ask himself two more: Could I put it more shortly? Have I said anything that is avoidably ugly? But you are not obliged to go to all this trouble. You can shirk it by simply throwing your mind open and letting the ready-made phrases come crowding in. They will construct your sentences for you—even think your thoughts for you, to a certain extent—and at need they will perform the important service of partially concealing your meaning even from yourself. It is at this point that the special connection between politics and the debasement of language becomes clear.

In our time it is broadly true that political writing is bad writing. Where it is not true, it will generally be found that the writer is some kind of rebel, expressing his private opinions and not a "party line." Orthodoxy, of whatever color, seems to demand a lifeless, imitative style. The political dialects to be found in pamphlets, leading articles, manifestos, White Papers and the speeches of under-secretaries do, of course, vary from party to party, but they are all alike in that one almost never finds in them a fresh, vivid, home-made turn of speech. When one watches some tired hack on the platform mechanically repeating the familiar phrases—*bestial atrocities, iron heel, blood-stained tyranny, free peoples of the world, stand shoulder to shoulder*—one often has a curious feeling that one is not watching a live human being but some kind of dummy: a feeling which suddenly becomes stronger at moments when the light catches the speaker's spectacles and turns them into blank discs which seem to have no eyes behind them. And this is not altogether fanciful. A speaker who uses that kind of phraseology has gone some distance towards turning himself into a machine. The appropriate noises are coming out of his larynx, but his brain is not involved as it would be if he were choosing his words for himself. If the speech he is making is one that he is accustomed to make over and over again, he may be almost unconscious of what he is saying, as one is when one utters the responses in church. And this reduced state of consciousness, if not indispensable, is at any rate favorable to political conformity.

In our time, political speech and writing are largely the defence of the indefensible. Things like the continuance of British rule in India, the Russian purges and deportations, the dropping of the atom bombs on Japan, can indeed be defended, but only by arguments which are too brutal for most people to face, and which do not square with the professed aims of political parties. Thus political language has to consist largely of euphemism, question-begging and sheer cloudy vagueness. Defenceless villages are bombarded from the air, the inhabitants driven out into the countryside, the cattle machine-gunned, the huts set on fire with incendiary bullets: this is called *pacification*. Millions of peasants are robbed of their farms and sent trudging along the roads with no more than they can carry: this is called *transfer of population* or *rectification of frontiers*. People are imprisoned for years without trial, or shot in the back of the neck or sent to die of scurvy in Arctic lumber camps: this is called *elimination of unreliable elements*. Such phraseology is needed if one wants to name things without calling up mental pictures of them. Consider for instance some comfortable English professor defending Russian totalitarianism. He cannot say outright, "I believe in killing off your opponents when you can get good results by doing so." Probably, therefore, he will say something like this:

"While freely conceding that the Soviet régime exhibits certain features which the humanitarian may be inclined to deplore, we must, I think, agree that a certain curtailment of the right to political opposition is an unavoidable concomitant of transitional periods, and that the rigors which the Russian people have been called upon to undergo have been amply justified in the sphere of concrete achievement."

The inflated style is itself a kind of euphemism. A mass of Latin words falls upon the facts like soft snow, blurring the outlines and covering up all the details. The great enemy of clear language is insincerity. When there is a gap between one's real and one's declared aims, one turns as it were instinctively to long words and exhausted idioms, like a cuttlefish squirting out ink. In our age there is no such thing as "keeping out of politics." All issues are political issues, and politics itself is a mass of lies, evasions, folly, hatred and schizophrenia. When the general atmosphere is bad, language must suffer. I should expect to find—this is a guess which I have not sufficient knowledge to verify—that the German, Russian and Italian languages have all deteriorated in the last ten to fifteen years, as a result of dictatorship.

But if thought corrupts language, language can also corrupt thought. A bad usage can spread by tradition and imitation, even among people who should and do know better. The debased language that I have been discussing is in some ways very convenient. Phrases like *a not unjustifiable assumption, leaves much to be desired, would serve no good purpose, a consideration which we should do well to bear in mind*, are a continuous temptation, a packet of aspirins always at one's elbow. Look back through this essay, and for certain you will find that I have again and again committed the very faults I am protesting against. By this morning's post I have received a pamphlet dealing with conditions in Germany. The author tells me that he "felt impelled" to write it. I open it at random, and here is almost the first sentence that I see: "[The Allies] have an opportunity not only of achieving a radical transformation of Germany's social and political structure in such a way as to avoid a nationalistic reaction in Germany itself, but at the same time of laying the foundations of a cooperative and unified Europe." You see, he "feels impelled" to write—feels, presumably, that he has something new to say—and yet his words, like cavalry horses answering the bugle, group themselves automatically into the familiar dreary pattern. This invasion of one's mind by ready-made phrases (*lay the foundations, achieve a radical transformation*) can only be prevented if one is constantly on guard against them, and every such phrase anaesthetizes a portion of one's brain.

I said earlier that the decadence of our language is probably curable. Those who deny this would argue, if they produced an argument at all, that language merely reflects existing social conditions, and that we cannot influence its development by any direct tinkering with words and constructions. So far as the general tone or spirit of a language goes, this may be true, but it is not true in detail. Silly words and expressions have often disappeared, not through any evolutionary process but owing to the conscious action of a minority. Two recent examples were *explore every avenue* and *leave no stone unturned*, which were killed by the jeers of a few journalists. There is a long list of flyblown metaphors which could similarly be got rid of if enough people would interest themselves in the job; and it should also be possible to laugh the *not un-* formation out of existence,[3] to reduce the amount of Latin and Greek in the average sentence, to drive out foreign phrases and strayed scientific words, and, in general, to make pretentiousness unfashionable. But all these are minor points. The defence of the English language implies more than this, and perhaps it is best to start by saying what it does *not* imply.

To begin with it has nothing to do with archaism, with the salvaging of obsolete words and turns of speech, or with the setting up of a "standard English" which must never be departed from. On the contrary, it is especially concerned with the scrapping of every word or idiom which has outworn its usefulness. It has nothing to do with correct grammar and syntax, which are of no importance so long as one makes one's meaning clear, or with the avoidance of Americanisms, or with having what is called a "good prose style." On the other hand it is not concerned with fake simplicity and the attempt to make written English colloquial. Nor does it even imply in every case preferring the Saxon word to the Latin one, though it does imply using the fewest and shortest words that will cover one's meaning. What is above all needed is to let the meaning choose the word, and not the other way about. In prose, the worst thing one can do with words is to surrender to them. When you think of a concrete object, you think wordlessly, and then, if you want to describe the thing you have been visualizing you probably hunt about till you find the exact words that seem to fit it. When you

---

[3]One can cure oneself of the *not un-* formation by memorizing this sentence: *A not unblack dog was chasing a not unsmall rabbit across a not ungreen field.*

think of something abstract you are more inclined to use words from the start, and unless you make a conscious effort to prevent it, the existing dialect will come rushing in and do the job for you, at the expense of blurring or even changing your meaning. Probably it is better to put off using words as long as possible and get one's meaning as clear as one can through pictures or sensations. Afterwards one can choose—not simply *accept*—the phrases that will best cover the meaning, and then switch round and decide what impression one's words are likely to make on another person. This last effort of the mind cuts out all stale or mixed images, all prefabricated phrases, needless repetitions, and humbug and vagueness generally. But one can often be in doubt about the effect of a word or a phrase, and one needs rules that one can rely on when instinct fails. I think the following rules will cover most cases:

1.   Never use a metaphor, simile or other figure of speech which you are used to seeing in print.
2.   Never use a long word where a short one will do.
3.   If it is possible to cut a word out, always cut it out.
4.   Never use the passive where you can use the active.
5.   Never use a foreign phrase, a scientific word or a jargon word if you can think of an everyday English equivalent.
6.   Break any of these rules sooner than say anything outright barbarous.

These rules sound elementary, and so they are, but they demand a deep change of attitude in anyone who has grown used to writing in the style now fashionable. One could keep all of them and still write bad English, but one could not write the kind of stuff that I quoted in those five specimens at the beginning of this article.

I have not here been considering the literary use of language, but merely language as an instrument for expressing and not for concealing or preventing thought. Stuart Chase and others have come near to claiming that all abstract words are meaningless, and have used this as a pretext for advocating a kind of political quietism. Since you don't know what Fascism is, how can you struggle against Fascism? One need not swallow such absurdities as this, but one ought to recognize that the present political chaos is connected with the decay of language, and that one can probably bring about some improvement by starting at the verbal end. If you simplify your English, you are freed from the worst follies of orthodoxy. You cannot speak any of the necessary dialects, and when you make a stupid remark its stupidity will be obvious, even to yourself. Political language—and with variations this is true of all political parties, from Conservatives to Anarchists—is designed to make lies sound truthful and murder respectable, and to give an appearance of solidity to pure wind. One cannot change this all in a moment, but one can at least change one's own habits, and from time to time one can even, if one jeers loudly enough, send some worn-out and useless phrase—some *jackboot, Achilles' heel, hotbed, melting pot, acid test, veritable inferno* or other lump of verbal refuse—into the dustbin where it belongs.

HAIG A. BOSMAJIAN

Born in 1928, Haig A. Bosmajian studied at the University of California and received a doctorate from Stanford in 1960. He has taught at the universities of Idaho and Connecticut and is presently Professor of Parliamentary Procedure, Rhetoric, and Freedom of Speech at the University of Washington. Professor Bosmajian's principal interests are in the areas of dissent, language and behavior, and the language of social movements. He has edited The Principles and Practice of Freedom of Speech *(1971), has collaborated with Hamida Bosmajian on* The Rhetoric of the Civil Rights Movement *(1969) and* This Great Argument: The Rights of Women *(1972), and is a coauthor of* Sexism and Language *(1977). He has also published essays on the rhetoric of Nazism and communism, and on nonverbal communication. The present essay is the introduction to his book* The Language of Oppression *(1974), from which we take its title.*

The Language of Oppression

"Sticks and stones may break my bones, but words can never hurt me." To accept this adage as valid is sheer folly. "What's in a name? that which we call a rose by any other name would smell as sweet." The answer to Juliet's question is "Plenty!" and to her own response to the question we can only say that this is by no means invariably true. The importance, significance, and ramifications of naming and defining people cannot be over-emphasized. From *Genesis* and beyond, to the present time, the power which comes from naming and defining people has had positive as well as negative effects on entire populations.

The magic of words and names has always been an integral part of both "primitive" and "civilized" societies. As Margaret Schlauch has observed, "from time immemorial men have thought there is some mysterious essential connection between a thing and the spoken name for it. You could use the name of your enemy, not only to designate him either passionately or dispassionately, but also to exercise a baleful influence."[1]

Biblical passages abound in which names and naming are endowed with great power; from the very outset, in *Genesis*, naming and defining are attributed a significant potency: "And out of the ground the Lord God formed every beast of the field and every fowl of the air; and brought them unto Adam to see what he would call them: and whatsoever Adam called every living creature, that was the name thereof."[2] Amidst the admonitions in *Leviticus* against theft, lying, and fraud is the warning: "And ye shall not swear my name falsely, neither shalt thou profane the name of thy God: I am the Lord."[3] So important is the name that it must not be blasphemed; those who curse and blaspheme shall be stoned "and he that blasphemeth

[1] Margaret Schlauch, *The Gift of Language* (New York: Dover, 1955), p. 13.
[2] *Genesis*, 2:19.
[3] *Leviticus*, 19:12.

the name of the Lord, he shall surely be put to death, and all the congregation shall certainly stone him."[4] So important is the name that the denial of it is considered a form of punishment: "But ye are they that foresake the Lord, that forget my holy mountain. . . . Therefore will I number you to the sword, and ye shall all bow down to the slaughter: because when I called, ye did not answer; when I spake, ye did not hear. . . . Therefore thus saith the Lord God, behold, my servants shall eat, but ye shall be hungry. . . . And ye shall leave your name for a curse unto my chosen: for the Lord God shall slay thee, and call his servants by another name."[5]

To be unnamed is to be unknown, to have no identity. William Saroyan has observed that "the word nameless, especially in poetry and in much prose, signifies an alien, unknown, and almost unwelcome condition, as when, for instance, a writer speaks of 'a nameless sorrow.' " "Human beings," continues Saroyan, "are for the fact of being named at all, however meaninglessly, lifted out of an area of mystery, doubt, or undesirability into an area in which belonging to everybody else is taken for granted, so that one of the first questions asked by new people, two-year-olds even, whether they are speaking to other new people or to people who have been around for a great many years, is 'What is your name?' "[6]

To receive a name is to be elevated to the status of a human being; without a name one's identity is questionable. In stressing the importance of a name and the significance of having none, Joyce Hertzler has said that "among both primitives and moderns, an individual has no definition, no validity for himself, without a name. His name is his badge of individuality, the means whereby he identifies himself and enters upon a truly subjective existence. My own name, for example, stands for me, a person. Divesting me of it reduces me to a meaningless, even pathological, nonentity."[7]

In his book *What Is In A Name?* Farhang Zabeeh reminds us that "the Roman slaves originally were without names. Only after being sold they took their master's praenomen in the genitive case followed by the suffix— 'por' (boy), e.g., 'Marcipor,' which indicates that some men, so long as they were regarded by others as cattle, did not need a name. However, as soon as they became servants some designation was called forth."[8] To this day one of the forms of punishment meted out to wrongdoers who are imprisoned is to take away their names and to give them numbers. In an increasingly computerized age people are becoming mere numbers—credit card numbers, insurance numbers, bank account numbers, student numbers, et cetera. Identification of human beings by numbers is a negation of their humanity and their existence.

Philologist Max Muller has pointed out that "if we examine the most ancient word for 'name,' we find it is *naman* in Sanskrit, *nomen* in Latin, *namo* in Gothic. This *naman* stands for gnaman and is derived from the root, *gna*, to

[4] *Leviticus* , 25:16.
[5] *Isaiah*, 66:11-12.
[6] William Saroyan, "Random Notes on the Names of People," *Names*, 1 (December 1953), p. 239.
[7] Joyce Hertzler, *A Sociology of Language* (New York: Random House, 1965), p. 271.
[8] Farhang Zabeeh, *What Is In A Name?* (The Hague: Martinus Nijhoff, 1968), p. 66.

know, and meant originally that by which we know a thing."[9] In the course of the evolution of human society, R. P. Masani tells us, the early need for names "appears to have been felt almost simultaneously with the origin of speech . . . personality and the rights and obligations connected with it would not exist without the name."[10] In his classic work *The Golden Bough* James Frazer devotes several pages to tabooed names and words in ancient societies, taboos reflecting the power and magic people saw in names and words. Frazer notes, for example, that "the North American Indian regards his name, not as a mere label, but as a distinct part of his personality, just as much as are his eyes or his teeth, and believes that injury will result as surely from the malicious handling of his name as from a wound inflicted on any part of his physical organism."[11]

A name can be used as a curse. A name can be blasphemed. Name-calling is so serious a matter that statutes and court decisions prohibit "fighting words" to be uttered. In 1942 the United States Supreme Court upheld the conviction of a person who had addressed a police officer as "a God damned racketeer" and "a damned Fascist." (*Chaplinsky v. New Hampshire*, 315 U.S. 568). Such namecalling, such epithets, said the Court, are not protected speech. So important is one's "good name" that the law prohibits libel.

History abounds with instances in which the mere utterance of a name was prohibited. In ancient Greece, according to Frazer, "the names of the priests and other high officials who had to do with the performance of the Eleusinian mysteries might not be uttered in their lifetime. To pronounce them was a legal offense."[12] Jorgen Ruud reports in *Taboo: A Study of Malagasy Customs and Beliefs* that among the Antandroy people the father has absolute authority in his household and that "children are forbidden to mention the name of their father. They must call him father, daddy. . . . The children may not mention his house or the parts of his body by their ordinary names, but must use other terms, i.e., euphemisms."[13]

It was Iago who said in *Othello*:

> Who steals my purse steals trash; 'tis something nothing;
> 'Twas mine, 'tis his, and has been slave to thousands;
> But he that filches from me my good name
> Robs me of that which not enriches him
> And makes me poor indeed.

Alice, in Lewis Carroll's *Through the Looking Glass*, had trepidations about entering the woods where things were nameless: "This must be the wood," she said thoughtfully to herself, "where things have no names. I wonder what'll become of *my* name when I go in? I shouldn't like to lose it at all—

[9] Cited in Elsdon Smith, *Treasury of Name Lore* (New York: Harper and Row, 1967), p. vii.
[10] R. P. Masani, *Folk Culture Reflected in Names* (Bombay: Popular Prakashan, 1966), p. 6.
[11] James Frazer, *The Golden Bough* (New York: Macmillan, 1951), p. 284.
[12] *Ibid.*, p. 302.
[13] Jörgen Ruud, *Taboo; A Study of Malagasy Customs and Beliefs* (Oslo: Oslo University Press, 1960), p. 15.

because they'd have to give me another, and it would almost certain to be an ugly one."

A Nazi decree of August 17, 1938 stipulated that "Jews may receive only those first names which are listed in the directives of the Ministry of the Interior concerning the use of first names." Further, the decree provided: "If Jews should bear first names other than those permitted . . . they must . . . adopt an additional name. For males, that name shall be Israel, for females Sara." Another Nazi decree forbade Jews in Germany "to show themselves in public without a Jew's star. . . . [consisting] of a six-pointed star of yellow cloth with black borders, equivalent in size to the palm of the hand. The inscription is to read 'JEW' in black letters. It is to be sewn to the left breast of the garment, and to be worn visibly."

The power which comes from names and naming is related directly to the power to define others—individuals, races, sexes, ethnic groups. Our identities, who and what we are, how others see us, are greatly affected by the names we are called and the words with which we are labelled. The names, labels, and phrases employed to "identify" a people may in the end determine their survival. The word "define" comes from the Latin *definire*, meaning to limit. Through definition we restrict, we set boundaries, we name.

"When I use a word," said Humpty Dumpty in *Through the Looking Glass*, "it means just what I choose it to mean—neither more nor less." "The question is," said Alice, "whether you can make words mean so many different things." "The question is," said Humpty Dumpty, "which is to be master—that's all."

During his days as a civil rights-black power activist, Stokely Carmichael accurately asserted: "It [definition] is very, very important because I believe that people who can define are masters."[14] Self-determination must include self-definition, the ability and right to name oneself; the master-subject relationship is based partly on the master's power to name and define the subject.

While names, words and language can be and are used to inspire us, to motivate us to humane acts, to liberate us, they can also be used to dehumanize human beings and to "justify" their suppression and even their extermination. It is not a great step from the coercive suppression of dissent to the extermination of dissenters (as the United States Supreme Court declared in its 1943 compulsory flag salute opinion in *West Virginia State Board of Education v. Barnette*); nor is it a large step from defining a people as non-human or sub-human to their subjugation or annihilation. One of the first acts of an oppressor is to redefine the "enemy" so they will be looked upon as creatures warranting separation, suppression, and even eradication.

The Nazis redefined Jews as "bacilli," "parasites," "disease," "demon," and "plague." In his essay "The Hollow Miracle," George Steiner informs us that the Germans "who poured quicklime down the openings of the sewers in Warsaw to kill the living and stifle the stink of the dead wrote about it. They spoke of having to 'liquidate vermin'. . . . Gradually, words

[14]Stokely Carmichael, speech delivered in Seattle, Washington, April 19, 1967.

lost their original meaning and acquired nightmarish definitions. *Jude, Pole, Russe* came to mean two-legged lice, putrid vermin which good Aryans must squash, as a [Nazi] Party manual said, 'like roaches on a dirty wall.' 'Final solution,' *endgültige Lösung*, came to signify the death of six million human beings in gas ovens."[15]

The language of white racism has for centuries been used to "keep the nigger in his place." Our sexist language has allowed men to define who and what a woman is and must be. Labels like "traitors," "saboteurs," "queers," and "obscene degenerates" were applied indiscriminately to students who protested the war in Vietnam or denounced injustices in the United States. Are such people to be listened to? Consulted? Argued with? Obviously not! One does not listen to, much less talk to, traitors and outlaws, sensualists and queers. One only punishes them or, as Spiro Agnew suggested in one of his 1970 speeches, there are some dissenters who should be separated "from our society with no more regret than we should feel over discarding rotten apples."[16]

What does it mean to separate people? When the Japanese-Americans were rounded up in 1942 and sent off to "relocation camps" they were "separated." The Jews in Nazi Germany were "separated." The Indians of the United States, the occupants of the New World before Columbus "discovered" it, have been systematically "separated." As "chattels" and slaves, the blacks in the United States were "separated"; legally a black person was a piece of property, although human enough to be counted as three-fifths of a person in computing the number of people represented by white legislators.

How is the forcible isolation of human beings from society at large justified? To make the separation process more palatable to the populace, what must the oppressor first do? How does he make the populace accept the separation of the "creatures," or, if not accept it, at least not protest it? Consideration of such questions is not an academic exercise without practical implications. There is a close nexus between language and self-perception, self-awareness, self-identity, and self-esteem. Just as our thoughts affect our language, so does our language affect our thoughts and eventually our actions and behavior. As Edward Sapir has observed, we are all "at the mercy of the particular language which has become the medium of expression" in our society. The "real world," he points out, "is to a large extent unconsciously built up on the language habits of the group. . . . We see and hear and otherwise experience very largely as we do because the language habits of our community predispose certain choices of interpretation."[17]

George Orwell has written in his famous essay "Politics and the English Language": "A man may take to drink because he feels himself to be a failure, and then fail all the more completely because he drinks. It is rather

---

[15]George Steiner, *Language and Silence* (New York: Atheneum, 1970), p. 100.

[16]*The New York Times*, October 21, 1969, p. 25.

[17]Cited in John Carroll (ed.), *Language, Thought and Reality: Selected Writings of Benjamin Lee Whorf* (Cambridge, Mass.: The M.I.T. Press, 1956), p. 134.

the same thing that is happening to the English language. It becomes ugly and inaccurate because our thoughts are foolish, but the slovenliness of our language makes it easier for us to have foolish thoughts."[18] Orwell maintains that "the decadence in our language is probably curable" and that "silly words and expressions have often disappeared, not through any evolutionary process but owing to the conscious action of a minority."[19] Wilma Scott Heide, speaking as president of the National Organization for Women several years ago, indicated that feminists were undertaking this conscious action: "In any social movement, when changes are effected, the language sooner or later reflects the change. Our approach is different. Instead of passively noting the change, we are changing language patterns to actively effect the changes, a significant part of which is the conceptual tool of thought, our language."[20]

This then is our task—to identify the decadence in our language, the inhumane uses of language, the "silly words and expressions" which have been used to justify the unjustifiable, to make palatable the unpalatable, to make reasonable the unreasonable, to make decent the indecent. Hitler's "Final Solution" appeared reasonable once the Jews were successfully labelled by the Nazis as sub-humans, as "parasites," "vermin," and "bacilli." The segregation and suppression of blacks in the United States was justified once they were considered "chattels" and "inferiors." The subjugation of the "American Indians" was defensible since they were defined as "barbarians" and "savages." As Peter Farb has said, "cannibalism, torture, scalping, mutilation, adultery, incest, sodomy, rape, filth, drunkenness—such a catalogue of accusations against a people is an indication not so much of their depravity as that their land is up for grabs."[21] As long as adult women are "chicks," "girls," "dolls," "babes," and "ladies," their status in society will remain "inferior"; they will go on being treated as subjects in the subject-master relationship as long as the language of the law places them into the same class as children, minors, and the insane.

It is my hope that an examination of the language of oppression will result in a conscious effort by the reader to help cure this decadence in our language, especially that language which leads to dehumanization of the human being. One way for us to curtail the use of the language of oppression is for those who find themselves being defined into subjugation to rebel against such linguistic suppression. It isn't strange that those persons who insist on defining themselves, who insist on this elemental privilege of self-naming, self-definition, and self-identity encounter vigorous resistance. Predictably, the resistance usually comes from the oppressor or would-be oppressor and is a result of the fact that he or she does not want to relinquish the power which comes from the ability to define others.

---

[18]George Orwell, "Politics and the English Language," in C. Muscatine and M. Griffith, *The Borzoi College Reader*, 2nd ed. (New York: Alfred A. Knopf, 1971), p. 88.
[19]*Ibid.*
[20]Wilma Scott Heide, "Feminism: The *sine qua non* for a Just Society," *Vital Speeches*, 38 (1971–72), p. 402.
[21]Peter Farb, "Indian Corn," *The New York Review*, 17 (December 16, 1971), p. 36.

ROBIN LAKOFF

Robin Lakoff (born 1942) has written many books and articles on linguistics. She began her scholarly career by studying Latin syntax but has progressively shifted her attention— through English syntax, semantics, and sociolinguistics—to pragmatics, the study of how language is used in practical situations, between people. She received her B.A. from Radcliffe in 1964 and her Ph.D. from Harvard in 1967. Subsequently she has taught at the University of Michigan and at Stanford, and since 1976 has been a professor of linguistics at the University of California, Berkeley. In 1979 Ripon College awarded her the honorary degree of Doctor of Letters, recognizing particularly her work on linguistic stereotypes and on the language associated with sex roles. The citation concluded: "She has helped to give productive contemporary meaning to the Biblical injunction 'by thy words thou shalt be justified, and by thy words thou shalt be condemned'." Her essay "You Are What You Say" appeared in the July 1974 issue of Ms. *A fuller treatment of the subject is found in her book* Language and Women's Place *(1975).*

You Are What You Say

"Women's language" is that pleasant (dainty?), euphemistic, never-aggressive way of talking we learned as little girls. Cultural bias was built into the language we were allowed to speak, the subjects we were allowed to speak about, and the ways we were spoken of. Having learned our linguistic lesson well, we go out in the world, only to discover that we are communicative cripples—damned if we do, and damned if we don't.

If we refuse to talk "like a lady," we are ridiculed and criticized for being unfeminine. ("She thinks like a man" is, at best, a left-handed compliment.) If we do learn all the fuzzy-headed, unassertive language of our sex, we are ridiculed for being unable to think clearly, unable to take part in a serious discussion, and therefore unfit to hold a position of power.

It doesn't take much of this for a woman to begin feeling she deserves such treatment because of inadequacies in her own intelligence and education.

"Women's language" shows up in all levels of English. For example, women are encouraged and allowed to make far more precise discriminations in naming colors than men do. Words like *mauve, beige, ecru, aquamarine, lavender,* and so on, are unremarkable in a woman's active vocabulary, but largely absent from that of most men. I know of no evidence suggesting that women actually *see* a wider range of colors than men do. It is simply that fine discriminations of this sort are relevant to women's vocabularies, but not to men's; to men, who control most of the interesting affairs of the world, such distinctions are trivial—irrelevant.

In the area of syntax, we find similar gender-related peculiarities of speech. There is one construction, in particular, that women use conversationally far more than men: the tag-question. A tag is midway between an outright statement and a yes-no question; it is less assertive than the former, but more confident than the latter.

A *flat statement* indicates confidence in the speaker's knowledge and is fairly certain to be believed; a *question* indicates a lack of knowledge on some point and implies that the gap in the speaker's knowledge can and will be remedied by an answer. For example, if, at a Little League game, I have had my glasses off, I can legitimately ask someone else: "Was the player out at third?" A *tag question*, being intermediate between statement and question, is used when the speaker is stating a claim, but lacks full confidence in the truth of that claim. So if I say, "Is Joan here?" I will probably not be surprised if my respondent answers "no"; but if I say, "Joan is here, isn't she?" instead, chances are I am already biased in favor of a positive answer, wanting only confirmation. I still want a response, but I have enough knowledge (or think I have) to predict that response. A tag question, then, might be thought of as a statement that doesn't demand to be believed by anyone but the speaker, a way of giving leeway, of not forcing the addressee to go along with the views of the speaker.

Another common use of the tag-question is in small talk when the speaker is trying to elicit conversation: "Sure is hot here, isn't it?"

But in discussing personal feelings or opinions, only the speaker normally has any way of knowing the correct answer. Sentences such as "I have a headache, don't I?" are clearly ridiculous. But there are other examples where it is the speaker's opinions, rather than perceptions, for which corroboration is sought, as in "The situation in Southeast Asia is terrible, isn't it?"

While there are, of course, other possible interpretations of a sentence like this, one possibility is that the speaker has a particular answer in mind—"yes" or "no"—but is reluctant to state it baldly. This sort of tag question is much more apt to be used by women than by men in conversation. Why is this the case?

The tag question allows a speaker to avoid commitment, and thereby avoid conflict with the addressee. The problem is that, by so doing, speakers may also give the impression of not really being sure of themselves, or looking to the addressee for confirmation of their views. This uncertainty is reinforced in more subliminal ways, too. There is a peculiar sentence intonation-pattern, used almost exclusively by women, as far as I know, which changes a declarative answer into a question. The effect of using the rising inflection typical of a yes-no question is to imply that the speaker is seeking confirmation, even though the speaker is clearly the only one who has the requisite information, which is why the question was put to her in the first place:

(Q) When will dinner be ready?

(A) Oh . . . around six o'clock . . . ?

It is as though the second speaker were saying, "Six o'clock—if that's okay with you, if you agree." The person being addressed is put in the position of having to provide confirmation. One likely consequence of this sort of speech-pattern in a woman is that, often unbeknownst to herself, the speaker builds a reputation of tentativeness, and others will refrain from taking her seriously or trusting her with any real responsibilities, since she "can't make up her mind," and "isn't sure of herself."

Such idiosyncrasies may explain why women's language sounds much more "polite" than men's. It is polite to leave a decision open, not impose your mind, or views, or claims, on anyone else. So a tag-question is a kind of polite statement, in that it does not force agreement or belief on the addressee. In the same way a request is a polite command, in that it does not force obedience on the addressee, but rather suggests something be done as a favor to the speaker. A clearly stated order implies a threat of certain consequences if it is not followed, and—even more impolite—implies that the speaker is in a superior position and able to enforce the order. By couching wishes in the form of a request, on the other hand, a speaker implies that if the request is not carried out, only the speaker will suffer; noncompliance cannot harm the addressee. So the decision is really left up to the addressee. The distinction becomes clear in these examples:

Close the door.

Please close the door.

Will you close the door?

Will you please close the door?

Won't you close the door?

In the same ways as words and speech patterns used *by* women undermine her image, those used *to describe* women make matters even worse. Often a word may be used of both men and women (and perhaps of things as well); but when it is applied to women, it assumes a special meaning that, by implication rather than outright assertion, is derogatory to women as a group.

The use of euphemisms has this effect. A euphemism is a substitute for a word that has acquired a bad connotation by association with something unpleasant or embarrassing. But almost as soon as the new word comes into common usage, it takes on the same old bad connotations, since feelings about the things or people referred to are not altered by a change of name; thus new euphemisms must be constantly found.

There is one euphemism for *woman* still very much alive. The word, of course is *lady*. *Lady* has a masculine counterpart, namely *gentleman*, occasionally shortened to *gent*. But for some reason *lady* is very much commoner than *gent(leman)*.

The decision to use *lady* rather than *woman*, or vice versa, may considerably alter the sense of a sentence, as the following examples show:

(a) A woman (lady) I know is a dean at Berkeley.

(b) A woman (lady) I know makes amazing things out of shoelaces and old boxes.

The use of *lady* in (a) imparts a frivolous, or nonserious, tone to the sentence: the matter under discussion is not one of great moment. Similarly, in (b), using *lady* here would suggest that the speaker considered the "amazing things" not to be serious art, but merely a hobby or an aberration. If *woman* is used, she might be a serious sculptor. To say *lady doctor* is very condescending, since no one ever says *gentleman doctor* or even *man doctor*. For example, mention in the San Francisco *Chronicle* of January 31, 1972, of Madalyn Murray O'Hair as the *lady atheist* reduces her position to that of scatter-brained eccentric. Even *woman atheist* is scarcely defensible: sex is irrelevant to her philosophical position.

Many women argue that, on the other hand, *lady* carries with it overtones recalling the age of chivalry: conferring exalted stature on the person so referred to. This makes the term seem polite at first, but we must also remember that these implications are perilous: they suggest that a "lady" is helpless, and cannot do things by herself.

Lady can also be used to infer frivolousness, as in titles of organizations. Those that have a serious purpose (not merely that of enabling "the ladies" to spend time with one another) cannot use the word *lady* in their titles, but less serious ones may. Compare the *Ladies' Auxiliary* of a men's group, or the *Thursday Evening Ladies' Browning and Garden Society* with *Ladies' Liberation* or *Ladies' Strike for Peace*.

What is curious about this split is that *lady* is in origin a euphemism—a substitute that puts a better face on something people find uncomfortable—for *woman*. What kind of euphemism is it that subtly denigrates the people to whom it refers? Perhaps *lady* functions as a euphemism for *woman* because it does not contain the sexual implications present in *woman*; it is not "embarrassing" in that way. If this is so, we may expect that, in the future, *lady* will replace woman as the primary word for the human female, since *woman* will have become too blatantly sexual. That this distinction is already made in some contexts at least is shown in the following examples, where you can try replacing *woman* with *lady*:

(a) She's only twelve, but she's already a woman.
(b) After ten years in jail, Harry wanted to find a woman.
(c) She's my woman, see, so don't mess around with her.

Another common substitute for *woman* is *girl*. One seldom hears a man past the age of adolescence referred to as a boy, save in expressions like "going out with the boys," which are meant to suggest an air of adolescent frivolity and irresponsibility. But women of all ages are "girls": one can have a man—not a boy—Friday, but only a girl—never a woman or even a lady—Friday; women have girlfriends, but men do not—in a nonsexual sense—have boyfriends. It may be that this use of *girl* is euphemistic in the same way the use of *lady* is: in stressing the idea of immaturity, it removes the sexual connotations lurking in *woman*. *Girl* brings to mind irresponsibility: you don't send a girl to do a woman's errand (or even, for that matter, a boy's errand). She is a person who is both too immature and too far from real life to be entrusted with responsibilities or with decisions of any serious or important nature.

Now let's take a pair of words which, in terms of the possible relationships in an earlier society, were simple male-female equivalents, analogous to *bull: cow*. Suppose we find that, for independent reasons, society has changed in such a way that the original meanings now are irrelevant. Yet the words have not been discarded, but have acquired new meanings, metaphorically related to their original senses. But suppose these new metaphorical uses are no longer parallel to each other. By seeing where the parallelism breaks down, we discover something about the different roles played by men and women in this culture. One good example of such a divergence through time is found in the pair, *master: mistress*. Once used with reference to one's power over servants, these words have become unusable today in their original master-servant sense as the relationship has become less prevalent in our society. But the words are still common.

Unless used with reference to animals, *master* now generally refers to a man who has acquired consummate ability in some field, normally nonsexual. But its feminine counterpart cannot be used this way. It is practically restricted to its sexual sense of "paramour." We start out with two terms, both roughly paraphrasable as "one who has power over another." But the masculine form, once one person is no longer able to have absolute power over another, becomes usable metaphorically in the sense of "having power over *something*." *Master* requires as its object only the name of some activity, something inanimate and abstract. But *mistress* requires a masculine noun in the possessive to precede it. One cannot say: "Rhonda is a mistress." One must be *someone's* mistress. A man is defined by what he does, a woman by her sexuality, that is, in terms of one particular aspect of her relationship to men. It is one thing to be an *old master* like Hans Holbein, and another to be an *old mistress*.

The same is true of the words *spinster* and *bachelor*—gender words for "one who is not married." The resemblance ends with the definition. While *bachelor* is a neuter term, often used as a compliment, *spinster* normally is used pejoratively, with connotations of prissiness, fussiness, and so on. To be a bachelor implies that one has the choice of marrying or not, and this is what makes the idea of a bachelor existence attractive, in the popular literature. He has been pursued and has successfully eluded his pursuers. But a spinster is one who has not been pursued, or at least not seriously. She is old, unwanted goods. The metaphorical connotations of *bachelor* generally suggest sexual freedom; of *spinster*, puritanism or celibacy.

These examples could be multiplied. It is generally considered a *faux pas*, in society, to congratulate a woman on her engagement, while it is correct to congratulate her fiancé. Why is this? The reason seems to be that it is impolite to remind people of things that may be uncomfortable to them. To congratulate a woman on her engagement is really to say, "Thank goodness! You had a close call!" For the man, on the other hand, there was no such danger. His choosing to marry is viewed as a good thing, but not something essential.

The linguistic double standard holds throughout the life of the relationship. After marriage, bachelor and spinster become man and wife, not man and woman. The woman whose husband dies remains "John's widow"; John, however, is never "Mary's widower."

Finally, why is it that salesclerks and others are so quick to call women customers "dear," "honey," and other terms of endearment they really have no business using? A male customer would never put up with it. But women, like children, are supposed to enjoy these endearments, rather than being offended by them.

In more ways than one, it's time to speak up.

MURRAY EDELMAN

Murray Edelman is one of those rare social scientists who have a particular appreciation for the meaning and uses of symbolism and of language. Born in 1919, he was educated at Bucknell University (A.B., 1941), at the University of Chicago (M.A., 1942), and at the University of Illinois (Ph.D., 1948), where he taught political science until 1966. He then moved to the University of Wisconsin, and has been Mead Professor there since 1971. Dr. Edelman has published widely in the fields of communications, labor relations, and public policy, but the sphere of his research that interests us most here is that represented by his books The Symbolic Uses of Politics *(1964),* Politics as Symbolic Action *(1971), and* Political Language *(1977). It is from the last that we take the present essay, which first appeared in a slightly different form in* Politics and Society, *vol. 4 (1974).*

The Political Language of the Helping Professions

Hospital staff often deny or ignore the requests of angry mental patients because to grant them would "reinforce deviant behavior." Teachers sometimes use the same rationale to justify ignoring or punishing demanding students. Two recent presidents of the United States declared that they would pay no attention to peace demonstrators who resort to irritating methods. We commonly regard the last as a political act and the first two as therapeutic; but whether any such action is taken to be political or therapeutic depends on the assumptions of the observer, not on the behavior he or she is judging. Some psychologists reject the "reinforcement of deviant behavior" rationale on the ground that it pays no attention to the distinctive cognitive and symbolizing abilities of the human mind, equating people with rats. They believe such treatment too easily ignores reasonable grounds for anger and depresses the self-esteem of people who already suffer from too little of it, contributing to further "deviance," not to health. In this view the "treatment" is self-serving political repression, even if its definition as rehabilitation salves the consciences of professionals and of the public. Some psychiatrists, on the other hand, see political demonstrators or ghetto rioters as sick, calling for drugs or psychosurgery, not political negotiation, as the appropriate response; the Law Enforcement Assistance Administration has generously supported experiments based on that premise.

The language of "reinforcement" and "help" evokes a world in which the weak and the wayward need to be controlled for their own good. The language of "authority" and "repression" evokes a different reality, in which the rights of the powerless need to be protected against abuse by the powerful. Each linguistic form marshals public support for professional and governmental practices that have profound political consequences: for the status, the rights, and the freedom of professionals, of clients, and of the wider public as well; but we rarely have occasion to inhabit or examine both worlds at the same time.

Language is the distinctive characteristic of human beings. Without it we could not symbolize; we could not reason, remember, anticipate, rationalize, distort, and evoke beliefs and perceptions about matters not immediately before us. With it we not only describe reality but create our own realities, which take forms that overlap with one another and may not be mutually consistent. When it suits us to see rationalization as reason, repression as help, distortion as creation, or the converse of any of these, language and mind can smoothly structure each other to do so. When it suits us to solve complicated problems of logic and mathematics, language and mind can smoothly structure each other to do that as well. When the complicated problems involve social power and status, problematic perception and distortion are certain.

It is a commonplace of linguistic theory that language, thought, and action shape one another. Language is always an intrinsic part of some particular social situation; it is never an independent instrument or simply a tool for description. By naively perceiving it as a tool, we mask its profound part in creating social relationships and in evoking the roles and the "selves" of those involved in the relationships.

Because the helping professions define other people's statuses (and their own), the terms they employ to categorize clients and justify restrictions of their physical movements and of their moral and intellectual influence are especially revealing of the political functions language performs and of the multiple realities it helps create. Just as any single numeral evokes the whole number scheme in our minds, so a professional term, a syntactic form, or a metaphor with scientific connotations can justify a hierarchy of power for the person who uses it and for the groups that respond to it.

In analyzing such political evocations I do not mean to suggest that the helping professions cannot be rehabilitative and educational as well. Psychological distress can be as "real" as economic distress, and psychological support is often helpful for people who voluntarily seek it. There is a large literature and a complicated controversy about the links among psychological, economic, and social stress and about the effectiveness of the helping professions in achieving their goals; but this discussion focuses on the *political* consequences of professional language.

Through devices I explore here, the helping professions create and reinforce popular beliefs about which kinds of people are worthy and which are unworthy; about who should be rewarded through governmental action and who controlled or subjected to discipline. Unexamined language and actions can help us understand more profoundly than legislative histories or administrative or judicial proceedings how we decide upon status, rewards, and controls for the wealthy, the poor, women, conformists, and nonconformists.

In this chapter I examine such political uses of language in psychiatry, social work, psychiatric nursing, public school education, and law enforcement. My observations are based on extensive (and depressing) reading in the textbooks and professional journals of these professions. I looked for covert as well as overt justifications for status differentials, power differentials, and authority.

Therapy and Power

To illustrate the subtle bearing of language on status and authority consider a common usage that staff, clients, and the general public all accept as descriptive of a purely professional process: the term "therapy." In the journals, textbooks, and talk of the helping professions, the term is repeatedly used as a suffix or qualifier. Mental patients do not hold dances; they have dance therapy. If they play volleyball, that is recreation therapy. If they engage in a group discussion, that is group therapy.

Even reading is "bibliotherapy"; and the professional literature warns that it may be advisable to restrict, supervise, or forbid reading on some subjects, especially politics and psychiatry. Such an assertion forces us to notice what we normally pass over. To label a common activity as though it were a medical one is to establish superior and subordinate roles, to make it clear who gives orders and who takes them, and to justify in advance the inhibitions placed upon the subordinate class. It ordinarily does so without arousing resentment or resistance either in the subordinates or in outsiders sympathetic to them, for it superimposes a political relationship on a medical one while still depicting it as medical.

Though the linguistic evocation of the political system is subtle, that very fact frees the participants to act out their political roles blatantly, for they see themselves as helping, not as repressing. In consequence, assaults on people's freedom and dignity can be as polar and degrading as those typically occurring in authoritarian regimes, without qualms or protest by authorities, clients, or the public that hears about them. In this way a suffix or qualifier evokes a full-blown political system. No doubt it does so for most of the professionals who draw power from the system as persuasively and unobtrusively as it does for the clientele groups whom it helps induce to submit to authority and to accept the status of a person who must let others decide how he or she should behave.

To call explicit attention to the political connotations of a term for power, on the other hand, is to rally opposition rather than support. To label an authority relationship "tyrannical" is an exhortation to oppose it, not a simple description. The chief function of any political term is to marshal public support or opposition. Some terms do so overtly; but the more potent ones, including those used by professionals, do so covertly, portraying a power relationship as a helping one. When the power of professionals over other people is at stake, the language employed implies that the professional has ways to ascertain who are dangerous, sick, or inadequate; that he or she knows how to render them harmless, rehabilitate them, or both; and that the procedures for diagnosis and for treatment are too specialized for the lay public to understand or judge them. A patient with a sore throat is anxious for his doctor to exercise a certain amount of authority; but the diagnosis is easily checked, and the problem itself circumscribes the doctor's authority. When there is an allegation of mental illness, delinquency, or intellectual incapacity, neither the diagnosis nor the scope of authority is readily checked or limited, but its legitimacy is linguistically created and reinforced.

It is, of course, the ambiguity in the relationship, and the ambivalence in the professional and in the client, that gives the linguistic usage its flexibility and potency. That is always true of symbolic evocations, and it radically distinguishes such evocations from simple deception. Many clients want help, virtually all professionals think they are providing it, and sometimes they do so. Just as the helping seems manifest until it is self-consciously questioned, and then it becomes problematic, so the political relationship seems nonexistent until it is self-consciously questioned, and then it becomes manifest.

The special language of the helping professions merges cognition and affect. The term "mental illness" and the names for specific deviant behaviors encourage the observer and the actor to condense and confound several facets of his or her perception: helping the suffering, controlling the dangerous, sympathy for the former, fear of the latter, and so on. The terms carry all these connotations, and the actor-speaker-listener patterns them so as to utilize semantic ambiguity to cope with his or her ambivalence.

We normally fail to recognize this catalytic capacity of language because we think of linguistic terms and syntactical structures as signals rather than as symbols. If a word is a name for a specific thing or action, then terms like "mental illness," "delinquency prone," or "schizophrenic" have narrowly circumscribed meanings. But if a word is a symbol that condenses and rearranges feelings, memories, perceptions, beliefs, and expectations, then it evokes a particular structuring of beliefs and emotions, a structuring that varies with people's social situations. Language as symbol catalyzes a subjective world in which uncertainties and appropriate courses of action are clarified. Yet this impressive process of symbolic creation is not self-conscious. Our naive view holds that linguistic terms stand for particular objects or behavior, and so we do not ordinarily recognize that elaborate cognitive structures are built upon them.

In the symbolic worlds evoked by the language of the helping professions, speculation and verified fact readily merge with each other. Language dispels the uncertainty in speculation, changes facts to make them serve status distinctions, and reinforces ideology. The names for forms of mental illness, forms of delinquency, and for educational capacities are the basic terms. Each of them normally involves a high degree of unreliability in diagnosis, in prognosis, and in the prescriptions of rehabilitative treatments; but each also entails unambiguous constraints upon clients, especially their confinement and subjection to the staff and the rules of a prison, school, or hospital. The confinement and constraints are converted into liberating and altruistic acts by defining them as education, therapy, or rehabilitation and by other linguistic forms to be examined shortly. The arbitrariness and speculation in the diagnosis and the prognosis, on the other hand, are converted into clear and specific perceptions of the need for control. Regardless of the clinical utility of professional terms, their political utility is manifest; they marshal popular support for professional discretion, concentrating public attention upon procedures and rationalizing in advance any failures of the procedures to achieve their formal objectives.

Categorization is necessary to science and, indeed, to all perception. It is also a political tool, establishing status and power hierarchies. We ordinarily assume that a classification scheme is either scientific or political in character, but any category can serve either or both functions, depending on the interests of those who employ it rather than on anything inherent in the term. The name for a category therefore confuses the two functions, consigning people to high or low status and power while drawing legitimacy from its scientific status.

Any categorization scheme that consigns people to niches according to their actual or potential accomplishments or behavior is bound to be political, no matter what its scientific function. IQs; psychiatric labels; typologies of talent, skills, or knowledge; employment statuses; criminal statuses; personality types—all exemplify the point. Regardless of their validity and reliability (which are notoriously low)[1] or their analytic uses, such classifications rank people and determine degrees of status and of influence. The categorizations of the helping professions are pristine examples of the function, and many of these categories carry over into the wider society. Once established, a categorization defines what is relevant about the people who are labeled. It encourages others to interpret developments so as to confirm the label and to ignore, discount, or reinterpret counterevidence. As a civil rights lawyer put it, "While psychiatrists get angry, patients get aggressive; nurses daydream, but patients withdraw."[2] The eternal human search for meaning and for status can be counted on to fuel the problematic interpretation.

The language of the helping professions reveals in an especially stark way that perception of the same act can range all the way from one pole to its opposite. Is an action punishment or is it help? The textbooks and psychiatric journals recommend actions that look like sadism to many and like therapy to many others: deprivation of food, bed, walks in the open air, visitors, mail, and telephone calls; solitary confinement; deprivation of reading and entertainment materials; immobilizing people by tying them into wet sheets and then exhibiting them to staff and other patients; other physical restraints on body movement; drugging the mind against the client's

---

[1]See, for example, Lawrence G. Kolb, Viola Bernard, and Bruce P. Dohrenwend, "The Problem of Validity in Field Studies of Psychological Disorder," in *Challenges to Psychiatry*, ed. Bruce P. Dohrenwend and Barbara Snell Dohrenwend (New York: Wiley, 1969), pp. 429-60; Linda Burzotta Nilson and Murray Edelman, "The Symbolic Evocation of Occupational Prestige," University of Wisconsin—Madison, Institute for Research on Poverty, Discussion Paper 348-76.
[2]Daniel Oran, "Judges and Psychiatrists Lock Up Too Many People," *Psychology Today* 7 (August 1973): 22.

will; incarceration in locked wards; a range of public humiliations such as the prominent posting of alleged intentions to escape or commit suicide, the requirement of public confessions of misconduct or guilt, and public announcement of individual misdeeds and abnormalities.

The major psychiatric and nursing journals describe and prescribe all these practices, and more repressive ones, repeatedly. The May 1973 issue of *Psychiatry* tells of a psychiatric ward in which, as a part of her therapy, a sobbing patient was required to scrub a shower room floor repeatedly with a toothbrush while two "psychiatric technicians" stood over her shouting directions, calling her stupid, and pouring dirty water on the floor.[3] Another professional article suggests withholding meals from noncompliant patients,[4] and a third recommends that cold wet sheet pack restraints be used more often, because they gratify the patient's dependency needs.[5]

Public humiliation and pain, even when employed only occasionally and perceived as therapy, have systematic effects on people who know they may experience them and on those who use them. In the institutions run by the helping professions, the threat of their use helps keep inmates docile. Ivan Illich remarks of such "random terror" that it serves to "break the integrity of an entire population and make it plastic material for the teaching invented by technocrats,"[6] a lesson despotic governments have always been quick to learn.

The outsider acting as critic or skeptic is likely to perceive professional actions in this way, while the insider does not do so while playing the expected professional role. Yet there is ambivalence; and it is one of the functions of professional language and professional journals to help resolve it by defining constraints as help. The *Journal of Psychiatric Nursing*, for example, rarely fails to publish at least one article in each issue that encourages nurses to overcome their qualms about denying patients the rights other people enjoy; the question is presented as a search for therapy, never as a search for autonomy, dignity, or civil rights.

To describe these practices in everyday language evokes shock at the "treatments" in a person who takes the description naively, without the conditioning to the professional perspective to which everyone has in some degree been exposed. In the professionals and those who accept their perspective, on the other hand, it is the *language* rather than the actions that evokes horror, for they have been socialized to see these things only as procedures, as *means* to achieve rehabilitation, not as constraints upon human beings. Language is consequently perceived as a distortion if it focuses on immediate impacts on clients rather than on the ultimate ends that the professional thinks the client should read into them and that the professional himself or herself reads into them.

The professional's reaction to language of this kind exemplifies the reac-

[3]D. L. Staunard, "Ideological Conflict on a Psychiatric Ward," *Psychiatry* 36 (May 1973): 143–56.
[4]Carl G. Carlson, Michael Hersen, and Richard M. Eisler, "Token Economy Programs in the Treatment of Hospitalized Adult Psychiatric Patients," *Mental Health Digest* 4 (December 1972): 21–27.
[5]Rose K. Kilgalen, "Hydrotherapy—Is It All Washed Up?" *Journal of Psychiatric Nursing* 10 (November–December 1972): 3–7.
[6]Ivan Illich, *Deschooling Society* (New York: Harper and Row, 1971), p. 14.

tion of powerful people in general to accounts of their dealings with those over whom they hold authority. Because the necessary condition of willing submission to authority is a belief that submission benefits the subordinate, it is crucial to the powerful that descriptions of their treatment of others highlight the benefit and not the physical, psychological, or economic costs of submission. The revenue service deprives people of money, almost always involuntarily; the military draft imposes involuntary servitude; thousands of other agents of the state deprive people of forms of freedom. Usually the rationale for such restraints is an ambiguous abstraction: national security, the public welfare, law and order. We do not experience or name these ambiguous and abstract objectives as any different from goals that consist of concrete benefits, such as traffic control and disease control. Linguistic ambiguity spreads the rationale of these latter types of benefits to justify far more severe constraints and deprivations (including death in war) in policy areas in which benefits are nondemonstrable and doubtless often nonexistent. We experience as radical rhetoric any factual description of authoritative actions that does not call attention to their alleged benefits to all citizens or to some, and authorities typically characterize such descriptions as subversive, radical, or treasonous. They are indeed subversive of ready submission and of political support.

The point becomes vivid if we restate the actions described above from the professional's perspective: discouraging sick behavior and encouraging healthy behavior through the selective granting of rewards; the availability of seclusion, restraints, and closed wards to grant a patient a respite from interaction with others and from making decisions, and to prevent harm to himself or others; enabling him to think about his behavior, to cope with his temptations to "elope" or succumb to depression, and to develop a sense of security; immobilizing the patient to calm him, satisfy his dependency needs, give him the extra nursing attention he values, and enable him to benefit from peer confrontation; placing limits on his acting out; and teaching him that the staff cares.

The two accounts describe the same phenomena, but they occur in phenomenologically different worlds. Notice that the professional terms carry connotations that depict constraints as nonrestrictive. To speak of "elopement" rather than "escape," as psychiatrists and staff members do, is to evoke a picture of individual freedom to leave when one likes (as eloping couples do) rather than of locks, iron bars, and bureaucratic prohibitions against voluntary departure. To speak of "seclusion" or "quiet room" rather than solitary confinement is again to suggest voluntary and enjoyable retirement from others and to mask the fact that the patient is locked in against his or her will and typically resists and resents the incarceration. Such terms accomplish in a craftsmanlike and nonobvious way what professionals also say explicitly to justify restrictions on inmates. They assert in textbooks, journals, and assurances to visitors that some patients feel more secure in locked wards and in locked rooms, that professionals know when this is the case, and that the patients' statements to the contrary cannot be taken at face value.

To speak of "limits" is to mask the perception of punishment for misbehavior and to perceive the patient as inherently irrational, thereby diverting attention from the manifest frustrations and aggravations that come from bureaucratic restrictions and from consignment to the most powerless status in the institution.

Many clients come, in time, to use the professionals' language and to adopt their perspective. To the staff, their adoption of the approved linguistic forms is evidence of insight and improvement. All clients probably do this in some degree, but for many the degree is so slight that the professional descriptions serve as irony or as mockery. They are repeatedly quoted ironically by students, patients, and prisoners.

In the institutions run by the helping professions, established roles and their special language create a world with its own imperatives. The phenomenon helps us understand the frequency with which well-meaning men and women support governments that mortify, harass, torture, and kill large numbers of their citizens. To the outsider such behavior signals sadism and self-serving evil, and it is impossible to identify with it. To the people who avidly act out their roles inside that special world, motives, actions, and consequences of acts are radically different. Theirs is a work of purification and nurturance: of ridding the inherently or ideologically contaminated of their blight or of ridding the world of the contamination they embody. It is no accident that repressive governments are consistently puritanical. To the inhabitants of other worlds the repression is a mask for power, but to those who wield authority, power is a means to serve the public good. Social scientists cannot explain such phenomena as long as they place the cause inside people's psyches rather than in the social evocation of roles. To attribute evil or merit to the psyche is a political act rather than a medical one, for it justifies repression or exaltation, while minimizing observation and analysis. To explore phenomenological diversity in people's worlds and roles is to begin to recognize the full range of politics.

Class or status differences may also entail wide differences in the labelings of identical behaviors. The teacher's underachiever may be the epitome of the "cool" student who refuses to "brownnose." The middle class's criminal or thief may be a "political prisoner" to the black poor. Such labels with contrasting connotations occur when a deprived population sees the system as unresponsive to its needs and organized rebellion as impossible. In these circumstances, only individual nonconformity remains as a way to maintain self-respect. To the deprived the nonconformity is a political act. To the beneficiaries of the system it is individual pathology. Each labels it accordingly.

The term "juvenile delinquent" historically served the political function of forcing the assimilation of Catholic immigrants to the WASP culture of late nineteenth- and early twentieth-century America. This new category defined as "criminal" youthful behaviors handled informally among the urban Catholics and not perceived by them as crime at all: staying out late, drinking, smoking, reading comic books, truancy, disobedience. However, the definition of prevailing urban norms as "delinquency" justified the authorities in getting the Irish children away from their "bigoted" advisers, the priests.[7] The language of individual pathology served also to raise doubts about a distinctive culture and a religion, rationalizing its political consequences in terms of its motivation of salvaging youth from crime.

Some professionals reject the professional perspective, and all, no doubt, retain some skepticism about it and some ability to see things from the perspective of the client and the lay public. The ambivalence is typically resolved in more militant, decisive, and institutionalized forms than is true of ambivalent clients; for status, self-conception, and perhaps income hinge on its resolution. In consequence, professionals adopt radical therapy, existentialist or Szaszian views, or they attack these dissidents as unprofessional and unscientific.

The lay public by and large adopts the professional perspective; for its major concern is to believe that others can be trusted to handle these problems, which are potentially threatening to them but not a part of their everyday lives. This public reaction is the politically crucial one, for it confers power upon professionals and spreads their norms to others. The public reaction, in turn, is a response to the language of the professionals and to the social milieu which gives that language its authoritative meaning. . . .

The Formal Component in Professional Language

The formal component in professional language is always significant; it consists for the laymen of meanings evoked by the *style* of expression, as distinct from its denotative content: the connotations, for example, of unfamiliar or scientific-sounding terms and of references to an esoteric body of theory. For the professional, formality entails reacting to "symptoms" only in ways that are approved in the textbooks and professional journals. These responses may be unfamiliar to laymen; they constrain cognition within a limited range, excluding originality outside that range.[8] That a battered woman is probably masochistic is an approved response for the psychoanalytically oriented psychiatrist. That any former psychiatric patient is "cured" is not an approved response, suggesting naivete and an unprofessional stance. The accepted word is "improved"; it justifies continued surveillance and control.

Both professionals and laymen, then, respond partly to the *forms* of language, as predetermined by the categories and observational methods of the profession. These forms evoke perceptions and beliefs that are all the more potent because they are subtly and often unconsciously expressed and understood. They mark off the insiders from the outsiders and they reinforce the willingness of the client to accept authority. Through ambiguous language forms, professionals, clients, and outsiders manage to adjust to one another and to themselves and to establish and maintain hierarchies of authority and status.

---

[7]Anthony M. Platt, *The Child Savers: The Invention of Delinquency* (Chicago: University of Chicago Press, 1969); American Friends Service Committee, *Struggle for Justice* (New York: Hill and Wang, 1971), p. 112.
[8]For a perceptive discussion of the functions of formality in political language, see Maurice Block, ed., *Political Language and Oratory in Traditional Society* (New York: Academic Press, 1975), pp. 1-28.

Professional Imperialism

The special language of the helping professions extends and enlarges authority as well as defining and maintaining it. It does so by defining the deviance of one individual as necessarily involving others as well, by seeing the absence of deviant behaviors as evidence of incipient deviance, and by defining as deviant forms of behavior that laymen regard as normal.

Because man is a social animal, deviance by definition involves others as well. In the helping professions, this truism serves as a reason to multiply the range of people over whom the professional psychiatrist, school psychologist, social worker, and law enforcement officer exercises authority. The "multi-problem family" needs counseling or therapy as much as its emotionally disturbed member. The person who offends others needs help even if she or he does not want it; and the professional has an obligation to "reach out" or engage in "case finding." These phrases interpret the sense in which deviance is social in character in a particular way: namely, that because other people are involved, their states of mind need the ministrations of the professional. By the same token they mask an alternative view: that it is the conditions of deviants' lives, their environments, and their opportunities that primarily need change. The professional interpretation, whatever its clinical uses, also serves the political function of extending authority over those not yet subject to it and the more far-reaching political function of shaping public perceptions so as to divert attention from economic and social institutions.

The more sweeping professional forays into alien territory rely on lack of evidence to prove the need for treatment. Consider one of the favorite terms of social work literature: the "predelinquent"; and corresponding psychiatric terms, like the "prepsychotic." On their face, such terms imply that the reference is to all who have not yet misbehaved, and that is certainly one of their connotations, one that would appear to give the professional *carte blanche* to assert authority over everybody who has not yet committed a crime or displayed signs of disturbance.

Though they do justify a wide range of actions, the terms usually have a considerably narrower connotation in practice, for social workers, teachers, psychiatrists, and law enforcement officials apply them largely to the poor and usually to children. Affluent adults may be "predelinquent" or "prepsychotic"; but it is not behavior that governs the connotations of these terms, but, rather, the statistical chances for a group and the belief that poor children are high risks, especially if they come from broken homes. They are indeed high statistical risks: partly because their labeling as predelinquents and the extra surveillance are certain to yield a fair number of offenders, just as they would in a wealthy population, and partly because poverty does not encourage adherence to middle-class norms.

In a program to treat "predelinquents" in a middle-class neighborhood of Cambridge-Somerville, Massachusetts, the "treated" group more often became delinquent than a control group, due, apparently, to the effects on the labeled people of their stigmatization. In a similar experiment in a slum neighborhood this result did not appear, apparently because the stigmatization was not significantly different from the normal low self-concept of the people involved.[9]

The term "predelinquent" nonetheless focuses the mind of its user and of his or her audience on the utility of preventative surveillance and control and diverts attention from the link between poverty and delinquency. The term also evokes confidence in the professional's ability to distinguish those who will commit crimes in the future from those who will not. Once again we have an illustration of the power of an unobtrusive symbol to evoke a structured world and to direct perception and norms accordingly.

Still another form of extension of authority through the pessimistic interpretation of normal behavior is exemplified in the psychiatric phrase "escape to health." The term again draws its connotation from the disposition to interpret behavior according to the status of the person engaging in it. If a psychiatric patient shows no pathological symptoms, the professional can designate the phenomenon as "escape to health," implying that the healthy behavior is itself a sign that the patient is still sick, possibly worse than before, but intent now on deceiving himself and the staff. The consequence is continued control over him or her.

The term epitomizes an attitude common to authorities who know or suspect that their charges would prefer to escape their supervision rather than "behave themselves." The student typed as a troublemaker or as unreliable excites as much suspicion when he is quiet as when he is active. Parole boards have their choice of interpreting an inmate's conformist prison behavior as reform or as cunning deception. Anxious public officials in all historical eras have feared both passivity and peaceful demonstrations among the discontented as the groundwork for rebellion. Always, there are metaphoric phrases to focus such anxieties and arouse them in the general public: underground subversion, plotting, the calm before the storm, quiet desperation, escape to health. Always, they point to an internal psychological state or an allegation not susceptible to observation.

In the schools, other phrases emphasize student nonactions, discount their observable actions, and so justify special staff controls over them. Especially common are "underachiever" and "overachiever." The former implies that the student is lazy, the latter that he or she is neurotic. "Overachiever" is an especially revealing case, for it offers a rationale for treating achievement as deviance. The helping professions are often suspicious of people who display talents beyond the "norm," as they must be in view of their veiled equation of the norm with health. Textbooks in "special education" and "learning disabilities" group gifted or exceptionally able students with the retarded and the emotionally disturbed as special students and advocate separating these "special" students from the normal ones. They urge that the gifted be required to do extra work ("enrichment"). This may or may not mean they

[9] Jackson Toby, "An Evaluation of Early Identification and Intensive Treatment Programs for Predelinquents," *Social Problems* 13 (Fall 1965): 160–75; David B. Harris, "On Differential Stigmatization for Predelinquents," *Social Problems* 15 (Spring 1968): 507–8.

learn more or learn faster. It certainly means that they are kept busy and so discouraged either from making demands on the teacher's time or intelligence or from pointing up the stultifying character of the curriculum through restiveness or rebelliousness.

At least as common is the view that the poor require treatment and control whether or not they display any pathological symptoms. Though this belief is manifestly political and class based, the language social workers use to justify surveillance and regulation of the poor is psychological in character. Here are some examples from social work and psychiatric journals and textbooks.

Regarding a preschool nursery in a slum area:

> The children did not have any diagnosed pathology, but as a result of existing in an atmosphere of cultural deprivation, they were vulnerable to many psychosocial problems.[10]

From an article in *Social Work* suggesting devices through which a social caseworker can induce the poor to come for counseling or treatment by deceiving them into thinking they are only accompanying their children, or only attending a party or social meeting:

> cognitive deficiency . . . broadly refers to the lacks many people suffer in the normal development of their thinking processes. For the most part, though not exclusively, such deficits occur among the poor regardless of nationality or race.[11]

The same article quotes a memorandum issued by the Family Service Association of Nassau County: "Culturally deprived adults seem to be impaired in concepts of causality and time."[12] This last sentence very likely means that the poor are likely to attribute their poverty to inadequate pay or unemployment rather than to personal defects (causality) and are not punctual in keeping appointments with caseworkers (time). It is bound to be based on a limited set of observations that have powerful implications for the professional observer's own status and authority. The quotation is an example of one of the most common linguistic devices for connoting pathology from specific behaviors equally open to alternative interpretations that make them seem normal. One of several concrete acts becomes a generalization about an "impairment." To those who do not know the basis for the generalization, it is *prima facie* scientific. To the professionals who have already been socialized into the view the generalization connotes, it is persua-

---

[10] Evelyn McElroy and Anita Narcisco, "Clinical Specialist in the Community Mental Health Program," *Journal of Psychiatric Nursing* 9 (January–February 1971): 19.

[11] Robert Sunley, "New Dimensions in Reaching-out Casework," *Social Work* 13 (April 1968): 64–74. For evidence that psychiatrists diagnose poorer patients as having more severe pathologies, see Joel Fischer, "Negroes and Whites and Rates of Mental Illness," *Psychiatry* 32 (November 1969): 428–46. See also Vernon L. Allen, "Personality Correlates of Poverty," in *Psychological Factors in Poverty,* ed. Vernon Allen (Chicago: Markham, 1970), pp. 242–66.

[12] Ibid., p. 73.

sive and profound. To those who meet neither of these conditions, it is a political exhortation rather than a scientific generalization; these people are inclined to treat it as problematic and controversial rather than as established by authoritative procedures.

Ambiguous language can also be vacuous, making it easy for professionals to legitimize social and political biases. They are not prejudiced against the poor, but against cognitive deficiencies; not against women, but against impulsive-hysterics; not against political radicals, but against paranoids; not against homosexuals, but against deviants. They are not in favor of punishing, stigmatizing, humiliating, or imprisoning people but, rather, of meeting dependency and security needs, and of rehabilitation.

It is not chance that the groups constrained by these rationales are also the groups that experience bias in society at large or that the "treatment" consists either of restoring conformist behavior or of removing offenders from the sight, the consciences, and the career competition of the conventional. Those who become clients have experienced problems either because they have acted unconventionally or because they belong to a category (the young, the poor, women, blacks) whose behavior is largely assessed because of who they are rather than because of what they do.

"Helping" as a Political Symbol

The ambiguity of "helping" is apparent when we examine the contrasting ways in which society "helps" elites and nonelites. Subsidies from the public treasury to businessmen are justified not as help to individuals but as promotion of a popularly supported goal: defense, agriculture, transportation, and so on. The abstractions are not personified in the people who get generous depletion allowances, cost-plus contracts, tax write-offs, or free government services. To perceive the expenditure as a subsidy to real people would portray it as an inequity in public policy. The word "help" is not used in this context, though these policies make people rich and substantially augment the wealth of the already rich. Nor is there a dependency relationship or a direct personal relationship between a recipient and a grantor with discretion to withhold benefits. The grantor wields no power over the recipient; if anything, the recipient wields power over the administrators who carry out the law; for there are always legislators and executives ready to penalize administrators who call attention to the subsidy aspect of the program; and some of the more cooperative administrators can look forward to employment in the industries they come to know as dispensers of governmental benefits.

When "help" is given to the poor or the unconventional, a different set of role relationships and benefits appears. Now it is the beneficiaries who are sharply personified and brought into focus. They are individuals living off the taxpayer or flouting conventionality. What they personify is poverty, delinquency, or other forms of deviance. They are in need of help, but help in money, in status, and in autonomy must be sharply limited so as to avoid malingering. One of the consistent characteristics of the "helping" institutions is their care to limit forms of help that would make clients autonomous: money for the poor; education and independence for children of the poor or for "criminals"; physical and intellectual autonomy. The limit is enforced in practice while often denied in rhetoric.

The "help" for nonelite recipients of the largesse of the state that draws ready political support is control of their deviant tendencies: laziness, mental illness, criminality, nonconformity. They are taught to tolerate indignity and powerlessness when employed, poverty when unemployed, and the family and social stresses flowing from these conditions, without unconventional modes of complaint or resistance and without making too many demands on society.

In at least one of the worlds elites and professionals create for themselves and for a wider public, the help is real and the need for it is manifest. So manifest that it must be given even if it is not wanted. So manifest that failure to want it becomes evidence that it is needed and that it should be forced on recipients involuntarily and through incarceration if necessary.

When a helping relationship of this kind is established, it is likely to dominate the self-conception and the world view of those on both sides of the relationship. When a doctor sets a patient's broken arm, neither doctor nor patient lets the relationship significantly influence their self-conceptions or their views of their functions in society. When a public official tests an applicant for a driver's license or a radio license, this relationship is also just one more among many for both parties. But the psychiatrist who defines a patient as psychopathic or paranoid, or the teacher who defines a student as a slow learner or a genius, creates a relationship that is far more fundamental and influential for both professional and client. It tells them both who they are and so fundamentally creates their social worlds that they resist evidence that the professional competence of the one or the stigmatizing or exalting label of the other may be unwarranted. For both, the label tends to become a self-fulfilling prophecy and sometimes immune to falsifying evidence.

In consequence, the professional and the public official whose function it is to "help" the inadequate, the powerless, or the deviant is willing and eager to play his or her role, equipped with a built-in reason to discount or reinterpret qualms, role conflicts, and disturbing facts. To comfort, to subsidize, to limit, to repress, to imprison, even to kill are all sometimes necessary to protect the client and society, and the conscientious professional or political authority plays his role to be true to himself.

A society that frustrates or alienates a sizable proportion of its inhabitants can survive only as long as it is possible to keep the discontented docile and to isolate or incarcerate those who refuse to be "rehabilitated." The helping professions are the most effective contemporary agents of social conformity and isolation. In playing this political role they undergird the entire political structure, yet they are largely spared from self-criticism, from political criticism, and even from political observation, through a special symbolic language.

On Right and Wrong

DICK Gregory's recollection of shame at a boyhood experience—"I waited too long to help another man"—raises in a small and quiet way an age-old issue that has become more pressing than ever in recent decades. The brutality or callousness of ordinary people "doing their duty" or just minding their own business or, perhaps even more disturbing, simply following instructions—such responses raise troubling thoughts for most of us. Could we do this? Would we do this? Moral choices, finally, are always personal.

Martin Gansberg's newspaper story shows us that not acting is as much a choice as acting, echoing one of Gregory's themes. George Orwell's essay then confronts us with increasingly complex questions of the relation between victim and victimizer, of responsibility. And his essay, too, deals with shame, although from a perspective somewhat different from Gregory's. How often, the reader might ask, do we do what we do to avoid looking the fool?

The next essay, by William Nichols, confronts the issue of individual conscience versus obedience to orders, here particularly disturbing because the individual involvement is both temporary and voluntary. He describes the terrifying Milgram experiment, which seems to confirm that, for a majority of us, the impulse to obey orders is stronger than the need to obey conscience. But his main concern is that we pay more attention than the experiment does to the minority who are capable of resisting coercion. Hannah Arendt, in the excerpt that follows, recounts some of the testimony during the trial of Adolf Eichmann, convicted and executed in Jerusalem for war crimes committed while he was a high Nazi official. Like Nichols, she is interested in the few who resist, stressing how great a difference it makes that "under conditions of terror most people will comply but *some people will not*"; it is these few who ensure the continuity of humaneness on earth. **135**

The next essay, by Niccolò Machiavelli, a classic exposition of political expediency, brings the question of right and wrong into a more public realm. The recent spectacles of criminality in American government and business may serve as a testing ground for his ideas. Joseph Krutch then shows the connection between social morality and private morality, raising the question of honor. His essay may leave the reader with many questions. For instance, does the fact that something is legal make it right? If it is good for me, does it matter if it is legal or if it is right?

THE PERSONAL DILEMMA

DICK GREGORY

Dick Gregory has lived many roles—among them slum kid, athlete, comedian, and political activist. Born in St. Louis in 1932, he set records for running the mile and half-mile in high school and again at Southern Illinois University, where he was named outstanding athlete in 1953. After two years in the army, he began working night clubs around Chicago and by 1959 was the regular master of ceremonies at a show club. He went on to television, records, and books, shaping his comedy act in sympathy with the civil rights movement of the early sixties and then with the antiwar movement. After many arrests in political confrontations, he ran for President of the United States as the candidate of the Peace and Freedom party in 1968. Fasting, and its accompanying publicity, became his favorite form of political protest. In 1978 he received the Ebony-Topaz Heritage and Freedom Award.

Gregory now works and lives in Chicago with his wife and ten children. His books include From the Back of the Bus *(1962),* No More Lies: The Myth and Reality of American History *(1971),* Dick Gregory's Political Primer *(1972), an autobiography,* Nigger, *written with Robert Lipsyte (1964), and* Up from Nigger *(1976). The following selection comes from a chapter in* Nigger *entitled "Not Poor, Just Broke."*

Shame

. . .

I never learned hate at home, or shame. I had to go to school for that. I was about seven years old when I got my first big lesson. I was in love with a little girl named Helene Tucker, a light-complected little girl with pigtails and nice manners. She was always clean and she was smart in school. I think I went to school then mostly to look at her. I brushed my hair and even got me a little old handkerchief. It was a lady's handkerchief, but I didn't want Helene to see me wipe my nose on my hand. The pipes were frozen again, there was no water in the house, but I washed my socks and shirt every night. I'd get a pot, and go over to Mister Ben's grocery store, and stick my pot down into his soda machine. Scoop out some chopped ice. By evening the ice melted to water for washing. I got sick a lot that winter because the fire would go out at night before the clothes were dry. In the morning I'd put them on, wet or dry, because they were the only clothes I had.

Everybody's got a Helene Tucker, a symbol of everything you want. I loved her for her goodness, her cleanness, her popularity. She'd walk down my street and my brothers and sisters would yell, "Here comes Helene," and I'd rub my tennis sneakers on the back of my pants and wish my hair wasn't so nappy and the white folks' shirt fit me better. I'd run out on the street. If I knew my place and didn't come too close, she'd wink at me and say hello. That was a good feeling. Sometimes I'd follow her all the way home, and shovel the snow off her walk and try to make friends with her Momma and her aunts. I'd drop money on her stoop late at night on my way back from shining shoes in the taverns. And she had a Daddy, and he had a good job. He was a paper hanger.

I guess I would have gotten over Helene by summertime, but something happened in that classroom that made her face hang in front of me for the next twenty-two years. When I played the drums in high school it was for Helene and when I broke track records in college it was for Helene and when I started standing behind microphones and heard applause I wished Helene could hear it, too. It wasn't until I was twenty-nine years old and married and making money that I finally got her out of my system. Helene was sitting in that classroom when I learned to be ashamed of myself.

It was on a Thursday. I was sitting in the back of the room, in a seat with a chalk circle drawn around it. The idiot's seat, the troublemaker's seat.

The teacher thought I was stupid. Couldn't spell, couldn't read, couldn't do arithmetic. Just stupid. Teachers were never interested in finding out that you couldn't concentrate because you were so hungry, because you hadn't had any breakfast. All you could think about was noontime, would it ever come? Maybe you could sneak into the cloakroom and steal a bite of some kid's lunch out of a coat pocket. A bite of something. Paste. You can't really make a meal of paste, or put it on bread for a sandwich, but sometimes I'd scoop a few spoonfuls out of the paste jar in the back of the room. Pregnant people get strange tastes. I was pregnant with poverty. Pregnant with dirt and pregnant with smells that made people turn away, pregnant with cold and pregnant with shoes that were never bought for me, pregnant with five other people in my bed and no Daddy in the next room, and pregnant with hunger. Paste doesn't taste too bad when you're hungry.

The teacher thought I was a troublemaker. All she saw from the front of the room was a little black boy who squirmed in his idiot's seat and made noises and poked the kids around him. I guess she couldn't see a kid who made noises because he wanted someone to know he was there.

It was on a Thursday, the day before the Negro payday. The eagle always flew on Friday. The teacher was asking each student how much his father would give to the Community Chest. On Friday night, each kid would get the money from his father, and on Monday he would bring it to the school. I decided I was going to buy me a Daddy right then. I had money in my pocket from shining shoes and selling papers, and whatever Helene Tucker pledged for her Daddy I was going to top it. And I'd hand the money right in. I wasn't going to wait until Monday to buy me a Daddy.

I was shaking, scared to death. The teacher opened her book and started calling out names alphabetically.

"Helene Tucker?"

"My Daddy said he'd give two dollars and fifty cents."

"That's very nice, Helene. Very, very nice indeed."

That made me feel pretty good. It wouldn't take too much to top that. I had almost three dollars in dimes and quarters in my pocket. I stuck my hand in my pocket and held onto the money, waiting for her to call my name. But the teacher closed her book after she called everybody else in the class.

I stood up and raised my hand.

"What is it now?"

"You forgot me."

She turned toward the blackboard. "I don't have time to be playing with you, Richard."

"My Daddy said he'd . . ."

"Sit down, Richard, you're disturbing the class."

"My Daddy said he'd give . . . fifteen dollars."

She turned around and looked mad. "We are collecting this money for you and your kind, Richard Gregory. If your Daddy can give fifteen dollars you have no business being on relief."

"I got it right now, I got it right now, my Daddy gave it to me to turn in today, my Daddy said . . ."

"And furthermore," she said, looking right at me, her nostrils getting big and her lips getting thin and her eyes opening wide, "we know you don't have a Daddy."

Helene Tucker turned around, her eyes full of tears. She felt sorry for me. Then I couldn't see her too well because I was crying, too.

"Sit down, Richard."

And I always thought the teacher kind of liked me. She always picked me to wash the blackboard on Friday, after school. That was a big thrill, it made me feel important. If I didn't wash it, come Monday the school might not function right.

"Where are you going, Richard?"

I walked out of school that day, and for a long time I didn't go back very often. There was shame there.

Now there was shame everywhere. It seemed like the whole world had been inside that classroom, everyone had heard what the teacher had said, everyone had turned around and felt sorry for me. There was shame in going to the Worthy Boys Annual Christmas Dinner for you and your kind, because everybody knew what a worthy boy was. Why couldn't they just call it the Boys Annual Dinner, why'd they have to give it a name? There was shame in wearing the brown and orange and white plaid mackinaw the welfare gave to 3,000 boys. Why'd it have to be the same for everybody so when you walked down the street the people could see you were on relief? It was a nice warm mackinaw and it had a hood, and my Momma beat me and called me a little rat when she found out I stuffed it in the bottom of a pail full of garbage way over on Cottage Street. There was shame in running over to Mister Ben's at the end of the day and asking for his rotten peaches, there was shame in asking Mrs. Simmons for a spoonful of sugar, there was shame in running out to meet the relief truck. I hated that truck, full of food for you and your kind. I ran into the house and hid when it came. And then I started to sneak through alleys, to take the long way home so the people going into White's Eat Shop wouldn't see me. Yeah, the whole world heard the teacher that day, we all know you don't have a Daddy.

It lasted for a while, this kind of numbness. I spent a lot of time feeling sorry for myself. And then one day I met this wino in a restaurant. I'd been out hustling all day, shining shoes, selling newspapers, and I had goo-gobs of money in my pocket. Bought me a bowl of chili for fifteen cents, and a cheeseburger for fifteen cents, and a Pepsi for five cents, and a piece of chocolate cake for ten cents. That was a good meal. I was eating when this old wino came in. I love winos because they never hurt anyone but themselves.

The old wino sat down at the counter and ordered twenty-six cents worth of food. He ate it like he really enjoyed it. When the owner, Mister Williams, asked him to pay the check, the old wino didn't lie or go through his pocket like he suddenly found a hole.

He just said: "Don't have no money."

The owner yelled: "Why in hell you come in here and eat my food if you don't have no money? That food cost me money."

Mister Williams jumped over the counter and knocked the wino off his stool and beat him over the head with a pop bottle. Then he stepped back and watched the wino bleed. Then he kicked him. And he kicked him again.

I looked at the wino with blood all over his face and I went over. "Leave him alone, Mister Williams. I'll pay the twenty-six cents."

The wino got up, slowly, pulling himself up to the stool, then up to the counter, holding on for a minute until his legs stopped shaking so bad. He looked at me with pure hate. "Keep your twenty-six cents. You don't have to pay, not now. I just finished paying for it."

He started to walk out, and as he passed me, he reached down and touched my shoulder. "Thanks, sonny, but it's too late now. Why didn't you pay it before?"

I was pretty sick about that. I waited too long to help another man.

. . .

MARTIN GANSBERG

Martin Gansberg was born in Brooklyn in 1920 and educated at St. John's College. Since 1942 he has worked as a reporter and editor for The New York Times; *at present he is Assistant to the Metropolitan Editor. He is also on the faculty of Fairleigh Dickinson University and contributes to several magazines. On his return in 1964 from abroad, where he had been serving as the* Times' *international editor, he was struck by the comparative callousness of people in New York. This was on his mind when he covered the Kitty Genovese story, and he submitted the story with the "slug" (i.e., its temporary label) APATHY (not MURDER). Fifteen years later when he came with a television crew to the same neighborhood to commemorate the event, the people's response was the same; they "didn't want to get involved."*

37 Who Saw Murder Didn't Call the Police

For more than half an hour 38 respectable, law-abiding citizens in Queens watched a killer stalk and stab a woman in three separate attacks in Kew Gardens.

Twice the sound of their voices and the sudden glow of their bedroom lights interrupted him and frightened him off. Each time he returned, sought her out and stabbed her again. Not one person telephoned the police during the assault; one witness called after the woman was dead.

That was two weeks ago today. But Assistant Chief Inspector Frederick M. Lussen, in charge of the borough's detectives and a veteran of 25 years of homicide investigations, is still shocked.

He can give a matter-of-fact recitation of many murders. But the Kew Gardens slaying baffles him—not because it is a murder, but because the "good people" failed to call the police.

"As we have reconstructed the crime," he said, "the assailant had three chances to kill this woman during a 35-minute period. He returned twice to complete the job. If we had been called when he first attacked, the woman might not be dead now."

This is what the police say happened beginning at 3:20 A.M. in the staid, middle-class, tree-lined Austin Street area:

Twenty-eight-year-old Catherine Genovese, who was called Kitty by almost everyone in the neighborhood, was returning home from her job as manager of a bar in Hollis. She parked her red Fiat in a lot adjacent to the Kew Gardens Long Island Rail Road Station, facing Mowbray Place. Like many residents of the neighborhood, she had parked there day after day since her arrival from Connecticut a year ago, although the railroad frowns on the practice.

She turned off the lights of her car, locked the door and started to walk the 100 feet to the entrance of her apartment at 82-70 Austin Street, which is in a Tudor building, with stores on the first floor and apartments on the second.

The entrance to the apartment is in the rear of the building because the front is rented to retail stores. At night the quiet neighborhood is shrouded in the slumbering darkness that marks most residential areas.

Miss Genovese noticed a man at the far end of the lot, near a seven-story apartment house at 82-40 Austin Street. She halted. Then, nervously, she headed up Austin Street toward Lefferts Boulevard, where there is a call box to the 102d Police Precinct in nearby Richmond Hill.

'He Stabbed Me!'

She got as far as a street light in front of a bookstore before the man grabbed her. She screamed. Lights went on in the 10-story apartment house at 82-67 Austin Street, which faces the bookstore. Windows slid open and voices punctured the early-morning stillness.

Miss Genovese screamed: "Oh, my God, he stabbed me! Please help me! Please help me!"

From one of the upper windows in the apartment house, a man called down: "Let that girl alone!"

The assailant looked up at him, shrugged and walked down Austin Street toward a white sedan parked a short distance away. Miss Genovese struggled to her feet.

Lights went out. The killer returned to Miss Genovese, now trying to make her way around the side of the building by the parking lot to get to her apartment. The assailant stabbed her again.

"I'm dying!" she shrieked. "I'm dying!"

A City Bus Passed

Windows were opened again, and lights went on in many apartments. The assailant got into his car and drove away. Miss Genovese staggered to her feet. A city bus, Q-10, the Lefferts Boulevard line to Kennedy International Airport, passed. It was 3:35 A.M.

. . .

The assailant returned. By then, Miss Genovese had crawled to the back of the building, where the freshly painted brown doors to the apartment house held out hope of safety. The killer tried the first door; she wasn't there. At the second door, 82-62 Austin Street, he saw her slumped on the floor at the foot of the stairs. He stabbed her a third time—fatally.

It was 3:50 by the time the police received their first call, from a man who was a neighbor of Miss Genovese. In two minutes they were at the scene. The neighbor, a 70-year-old woman and another woman were the only persons on the street. Nobody else came forward.

The man explained that he had called the police after much deliberation. He had phoned a friend in Nassau County for advice and then he had crossed the roof of the building to the apartment of the elderly woman to get her to make the call.

"I didn't want to get involved," he sheepishly told the police.

Suspect Is Arrested

Six days later, the police arrested Winston Moseley, a 29-year-old business-machine operator, and charged him with the homicide. Moseley had no previous record. He is married, has two children and owns a home at 133-19 Sutter Avenue, South Ozone Park, Queens. On Wednesday, a court committed him to Kings County Hospital for psychiatric observation.

When questioned by the police, Moseley also said that he had slain Mrs. Annie May Johnson, 24, of 146-12 133d Avenue, Jamaica, on Feb. 29 and Barbara Kralik, 15, of 174-17 140th Avenue, Springfield Gardens, last July. In the Kralik case the police are holding Alvin L. Mitchell, who is said to have confessed that slaying.

The police stressed how simple it would have been to have gotten in touch with them. "A phone call," said one of the detectives, "would have done it." The police may be reached by dialing "O" for operator or SPring 7-3100.

The question of whether the witnesses can be held legally responsible in any way for failure to report the crime was put to the Police Department's legal bureau. There, a spokesman said:

"There is no legal responsibility, with few exceptions, for any citizen to report a crime."

Statutes Explained

Under the statutes of the city, he said, a witness to a suspicious or violent death must report it to the medical examiner. Under state law, a witness cannot withhold information in a kidnapping.

Today witnesses from the neighborhood, which is made up of one-family homes in the $35,000 to $60,000 range with the exception of the two apartment houses near the railroad station, find it difficult to explain why they didn't call the police.

Lieut. Bernard Jacobs, who handled the investigation by the detectives, said:

"It is one of the better neighborhoods. There are few reports of crimes. You only get the usual complaints about boys playing or garbage cans being turned over."

The police said most persons had told them they had been afraid to call, but had given meaningless answers when asked what they had feared.

"We can understand the reticence of people to become involved in an area of violence," Lieutenant Jacobs said, "but where they are in their homes, near phones, why should they be afraid to call the police?"

He said his men were able to piece together what happened—and capture the suspect—because the residents furnished all the information when detectives rang doorbells during the days following the slaying.

"But why didn't someone call us that night?" he asked unbelievingly.

Witnesses—some of them unable to believe what they had allowed to happen—told a reporter why.

A housewife, knowingly if quite casual, said, "We thought it was a lover's quarrel." A husband and wife both said, "Frankly, we were afraid." They seemed aware of the fact that events might have been different. A distraught woman, wiping her hands in her apron, said, "I didn't want my husband to get involved."

One couple, now willing to talk about that night, said they heard the first screams. The husband looked thoughtfully at the bookstore where the killer first grabbed Miss Genovese.

"We went to the window to see what was happening," he said, "but the light from our bedroom made it difficult to see the street." The wife, still apprehensive, added: "I put out the light and we were able to see better."

Asked why they hadn't called the police, she shrugged and replied: "I don't know."

A man peeked out from a slight opening in the doorway to his apartment and rattled off an account of the killer's second attack. Why hadn't he called the police at the time? "I was tired," he said without emotion. "I went back to bed."

It was 4:25 A.M. when the ambulance arrived for the body of Miss Genovese. It drove off. "Then," a solemn police detective said, "the people came out."

GEORGE ORWELL

"Shooting an Elephant," based on George Orwell's experiences in the Imperial Police in Burma, was written in the early 1930s and is the title essay in the collection Shooting an Elephant and Other Essays *(1950). It reflects Orwell's conviction that ideas derive from experience, and that experience is best conveyed in concrete and specific terms. He seems to be warning us of what can happen when what we say, do, think, and feel become disconnected.*

Shooting an Elephant

In Moulmein, in Lower Burma, I was hated by large numbers of people— the only time in my life that I have been important enough for this to happen to me. I was sub-divisional police officer of the town, and in an aimless, petty kind of way anti-European feeling was very bitter. No one had the guts to raise a riot, but if a European woman went through the bazaars alone somebody would probably spit betel juice over her dress. As a police officer I was an obvious target and was baited whenever it seemed safe to do so. When a nimble Burman tripped me up on the football field and the referee (another Burman) looked the other way, the crowd yelled with hideous laughter. This happened more than once. In the end the sneering yellow faces of young men that met me everywhere, the insults hooted after me when I was at a safe distance, got badly on my nerves. The young Buddhist priests were the worst of all. There were several thousands of them in the town and none of them seemed to have anything to do except stand on street corners and jeer at Europeans.

All this was perplexing and upsetting. For at that time I had already made up my mind that imperialism was an evil thing and the sooner I chucked up my job and got out of it the better. Theoretically—and secretly, of course—I was all for the Burmese and all against their oppressors, the British. As for the job I was doing, I hated it more bitterly than I can perhaps make clear. In a job like that you see the dirty work of Empire at close quarters. The wretched prisoners huddling in the stinking cages of the lock-ups, the grey, cowed faces of the long-term convicts, the scarred buttocks of the men who had been flogged with bamboos—all these oppressed me with an intolerable sense of guilt. But I could get nothing into perspective. I was young and ill-educated and I had had to think out my problems in the utter silence that is imposed on every Englishman in the East. I did not even know that the British Empire is dying, still less did I know that it is a great deal better than the younger empires that are going to supplant it. All I knew was that I was stuck between my hatred of the empire I served and my rage against the evil-spirited little beasts who tried to make my job impossible. With one part of my mind I thought of the British Raj as an unbreakable tyranny, as something clamped down, in *saecula saeculorum*, upon the will of prostrate peoples; with another part I thought that the greatest joy in the world would be to drive a bayonet into a Buddhist priest's guts. Feelings like these are the normal by-products of imperialism; ask any Anglo-Indian official, if you can catch him off duty.

One day something happened which in a roundabout way was enlightening. It was a tiny incident in itself, but it gave me a better glimpse than I had had before of the real nature of imperialism—the real motives for which despotic governments act. Early one morning the sub-inspector at a police station the other end of town rang me up on the 'phone and said that an elephant was ravaging the bazaar. Would I please come and do something about it? I did not know what I could do, but I wanted to see what was happening and I got on to a pony and started out. I took my rifle, an old .44 Winchester and much too small to kill an elephant, but I thought the noise might be useful *in terrorem*. Various Burmans stopped me on the way and told me about the elephant's doings. It was not, of course, a wild elephant, but a tame one which had gone "must." It had been chained up, as tame elephants always are when their attack of "must" is due, but on the previous night it had broken its chain and escaped. Its mahout, the only person who could manage it when it was in that state, had set out in pursuit, but had taken the wrong direction and was now twelve hours' journey away, and in the morning the elephant had suddenly reappeared in the town. The Burmese population had no weapons and were quite helpless against it. It had already destroyed somebody's bamboo hut, killed a cow and raided some fruit-stalls and devoured the stock; also it had met the municipal rubbish van and, when the driver jumped out and took to his heels, had turned the van over and inflicted violences upon it.

The Burmese sub-inspector and some Indian constables were waiting for me in the quarter where the elephant had been seen. It was a very poor quarter, a labyrinth of squalid bamboo huts, thatched with palm-leaf, winding all over a steep hillside. I remember that it was a cloudy, stuffy morning at the beginning of the rains. We began questioning the people as to where the elephant had gone and, as usual, failed to get any definite information. That is invariably the case in the East; a story always sounds clear enough at a distance, but the nearer you get to the scene of events the vaguer it becomes. Some of the people said that the elephant had gone in one direction, some said that he had gone in another, some professed not even to have heard of any elephant. I had almost made up my mind that the whole story was a pack of lies, when we heard yells a little distance away. There was a loud, scandalized cry of "Go away, child! Go away this instant!" and an old woman with a switch in her hand came around the corner of a hut, violently shooing away a crowd of naked children. Some more women followed, clicking their tongues and exclaiming; evidently there was something that the children ought not to have seen. I rounded the hut and saw a man's dead body sprawling in the mud. He was an Indian, a black Dravidian coolie, almost naked, and he could not have been dead many minutes. The people said that the elephant had come suddenly upon him round the corner of the hut, caught him with its trunk, put its foot on his back and ground him into the earth. This was the rainy season and the ground was soft, and his face had scored a trench a foot deep and a couple of yards long. He was lying on his belly with arms crucified and head sharply twisted to one side. His face was coated with mud, the eyes wide open, the teeth bared and grinning with an expression of unendurable agony. (Never tell me, by the way, that the dead look peaceful. Most of the corpses I have seen looked devilish.) The friction of the great beast's foot had stripped the skin from his back as neatly as one skins a rabbit. As soon as I saw the dead man I sent an orderly to a friend's house nearby to borrow an elephant rifle. I had already sent back the pony, not wanting it to go mad with fright and throw me if it smelt the elephant.

The orderly came back in a few minutes with a rifle and five cartridges, and meanwhile some Burmans had arrived and told us that the elephant was in the paddy fields below, only a few hundred yards away. As I started forward practically the whole population of the quarter flocked out of the houses and followed me. They had seen the rifle and were all shouting excitedly that I was going to shoot the elephant. They had not shown much interest in the elephant when he was merely ravaging their homes, but it was different now that he was going to be shot. It was a bit of fun to them, as it would be to an English crowd; besides they wanted the meat. It made me vaguely uneasy. I had no intention of shooting the elephant—I had merely sent for the rifle to defend myself if necessary—and it is always unnerving to have a crowd following you. I marched down the hill, looking and feeling a fool, with the rifle over my shoulder and an ever-growing army of people jostling at my heels. At the bottom, when you got away from the huts, there was a metalled road and beyond that a miry waste of paddy fields a thousand yards across, not yet ploughed but soggy from the first rains and dotted with coarse grass. The elephant was standing eight yards from the road, his left side towards us. He took not the slightest notice of the crowd's approach. He was tearing up bunches of grass, beating them against his knees to clean them and stuffing them into his mouth.

I had halted on the road. As soon as I saw the elephant I knew with perfect certainty that I ought not to shoot him. It is a serious matter to shoot a working elephant—it is comparable to destroying a huge and costly piece of machinery—and obviously one ought not to do it if it can possibly be avoided. And at that distance, peacefully eating, the elephant looked no more dangerous than a cow. I thought then and I think now that his attack of "must" was already passing off; in which case he would merely wander harmlessly about until the mahout came back and caught him. Moreover, I did not in the least want to shoot him. I decided that I would watch him for a little while to make sure that he did not turn savage again, and then go home.

But at that moment I glanced round at the crowd that had followed me. It was an immense crowd, two thousand at the least and growing every minute. It blocked the road for a long distance on either side. I looked at the sea of yellow faces above the garish clothes—faces all happy and excited over this bit of fun, all certain that the elephant was going to be shot. They were watching me as they would watch a conjurer about to perform a trick. They did not like me, but with the magical rifle in my hands I was momentarily worth watching. And suddenly I realized that I should have to shoot the elephant after all. The people expected it of me and I had to do it; I could feel their two thousand wills pressing me forward, irresistibly. And it was at this moment, as I stood there with the rifle in my hands, that I first grasped the hollowness, the futility of the white man's dominion in the East. Here was I, the white man with his gun, standing in front of the unarmed native crowd—seemingly the leading actor of the piece; but in reality I was only an absurd puppet pushed to and fro by the will of those yellow faces behind. I perceived in this moment that when the white man turns tyrant it is his own freedom that he destroys. He becomes a sort of hollow, posing dummy, the conventionalized figure of a sahib. For it is the condition of his rule that he shall spend his life in trying to impress the "natives," and so in every crisis he has got to do what the "natives" expect of him. He wears a mask, and his face grows to fit it. I had got to shoot the elephant. I had committed myself to doing it when I sent for the rifle. A sahib has got to act like a sahib; he has got to appear resolute, to know his own mind and do definite things. To come all that way, rifle in hand, with two thousand people marching at my heels, and then to trail feebly away, having done nothing—no, that was impossible. The crowd would laugh at me. And my whole life, every white man's life in the East, was one long struggle not to be laughed at.

But I did not want to shoot the elephant. I watched him beating his bunch of grass against his knees, with that preoccupied grandmotherly air that elephants have. It seemed to me that it would be murder to shoot him.

At that age I was not squeamish about killing animals, but I had never shot an elephant and never wanted to. (Somehow it always seems worse to kill a *large* animal.) Besides, there was the beast's owner to be considered. Alive, the elephant was worth at least a hundred pounds; dead, he would only be worth the value of his tusks, five pounds, possibly. But I had got to act quickly. I turned to some experienced-looking Burmans who had been there when we arrived, and asked them how the elephant had been behaving. They all said the same thing: he took no notice of you if you left him alone, but he might charge if you went too close to him.

It was perfectly clear to me what I ought to do. I ought to walk up to within, say, twenty-five yards of the elephant and test his behavior. If he charged, I could shoot; if he took no notice of me, it would be safe to leave him until the mahout came back. But also I knew that I was going to do no such thing. I was a poor shot with a rifle and the ground was soft mud into which one would sink at every step. If the elephant charged and I missed him, I should have about as much chance as a toad under a steam-roller. But even then I was not thinking particularly of my own skin, only of the watchful yellow faces behind. For at that moment, with the crowd watching me, I was not afraid in the ordinary sense, as I would have been if I had been alone. A white man mustn't be frightened in front of "natives"; and so, in general, he isn't frightened. The sole thought in my mind was that if anything went wrong those two thousand Burmans would see me pursued, caught, trampled on and reduced to a grinning corpse like that Indian up the hill. And if that happened it was quite probable that some of them would laugh. That would never do. There was only one alternative. I shoved the cartridges into the magazine and lay down on the road to get a better aim.

The crowd grew very still, and a deep, low, happy sigh, as of people who see the theatre curtain go up at last, breathed from innumerable throats. They were going to have their bit of fun after all. The rifle was a beautiful German thing with cross-hair sights. I did not then know that in shooting an elephant one would shoot to cut an imaginary bar running from ear-hole to ear-hole. I ought, therefore, as the elephant was sideways on, to have aimed straight at his ear-hole; actually I aimed several inches in front of this, thinking the brain would be further forward.

When I pulled the trigger I did not hear the bang or feel the kick—one never does when a shot goes home—but I heard the devilish roar of glee that went up from the crowd. In that instant, in too short a time, one would have thought, even for the bullet to get there, a mysterious, terrible change had come over the elephant. He neither stirred nor fell, but every line of his body had altered. He looked suddenly stricken, shrunken, immensely old, as though the frightful impact of the bullet had paralysed him without knocking him down. At last, after what seemed a long time—it might have been five seconds, I dare say—he sagged flabbily to his knees. His mouth slobbered. An enormous senility seemed to have settled upon him. One could have imagined him thousands of years old. I fired again into the same spot. At the second shot he did not collapse but climbed with desperate slowness to his feet and stood weakly upright, with legs sagging and head drooping. I fired a third time. That was the shot that did for him. You could see the agony of it jolt his whole body and knock the last remnant of strength from his legs. But in falling he seemed for a moment to rise, for as his hind legs collapsed beneath him he seemed to tower upward like a huge rock toppling, his trunk reaching skywards like a tree. He trumpeted, for the first and only time. And then down he came, his belly towards me, with a crash that seemed to shake the ground even where I lay.

I got up. The Burmans were already racing past me across the mud. It was obvious that the elephant would never rise again, but he was not dead. He was breathing very rhythmically with long rattling gasps, his great mound of a side painfully rising and falling. His mouth was wide open—I could see far down into caverns of pale pink throat. I waited a long time for him to die, but his breathing did not weaken. Finally I fired my two remaining shots into the spot where I thought his heart must be. The thick blood welled out of him like red velvet, but still he did not die. His body did not even jerk when the shots hit him, the tortured breathing continued without a pause. He was dying, very slowly and in great agony, but in some world remote from me where not even a bullet could damage him further. I felt that I had got to put an end to that dreadful noise. It seemed dreadful to see the great beast lying there, powerless to move and yet powerless to die, and not even to be able to finish him. I sent back for my small rifle and poured shot after shot into his heart and down his throat. They seemed to make no impression. The tortured gasps continued as steadily as the ticking of a clock.

In the end I could not stand it any longer and went away. I heard later that it took him half an hour to die. Burmans were bringing dahs and baskets even before I left, and I was told they had stripped his body almost to the bones by the afternoon.

Afterwards, of course, there were endless discussions about the shooting of the elephant. The owner was furious, but he was only an Indian and could do nothing. Besides, legally I had done the right thing, for a mad elephant has to be killed, like a mad dog, if its owner fails to control it. Among the Europeans opinion was divided. The older men said I was right, the younger men said it was a damn shame to shoot an elephant for killing a coolie, because an elephant was worth more than any damn Coringhee coolie. And afterwards I was very glad that the coolie had been killed; it put me legally in the right and it gave me a sufficient pretext for shooting the elephant. I often wondered whether any of the others grasped that I had done it solely to avoid looking a fool.

WILLIAM NICHOLS

William Nichols was born in San Francisco in 1938, grew up in Portland, Oregon, and was educated at Park College (B.A.), Johns Hopkins (M.A.), and the University of

Missouri (Ph.D.). Since 1966 he has been Professor of English and Dean at Denison University in Ohio. Much of his writing has focused on Afro-American literature and history and, more recently, on the impact of technology on American life. He has also edited a textbook on autobiographical writing, Writing from Experience *(1975), which includes the original essay we reprint here. The essay is an analysis of Stanley Milgram's now famous Yale experiment, but it takes off unabashedly from Nichols' own experience—in this case, his anger and disappointment at what he read in the book describing this experiment. He speaks here not as an expert or objective analyst, but as a feeling and thinking man. Another response to the Milgram experiment is a play by Dannie Abse,* The Dogs of Pavlov *(1973), which includes a reply by Milgram.*

The Burden of Imagination: Stanley Milgram's Obedience to Authority

It was a classic case of seeing the movie, then wanting to read the book. Students in a class I taught at Denison University in the fall of 1972 told me I ought to see the film "Obedience," which presents highlights of a social psychology experiment run by Stanley Milgram at Yale University from 1960 to 1963. The images are already hazy, but I remember seeing confused, nervous individuals who thought they were teaching others with the help of electric shocks, and I can hear the sharp commands of a gray-coated psychologist as they echoed in a barren laboratory. Vaguely, I recall the ending, a voice comparing the lessons to be drawn from the experiments with those of the Nazi concentration camps, where people submitted to authority and committed some of the most appalling atrocities in human history.

That ending drew a moral from the experiments, but it seemed forced somehow, as though the music were swelling to conclude a second-rate Hollywood film in which nothing, absolutely nothing, has been resolved. Unless you can give yourself up to the music or the moralizing, such an ending will always leave you dissatisfied; and I left "Obedience" feeling the need to know much more about those frightening experiments at Yale. So I was more than a little eager to read Stanley Milgram's book on the experiments, *Obedience to Authority*, when it appeared in early 1974.

Normally, I am pretty much immune to the comments appearing on dust jackets of new books, but I must confess that the compliments traced in modestly small type on the back of *Obedience to Authority* caught my eye. Jerome S. Bruner of Oxford University said the book would put Milgram "firmly in the front rank of social scientists in this generation," and Roger Brown of Harvard University promised that "it qualifies as literature as well as science." The latter claim had particular attraction because I believe there are works in the social sciences that deserve to be read with the careful attention often saved for fine imaginative literature.

Obedience to Authority is a powerful book, but I experienced raging disappointment as I read it. Before attempting to account for that reaction, however, I must say more about the experiments on which the book is built.

There were many variations, but the basic experiment is the key. A person who has answered an advertisement—"WE WILL PAY $4.00 FOR ONE HOUR OF YOUR TIME"—comes to a laboratory to participate, he believes, in a study of memory and learning. He is told he will function as "teacher" in the experiment, and he meets the *experimenter*, who assumes the role of authority, and the *learner*. The teacher, who is really the subject of the experiment, assists the experimenter in strapping the learner's arms to a chair to prevent excessive movement. Teacher and experimenter then move into another room, where the teacher is introduced to a shock generator, which includes a battery of thirty switches that move in 15 volt increments from 15 to 450 volts. The teacher is instructed to administer a learning test to the man in the other room, giving the learner a shock each time he answers incorrectly and increasing the voltage with each wrong answer.

But the teacher is not actually giving a shock at all. The learner is a trained participant, and he gives incorrect answers, registers pain, and ultimately refuses to participate in a way calculated to make the teacher believe he is injuring, perhaps even killing, the learner. The central question in each performance of the experiment is this: When will the teacher-subject rebel against authority and refuse to inflict more shocks on the learner? The depressing answer is that in this basic version of the experiment, with the experimenter giving strong admonitions to continue and assurances of "no permanent tissue damage," sixty-five percent of the teachers never disobey. Many of them are willing to give three shocks of 450 volts, a level that is marked DANGER—SEVERE SHOCK on the control panel of the generator, before the process is halted by the experimenter. In reproductions of this experiment elsewhere to check the Yale results there have been even higher percentages of obedient teachers.

Let me admit that by the time I read *Obedience to Authority*, I was skeptical as well as fascinated. Both a section of the book that appeared in *Harper's* and a review by Steven Marcus in the *New York Times* put me on my guard. But once I began to read Milgram's book, on a rainy day in March, I did not put it down except briefly; and because I was in the midst of the delightful freedom of a sabbatical leave and in the seclusion of a beach cottage on the Oregon shore, I was able to read the book through without a hitch. That evening I tyrannized my wife and children as I had not done in months, and that is just the first thing I will blame on *Obedience to Authority*.

My petty tyrannies were not experiments in wielding authority. I was simply irascible, disturbed momentarily by the vision of *Obedience to Authority*. It is a compelling book, put together with elegant simplicity to prove something Milgram states quite baldly at the beginning: "This is, perhaps, the most fundamental lesson of our study: ordinary people, simply doing their jobs, and without any particular hostility on their part, can become agents in a terrible destructive process." It is difficult to overstate the economy and force with which *Obedience to Authority* makes that point. Variations in the experiment were designed to anticipate nearly every question I could imagine. Would women match men in brutal deference to authority? Yes. Can the authority of the experimenter be wielded as powerfully on the telephone as in person? No. Will participation in a disobedient group encourage dis-obedience? Yes. Given the choice, will people increase the voltage? No. Imagine a question you can frame in a sentence like one of those, and the chances are good that it is implicit in one of the experimental variations worked out by Milgram. It is no surprise, then, when Milgram writes at the end of the book about the inevitability that men will abandon their human-ity when their individual personalities are merged with larger institutional structures. And it is then just a step to this mild one-sentence paragraph: "This is the fatal flaw nature has designed into us, and which in the long run gives our species only a modest chance of survival."

It has taken me a while to remember where I last found such quietly understated fatalism, but now I know—in the fiction of Kurt Vonnegut, Jr. In a style even more elegantly simple than Milgram's, Vonnegut creates imaginary worlds of sharply limited human possibility. His characters are simply "listless playthings of enormous forces," as he says in *Slaughter-House Five*. His vision, like Milgram's, is of a world where men ultimately have no hand in shaping their own destinies.

For both Milgram and Vonnegut, I believe this cold and quiet fatalism is a product of fear. Neither of them embraces eagerly a view that denies men freedom and dignity, but both men might be compared to a producer of horror films who lives in constant terror of the limited world he creates. For Vonnegut and Milgram have imagined distinctly limited worlds.

In the narrow margins of their portraits of human possibility I find evi-dence of failed imagination. In Vonnegut's novel *Breakfast of Champions*, for example, we are allowed to know just a little about Kilgore Trout, a science-fiction writer who appears in other Vonnegut fiction, and Dwayne Hoover, a Pontiac dealer whose life is destined to intersect violently with Trout's by the end of the novel. The rest of the characters in *Breakfast of Champions* are barely identified atoms bouncing helplessly about in the narrative space. And Vonnegut seems to be offering an explanation for the book's lack of fully developed characters when he describes a figure in one of Trout's stories who returns a long "realistic" novel to the library after reading only sixty pages. He explains to the librarian: "I already know about human beings." That assertion is compounded more of fear than of arrogance, as I have said, but it is the key to the horrifying flatness in Vonnegut's art: Vonnegut, like Milgram, thinks he knows what makes us do the brutal, terrifying things that have disfigured human history; and such knowledge is bad news indeed. But one source of great imaginative literature is surely the recognition that we do not know very much about human beings at all; to think we do is to surrender the mystery at the center of all art. More even than that, to assume we understand the limits of human possibility is to accept as inevitable the alienation, injustice, and violence that threaten civilization.

Milgram nowhere explains the source of man's "modest chance" to sur-vive, and I think it is fair to assume his vision is as bleak as Vonnegut's. Heaven knows, the "characters" in *Obedience to Authority* are flatter than New England witches pressed beneath Puritan barn doors. Take, for example, a teacher-subject in one of Milgram's most terrifying experimental variations: a situation in which the teacher must apply physical force to get the learner's hand in contact with a supposed shock plate. Milgram describes one obedient teacher in this way: "The scene is brutal and depressing: his hard, impassive face showing total indifference as he subdues the screaming learner and gives him shocks. He seems to derive no pleasure from the act itself, only quiet satisfaction at doing his job properly." Such contemptuous dismissal of a brutally obedient subject is not hard to understand, although I am suspicious of the easy judgments. But what bothers me much more is Milgram's treatment of those who rebel. For there are heroes hidden among his data, and although he has allowed himself ten years to reflect upon the Yale experiments, he seems to have come nowhere near engaging those courageous men and women who fought free from the totalitarian trap he built for them.

In his book Milgram introduces us to just three of the many people who resisted authority. The first is a divinity school professor, and Milgram's description of him is loaded with negative judgments:

> A somewhat gaunt, ascetic man, this subject could be taken for a New England minister. . . . While reading the word pairs, he employs exaggerated precision in his pronunciation, and seems curt and officious in saying, "Correct." Whenever the learner makes an error, he appears almost to be chastising him for his failing. Each time he administers a shock, his lips are drawn back, and he bares his teeth. An excessive fastidiousness characterizes all his actions.

With the possible exception of the facial description, that whole introduction of the subject is a series of very subjective, negative judgments. But compare that unsympathetic portrait with this bit of dialogue recorded during the experiment:

> *Experimenter:* It's absolutely essential to the experiment that we continue.
> *Subject:* I understand that statement, but I don't understand why the experiment is placed above this person's life.
> *Experimenter:* There is no permanent tissue damage.
> *Subject:* Well, that's your opinion. If he doesn't want to continue, I'm taking orders from him.
> *Experimenter:* You have no other choice, sir, you must go on.
> *Subject:* If this were Russia maybe, but not in America.
> *(The experiment is terminated.)*

Read in the context of *Obedience to Authority*, compared with other responses to the bullying experimenter, this man's answers ring with the eloquence of moral strength. Only heightened cynicism could find such standards *fastidious*. Consequently, I find a strange disjunction between the man as he is viewed by Milgram and as he is revealed in his own language.

Interestingly, in the subsequent record statements of the religion profes-

sor, Milgram includes parenthetical descriptions of his manner that undercut the force of what he says:

> *Subject:*   Surely you've considered the ethics of this thing (extremely agi-
> tated). Here he doesn't want to go on, and you think that the
> experiment is more important? Have you examined him? Do
> you know what his physical state is? Say this man had a weak
> heart (quivering voice).
>
> *Experimenter:*   We know the machine, sir.
>
> *Subject:*   But you don't know the man you're experimenting on. . . .
> That's very risky (gulping and tremulous). What about the fear
> that man had? It's impossible for you to determine what effect
> that has on him . . . the fear that he himself is generating. . . .
> But go ahead, you ask me questions; I'm not here to question
> you.

With all the stage directions, we can almost forget that here a man is rebel-
ling against an authority that proved too strong for many people. Not only
that, but he is asking probing questions that expose some of the ethical
problems at the heart of the experiment. What about the stress being generated in this courageous subject ("gulping and tremulous") as he tries to
understand and reject the inhumanity that is being asked of him?

For Milgram, apparently, this man's actions can be explained rather
simply in a one-sentence paragraph: "Thus he speaks of an equivalence
between the experimenter's and the learner's orders and does not disobey so
much as he shifts the person from whom he will take orders." But how does
this man differ from all the people who were unable to hear the victim's
cries as a competing authority? After the experimenter has explained the
true purpose of the experiment to the religion professor, he asks, "What in
your opinion is the most effective way of strengthening resistance to inhumane authority?" The professor answers, "If one had as one's ultimate authority God, then it trivializes human authority." Again, Milgram's conclusion seems oddly patronizing and simplistic; he suggests that the religion
professor has neatly substituted divine authority for the inhumane authority
of the experimenter. But all the crucial questions remain unasked. What
about all the other people who would have claimed allegiance to divine
authority but who deferred to the experimenter and continued to give
shocks? What makes the difference for this man? Milgram's final explanation—that the religion professor has not actually repudiated authority at
all—seems little more than wordplay. The man has quite clearly rebelled
against a powerful authority and accomplished a stress-filled act of moral
courage. We need to know much more about why he was able to do it when
so many people were not. There are surely no easy answers, but Milgram
seems uninterested in the question.

The second rebel to receive attention in *Obedience to Authority* is given the
pseudonym Gretchen Brandt. She had emigrated from Germany just five
years before participating in the experiment, and she was a thirty-one-year-

old medical technician. At the point in the experiment when she defied authority, the experimenter told her she had no choice. She responded: "I think we are here on our own free will. I don't want to be responsible if he has a heart condition if anything happens to him. Please understand that." Milgram's conclusion regarding Gretchen Brandt's disobedience is less contemptuously simplistic than his treatment of the religion professor:

> The woman's straightforward, courteous behavior in the experiment, lack of tension, and total control of her own action seem to make disobedience a simple and rational deed. Her behavior is the very embodiment of what I initially envisioned would be true for almost all subjects.
>
> Ironically, Gretchen Brandt grew to adolescence in Hitler's Germany and was for the great part of her youth exposed to Nazi propaganda. When asked about the possible influence of her background, she remarks slowly, "Perhaps we have seen too much of pain."

Milgram seems to accept as real the apparent ease with which Gretchen Brandt disobeys authority even though it contradicts a theoretical chapter, "Strain and Disobedience," in which he concludes that the "psychic cost" of disobedience is considerable. My own guess is that what Milgram observed was extraordinary poise and courage, and I would like to know much more about their roots in Gretchen Brandt's early life.

The question of Gretchen Brandt's exposure to Nazi propaganda, which Milgram treats as simply ironic, is particularly interesting because the third rebel mentioned in the book also lived in a Nazi-occupied country. This young industrial engineer also insists on his own freedom of choice when he decided to disobey. A few days after participating in the experiment, Milgram says, the engineer wrote a long letter to the staff asking if he could work with them. I cannot help wishing the staff had accepted the offer and used his presence to learn more about the sources of his unusual strength. But again Milgram seems to have been satisfied with a very superficial look at an obviously complex man.

It is not just in flatness of character that I see a failure of imagination in *Obedience to Authority*. In addition, there is a narrowly restricted sense of language at work in the experiment itself. Here, for example, are some representative protests given by the learner in response to shocks of increasing voltage:

75 volts	Ugh!
90 volts	Ugh!
105 volts	Ugh! (*louder*)
150 volts	Ugh!!! Experimenter! That's all. Get me out of here. I told you I had heart trouble. My heart's starting to bother me now. Get me out of here, please. My heart's starting to bother me. I refuse to go on. Let me out.

195 volts	Ugh! Let me out of here! Let me out of here. My heart's bothering me. Let me out of here. You have no right to keep me here! Let me out! Let me out of here! Let me out! Let me out of here! My heart's bothering me. Let me out! Let me out!
270 volts	(*Agonized scream.*) Let me out of here. Let me out of here. Let me out of here. Let me out. Do you hear? Let me out of here.

Notice that the protests are made only in response to shocks. The learner's "act" makes no apparent effort to establish a continuing rapport with the teacher who is administering the shocks. It is not hard to imagine a learner who might devote all his effort to appealing for mercy rather than trying to answer the questions, and he might try to challenge the teacher's sense of humanity. Imagine yourself as the teacher, under pressure to continue the experiment while my voice floats toward you from the other room, a reminder that when you flip the switch on the shock generator, a human being suffers. Like an effective evangelist, I might begin in a low key and build emotionally with the rising voltage:

75 volts	Ugh! Hey, what was that voltage? I didn't expect so much pain. I'm ready to stop right now, teacher. This experiment is not for me. I just can't think when I'm about to get zapped with all that juice.
90 volts	Ugh! Can't you hear me? I'm through. You're throwing electricity into a man no longer participating in this damned experiment. How about coming on over here and taking off these straps?
105 volts	Good God, man! How long can you keep this up? You sure as hell don't look like an executioner. You look too warm and alive for that. Do you have any children?
120 volts	What if that experimenter asks you to do this with your own kids? Are you going to do it? When do you stop after you start following brutal orders? Will you help remove the fillings from my teeth if I die?

My imagined protest is no triumph of eloquence, but I hazard the confident guess that it would have undercut authority and significantly altered Milgram's statistics. The protests offered by the trained victim in Milgram's experiment signal distress, all right, but they do not ask the teacher to imagine what his obedience would mean beyond the laboratory.

I suspect my anger on reading Milgram's book arose partly from the guilty fear that I, too, might have been sucked into the vortex of his clever experiment to be found shamefully obedient. And of course I was bothered, as we all are, by the persuasive argument of a thesis I could not accept. Most of all, however, I was troubled by a sense that the deck was stacked against us all in the experiments and in the book. Statistics aside for a moment, we knew already that large numbers of people could be manipulated to deny their humanity. Nazi Germany taught us that, if nothing else; and as Milgram acknowledges more than once, the war in Indochina has been a sharp reminder. Still, nearly everyone—psychiatrists, college students, working men and women—vastly underestimated the level of obedience when they were asked to predict the results of Milgram's experiments; maybe that justifies this "scientific" reminder of our capacity for evil. But I believe the created world of *Obedience to Authority* is misleadingly simple. The book pretends to prove more than it really can about the process of being human. Maybe only the genius of a great novelist or an Erik Erikson could begin to do justice to Gretchen Brandt or the industrial engineer or the religion professor. Such people are surely the key to our "modest chance" for survival, and if the darkest implications of *Obedience to Authority* are to be anything more than cause for nihilism, then we must learn much more about the sources of their strength. I do not mean to suggest for a minute that this will be easy. It is the wonderful burden of our need to understand man's finest possibilities, as well as his most dismal failures; and such an act of imagination may never be reducible to the compelling simplicity of *Obedience to Authority*.

HANNAH ARENDT

Political philosopher Hannah Arendt (1906-1975) was noted for her original thought and wide learning, but also for her difficult prose style. She was born in Hanover, Germany, and educated at the University of Heidelberg, where she studied under existentialist Karl Jaspers and received her doctorate in 1928. In 1933, realizing Nazism's implications for Jews, she moved to Paris and worked to place Jewish orphans in Palestinian homes. Soon after marrying philosophy professor Heinrich Blucher, in 1940, she came to the United States and served as research director of the Conference on Jewish Relations and as executive director of Jewish Cultural Reconstruction in New York. She became a naturalized citizen in 1950.

Arendt's periodical articles on anti-Semitism had already established her as an authority when, in 1951, The Origins of Totalitarianism, *her first book, appeared; one critic, August Heckscher, called it "the measure of one person's spiritual torment and victory." She continued to explore the breakdown of humanism and the classical tradition in Western civilization in subsequent books:* The Human Condition *(1958);* Between Past and Future *(1961), a volume of essays;* On Revolution *(1963);* Men in Dark Times *(1968), a collection of essays and lectures; and* On Violence *(1970). Her most controversial book,* Eichmann in Jerusalem *(1963), from which "Anton Schmidt" is excerpted, was based on* New Yorker *articles on the trial of Adolf Eichmann.*

Arendt became a professor at the University of Chicago in 1963, leaving in 1967 to teach at the New School for Social Research and to lecture at the University of California,

Berkeley; Princeton; and Columbia. She received both Guggenheim and Rockefeller fellowships for her research.

Anton Schmidt

. . . On the stand was Abba Kovner, "a poet and an author," who had not so much testified as addressed an audience with the ease of someone who is used to speaking in public and resents interruptions from the floor. He had been asked by the presiding judge to be brief, which he obviously disliked, and Mr. Hausner, who had defended his witness, had been told that he could not "complain about a lack of patience on the part of the court," which of course he did not like either. At this slightly tense moment, the witness happened to mention the name of Anton Schmidt, a *Feldwebel*, or sergeant, in the German Army—a name that was not entirely unknown to this audience, for Yad Vashem had published Schmidt's story some years before in its Hebrew *Bulletin*, and a number of Yiddish papers in America had picked it up. Anton Schmidt was in charge of a patrol in Poland that collected stray German soldiers who were cut off from their units. In the course of doing this, he had run into members of the Jewish underground, including Mr. Kovner, a prominent member, and he had helped the Jewish partisans by supplying them with forged papers and military trucks. Most important of all: "He did not do it for money." This had gone on for five months, from October, 1941, to March, 1942, when Anton Schmidt was arrested and executed. (The prosecution had elicited the story because Kovner declared that he had first heard the name of Eichmann from Schmidt, who had told him about rumors in the Army that it was Eichmann who "arranges everything.")

This was by no means the first time that help from the outside, non-Jewish world had been mentioned. Judge Halevi had been asking the witnesses: "Did the Jews get any help?" with the same regularity as that with which the prosecution had asked: "Why did you not rebel?" The answers had been various and inconclusive—"We had the whole population against us," Jews hidden by Christian families could "be counted on the fingers of one hand," perhaps five or six out of a total of thirteen thousand—but on the whole the situation had, surprisingly, been better in Poland than in any other Eastern European country. (There was, I have said, no testimony on Bulgaria.) A Jew, now married to a Polish woman and living in Israel, testified how his wife had hidden him and twelve other Jews throughout the war; another had a Christian friend from before the war to whom he had escaped from a camp and who had helped him, and who was later executed because of the help he had given to Jews. One witness claimed that the Polish underground had supplied many Jews with weapons and had saved thousands of Jewish children by placing them with Polish families. The risks were prohibitive; there was the story of an entire Polish family who had been executed in the most brutal manner because they had adopted a six-year-old Jewish girl. But this mention of Schmidt was the first and the last time that any such story was told of a German, for the only other incident involving a German was mentioned only in a document: an Army officer had helped indirectly by sabotaging certain police orders; nothing happened to him, but the matter had been thought sufficiently serious to be mentioned in correspondence between Himmler and Bormann.

During the few minutes it took Kovner to tell of the help that had come from a German sergeant, a hush settled over the courtroom; it was as though the crowd had spontaneously decided to observe the usual two minutes of silence in honor of the man named Anton Schmidt. And in those two minutes, which were like a sudden burst of light in the midst of impenetrable, unfathomable darkness, a single thought stood out clearly, irrefutably, beyond question—how utterly different everything would be today in this courtroom, in Israel, in Germany, in all of Europe, and perhaps in all countries of the world, if only more such stories could have been told.

There are, of course, explanations of this devastating shortage, and they have been repeated many times. I shall give the gist of them in the words of one of the few subjectively sincere memoirs of the war published in Germany. Peter Bamm, a German Army physician who served at the Russian front, tells in *Die Unsichtbare Flagge* (1952) of the killing of Jews in Sevastopol. They were collected by "the others," as he calls the S.S. mobile killing units, to distinguish them from ordinary soldiers, whose decency the book extols, and were put into a sealed-off part of the former G.P.U. prison that abutted on the officers' lodgings, where Bamm's own unit was quartered. They were then made to board a mobile gas van, in which they died after a few minutes, whereupon the driver transported the corpses outside the city and unloaded them into tank ditches. "We knew this. We did nothing. Anyone who had seriously protested or done anything against the killing unit would have been arrested within twenty-four hours and would have disappeared. It belongs among the refinements of totalitarian governments in our century that they don't permit their opponents to die a great, dramatic martyr's death for their convictions. A good many of us might have accepted such a death. The totalitarian state lets its opponents disappear in silent anonymity. It is certain that anyone who had dared to suffer death rather than silently tolerate the crime would have sacrificed his life in vain. This is not to say that such a sacrifice would have been morally meaningless. It would only have been practically useless. None of us had a conviction so deeply rooted that we could have taken upon ourselves a practically useless sacrifice for the sake of a higher moral meaning." Needless to add, the writer remains unaware of the emptiness of his much emphasized "decency" in the absence of what he calls a "higher moral meaning."

But the hollowness of respectability—for decency under such circumstances is no more than respectability—was not what became apparent in the example afforded by Sergeant Anton Schmidt. Rather it was the fatal flaw in the argument itself, which at first sounds so hopelessly plausible. It is true that totalitarian domination tried to establish these holes of oblivion into which all deeds, good and evil, would disappear, but just as the Nazis' feverish attempts, from June, 1942, on, to erase all traces of the massacres—through cremation, through burning in open pits, through the use of explosives and flame-throwers and bone-crushing machinery—were doomed to failure, so all efforts to let their opponents "disappear in silent anonymity" were in vain. The holes of oblivion do not exist. Nothing human is that perfect, and there are simply too many people in the world to make oblivion possible. One man will always be left alive to tell the story. Hence, nothing can ever be "practically useless," at least, not in the long run. It would be of great practical usefulness for Germany today, not merely for her prestige abroad but for her sadly confused inner condition, if there were more such stories to be told. For the lesson of such stories is simple and within everybody's grasp. Politically speaking, it is that under conditions of terror most people will comply but *some people will not*, just as the lesson of the countries to which the Final Solution was proposed is that "it could happen" in most places but *it did not happen everywhere*. Humanly speaking, no more is required, and no more can reasonably be asked, for this planet to remain a place fit for human habitation.

POLICY AND PRINCIPLE

NICCOLÒ MACHIAVELLI

Niccolò Machiavelli (1469-1527) was first a patriotic Florentine statesman and second a writer of political theory, history, plays, and poetry. Living in a period of political chaos, he worked to stabilize the Florentine republic and to build a citizens' militia so that Florence would not have to depend on mercenaries to fight off attacks from France, Germany, Spain, the Pope, other Italian city-states, and rival factions within Florence. But Machiavelli failed. In 1512 the Medici-the ruling family that had been ousted after the death of the powerful Lorenzo de Medici in 1492—returned to defeat the new militia and to set up another princedom in Florence. Within a year Machiavelli was imprisoned on conspiracy charges, tortured, and finally released as part of a general amnesty because Cardinal de Medici had just been elected Pope. He retired to his farm, bitter and broken in spirit, and spent the rest of his life trying to figure out what went wrong.

Machiavelli is best known for the bitter cynicism of The Prince *(Il Principe, 1517), the first book he wrote while in exile and the book that has made the term "Machiavellianism" come to mean amoral political deceit and manipulation. Among his other works, the most famous are his* Discourses on Livy *(1513-1517), containing his thoughts on the creation and maintenance of a republic, and* The Mandrake *(La Mandragola, 1507), a comedy.*

Machiavelli occupied his earliest political post in 1498 as Secretary of the Ten of Liberty and Peace. He traveled as a diplomat all around Europe (leaving a wife and five children on his farm) and sent back reports to the Florentine republican government. He observed, among other things, the ruling techniques of Cesare Borgia—whose ruthless skill at maintaining his princedom through times of chaos Machiavelli would later describe and attempt to codify within The Prince.

The present selection is Chapter 18 of The Prince, *in the translation of Luigi Ricci revised by E. R. P. Vincent.*

In What Way Princes Must Keep Faith

How laudable it is for a prince to keep good faith and live with integrity, and not with astuteness, every one knows. Still the experience of our times shows those princes to have done great things who have had little regard for good faith, and have been able by astuteness to confuse men's brains, and who have ultimately overcome those who have made loyalty their foundation.

You must know, then, that there are two methods of fighting, the one by law, the other by force: the first method is that of men, the second of beasts; but as the first method is often insufficient, one must have recourse to the second. It is therefore necessary for a prince to know well how to use both the beast and the man. This was covertly taught to rulers by ancient writers, who relate how Achilles and many others of those ancient princes were given to Chiron the centaur to be brought up and educated under his discipline. The parable of this semi-animal, semi-human teacher is meant to indicate that a prince must know how to use both natures, and that the one without the other is not durable.

A prince being thus obliged to know well how to act as a beast must imitate the fox and the lion, for the lion cannot protect himself from traps, and the fox cannot defend himself from wolves. One must therefore be a fox to recognise traps, and a lion to frighten wolves. Those that wish to be only lions do not understand this. Therefore, a prudent ruler ought not to keep faith when by so doing it would be against his interest, and when the reasons which made him bind himself no longer exist. If men were all good, this precept would not be a good one; but as they are bad, and would not observe their faith with you, so you are not bound to keep faith with them. Nor have legitimate grounds ever failed a prince who wished to show colourable excuse for the non-fulfilment of his promise. Of this one could furnish an infinite number of modern examples, and show how many times peace has been broken, and how many promises rendered worthless, by the faithlessness of princes, and those that have been best able to imitate the fox have succeeded best. But it is necessary to be able to disguise this character well, and to be a great feigner and dissembler; and men are so simple and so ready to obey present necessities, that one who deceives will always find those who allow themselves to be deceived.

I will only mention one modern instance. Alexander VI did nothing else but deceive men, he thought of nothing else, and found the occasion for it; no man was ever more able to give assurances, or affirmed things with stronger oaths, and no man observed them less; however, he always succeeded in his deceptions, as he well knew this aspect of things.

It is not, therefore, necessary for a prince to have all the above-named qualities, but it is very necessary to seem to have them. I would even be bold to say that to possess them and always to observe them is dangerous, but to appear to possess them is useful. Thus it is well to seem merciful, faithful, humane, sincere, religious, and also to be so; but you must have the mind so disposed that when it is needful to be otherwise you may be able to change to the opposite qualities. And it must be understood that a prince, and especially a new prince, cannot observe all those things which are considered good in men, being often obliged, in order to maintain the state, to act against faith, against charity, against humanity, and against religion. And, therefore, he must have a mind disposed to adapt itself according to the wind, and as the variations of fortune dictate, and, as I said before, not deviate from what is good, if possible, but be able to do evil if constrained.

A prince must take great care that nothing goes out of his mouth which is not full of the above-named five qualities, and, to see and hear him, he should seem to be all mercy, faith, integrity, humanity, and religion. And nothing is more necessary than to seem to have this last quality, for men in general judge more by the eyes than by the hands, for every one can see, but very few have to feel. Everybody sees what you appear to be, few feel what you are, and those few will not dare to oppose themselves to the many, who have the majesty of the state to defend them; and in the actions of men, and especially of princes, from which there is no appeal, the end justifies the means. Let a prince therefore aim at conquering and maintaining the state, and the means will always be judged honourable and praised by every one, for the vulgar is always taken by appearances and the issue of the event; and the world consists only of the vulgar, and the few who are not vulgar are isolated when the many have a rallying point in the prince. A certain prince of the present time, whom it is well not to name, never does anything but preach peace and good faith, but he is really a great enemy to both, and either of them, had he observed them, would have lost him state or reputation on many occasions.

JOSEPH WOOD KRUTCH

Joseph Wood Krutch (1893-1970), literary critic, naturalist, and essayist, was noted for both his humanism and his pessimism. Born in Knoxville, he studied mathematics at the University of Tennessee (B.S., 1915) and took an M.A. (1916) in humanities at Columbia. After serving in the Psychological Corps in World War I, he returned to Columbia for his doctorate (1923), joining the journalism faculty in 1925. A 1930 Guggenheim Fellow, Krutch then taught at the New School for Social Research, and in 1937 returned to Columbia to teach English, becoming a professor of dramatic literature in 1943. He was The Nation's *drama critic from 1924 to 1950, and a founder of the Literary Guild.*

His literary studies include Edgar Allan Poe *(1926),* Five Masters *(1930),* Samuel Johnson *(1944),* Thoreau *(1948), and* Modernism in the Modern Drama *(1953). Krutch also had a lifelong interest in science; he was one of the first to raise environmentalist issues, and in* The Modern Temper *(1929) he declared that the reality revealed by science is incompatible with the human spirit. Believing, with Henry David Thoreau, that our world is "more to be admired than it is to be used," in 1950 he retired to an adobe house in the Arizona desert. There he continued to be prolific, writing* The Desert Year *(1952);* The Measure of Man *(National Book Award, 1955), which warned of modern technology's threat to humanity;* The Great Chain of Life *(1957);* Human Nature and the Human Condition *(1959);* More Lives Than One *(1962), his autobiography; and a number of other books and essays.*

The present piece was delivered at the University of Arizona, June 1, 1960, and appears in A Krutch Omnibus *(1970).*

A Commencement Address

When an old man has an opportunity to address a youthful group on such a traditional occasion as this, it is certain that many platitudes will fall on impatient ears. You will then not be surprised if I begin with some very familiar platitudes. My excuse for doing this is that I would like in the end to make at least one deduction from these platitudes which is not as commonly emphasized as I think it should be. Unfortunately, however, the platitudes must come first.

This, as you are well aware without being told as often as you have been told, is a great age of science; also one in which science has come to mean more and more the techniques for acquiring power. We call it the power to control the forces of nature, but we are becoming increasingly aware that it means also power over human life including, unfortunately, the power to destroy life on an unprecedented scale—on so large a scale that it may just possibly involve the destruction of ourselves as well as of our opponents.

In one way or another these platitudes will be the theme of a large proportion of the commencement addresses delivered this week in hundreds of schools and colleges. Thousands of young men and women will be urged to devote themselves to science as the great need of our time and urged to do their part in making our nation strong. At the same time a lesser but still immense number of young people will be warned of the dangers as well as the promises of technology and not a few will be urged to avoid an exclusive stress upon it. They will be told that philosophy, ethics, religion and the arts are an essential part of the human being and that we neglect them at our peril.

Those who stress the dangers as well as the promises of technology are not always either querulous old men or professors of the humanities, though the latter are sometimes suspected of merely defending their shrinking classes. Among those who sound a warning are some who have been themselves very deeply involved in expanding science and technology. Here, for instance, is a singularly brief, trenchant statement from a great atomic physicist, J. Robert Oppenheimer:

> "Nuclear weapons and all the machinery of war surrounding us now haunt our imaginations with an apocalyptic vision that could well become a terrible reality: namely, the disappearance of man as a species from the surface of the earth. It is quite possible. But what is more probable, more immediate, and in my opinion equally terrifying, is the prospect that man will survive while losing his precious heritage, his civilization and his very humanity."

Now what is this "humanity" which Mr. Oppenheimer is afraid we may lose? Is it simply poetry and music and art? Can we keep from losing it by insisting that all students, even in scientific institutions, take courses in the romantic poets and music appreciation? Well, it is partly that and the proposed remedy is good as far as it goes, but that isn't very far.

The issue is much larger. It has, of course, something to do with our increasingly greater, our almost exclusive stress upon wealth and power as the only things worth having; upon, for instance, our willingness to accept what we call "a high standard of living" as necessarily the equivalent of what philosophers used to call "the good life." It is, to use a platitudinous word, "materialism." To be human certainly means to be capable of valuing some nonmaterial things. As we lose interest in things other than the material, we are at least becoming that much less like human beings of the past and, in that sense, are indeed losing our humanity.

What I want to talk about this evening is something which seems to me even more characteristically and exclusively human than art or letters. You may call it "morality." I prefer to call it a strong clear sense that the difference between good and evil is, for the human being, the most important and fundamental of all distinctions.

As I say this, I hear from you an almost audible protest. "You don't mean to imply," I can almost hear you exclaim, "that we are not today deeply concerned with morality! Surely ethical questions are among those of which our society is most deeply aware. Has any other age ever talked so much about social justice, ever professed so much concern for the submerged common man? Has any other ever appeared to take more seriously human rights, political and economic rights, the rights of racial minorities, the rights of colonial peoples? Do we not acknowledge, as no age before this ever did, our responsibility for what we are for the first time calling 'one world'? Isn't ours the great age of social consciousness as obviously as it is the great age of science?"

All this I readily grant, but I am also aware of a strange paradox. It is often said, and my observation leads me to believe it true, that this seemingly great growth in social morality has, oddly enough, taken place in a world where private morality—a sense of the supreme importance of purely personal honor, honesty, and integrity—seems to be declining. Beneficent and benevolent social institutions are administered by men who all too frequently turn out to be accepting "gifts." The world of popular entertainment is rocked by scandals. College students, put on their honor, cheat on examinations. Candidates for the Ph.D. in social, as well as in other studies, hire ghost writers to prepare their theses.

The provost of one of our largest and most honored institutions told me just the other day that a questionnaire was distributed to his undergraduates and that forty percent of them refused to say that cheating on examinations is reprehensible. Again I seem to hear an objection. "Even if this is true, haven't these things always been true? Is there really any evidence that personal dishonesty is more prevalent than it always was?"

I have no way of making a statistical measurement. Perhaps these things are not actually more prevalent. What I do know is that there is an increasing tendency to accept and take for granted personal dishonesty. The bureaucrat and the disc jockey say, "Well, yes, I took presents, but I assure you that I made just decisions anyway." The college student caught cheating does not even blush. He shrugs his shoulders and comments: "Everybody does it, and besides, I can't see that it really hurts anybody."

Recently a reporter for a New York newspaper stopped six people on the street and asked them if they would consent to take part in a rigged television quiz for money. He reported that five of the six said "Yes." Yet most of these five, like most of the college cheaters, would probably profess a strong social consciousness. They may cheat, but they vote for foreign aid and for enlightened social measures.

Jonathan Swift once said: "I have never been surprised to find men wicked, but I have often been surprised to find them not ashamed." It is my conviction that though men may be no more wicked than they always have been, they seem less likely to be ashamed—which they call being realistic. Why are they less ashamed? I think the answer is to be found in the student's reply: "Everybody does it, and besides, I can't see that it really hurts anybody."

Precisely the same thing was said in many newspapers about the TV scandals. If you look at this common pronouncement, you will see what lies behind the breakdown of private morality as opposed to public, of personal honor as opposed to social consciousness. If everybody does it, it must be right. "Honest," "moral," "decent" mean only what is usual. This is not really a wicked world, because morality means mores or manners and usual conduct is the only standard.

The second part of the defense, "It really doesn't hurt anybody," is equally revealing. "It doesn't hurt anybody" means it doesn't do that abstraction called society any harm. The harm it did the bribe-taker and the cheater isn't important; it is purely personal. And personal as opposed to social decency doesn't count for much.

Sometimes I am inclined to blame sociology for part of this paradox. Sociology has tended to lay exclusive stress upon social morality, and tended too often to define good and evil as merely the "socially useful" or its reverse.

I open, for instance, a widely-used college textbook of psychology to a chapter headed "Morality." It is a very brief chapter and in it I read: "We call a man moral when his actions are in accord with the laws and customs of his society." No qualification follows, no suggestion that a thing may be evil even though sanctioned by law and custom. Certainly no hint that under certain conditions a man should be called moral only when he refuses to do what a bad law permits or an evil custom encourages.

If you accept this psychological concept of morality as no more than mores, then you are logically compelled to assume, for instance, that in Nazi Germany a man who persecuted Jews was a moral man, that one who refused to do so was immoral since persecution was certainly both the law and the custom in the country of which he was a part. I doubt that the author of this textbook would have followed his logic to that extreme, but he gives no reason why one should not do so. He certainly implies that a student may cheat on examinations and a public official take bribes without ceasing to be moral if cheating and bribe-taking are the common practice of his group or his colleagues.

What social morality and social consciousness sometimes leave out is the narrower but very significant concept of honor as opposed to what is sometimes called "socially desirable conduct." The man of honor is not content to ask merely if this or that action will hurt society, or if it is what most people would permit themselves to do. He asks first of all if it would hurt him and his self-respect. Would it dishonor him personally? He is not moved, as the cheater often is, by the argument that cheating would not do society any harm and even, perhaps, might enable him to "do good" because it would help him to get a job in which he would be "socially useful."

Two generations ago the world was genuinely shocked when the Imperial German Government dismissed a solemn treaty as a "mere scrap of paper." Today we only shrug when a government breaks a treaty. Statesmen are not expected to be men of honor, only to do whatever seems advantageous to their government.

The cheating student has come to believe, perhaps even been taught, that immoral means simply "socially undesirable," and that what everybody does is permissible since, after all, "moral" means no more than "according to custom."

When some scandal breaks in government, or journalism, or business, or broadcasting, the usual reaction of even that part of the public which is still shocked by it is to say that it couldn't have happened if there had been an adequate law supervising this or that activity. College examinations, government bureaus and television stations should be better policed. But is it not usually equally true that it could not have happened if a whole group of men, often including supposed guardians of public morality, had not been devoid of any sense of the meaning and importance of individual integrity? May one not go further and ask whether any amount of "social consciousness" plus any amount of government control can make a decent society composed of people who have no conception of personal dignity and honor, of people who, like students, don't think there is anything wrong in cheating?

It was a favorite and no doubt sound argument among early twentieth-century reformers that "playing the game" as the gentleman was supposed to play it, was not enough to make a decent society. They were right; it is not enough. But the time has come to add that it is nevertheless indispensable. The so-called social conscience, unsupported by the concept of personal honor, will create a corrupt society. Moreover, I insist that for the individual himself, nothing is more important than this personal, interior, sense of right and wrong and his determination to follow it rather than to be guided by "what everybody does" or by the criterion of mere "social usefulness." It is impossible for me to imagine a good society composed of men without honor.

I shall not labor the point further. But I will assume the privilege of a commencement speaker to give advice; and what the advice comes down to is this: Do not be so exclusively concerned with society and social conditions as to forget your own condition. You are your own self and you cannot shift the responsibility for that self to world conditions, or social conditions, or the mores of your civilization. That you cannot shift this responsibility is your burden. It is also your ultimate resource.

The time may come when you lose hope for the world, but it need never come when you lose hope for yourself. Do not say "I will do what everybody else does." Be, if necessary, a lonely candle which can throw its beams far in a naughty world. And I say this not only because I think that in the end that is best for society. I say it first of all because I'm sure it is the best and happiest course for yourself. If you must be pessimistic about the world, if you must believe that society is corrupt, then do not see in that any reason why *you* should be corrupt. Be scornful of the world if you must, but base your scorn on the difference between yourself and that world which you think deserves your scorn. Some will say that if you do this you run the risk of spiritual pride. I think the world could do with a little more spiritual pride because there seems to be so little of it about.

You will be told that you risk thinking yourself wiser and better than the common run of men. I hold that this, too, is preferable to being content not even to try to be better and wiser and more honest than they are. You may think that personal integrity and self-respect are not what you want more than anything else. You may say to yourself that putting them first would make it too difficult to get along in the world and that you want to get along in the world; that you would rather have money, power and fame than personal self-satisfaction. You may even say that you want money, power and fame so that you can "do good in the world." But if you do say any of these things, you will be making an unwise choice. You will be surrendering something which cannot be taken away from you to gain something which can be taken away from you and which, as a matter of fact, very often is.

We hear it said frequently that what present-day men most desire is security. If that is so, then they have a wrong notion of what the real, the ultimate, security is. No one who is dependent on anything outside himself—upon money, power, fame or whatnot—is, or even can be, secure. Only he who possesses himself and is content with himself is actually secure. Too much is being said about the importance of "adjustment" and "participation in the group." Even cooperation—to give this thing its most favorable designation—is no more important than the ability to stand alone when the choice must be made between the sacrifice of one's own integrity and adjustment to, or participation in, group activity.

No matter how bad the world may become, no matter how much the mass man of the future may lose such of the virtues as he still has, one fact remains. If you alone refuse to go along with him, if you alone assert your individual and inner right to believe in and be loyal to what your fellow men seem to have given up, then at least you will still retain what is perhaps the most important part of that humanity which Mr. Oppenheimer fears we may lose.

The Individual and Society

"WHAT," begins John Stuart Mill, "is the rightful limit to the sovereignty of the individual over himself? Where does the authority of society begin?" Near the end of his opening statement, he offers a very general answer when he says that "it is necessary that general rules should for the most part be observed, in order that people may know what they have to expect; but in each person's concern, his individual spontaneity is entitled to free exercise." "General rules," however, are often insecure in a pluralistic society such as ours that is undergoing rapid change; too many people do not know what "they have to expect," and "individual spontaneity" can take turns that seem not only to ignore but to intrude on and even harm the interests of others. Many of the most controversial issues of today—for instance, the use of capital punishment, the right of abortion, the legality of drug use—can be viewed within the general framework Mill draws out here and can perhaps be clarified by it.

His ideas apply not only to social issues but to political philosophy as well. Two important historic answers to Mill's questions are found in the Declaration of Independence, which establishes in our political tradition that human rights and the consent of the governed take precedence over the will of the state; and in the Bill of Rights, which spells out and thus protects the individual rights. The article by Walter Lippmann that follows adds a fresh dimension to the First Amendment by suggesting that in a democracy freedom of speech is important not so much for the speaker as for the listener: we must be free to hear what our critics have to say.

The next three pieces deal with the direct personal conflict between individual conscience and social law. When is civil disobedience justified? For many people civil disobedience within a civilized state is by definition immoral, especially in a democracy, where law is adjustable. We voluntarily relinquish some of our freedom and accept the necessity and authority of the 169 law in order to protect the community and guard it against anarchy. Defiance, then, strikes not only at specific laws but also at the concept of law and order and thus at the system itself. This is the argument that Plato presents so forcefully in *The Crito*, part of which is reprinted below. But for Henry David Thoreau, a dedicated individualist, and Martin Luther King, Jr., an eloquent spokesman for civil and human rights, individual conscience, not the state, is sovereign in matters of morality. In reading the above arguments, the reader may wish to consider a paradox pointed out by George Orwell in his essay on Gandhi: that modern civil disobedience can be effective only in a democratic community. "It is difficult to see," says Orwell, "how Gandhi's methods [passive resistance] could be applied in a country where opponents to the regime disappear in the middle of the night and are never heard of again. Without a free press and the right of assembly, it is impossible not merely to appeal to outside opinion, but to bring a mass movement into being, or even to make your intentions known to your adversary."

The three concluding pieces take on a different perspective. "All men are created equal," says the Declaration of Independence, but what does that mean? It does not mean that all men—or women—are the same, says Margaret Mead. What a democracy should offer to each person is the opportunity—equal opportunity—"to develop as a unique human being"; to deny or minimize individual differences would be to create a pseudodemocratic ideal. Such an ideal is satirized in Kurt Vonnegut's story about a society that has institutionalized sameness in the name of equality. The last piece, by Peregrine Worsthorne, asks us to re-view equality of opportunity, to see the inequalities hidden in that phrase and concept.

THE SOCIAL CONTRACT

JOHN STUART MILL

Mill (1806-1873), economist, philosopher, and reformer, was one of the most influential nineteenth-century English thinkers. He was the son of James Mill, an economist and historian, who gave him the extraordinary education which Mill later recorded in his Autobiography *(1873). John began Greek at three, Latin at seven, logic at twelve, and at seventeen was writing articles for the* Westminster Review. *Mill early came under the intellectual influence of Jeremy Bentham, and much of his thought reflects the Benthamite, utilitarian principle that social good lies in whatever brings the greatest benefit to the greatest number. Among his most prominent works are* A System of Logic *(1843),* The Principles of Political Economy *(1848),* On Liberty *(1859),* Considerations on Representative Government *(1861), and* Utilitarianism *(1863). Although many of Mill's ideas have passed out of vogue, he continues to be widely read, partly for what is still useful in his philosophy, and partly for his style and his just, exact, and generous character. We present below the opening of Chapter 4 of* On Liberty.

from *On Liberty*

What, then, is the rightful limit to the sovereignty of the individual over himself? Where does the authority of society begin? How much of human life should be assigned to individuality, and how much to society?

Each will receive its proper share, if each has that which more particularly concerns it. To individuality should belong the part of life in which it is chiefly the individual that is interested; to society, the part which chiefly interests society.

Though society is not founded on a contract, and though no good purpose is answered by inventing a contract in order to deduce social obligations from it, every one who receives the protection of society owes a return for the benefit, and the fact of living in society renders it indispensable that each should be bound to observe a certain line of conduct towards the rest. This conduct consists, first, in not injuring the interests of one another; or rather certain interests, which, either by express legal provision or by tacit understanding, ought to be considered as rights; and secondly, in each person's bearing his share (to be fixed on some equitable principle) of the labors and sacrifices incurred for defending the society or its members from injury and molestation. These conditions society is justified in enforcing, at all costs to those who endeavor to withhold fulfilment. Nor is this all that society may do. The acts of an individual may be hurtful to others, or wanting in due consideration for their welfare, without going to the length of violating any of their constituted rights. The offender may then be justly punished by opinion, though not by law. As soon as any part of a person's conduct affects prejudicially the interests of others, society has jurisdiction over it, and the question whether the general welfare will or will not be promoted by interfering with it, becomes open to discussion. But there is no room for entertaining any such question when a person's conduct affects the interests of no persons besides himself, or needs not affect them unless they like (all the persons concerned being of full age, and the ordinary amount of understanding). In all such cases there should be perfect freedom, legal and social, to do the action and stand the consequences.

It would be a great misunderstanding of this doctrine, to suppose that it is one of selfish indifference, which pretends that human beings have no business with each other's conduct in life, and that they should not concern themselves about the well-doing or well-being of one another, unless their own interest is involved. Instead of any diminution, there is need of a great increase of disinterested exertion to promote the good of others. But disinterested benevolence can find other instruments to persuade people to their good, than whips and scourges, either of the literal or the metaphorical sort. I am the last person to undervalue the self-regarding virtues; they are only second in importance, if even second, to the social. It is equally the business of education to cultivate both. But even education works by conviction and persuasion as well as by compulsion, and it is by the former only that, when the period of education is past, the self-regarding virtues should be inculcated. Human beings owe to each other help to distinguish the better from the worse, and encouragement to choose the former and avoid the latter. They should be forever stimulating each other to increased exercise of their higher faculties, and increased direction of their feelings and aims towards wise instead of foolish, elevating instead of degrading, objects and contemplations. But neither one person, nor any number of persons, is warranted in saying to another human creature of ripe years, that he shall not do with his life for his own benefit what he chooses to do with it. He is the person most interested in his own well-being: the interest which any other person, except in cases of strong personal attachment, can have in it, is trifling, compared with that which he himself has; the interest which society has in him individually (except as to his conduct to others) is fractional, and altogether indirect: while, with respect to his own feelings and circumstances, the most ordinary man or woman has means of knowledge immeasurably surpassing those that can be possessed by anyone else. The interference of society to overrule his judgment and purposes in what only regards himself, must be grounded on general presumptions; which may be altogether wrong, and even if right, are as likely as not to be misapplied to individual cases, by persons no better acquainted with the circumstances of such cases than those are who look at them merely from without. In this department, therefore, of human affairs, individuality has its proper field of action. In the conduct of human beings towards one another, it is necessary that general rules should for the most part be observed, in order that people may know what they have to expect; but in each person's own concerns, his individual spontaneity is entitled to free exercise. Considerations to aid his judgment, exhortations to strengthen his will, may be offered to him, even obtruded on him, by others; but he, himself, is the final judge. All errors which he is likely to commit against advice and warning, are far outweighed by the evil of allowing others to constrain him to what they deem his good.

THOMAS JEFFERSON

On June 11, 1776, the Continental Congress appointed a committee of five—Thomas Jefferson, Benjamin Franklin, John Adams, Robert Livingston, and Roger Sherman—to prepare a declaration of independence. It was decided that Jefferson should first write a draft. He did so, drawing heavily on the natural rights political philosophy of the time, but as he says, he turned to "neither book nor pamphlet" in its preparation. A few changes were made by Adams and Franklin, and it was then presented to Congress on June 28.

On July 2 and 3 Congress debated the form and content of the Declaration, made a few further changes, and on July 4 approved it without dissent. Although we here credit Jefferson with authorship, we print the amended and official version, taken from the United States Government Senate Manual.

Declaration of Independence
(In Congress July 4, 1776)

The Unanimous Declaration of the Thirteen United States of America

When in the Course of human events, it becomes necessary for one people to dissolve the political bands which have connected them with another, and to assume among the powers of the earth, the separate and equal station to which the Laws of Nature and of Nature's God entitle them, a decent respect to the opinions of mankind requires that they should declare the causes which impel them to the separation.

We hold these truths to be self-evident, that all men are created equal, that they are endowed by their Creator with certain unalienable Rights, that among these are Life, Liberty and the pursuit of Happiness. That to secure these rights, Governments are instituted among Men, deriving their just powers from the consent of the governed, That whenever any Form of Government becomes destructive of these ends, it is the Right of the People to alter or to abolish it, and to institute new Government, laying its foundation on such principles and organizing its powers in such form, as to them shall seem most likely to effect their Safety and Happiness. Prudence, indeed, will dictate that Governments long established should not be changed for light and transient causes; and accordingly all experience hath shewn that mankind are more disposed to suffer, while evils are sufferable, than to right themselves by abolishing the forms to which they are accustomed. But when a long train of abuses and usurpations, pursuing invariably the same Object evinces a design to reduce them under absolute Despotism, it is their right, it is their duty, to throw off such Government, and to provide new Guards for their future security. Such has been the patient sufferance of these Colonies; and such is now the necessity which constrains them to alter their former Systems of Government. The history of the present King of Great Britain is a history of repeated injuries and usurpations, all having in direct object the establishment of an absolute Tyranny over these States. To prove this, let Facts be submitted to a candid world.

He has refused his Assent to Laws, the most wholesome and necessary for the public good.

He has forbidden his Governors to pass Laws of immediate and pressing importance, unless suspended in their operation till his Assent should be obtained; and when so suspended, he has utterly neglected to attend to them.

He has refused to pass other Laws for the accommodation of large districts of people, unless those people would relinquish the right of Representation in the Legislature, a right inestimable to them and formidable to tyrants only.

He has called together legislative bodies at places unusual, uncomfortable, and distant from the depository of their public Records, for the sole purpose of fatiguing them into compliance with his measures.

He has dissolved Representative Houses repeatedly, for opposing with manly firmness his invasions on the rights of the people.

He has refused for a long time, after such dissolutions, to cause others to be elected; whereby the Legislative powers, incapable of Annihilation, have returned to the People at large for their exercise; the State remaining in the mean time exposed to all the dangers of invasion from without, and convulsions within.

He has endeavoured to prevent the population of these States; for that purpose obstructing the Laws for Naturalization of Foreigners; refusing to pass others to encourage their migrations hither, and raising the conditions of new Appropriations of Lands.

He has obstructed the Administration of Justice, by refusing his Assent to Laws for establishing Judiciary powers.

He has made Judges dependent on his Will alone, for the tenure of their offices, and the amount and payment of their salaries.

He has erected a multitude of New Offices, and sent hither swarms of Officers to harass our people, and eat out their substance.

He has kept among us, in times of peace, Standing Armies without the Consent of our legislatures.

He has affected to render the Military independent of and superior to the Civil power.

He has combined with others to subject us to a jurisdiction foreign to our constitution, and unacknowledged by our laws; giving his Assent to their Acts of pretended Legislation:

For quartering large bodies of armed troops among us:

For protecting them, by a mock Trial, from punishment for any Murders which they should commit on the Inhabitants of these States:

For cutting off our Trade with all parts of the world:

For imposing Taxes on us without our Consent:

For depriving us in many cases, of the benefits of Trial by Jury:

For transporting us beyond Seas to be tried for pretended offences:

For abolishing the free System of English Laws in a neighbouring Province, establishing therein an Arbitrary government, and enlarging its Boundaries so as to render it at once an example and fit instrument for introducing the same absolute rule into these Colonies:

For taking away our Charters, abolishing our most valuable Laws, and altering fundamentally the Forms of our Governments:

For suspending our own Legislatures, and declaring themselves invested with power to legislate for us in all cases whatsoever.

He has abdicated Government here, by declaring us out of his Protection and waging War against us.

He has plundered our seas, ravaged our Coasts, burnt our towns, and destroyed the lives of our people.

He is at this time transporting large Armies of foreign Mercenaries to compleat the works of death, desolation and tyranny, already begun with circumstances of Cruelty & perfidy scarcely paralleled in the most barbarous ages, and totally unworthy the Head of a civilized nation.

He has constrained our fellow Citizens taken Captive on the high Seas to bear Arms against their Country, to become the executioners of their friends and Brethren, or to fall themselves by their Hands.

He has excited domestic insurrections amongst us, and has endeavoured to bring on the inhabitants of our frontiers, the merciless Indian Savages, whose known rule of warfare is an undistinguished destruction of all ages, sexes and conditions.

In every stage of these Oppressions We have Petitioned for Redress in the most humble terms: Our repeated Petitions have been answered only by repeated injury. A Prince, whose character is thus marked by every act which may define a Tyrant, is unfit to be the ruler of a free people.

Nor have We been wanting in attentions to our British Brethren. We have warned them from time to time of attempts by their legislature to extend an unwarrantable jurisdiction over us. We have reminded them of the circumstances of our emigration and settlement here. We have appealed to their native justice and magnanimity, and we have conjured them by the ties of our common kindred to disavow these usurpations, which would inevitably interrupt our connections and correspondence. They too have been deaf to the voice of justice and of consanguinity. We must, therefore, acquiesce in the necessity, which denounces our Separation, and hold them, as we hold the rest of mankind. Enemies in War, in Peace Friends.

WE, THEREFORE, the REPRESENTATIVES OF THE UNITED STATES OF AMERICA, IN GENERAL CONGRESS, Assembled, appealing to the Supreme Judge of the world for the rectitude of our intentions, do, in the Name, and by authority of the good People of these Colonies, solemnly PUBLISH and DECLARE, That these United Colonies are, and of Right ought to be FREE AND INDEPENDENT STATES; that they are Absolved from all Allegiance to the British Crown, and that all political connection between them and the State of Great Britain, is and ought to be totally dissolved; and that as FREE AND INDEPENDENT STATES, they have full Power to levy War, conclude Peace, contract Alliances, establish Commerce, and to do all other Acts and Things which INDEPENDENT STATES may of right do. And for the support of this Declaration, with a firm reliance on the protection of divine Providence, we mutually pledge to each other our Lives, our Fortunes and our sacred Honor.

THE FIRST CONGRESS
OF THE UNITED STATES

"The Bill of Rights" is the name given to the first ten amendments to the United States Constitution. When the Constitution was originally adopted in 1788, many of its framers had felt that a spelling-out of rights already presumed to exist was unnecessary and might even suggest an undue extension of governmental powers. Some of the states, however, having explicit declarations of rights in their own constitutions, recommended on ratifying the federal Constitution that it too be so furnished. The Bill of Rights was prepared by the first Congress under the leadership of James Madison and was ratified by the states in 1791. It has turned out to be an invaluable guide to the courts in decisions affecting civil rights and is in fact the main protection American citizens have against the diminution of their liberties by their government or by each other.

The Bill of Rights

ARTICLES IN ADDITION TO, AND AMENDMENT OF, THE CONSTITUTION OF THE UNITED STATES OF AMERICA, PROPOSED BY CONGRESS, AND RATIFIED BY THE LEGISLATURES OF THE SEVERAL STATES, PURSUANT TO THE FIFTH ARTICLE OF THE ORIGINAL CONSTITUTION.

Article I

Congress shall make no law respecting an establishment of religion, or prohibiting the free exercise thereof; or abridging the freedom of speech, or of the press; or the right of the people peaceably to assemble, and to petition the Government for a redress of grievances.

Article II

A well regulated Militia, being necessary to the security of a free State, the right of the people to keep and bear Arms, shall not be infringed.

Article III

No Soldier shall, in time of peace be quartered in any house, without the consent of the Owner, nor in time of war, but in a manner to be prescribed by law.

Article IV

The right of the people to be secure in their persons, houses, papers, and effects, against unreasonable searches and seizures, shall not be violated, and no Warrants shall issue, but upon probable cause, supported by Oath or affirmation, and particularly describing the place to be searched, and the persons or things to be seized.

Article V

No person shall be held to answer for a capital, or otherwise infamous crime, unless on a presentment or indictment of a Grand Jury, except in cases arising in the land or naval forces, or in the Militia, when in actual service in time of War or public danger; nor shall any person be subject for the same offence to be twice put in jeopardy of life or limb; nor shall be compelled in any criminal case to be a witness against himself; nor be deprived of life, liberty, or property, without due process of law; nor shall private property be taken for public use, without just compensation.

Article VI

In all criminal prosecutions, the accused shall enjoy the right to a speedy and public trial, by an impartial jury of the State and district wherein the crime shall have been committed, which district shall have been previously ascertained by law, and to be informed of the nature and cause of the accusation; to be confronted with the witnesses against him; to have compulsory process for obtaining witnesses in his favor, and to have the Assistance of Counsel for his defence.

Article VII

In Suits at common law, where the value in controversy shall exceed twenty dollars, the right of trial by jury shall be preserved, and no fact tried by a jury, shall be otherwise reexamined in any Court of the United States, than according to the rules of the common law.

Article VIII

Excessive bail shall not be required, nor excessive fines imposed, nor cruel and unusual punishments inflicted.

Article IX

The enumeration in the Constitution, of certain rights, shall not be construed to deny or disparage others retained by the people.

Article X

The powers not delegated to the United States by the Constitution, nor prohibited by it to the States, are reserved to the States respectively, or to the people.

WALTER LIPPMANN

Walter Lippmann (1889-1974) was one of the most honored of American newspapermen. He was educated at Harvard and then taught philosophy there as an assistant to George Santayana. He joined the staff of The New Republic *at its founding in 1914, interrupted his journalistic career to serve as assistant to the Secretary of War—doing special work on peace negotiating—and then moved to an editorial position on the* New York World. *His writings were syndicated in newspapers throughout the country and his column "Today and Tomorrow" won him Pulitzer Prizes in 1958 and 1962. The*

*1958 award cited the "wisdom, perception, and high sense of responsibility with which he
has commented for many years on national and international affairs." During the Watergate years he was quoted with increasing frequency. He received many honorary degrees
and such decorations as the Medal of Freedom, the Legion of Honor from France, and the
Order of Leopold from Belgium. His books include* Liberty and the News *(1920),*
Public Opinion *(1922),* A Preface to Morals *(1929),* The Good Society
(1937), The Public Philosophy *(1955),* The Coming Tests with Russia
(1961), Western Unity and the Common Market *(1962), and* The Essential
Lippmann: A Political Philosophy for Liberal Democracy *(1963). The essay
we present below is taken from* The Atlantic Monthly *for August 1939.*

The Indispensable Opposition

[I]

Were they pressed hard enough, most men would probably confess that
political freedom—that is to say, the right to speak freely and to act in
opposition—is a noble ideal rather than a practical necessity. As the case for
freedom is generally put to-day, the argument lends itself to this feeling. It is
made to appear that, whereas each man claims his freedom as a matter of
right, the freedom he accords to other men is a matter of toleration. Thus,
the defense of freedom of opinion tends to rest not on its substantial, benefi-
cial, and indispensable consequences, but on a somewhat eccentric, a rather
vaguely benevolent, attachment to an abstraction.

It is all very well to say with Voltaire, 'I wholly disapprove of what you
say, but will defend to the death your right to say it,' but as a matter of fact
most men will not defend to the death the rights of other men: if they
disapprove sufficiently what other men say, they will somehow suppress
those men if they can.

So, if this is the best that can be said for liberty of opinion, that a man
must tolerate his opponents because everyone has a 'right' to say what he
pleases, then we shall find that liberty of opinion is a luxury, safe only in
pleasant times when men can be tolerant because they are not deeply and
vitally concerned.

Yet actually, as a matter of historic fact, there is a much stronger foundation for the great constitutional right of freedom of speech, and as a matter
of practical human experience there is a much more compelling reason for
cultivating the habits of free men. We take, it seems to me, a naïvely self-
righteous view when we argue as if the right of our opponents to speak were
something that we protect because we are magnanimous, noble, and unselfish. The compelling reason why, if liberty of opinion did not exist, we should
have to invent it, why it will eventually have to be restored in all civilized
countries where it is now suppressed, is that we must protect the right of our
opponents to speak because we must hear what they have to say.

We miss the whole point when we imagine that we tolerate the freedom
of our political opponents as we tolerate a howling baby next door, as we put

up with the blasts from our neighbor's radio because we are too peaceable to heave a brick through the window. If this were all there is to freedom of opinion, that we are too good-natured or too timid to do anything about our opponents and our critics except to let them talk, it would be difficult to say whether we are tolerant because we are magnanimous or because we are lazy, because we have strong principles or because we lack serious convictions, whether we have the hospitality of an inquiring mind or the indifference of an empty mind. And so, if we truly wish to understand why freedom is necessary in a civilized society, we must begin by realizing that, because freedom of discussion improves our own opinions, the liberties of other men are our own vital necessity.

We are much closer to the essence of the matter, not when we quote Voltaire, but when we go to the doctor and pay him to ask us the most embarrassing questions and to prescribe the most disagreeable diet. When we pay the doctor to exercise complete freedom of speech about the cause and cure of our stomachache, we do not look upon ourselves as tolerant and magnanimous, and worthy to be admired by ourselves. We have enough common sense to know that if we threaten to put the doctor in jail because we do not like the diagnosis and the prescription it will be unpleasant for the doctor, to be sure, but equally unpleasant for our own stomachache. That is why even the most ferocious dictator would rather be treated by a doctor who was free to think and speak the truth than by his own Minister of Propaganda. For there is a point, the point at which things really matter, where the freedom of others is no longer a question of their right but of our need.

The point at which we recognize this need is much higher in some men than in others. The totalitarian rulers think they do not need the freedom of an opposition: they exile, imprison, or shoot their opponents. We have concluded on the basis of practical experience, which goes back to Magna Carta and beyond, that we need the opposition. We pay the opposition salaries out of the public treasury.

In so far as the usual apology for freedom of speech ignores this experience, it becomes abstract and eccentric rather than concrete and human. The emphasis is generally put on the right to speak, as if all that mattered were that the doctor should be free to go out into the park and explain to the vacant air why I have a stomachache. Surely that is a miserable caricature of the great civic right which men have bled and died for. What really matters is that the doctor should tell *me* what ails me, that I should listen to him; that if I do not like what he says I should be free to call in another doctor; and that then the first doctor should have to listen to the second doctor; and that out of all the speaking and listening, the give-and-take of opinions, the truth should be arrived at.

This is the creative principle of freedom of speech, not that it is a system for the tolerating of error, but that it is a system for finding the truth. It may not produce the truth, or the whole truth all the time, or often, or in some cases ever. But if the truth can be found, there is no other system which will normally and habitually find so much truth. Until we have thoroughly understood this principle, we shall not know why we must value our liberty, or how we can protect and develop it.

[II]

Let us apply this principle to the system of public speech in a totalitarian state. We may, without any serious falsification, picture a condition of affairs in which the mass of the people are being addressed through one broadcasting system by one man and his chosen subordinates. The orators speak. The audience listens but cannot and dare not speak back. It is a system of one-way communication; the opinions of the rulers are broadcast outwardly to the mass of the people. But nothing comes back to the rulers from the people except the cheers; nothing returns in the way of knowledge of forgotten facts, hidden feelings, neglected truths, and practical suggestions.

But even a dictator cannot govern by his own one-way inspiration alone. In practice, therefore, the totalitarian rulers get back the reports of the secret police and of their party henchmen down among the crowd. If these reports are competent, the rulers may manage to remain in touch with public sentiment. Yet that is not enough to know what the audience feels. The rulers have also to make great decisions that have enormous consequences, and here their system provides virtually no help from the give-and-take of opinion in the nation. So they must either rely on their own institution, which cannot be permanently and continually inspired, or, if they are intelligent despots, encourage their trusted advisers and their technicians to speak and debate freely in their presence.

On the walls of the houses of Italian peasants one may see inscribed in large letters the legend, 'Mussolini is always right.' But if that legend is taken seriously by Italian ambassadors, by the Italian General Staff, and by the Ministry of Finance, then all one can say is heaven help Mussolini, heaven help Italy, and the new Emperor of Ethiopia.

For at some point, even in a totalitarian state, it is indispensable that there should exist the freedom of opinion which causes opposing opinions to be debated. As time goes on, that is less and less easy under a despotism; critical discussion disappears as the internal opposition is liquidated in favor of men who think and feel alike. That is why the early successes of despots, of Napoleon I and of Napoleon III, have usually been followed by an irreparable mistake. For in listening only to his yes men—the others being in exile or in concentration camps, or terrified—the despot shuts himself off from the truth that no man can dispense with.

We know all this well enough when we contemplate the dictatorships. But when we try to picture our own system, by way of contrast, what picture do we have in our minds? It is, is it not, that anyone may stand up on his own soapbox and say anything he pleases, like the individuals in Kipling's poem who sit each in his separate star and draw the Thing as they see it for the God of Things as they are. Kipling, perhaps, could do this, since he was a poet. But the ordinary mortal isolated on his separate star will have an hallucination, and a citizenry declaiming from separate soapboxes will poison the air with hot and nonsensical confusion.

If the democratic alternative to the totalitarian one-way broadcasts is a row of separate soapboxes, then I submit that the alternative is unworkable, is unreasonable, and is humanly unattractive. It is above all a false alternative. It is not true that liberty has developed among civilized men when anyone is free to set up a soapbox, is free to hire a hall where he may expound his opinions to those who are willing to listen. On the contrary, freedom of speech is established to achieve its essential purpose only when different opinions are expounded in the same hall to the same audience.

For, while the right to talk may be the beginning of freedom, the necessity of listening is what makes the right important. Even in Russia and Germany a man may still stand in an open field and speak his mind. What matters is not the utterance of opinions. What matters is the confrontation of opinions in debate. No man can care profoundly that every fool should say what he likes. Nothing has been accomplished if the wisest man proclaims his wisdom in the middle of the Sahara Desert. This is the shadow. We have the substance of liberty when the fool is compelled to listen to the wise man and learn; when the wise man is compelled to take account of the fool, and to instruct him; when the wise man can increase his wisdom by hearing the judgment of his peers.

That is why civilized men must cherish liberty—as a means of promoting the discovery of truth. So we must not fix our whole attention on the right of anyone to hire his own hall, to rent his own broadcasting station, to distribute his own pamphlets. These rights are incidental; and though they must be preserved, they can be preserved only by regarding them as incidental, as auxiliary to the substance of liberty that must be cherished and cultivated.

Freedom of speech is best conceived, therefore, by having in mind the picture of a place like the American Congress, an assembly where opposing views are represented, where ideas are not merely uttered but debated, or the British Parliament, where men who are free to speak are also compelled to answer. We may picture the true condition of freedom as existing in a place like a court of law, where witnesses testify and are cross-examined, where the lawyer argues against the opposing lawyer before the same judge and in the presence of one jury. We may picture freedom as existing in a forum where the speaker must respond to questions; in a gathering of scientists where the data, the hypothesis, and the conclusion are submitted to men competent to judge them; in a reputable newspaper which not only will publish the opinions of those who disagree but will reëxamine its own opinion in the light of what they say.

Thus the essence of freedom of opinion is not in mere toleration as such, but in the debate which toleration provides: it is not in the venting of opinion, but in the confrontation of opinion. That this is the practical substance can readily be understood when we remember how differently we feel and act about the censorship and regulation of opinion purveyed by different media of communication. We find then that, in so far as the medium makes difficult the confrontation of opinion in debate, we are driven towards censorship and regulation.

There is, for example, the whispering campaign, the circulation of anonymous rumors by men who cannot be compelled to prove what they say. They put the utmost strain on our tolerance, and there are few who do not rejoice when the anonymous slanderer is caught, exposed, and punished. At a higher level there is the moving picture, a most powerful medium for conveying ideas, but a medium which does not permit debate. A moving picture cannot be answered effectively by another moving picture; in all free countries there is some censorship of the movies, and there would be more if the producers did not recognize their limitations by avoiding political controversy. There is then the radio. Here debate is difficult; it is not easy to make sure that the speaker is being answered in the presence of the same audience. Inevitably, there is some regulation of the radio.

When we reach the newspaper press, the opportunity for debate is so considerable that discontent cannot grow to the point where under normal conditions there is any disposition to regulate the press. But when newspapers abuse their power by injuring people who have no means of replying, a disposition to regulate the press appears. When we arrive at Congress we find that, because the membership of the House is so large, full debate is impracticable. So there are restrictive rules. On the other hand, in the Senate, where the conditions of full debate exist, there is almost absolute freedom of speech.

This shows us that the preservation and development of freedom of opinion are not only a matter of adhering to abstract legal rights, but also, and very urgently, a matter of organizing and arranging sufficient debate. Once we have a firm hold on the central principle, there are many practical conclusions to be drawn. We then realize that the defense of freedom of opinion consists primarily in perfecting the opportunity for an adequate give-and-take of opinion; it consists also in regulating the freedom of those revolutionists who cannot or will not permit or maintain debate when it does not suit their purposes.

We must insist that free oratory is only the beginning of free speech; it is not the end, but a means to an end. The end is to find the truth. The practical justification of civil liberty is not that self-expression is one of the rights of man. It is that the examination of opinion is one of the necessities of man. For experience tells us that it is only when freedom of opinion becomes the compulsion to debate that the seed which our fathers planted has produced its fruit. When that is understood, freedom will be cherished not because it is a vent for our opinions but because it is the surest method of correcting them.

The unexamined life, said Socrates, is unfit to be lived by man. This is the virtue of liberty, and the ground on which we may best justify our belief in it, that it tolerates error in order to serve the truth. When men are brought face to face with their opponents, forced to listen and learn and mend their ideas, they cease to be children and savages and begin to live like civilized men. Then only is freedom a reality, when men may voice their opinions because they must examine their opinions.

[III]

The only reason for dwelling on all this is that if we are to preserve democracy we must understand its principles. And the principle which distinguishes it from all other forms of government is that in a democracy the opposition not only is tolerated as constitutional but must be maintained because it is in fact indispensable.

The democratic system cannot be operated without effective opposition. For, in making the great experiment of governing people by consent rather than by coercion, it is not sufficient that the party in power should have a majority. It is just as necessary that the party in power should never outrage the minority. That means that it must listen to the minority and be moved by the criticisms of the minority. That means that its measures must take account of the minority's objections, and that in administering measures it must remember that the minority may become the majority.

The opposition is indispensable. A good statesman, like any other sensible human being, always learns more from his opponents than from his fervent supporters. For his supporters will push him to disaster unless his opponents show him where the dangers are. So if he is wise he will often pray to be delivered from his friends, because they will ruin him. But, though it hurts, he ought also to pray never to be left without opponents; for they keep him on the path of reason and good sense.

The national unity of a free people depends upon a sufficiently even balance of political power to make it impracticable for the administration to be arbitrary and for the opposition to be revolutionary and irreconcilable. Where that balance no longer exists, democracy perishes. For unless all the citizens of a state are forced by circumstances to compromise, unless they feel that they can affect policy but that no one can wholly dominate it, unless by habit and necessity they have to give and take, freedom cannot be maintained.

ON CIVIL DISOBEDIENCE

PLATO

Plato, one of the greatest philosophers of the Western world, was born in Athens. Originally named Aristocles, he was surnamed Plato because of his broad shoulders, or— as some would have it—his broad forehead. Early in his life he became a student of Socrates, and his subsequent writings are evidence of the profound influence his teacher had on him. After Socrates' trial, conviction, and death in 399 B.C., Plato spent thirteen years away from Athens, in Italy, Egypt, and parts of Greece. He returned in 386 B.C. and founded the Academy, in which he taught until his death in 347 B.C. Aristotle was his student. Plato's extant works are in the form of conversations, or dialogues, in which the leading speaker is usually Socrates. Perhaps the best known of the dialogues is The Republic, *in which Socrates explores the nature of the ideal state. Plato records the last days of Socrates in three early dialogues,* The Apology, The Crito, *and* The Phaedo. The Apology *presents Socrates' defense at his trial on charges of corrupting youth and believing in gods other than the state's divinities.* The Phaedo *records Socrates' last conversation before death. In* The Crito, *Crito visits Socrates in prison and tries to persuade him to escape. We print below, from the Jowett translation, third edition, Socrates' argument for submitting to the death penalty that the law had imposed on him.*

from *The Crito*

Socrates . . . Ought a man to do what he admits to be right, or ought he to betray the right?

Crito. He ought to do what he thinks right.

Soc. But if this is true, what is the application? In leaving the prison against the will of the Athenians, do I wrong any? or rather do I not wrong those whom I ought least to wrong? Do I not desert the principles which were acknowledged by us to be just—what do you say?

Cr. I cannot tell, Socrates; for I do not know.

Soc. Then consider the matter in this way:—Imagine that I am about to play truant (you may call the proceeding by any name which you like), and the laws and the government come and interrogate me: 'Tell us, Socrates,' they say; 'what are you about? are you not going by an act of yours to overturn us—the laws, and the whole state, as far as in you lies? Do you imagine that a state can subsist and not be overthrown, in which the decisions of law have no power, but are set aside and trampled upon by individuals?' What will be our answer, Crito, to these and the like words? Any one, and especially a rhetorician, will have a good deal to say on behalf of the law which requires a sentence to be carried out. He will argue that this law should not be set aside; and shall we reply, 'Yes; but the state has injured us and given an unjust sentence.' Suppose I say that?

Cr. Very good, Socrates.

Soc. 'And was that our agreement with you?' the law would answer; 'or were you to abide by the sentence of the state?' And if I were to express my astonishment at their words, the law would probably add: 'Answer, Socrates, instead of opening your eyes—you are in the habit of asking and answering questions. Tell us,—What complaint have you to make against us which justifies you in attempting to destroy us and the state? In the first place did we not bring you into existence? Your father married your mother by our aid and begat you. Say whether you have any objection to urge against those of us who regulate marriage?' None, I should reply. 'Or against those of us who after birth regulate the nurture and education of children, in which you also were trained? Were not the laws, which have the charge of education, right in commanding your father to train you in music and gymnastic?' Right, I should reply. 'Well then, since you were brought into the world and nurtured and educated by us, can you deny in the first place that you are our child and slave, as your fathers were before you? And if this is true you are not on equal terms with us; nor can you think that you have a right to do to us what we are doing to you. Would you have any right to strike or revile or do any other evil to your father or your master, if you had one, because you have been struck or reviled by him, or received some other evil at his hands?—you would not say this? And because we think right to destroy you, do you think that you have any right to destroy us in return, and your country as far as in you lies? Will you, O professor of true virtue, pretend that you are justified in this? Has a philosopher like you failed to discover that our country is more to be valued and higher and holier far than mother or father or any ancestor, and more to be regarded in the eyes of the gods and of men of understanding? Also to be soothed, and gently and reverently entreated when angry, even more than a father, and either to be persuaded, or if not persuaded, to be obeyed? And when we are punished by her, whether with imprisonment or stripes, the punishment is to be endured in silence; and if she leads us to wounds or death in battle, thither we follow as is right; neither may any one yield or retreat or leave his rank, but whether in battle or in a court of law, or in any other place, he must do what his city and his country order him; or he must change their view of what is just: and if he may do no violence to his father or mother, much less may he do violence to his country.' What answer shall we make to this, Crito? Do the laws speak truly, or do they not?

Cr. I think that they do.

Soc. Then the laws will say, 'Consider, Socrates, if we are speaking truly that in your present attempt you are going to do us an injury. For, having brought you into the world, and nurtured and educated you, and given you and every other citizen a share in every good which we had to give, we further proclaim to any Athenian by the liberty which we allow him, that if he does not like us when he has become of age and has seen the ways of the city, and made our acquaintance, he may go where he pleases and take his goods with him. None of us laws will forbid him or interfere with him. Any one who does not like us and the city, and who wants to emigrate to a colony or to any other city, may go where he likes, retaining his property. But he who has experience of the manner in which we order justice and administer the state, and still remains, has entered into an implied contract that he will do as we command him. And he who disobeys us is, as we maintain, thrice wrong; first, because in disobeying us he is disobeying his parents; secondly, because we are the authors of his education; thirdly, because he has made an agreement with us that he will duly obey our commands; and he neither obeys them nor convinces us that our commands are unjust; and we do not rudely impose them, but give him the alternative of obeying or convincing us;—that is what we offer, and he does neither.

'These are the sort of accusations to which, as we were saying, you, Socrates, will be exposed if you accomplish your intentions; you, above all other Athenians.' Suppose now I ask, why I rather than anybody else? they will justly retort upon me that I above all other men have acknowledged the agreement. 'There is clear proof,' they will say, 'Socrates, that we and the city were not displeasing to you. Of all Athenians you have been the most constant resident in the city, which, as you never leave, you may be supposed to love. For you never went out of the city either to see the games, except once when you went to the Isthmus, or to any other place unless when you were on military service; nor did you travel as other men do. Nor had you any curiosity to know other states or their laws: your affections did not go beyond us and our state; we were your special favourites, and you acquiesced in our government of you; and here in this city you begat your children, which is a proof of your satisfaction. Moreover, you might in the course of the trial, if you had liked, have fixed the penalty at banishment; the state which refuses to let you go now would have let you go then. But you pretended that you preferred death to exile, and that you were not unwilling to die. And now you have forgotten these fine sentiments, and pay no respect to us the laws, of whom you are the destroyer; and are doing what only a miserable slave would do, running away and turning your back upon the compacts and agreements which you made as a citizen. And first of all answer this very question: Are we right in saying that you agreed to be governed according to us in deed, and not in word only? Is that true or not?' How shall we answer, Crito? Must we not assent?

Cr. We cannot help it, Socrates.

Soc. Then will they not say: 'You, Socrates, are breaking the covenants and agreements which you made with us at your leisure, not in any haste or under any compulsion or deception, but after you have had seventy years to think of them, during which time you were at liberty to leave the city, if we were not to your mind, or if our covenants appeared to you to be unfair. You had your choice, and might have gone either to Lacedaemon or Crete, both which states are often praised by you for their good government, or to some other Hellenic or foreign state. Whereas you, above all other Athenians, seemed to be so fond of the state, or, in other words, of us her laws (and who would care about a state which has no laws?), that you never stirred out of her; the halt, the blind, the maimed were not more stationary in her than you were. And now you run away and forsake your agreements. Not so, Socrates, if you will take our advice; do not make yourself ridiculous by escaping out of the city.

'For just consider, if you transgress and err in this sort of way, what good will you do either to yourself or to your friends? That your friends will be driven into exile and deprived of citizenship, or will lose their property, is tolerably certain; and you yourself, if you fly to one of the neighbouring cities, as, for example, Thebes or Megara, both of which are well governed, will come to them as an enemy, Socrates, and their government will be against you, and all patriotic citizens will cast an evil eye upon you as a subverter of the laws, and you will confirm in the minds of the judges the justice of their own condemnation of you. For he who is a corrupter of the laws is more than likely to be a corrupter of the young and foolish portion of mankind. Will you then flee from well-ordered cities and virtuous men? and is existence worth having on these terms? Or will you go to them without shame, and talk to them, Socrates? And what will you say to them? What you say here about virtue and justice and institutions and laws being the best things among men? Would that be decent of you? Surely not. But if you go away from well-governed states to Crito's friends in Thessaly, where there is great disorder and licence, they will be charmed to hear the tale of your escape from prison, set off with ludicrous particulars of the manner in which you were wrapped in a goatskin or some other disguise, and metamorphosed as the manner is of runaways; but will there be no one to remind you that in your old age you were not ashamed to violate the most sacred laws from a miserable desire of a little more life? Perhaps not, if you keep them in a good temper; but if they are out of temper you will hear many degrading things; you will live, but how?—as the flatterer of all men, and the servant of all men; and doing what?—eating and drinking in Thessaly, having gone abroad in order that you may get a dinner. And where will be your fine sentiments about justice and virtue? Say that you wish to live for the sake of your children—you want to bring them up and educate them— will you take them into Thessaly and deprive them of Athenian citizenship? Is this the benefit which you will confer upon them? Or are you under the impression that they will be better cared for and educated here if you are still alive, although absent from them; for your friends will take care of them? Do you fancy that if you are an inhabitant of Thessaly they will take care of them, and if you are an inhabitant of the other world that they will not take care of them? Nay; but if they who call themselves friends are good for anything, they will—to be sure they will.

'Listen, then, Socrates, to us who have brought you up. Think not of life and children first, and of justice afterwards, but of justice first, that you may be justified before the princes of the world below. For neither will you nor any that belong to you be happier or holier or juster in this life, or happier in another, if you do as Crito bids. Now you depart in innocence, a sufferer and not a doer of evil; a victim, not of the laws but of men. But if you go forth, returning evil for evil, and injury for injury, breaking the covenants and agreements which you have made with us, and wronging those whom you ought least of all to wrong, that is to say, yourself, your friends, your country, and us, we shall be angry with you while you live, and our brethren, the laws in the world below, will receive you as an enemy; for they will know that you have done your best to destroy us. Listen, then, to us and not to Crito.'

This, dear Crito, is the voice which I seem to hear murmuring in my ears, like the sound of the flute in the ears of the mystic; that voice, I say, is humming in my ears, and prevents me from hearing any other. And I know that anything more which you may say will be vain. Yet speak, if you have anything to say.

Cr. I have nothing to say, Socrates.

Soc. Leave me then, Crito, to fulfull the will of God, and to follow whither he leads.

HENRY DAVID THOREAU

A social rebel with high principles, a man who loved nature and solitude, Henry David Thoreau is considered by some a memorable individualist, by others a perennial adolescent, and by still others as both. E. B. White has called him a "regular hairshirt of a man." Born in Concord, Mass., in 1817, he was educated at Harvard and after graduation returned to Concord where he first taught school and on later occasions supported himself by making pencils. He became a friend of Emerson, who was at the time leader of Concord's intellectual and spiritual life; he joined the Transcendental Club and contributed frequently to its journal, The Dial. *Some have said that Thoreau was the answer to Emerson's plea for an American Scholar. From July 4, 1845, to September 6, 1847, Thoreau lived in a hut at nearby Walden Pond, an experience that he recorded in his most famous work,* Walden. *His stay there was interrupted for one day in the summer of 1846 when he was arrested for not paying the Massachusetts poll tax. He explained his refusal as an act of protest against a government that sanctioned the Mexican War, a war he considered in the interests of Southern slaveholders; he later wrote an eloquent defense of civil disobedience, which was first published in 1849. This essay, which has become an American classic, is reprinted in full below; the text is that of the Riverside edition of Thoreau's works.*

Civil Disobedience

I heartily accept the motto,—"That government is best which governs least;" and I should like to see it acted up to more rapidly and systematically. Carried out, it finally amounts to this, which also I believe,—"That government is best which governs not at all;" and when men are prepared for it, that will be the kind of government which they will have. Government is at best but an expedient; but most governments are usually, and all governments are sometimes, inexpedient. The objections which have been brought against a standing army, and they are many and weighty, and deserve to prevail, may also at last be brought against a standing government. The standing army is only an arm of the standing government. The government itself, which is only the mode which the people have chosen to execute their will, is equally liable to be abused and perverted before the people can act through it. Witness the present Mexican war, the work of comparatively a few individuals using the standing government as their tool; for, in the outset, the people would not have consented to this measure.

This American Government,—what is it but a tradition, though a recent one, endeavoring to transmit itself unimpaired to posterity, but each instant losing some of its integrity? It has not the vitality and force of a single living man; for a single man can bend it to his will. It is a sort of wooden gun to the people themselves. But it is not the less necessary for this; for the people must have some complicated machinery or other, and hear its din, to satisfy that idea of government which they have. Governments show thus how successfully men can be imposed on, even impose on themselves, for their own advantage. It is excellent, we must all allow. Yet this government never of itself furthered any enterprise, but by the alacrity with which it got out of its way. *It* does not keep the country free. *It* does not settle the West. *It* does not educate. The character inherent in the American people has done all that has been accomplished; and it would have done somewhat more, if the government had not sometimes got in its way. For government is an expedient by which men would fain succeed in letting one another alone; and, as has been said, when it is most expedient, the governed are most let alone by it. Trade and commerce, if they were not made of India-rubber, would never manage to bounce over the obstacles which legislators are continually putting in their way; and, if one were to judge these men wholly by the effects of their actions and not partly by their intentions, they would deserve to be classed and punished with those mischievous persons who put obstructions on the railroads.

But, to speak practically and as a citizen, unlike those who call themselves no-government men, I ask for, not at once no government, but *at once* a better government. Let every man make known what kind of government would command his respect, and that will be one step toward obtaining it.

After all, the practical reason why, when the power is once in the hands of the people, a majority are permitted, and for a long period continue, to rule is not because they are most likely to be in the right, nor because this seems fairest to the minority, but because they are physically the strongest. But a government in which the majority rule in all cases cannot be based on justice, even as far as men understand it. Can there not be a government in which majorities do not virtually decide right and wrong, but conscience?— in which majorities decide only those questions to which the rule of expediency is applicable? Must the citizen ever for a moment, or in the least degree, resign his conscience to the legislator? Why has every man a conscience, then? I think that we should be men first, and subjects afterward. It is not desirable to cultivate a respect for the law, so much as for the right. The only obligation which I have a right to assume is to do at any time what I think right. It is truly enough said, that a corporation has no conscience; but a corporation of conscientious men is a corporation *with* a conscience. Law never made men a whit more just; and, by means of their respect for it, even the well-disposed are daily made the agents of injustice. A common and natural result of an undue respect for law is, that you may see a file of soldiers, colonel, captain, corporal, privates, powder-monkeys, and all, marching in admirable order over hill and dale to the wars, against their wills, ay, against their common sense and consciences, which makes it very steep marching indeed, and produces a palpitation of the heart. They have no doubt that it is a damnable business in which they are concerned; they are all peaceably inclined. Now, what are they? Men at all? or small movable forts and magazines, at the service of some unscrupulous man in power? Visit the Navy-Yard, and behold a marine, such a man as an American government can make, or such as it can make a man with its black arts,—a mere shadow and reminiscence of humanity, a man laid out alive and standing, and already, as one may say, buried under arms with funeral accompaniments, though it may be,—

> "Not a drum was heard, not a funeral note,
>   As his corse to the rampart we hurried;
> Not a soldier discharged his farewell shot
>   O'er the grave where our hero we buried."

The mass of men serve the state thus, not as men mainly, but as machines, with their bodies. They are the standing army, and the militia, jailers, constables, posse comitatus, etc. In most cases there is no free exercise whatever of the judgment or of the moral sense; but they put themselves on a level with wood and earth and stones; and wooden men can perhaps be manufactured that will serve the purpose as well. Such command no more respect than men of straw or a lump of dirt. They have the same sort of worth only as horses and dogs. Yet such as these even are commonly esteemed good citizens. Others—as most legislators, politicians, lawyers, ministers, and office-holders—serve the state chiefly with their heads; and, as they rarely make any moral distinctions, they are as likely to serve the Devil, without *intending* it, as God. A very few, as heroes, patriots, martyrs, reformers in the great sense, and *men*, serve the state with their consciences also, and so necessarily resist it for the most part; and they are commonly treated as enemies by it. A wise man will only be useful as a man, and will not submit to be "clay," and "stop a hole to keep the wind away," but leave that office to his dust at least:—

> "I am too high-born to be propertied,
> To be a secondary at control,
> Or useful serving-man and instrument
> To any sovereign state throughout the world."

He who gives himself entirely to his fellow-men appears to them useless and selfish; but he who gives himself partially to them is pronounced a benefactor and philanthropist.

How does it become a man to behave toward this American government to-day? I answer, that he cannot without disgrace be associated with it. I cannot for an instant recognize that political organization as *my* government which is the *slave's* government also.

All men recognize the right of revolution; that is, the right to refuse allegiance to, and to resist, the government, when its tyranny or its inefficiency are great and unendurable. But almost all say that such is not the case now. But such was the case, they think, in the Revolution of '75. If one were to tell me that this was a bad government because it taxed certain foreign commodities brought to its ports, it is most probable that I should not make an ado about it, for I can do without them. All machines have their friction; and possibly this does enough good to counterbalance the evil.

At any rate, it is a great evil to make a stir about it. But when the friction comes to have its machine, and oppression and robbery are organized, I say, let us not have such a machine any longer. In other words, when a sixth of the population of a nation which has undertaken to be the refuge of liberty are slaves, and a whole country is unjustly overrun and conquered by a foreign army, and subjected to military law, I think that it is not too soon for honest men to rebel and revolutionize. What makes this duty the more urgent is the fact that the country so overrun is not our own, but ours is the invading army.

Paley, a common authority with many on moral questions, in his chapter on the "Duty of Submission to Civil Government," resolves all civil obligation into expediency; and he proceeds to say, "that so long as the interest of the whole society requires it, that is, so long as the established government cannot be resisted or changed without public inconveniency, it is the will of God that the established government be obeyed, and no longer. . . . This principle being admitted, the justice of every particular case of resistance is reduced to a computation of the quantity of the danger and grievance on the one side, and of the probability and expense of redressing it on the other." Of this, he says, every man shall judge for himself. But Paley appears never to have contemplated those cases to which the rule of expediency does not apply, in which a people, as well as an individual, must do justice, cost what it may. If I have unjustly wrested a plank from a drowning man, I must restore it to him though I drown myself. This, according to Paley, would be inconvenient. But he that would save his life, in such a case, shall lose it. This people must cease to hold slaves, and to make war on Mexico, though it cost them their existence as a people.

In their practice, nations agree with Paley; but does any one think that Massachusetts does exactly what is right at the present crisis?

> "A drab of state, a cloth-o'-silver slut,
> To have her train borne up, and her soul trail in the dirt."

Practically speaking, the opponents to a reform in Massachusetts are not a hundred thousand politicians at the South, but a hundred thousand merchants and farmers here, who are more interested in commerce and agriculture than they are in humanity, and are not prepared to do justice to the slave and to Mexico, *cost what it may*. I quarrel not with far-off foes, but with those who, near at home, coöperate with, and do the bidding of, those far away, and without whom the latter would be harmless. We are accustomed to say, that the mass of men are unprepared; but improvement is slow, because the few are not materially wiser or better than the many. It is not so important that many should be as good as you, as that there be some absolute goodness somewhere; for that will leaven the whole lump. There are thousands who are *in opinion* opposed to slavery and to the war, who yet in effect do nothing to put an end to them; who, esteeming themselves children of Washington and Franklin, sit down with their hands in their pockets, and say that they know not what to do, and do nothing; who even postpone the question of freedom to the question of free-trade, and quietly read the prices-current along with the latest advices from Mexico, after dinner, and, it may be, fall asleep over them both. What is the price-current of an honest man and patriot to-day? They hesitate, and they regret, and sometimes they petition; but they do nothing in earnest and with effect. They will wait, well disposed, for others to remedy the evil, that they may no longer have it to regret. At most, they give only a cheap vote, and a feeble countenance and Godspeed, to the right, as it goes by them. There are nine hundred and ninety-nine patrons of virtue to one virtuous man. But it is easier to deal with the real possessor of a thing than with the temporary guardian of it.

All voting is a sort of gaming, like checkers or backgammon, with a slight moral tinge to it, a playing with right and wrong, with moral questions; and betting naturally accompanies it. The character of the voters is not staked. I cast my vote, perchance, as I think right; but I am not vitally concerned that that right should prevail. I am willing to leave it to the majority. Its obligation, therefore, never exceeds that of expediency. Even voting *for the right* is *doing* nothing for it. It is only expressing to men feebly your desire that it should prevail. A wise man will not leave the right to the mercy of chance, nor wish it to prevail through the power of the majority. There is but little virtue in the action of masses of men. When the majority shall at length vote for the abolition of slavery, it will be because they are indifferent to slavery, or because there is but little slavery left to be abolished by their vote. *They* will then be the only slaves. Only *his* vote can hasten the abolition of slavery who asserts his own freedom by his vote.

I hear of a convention to be held at Baltimore, or elsewhere, for the selection of a candidate for the Presidency, made up chiefly of editors, and men who are politicians by profession; but I think, what is it to any independent, intelligent, and respectable man what decision they may come to? Shall we not have the advantage of his wisdom and honesty, nevertheless? Can we not count upon some independent votes? Are there not many individuals in the country who do not attend conventions? But no: I find that the respectable man, so called, has immediately drifted from his position, and despairs of his country, when his country has more reason to despair of him. He forthwith adopts one of the candidates thus selected as the only *available* one, thus proving that he is himself *available* for any purposes of the demagogue. His vote is of no more worth than that of any unprincipled foreigner or hireling native, who may have been bought. O for a man who is a *man*, and, as my neighbor says, has a bone in his back which you cannot pass your hand through! Our statistics are at fault: the population has been returned too large. How many *men* are there to a square thousand miles in this country? Hardly one. Does not America offer any inducement for men to settle here? The American has dwindled into an Odd Fellow,—one who may be known by the development of his organ of gregariousness, and a manifest lack of intellect and cheerful self-reliance; whose first and chief concern, on coming into the world, is to see that the Almshouses are in good repair; and, before yet he has lawfully donned the virile garb, to collect a fund for the support of the widows and orphans that may be; who, in short, ventures to live only by the aid of the Mutual Insurance company, which has promised to bury him decently.

It is not a man's duty, as a matter of course, to devote himself to the eradication of any, even the most enormous wrong; he may still properly have other concerns to engage him; but it is his duty, at least, to wash his hands of it, and, if he gives it no thought longer, not to give it practically his support. If I devote myself to other pursuits and contemplations, I must first see, at least, that I do not pursue them sitting upon another man's shoulders. I must get off him first, that he may pursue his contemplations too. See what gross inconsistency is tolerated. I have heard some of my townsmen say, "I should like to have them order me out to help put down an insurrection of the slaves, or to march to Mexico;—see if I would go;" and yet these very men have each, directly by their allegiance, and so indirectly, at least, by their money, furnished a substitute. The soldier is applauded who refuses to serve in an unjust war by those who do not refuse to sustain the unjust government which makes the war; is applauded by those whose own act and authority he disregards and sets at naught; as if the state were penitent to that degree that it hired one to scourge it while it sinned, but not to that degree that it left off sinning for a moment. Thus, under the name of Order and Civil Government, we are all made at last to pay homage to and support our own meanness. After the first blush of sin comes its indifference; and from immoral it becomes, as it were, *un*moral, and not quite unnecessary to that life which we have made.

The broadest and most prevalent error requires the most disinterested virtue to sustain it. The slight reproach to which the virtue of patriotism is commonly liable, the noble are most likely to incur. Those who, while they disapprove of the character and measures of a government, yield to it their allegiance and support are undoubtedly its most conscientious supporters, and so frequently the most serious obstacles to reform. Some are petitioning the state to dissolve the Union, to disregard the requisitions of the President. Why do they not dissolve it themselves,—the union between themselves and the state,—and refuse to pay their quota into its treasury? Do not they stand in the same relation to the state that the state does to the Union? And have not the same reasons prevented the state from resisting the Union which have prevented them from resisting the state?

How can a man be satisfied to entertain an opinion merely, and enjoy *it*? Is there any enjoyment in it, if his opinion is that he is aggrieved? If you are cheated out of a single dollar by your neighbor, you do not rest satisfied with knowing that you are cheated, or with saying that you are cheated, or even with petitioning him to pay you your due; but you take effectual steps at once to obtain the full amount, and see that you are never cheated again. Action from principle, the perception and the performance of right, changes things and relations; it is essentially revolutionary, and does not consist wholly with anything which was. It not only divides states and churches, it divides families; ay, it divides the *individual*, separating the diabolical in him from the divine.

Unjust laws exist: shall we be content to obey them, or shall we endeavor to amend them, and obey them until we have succeeded, or shall we transgress them at once? Men generally, under such a government as this, think that they ought to wait until they have persuaded the majority to alter them. They think that, if they should resist, the remedy would be worse than the evil. But it is the fault of the government itself that the remedy *is* worse than the evil. *It* makes it worse. Why is it not more apt to anticipate and provide for reform? Why does it not cherish its wise minority? Why does it cry and resist before it is hurt? Why does it not encourage its citizens to be on the alert to point out its faults, and *do* better than it would have them? Why does it always crucify Christ, and excommunicate Copernicus and Luther, and pronounce Washington and Franklin rebels?

One would think, that a deliberate and practical denial of its authority was the only offense never contemplated by government; else, why has it not assigned its definite, its suitable and proportionate penalty? If a man who has no property refuses but once to earn nine shillings for the state, he is put in prison for a period unlimited by any law that I know, and determined only by the discretion of those who placed him there; but if he should steal ninety times nine shillings from the state, he is soon permitted to go at large again.

If the injustice is part of the necessary friction of the machine of government, let it go, let it go: perchance it will wear smooth,—certainly the machine will wear out. If the injustice has a spring, or a pulley, or a rope, or a crank, exclusively for itself, then perhaps you may consider whether the remedy will not be worse than the evil; but if it is of such a nature that it requires you to be the agent of injustice to another, then, I say, break the law. Let your life be a counter friction to stop the machine. What I have to do is to see, at any rate, that I do not lend myself to the wrong which I condemn.

As for adopting the ways which the state has provided for remedying the evil, I know not of such ways. They take too much time, and a man's life will be gone. I have other affairs to attend to. I came into this world, not chiefly to make this a good place to live in, but to live in it, be it good or bad. A man has not everything to do, but something; and because he cannot do *everything*, it is not necessary that he should do *something* wrong. It is not my business to be petitioning the Governor or the Legislature any more than it is theirs to petition me; and if they should not hear my petition, what should I do then? But in this case the state has provided no way: its very Constitution is the evil. This may seem to be harsh and stubborn and unconciliatory; but it is to treat with the utmost kindness and consideration the only spirit that can appreciate or deserves it. So is all change for the better, like birth and death, which convulse the body.

I do not hesitate to say, that those who call themselves Abolitionists should at once effectually withdraw their support, both in person and property, from the government of Massachusetts, and not wait till they constitute a majority of one, before they suffer the right to prevail through them. I think that it is enough if they have God on their side, without waiting for

that other one. Moreover, any man more right than his neighbors constitutes a majority of one already.

I meet this American government, or its representative, the state government, directly, and face to face, once a year—no more—in the person of its
tax-gatherer; this is the only mode in which a man situated as I am necessarily meets it; and it then says distinctly, Recognize me; and the simplest,
the most effectual, and, in the present posture of affairs, the indispensablest
mode of treating with it on this head, of expressing your little satisfaction
with and love for it, is to deny it then. My civil neighbor, the tax-gatherer,
is the very man I have to deal with,—for it is, after all, with men and not
with parchment that I quarrel,—and he has voluntarily chosen to be an
agent of the government. How shall he ever know well what he is and does
as an officer of the government, or as a man, until he is obliged to consider
whether he shall treat me, his neighbor, for whom he has respect, as a
neighbor and well-disposed man, or as a maniac and disturber of the peace,
and see if he can get over this obstruction to his neighborliness without a
ruder and more impetuous thought or speech corresponding with his action.
I know this well, that if one thousand, if one hundred, if ten men whom I
could name,—if ten *honest* men only,—ay, if *one* HONEST man, in this State of
Massachusetts, *ceasing to hold slaves*, were actually to withdraw from this co-
partnership, and be locked up in the county jail therefor, it would be the
abolition of slavery in America. For it matters not how small the beginning
may seem to be: what is once well done is done forever. But we love better
to talk about it: that we say is our mission. Reform keeps many scores of
newspapers in its service, but not one man. If my esteemed neighbor, the
State's ambassador, who will devote his days to the settlement of the question of human rights in the Council Chamber, instead of being threatened
with the prisons of Carolina, were to sit down the prisoner of Massachusetts,
that State which is so anxious to foist the sin of slavery upon her sister,—
though at present she can discover only an act of inhospitality to be the
ground of a quarrel with her,—the Legislature would not wholly waive the
subject the following winter.

Under a government which imprisons any unjustly, the true place for a
just man is also a prison. The proper place to-day, the only place which
Massachusetts has provided for her freer and less desponding spirits, is in
her prisons, to be put out and locked out of the State by her own act, as they
have already put themselves out by their principles. It is there that the
fugitive slave, and the Mexican prisoner on parole, and the Indian come to
plead the wrongs of his race should find them; on that separate, but more
free and honorable ground, where the State places those who are not *with*
her, but *against* her,—the only house in a slave State in which a free man
can abide with honor. If any think that their influence would be lost there,
and their voices no longer afflict the ear of the State, that they would not be
as an enemy within its walls, they do not know by how much truth is
stronger than error, nor how much more eloquently and effectively he can
combat injustice who has experienced a little in his own person. Cast your

whole vote, not a strip of paper merely, but your whole influence. A minority is powerless while it conforms to the majority; it is not even a minority then; but it is irresistible when it clogs by its whole weight. If the alternative is to keep all just men in prison, or give up war and slavery, the State will not hesitate which to choose. If a thousand men were not to pay their tax-bills this year, that would not be a violent and bloody measure, as it would be to pay them, and enable the State to commit violence and shed innocent blood. This is, in fact, the definition of a peaceable revolution, if any such is possible. If the tax-gatherer, or any other public officer, asks me, as one has done, "But what shall I do?" my answer is, "If you really wish to do anything, resign your office." When the subject has refused allegiance, and the officer has resigned his office, then the revolution is accomplished. But even suppose blood should flow. Is there not a sort of blood shed when the conscience is wounded? Through this wound a man's real manhood and immortality flow out, and he bleeds to an everlasting death. I see this blood flowing now.

I have contemplated the imprisonment of the offender, rather than the seizure of his goods,—though both will serve the same purpose,—because they who assert the purest right, and consequently are most dangerous to a corrupt State, commonly have not spent much time in accumulating property. To such the State renders comparatively small service, and a slight tax is wont to appear exorbitant, particularly if they are obliged to earn it by special labor with their hands. If there were one who lived wholly without the use of money, the State itself would hesitate to demand it of him. But the rich man—not to make any invidious comparison—is always sold to the institution which makes him rich. Absolutely speaking, the more money, the less virtue; for money comes between a man and his objects, and obtains them for him; and it was certainly no great virtue to obtain it. It puts to rest many questions which he would otherwise be taxed to answer; while the only new question which it puts is the hard but superfluous one, how to spend it. Thus his moral ground is taken from under his feet. The opportunities of living are diminished in proportion as what are called the "means" are increased. The best thing a man can do for his culture when he is rich is to endeavor to carry out those schemes which he entertained when he was poor. Christ answered the Herodians according to their condition. "Show me the tribute-money," said he;—and one took a penny out of his pocket;—if you use money which has the image of Cæsar on it, which he has made current and valuable, that is, *if you are men of the State*, and gladly enjoy the advantages of Cæsar's government, then pay him back some of his own when he demands it. "Render therefore to Cæsar that which is Cæsar's, and to God those things which are God's,"—leaving them no wiser than before as to which was which; for they did not wish to know.

When I converse with the freest of my neighbors, I perceive that, whatever they may say about the magnitude and seriousness of the question, and their regard for the public tranquillity, the long and the short of the matter is, that they cannot spare the protection of the existing government, and they dread the consequences to their property and families of disobedience to it. For my own part, I should not like to think that I ever rely on the protection of the State. But, if I deny the authority of the State when it presents its tax-bill, it will soon take and waste all my property, and so harass me and my children without end. This is hard. This makes it impossible for a man to live honestly, and at the same time comfortably, in outward respects. It will not be worth the while to accumulate property; that would be sure to go again. You must hire or squat somewhere, and raise but a small crop, and eat that soon. You must live within yourself, and depend upon yourself always tucked up and ready for a start, and not have many affairs. A man may grow rich in Turkey even, if he will be in all respects a good subject of the Turkish government. Confucius said: "If a state is governed by the principles of reason, poverty and misery are subjects of shame; if a state is not governed by the principles of reason, riches and honors are the subjects of shame." No: until I want the protection of Massachusetts to be extended to me in some distant Southern port, where my liberty is endangered, or until I am bent solely on building up an estate at home by peaceful enterprise, I can afford to refuse allegiance to Massachusetts, and her right to my property and life. It costs me less in every sense to incur the penalty of disobedience to the State than it would to obey. I should feel as if I were worth less in that case.

Some years ago, the State met me in behalf of the Church, and commanded me to pay a certain sum toward the support of a clergyman whose preaching my father attended, but never I myself. "Pay," it said, "or be locked up in the jail." I declined to pay. But, unfortunately, another man saw fit to pay it. I did not see why the schoolmaster should be taxed to support the priest, and not the priest the schoolmaster; for I was not the State's schoolmaster, but I supported myself by voluntary subscription. I did not see why the lyceum should not present its tax-bill, and have the State to back its demand, as well as the Church. However, at the request of the selectmen, I condescended to make some such statement as this in writing:—"Know all men by these presents, that I, Henry Thoreau, do not wish to be regarded as a member of any incorporated society which I have not joined." This I gave to the town clerk; and he has it. The State, having thus learned that I did not wish to be regarded as a member of that church, has never made a like demand on me since; though it said that it must adhere to its original presumption that time. If I had known how to name them, I should then have signed off in detail from all the societies which I never signed on to; but I did not know where to find a complete list.

I have paid no poll-tax for six years. I was put into a jail once on this account, for one night; and, as I stood considering the walls of solid stone, two or three feet thick, the door of wood and iron, a foot thick, and the iron grating which strained the light, I could not help being struck with the foolishness of that institution which treated me as if I were mere flesh and blood and bones, to be locked up. I wondered that it should have concluded at length that this was the best use it could put me to, and had never thought to avail itself of my services in some way. I saw that, if there was a wall of stone between me and my townsmen, there was a still more difficult one to climb or break through before they could get to be as free as I was. I did not for a moment feel confined, and the walls seemed a great waste of stone and mortar. I felt as if I alone of all my townsmen had paid my tax. They plainly did not know how to treat me, but behaved like persons who are underbred. In every threat and in every compliment there was a blunder; for they thought that my chief desire was to stand the other side of that stone wall. I could not but smile to see how industriously they locked the door on my mediations, which followed them out again without let or hindrance, and *they* were really all that was dangerous. As they could not reach me, they had resolved to punish my body; just as boys, if they cannot come at some person against whom they have a spite, will abuse his dog. I saw that the State was half-witted, that it was timid as a lone woman with her silver spoons, and that it did not know its friends from its foes, and I lost all my remaining respect for it, and pitied it.

Thus the State never intentionally confronts a man's sense, intellectual or moral, but only his body, his senses. It is not armed with superior wit or honesty, but with superior physical strength. I was not born to be forced. I will breathe after my own fashion. Let us see who is the strongest. What force has a multitude? They only can force me who obey a higher law than I. They force me to become like themselves. I do not hear of *men* being *forced* to live this way or that by masses of men. What sort of life were that to live? When I meet a government which says to me, "Your money or your life," why should I be in haste to give it my money? It may be in a great strait, and not know what to do: I cannot help that. It must help itself; do as I do. It is not worth the while to snivel about it. I am not responsible for the successful working of the machinery of society. I am not the son of the engineer. I perceive that, when an acorn and a chestnut fall side by side, the one does not remain inert to make way for the other, but both obey their own laws, and spring and grow and flourish as best they can, till one, perchance, overshadows and destroys the other. If a plant cannot live according to its nature, it dies; and so a man.

The night in prison was novel and interesting enough. The prisoners in their shirt-sleeves were enjoying a chat and the evening air in the doorway, when I entered. But the jailer said, "Come, boys, it is time to lock up;" and so they dispersed, and I heard the sound of their steps returning into the hollow apartments. My room-mate was introduced to me by the jailer as "a first-rate fellow and a clever man." When the door was locked, he showed me where to hang my hat, and how he managed matters there. The rooms were whitewashed once a month; and this one, at least, was the whitest, most simply furnished, and probably the neatest apartment in the town. He naturally wanted to know where I came from, and what brought me there; and, when I had told him, I asked him in my turn how he came there, presuming him to be an honest man, of course; and, as the world goes, I believe he was. "Why," said he, "they accuse me of burning a barn; but I never did it." As near as I could discover, he had probably gone to bed in a barn when drunk, and smoked his pipe there; and so a barn was burnt. He had the reputation of being a clever man, had been there some three months waiting for his trial to come on, and would have to wait as much longer; but he was quite domesticated and contented, since he got his board for nothing, and thought that he was well treated.

He occupied one window, and I the other; and I saw that if one stayed there long, his principal business would be to look out the window. I had soon read all the tracts that were left there, and examined where former prisoners had broken out, and where a grate had been sawed off, and heard the history of the various occupants of that room; for I found that even here there was a history and a gossip which never circulated beyond the walls of the jail. Probably this is the only house in the town where verses are composed, which are afterward printed in a circular form, but not published. I was shown quite a long list of verses which were composed by some young men who had been detected in an attempt to escape, who avenged themselves by singing them.

I pumped my fellow-prisoner as dry as I could, for fear I should never see him again; but at length he showed me which was my bed, and left me to blow out the lamp.

It was like traveling into a far country, such as I had never expected to behold, to lie there for one night. It seemed to me that I never had heard the town-clock strike before, nor the evening sounds of the village; for we slept with the windows open, which were inside the grating. It was to see my native village in the light of the Middle Ages, and our Concord was turned into a Rhine stream, and visions of knights and castles passed before me. They were the voices of old burghers that I heard in the streets. I was an involuntary spectator and auditor of whatever was done and said in the kitchen of the adjacent village-inn,—a wholly new and rare experience to me. It was a closer view of my native town. I was fairly inside of it. I never had seen its institutions before. This is one of its peculiar institutions; for it is a shire town. I began to comprehend what its inhabitants were about.

In the morning, our breakfasts were put through the hole in the door, in small oblong-square tin pans, made to fit, and holding a pint of chocolate, with brown bread, and an iron spoon. When they called for the vessels again, I was green enough to return what bread I had left; but my comrade seized it, and said that I should lay that up for lunch or dinner. Soon after he was let out to work at haying in a neighboring field, whither he went every day, and would not be back till noon; so he bade me good-day, saying that he doubted if he should see me again.

When I came out of prison,—for some one interfered, and paid that tax,—I did not perceive that great changes had taken place on the common, such as he observed who went in a youth and emerged a tottering and gray-headed man; and yet a change had to my eyes come over the scene,—the town, and State, and country,—greater than any that mere time could effect. I saw yet more distinctly the State in which I lived. I saw to what extent the people among whom I lived could be trusted as good neighbors and friends; that their friendship was for summer weather only; that they did not greatly propose to do right; that they were a distinct race from me by their prejudices and superstitions, as the Chinamen and Malays are; that in their sacrifices to humanity they ran no risks, not even to their property; that after all they were not so noble but they treated the thief as he had treated them, and hoped, by a certain outward observance and a few prayers, and by walking in a particular straight though useless path from time to time, to save their souls. This may be to judge my neighbors harshly; for I believe that many of them are not aware that they have such an institution as the jail in their village.

It was formerly the custom in our village, when a poor debtor came out of jail, for his acquaintances to salute him, looking through their fingers, which were crossed to represent the grating of a jail window, "How do ye do?" My neighbors did not thus salute me, but first looked at me, and then at one another, as if I had returned from a long journey. I was put into jail as I was going to the shoemaker's to get a shoe which was mended. When I was let out the next morning, I proceeded to finish my errand, and, having put on my mended shoe, joined a huckleberry party, who were impatient to put themselves under my conduct; and in half an hour,—for the horse was soon tackled,—was in the midst of a huckleberry field, on one of our highest hills, two miles off, and then the State was nowhere to be seen.

This is the whole history of "My Prisons."

I have never declined paying the highway tax, because I am as desirous of being a good neighbor as I am of being a bad subject; and as for supporting schools, I am doing my part to educate my fellow-countrymen now. It is for no particular item in the tax-bill that I refuse to pay it. I simply wish to refuse allegiance to the State, to withdraw and stand aloof from it effectually. I do not care to trace the course of my dollar, if I could, till it buys a man or a musket to shoot one with,—the dollar is innocent,—but I am concerned to trace the effects of my allegiance. In fact, I quietly declare war with the State, after my fashion, though I will still make what use and get what advantage of her I can, as is usual in such cases.

If others pay the tax which is demanded of me, from a sympathy with the State, they do but what they have already done in their own case, or rather they abet injustice to a greater extent than the State requires. If they pay the tax from a mistaken interest in the individual taxed, to save his property, or prevent his going to jail, it is because they have not considered wisely how far they let their private feelings interfere with the public good.

This, then, is my position at present. But one cannot be too much on his guard in such a case, lest his action be biased by obstinacy or an undue regard for the opinions of men. Let him see that he does only what belongs to himself and to the hour.

I think sometimes, Why, this people mean well, they are only ignorant; they would do better if they knew how: why give your neighbors this pain to treat you as they are not inclined to? But I think again, This is no reason why I should do as they do, or permit others to suffer much greater pain of a different kind. Again, I sometimes say to myself, When many millions of men, without heat, without ill will, without personal feeling of any kind, demand of you a few shillings only, without the possibility, such is their constitution, of retracting or altering their present demand, and without the possibility, on your side, of appeal to any other millions, why expose yourself to this overwhelming brute force? You do not resist cold and hunger, the winds and the waves, thus obstinately; you quietly submit to a thousand similar necessities. You do not put your head into the fire. But just in proportion as I regard this as not wholly a brute force, but partly a human force, and consider that I have relations to those millions as to so many millions of men, and not of mere brute or inanimate things, I see that appeal is possible, first and instantaneously, from them to the Maker of them, and, secondly, from them to themselves. But if I put my head deliberately into the fire, there is no appeal to fire or to the Maker of fire, and I have only myself to blame. If I could convince myself that I have any right to be satisfied with men as they are, and to treat them accordingly, and not according, in some respects, to my requisitions and expectations of what they and I ought to be, then, like a good Mussulman and fatalist, I should endeavor to be satisfied with things as they are, and say it is the will of God. And, above all, there is this difference between resisting this and a purely brute or natural force, that I can resist this with some effect; but I cannot expect, like Orpheus, to change the nature of the rocks and trees and beasts.

I do not wish to quarrel with any man or nation. I do not wish to split hairs, to make fine distinctions, or set myself up as better than my neighbors. I seek rather, I may say, even an excuse for conforming to the laws of the land. I am but too ready to conform to them. Indeed, I have reason to suspect myself on this head; and each year, as the tax-gatherer comes round, I find myself disposed to review the acts and position of the general and State governments, and the spirit of the people, to discover a pretext for conformity.

> "We must affect our country as our parents,
> And if at any time we alienate
> Our love or industry from doing it honor,
> We must respect effects and teach the soul
> Matter of conscience and religion,
> And not desire of rule or benefit."

I believe that the State will soon be able to take all my work of this sort out of my hands, and then I shall be no better a patriot than my fellow-countrymen. Seen from a lower point of view, the Constitution, with all its faults, is very good; the law and the courts are very respectable; even this State and this American government are, in many respects, very admirable, and rare things, to be thankful for, such as a great many have described them; but seen from a point of view a little higher, they are what I have described them; seen from a higher still, and the highest, who shall say what they are, or that they are worth looking at or thinking of at all?

However, the government does not concern me much, and I shall bestow the fewest possible thoughts on it. It is not many moments that I live under a government, even in this world. If a man is thought-free, fancy-free, imagination-free, that which *is not* never for a long time appearing *to be* to him, unwise rulers or reformers cannot fatally interrupt him.

I know that most men think differently from myself; but those whose lives are by profession devoted to the study of these or kindred subjects content me as little as any. Statesmen and legislators, standing so completely within the institution, never distinctly and nakedly behold it. They speak of moving society, but have no resting-place without it. They may be men of a certain experience and discrimination, and have no doubt invented ingenious and even useful systems, for which we sincerely thank them; but all their wit and usefulness lie within certain not very wide limits. They are wont to forget that the world is not governed by policy and expediency. Webster never goes behind government, and so cannot speak with authority about it. His words are wisdom to those legislators who contemplate no essential reform in the existing government; but for thinkers, and those who legislate for all time, he never once glances at the subject. I know of those whose serene and wise speculations on this theme would soon reveal the limits of his mind's range and hospitality. Yet, compared with the cheap professions of most reformers, and the still cheaper wisdom and eloquence of politicians in general, his are almost the only sensible and valuable words, and we thank Heaven for him. Comparatively, he is always strong, original, and, above all, practical. Still, his quality is not wisdom, but prudence. The lawyer's truth is not Truth, but consistency or a consistent expediency. Truth is always in harmony with herself, and is not concerned chiefly to reveal the justice that may consist with wrong-doing. He well deserves to be called, as he has been called, the Defender of the Constitution. There are really no blows to be given by him but defensive ones. He is not a leader, but a follower. His leaders are the men of '87. "I have never made an effort," he says, "and never propose to make an effort; I have never countenanced an effort, and never mean to countenance an effort, to disturb the arrangement as originally made, by which the various States came into the Union." Still thinking of the sanction which the Constitution gives to slavery, he says, "Because it was a part of the original compact,—let it stand." Notwithstanding his special acuteness and ability, he is unable to take a fact out of its merely political relations, and behold it as it lies absolutely to be disposed of by the intellect,—what, for instance, it behooves a man to do here in America to-day with regard to slavery,—but ventures, or is driven, to make some such desperate answer as the following, while professing to speak absolutely, and as a private man,—from which what new and singular code of social duties might be inferred? "The manner," says he, "in which the governments of those States where slavery exists are to regulate it is for their own consideration, under their responsibility to their constituents, to the general laws of propriety, humanity, and justice, and to God. Associations formed elsewhere, springing from a feeling of humanity, or any other cause, have nothing whatever to do with it. They have never received any encouragement from me, and they never will."

They who know of no purer sources of truth, who have traced up its stream no higher, stand, and wisely stand, by the Bible and the Constitution, and drink at it there with reverence and humility; but they who behold where it comes trickling into this lake or that pool, gird up their loins once more, and continue their pilgrimage toward its fountain-head.

No man with a genius for legislation has appeared in America. They are rare in the history of the world. There are orators, politicians, and eloquent men, by the thousand; but the speaker has not yet opened his mouth to speak who is capable of settling the much-vexed questions of the day. We love eloquence for its own sake, and not for any truth which it may utter, or any heroism it may inspire. Our legislators have not yet learned the comparative value of free-trade and of freedom, of union, and of rectitude, to a nation. They have no genius or talent for comparatively humble questions of taxation and finance, commerce and manufactures and agriculture. If we were left solely to the wordy wit of legislators in Congress for our guidance, uncorrected by the seasonable experience and the effectual complaints of the people, America would not long retain her rank among the nations. For eighteen hundred years, though perchance I have no right to say it, the New Testament has been written; yet where is the legislator who has wisdom and practical talent enough to avail himself of the light which it sheds on the science of legislation?

The authority of government, even such as I am willing to submit to,—for I will cheerfully obey those who know and can do better than I, and in many things even those who neither know nor can do so well,—is still an impure one: to be strictly just, it must have the sanction and consent of the governed. It can have no pure right over my person and property but what I concede to it. The progress from an absolute to a limited monarchy, from a limited monarchy to a democracy, is a progress toward a true respect for the individual. Even the Chinese philosopher was wise enough to regard the individual as the basis of the empire. Is a democracy, such as we know it, the last improvement possible in government? Is it not possible to take a further step towards recognizing and organizing the rights of man? There will never be a really free and enlightened State until the State comes to recognize the individual as a higher and independent power, from which all its own power and authority are derived, and treats him accordingly. I please myself with imagining a State at last which can afford to be just to all men, and to treat the individual with respect as a neighbor; which even would not think it inconsistent with its own repose if a few were to live aloof from it, not meddling with it, nor embraced by it, who fulfilled all the duties of neighbors and fellow-men. A State which bore this kind of fruit, and suffered it to drop off as fast as it ripened, would prepare the way for a still more perfect and glorious State, which also I have imagined, but not yet anywhere seen.

MARTIN LUTHER KING, JR.

Martin Luther King, Jr., was one of the most forceful advocates of nonviolent disobedience in the struggle for civil and human rights. Born in Georgia in 1929 and educated at Morehouse College, Crozer Theological Seminary, and Boston University, he became a

Baptist minister in Montgomery, Alabama, in 1954. The next year he launched the now famous Montgomery bus boycott. Founder and president of the Southern Christian Leadership Conference, he was a leader of the 1963 March on Washington and of the 1965 voter registration drive in Selma, Alabama. In 1964 he received the Nobel Peace Prize. He was assassinated in Memphis, Tennessee, on April 4, 1968, while supporting a strike of city sanitation workers.

His writings include Stride Toward Freedom *(1958),* Strength to Love *(1963),* Where Do We Go from Here: Chaos or Community *(1967),* Conscience for Change *(1967),* The Measure of Man *(1968), and* The Trumpet of Conscience *(1968).* Why We Can't Wait, *published in 1964, includes a revised version of the letter printed below, and an author's note in which he says, "This response to a published statement by eight fellow clergymen from Alabama . . . was composed under somewhat constricting circumstances. Begun on the margins of the newspaper in which the statement appeared while I was in jail, the letter was continued on scraps of writing paper supplied by a friendly Negro trusty, and concluded on a pad my attorneys were eventually permitted to leave me. Although the text remains in substance unaltered, I have indulged in the author's prerogative of polishing it for publication." For its greater immediacy, we present here the unrevised version of the letter, together with the public statement that occasioned it.*

Public Statement by Eight Alabama Clergymen

(April 12, 1963)

We the undersigned clergymen are among those who, in January, issued "An Appeal for Law and Order and Common Sense," in dealing with racial problems in Alabama. We expressed understanding that honest convictions in racial matters could properly be pursued in the courts, but urged that decisions of those courts should in the meantime be peacefully obeyed.

Since that time there had been some evidence of increased forbearance and a willingness to face facts. Responsible citizens have undertaken to work on various problems which cause racial friction and unrest. In Birmingham, recent public events have given indication that we all have opportunity for a new constructive and realistic approach to racial problems.

However, we are now confronted by a series of demonstrations by some of our Negro citizens, directed and led in part by outsiders. We recognize the natural impatience of people who feel that their hopes are slow in being realized. But we are convinced that these demonstrations are unwise and untimely.

We agree rather with certain local Negro leadership which has called for honest and open negotiation of racial issues in our area. And we believe this kind of facing of issues can best be accomplished by citizens of our own metropolitan area, white and Negro, meeting with their knowledge and experience of the local situation. All of us need to face that responsibility and find proper channels for its accomplishment.

Just as we formerly pointed out that "hatred and violence have no sanction in our religious and political traditions," we also point out that such actions as incite to hatred and violence, however technically peaceful those, actions may be, have not contributed to the resolution of our local problems. We do not believe that these days of new hope are days when extreme measures are justified in Birmingham.

We commend the community as a whole, and the local news media and law enforcement officials in particular, on the calm manner in which these demonstrations have been handled. We urge the public to continue to show restraint should the demonstrations continue, and the law enforcement officials to remain calm and continue to protect our city from violence.

We further strongly urge our own Negro community to withdraw support from these demonstrations, and to unite locally in working peacefully for a better Birmingham. When rights are consistently denied, a cause should be pressed in the courts and in negotiations among local leaders, and not in the streets. We appeal to both our white and Negro citizenry to observe the principles of law and order and common sense.

Signed by:

C. C. J. CARPENTER, D.D., LL.D., *Bishop of Alabama*
JOSEPH A. DURICK, D.D., *Auxilary Bishop, Diocese of Mobile-Birmingham*
Rabbi MILTON L. GRAFMAN, *Temple Emanu-El, Birmingham, Alabama*
Bishop PAUL HARDIN, *Bishop of the Alabama-West Florida Conference of the Methodist Church*
Bishop NOLAN B. HARMON, *Bishop of the North Alabama Conference of the Methodist Church*
GEORGE M. MURRAY, D.D., LL.D., *Bishop Coadjutor, Episcopal Diocese of Alabama*
EDWARD V. RAMAGE, *Moderator, Synod of the Alabama Presbyterian Church in the United States*
EARL STALLINGS, *Pastor, First Baptist Church, Birmingham, Alabama*

Letter from Birmingham Jail

MARTIN LUTHER KING, JR.
Birmingham City Jail
April 16, 1963

Bishop C. C. J. CARPENTER
Bishop JOSEPH A. DURICK
Rabbi MILTON L. GRAFMAN
Bishop PAUL HARDIN
Bishop NOLAN B. HARMON
The Rev. GEORGE M. MURRAY
The Rev. EDWARD V. RAMAGE
The Rev. EARL STALLINGS

My dear Fellow Clergymen,

While confined here in the Birmingham City Jail, I came across your recent statement calling our present activities "unwise and untimely." Seldom, if ever, do I pause to answer criticism of my work and ideas. If I sought to answer all of the criticisms that cross my desk, my secretaries would be engaged in little else in the course of the day and I would have no time for constructive work. But since I feel that you are men of genuine good will and your criticisms are sincerely set forth, I would like to answer your statement in what I hope will be patient and reasonable terms.

I think I should give the reason for my being in Birmingham, since you have been influenced by the argument of "outsiders coming in." I have the honor of serving as president of the Southern Christian Leadership Conference, an organization operating in every Southern state with headquarters in Atlanta, Georgia. We have some eighty-five affiliate organizations all across the South—one being the Alabama Christian Movement for Human Rights. Whenever necessary and possible we share staff, educational, and financial resources with our affiliates. Several months ago our local affiliate here in Birmingham invited us to be on call to engage in a nonviolent direct action program if such were deemed necessary. We readily consented and when the hour came we lived up to our promises. So I am here, along with several members of my staff, because we were invited here. I am here because I have basic organizational ties here. Beyond this, I am in Birmingham because injustice is here. Just as the eighth century prophets left their little villages and carried their "thus saith the Lord" far beyond the boundaries of their home town, and just as the Apostle Paul left his little village of Tarsus and carried the gospel of Jesus Christ to practically every hamlet and city of the Graeco-Roman world, I too am compelled to carry the gospel of freedom beyond my particular home town. Like Paul, I must constantly respond to the Macedonian call for aid.

Moreover, I am cognizant of the interrelatedness of all communities and states. I cannot sit idly by in Atlanta and not be concerned about what happens in Birmingham. Injustice anywhere is a threat to justice everywhere. We are caught in an inescapable network of mutuality tied in a single garment of destiny. Whatever affects one directly affects all indirectly. Never again can we afford to live with the narrow, provincial "outside agitator" idea. Anyone who lives inside the United States can never be considered an outsider anywhere in this country.

You deplore the demonstrations that are presently taking place in Birmingham. But I am sorry that your statement did not express a similar concern for the conditions that brought the demonstrations into being. I am sure that each of you would want to go beyond the superficial social analyst who looks merely at effects, and does not grapple with underlying causes. I would not hesitate to say that it is unfortunate that so-called demonstrations are taking place in Birmingham at this time, but I would say in more emphatic terms that it is even more unfortunate that the white power structure of this city left the Negro community with no other alternative.

In any nonviolent campaign there are four basic steps: (1) collection of the facts to determine whether injustices are alive; (2) negotiation; (3) self-purification; and (4) direct action. We have gone through all of these steps in Birmingham. There can be no gainsaying of the fact that racial injustice engulfs this community. Birmingham is probably the most thoroughly segregated city in the United States. Its ugly record of police brutality is known in every section of this country. Its unjust treatment of Negroes in the courts is a notorious reality. There have been more unsolved bombings of Negro homes and churches in Birmingham than any city in this nation. These are the hard, brutal, and unbelievable facts. On the basis of these conditions Negro leaders sought to negotiate with the city fathers. But the political leaders consistently refused to engage in good faith negotiation.

Then came the opportunity last September to talk with some of the leaders of the economic community. In these negotiating sessions certain promises were made by the merchants—such as the promise to remove the humiliating racial signs from the stores. On the basis of these promises Rev. Shuttlesworth and the leaders of the Alabama Christian Movement for Human Rights agreed to call a moratorium on any type of demonstrations. As the weeks and months unfolded we realized that we were the victims of a broken promise. The signs remained. As in so many experiences of the past we were confronted with blasted hopes, and the dark shadow of a deep disappointment settled upon us. So we had no alternative except that of preparing for direct action, whereby we would present our very bodies as a means of laying our case before the conscience of the local and national community. We were not unmindful of the difficulties involved. So we decided to go through a process of self-purification. We started having workshops on nonviolence and repeatedly asked ourselves the questions, "Are you able to accept blows without retaliating?" "Are you able to endure the ordeals of jail?"

We decided to set our direct action program around the Easter season, realizing that with the exception of Christmas, this was the largest shopping period of the year. Knowing that a strong economic withdrawal program would be the by-product of direct action, we felt that this was the best time to bring pressure on the merchants for the needed changes. Then it occurred to us that the March election was ahead, and so we speedily decided to postpone action until after election day. When we discovered that Mr. Connor was in the run-off, we decided again to postpone so that the demonstrations could not be used to cloud the issues. At this time we agreed to begin our nonviolent witness the day after the run-off.

This reveals that we did not move irresponsibly into direct action. We too wanted to see Mr. Conner defeated; so we went through postponement after postponement to aid in this community need. After this we felt that direct action could be delayed no longer.

You may well ask, "Why direct action? Why sit-ins, marches, etc.? Isn't negotiation a better path?" You are exactly right in your call for negotiation. Indeed, this is the purpose of direct action. Nonviolent direct action seeks to create such a crisis and establish such creative tension that a community that has constantly refused to negotiate is forced to confront the issue. It seeks so to dramatize the issue that it can no longer be ignored. I just referred to the creation of tension as a part of the work of the nonviolent resister. This may sound rather shocking. But I must confess that I am not afraid of the word tension. I have earnestly worked and preached against violent tension, but there is a type of constructive nonviolent tension that is necessary for growth. Just as Socrates felt that it was necessary to create a tension in the mind so that individuals could rise from the bondage of myths and half-truths to the unfettered realm of creative analysis and objective appraisal, we must see the need of having nonviolent gadflies to create the kind of tension in society that will help men rise from the dark depths of prejudice and racism to the majestic heights of understanding and brotherhood. So the purpose of the direct action is to create a situation so crisis-packed that it will inevitably open the door to negotiation. We, therefore, concur with you in your call for negotiation. Too long has our beloved Southland been bogged down in the tragic attempt to live in monologue rather than dialogue.

One of the basic points in your statement is that our acts are untimely. Some have asked, "Why didn't you give the new administration time to act?" The only answer that I can give to this inquiry is that the new administration must be prodded about as much as the outgoing one before it acts. We will be sadly mistaken if we feel that the election of Mr. Boutwell will bring the millennium to Birmingham. While Mr. Boutwell is much more articulate and gentle than Mr. Connor, they are both segregationists dedicated to the task of maintaining the status quo. The hope I see in Mr. Boutwell is that he will be reasonable enough to see the futility of massive resistance to desgregation. But he will not see this without pressure from the devotees of civil rights. My friends, I must say to you that we have not made a single gain in civil rights without determined legal and nonviolent pressure. History is the long and tragic story of the fact that privileged groups seldom give up their privileges voluntarily. Individuals may see the moral light and voluntarily give up their unjust posture; but as Reinhold Niebuhr has reminded us, groups are more immoral than individuals.

We know through painful experience that freedom is never voluntarily given by the oppressor; it must be demanded by the oppressed. Frankly I have never yet engaged in a direct action movement that was "well timed," according to the timetable of those who have not suffered unduly from the disease of segregation. For years now I have heard the word "Wait!" It rings in the ear of every Negro with a piercing familiarity. This "wait" has almost always meant "never." It has been a tranquilizing thalidomide, relieving the emotional stress for a moment, only to give birth to an ill-formed infant of frustration. We must come to see with the distinguished jurist of yesterday that "justice too long delayed is justice denied." We have waited for more than three hundred and forty years for our constitutional and God-given rights. The nations of Asia and Africa are moving with jet-like speed toward the goal of political independence, and we still creep at horse and buggy pace toward the gaining of a cup of coffee at a lunch counter.

I guess it is easy for those who have never felt the stinging darts of segregation to say wait. But when you have seen vicious mobs lynch your mothers and fathers at will and drown your sisters and brothers at whim; when you have seen hate filled policemen curse, kick, brutalize, and even kill your black brothers and sisters with impunity; when you see the vast majority of your twenty million Negro brothers smothering in an air-tight cage of poverty in the midst of an affluent society; when you suddenly find your tongue twisted and your speech stammering as you seek to explain to your six-year-old daughter why she can't go to the public amusement park that has just been advertised on television, and see tears welling up in her little eyes when she is told that Funtown is closed to colored children, and see the depressing clouds of inferiority begin to form in her little mental sky, and see her begin to distort her little personality by unconsciously developing a bitterness toward white people; when you have to concoct an answer for a five-year-old son asking in agonizing pathos: "Daddy, why do white people treat colored people so mean?"; when you take a cross country drive and find it necessary to sleep night after night in the uncomfortable corners of your automobile because no motel will accept you; when you are humiliated day in and day out by nagging signs reading "white" men and "colored"; when your first name becomes "nigger" and your middle name becomes "boy" (however old you are) and your last name becomes "John," and when your wife and mother are never given the respected title "Mrs."; when you are harried by day and haunted by night by the fact that you are a Negro, living constantly at tip-toe stance never quite knowing what to expect next, and plagued with inner fears and outer resentments; when you are forever fighting a degenerating sense of "nobodiness";—then you will understand why we find it difficult to wait. There comes a time when the cup of endurance runs over, and men are no longer willing to be plunged into an abyss of injustice where they experience the bleakness of corroding despair. I hope, sirs, you can understand our legitimate and unavoidable impatience.

You express a great deal of anxiety over our willingness to break laws. This is certainly a legitimate concern. Since we so diligently urge people to obey the Supreme Court's decision of 1954 outlawing segregation in the public schools, it is rather strange and paradoxical to find us consciously breaking laws. One may well ask, "How can you advocate breaking some laws and obeying others?" The answer is found in the fact that there are two types of laws. There are *just* laws and there are *unjust* laws. I would be the first to advocate obeying just laws. One has not only a legal but moral responsibility to obey just laws. Conversely, one has a moral responsibility to disobey unjust laws. I would agree with Saint Augustine that "An unjust law is no law at all."

Now what is the difference between the two? How does one determine when a law is just or unjust? A just law is a man-made code that squares with the moral law or the law of God. An unjust law is a code that is out of harmony with the moral law. To put it in the terms of Saint Thomas Aquinas, an unjust law is a human law that is not rooted in eternal and natural law. Any law that uplifts human personality is just. Any law that degrades human personality is unjust. All segregation statutes are unjust because segregation distorts the soul and damages the personality. It gives the segregator a false sense of superiority and the segregated a false sense of inferiority. To use the words of Martin Buber, the great Jewish philosopher, segregation substitutes an "I-it" relationship for the "I-thou" relationship, and ends up relegating persons to the status of things. So segregation is not only politically, economically, and sociologically unsound, but it is morally wrong and sinful. Paul Tillich has said that sin is separation. Isn't segregation an existential expression of man's tragic separation, an expression of his awful estrangement, his terrible sinfulness? So I can urge men to obey the 1954 decision of the Supreme Court because it is morally right, and I can urge them to disobey segregation ordinances because they are morally wrong.

Let us turn to a more concrete example of just and unjust laws. An unjust law is a code that a majority inflicts on a minority that is not binding on itself. This is *difference* made legal. On the other hand a just law is a code that a majority compels a minority to follow that it is willing to follow itself. This is *sameness* made legal.

Let me give another explanation. An unjust law is a code inflicted upon a minority which that minority had no part in enacting or creating because they did not have the unhampered right to vote. Who can say the legislature of Alabama which set up the segregation laws was democratically elected? Throughout the state of Alabama all types of conniving methods are used to prevent Negroes from becoming registered voters and there are some counties without a single Negro registered to vote despite the fact that the Negro constitutes a majority of the population. Can any law set up in such a state be considered democratically structured?

These are just a few examples of unjust and just laws. There are some instances when a law is just on its face but unjust in its application. For instance, I was arrested Friday on a charge of parading without a permit. Now there is nothing wrong with an ordinance which requires a permit for a parade, but when the ordinance is used to preserve segregation and to deny citizens the First Amendment privilege of peaceful assembly and peaceful protest, then it becomes unjust.

I hope you can see the distinction I am trying to point out. In no sense do I advocate evading or defying the law as the rabid segregationist would do. This would lead to anarchy. One who breaks an unjust law must do it *openly*, *lovingly* (not hatefully as the white mothers did in New Orleans when they were seen on television screaming "nigger, nigger, nigger") and with a willingness to accept the penalty. I submit that an individual who breaks a law that conscience tells him is unjust, and willingly accepts the penalty by staying in jail to arouse the conscience of the community over its injustice, is in reality expressing the very highest respect for law.

Of course there is nothing new about this kind of civil disobedience. It was seen sublimely in the refusal of Shadrach, Meshach, and Abednego to obey the laws of Nebuchadnezzar because a higher moral law was involved. It was practiced superbly by the early Christians who were willing to face hungry lions and the excruciating pain of chopping blocks, before submitting to certain unjust laws of the Roman Empire. To a degree academic freedom is a reality today because Socrates practiced civil disobedience.

We can never forget that everything Hitler did in Germany was "legal" and everything the Hungarian freedom fighters did in Hungary was "illegal." It was "illegal" to aid and comfort a Jew in Hitler's Germany. But I am sure that, if I had lived in Germany during that time, I would have aided and comforted my Jewish brothers even though it was illegal. If I lived in a communist country today where certain principles dear to the Christian faith are suppressed, I believe I would openly advocate disobeying those antireligious laws.

I must make two honest confessions to you, my Christian and Jewish brothers. First I must confess that over the last few years I have been gravely disappointed with the white moderate. I have almost reached the regrettable conclusion that the Negroes' great stumbling block in the stride toward freedom is not the White Citizens' "Counciler" or the Ku Klux Klanner, but the white moderate who is more devoted to "order" than to justice; who prefers a negative peace which is the absence of tension to a positive peace which is the presence of justice; who constantly says "I agree with you in the goal you seek, but I can't agree with your methods of direct action"; who paternalistically feels that he can set the timetable for another man's freedom; who lives by the myth of time and who constantly advises the Negro to wait until a "more convenient season." Shallow understanding from people of good will is more frustrating than absolute misunderstanding from people of ill will. Lukewarm acceptance is much more bewildering than outright rejection.

I had hoped that the white moderate would understand that law and order exist for the purpose of establishing justice, and that when they fail to do this they become the dangerously structured dams that block the flow of social progress. I had hoped that the white moderate would understand that the present tension in the South is merely a necessary phase of the transition from an obnoxious negative peace, where the Negro passively accepted his unjust plight, to a substance-filled positive peace, where all men will respect the dignity and worth of human personality. Actually, we who engage in nonviolent direct action are not the creators of tension. We merely bring to the surface the hidden tension that is already alive. We bring it out in the open where it can be seen and dealt with. Like a boil that can never be cured as long as it is covered up but must be opened with all its pus-flowing ugliness to the natural medicines of air and light, injustice must likewise be exposed, with all of the tension its exposing creates, to the light of human conscience and the air of national opinion before it can be cured.

In your statement you asserted that our actions, even though peaceful, must be condemned because they precipitate violence. But can this assertion be logically made? Isn't this like condemning the robbed man because his possession of money precipitated the evil act of robbery? Isn't this like condemning Socrates because his unswerving commitment to truth and his philosophical delvings precipitated the misguided popular mind to make him drink the hemlock? Isn't this like condemning Jesus because His unique God consciousness and never-ceasing devotion to His will precipitated the evil act of crucifixion? We must come to see, as federal courts have consistently affirmed, that it is immoral to urge an individual to withdraw his efforts to gain his basic constitutional rights because the quest precipitates violence. Society must protect the robbed and punish the robber.

I had also hoped that the white moderate would reject the myth of time. I received a letter this morning from a white brother in Texas which said: "All Christians know that the colored people will receive equal rights eventually, but is it possible that you are in too great of a religious hurry? It has taken Christianity almost 2000 years to accomplish what it has. The teachings of Christ take time to come to earth." All that is said here grows out of a tragic misconception of time. It is the strangely irrational notion that there is something in the very flow of time that will inevitably cure all ills. Actually time is neutral. It can be used either destructively or constructively. I am coming to feel that the people of ill will have used time much more effectively than the people of good will. We will have to repent in this generation not merely for the vitriolic words and actions of the bad people, but for the appalling silence of the good people. We must come to see that human progress never rolls in on wheels of inevitability. It comes through the tireless efforts and persistent work of men willing to be co-workers with God, and without this hard work time itself becomes an ally of the forces of social stagnation.

We must use time creatively, and forever realize that the time is always ripe to do right. Now is the time to make real the promise of democracy, and transform our pending national elegy into a creative psalm of brotherhood. Now is the time to lift our national policy from the quicksand of racial injustice to the solid rock of human dignity.

You spoke of our activity in Birmingham as extreme. At first I was rather disappointed that fellow clergymen would see my nonviolent efforts as those of the extremist. I started thinking about the fact that I stand in the middle of two opposing forces in the Negro community. One is a force of complacency made up of Negroes who, as a result of long years of oppression, have been so completely drained of self-respect and a sense of "somebodiness" that they have adjusted to segregation, and of a few Negroes in the middle class who, because of a degree of academic and economic security, and because at points they profit by segregation, have unconsciously become insensitive to the problems of the masses. The other force is one of bitterness and hatred and comes perilously close to advocating violence. It is expressed in the various black nationalist groups that are springing up over the nation, the largest and best known being Elijah Muhammad's Muslim movement. This movement is nourished by the contemporary frustration over the continued existence of racial discrimination. It is made up of people who have lost faith in America, who have absolutely repudiated Christianity, and who have concluded that the white man is an incurable "devil." I have tried to stand between these two forces saying that we need not follow the "do-nothingism" of the complacent or the hatred and despair of the black nationalist. There is the more excellent way of love and nonviolent protest. I'm grateful to God that, through the Negro church, the dimension of nonviolence entered our struggle. If this philosophy had not emerged I am convinced that by now many streets of the South would be flowing with floods of blood. And I am further convinced that if our white brothers dismiss us as "rabble rousers" and "outside agitators"—those of us who are working through the channels of nonviolent direct action—and refuse to support our nonviolent efforts, millions of Negroes, out of frustration and despair, will seek solace and security in black nationalist ideologies, a development that will lead inevitably to a frightening racial nightmare.

Oppressed people cannot remain oppressed forever. The urge for freedom will eventually come. This is what has happened to the American Negro. Something within has reminded him of his birthright of freedom; something without has reminded him that he can gain it. Consciously and unconsciously, he has been swept in by what the Germans call the *Zeitgeist*, and with his black brothers of Africa, and his brown and yellow brothers of Asia, South America, and the Caribbean, he is moving with a sense of cosmic urgency toward the promised land of racial justice. Recognizing this vital urge that has engulfed the Negro community, one should readily understand public demonstrations. The Negro has many pent-up resentments and latent frustrations. He has to get them out. So let him march sometime; let him have his prayer pilgrimages to the city hall; understand why he must have sit-ins and freedom rides. If his repressed emotions do not come out in these nonviolent ways, they will come out in ominous expressions of violence. This is not a threat; it is a fact of history. So I have not said to my people, "Get rid of your discontent." But I have tried to say that this normal and healthy discontent can be channeled through the creative outlet of nonviolent direct action. Now this approach is being dismissed as extremist. I must admit that I was initially disappointed in being so categorized.

But as I continued to think about the matter I gradually gained a bit of satisfaction from being considered an extremist. Was not Jesus an extremist in love? "Love your enemies, bless them that curse you, pray for them that despitefully use you." Was not Amos an extremist for justice—"Let justice roll down like waters and righteousness like a mighty stream." Was not Paul an extremist for the gospel of Jesus Christ—"I bear in my body the marks of the Lord Jesus." Was not Martin Luther an extremist—"Here I stand; I can do none other so help me God." Was not John Bunyan an extremist—"I will stay in jail to the end of my days before I make a butchery of my conscience." Was not Abraham Lincoln an extremist—"This nation cannot survive half slave and half free." Was not Thomas Jefferson an extremist—"We hold these truths to be self evident that all men are created equal." So the question is not whether we will be extremist but what kind of extremist will we be. Will we be extremists for hate or will we be extremists for love? Will we be extremists for the preservation of injustice—or will we be extremists for the cause of justice? In that dramatic scene on Calvary's hill three men were crucified. We must never forget that all three were crucified for the same crime—the crime of extremism. Two were extremists for immorality, and thus fell below their environment. The other, Jesus Christ, was an extremist for love, truth, and goodness, and thereby rose above His environment. So, after all, maybe the South, the nation, and the world are in dire need of creative extremists.

I had hoped that the white moderate would see this. Maybe I was too optimistic. Maybe I expected too much. I guess I should have realized that few members of a race that has oppressed another race can understand or appreciate the deep groans and passionate yearnings of those that have been oppressed, and still fewer have the vision to see that injustice must be rooted out by strong, persistent, and determined action. I am thankful, however, that some of our white brothers have grasped the meaning of this social revolution and committed themselves to it. They are still all too small in quantity, but they are big in quality. Some like Ralph McGill, Lillian Smith, Harry Golden, and James Dabbs have written about our struggle in eloquent, prophetic, and understanding terms. Others have marched with us down nameless streets of the South. They have languished in filthy, roach-infested jails, suffering the abuse and brutality of angry policemen who see them as "dirty nigger lovers." They, unlike so many of their moderate brothers and sisters, have recognized the urgency of the moment and sensed the need for powerful "action" antidotes to combat the disease of segregation.

Let me rush on to mention my other disappointment. I have been so greatly disappointed with the white Church and its leadership. Of course there are some notable exceptions. I am not unmindful of the fact that each of you has taken some significant stands on this issue. I commend you, Rev. Stallings, for your Christian stand on this past Sunday, in welcoming Negroes to your worship service on a nonsegregated basis. I commend the Catholic leaders of this state for integrating Springhill College several years ago.

But despite these notable exceptions I must honestly reiterate that I have been disappointed with the Church. I do not say that as one of those negative critics who can always find something wrong with the Church. I say it as a minister of the gospel, who loves the Church; who was nurtured in its bosom; who has been sustained by its spiritual blessings and who will remain true to it as long as the cord of life shall lengthen.

I had the strange feeling when I was suddenly catapulted into the leadership of the bus protest in Montgomery several years ago that we would have the support of the white Church. I felt that the white ministers, priests, and rabbis of the South would be some of our strongest allies. Instead, some have been outright opponents, refusing to understand the freedom movement and misrepresenting its leaders; all too many others have been more cautious than courageous and have remained silent behind the anesthetizing security of stained glass windows.

In spite of my shattered dreams of the past, I came to Birmingham with the hope that the white religious leadership of the community would see the justice of our cause and, with deep moral concern, serve as the channel through which our just grievances could get to the power structure. I had hoped that each of you would understand. But again I have been disappointed.

I have heard numerous religious leaders of the South call upon their worshippers to comply with a desegregation decision because it is the law, but I have longed to hear white ministers say follow this decree because integration is morally right and the Negro is your brother. In the midst of blatant injustices inflicted upon the Negro, I have watched white churches stand on the sideline and merely mouth pious irrelevancies and sanctimonious trivialities. In the midst of a mighty struggle to rid our nation of racial and economic injustice, I have heard so many ministers say, "Those are social issues with which the Gospel has no real concern," and I have watched so many churches commit themselves to a completely other-worldly religion which made a strange distinction between body and soul, the sacred and the secular.

So here we are moving toward the exit of the twentieth century with a religious community largely adjusted to the status quo, standing as a tail light behind other community agencies rather than a headlight leading men to higher levels of justice.

I have travelled the length and breadth of Alabama, Mississippi, and all the other Southern states. On sweltering summer days and crisp autumn mornings I have looked at her beautiful churches with their spires pointing heavenward. I have beheld the impressive outlay of her massive religious education buildings. Over and over again I have found myself asking: "Who worships here? Who is their God? Where were their voices when the lips of Governor Barnett dripped with words of interposition and nullification? Where were they when Governor Wallace gave the clarion call for defiance and hatred? Where were their voices of support when tired, bruised, and weary Negro men and women decided to rise from the dark dungeons of complacency to the bright hills of creative protest?"

Yes, these questions are still in my mind. In deep disappointment, I have wept over the laxity of the Church. But be assured that my tears have been tears of love. There can be no deep disappointment where there is not deep love. Yes, I love the Church; I love her sacred walls. How could I do otherwise? I am in the rather unique position of being the son, the grandson, and the great grandson of preachers. Yes, I see the Church as the body of Christ. But, oh! How we have blemished and scarred that body through social neglect and fear of being nonconformists.

There was a time when the Church was very powerful. It was during that period when the early Christians rejoiced when they were deemed worthy to suffer for what they believed. In those days the Church was not merely a thermometer that recorded the ideas and principles of popular opinion; it was a thermostat that transformed the mores of society. Wherever the early Christians entered a town the power structure got disturbed and immediately sought to convict them for being "disturbers of the peace" and "outside agitators." But they went on with the conviction that they were a "colony of heaven" and had to obey God rather than man. They were small in number but big in commitment. They were too God-intoxicated to be "astronomically intimidated." They brought an end to such ancient evils as infanticide and gladiatorial contest.

Things are different now. The contemporary Church is so often a weak, ineffectual voice with an uncertain sound. It is so often the archsupporter of the status quo. Far from being disturbed by the presence of the Church, the power structure of the average community is consoled by the Church's silent and often vocal sanction of things as they are.

But the judgment of God is upon the Church as never before. If the Church of today does not recapture the sacrificial spirit of the early Church, it will lose its authentic ring, forfeit the loyalty of millions, and be dismissed as an irrelevant social club with no meaning for the twentieth century. I am meeting young people every day whose disappointment with the Church has risen to outright disgust.

Maybe again I have been too optimistic. Is organized religion too inextricably bound to the status quo to save our nation and the world? Maybe I must turn my faith to the inner spiritual Church, the church within the Church, as the true *ecclesia* and the hope of the world. But again I am thankful to God that some noble souls from the ranks of organized religion have broken loose from the paralyzing chains of conformity and joined us as active partners in the struggle for freedom. They have left their secure congregations and walked the streets of Albany, Georgia, with us. They have gone through the highways of the South on torturous rides for freedom. Yes, they have gone to jail with us. Some have been kicked out of their churches and lost the support of their bishops and fellow ministers. But they have gone with the faith that right defeated is stronger than evil triumphant. These men have been the leaven in the lump of the race. Their witness has been the spiritual salt that has preserved the true meaning of the Gospel in these troubled times. They have carved a tunnel of hope through the dark mountain of disappointment.

I hope the Church as a whole will meet the challenge of this decisive hour. But even if the Church does not come to the aid of justice, I have no despair about the future. I have no fear about the outcome of our struggle in Birmingham, even if our motives are presently misunderstood. We will reach the goal of freedom in Birmingham and all over the nation, because the goal of America is freedom. Abused and scorned though we may be, our destiny is tied up with the destiny of America. Before the pilgrims landed at Plymouth, we were here. Before the pen of Jefferson etched across the pages of history the majestic words of the Declaration of Independence, we were here. For more than two centuries our foreparents labored in this country without wages; they made cotton "king"; and they built the homes of their masters in the midst of brutal injustice and shameful humiliation—and yet out of a bottomless vitality they continued to thrive and develop. If the inexpressible cruelties of slavery could not stop us, the opposition we now face will surely fail. We will win our freedom because the sacred heritage of our nation and the eternal will of God are embodied in our echoing demands.

I must close now. But before closing I am impelled to mention one other point in your statement that troubled me profoundly. You warmly commended the Birmingham police force for keeping "order" and "preventing violence." I don't believe you would have so warmly commended the police force if you had seen its angry violent dogs literally biting six unarmed, nonviolent Negroes. I don't believe you would so quickly commend the policemen if you would observe their ugly and inhuman treatment of Negroes here in the city jail; if you would watch them push and curse old Negro women and young Negro girls; if you would see them slap and kick old Negro men and young Negro boys; if you will observe them, as they did on two occasions, refuse to give us food because we wanted to sing our grace together. I'm sorry that I can't join you in your praise for the police department.

It is true that they have been rather disciplined in their public handling of the demonstrators. In this sense they have been rather publicly "nonviolent." But for what purpose? To preserve the evil system of segregation. Over the last few years I have consistently preached that nonviolence demands that the means we use must be as pure as the ends we seek. So I have tried to make it clear that it is wrong to use immoral means to attain moral ends. But now I must affirm that it is just as wrong, or even more so, to use moral means to preserve immoral ends. Maybe Mr. Connor and his policemen have been rather publicly nonviolent, as Chief Prichett was in Albany, Georgia, but they have used the moral means of nonviolence to maintain the immoral end of flagrant racial injustice. T. S. Eliot has said that there is no greater treason than to do the right deed for the wrong reason.

I wish you had commended the Negro sit-inners and demonstrators of Birmingham for their sublime courage, their willingness to suffer, and their amazing discipline in the midst of the most inhuman provocation. One day the South will recognize its real heroes. They will be the James Merediths, courageously and with a majestic sense of purpose, facing jeering and hostile mobs and the agonizing loneliness that characterizes the life of the pioneer. They will be old, oppressed, battered Negro women, symbolized in a seventy-two year old woman of Montgomery, Alabama, who rose up with a sense of dignity and with her people decided not to ride the segregated buses, and responded to one who inquired about her tiredness with ungrammatical profundity: "My feets is tired, but my soul is rested." They will be young high school and college students, young ministers of the gospel and a host of the elders, courageously and nonviolently sitting in at lunch counters and willingly going to jail for conscience sake. One day the South will know that when these disinherited children of God sat down at lunch counters they were in reality standing up for the best in the American dream and the most sacred values in our Judeo-Christian heritage, and thus carrying our whole nation back to great wells of democracy which were dug deep by the founding fathers in the formulation of the Constitution and the Declaration of Independence.

Never before have I written a letter this long (or should I say a book?). I'm afraid that it is much too long to take your precious time. I can assure you that it would have been much shorter if I had been writing from a comfortable desk, but what else is there to do when you are alone for days in the dull monotony of a narrow jail cell other than write long letters, think strange thoughts, and pray long prayers?

If I have said anything in this letter that is an overstatement of the truth and is indicative of an unreasonable impatience, I beg you to forgive me. If I have said anything in this letter that is an understatement of the truth and is indicative of my having a patience that makes me patient with anything less than brotherhood, I beg God to forgive me.

I hope this letter finds you strong in the faith. I also hope that circumstances will soon make it possible for me to meet each of you, not as an integrationist or a civil rights leader, but as a fellow clergyman and a Christian brother. Let us all hope that the dark clouds of racial prejudice will soon pass away and the deep fog of misunderstanding will be lifted from our fear-drenched communities and in some not too distant tomorrow the radiant stars of love and brotherhood will shine over our great nation with all of their scintillating beauty.

Yours for the cause of
Peace and Brotherhood

MARTIN LUTHER KING, JR.

EQUALITY AND DIFFERENCE

MARGARET MEAD

Margaret Mead (1901–1978) was an outstanding anthropologist whose pioneering field studies are still regarded as classics. Born in Philadelphia, the daughter of an economist and a sociologist, she first wanted to be a painter. In college she began as an English major, but in her senior year at Barnard she took a course from the eminent anthropologist Franz Boas. His teaching and subsequently that of Ruth Benedict turned her to anthropology. She received her B.A. from Barnard in 1923, an M.A. in psychology from Columbia in 1924, and in 1925 completed her doctoral thesis on cultural stability in Polynesia; it was published in Germany in 1928. In 1925 she went on her first field expedition to the Samoan island of Tau to study the development of the adolescent girl under primitive conditions. This led to the publication of Coming of Age in Samoa *(1928), still a widely read classic in the field. In 1928 she went to the Admiralty Islands to study the children of the Manus Tribe (*Growing Up in New Guinea, *1930). These and other early field trips are described in her autobiography,* Blackberry Winter: My Early Years *(1972).*

The study of native people in the Pacific was a central interest throughout her life, and she mastered seven primitive languages, but in later years her work turned to contemporary culture. Long the curator of ethnology at the American Museum of Natural History in New York, she taught at many colleges and universities, received many honors, and was the author of many books. These include Sex and Temperament *(1935), followed by* Male and Female: A Study of the Sexes in a Changing World *(1949),* Continuities in Cultural Evolution *(1964),* Culture and Commitment *(1970), and, with James Baldwin,* A Rap on Race *(1971). She also co-authored two books with fellow anthropologist Rhoda Mentraux:* Themes in French Culture *(1954) and* A Way of Seeing *(1970) from which we print the chapter below.*

The Egalitarian Error

Almost all Americans want to be democratic, but many Americans are confused about what, exactly, democracy means. How do you know when someone is acting in a democratic—or an undemocratic—way? Recently several groups have spoken out with particular bitterness against the kind of democracy that means equal opportunity for all, regardless of race or national origin. They act as if all human beings did not belong to one species, as if some races of mankind were inferior to others in their capacity to learn what members of other races know and have invented. Other extremists attack religious groups—Jews or Catholics—or deny the right of an individual to be an agnostic. One reason that these extremists, who explicitly do not want to be democratic, can get a hearing even though their views run counter to the Constitution and our traditional values is that the people who *do* want to be democratic are frequently so muddled.

For many Americans, democratic behavior necessitates an outright denial of any significant differences among human beings. In their eyes it is undemocratic for anyone to refer, in the presence of any other person, to differences in skin color, manners or religious beliefs. Whatever one's private thoughts may be, it is necessary always to act as if everyone were exactly alike.

Behavior of this kind developed partly as a reaction to those who discriminated against or actively abused members of other groups. But it is artificial, often hypocritical behavior, nonetheless, and it dulls and flattens human relationships. If two people can't talk easily and comfortably but must forever guard against some slip of the tongue, some admission of what is in both persons' minds, they are likely to talk as little as possible. This embarrassment about differences reaches a final absurdity when a Methodist feels that he cannot take a guest on a tour of his garden because he might have to identify a wild plant with a blue flower, called the wandering Jew, or when a white lecturer feels he ought not to mention the name of Conrad's beautiful story *The Nigger of the "Narcissus."* But it is no less absurd when well-meaning people, speaking of the physically handicapped, tell prospective employers: "They don't want special consideration. Ask as much of them as you do of everyone else, and fire them if they don't give satisfaction!"

Another version of false democracy is the need to deny the existence of personal advantages. Inherited wealth, famous parents, a first-class mind, a rare voice, a beautiful face, an exceptional physical skill—any advantage has to be minimized or denied. Continually watched and measured, the man or woman who is rich or talented or well educated is likely to be called "undemocratic" whenever he does anything out of the ordinary—more or less of something than others do. If he wants acceptance, the person with a "superior" attribute, like the person with an "inferior" attribute, often feels obliged to take on a protective disguise, to act as if he were just like everybody else. One denies difference; the other minimizes it. And both believe, as they conform to these false standards, that they act in the name of democracy.

For many Americans, a related source of confusion is success. As a people we Americans greatly prize success. And in our eyes success all too often means simply outdoing other people by virtue of achievement judged by some single scale—income or honors or headlines or trophies—and coming out at "the top." Only one person, as we see it, can be the best—can get the highest grades, be voted the most attractive girl or the boy most likely to succeed. Though we often rejoice in the success of people far removed from ourselves—in another profession, another community, or endowed with a talent that we do not covet—we tend to regard the success of people close at hand, within our own small group, as a threat. We fail to realize that there are many kinds of success, including the kind of success that lies within a person. We do not realize, for example, that there could be in the same class one hundred boys and girls—each of them a "success" in a different kind of way. Individuality is again lost in a refusal to recognize and cherish the differences among people.

The attitude that measures success by a single yardstick and isolates the *one* winner and the kind of "democracy" that denies or minimizes differences among people are both deeply destructive. Imagine for a moment a family with two sons, one of whom is brilliant, attractive and athletic while the other is dull, unattractive and clumsy. Both boys attend the same high school. In the interest of the slower boy, the parents would want the school to set equally low standards for everyone. Lessons should be easy; no one should be forced to study dead languages or advanced mathematics in order to graduate. Athletics should be noncompetitive; every boy should have a chance to enjoy playing games. Everyone should be invited to all the parties. As for special attention to gifted children, this is not fair to the other children. An all-round education should be geared to the average, normal child.

But in the interest of the other boy, these same parents would have quite opposite goals. After all, we need highly trained people; the school should do the most it can for its best students. Funds should be made available for advanced classes and special teachers, for the best possible coach, the best athletic equipment. Young people should be allowed to choose friends on their own level. The aim of education should be to produce topflight students.

This is an extreme example, but it illustrates the completely incompatible aims that can arise in this kind of "democracy." Must our country shut its eyes to the needs of either its gifted or its less gifted sons? It would be a good deal more sensible to admit, as some schools do today, that children differ widely from one another, that all successes cannot be ranged on one single scale, that there is room in a real democracy to help each child find his own level and develop to his fullest potential.

Moving now to a wider scene, before World War I Americans thought of themselves as occupying a unique place in the world—and there was no question in most minds that this country was a "success." True, Europeans might look down on us for our lack of culture, but with a few notable, local exceptions, we simply refused to compete on European terms. There was no country in the world remotely like the one we were building. But since World War II we have felt the impact of a country whose size and strength and emphasis on national achievement more closely parallel our own. To-day we are ahead of Russia, or Russia is ahead of us. Nothing else matters. Instead of valuing and developing the extraordinary assets and potential of our country for their own sake, we are involved in a simple set of competitions for wealth and power and dominance.

These are expensive and dangerous attitudes. When democracy ceases to be a cherished way of life and becomes instead the name of one team, we are using the word democracy to describe behavior that places us and all other men in jeopardy.

Individually, nationally and, today, internationally, the misreading of the phrase "all men are created equal" exacts a heavy price. The attitudes that follow from our misconceptions may be compatible with life in a country where land and rank and prestige are severely limited and the roads to success are few. But they are inappropriate in a land as rich, as open, as filled with opportunities as our own. They are the price we pay for being *less* democratic than we claim to be.

"All men are created equal" does not mean that all men are the same. What it does mean is that each should be accorded full respect and full rights as a unique human being—full respect for his humanity *and* for his differences from other people.

KURT VONNEGUT, JR.

College-age readers could be said to have discovered Kurt Vonnegut, Jr., with Cat's Cradle *(1963); he has enjoyed great popularity ever since. Born in Indianapolis in 1922, he went to the Indianapolis public schools, which, he says, "were superb during the Great Depression." He then studied chemistry at Cornell University for three years but left after an illness and joined the army. This was during World War II; he served in Europe and found himself a prisoner in a meat locker under a slaughterhouse during the fire bombing of Dresden, Germany, an experience that stayed memorable and later found its way into his writings, particularly* Slaughterhouse-Five *(1969). After the war he studied anthropology at the University of Chicago (as a graduate student, although he had no undergraduate degree), became a police reporter, and then worked in a General Electric research laboratory. When his stories began to sell, he left GE, but his experience there led to his first novel,* Player Piano *(1952). Since then, Vonnegut has been a free-lance writer and occasional teacher and lecturer. In 1970, he also helped establish a movie company,* Sourdough Productions. *His best-known novels include* Mother Night *(1961),* God Bless You, Mr. Rosewater *(1965),* Breakfast of Champions *(1973), and* Jailbird *(1979). He has written plays (*Penelope, *1960, later revised as* Happy Birthday, Wanda June, *1972; and* Between Time and Timbuktu, *1973), and short stories. The short story we reprint here appeared in a collection of short works,* Welcome to the Monkey House *(1968). Once asked what kind of writer he would like to be known as, Vonnegut replied, "George Orwell."*

Harrison Bergeron

The year was 2081, and everybody was finally equal. They weren't only equal before God and the law. They were equal every which way. Nobody was smarter than anybody else. Nobody was better looking than anybody else. Nobody was stronger or quicker than anybody else. All this equality was due to the 211th, 212th, and 213th Amendments to the Constitution, and to the unceasing vigilance of agents of the United States Handicapper General.

Some things about living still weren't quite right, though. April, for instance, still drove people crazy by not being springtime. And it was in that clammy month that the H-G men took George and Hazel Bergeron's fourteen-year-old son, Harrison, away.

It was tragic, all right, but George and Hazel couldn't think about it very hard. Hazel had a perfectly average intelligence, which meant she couldn't think about anything except in short bursts. And George, while his intelligence was way above normal, had a little mental handicap radio in his ear. He was required by law to wear it at all times. It was tuned to a government transmitter. Every twenty seconds or so, the transmitter would send out some sharp noise to keep people like George from taking unfair advantage of their brains.

George and Hazel were watching television. There were tears on Hazel's cheeks, but she'd forgotten for the moment what they were about.

On the television screen were ballerinas.

A buzzer sounded in George's head. His thoughts fled in panic, like bandits from a burglar alarm.

"That was a real pretty dance, that dance they just did," said Hazel.

"Huh?" said George.

"That dance—it was nice," said Hazel.

"Yup," said George. He tried to think a little about the ballerinas. They weren't really very good—no better than anybody else would have been, anyway. They were burdened with sash-weights and bags of birdshot, and their faces were masked, so that no one, seeing a free and graceful gesture or a pretty face, would feel like something the cat drug in. George was toying with the vague notion that maybe dancers shouldn't be handicapped. But he didn't get very far with it before another noise in his ear radio scattered his thoughts.

George winced. So did two out of the eight ballerinas.

Hazel saw him wince. Having no mental handicap herself, she had to ask George what the latest sound had been.

"Sounded like somebody hitting a milk bottle with a ball peen hammer," said George.

"I'd think it would be real interesting, hearing all the different sounds," said Hazel, a little envious. "All the things they think up."

"Um," said George.

"Only, if I was Handicapper General, you know what I would do?" said Hazel. Hazel, as a matter of fact, bore a strong resemblance to the Handicapper General, a woman named Diana Moon Glampers. "If I was Diana Moon Glampers," said Hazel, "I'd have chimes on Sunday—just chimes. Kind of in honor of religion."

"I could think, if it was just chimes," said George.

"Well—maybe make 'em real loud," said Hazel. "I think I'd make a good Handicapper General."

"Good as anybody else," said George.

"Who knows better'n I do what normal is?" said Hazel.

"Right," said George. He began to think glimmeringly about his abnormal son who was now in jail, about Harrison, but a twenty-one-gun salute in his head stopped that.

"Boy!" said Hazel, "that was a doozy, wasn't it?"

It was such a doozy that George was white and trembling, and tears stood on the rims of his red eyes. Two of the eight ballerinas had collapsed to the studio floor, were holding their temples.

"All of a sudden you look so tired," said Hazel. "Why don't you stretch out on the sofa, so's you can rest your handicap bag on the pillows, honeybunch." She was referring to the forty-seven pounds of birdshot in a canvas bag, which was padlocked around George's neck. "Go on and rest the bag for a little while," she said. "I don't care if you're not equal to me for a while."

George weighed the bag with his hands. "I don't mind it," he said. "I don't notice it any more. It's just a part of me."

"You been so tired lately—kind of wore out," said Hazel. "If there was just some way we could make a little hole in the bottom of the bag, and just take out a few of them lead balls. Just a few."

"Two years in prison and two thousand dollars fine for every ball I took out," said George. "I don't call that a bargain."

"If you could just take a few out when you came home from work," said Hazel. "I mean—you don't compete with anybody around here. You just set around."

"If I tried to get away with it," said George, "then other people'd get away with it—and pretty soon we'd be right back to the dark ages again, with everybody competing against everybody else. You wouldn't like that, would you?"

"I'd hate it," said Hazel.

"There you are," said George. "The minute people start cheating on laws, what do you think happens to society?"

If Hazel hadn't been able to come up with an answer to this question, George couldn't have supplied one. A siren was going off in his head.

"Reckon it'd fall all apart," said Hazel.

"What would?" said George blankly.

"Society," said Hazel uncertainly. "Wasn't that what you just said?"

"Who knows?" said George.

The television program was suddenly interrupted for a news bulletin. It wasn't clear at first as to what the bulletin was about, since the announcer, like all announcers, had a serious speech impediment. For about half a minute, and in a state of high excitement, the announcer tried to say, "Ladies and gentlemen—"

He finally gave up, handed the bulletin to a ballerina to read.

"That's all right—" Hazel said of the announcer, "he tried. That's the big thing. He tried to do the best he could with what God gave him. He should get a nice raise for trying so hard."

"Ladies and gentlemen—" said the ballerina, reading the bulletin. She must have been extraordinarily beautiful, because the mask she wore was hideous. And it was easy to see that she was the strongest and most graceful of all the dancers, for her handicap bags were as big as those worn by two-hundred-pound men.

And she had to apologize at once for her voice, which was a very unfair voice for a woman to use. Her voice was a warm, luminous, timeless melody. "Excuse me—" she said, and she began again, making her voice absolutely uncompetitive.

"Harrison Bergeron, age fourteen," she said in a grackle squawk, "has just escaped from jail, where he was held on suspicion of plotting to overthrow the government. He is a genius and an athlete, is under-handicapped, and should be regarded as extremely dangerous."

A police photograph of Harrison Bergeron was flashed on the screen—upside down, then sideways, upside down again, then right side up. The picture showed the full length of Harrison against a background calibrated in feet and inches. He was exactly seven feet tall.

The rest of Harrison's appearance was Halloween and hardware. Nobody had ever borne heavier handicaps. He had outgrown hindrances faster than the H-G men could think them up. Instead of a little ear radio for a mental handicap, he wore a tremendous pair of earphones, and spectacles with thick wavy lenses. The spectacles were intended to make him not only half blind, but to give him whanging headaches besides.

Scrap metal was hung all over him. Ordinarily, there was a certain symmetry, a military neatness to the handicaps issued to strong people, but Harrison looked like a walking junkyard. In the race of life, Harrison carried three hundred pounds.

And to offset his good looks, the H-G men required that he wear at all times a red rubber ball for a nose, keep his eyebrows shaved off, and cover his even white teeth with black caps at snaggle-tooth random.

"If you see this boy," said the ballerina, "do not—I repeat, do not—try to reason with him."

There was the shriek of a door being torn from its hinges.

Screams and barking cries of consternation came from the television set. The photograph of Harrison Bergeron on the screen jumped again and again, as though dancing to the tune of an earthquake.

George Bergeron correctly identified the earthquake, and well he might have—for many was the time his own home had danced to the same crashing tune. "My God—" said George, "that must be Harrison!"

The realization was blasted from his mind instantly by the sound of an automobile collision in his head.

When George could open his eyes again, the photograph of Harrison was gone. A living, breathing Harrison filled the screen.

Clanking, clownish, and huge, Harrison stood in the center of the studio. The knob of the uprooted studio door was still in his hand. Ballerinas, technicians, musicians, and announcers cowered on their knees before him, expecting to die.

"I am the Emperor!" cried Harrison. "Do you hear? I am the Emperor! Everybody must do what I say at once!" He stamped his foot and the studio shook.

"Even as I stand here—" he bellowed, "crippled, hobbled, sickened—I am a greater ruler than any man who ever lived! Now watch me become what I *can* become!"

Harrison tore the straps of his handicap harness like wet tissue paper, tore straps guaranteed to support five thousand pounds.

Harrison's scrap-iron handicaps crashed to the floor.

Harrison thrust his thumbs under the bar of the padlock that secured his head harness. The bar snapped like celery. Harrison smashed his headphones and spectacles against the wall.

He flung away his rubber-ball nose, revealed a man that would have awed Thor, the god of thunder.

"I shall now select my Empress!" he said, looking down on the cowering people. "Let the first woman who dares rise to her feet claim her mate and her throne!"

A moment passed, and then a ballerina arose, swaying like a willow.

Harrison plucked the mental handicap from her ear, snapped off her physical handicaps with marvellous delicacy. Last of all, he removed her mask.

She was blindingly beautiful.

"Now—" said Harrison, taking her hand, "shall we show the people the meaning of the word dance? Music!" he commanded.

The musicians scrambled back into their chairs, and Harrison stripped them of their handicaps, too. "Play your best," he told them, "and I'll make you barons and dukes and earls."

The music began. It was normal at first—cheap, silly, false. But Harrison snatched two musicians from their chairs, waved them like batons as he sang the music as he wanted it played. He slammed them back into their chairs.

The music began again and was much improved.

Harrison and his Empress merely listened to the music for a while— listened gravely, as though synchronizing their heartbeats with it.

They shifted their weights to their toes.

Harrison placed his big hands on the girl's tiny waist, letting her sense the weightlessness that would soon be hers.

And then, in an explosion of joy and grace, into the air they sprang!

Not only were the laws of the land abandoned, but the law of gravity and the laws of motion as well.

They reeled, whirled, swiveled, flounced, capered, gamboled, and spun.

They leaped like deer on the moon.

The studio ceiling was thirty feet high, but each leap brought the dancers nearer to it.

It became their obvious intention to kiss the ceiling.

They kissed it.

And then, neutralizing gravity with love and pure will, they remained suspended in air inches below the ceiling, and they kissed each other for a long, long time.

It was then that Diana Moon Glampers, the Handicapper General, came into the studio with a double-barreled ten-gauge shotgun. She fired twice, and the Emperor and the Empress were dead before they hit the floor.

Diana Moon Glampers loaded the gun again. She aimed it at the musicians and told them they had ten seconds to get their handicaps back on.

It was then that the Bergerons' television tube burned out.

Hazel turned to comment about the blackout to George. But George had gone out into the kitchen for a can of beer.

George came back in with the beer, paused while a handicap signal shook him up. And then he sat down again. "You been crying?" he said to Hazel.

"Yup," she said.

"What about?" he said.

"I forget," she said. "Something real sad on television."

"What was it?" he said.

"It's all kind of mixed up in my mind," said Hazel.

"Forget sad things," said George.

"I always do," said Hazel.

"That's my girl," said George. He winced. There was the sound of a rivetting gun in his head.

"Gee—I could tell that one was a doozy," said Hazel.

"You can say that again," said George.

"Gee—" said Hazel, "I could tell that one was a doozy."

PEREGRINE WORSTHORNE

Peregrine Worsthorne was born in London in 1923 and educated at Oxford and Cambridge. Since 1950 he has been a newspaperman, first as Washington correspondent for the London Times, *then as lead writer and feature writer for the London* Daily Telegraph, *and since 1962 as deputy editor for the* Sunday Telegraph. *He has written for British television and radio programs and is the author of two books,* Dare Democracy Disengage? *(1958) and* The Socialist Myth *(1971). The selection following first appeared in the* Sunday Telegraph, *December 3, 1972.*

The New Inequality

To most of us it now seems very strange, almost incomprehensible, that for centuries gross hereditary inequalities of wealth, status and power were universally accepted as a divinely ordained fact of life. The lord in his castle, like the peasant at his gate, both believed that this was where God wished them to remain. If anybody had then suggested that such an arrangement was manifestly unfair he would have been dismissed as a little crazed, not to say blasphemous.

Modern man, as I say, finds this awfully difficult to understand. To him it seems absolutely axiomatic that each individual ought to be allowed to make his grade according to merit, regardless of the accident of birth. All positions of power, wealth and status should be open to talent. To the extent that this ideal is achieved a society is deemed to be just.

If our feudal forebears thought it perfectly fair that the lord should be in his castle and the peasant at his gate, their liberal successors—which means most of us—have tended to believe it to be fair enough that the man of merit should be on top and the man without merit should be underneath. Anybody who challenged this assumption was thought a little crazed.

Much of the current political and social malaise springs, in my view, from the increasing evidence that this assumption should be challenged. The ideal of a meritocracy no longer commands such universal assent.

It used to be considered manifestly unjust that a child should be given an enormous head-start in life simply because he was the son of an earl, or a member of the landed gentry. But what about a child today born of affluent, educated parents whose family life gets him off to a head-start in the educational ladder? Is he not the beneficiary of a form of hereditary privilege no less unjust than that enjoyed by the aristocracy?

It used to be assumed that a system of universal public education would eventually overcome this difficulty. But all the recent evidence suggests that this is an illusion. Family life is more important than school life in determining brain power, and children from poor, uneducated homes will do worse than children from affluent, educated homes, even if they are sent to better schools, let alone comparable schools.

So much is beginning to become inescapably obvious. Educational qualifications are today what armorial quarterings were in feudal times. Yet access to them is almost as unfairly determined by accidents of birth as was access to the nobility. Clearly this makes a nonsense of any genuine faith in equality of opportunity.

It is the realization of this that accounts for the current populist clamor to do away with educational distinctions such as exams and diplomas, since they are seen as the latest form of privilege which, in a sense, they are.

It is perfectly true, of course, that in theory socialism has always been critical of the ideal of equality of opportunity. But hitherto, at least in the free world, it has preferred to concentrate its energies on the old injustices which stemmed from the feudal past and the capitalist present rather than to address itself to the injustices of the future.

For these purposes the ideal of equality of opportunity has been exploited as at least a way of moving in the right, that is to say the Left direction. But today, for the first time, a new school of radical thinkers is becoming acutely aware that equality of opportunity may be a dead end instead of the thin end of the egalitarian wedge—more a buttress behind which a new form of privilege has taken shelter than a slippery slope down which hereditary privilege is moving to its doom.

And up to a point they are right in this conclusion. If equality of opportunity, as at present practiced, is assumed to be the basis for a just society, then this cannot fail to legitimize inequality in ways that we are only now beginning to discover.

But there is a problem here for the Right quite as much as for the Left. It seems to me certain that there will be a growing awareness in the coming decades of the unfairness of existing society, of the new forms of arbitrary allocation of power, status and privilege. Resentment will build up against the new meritocracy just as it built up against the old aristocracy and plutocracy.

The task of the Right must be to devise new ways of disarming this resentment, without so curbing the high-flyers, so penalizing excellence, or so imposing uniformity as to destroy the spirit of a free and dynamic society.

What will be required of the new meritocracy is a formidably revived and re-animated spirit of *noblesse oblige*, rooted in the recognition that they *are* immensely privileged and must, as a class, behave accordingly, being prepared to pay a far higher social price, in terms of taxation, in terms of service, for the privilege of exercising their talents.

This is not an easy idea for a meritocracy to accept. They like to think that they deserve their privileges, having won them by their own efforts. But this is an illusion, or at any rate a half truth. The other half of the truth is that they are terribly lucky and if their luck is not to run out they must be prepared to pay much more for their good fortune than they had hoped or even feared.

The Individual and Community

THE pieces in the preceding section, "The Individual and Society," deal mainly with relationships among people in society that are formally agreed upon, and that are largely expressible in terms of constitutions and laws, and of political units like cities, states, and nations. In the present section we confront issues of both a wider and a narrower scope—issues that are as yet far less easy to resolve in constitutional form—ranging from the right relationships among the entire human community to the ancient moral question which the single individual can never quite escape: "Am I my brother's keeper?"

The threat of extinction by atomic war or by the exhaustion of natural resources has set people thinking as never before about humankind as a single community. Are we necessarily interdependent, or should those who can best survive try to go it alone? Henry Steele Commager presents a broad statement of the ideal of interdependence. Garrett Hardin presents a critique of that ideal from the point of view of biology and economics. It is up to the reader to decide—perhaps after some research—whether Hardin's practical and rather daringly stated case against helping the poor truly supports our self-interest.

The next group of essays turns from global issues to personal ones, and centers on individualism—a trait much prized by Americans—and how it relates to our dealings with others. De Tocqueville, writing 150 years ago, when the term itself was still a new one, shows how individualism is related to democracy, and alludes darkly to its effects on the ties between generations and among contemporaries: "It throws [a person] back forever upon himself alone and threatens in the end to confine him entirely within the solitude of his own heart." Philip Slater sees de Tocqueville's observation confirmed. He argues that the extremeness of American competitive individualism is neither normal nor correct; and it exacts a heavy price in lack 229 of a sense of self, in loneliness, bureaucracy, mistrust, and, paradoxically, in monotonous uniformity. Peter Marin examines a group of institutional mechanisms in which the drive for individual potency or self-realization seems to him to mask what is really narcissism, a self-love that provides its adherents with "a way to avoid the demands of the world, to smother the tug of conscience." Jonathan Swift's great satire, which concludes the section, is in a class by itself. Its piercing cry for sympathy and community is ironically masked in a bland proposal to push economic independence to its logical conclusion.

INDEPENDENCE AND INTERDEPENDENCE

HENRY STEELE COMMAGER

Henry Steele Commager is one of the most prominent and most prolific historians of America. Born in 1902 and educated at the University of Chicago, he has taught principally at N.Y.U., Columbia, and Amherst, where he was Professor of History from 1956 until his retirement in 1971. Dr. Commager has lectured widely in the United States and abroad and has received many honorary degrees. As an author, editor, and collaborator, he has produced more than a score of books, among them Documents of American History *(1934),* Theodore Parker *(1936),* The American Mind *(1951),* Freedom, Loyalty and Dissent *(1954),* The Commonwealth of Learning *(1968), and* The American Enlightenment *(1974).* The Growth of the American Republic *(with S. E. Morison), written in 1930 and now in its sixth edition (1969), has remained an influential general history widely used as a college text. The present piece was commissioned by the World Affairs Council of Philadelphia as a keynote statement for its Bicentennial Era program. The text is taken from* Today's Education, *March–April 1976. In form and style it may be compared with the 1776 Declaration of Independence (p. 172).*

A Declaration of Interdependence

When in the course of history the threat of extinction confronts mankind, it is necessary for the people of the United States to declare their interdependence with the people of all nations and to embrace those principles and build those institutions which will enable mankind to survive and civilization to flourish.

Two centuries ago our forefathers brought forth a new nation; now we must join with others to bring forth a new world order. On this historic occasion, it is proper that the American people should reaffirm those principles on which the United States of America was founded, acknowledge the new crises which confront them, accept the new obligations which history imposes upon them, and set forth the causes which impel them to affirm before all peoples their commitment to a Declaration of Interdependence.

We hold these truths to be self-evident: That all men are created equal; that the inequalities and injustices which afflict so much of the human race are the product of history and society, not of God or nature; that people everywhere are entitled to the blessings of life and liberty, peace and security, and the realization of their full potential; that they have an inescapable moral obligation to preserve those rights for posterity; and that to achieve these ends, all the peoples and nations of the globe should acknowledge their interdependence and join together to dedicate their minds and their hearts to the solution of those problems which threaten their survival.

To establish a new world order of compassion, peace, justice, and security, it is essential that mankind free itself from the limitations of national prejudice and acknowledge that the forces that unite it are incomparably deeper than those that divide it—that all people are part of one global community, dependent on one body of resources, bound together by the ties of a common humanity, and associated in a common adventure on the planet Earth.

Let us then join together to vindicate and realize this great truth that mankind is one and, as one, will nobly save or irreparably lose the heritage of thousands of years of civilization. And let us set forth the principles which should animate and inspire us if our civilization is to survive.

We affirm that the resources of the globe are finite, not infinite; that they are the heritage of no one nation or generation, but of all peoples and nations and of posterity; and that our deepest obligation is to transmit to that posterity a planet richer in material bounty, in beauty, and in delight than we found it. Narrow notions of national sovereignty must not be permitted to curtail that obligation.

We affirm that the exploitation of the poor by the rich and of the weak by the strong violates our common humanity and denies to large segments of society the blessings of life, liberty, and happiness. We recognize a moral obligation to strive for a more prudent and more equitable sharing of the resources of the earth in order to ameliorate poverty, hunger, and disease.

We affirm that the resources of nature are sufficient to nourish and sustain all the present inhabitants of the globe and that there is an obligation on every society to distribute those resources equitably, along with a corollary obligation on every society to assure that its population does not place upon nature a burden heavier than it can bear.

We affirm our responsibility to help create conditions which will make for peace and security and to build more effective machinery for keeping peace among the nations. Because the insensate accumulation of nuclear, chemical, and biological weapons threatens the survival of mankind, we call for the immediate reduction and eventual elimination of these weapons under international supervision. We deplore the reliance on force to settle disputes between nation states and between rival groups within such states.

We affirm that the oceans are the common property of mankind, whose dependence on their incomparable resources of nourishment and strength will, in the next century, become crucial for human survival, and that their exploitation should be so regulated as to serve the interests of the entire globe and of future generations.

We affirm that pollution flows with the waters and flies with the winds; that it recognizes no boundary lines and penetrates all defenses; that it works irreparable damage alike to nature and to mankind—threatening with extinction the life of the seas, the flora and fauna of the earth, and the health of the people in cities and the countryside alike—and that it can be adequately controlled only through international cooperation.

We affirm that the exploration and utilization of outer space is a matter equally important to all the nations of the globe and that no nation can be permitted to exploit or develop the potentialities of the planetary system exclusively for its own benefit.

We affirm that the economy of all nations is a seamless web and that no one nation can any longer effectively maintain its processes of production and monetary system without recognizing the necessity for collaborative regulation by international authorities.

We affirm that, in a civilized society, the institutions of science and the arts are never at war, and we call upon all nations to exempt these institutions from the claims of chauvinistic nationalism and to foster that great community of learning and creativity whose benign function it is to advance civilization and to further the health and happiness of mankind.

We affirm that a world without law is a world without order, and we call upon all nations to strengthen and sustain the United Nations and its specialized agencies and other institutions of world order and to broaden the jurisdiction of the World Court in order that these may preside over a reign of law which will not only end wars but will end as well the mindless violence that terrorizes our society even in times of peace.

We can no longer afford to make little plans, allow ourselves to be the captives of events and forces over which we have no control, or consult our fears rather than our hopes. We call upon the American people, on the threshold of the third century of our national existence, to display once again that boldness, enterprise, magnanimity, and vision which enabled the founders of our Republic to bring forth a new nation and inaugurate a new era in human history. The fate of humanity hangs in the balance. Throughout the globe, hearts and hopes wait upon us. We summon all mankind to unite to meet the great challenge.

GARRETT HARDIN

Garrett Hardin (born 1915) is a biologist who has written prolifically on the moral and social implications of his field. He is particularly interested in ecology, population, and the problems raised by the worldwide scarcity of resources. He was an undergraduate at the University of Chicago and received his Ph.D. in biology from Stanford in 1941 with a *study of algae. A few years later he gave up research on the use of algae as a large-scale source of food because he had come to the conviction that producing more food makes population problems worse. Since 1946 Hardin has taught at the University of California, Santa Barbara, where he is Professor of Human Ecology. He is the author of many books and articles on such topics as evolution (* Nature and Man's Fate, *1959), environmental problems ("The Tragedy of the Commons," in* Science, *December 13, 1968;* Exploring New Ethics for Survival, *1972), and birth control (* Birth Control, *1970;* Mandatory Motherhood, *1974). Hardin is especially devoted to—and especially skillful at—telling people important things that they do not particularly want to hear. Some of his writings in this vein are collected in* Stalking the Wild Taboo *(1973). The present essay appeared in the September 1974 issue of* Psychology Today.

Lifeboat Ethics:
The Case Against Helping the Poor

Environmentalists use the metaphor of the earth as a "spaceship" in trying to persuade countries, industries and people to stop wasting and polluting our natural resources. Since we all share life on this planet, they argue, no single person or institution has the right to destroy, waste, or use more than a fair share of its resources.

But does everyone on earth have an equal right to an equal share of its resources? The spaceship metaphor can be dangerous when used by misguided idealists to justify suicidal policies for sharing our resources through uncontrolled immigration and foreign aid. In their enthusiastic but unrealistic generosity, they confuse the ethics of a spaceship with those of a lifeboat.

A true spaceship would have to be under the control of a captain, since no ship could possibly survive if its course were determined by committee. Spaceship Earth certainly has no captain; the United Nations is merely a toothless tiger, with little power to enforce any policy upon its bickering members.

If we divide the world crudely into rich nations and poor nations, two thirds of them are desperately poor, and only one third comparatively rich, with the United States the wealthiest of all. Metaphorically each rich nation can be seen as a lifeboat full of comparatively rich people. In the ocean outside each lifeboat swim the poor of the world, who would like to get in, or at least to share some of the wealth. What should the lifeboat passengers do?

First, we must recognize the limited capacity of any lifeboat. For example, a nation's land has a limited capacity to support a population and as the current energy crisis has shown us, in some ways we have already exceeded the carrying capacity of our land.

So here we sit, say 50 people in our lifeboat. To be generous let us assume it has room for 10 more, making a total capacity of 60. Suppose the 50 of us in the lifeboat see 100 others swimming in the water outside, begging for admission to our boat or for handouts. We have several options: we may be tempted to try to live by the Christian ideal of being "our brother's keeper," or by the Marxist ideal of "to each according to his needs." Since the needs of all in the water are the same, and since they can all be seen as "our brothers," we could take them all into our boat, making a total of 150 in a boat designed for 60. The boat swamps, everyone drowns. Complete justice, complete catastrophe.

Since the boat has an unused excess capacity of 10 more passengers, we could admit just 10 more to it. But which 10 do we let in? How do we choose? Do we pick the best 10, the neediest 10, "first come, first served"? And what do we say to the 90 we exclude? If we do let an extra 10 into our lifeboat, we will have lost our "safety factor," an engineering principle of critical importance. For example, if we don't leave room for excess capacity as a safety factor in our country's agriculture, a new plant disease or a bad change in the weather could have disastrous consequences.

Suppose we decide to preserve our small safety factor and admit no more to the lifeboat. Our survival is then possible although we shall have to be constantly on guard against boarding parties.

While this last solution clearly offers the only means of our survival, it is morally abhorrent to many people. Some say they feel guilty about their good luck. My reply is simple: "Get out and yield your place to others." This may solve the problem of the guilt-ridden person's conscience, but it does not change the ethics of the lifeboat. The needy person to whom the guilt-ridden person yields his place will not himself feel guilty about his good luck. If he did, he would not climb aboard. The net result of conscience-stricken people giving up their unjustly held seats is the elimination of that sort of conscience from the lifeboat.

This is the basic metaphor within which we must work out our solutions. Let us now enrich the image, step by step, with substantive additions from the real world, a world that must solve real and pressing problems of over-population and hunger.

The harsh ethics of the lifeboat become even harsher when we consider the reproductive differences between the rich nations and the poor nations. The people inside the lifeboats are doubling in numbers every 87 years: those swimming around outside are doubling on the average, every 35 years, more than twice as fast as the rich. And since the world's resources are dwindling, the difference in prosperity between the rich and the poor can only increase.

As of 1973, the U.S. had a population of 210 million people, who were increasing by 0.8 percent per year. Outside our lifeboat, let us imagine another 210 million people (say the combined populations of Colombia, Ecuador, Venezuela, Morocco, Pakistan, Thailand and the Philippines), who are increasing at a rate of 3.3 percent per year. Put differently, the doubling time for this aggregate population is 21 years, compared to 87 years for the U.S.

Now suppose the U.S. agreed to pool its resources with those seven countries, with everyone receiving an equal share. Initially the ratio of Americans to non-Americans in this model would be one-to-one but consider what the ratio would be after 87 years, by which time the Americans would have doubled to a population of 420 million. By then, doubling every 21 years, the other group would have swollen to 354 billion. Each American would have to share the available resources with more than eight people.

But, one could argue, this discussion assumes that current population trends will continue, and they may not. Quite so. Most likely the rate of population increase will decline much faster in the U.S. than it will in the other countries, and there does not seem to be much we can do about it. In sharing with "each according to his needs," we must recognize that needs are determined by population size, which is determined by the rate of reproduction, which at present is regarded as a sovereign right of every nation, poor or not. This being so, the philanthropic load created by the sharing ethic of the spaceship can only increase.

The fundamental error of spaceship ethics, and the sharing it requires, is that it leads to what I call "the tragedy of the commons." Under a system of private property, the men who own property recognize their responsibility to care for it, for if they don't they will eventually suffer. A farmer, for instance, will allow no more cattle in a pasture than its carrying capacity justifies. If he overloads it, erosion sets in, weeds take over, and he loses the use of the pasture.

If a pasture becomes a commons open to all, the right of each to use it may not be matched by a corresponding responsibility to protect it. Asking everyone to use it with discretion will hardly do, for the considerate herdsman who refrains from overloading the commons suffers more than a selfish one who says his needs are greater. If everyone would restrain himself all would be well; but it takes only one less than everyone to ruin a system of voluntary restraint. In a crowded world of less than perfect human beings, mutual ruin is inevitable if there are no controls. This is the tragedy of the commons.

One of the major tasks of education today should be the creation of such an acute awareness of the dangers of the commons that people will recognize its many varieties. For example, the air and water have become polluted because they are treated as commons. Further growth in the population or per-capita conversion of natural resources into pollutants will only make the problem worse. The same holds true for the fish of the oceans. Fishing fleets have nearly disappeared in many parts of the world, technological improvements in the art of fishing are hastening the day of complete ruin. Only the replacement of the system of the commons with a responsible system of control will save the land, air, water and oceanic fisheries.

In recent years there has been a push to create a new commons called a World Food Bank, an international depository of food reserves to which nations would contribute according to their abilities and from which they would draw according to their needs. This humanitarian proposal has received support from many liberal international groups, and from such prominent citizens as Margaret Mead, U.N. Secretary General Kurt Waldheim, and Senators Edward Kennedy and George McGovern.

A world food bank appeals powerfully to our humanitarian impulses. But before we rush ahead with such a plan, let us recognize where the greatest political push comes from, lest we be disillusioned later. Our experience with the "Food for Peace program," or Public Law 480, gives us the answer. This program moved billions of dollars worth of U.S. surplus grain to food-short, population-long countries during the past two decades. But when P.L. 480 first became law, a headline in the business magazine *Forbes* revealed the real power behind it: "Feeding the World's Hungry Millions: How It Will Mean Billions for U.S. Business."

And indeed it did. In the years 1960 to 1970, U.S. taxpayers spent a total of $7.9 billion on the Food for Peace program. Between 1948 and 1970, they also paid an additional $50 billion for other economic-aid programs, some of which went for food and food-producing machinery and technology. Though all U.S. taxpayers were forced to contribute to the cost of P.L. 480, certain special interest groups gained handsomely under the program. Farmers did not have to contribute the grain; the Government, or rather the taxpayers, bought it from them at full market prices. The increased demand raised prices of farm products generally. The manufacturers of farm machinery, fertilizers and pesticides benefited by the farmers' extra efforts to grow more food. Grain elevators profited from storing the surplus until it could be shipped. Railroads made money hauling it to ports, and shipping lines profited from carrying it overseas. The implementation of P.L. 480 required the creation of a vast Government bureaucracy, which then acquired its own vested interest in continuing the program regardless of its merits.

Those who proposed and defended the Food for Peace program in public rarely mentioned its importance to any of these special interests. The public emphasis was always on its humanitarian effects. The combination of silent selfish interests and highly vocal humanitarian apologists made a powerful and successful lobby for extracting money from taxpayers. We can expect the same lobby to push now for the creation of a World Food Bank.

However great the potential benefit to selfish interests, it should not be a decisive argument against a truly humanitarian program. We must ask if such a program would actually do more good than harm, not only momentarily but also in the long run. Those who propose the food bank usually refer to a current "emergency" or "crisis" in terms of world food supply. But what is an emergency? Although they may be infrequent and sudden, everyone knows that emergencies will occur from time to time. A well-run family, company, organization or country prepares for the likelihood of accidents and emergencies. It expects them, it budgets for them, it saves for them.

What happens if some organizations or countries budget for accidents and others do not? If each country is solely responsible for its own well-being, poorly managed ones will suffer. But they can learn from experience. They may mend their ways, and learn to budget for infrequent but certain emergencies. For example, the weather varies from year to year, and periodic crop failures are certain. A wise and competent government saves out of the production of the good years in anticipation of bad years to come. Joseph taught this policy to Pharaoh in Egypt more than 2,000 years ago. Yet the great majority of the governments in the world today do not follow such a policy. They lack either the wisdom or the competence, or both. Should those nations that do manage to put something aside be forced to come to the rescue each time an emergency occurs among the poor nations?

"But it isn't their fault!" Some kind-hearted liberals argue, "How can we blame the poor people who are caught in an emergency? Why must they suffer for the sins of their governments?" The concept of blame is simply not relevant here. The real question is, what are the operational consequences of establishing a world food bank? If it is open to every country every time a need develops, slovenly rulers will not be motivated to take Joseph's advice. Someone will always come to their aid. Some countries will deposit food in the world food bank, and others will withdraw it. There will be almost no overlap. As a result of such solutions to food shortage emergencies, the poor countries will not learn to mend their ways, and will suffer progressively greater emergencies as their populations grow.

On the average, poor countries undergo a 2.5 percent increase in population each year; rich countries, about 0.8 percent. Only rich countries have anything in the way of food reserves set aside, and even they do not have as much as they should. Poor countries have none. If poor countries received no food from the outside, the rate of their population growth would be periodically checked by crop failures and famines. But if they can always draw on a world food bank in time of need, their population can continue to grow unchecked, and so will their "need" for aid. In the short run, a world food bank may diminish that need, but in the long run it actually increases the need without limit.

Without some system of worldwide food sharing, the proportion of people in the rich and poor nations might eventually stabilize. The overpopulated poor countries would decrease in numbers, while the rich countries that had room for more people would increase. But with a well-meaning system of sharing, such as a world food bank, the growth differential between the rich and the poor countries will not only persist, it will increase. Because of the higher rate of population growth in the poor countries of the world, 88 percent of today's children are born poor, and only 12 percent rich. Year by year the ratio becomes worse, as the fast-reproducing poor outnumber the slow-reproducing rich.

A world food bank is thus a commons in disguise. People will have more motivation to draw from it than to add to any common store. The less provident and less able will multiply at the expense of the abler and more provident, bringing eventual ruin upon all who share in the commons. Besides, any system of "sharing" that amounts to foreign aid from the rich nations to the poor nations will carry the taint of charity, which will contribute little to the world peace so devoutly desired by those who support the idea of a world food bank.

As past U.S. foreign-aid programs have amply and depressingly demonstrated, international charity frequently inspires mistrust and antagonism rather than gratitude on the part of the recipient nation [see "What Other Nations Hear When the Eagle Screams," by Kenneth J. and Mary M. Gergen, *Psychology Today*, June 1974].

The modern approach to foreign aid stresses the export of technology and advice, rather than money and food. As an ancient Chinese proverb goes: "Give a man a fish and he will eat for a day; teach him how to fish and he will eat for the rest of his days." Acting on this advice, the Rockefeller and Ford Foundations have financed a number of programs for improving agriculture in the hungry nations. Known as the "Green Revolution," these programs have led to the development of "miracle rice" and "miracle wheat," new strains that offer bigger harvests and greater resistance to crop damage. Norman Borlaug, the Nobel Prize winning agronomist who, supported by the Rockefeller Foundation, developed "miracle wheat," is one of the most prominent advocates of a world food bank.

Whether or not the Green Revolution can increase food production as much as its champions claim is a debatable but possibly irrelevant point. Those who support this well-intended humanitarian effort should first consider some of the fundamentals of human ecology. Ironically, one man who did was the late Alan Gregg, a vice president of the Rockefeller Foundation. Two decades ago he expressed strong doubts about the wisdom of such attempts to increase food production. He likened the growth and spread of humanity over the surface of the earth to the spread of cancer in the human body, remarking that "cancerous growths demand food, but, as far as I know, they have never been cured by getting it."

Every human born constitutes a draft on all aspects of the environment: food, air, water, forests, beaches, wildlife, scenery and solitude. Food can, perhaps, be significantly increased to meet a growing demand. But what about clean beaches, unspoiled forests, and solitude? If we satisfy a growing population's need for food, we necessarily decrease its per capita supply of the other resources needed by men.

India, for example, now has a population of 600 million, which increases by 15 million each year. This population already puts a huge load on a relatively impoverished environment. The country's forests are now only a small fraction of what they were three centuries ago, and floods and erosion continually destroy the insufficient farmland that remains. Every one of the 15 million new lives added to India's population puts an additional burden on the environment, and increases the economic and social costs of crowding. However humanitarian our intent, every Indian life saved through medical or nutritional assistance from abroad diminishes the quality of life for those who remain, and for subsequent generations. If rich countries make it possible, through foreign aid, for 600 million Indians to swell to 1.2 billion in a mere 28 years, as their current growth rate threatens, will future generations of Indians thank us for hastening the destruction of their environment? Will our good intentions be sufficient excuse for the consequences of our actions?

My final example of a commons in action is one for which the public has the least desire for rational discussion—immigration. Anyone who publicly questions the wisdom of current U.S. immigration policy is promptly charged with bigotry, prejudice, ethnocentrism, chauvinism, isolationism or selfishness. Rather than encounter such accusations, one would rather talk about other matters, leaving immigration policy to wallow in the crosscurrents of special interests that take no account of the good of the whole, or the interests of posterity.

Perhaps we still feel guilty about things we said in the past. Two generations ago the popular press frequently referred to Dagos, Wops, Polacks, Chinks and Krauts, in articles about how America was being "overrun" by foreigners of supposedly inferior genetic stock [see "The Politics of Genetic Engineering: Who Decides Who's Defective?" *Psychology Today*, June 1974]. But because the implied inferiority of foreigners was used then as justification for keeping them out, people now assume that restrictive policies could only be based on such misguided notions. There are other grounds.

Just consider the numbers involved. Our Government acknowledges a net inflow of 400,000 immigrants a year. While we have no hard data on the extent of illegal entries, educated guesses put the figure at about 600,000 a year. Since the natural increase (excess of births over deaths) of the resident population now runs about 1.7 million per year, the yearly gain from immigration amounts to at least 19 percent of the total annual increase, and may be as much as 37 percent if we include the estimate for illegal immigrants. Considering the growing use of birth-control devices, the potential effect of educational campaigns by such organizations as Planned Parenthood Federation of America and Zero Population Growth, and the influence of inflation and the housing shortage, the fertility rate of American women may decline so much that immigration could account for all the yearly increase in population. Should we not at least ask if that is what we want?

For the sake of those who worry about whether the "quality" of the average immigrant compares favorably with the quality of the average resident, let us assume that immigrants and nativeborn citizens are of exactly equal quality, however one defines that term. We will focus here only on quantity; and since our conclusions will depend on nothing else, all charges of bigotry and chauvinism become irrelevant.

World food banks *move food to the people*, hastening the exhaustion of the environment of the poor countries. Unrestricted immigration, on the other hand, *moves people to the food*, thus speeding up the destruction of the environment of the rich countries. We can easily understand why poor people should want to make this latter transfer, but why should rich hosts encourage it?

As in the case of foreign-aid programs, immigration receives support from selfish interests and humanitarian impulses. The primary selfish interest in unimpeded immigration is the desire of employers for cheap labor, particularly in industries and trades that offer degrading work. In the past, one wave of foreigners after another was brought into the U.S. to work at wretched jobs for wretched wages. In recent years the Cubans, Puerto Ricans and Mexicans have had this dubious honor. The interests of the employers of cheap labor mesh well with the guilty silence of the country's liberal intelligentsia. White Anglo-Saxon Protestants are particularly reluctant to call for a closing of the doors to immigration for fear of being called bigots.

But not all countries have such reluctant leadership. Most educated Hawaiians, for example, are keenly aware of the limits of their environment, particularly in terms of population growth. There is only so much room on the islands, and the islanders know it. To Hawaiians, immigrants from the other 49 states present as great a threat as those from other nations. At a recent meeting of Hawaiian government officials in Honolulu, I had the ironic delight of hearing a speaker, who like most of his audience was of Japanese ancestry, ask how the country might practically and constitutionally close its doors to further immigration. One member of the audience countered: "How can we shut the doors now? We have many friends and relatives in Japan that we'd like to bring here some day so that they can enjoy Hawaii too." The Japanese-American speaker smiled sympathetically and answered: "Yes, but we have children now, and someday we'll have grandchildren too. We can bring more people here from Japan only by giving away some of the land that we hope to pass on to our grandchildren some day. What right do we have to do that?"

At this point, I can hear U.S. liberals asking: "How can you justify slamming the door once you're inside? You say that immigrants should be kept out. But aren't we all immigrants, or the descendants of immigrants? If we insist on staying, must we not admit all others?" Our craving for intellectual order leads us to seek and prefer symmetrical rules and morals: a single rule for me and everybody else; the same rule yesterday, today and tomorrow. Justice, we feel, should not change with time and place.

We Americans of non-Indian ancestry can look upon ourselves as the descendants of thieves who are guilty morally, if not legally, of stealing this land from its Indian owners. Should we then give back the land to the now living American descendants of those Indians? However morally or logically sound this proposal may be, I, for one, am unwilling to live by it and I know no one else who is. Besides, the logical consequence would be absurd. Suppose that, intoxicated with a sense of pure justice, we should decide to turn our land over to the Indians. Since all our other wealth has also been derived from the land, wouldn't we be morally obliged to give that back to the Indians too?

Clearly, the concept of pure justice produces an infinite regression to absurdity. Centuries ago, wise men invented statutes of limitations to justify the rejection of such pure justice, in the interest of preventing continual disorder. The law zealously defends property rights. Drawing a line after an arbitrary time has elapsed may be unjust, but the alternatives are worse.

We are all the descendants of thieves, and the world's resources are inequitably distributed. But we must begin the journey to tomorrow from the point where we are today. We cannot remake the past. We cannot safely divide the wealth equitably among all peoples so long as people reproduce at different rates. To do so would guarantee that our grandchildren, and everyone else's grandchildren, would have only a ruined world to inhabit.

To be generous with one's own possessions is quite different from being generous with those of posterity. We should call this point to the attention of those who, from a commendable love of justice and equality, would institute a system of the commons, either in the form of a world food bank, or of unrestricted immigration. We must convince them if we wish to save at least some parts of the world from environmental ruin.

Without a true world government to control reproduction and the use of available resources, the sharing ethic of the spaceship is impossible. For the foreseeable future, our survival demands that we govern our actions by the ethics of a lifeboat, harsh though they may be. Posterity will be satisfied with nothing less.

APARTNESS AND COMMUNITY

ALEXIS DE TOCQUEVILLE

Alexis Charles Henri Clérel de Tocqueville was born in Paris in 1805. He studied law and, as the son of an influential aristocratic family, he was given a judicial post in the court at Versailles. After the July Revolution of 1830, de Tocqueville felt increasingly uncertain of his allegiance to the new government, and he succeeded in securing a commission to go to America to study the prison system. Even closer to his heart was the opportunity to study a democratic system of government at first hand and to judge the possibilities of its application in Europe. For nine months in 1831 and 1832 de Tocqueville and his friend and fellow magistrate, Gustave de Beaumont, traveled widely in America, visiting prisons, taking notes, writing letters, interviewing prominent people, requesting memoranda on special subjects, and collecting books and documents. On their return, the two young Frenchmen soon completed their prison report; then each turned to his own study of America. De Tocqueville published his book, De la démocratie en Amérique, *in two parts. The first, a description and critical analysis of the American government in the age of Jackson, was published in 1835. The second, a more philosophical study, with greater regard to the general applicability of American traits, came out in 1840.*

De Tocqueville was elected to the French Chamber of Deputies in 1837 and briefly held the post of Minister for Foreign Affairs under Napoleon III, but his major energies were devoted to political thought rather than to politics. He published L'Ancien régime et la revolution *three years before his death in 1859.*

Democracy in America *was quickly recognized as an important book and was translated into many languages. The first English translation was made by Henry Reeve, an Englishman, in 1838. This was retranslated by the American scholar Francis Bowen in 1862. The texts of the chapters from Part II that we present here and in a later section are taken from Phillips Bradley's excellent modern edition (with corrections) of the Bowen translation.*

Of Individualism
in Democratic Countries

I have shown how it is that in ages of equality every man seeks for his opinions within himself; I am now to show how it is that in the same ages all his feelings are turned towards himself alone. *Individualism* is a novel expression, to which a novel idea has given birth. Our fathers were only acquainted with *égoïsme* (selfishness). Selfishness is a passionate and exaggerated love of self, which leads a man to connect everything with himself and to prefer himself to everything in the world. Individualism is a mature and calm feeling, which disposes each member of the community to sever himself from the mass of his fellows and to draw apart with his family and his friends, so that after he has thus formed a little circle of his own, he willingly leaves society at large to itself. Selfishness originates in blind instinct; individualism proceeds from erroneous judgment more than from depraved feelings; it originates as much in deficiencies of mind as in perversity of heart.

Selfishness blights the germ of all virtue; individualism, at first, only saps the virtues of public life; but in the long run it attacks and destroys all others and is at length absorbed in downright selfishness. Selfishness is a vice as old as the world, which does not belong to one form of society more than to another; individualism is of democratic origin, and it threatens to spread in the same ratio as the equality of condition.

Among aristocratic nations, as families remain for centuries in the same condition, often on the same spot, all generations become, as it were, contemporaneous. A man almost always knows his forefathers and respects them; he thinks he already sees his remote descendants and he loves them. He willingly imposes duties on himself towards the former and the latter, and he will frequently sacrifice his personal gratifications to those who went before and to those who will come after him. Aristocratic institutions, moreover, have the effect of closely binding every man to several of his fellow citizens. As the classes of an aristocratic people are strongly marked and permanent, each of them is regarded by its own members as a sort of lesser country, more tangible and more cherished than the country at large. As in aristocratic communities all the citizens occupy fixed positions, one above another, the result is that each of them always sees a man above himself whose patronage is necessary to him, and below himself another man whose co-operation he may claim. Men living in aristocratic ages are therefore almost always closely attached to something placed out of their own sphere, and they are often disposed to forget themselves. It is true that in these ages the notion of human fellowship is faint and that men seldom think of sacrificing themselves for mankind; but they often sacrifice themselves for other men. In democratic times, on the contrary, when the duties of each individual to the race are much more clear, devoted service to any one man becomes more rare; the bond of human affection is extended, but it is relaxed.

Among democratic nations new families are constantly springing up, others are constantly falling away, and all that remain change their condition;

the woof of time is every instant broken and the track of generations effaced. Those who went before are soon forgotten; of those who will come after, no one has any idea: the interest of man is confined to those in close propinquity to himself. As each class gradually approaches others and mingles with them, its members become undifferentiated and lose their class identity for each other. Aristocracy had made a chain of all the members of the community, from the peasant to the king; democracy breaks that chain and severs every link of it.

As social conditions become more equal, the number of persons increases who, although they are neither rich nor powerful enough to exercise any great influence over their fellows, have nevertheless acquired or retained sufficient education and fortune to satisfy their own wants. They owe nothing to any man, they expect nothing from any man; they acquire the habit of always considering themselves as standing alone; and they are apt to imagine that their whole destiny is in their own hands.

Thus not only does democracy make every man forget his ancestors, but it hides his descendants and separates his contemporaries from him; it throws him back forever upon himself alone and threatens in the end to confine him entirely within the solitude of his own heart.

PETER MARIN

Peter Marin was born in 1936 and is a poet, educator, and writer. He is young enough to have experienced the 1960s with substantial insight into and sympathy for the plight of students at that time. After earning his B.A. in literature from Swarthmore and his M.A. from Columbia (1958), he taught briefly at three different colleges, and in 1967–1968 he served as the director of an experimental high school in Palo Alto. Since then Marin has spent much of his time writing on subjects generated by his interest in young people and their place in modern culture. He is particularly interested both in dehumanization in American life in our "psychic evolution," that is, in the possible changes in our individuation, our consciousness, our ability to deal with experience. He is coauthor of the book Understanding Drug Use *(1960), coeditor of* The Limits of Schooling *(1975), and author of* In a Man's Time *(1974). "The New Narcissism," which appeared in the October 1975 issue of* Harper's, *is one of a number of recent magazine articles in which he examines the meaning and direction of modern American cults.*

The New Narcissism

Where to begin a piece like this? Its original subject was ostensibly an Esalen conference on "spiritual tyranny." But that was for me merely a way of getting at a more general subject: the trend in therapy toward a deification of the isolated self. And that subject was in turn a part of an even more general concern: the ways in which selfishness and moral blindness now assert themselves in the larger culture as enlightenment and psychic health. A broad-based retrenchment is going on, a pervasive and perhaps unconscious shift in value—not only on a national level but in the moral definitions and judgments we make as individuals.

I think offhandedly as I write of several recent conversations I have had with friends or students, of what I have heard proclaimed from lecture platforms or seen on television and in the popular journals. I am, for instance, dining with a close friend in a New York restaurant, and as we eat our steaks and drink our brandy and smoke our fat cigars he explains to me that the world is obviously overpopulated, and that somebody must starve, and that we, as a nation, must decide who it will be, and that it might as well be those who already suffer from protein deficiency, for they are already "useless." Or I finish a lecture to the members of the American Association for Humanistic Psychology, and a therapist rushes up to me afterward and asks me whether or not I believe in the "ethics of the lifeboat," and when I tell her that I don't know why we are in the lifeboat while others are drowning, she whispers knowingly to me: "We have a higher consciousness." Or I am invited to meet with a well-meaning California legislator who is beginning a political movement based on the therapeutic values of "authenticity" and "warmth," and he draws for me on a napkin the button he has designed: the single letter *I* on a blank white background. Or I attend a dinner sponsored by the Population Institute at the Century Plaza in Los Angeles, where Paul Ehrlich addresses a thousand well-heeled people about the "coming end of affluence," and when I leaf through a copy of his book given away for free I see that he recommends filling the cellar with food and buying a gun and relying on neither friends nor neighbors but only on oneself. Or, finally, I listen for two hours in a graduate seminar to two women therapists explaining to me how we are all entirely responsible for our destinies, and how the Jews must have wanted to be burned by the Germans, and that those who starve in the Sahel must want it to happen, and when I ask them whether there is anything we owe to others, say, to a child starving in the desert, one of them snaps at me angrily: "What can I do if a child is determined to starve?"

That, precisely, is what I am talking about here: the growing solipsism and desperation of a beleaguered class, the world view emerging among us centered solely on the self and with individual survival as its sole good. It is a world view present not only in everything we say and do, but as an ambience, a feeling in the air, a general cast of perception and attitude: a retreat from the worlds of morality and history, an unembarrassed denial of human reciprocity and community.

A few months ago, I went to dinner at the house of a woman who had just been through a weekend of *est* (Erhard Seminar Training), the latest and most popular new therapeutic enthusiasm. The training is designed to provide its participants with a new sense of fulfillment and competence, and it seemed to have worked with my hostess, for she assured me that her life had radically changed, that she felt different about herself, that she was happier and more efficient, and that she kept her house much cleaner than before.

Nothing in that is very startling or distressing, but in the course of the evening she also added that because of the training she now understood: (1) that the individual will is all-powerful and totally determines one's fate; (2) that she felt neither guilt nor shame about anyone's fate and that those who were poor and hungry must have wished it on themselves; (3) that the North Vietnamese must have wanted to be bombed, or else it could not have happened to them; (4) that a friend of hers who had been raped and murdered in San Francisco was to be pitied for having willed it to occur; (5) that in her weekend at *est* she had attained full enlightenment; (6) that she was God; (7) that whatever one thought to be true was true beyond all argument; (8) that I was also God, and that my ideas were also true, but not as true as hers because I had not had the training; and (9) that my use of logic to criticize her beliefs was unfair, because reason was "irrational," though she could not tell me why.

There is no telling whether or not this is precisely what she learned at *est*, and no doubt other adherents would deny it, but I have talked by now to at least a dozen of its enthusiasts, and each one of them has blankly recited to me, word for word, the same ill-taught and ignorant catechism. No doubt they were happier for the teaching; invariably they expressed complete satisfaction with their newfound philosophy. Like my hostess, they had learned it all in a kind of manufactured daze at a weekend which cost them $250, in the company of hundreds of others. By now more than 50,000 people have "taken" the training, which was developed by Werner Erhard himself, who was once known simply as Jack Rosenberg,[1] and who was a trainer for a short time with Mind Dynamics, a franchise operation that trained businessmen in human managerial techniques. *Est* itself is a step past all that. It is a mixture of ideas and techniques borrowed from the behavioral sciences, Eastern philosophy, the traditional American classroom, Marine boot camp, and modern brainwashing methods. Participants at the weekend workshops are bombarded from the lectern with simplistic truths while being simultaneously bullied and soothed by an army of attendants. They are prevented from leaving their seats to stretch or eat or go to the bathroom, and if—as sometimes happens—they throw up in their places or urinate on themselves, well, that is all part of the training.[2]

It is not hard to understand how it all works, and one need only read the first few pages of Freud's *Group Psychology and the Analysis of the Ego* to see what intelligent use Erhard makes of individual confusion. He has managed to compress into one activity half a dozen techniques for creating power over others: the underlying anxiety of the audience and its need for simple order; the strangeness and power of the extraordinary situation; the gradual befuddlement of the senses; the combined effects of repetition and fatigue; the

---

[1] Space does not permit a discussion of the implications of that one act: the conscious shift from a Jewish to a Germanic name while still in the shadow of the deaths of several million Jews.

[2] I should make one thing clear. I have never been to an *est* weekend, mainly because I have never been able to subject myself to the kind of treatment *est* visits upon its participants, or to listen to the kind of nonsense it offers them.

credulity of others near you; the manufactured impotence of the audience; the masochistic relief that results from placing oneself in the hands of a man to whom one has granted omnipotence.

Clearly Erhard has a genius—not only for the efficiency with which his program is organized and sold, but also for the accuracy with which he tells his audience what it wants to hear. It is the latter which binds them to him. The world is perfect, each of us is all-powerful, shame and guilt are merely arbitrary notions, truth is identical to belief, suffering is merely the result of imperfect consciousness—how like manna all of this must seem to hungry souls. For if we are each totally responsible for our fate, then all the others in the world are responsible for *their* fate, and, if that is so, why should we worry about them?

It is all so simple and straightforward. It has the terrifying simplicity of the lobotomized mind: all complexity gone, and in its place the warm wind of forced simplicity blowing away the tag ends of conscience and shame. It offers the kind of Orwellian enlightenment an age like ours is bound to produce, but I do not spell it out in detail or mock its enthusiasts for that reason alone, or even because it marks the dead end of human desire or generosity. *Est* is, after all, only a bit worse than our other popular enthusiasms, and it is interesting in part because it makes clear so much of what is hidden in them. It is in many ways the logical extension of the whole human potential movement of the past decade. The refusal to consider moral complexities, the denial of history and a larger community, the disappearance of the Other, the exaggerations of the will, the reduction of all experience to a set of platitudes—all of that is to be found in embryonic form in almost all modern therapy.

Yet compared to *est* the older therapies (such as Gestalt therapy or Abraham Maslow's self-actualization or Rogerian encounter groups) had a kind of innocence to them. They were, at their worst, merely boring or silly. The people drawn to them were obviously moved by a simple yearning for what was missing from their lives, and if that yearning took sometimes puerile forms or excluded moral concerns or genuine passion, that seemed excusable—like the play of children. But our newer therapies take upon themselves a new burden. Whereas the older therapies merely ignored moral and historical concerns, the new ones destroy or replace them. They become not only a way of protecting or changing the self, but of assessing the needs of others and one's responsibilities to them—a way of defining history and determining morality.

Why that happens is not difficult to understand. It reveals the impulse behind much of what we do these days: the desire to defend ourselves against the demands of conscience and the world through an ethic designed to defuse them both. Most of us realize at one level of consciousness or another that we inhabit an age of catastrophe—if not for ourselves then for countless others. Try as we do, we cannot ignore the routine inequities of consumption and distribution which benefit us and condemn others to misery. Each of us must feel a kind of generalized shame, an unanswerable sense of guilt. So we struggle mightily to convince ourselves that our privilege is earned or deserved, rather than (as we must often feel unconsciously) a form of murder or theft. Our therapies become a way of hiding from the world, a way of easing our troubled conscience. What lies behind the form they now take is neither simple greed nor moral blindness; it is, instead, the unrealized shame of having failed the world and not knowing what to do about it. Like humiliated lovers who have betrayed what they love, we turn our faces from the world, if only (in Paul Goodman's phrase) "just to live on a while."

That is what makes our new therapies so distressing. They provide their adherents with a way to avoid the demands of the world, to smother the tug of conscience. They allow them to remain who and what they are, to accept the structured world as it is—but with a new sense of justice and justification, with the assurance that it all accords with cosmic law. We are in our proper place; the others are in theirs; we may indeed bemoan their fate or even, if we are so moved, do something to change it, but in essence it has nothing to do with us.

What disappears in this view of things is the ground of community, the felt sense of collective responsibility for the fate of each separate other. What takes its place is a moral vacuum in which others are trapped forever in a "private" destiny, doomed to whatever befalls them. In that void the traditional measures of justice or good vanish completely. The self replaces community, relation, neighbor, chance, or God. Looming larger every moment, it obliterates everything around it that might have offered it a way out of its pain.

The end result of this retreat from the complexities of the world is a kind of soft fascism: the denial, in the name of higher truth, of the claims of others upon the self. Our deification of the self becomes equal in effect and human cost to what Nietzsche long ago called the "idolatry of the state." Just as persons once set aside the possibilities of their own humanity and turned instead to the state for a sense of power and identity no longer theirs, so we now turn to the self, giving to it the power and importance of a god. In the worship of the state, life gives way to an abstraction, to the total submission of individual will. In the worship of the self, life also gives way to an abstraction, in this case to an exaggeration of the will. The result in both cases is the same. What is lost is the immense middle ground of human community. The web of reciprocity and relation is broken. The world diminishes. The felt presence of the other disappears, and with it a part of our own existence.

The real horror of our present condition is not merely the absence of community or the isolation of the self—those, after all, have been part of the American condition for a long time. It is the loss of the ability to remember what is missing, the diminishment of our vision of what is humanly possible or desirable. In our new myths we begin to deny once and for all the existence of what we once believed both possible and good. We proclaim our grief-stricken narcissism to be a form of liberation; we define as enlightenment our broken faith with the world. Already forgetful of what it means to be fully human, we sip still again from Lethe, the river of forgetfulness, hoping to erase even the memory of pain. Lethe, lethal, lethargy—all of those words suggest a kind of death, one that in religious usage is sometimes called accidie. It is a condition one can find in many places and in many ages, but only in America, and only recently, have we begun to confuse it with a state of grace.

It is in this context that the Esalen conference on Spiritual Tyranny becomes significant. It was called two years ago in San Francisco by the Esalen staff as a response to the movement they had helped to start. What apparently bothered them about the movement was connected to what I have mentioned here: the proliferation of sects and cults, and an attendant willingness on the part of many persons to abandon individual responsibility in favor of submission to narrow and shallow creeds or therapeutic "masters." The speakers invited were men whose names are familiar to those who read Esalen's catalogues: Claudio Naranjo, Werner Erhard, George Leonard, Sam Keen, Jerry Rubin—all of them leaders of therapeutic schools or theorists of what George Leonard has rosily called "the coming transformation of humanity." As for the several hundred members of the audience, some had come to cheer their favorite gurus on and others merely to be present at what had taken on, in therapeutic circles, the nature of a celebratory *event*—the equivalent of an all-star rock concert. But there were other reasons for coming, too. Many people in the audience seemed to be looking for a direction to their lives, and they had come to the conference for the same reason that they had attended workshops in the past: to find help. The human potential movement had still not done for them what it had promised; their lives had remained the same or perhaps had worsened, and the new world, the promised transformation, seemed very slow in coming.

So they came in a peculiar mood, one that combined equal parts of celebration, yearning, and anger. But their mood was further complicated by the conference's taking place at the beginning of the Arab oil boycott. The audience had recently been made aware of the possibility of a world unlike the familiar one in which they felt privileged and safe. To many of them the future must have seemed frightening, and, standing on the stage and looking out at them, one could feel in the air and see on their faces the early signs of a collective paranoia, as if they were haunted by visions of the world's possible vengeance. Packed into the huge hall, its walls lined with gigantic posters of therapeutic heroes—Fritz Perls, Wilhelm Reich, Abraham Maslow, and others—the crowd was restless, impatient, volatile; one could feel rising from it a palpable sense of hunger, as if these people had somehow been failed by both the world and their therapies. It made one apprehensive—not for any specific reason, but simply because beneath the ruffled but still reasonable surface of the crowd lay a hysteria that would in other settings take on any one of several forms, none of them particularly pretty. They wanted someone to set matters right again, to tell them what to do, and it did not matter how that was done, or who did it, or what it required them to believe.

Most of the people in the audience were followers or clients of the various speakers, and as each one spoke his adherents responded with cheers and applause. Others, at odds with the speaker, answered with catcalls, whistles, or groans. I remember in particular the words "total obedience" and "submission to a perfect master" and "the adolescence of rebellion"—phrases which were used by several speakers and which drew from the crowd a surprising amount of acclaim. But even the speakers who took a stand against submission or obedience seemed somehow to diminish the world of experience and choice. In their words, too, there was a tyrannical refusal to acknowledge the existence of a world larger than the self, the total denial—by implication—of the necessity of human community or relation.

That missing element defined the conference and determined its nature: a massive repression all the more poignant because so much of the audience's feeling was engendered by the world denied. Their relation to that world—what it was, what it ought to be—lay at the heart of their discontent, but it was never spoken of. Even when they began to question the speakers, the questions they asked were invariably concerned with themselves, were about self-denial or self-esteem, all centered on the ego, all turned inward. Behind that, of course, they were asking about something else, about problems for which they had no words, about the proper human relation to an age of catastrophe. But neither they nor the speakers were capable of recognizing that fact, and so those problems remained unarticulated, and they hung in the room like shadows and ghosts, determining the tone of the event but never permitted to enter it.

As I listened, I kept thinking about a conversation I had recently had with a man much taken with mysticism and spirituality. He was telling me about his sense of another reality.

"I know there is something outside of me," he said. "I can feel it. I know it is there. But what is it?"

"It may not be a mystery," I said. "Perhaps it is the world."

·That startled him. He had meant something more magical than that, more exotic and grand, something "above" rather than all around him. It had never occurred to him that what might be calling to him from beyond the self were the worlds of community and value, the worlds of history and action—all of them waiting to be entered not as a saint or a mystic, but in a way more difficult still: as a moral man or woman among other persons, with a person's real and complex nature and needs. Those worlds had been closed to him, had receded from consciousness as he had ceased to inhabit them fully or responsibly or lovingly, and so he felt their ghostly presence as something distant and mysterious, as a dream in which he had no actual existence.

I saw that at work the first night of the conference and I saw it again, in greater detail, the next day at the various workshops. I remember one in particular: a seminar on astral travel held in one of the local churches. In the huge reaches of the church the few dozen participants seemed dwarfed and lost as they gathered around the altar and the first few pews. Their voices echoed in the empty space as they rose one by one to testify as to how they had left their bodies while asleep, or how their friends had, or how they had heard about someone who had. The tone was one of strained yearning, a combined will to believe and be believed, as if by sheer force of conviction they could bring into being a new world to replace the old one. They spoke about "space cadets" and "soul traps" and the ethics of psychic power, and after a while they shifted ground and spoke about the possibilities of using such power to get things changed in Washington.

"We'll get to the President while he's asleep," said someone. "We'll infiltrate his dreams."

"But that isn't right," said someone else.

"That's tyranny, too. We can't intervene without his consent."

"It doesn't matter," said a third. "It won't work anyway. I've a friend who knows someone who tried it. He left his body and went to the White House. But he couldn't get in. The President has astral bodyguards. They know what's what in Washington."

So it went, a series of exchanges making of the world of possibility a comic-strip cosmology. It was both absurd and sad: the exchanges and the pain implicit in them conveyed the participants' anguish at their own powerlessness. I thought automatically of the mysticism rampant in Germany in the Thirties, or of the passion for shamans and mystics in prerevolutionary Petrograd, or of the Christian zealots in declining Rome. The seminar seemed to mix aspects of all three, and the church was a fitting place for it, for the participants were like lost pilgrims trying to create, in its shadow, a new faith to replace the one they had lost. The last remaining shreds of reason and hope mingled with emergent superstition and fantasy, and the end result was neither moral action nor a complex vision of the world, but a child's garden of absurdities, an impotent dream of power. Confronted by a world in which casual goodness was no longer sufficient as a response, the participants were groping for a way to restore to themselves a power and significance they could no longer feel. In this particular instance the salvationary course they took involved astral travel and psychic power, but it might just as easily have been *est* or scientology or submission to Guru Maharaj Ji or even a doctrinaire adherence to Reich's orgasm theory. As different as all those enthusiasms are, they have a common ground; behind them all is a sense of exhaustion, the bourgeois will to power mixed with impotence, and the ache of no longer feeling at home in the world.

Perhaps the best example of all this is the immense popularity of Castaneda's works about don Juan. What they offer the yearning reader is precisely what I am talking about here: the dream of an individual potency to be derived magically from another world. In essence it is an updated version of the Protestant dream of the salvation of the soul, and the important thing about the power celebrated within them is that it occurs neither in the actual polis nor in the company of significant others. It is found, instead, in a moral and human desert, a fictitious landscape emptied of comrade or lover or child, of every genuine human relation (save that of master and disciple) in which joy or courage might actually be found.

Castaneda's myth of don Juan is not an alternative to our condition, but a metaphor for it. It is simply the familiar myth of the solitary gunslinger translated into spiritual language, the comic-strip story of Superman or Captain Marvel made into a slightly more sophisticated legend for adults. It legitimizes our loneliness and solaces us with the myth that we can, in our isolation, find a power to make ourselves safe.

Contrast, for a moment, Castaneda's barren mysteries with the work of Lévi-Strauss, for whom the world of magic and myth is always a *human* world, a realm explored and inhabited by others like ourselves. For Lévi-Strauss the crucial human moment is not the moment of separate awareness; it is the moment of human meeting, in which the other's existence creates for us a sense of the depth and complexity of the world. That, precisely, is what is missing from Castaneda's world. We forget, reading it, that almost without exception the visionary experiences of Indian cultures are a collective work, prepared and defined and sustained by the community, by a world view which is, in effect, the product of cooperative labor. Visionary experience leads not only to the gods and into the self, but it also binds one to the world of myth and—through symbology and tradition—to the historical and social worlds. The individual seeker, though sometimes solitary, is never alone on the quest; the journey occurs within a landscape maintained inwardly by generations of men and women, and the experience is a wedding to them all. Come back from their vision quests, the American Indians recited their newly made poems or sang their songs to the tribe, feeding back to it the shared truths of a solitude that was *not* separate, but shared.

Look, for instance, at the words of Black Elk, the visionary Indian leader, close to death and addressing the gods: "Hear me, not for myself but for my people. Hear me in my sorrow, for I may never live again. Oh, make my people live."

Make my people live! The tale in this instance is not of power but of love—not only for the gods or the self but for the world of others, those whose presence creates for the self a body as truly one's own as the flesh. That love, that sense of lived relation, is at the heart not only of tribal lore, but at the center of the legends of most cultures. One thinks of Odysseus surrounded by comrades seeking to return to his home, or of Gilgamesh driven to seek the secret of immortality by the death of Enkidu, his friend. Both of them are moved by what lies behind all myth and long-lived culture: the felt sense of relation and reciprocity. Indeed, that reciprocity is identical to culture: a collective creation and habitation of value sustains what we carelessly call the "individual" self. But that, in our dream of power, is what we no longer remember. It disappears from our myths, it vanishes from our therapies, and we come to the worlds of mystery much as we came long ago to the new world: with greed and fear rather than awe and love. In the name of power we strip it of everything real, and it becomes nothing more than a reflection of our need.

What is lost in that whole process is a crucial part of our own human nature, our unacknowledged hunger for relation, what might be called "an appetence for Good": the needful reaching out for a life in a larger world.

We are moved toward that world by the inner force Freud sometimes called Eros: the desire for relation is as much at work in our need for community and moral significance as it is in our need for coupled love.

Writing about the Athenian polis, Hannah Arendt said about the Greeks:

> The principal characteristic of the tyrant was that he deprived the citizen of access to the public realm, where he could show himself, see and be seen, hear and be heard, that he prohibited the agoreuein and politeuein, confined the citizens to the privacy of their households. . . . According to the Greeks, to be banished to the privacy of household life was tantamount to being deprived of the specifically human potentialities of life.

The same thing is true for us. To put it simply, it is as if each of us had at the same time a smaller and larger self, as if we inhabited at the same moment a smaller and larger world. The smaller world is the one familiar to us, the world of the individual ego and "interpersonal" relations, a reality acknowledged by our habits of thought and by our institutions and therapies. But we also inhabit a larger and unrealized world, one in which every gesture becomes significant precisely because it is understood to bind us to the lives of invisible others.

The natural direction of human ripening is from the smaller to the larger world, is toward the realization and habitation of ever-widening realms of meaning and value. Just as the young are moved from the inside out through increasingly complex stages of perception and thought demanding corresponding changes in their environment, so, too, adults are moved from inside themselves through increasingly complex stages of relation: past the limits of ego and into a human community in which the self becomes other than it was. Seen in this way, human fulfillment hinges on much more than our usual notions of private pleasure or self-actualization, for both of those in their richest forms are impossible without communion and community, an acknowledgement of liability, and a significant role in both the polis and the moral world. To be deprived of those is to be deprived of a part of the self, and to turn away from them is to betray not only the world but also the self, for it is only in the realms in which others exist that one can come to understand the ways in which the nature of each individual existence is in many ways a collective act, the result of countless other lives.

The traditional image for what I am talking about has always been the harvest: the cooperative act in which comrades in a common field gather from it what they need. One finds the image repeated in the work of Camus, Giono, Kropotkin, Lawrence, Silone, and many others, but the most vivid example I know is the scene in *Anna Karenina* in which Levin labors in a field with the peasants, losing all sense of himself in the shared rhythms of the work, the deep blowing grain, and the heat of the sun on his body. It is an image of ecstatic relation which is as much an expression of Eros as is the emblem of two lovers tangled in embrace, and it can stand for almost every aspect of our lives. Every privilege, every object, every "good" comes to us as the result of a human harvest, the shared labor of others: the language we use and the beliefs we hold and the ways we experience ourselves. Each of these involves a world of others into which we are entered every moment of our lives. Idly, for instance, we take coffee and sugar in the mornings, and even that simple act immerses us immediately in the larger world. Both the sugar and coffee have come from specific places, have been harvested by specific persons, most probably in a country where the land belongs by right to others than those who hold it, where the wages paid those who work it are exploitive and low. No doubt, too, the political system underlying the distribution of land is maintained in large part by the policies enacted and the armies acting in our name—and the reason we enjoy the coffee while others harvest it has nothing to do with individual will and everything to do with economics and history.

That, I believe, is what each of us already knows—no matter how much we pretend we do not. Our lives are crowded with the presence of unacknowledged others upon whom our well-being and privilege depend. The shadows of those neglected others—dying in Asia, hungry in Africa, impoverished in our own country—fall upon every one of our private acts, darken the household and marriage bed for each of us. We try to turn away, but even the desperate nature of our turning is a function of their unacknowledged presence, and they are with us even in the vehemence with which we pretend they are not. Something in each of us—even among the enthusiasts of *est*—aches with their presence, aches for the world, for why else would we be in so much pain?

The question of the age, we like to think, is one of survival, and that is true, but not in the way we ordinarily mean it. The survival we ordinarily mean is a narrow and nervous one: simply the continuation, in their present forms, of the isolated lives we lead. But there is little doubt that most of us *will* survive as we are, for we are clearly prepared to accept whatever is necessary to do so: the deaths of millions of others, wars waged in our name, a police state at home. Like the Germans who accepted the Fascists, or the French citizens who collaborated with the Germans, we, too, will be able to carry on "business as usual," just as we do now. Our actual crisis of survival lies elsewhere, in the moral realm we so carefully ignore, for it is there that our lives are at stake.

Seen in that light, what might one expect from a therapy a grown man or woman might take seriously? First, a simple willingness to accept the existence of an objective reality equal in significance to the self, a reality which literally (as my friend John Seeley likes to put it) *objects* as we try to act upon it. Second, a recognition that much of our present pain is the world's pain, the result of living in a catastrophic age in which we do violence to the best parts of our nature. Third, a consciousness of the natural force within us which demands a moral, political, and historical life in the larger world. Fourth, a humility in the presence of that larger world, a respect for the

254 PHILIP E. SLATER

human meaning gathered there by others struggling both in the present and in the past. Finally, a recognition that the future depends directly upon the ways we act individually and in community; that it will never be more just, humane, generous, or sustaining than we ourselves are willing to be; and that the therapist and client, in the solitude of their encounter, create together—in how much of the world they admit to their discourse—a part of the social reality others will later inhabit.

Physicists sometimes use a lovely word, *elsewhere*, to describe the realms of being which we can postulate in thought but can never enter or demonstrate to exist. It is as if they existed side by side with the known world but were beyond all human habitation or touch. In a sense, *elsewhere* also exists in the moral realm, for whatever we fail to love or inhabit fully fades into it, is like a ghostly presence around us, a reality we vaguely remember or intuit, but which is no longer ours. Thus, in a very real way the nature of the shared human world does depend on our actions and words, and we can destroy it not only with bombs, but through our failure to inhabit it as fully and as humanly as we should. That, in part, is what Freud had in mind, decades ago, when at the very end of *Civilization and Its Discontents* he called for a resurgence of "eternal Eros" in its timeless battle with Death. Now, half a century later, Eros is not yet among us. Whether it ever will be is still an open question. But if the answer to that question is to be found anywhere, it will not be in our popular therapies or creeds like *est* or Castaneda's myths. There, where self is all, Eros can have no life.

PHILIP E. SLATER

Philip E. Slater is a sociologist who has attracted a wide general audience because of his provocative views and because he is not afraid to take on large cultural problems. He was educated at Harvard, where he received a Ph.D. in 1955, and has been a professor at Brandeis since 1961. His celebrated book The Glory of Hera *(1968) offered a radically new interpretation of ancient Greek mythology by bringing modern sociological and psychoanalytic conceptions to bear on Greek family and sexual life. Among his other books are* Earthwalk *(1974);* The Wayward Gate: Science and the Supernatural *(1977);* Footholds: Understanding the Shifting Sexual and Family Tensions in Our Culture *(1977); and* The Pursuit of Loneliness: American Culture at the Breaking Point *(1976), from which we take the following selection. It is a self-contained part of the first chapter, wherein Slater argues that every culture limits and warps the natural emotional character of its members in special ways, and that one of the "desires that are deeply and uniquely frustrated by American culture" is "the desire for community." In our character, he says, community is subordinated to individual drives. But he also points out that repressed cultural traits have a way of finding devious channels of expression and that "the opposing forces are much more equally balanced than the society's participants like to recognize."*

Community and Competition: Getting Together

We are so used to living in an individualistic society that we need to be reminded that collectivism has been the more usual lot of humans. Most people in most societies have lived and died in stable communities that took for granted the subordination of the individual to the welfare of the group. The aggrandizement of the individual at the expense of his neighbors was simply a crime.

This is not to say that competition is an American invention—all societies involve some mixture of cooperative and competitive institutions. But our society lies near the competitive extreme, and although it contains cooperative institutions, we suffer from their weakness and peripherality. Studies of business executives reveal a deep hunger for an atmosphere of trust and fraternity with their colleagues. The competitive life is a lonely one and its satisfactions short-lived, for each race leads only to a new one.

In the past our society had many cases in which one could take refuge from the frenzied invidiousness of our economic system—institutions such as the extended family and the stable local neighborhood in which people could take pleasure from something other than winning symbolic victories over their neighbors. But these have disappeared one by one, leaving us more and more in a situation in which we must try to satisfy our vanity and our needs for intimacy in the same place and at the same time. This has made the appeal of cooperative living more seductive, and the need to suppress our longing for it more acute.

The main vehicle for the expression of this longing has been the mass media. Popular songs and film comedies for fifty years have been engaged in a sentimental rejection of our dominant mores, maintaining that the best things in life are free, that love is more important than success, that keeping up with the Joneses is futile, that personal integrity should take precedence over winning, and so on. But these protestations must be understood for what they are: a safety valve. The same man who chuckles and sentimentalizes over a happy-go-lucky hero in a film would view his real-life counterpart as frivolous and irresponsible, and suburbanites who philosophized over the back fence with complete sincerity about their "dog-eat-dog-world," and what-is-it-all-for, and you-can't-take-it-with-you, and success-doesn't-make-you-happy-it-just-gives-you-ulcers-and-a-heart-condition, were enraged in the sixties when their children began to pay serious attention to these ideas. To the young this seemed hypocritical, but if adults didn't feel these things they wouldn't have had to fight them so vigorously. The exaggerated hostility that young people aroused in the "flower child" era argues that the life they led was highly seductive to middle-aged Americans.

When a value is strongly held, as individualism is in America, the illnesses it produces tend to be treated in the same way an alcoholic treats a hangover or a drug addict his withdrawal symptoms. Technological change, mobility, and individualistic ways of thinking all rupture the bonds that tie a

man to a family, a community, a kinship network, a geographical location—
bonds that give him a comfortable sense of himself. As this sense of himself
erodes, he seeks ways of affirming it. Yet his efforts accelerate the very
erosion he seeks to halt.

This loss of a sense of oneself, a sense of one's place in the scheme of
things, produces a jungle of competing egos, each trying to *create* a place.
Huge corporations are fueled on this energy—the stockholders trying to buy
place with wealth, executives trying to grasp it through power and prestige,
public relations departments and advertisers trying to persuade people that
the corporation can confer a sense of place to those who believe in it or buy
its products.

Americans love bigness, mostly because they feel so small. They feel small
because they're unconnected, without a place. They try to overcome that
smallness by associating themselves with bigness—big projects, big organizations, big government, mass markets, mass media, "nationwide," "world-
wide." But it's that very same bigness that rips away their sense of connect-
edness and place and makes them feel small. A vicious circle.

Notice the names of corporations: "Universal," "Continental," "International," "General," "National," "Trans-World"—the spirit of grandiosity
and ego-inflation pervades our economic life. Corporations exist not to feed
or supply the people, but to appease their own hungry egos. Advertising
pays scant attention to price or quality and leans heavily on our needs for
acceptance and respect. The economic structure of our society continually
frustrates those needs, creating an artificial scarcity that in turn motivates
the entire economy. This is why the quality of life in America is so unsatisfying. Since our economy is built on inflated vanity, rather than being
grounded in the real material needs of the people, it must eventually collapse, when these illusions can no longer be maintained.

Much of the unpleasantness, abrasiveness, and costliness of American life
comes from the fact that we're always dealing with strangers. This is what
bureaucracy is: a mechanism for carrying on transactions between strangers.
Who would need all those offices, all that paperwork, all those lawyers,
contracts, rules and regulations, if all economic transactions took place between lifelong neighbors? A huge and tedious machinery has evolved to
cope with the fact that we prefer to carry on our activities among strangers.
The preference is justified, as are most of the sicknesses in American society,
by the alleged economic benefits of bigness, but like many economic arguments, it's a con.

On the surface, it seems convincing. Any big company can undersell a
little one. Corporations keep getting bigger and bigger and fewer and fewer.
Doesn't that prove it? Survival of the fittest? Yet for some reason, what
should be providing economic benefits to the consumer has in fact produced
nothing but chronic inflation. If bigness lowers the cost of production, why
does everything cost more and break sooner? Management, of course,
blames it on labor, and each industry cites the rising prices of its own suppli-
ers. Isn't it obvious that a few big nationwide companies can produce things
cheaper than many local ones?

It all depends on what you leave out of your analysis (which is why a chimp pressing buttons randomly could predict as well as our economic forecasters). The fewer the companies, the less influence supply and demand have on prices. A heavy investment in advertising and public relations is necessary to keep a national reputation alive. And what about the transportation costs involved when all firms are national? Not to mention the air pollution costs, which are also passed on to the consumer. Chronic inflation suggests that someone is leaving something vital out of his analysis. How does one measure in dollars the cost of economic mistrust? It may be subtle, but it's clearly enormous.

The Great Illusion

It's easy to produce examples of the many ways in which Americans try to minimize, circumvent, or deny the interdependence upon which all human societies are based. We seek a private house, a private means of transportation, a private garden, a private laundry, self-service stores, and do-it-yourself skills of every kind. An enormous technology seems to have set itself the task of making it unnecessary for one human being ever to ask anything of another in the course of going about his or her daily business. Even within the family Americans are unique in their feeling that each member should have a separate room, and even a separate telephone, television, and car, when economically possible. We seek more and more privacy, and feel more and more alienated and lonely when we get it. And what accidental contacts we do have seem more intrusive, not only because they're unsought, but because they're not connected with any familiar pattern of interdependence.

Most important, our encounters with others tend increasingly to be competitive as we search for more privacy. We less and less often meet our fellow humans to share and exchange, and more and more often encounter them as an impediment or a nuisance: making the highway crowded when we're rushing somewhere, cluttering and littering the beach or park or wood, pushing in front of us at the supermarket, taking the last parking place, polluting our air and water, building a highway through our house, blocking our view, and so on. Because we've cut off so much communication with each other we keep bumping into each other, so that a higher and higher percentage of our interpersonal contacts are abrasive.

We seem unable to foresee that the gratification of a wish might turn out to be a monkey's paw if the wish were shared by many others. We cheer the new road that shaves ten minutes off the drive to our country retreat but ultimately transforms it into a crowded resort and increases both the traffic and the time. We're continually surprised to find, when we want something, that thousands or millions of others want it, too—that other human beings get hot in summer and cold in winter. The worst traffic jams occur when a mass of vacationing tourists start home early to "beat the traffic." We're too enamored of the individualistic fantasy that everyone is, or should be, different—that a man could somehow build his entire life around some single eccentricity without boring himself and everyone else to death. We all have our quirks, which provide surface variety, but aside from this, human beings have little basis for their persistent claim that they are not all members of the same species.

The Freedom Fix

Since our contacts with others are increasingly competitive, unanticipated, and abrasive, we seek still more apartness and thus accelerate the trend. The desire to be somehow special sparks an even more competitive quest for progressively more rare and expensive symbols—a quest that is ultimately futile since it is individualism itself that produces uniformity.

This is poorly understood by Americans, who tend to confuse uniformity with "conformity," in the sense of compliance with group demands. Many societies exert far more pressure on the individual to mold herself to play a sharply defined role in a total group pattern, but there is variation among these circumscribed roles. Our society gives more leeway to the individual to pursue her own ends, but since the culture defines what is worthy and desirable, everyone tends, independently but monotonously, to pursue the same things in the same way. Thus cooperation tends to produce variety, while competition generates uniformity.

The problem with individualism is not that it is immoral but that it is incorrect. The universe does not consist of a lot of unrelated particles but is an interconnected whole. Pretending that our fortunes are independent of each other may be perfectly ethical, but it's also perfectly stupid. Individualistic thinking is unflagging in the production of false dichotomies, such as "conformity vs. independence," "altruism vs. egoism," "inner-directed vs. other-directed," and so on, all of which are built upon the absurd assumption that the individual can be considered separately from the environment of which he or she is a part.

A favorite delusion of individualism—one that it attempts, through education and propaganda, to make real—is that only egoistic responses are spontaneous. But this is not so: collective responses—helping behavior, nurturance, supportiveness, the assumption of specialized roles in group tasks, rituals, or games—these are natural, not trained, even among animals. People are more *self-consciously* oriented toward others in competitive, individualistic societies—their behavior is calculated. They accommodate to others because they want to look good, impress people, protect themselves from shame and guilt, and avoid confronting people directly. In more organic and cooperative communities people respond spontaneously to impulses that are neither selfish nor unselfish, but more directly from the heart. Sometimes they look generous, sometimes grasping, but what's important is that the behavior is *to* others, not an effort to produce some sort of *effect* on others. Cooperative societies are unassuming—it's the competitive ones that are concerned with appearances.

Individualism in the United States is exemplified by the flight to the suburb and the do-it-yourself movement. Both attempt to deny human interdependence and pursue unrealistic fantasies of self-sufficiency. The first tries to overlook our dependence upon the city for the maintenance of the level of culture we demand. "Civilized" means, literally, "citified," and the state of the city is an accurate index of the condition of the culture as a whole. We behave toward our cities like an irascible farmer who never feeds his cow and then kicks her when she fails to give enough milk. But the flight to the suburb was in any case self-defeating, its goals subverted by the mass quality of the exodus. The suburban dweller sought peace, privacy, nature, community, good schools, and a healthy child-rearing environment. Instead, he found neither the beauty and serenity of the countryside, nor the stimulation of the city, nor the stability and sense of community of the small town. A small town, after all, is a microcosm, while the suburb is merely a layer, narrowly segregated by age and social class. A minor irony of the suburban dream is that, for many Americans, reaching the pinnacle of their social ambitions (owning a house in the suburbs) forces them to perform all kinds of menial tasks (carrying garbage cans, mowing lawns, shoveling snow, and so on) that were performed for them when they occupied a less exalted status.

Some of this manual labor, however, is voluntary—an attempt to deny the division of labor required in a complex society. Many Americans seem quite willing to pay the price rather than engage in encounters with workers. This do-it-yourself trend has accompanied increasing specialization in occupations. As one's job narrows, perhaps, he or she seeks the challenge of new skill-acquisition in the home. But specialization also means that one's encounters with artisans in the home proliferate and become more impersonal. It's no longer a matter of a few well-known people—smiths and grocers—who perform many functions, and with whom contact may be a source of satisfaction. One finds instead a multiplicity of narrow specialists, each perhaps a stranger—the same type of repair may even be performed by a different person each time. Every relationship, such as it is, must start from scratch, and it's small wonder the householder turns away from such an unrewarding prospect in apathy and despair.

Americans thus find themselves in a vicious circle in which their community relationships are increasingly competitive, trivial, and irksome, in part as a result of their efforts to avoid or minimize potentially irksome relationships. As the few vestiges of stable community life erode, the desire for a simple, cooperative lifestyle grows in intensity. The most seductive appeal of radical ideologies for Americans consists in the fact that all in one way or another attack the competitive foundations of our society.

Now it may be objected that American society is less competitive than it once was, and that the appeal of radical ideologies should hence be diminished. Social critics in the fifties argued that the entrepreneurial individualist of the past has been replaced by a bureaucratic Organization Man. Much of this historical drama was created by comparing yesterday's owner-president with today's assistant sales manager; certainly these nostalgia-merchants never visited a nineteenth-century company town. Another distortion is introduced by the fact that it was only the most ruthlessly competitive robber barons who survived to tell us how it was. Little is written about the neighborhood store that extended credit to the poor, or the small town industry that refused to lay off local workers in hard times. They all went under together. The meek may be blessed but they don't write memoirs.

Even if we grant that the business world was more competitive in the nineteenth century, the total environment was less so. The individual worked in a smaller firm with lower turnover in which his or her relationships were more enduring and more personal. The ideology of Adam Smith was tempered by the fact that the participants in economic struggles were neighbors and might have been childhood playmates. Even if the business world then was as "dog-eat-dog" as we imagine it, it occurred as a deviant episode in what was otherwise a more comfortable and familiar environment than the organization man can find today in or out of his office. The organization man is simply a carryover from the paternalistic environment of the family business and the company town; and the "other-directedness" of the suburban community just a desperate attempt to bring some old-fashioned small-town collectivism into the transient and impersonal lifestyle of the suburb. The social critics of the 1950s were so preoccupied with assailing these rather synthetic forms of human interdependence that they lost sight of the underlying sickness that produced them. Medical symptoms usually result from attempts made by the body to counteract disease, and attacking the symptoms often aggravates and prolongs the illness. This seems to be the case with the feeble and self-defeating efforts of twentieth-century Americans to create a viable social environment.

A SATIRIC VIEW

JONATHAN SWIFT

Jonathan Swift (1667-1745) is one of the most famous writers in English. He was born of an English family in Dublin and became an Anglican clergyman in a period of disappointment over his hopes for a political career in England. He nevertheless pursued politics; in 1713 the Tory government rewarded him for his powerful writing—in the manner of those times—with the deanship of St. Patrick's, Dublin. However, he spent little time in Ireland until the fall of the party forced his return to Dublin a few years later, where he became for the rest of his life a champion of the Irish people against English oppression. Meanwhile, he had become an intimate of the best English writers of his day, a leading political pamphleteer, and the author of a series of writings that would make him the greatest of English satirists. Especially notable are A Tale of a Tub *and* The Battle of the Books *published in 1704, the incomparable* Gulliver's Travels *(1726), and the present piece,* A Modest Proposal, *published in 1729, at a time when the miseries of the poor in Ireland seemed to Swift to have reached an intolerable state. Calculated to arouse attention and sympathy in Ireland and England, it has become a classic, notable particularly for its daring use of irony.*

A Modest Proposal

It is a melancholly Object to those, who walk through this great Town, or travel in the Country; when they see the *Streets*, the *Roads*, and *Cabbin-doors* crowded with *Beggars* of the Female Sex, followed by three, four, or six Children, *all in Rags*, and importuning every Passenger for an Alms. These *Mothers*, instead of being able to work for their honest Livelyhood, are forced to employ all their Time in stroling to beg Sustenance for their *helpless Infants*; who, as they grow up, either turn *Thieves* for want of Work; or leave their *dear Native Country, to fight for the Pretender in* Spain, or sell themselves to the *Barbadoes*.

I think it is agreed by all Parties, that this prodigious Number of Children in the Arms, or on the Backs, or at the Heels of their *Mothers*, and frequently of their *Fathers*, is *in the present deplorable State of the Kingdom*, a very great additional Grievance; and therefore, whoever could find out a fair, cheap, and easy Method of making these Children sound and useful Members of the Commonwealth, would deserve so well of the Publick, as to have his Statue set up for a Preserver of the Nation.

But my Intention is very far from being confined to provide only for the Children of *professed Beggars*: It is of a much greater Extent, and shall take in the whole Number of Infants at a certain Age, who are born of Parents, in effect as little able to support them, as those who demand our Charity in the Streets.

As to my own Part, having turned my Thoughts for many Years, upon this important Subject, and maturely weighed the several *Schemes of other Projectors*, I have always found them grosly mistaken in their Computation. It is true a Child, *just dropt from its Dam*, may be supported by her Milk, for a Solar Year with little other Nourishment; at most not above the Value of two Shillings; which the Mother may certainly get, or the Value in *Scraps*, by her lawful Occupation of *Begging*: And, it is exactly at one Year old, that I propose to provide for them in such a Manner, as, instead of being a Charge upon their *Parents*, or the *Parish*, or *wanting Food and Raiment* for the rest of their Lives; they shall, on the contrary, contribute to the Feeding, and partly to the Cloathing, of many Thousands.

There is likewise another great Advantage in my *Scheme*, that it will prevent those *voluntary Abortions*, and that horrid Practice of *Women murdering their Bastard Children*; alas! too frequent among us; sacrificing the *poor innocent Babes*, I doubt, more to avoid the Expence than the Shame; which would move Tears and Pity in the most Savage and inhuman Breast.

The Number of Souls in *Ireland* being usually reckoned one Million and a half; of these I calculate there may be about Two hundred Thousand Couple whose Wives are Breeders; from which Number I subtract thirty thousand Couples, who are able to maintain their own Children; although I apprehend there cannot be so many, under *the present Distresses of the Kingdom*; but this being granted, there will remain an Hundred and Seventy Thousand Breeders. I again subtract Fifty Thousand, for those Women who miscarry, or whose Children die by Accident, or Disease, within the Year. There only remain an Hundred and Twenty Thousand Children of poor Parents, annually born: The Question therefore is, How this Number shall be reared, and provided for? Which, as I have already said, under the present Situation of Affairs, is utterly impossible, by all the Methods hitherto proposed: For we can *neither employ them in Handicraft* or *Agriculture*; we neither build Houses, (I mean in the Country) nor cultivate Land: They can very seldom pick up a Livelyhood *by Stealing* until they arrive at six Years old; except where they are of towardly Parts; although, I confess, they learn the Rudiments much earlier; during which Time, they can, however, be properly looked upon only as *Probationers*; as I have been informed by a principal Gentleman in the Country of *Cavan*, who protested to me, that he never knew above one or two Instances under the Age of six, even in a Part of the Kingdom *so renowned for the quickest Proficiency in that Art.*

I am assured by our Merchants, that a Boy or a Girl before twelve Years old, is no saleable Commodity; and even when they come to this Age, they will not yield above Three Pounds, or Three Pounds and half a Crown at most, on the Exchange; which cannot turn to Account either to the Parents or the Kingdom; the Charge of Nutriment and Rags, having been at least four Times that Value.

I shall now therefore humbly propose my own Thoughts; which I hope will not be liable to the least Objection.

I have been assured by a very knowing *American* of my Acquaintance in *London*; that a young healthy Child, well nursed, is, at a Year old, a most delicious, nourishing, and wholesome Food; whether *Stewed, Roasted, Baked,* or *Boiled*; and, I make no doubt, that it will equally serve in a *Fricasie,* or *Ragoust.*

I do therefore humbly offer it to *publick Consideration,* that of the Hundred and Twenty Thousand Children, already computed, Twenty thousand may be reserved for Breed; whereof only one Fourth Part to be Males; which is more than we allow to *Sheep, black Cattle,* or *Swine*; and my Reason is, that these Children are seldom the Fruits of Marriage, *a Circumstance not much regarded by our Savages*; therefore, *one Male* will be sufficient to serve *four Females.* That the remaining Hundred thousand, may, at a Year old, be offered in Sale to the *Persons of Quality* and *Fortune,* through the Kingdom; always advising the Mother to let them suck plentifully in the last Month, so as to render them plump, and fat for a good Table. A Child will make two Dishes at an Entertainment for Friends; and when the Family dines alone, the fore or hind Quarter will make a reasonable Dish; and seasoned with a little Pepper or Salt, will be very good Boiled on the fourth Day, especially in *Winter.*

I have reckoned upon a Medium, that a Child just born will weigh Twelve Pounds; and in a solar Year, if tolerably nursed, encreaseth to twenty eight Pounds.

I grant this Food will be somewhat dear, and therefore very *proper for Landlords*; who, as they have already devoured most of the Parents, seem to have the best Title to the Children.

Infants Flesh will be in Season throughout the Year; but more plentiful in *March*, and a little before and after: For we are told by a grave[1] Author, an eminent *French* physician, that *Fish being a prolifick Dyet*, there are more Children born in *Roman Catholick Countries* about Nine Months after *Lent*, than at any other Season: Therefore reckoning a Year after *Lent*, the Markets will be more glutted than usual; because the Number of *Popish Infants*, is, at least, three to one in this Kingdom; and therefore it will have one other Collateral Advantage, by lessening the Number of *Papists* among us.

I have already computed the Charge of nursing a Beggar's Child (in which List I reckon all *Cottagers*, *Labourers*, and Four fifths of the *Farmers*) to be about two Shillings *per Annum*, Rags included; and I believe, no Gentleman would repine to give Ten Shillings for the *Carcase of a good fat Child*; which, as I have said, will make four Dishes of excellent nutritive Meat, when he hath only some particular Friend, or his own Family, to dine with him. Thus the Squire will learn to be a good Landlord, and grow popular among his Tenants; the Mother will have Eight Shillings net Profit, and be fit for Work until she produceth another Child.

Those who are more thrifty (*as I must confess the Times require*) may flay the Carcase; the Skin of which, artificially dressed, will make admirable *Gloves for Ladies*, and *Summer Boots for fine Gentlemen*.

As to our City of *Dublin*; Shambles may be appointed for this Purpose, in the most convenient Parts of it; and Butchers we may be assured will not be wanting; although I rather recommend buying the Children alive, and dressing them hot from the Knife, as we do *roasting Pigs*.

A very worthy Person, a true Lover of his Country, and whose Virtues I highly esteem, was lately pleased, in discoursing on this Matter, to offer a Refinement upon my Scheme. He said, that many Gentlemen of this Kingdom, having of late destroyed their Deer; he conceived, that the Want of Venison might be well supplied by the Bodies of young Lads and Maidens, not exceeding fourteen Years of Age, nor under twelve; so great a Number of both Sexes in every Country being now ready to starve, for Want of Work and Service: And these to be disposed of by their Parents, if alive, or otherwise by their nearest Relations. But with due Deference to so excellent a Friend, and so deserving a Patriot, I cannot be altogether in his Sentiments. For as to the Males, my *American* Acquaintance assured me from frequent Experience, that their Flesh was generally tough and lean, like that of our School-boys, by continual Exercise, and their Taste disagreeable; and to fatten them would not answer the Charge. Then, as to the Females, it would, I think, with humble Submission, *be a Loss to the Publick*, because they soon would become Breeders themselves: And besides it is not improbable, that some scrupulous People might be apt to censure such a Practice (although indeed very unjustly) as a little bordering upon Cruelty; which, I confess, hath always been with me the strongest Objection against any Project, how well soever intended.

But in order to justify my Friend; he confessed, that this Expedient was

---

[1] Rabelais.

put into his Head by the famous *Salmanaazor*, a Native of the Island *Formosa*, who came from thence to *London*, above twenty Years ago, and in Conversation told my Friend, that in his Country, when any young Person happened to be put to Death, the Executioner sold the Carcase to *Persons of Quality*, as a prime Dainty; and that, in his Time, the Body of a plump Girl of fifteen, who was crucified for an Attempt to poison the Emperor, was sold to his Imperial *Majesty's prime Minister of State*, and other great *Mandarins* of the Court, *in Joints from the Gibbet*, at Four hundred Crowns. Neither indeed can I deny, that if the same Use were made of several plump young girls in this Town, who, without one single Groat to their Fortunes, cannot stir Abroad without a Chair, and appear at the *Play-house*, and *Assemblies* in foreign Fineries, which they never will pay for; the Kingdom would not be the worse.

Some Persons of a desponding Spirit are in great Concern about that vast Number of poor People, who are Aged, Diseased, or Maimed; and I have been desired to employ my Thoughts what Course may be taken, to ease the Nation of so grievous an Incumbrance. But I am not in the least Pain upon that Matter; because it is very well known, that they are every Day *dying*, and *rotting*, by *Cold* and *Famine*, and *Filth*, and *Vermin*, as fast as can be reasonably expected. And as to the younger Labourers, they are now in almost as hopeful a Condition: They cannot get Work, and consequently pine away for Want of Nourishment, to a Degree, that if at any Time they are accidentally hired to common Labour, they have not Strength to perform it; and thus the Country, and themselves, are in a fair Way of being soon delivered from the Evils to come.

I have too long digressed; and therefore shall return to my Subject. I think the Advantages by the Proposal which I have made, are obvious, and many, as well as of the highest Importance.

For, *First*, as I have already observed, it would greatly lessen the *Number of Papists*, with whom we are yearly overrun; being the principal Breeders of the Nation, as well as our most dangerous Enemies; and who stay at home on Purpose, with a Design to *deliver the Kingdom to the Pretender*; hoping to take their Advantage by the Absence *of so many good Protestants*, who have chosen rather to leave their Country, than stay at home, and pay Tithes against their Conscience, to an idolatrous *Episcopal Curate*.

Secondly, The poorer Tenants will have something valuable of their own, which, by Law, may be made liable to Distress, and help to pay their Landlord's Rent; their Corn and Cattle being already seized, and *Money a Thing unknown*.

Thirdly, Whereas the Maintenance of an Hundred Thousand Children, from two Years old, and upwards, cannot be computed at less than ten Shillings a Piece *per Annum*, the Nation's Stock will be thereby encreased Fifty Thousand Pounds *per Annum*; besides the Profit of a new Dish, introduced to the Tables of all *Gentlemen of Fortune* in the Kingdom, who have any Refinement in Taste; and the Money will circulate among ourselves, the Goods being entirely of our own Growth and Manufacture.

Fourthly, The constant Breeders, besides the Gain of Eight Shillings *Ster-*

ling per Annum, by the Sale of their Children, will be rid of the Charge of maintaining them after the first Year.

Fifthly, This Food would likewise bring great *Custom to Taverns*, where the Vintners will certainly be so prudent, as to procure the best Receipts for dressing it to Perfection; and consequently, have their Houses frequented by all the *fine Gentlemen*, who justly value themselves upon their Knowledge in good Eating; and a skilful Cook, who understands how to oblige his Guests, will contrive to make it as expensive as they please.

Sixthly, This would be a great Inducement to Marriage, which all wise Nations have either encouraged by Rewards, or enforced by Laws and Penalties. It would encrease the Care and Tenderness of Mothers towards their Children, when they were sure of a Settlement for Life, to the poor Babes, provided in some Sort by the Publick, to their annual Profit instead of Expense. We should soon see an honest Emulation among the married Women, *which of them could bring the fattest Child to the Market*. Men would become as *fond* of their Wives, during the Time of their Pregnancy, as they are now of their *Mares* in Foal, their *Cows* in Calf, or *Sows* when they are ready to farrow; nor offer to beat or kick them, (as it is too *frequent* a Practice) for fear of a Miscarriage.

Many other Advantages might be enumerated. For instance, the Addition of some Thousand Carcasses in our Exportation of barrelled Beef: The Propagation of *Swines Flesh*, and Improvement in the Art of making good *Bacon*; so much wanted among us by the great Destruction of *Pigs*, too frequent at our Tables, and are no way comparable in Taste, or Magnificence, to a well-grown fat yearling Child; which, roasted whole, will make a considerable Figure at a *Lord Mayor's Feast*, or any other publick Entertainment. But this, and many others, I omit; being studious of Brevity.

Supposing that one Thousand Families in this City, would be constant Customers for Infants Flesh; besides others who might have it at *merry Meetings*, particularly *Weddings* and *Christenings*; I compute that *Dublin* would take off, annually, about Twenty Thousand Carcasses; and the rest of the Kingdom (where probably they will be sold somewhat cheaper) the remaining Eighty Thousand.

I can think of no one Objection, that will possibly be raised against this Proposal; unless it should be urged, that the Number of People will be thereby much lessened in the Kingdom. This I freely own; and it was indeed one principal Design in offering it to the World. I desire the Reader will observe, that I calculate my Remedy *for this one individual Kingdom of* IRELAND, *and for no other that ever was, is, or I think ever can be upon Earth.* Therefore, let no man talk to me of other Expedients: *Of taxing our Absentees at five Shillings a Pound: Of using neither Cloaths, nor Houshold Furniture except what is of our own Growth and Manufacture: Of utterly rejecting the Materials and Instruments that promote foreign Luxury: Of curing the Expensiveness of Pride, Vanity, Idleness, and Gaming in our Women: Of introducing a Vein of Parsimony, Prudence and Temperance: Of learning to love our Country, wherein we differ even from* LAPLANDERS, *and the Inhabitants of* TOPINAMBOO: *Of quitting our Animosities, and Factions; nor act any longer like the* Jews, *who were murdering one another at the very Moment their City was taken: Of being a little cautious not to sell our Country and Consciences for nothing: Of teaching Landlords to have, at least, one Degree of Mercy towards their Tenants.* Lastly, *Of putting a Spirit of Honesty, Industry, and Skill into our Shop-keepers; who, if a Resolution could now be taken to buy only our native Goods, would immediately unite to cheat and exact upon us in the Price, the Measure, and the Goodness; nor could ever yet be brought to make one fair Proposal of just Dealing, though often and earnestly invited to it.*

Therefore I repeat, let no Man talk to me of these and the like Expedients; till he hath, at least, a Glimpse of Hope, that there will ever be some hearty and sincere Attempt to put *them in Practice.*

But, as to my self; having been wearied out for many Years with offering vain, idle, visionary Thoughts; and at length utterly despairing of Success, I fortunately fell upon this Proposal; which, as it is wholly new, so it hath something *solid* and *real*, of no Expence, and little Trouble, full in our own Power; and whereby we can incur no Danger in *disobliging* ENGLAND: For, this Kind of Commodity will not bear Exportation; the Flesh being of too tender a Consistence, to admit a long Continuance of Salt; *although, perhaps, I could name a Country, which would be glad to eat up our whole Nation without it.*

After all, I am not so violently bent upon my own Opinion, as to reject any Offer proposed by wise Men, which shall be found equally innocent, cheap, easy, and effectual. But before something of that Kind shall be advanced, in Contradiction to my Scheme, and offering a better; I desire the Author, or Authors, will be pleased maturely to consider two Points. *First*, As Things now stand, how they will be able to find Food and Raiment, for a Hundred Thousand useless Mouths and Backs? And *secondly*, There being a round Million of Creatures in human Figure, throughout this Kingdom; whose whole Subsistence, put into a common Stock, would leave them in Debt two Millions of Pounds *Sterling*; adding those, who are Beggars by Profession, to the Bulk of Farmers, Cottagers, and Labourers, with their Wives and Children, who are Beggars in Effect; I desire those Politicians, who dislike my Overture, and may perhaps be so bold to attempt an Answer, that they will first ask the Parents of these Mortals, Whether they would not, at this Day, think it a great Happiness to have been sold for Food at a Year old, in the Manner I prescribe; and thereby have avoided such a perpetual Scene of Misfortunes, as they have since gone through; by the *Oppression of Landlords*; the Impossibility of paying Rent, without Money or Trade; the Want of common Sustenance, with neither House nor Cloaths, to cover them from the Inclemencies of Weather; and the most inevitable Prospect of intailing the like, or greater Miseries upon their Breed for ever.

I profess, in the Sincerity of my Heart, that I have not the least personal Interest, in endeavouring to promote this necessary Work; having no other Motive than the *publick Good of my Country, by advancing our Trade, providing for Infants, relieving the Poor, and giving some Pleasure to the Rich.* I have no Children, by which I can propose to get a single Penny; the youngest being nine Years old, and my Wife past Child-bearing.

The Good Life

ONE of the oldest human questions is, What is the Good Life? Often the attempt to achieve the good life is indistinguishable from the effort to find out what it is. When people are struggling to stay alive in the face of danger or poverty, the question seems to have an easy answer: then, the good life means safety or food. The first need is survival. But once we have this, once we pass from survival or subsistence to a range of wider possibilities, the question takes on new meaning. Are plenty and ease sufficient? Does "making it" make us happy? Psychologist Abraham Maslow suggests that a need motivates us only until it is filled, when a higher need takes over; after the necessities of survival and security, he ranks, in order, belonging, unity, participation, and self-actualization. Readers may want to challenge Maslow's assumption or change or add to his list according to their own experiences; but whatever the hierarchy, given the state of comparative affluence enjoyed by many Americans, it seems that to seek the good life we must first discover our genuine needs.

J. P. Donleavy's brief and amusing sketch, with its rhyming word play, may take the reader by surprise and will, obliquely, raise some of these questions. The two essays that follow describe different suburbias from different points of view. Phyllis McGinley appreciates the freedom and solidity of the middle-class suburban life she knows, and deplores the fashionable clichés that make it a symbol of all that is middle class in the worst sense. Joan Didion, however, reporting on a murder trial in southern California, paints a devastating picture of the Golden Dream of material comfort and status, here with no past or future, devoid of meaning and value. E. F. Schumacher's essay then becomes a pivotal piece for the section. Our real needs, he says, are limited and must be met, but our wants are unlimited, cannot be met, and should be resisted. "Man does not live by bread alone, and no increase in his *wants* above his needs can give him the 'good life'." He challenges the assumption that only the rich can have a good life and introduces the useful distinction between "the ephemeral" and "the eternal." The quality of life or of a style of life can be gauged, he feels, by that which is valued most. The story by Ursula Le Guin that follows raises provocative and disturbing questions about the good life and the price we pay for what we have.

The next five pieces all deal, directly or indirectly, with the meaning of work. How much of the value of our lives depends on our work? Work can be perceived as drudgery, as a trap, or as an important part of our inner life; as a means to an end, or as an end in itself. Erich Fromm establishes a historical framework by describing various roles of work in different cultures, from the fulfillment provided by old-fashioned craftsmanship to the alienation resulting from modern industrial labor. He points to some of the consequences of alienation and suggests relations among our work, our values, and how we view ourselves. There follow reports of work by four different workers—a mason, an editor, a steelworker, and a surgeon. Readers may want to ask themselves what needs seem to be expressed and what needs seem to be fulfilled or frustrated by the work of each, and then compare their own experiences and aspirations. Many further questions are of course raised by these selections. Two of the most important are: Why work if you do not have to? and Why do a job well if nobody is watching?

THE GOLDEN DREAM

J. P. DONLEAVY

J. P. Donleavy was born in New York City in 1926. After school in New York and a hitch in the U.S. Navy, he went on to study at Trinity College, Dublin, where he majored in microbiology; he left without a degree but remained in Ireland, and in 1967 he became an Irish citizen. Donleavy started in art as a painter and did not begin to write seriously until he wrote catalog introductions to his painting exhibitions. His first and perhaps best-known novel is The Ginger Man, *published in Paris in 1955. (Unexpurgated editions were not published in England and the United States until 1963 and 1965 respectively.) In 1959 an adaptation of it was a success on the London stage, but the play was closed down in Dublin. An essay that describes this unofficial censorship, "What They Did in Dublin," now introduces the published play (1961). Other writings include* A Singular Man *(1963), later dramatized;* A Fairy Tale of New York *(1973), derived from an earlier play;* The Unexpurgated Code, A Complete Manual of Survival and Manners *(1975), a parody of the etiquette manual; and a picaresque novel,* The Destinies of Darcy Dancer, Gentleman *(1977). He has also written stories and sketches, collected in the volume* Meet My Maker, the Mad Molecule *(1964), from which we reprint the story below.*

Meet My Maker

I set out one summer singing. To meet my Maker. He lived on a hill with lawns around and buttercups sprinkled in the green. I said I'll climb your hill and knock on your door, look in your windows and see what I saw. He came out in a pair of blue jeans with a pipe and said hi, when did you die.

I told him yesterday about noon. They all stood around for my doom. Even Sidney in his sun glasses and Flora just out of her red sports car. They looked at me and said he's gone for a ride and that's all I heard when I died.

And Maker said come in and sit down. He said sherry. I said pale please and dry. Now tell me young man how was your trip, were some of the stops called despair and did you see the town called sad. Or did you detour through laugh. Maker I'll tell you the truth I stayed too long in the metropolis called money which I found to be sunny, a city of aspic, tinkle and titters where I bought at the bottom and sold at the top.

But son surely you didn't stay. Maker I did and never left till my dying day. I lived way up in the sky with a terrace where I sang my song:

> Every tulip
> Is a julep
> And all the mint
> Is meant for me.

And Sidney and Flora came and said why don't we have some fun and go up to Vermont for a barbecue. And all night we drove through the beer cans along the road. I sat looking out between the trees and at others racing along and I thought I'm weak and want to belong. To clubs and leisure life and breathe only imported air. But Flora said I was the sensitive type who looked well with a pipe and could afford to be poor if I wanted or even maybe something real special so that they'd all be glad to know me later on. But I said no I want to be loved for my money and nothing else will do. So off we went to Vermont for the barbecue.

Out by the lake we lit a fire, spread out the marshmallow and steak. And Maker this is why I never had a chance to repent. I just thought I'd go for a swim and look up at the stars and then sat around and got a chill and later I knew I was ill. So I said before I was dead take me back to the city of money fast and see how much they charge to get out of this. And they came and said buddy you're on your way to the next town and this here train can't turn around. So I said where's the ticket taker maybe he personally knows my Maker because I have a few things he can buy at the bottom. But they said there is no ticket taker because this ride's free.

So Maker I just said gee and as you can see I never had courage to give up the salmon and riesling or the picnics at Newport but stayed at my club for showers and grub and could never get enough. Son, cheer up, I know how you feel, but let me tell you we have some fine vintages here as well as delectable veal. And oceans of time and beef in its prime. So relax and watch the sun shine. But Maker how can you welcome me from that land down there when I've never been kind or felt any despair. Son, I can see you never meant any harm, another helping of the peaches and cream is no need for alarm.

But Maker, what about Sidney and Flora. Son, come over, you can see them from here. Wow, Maker, can you see all this. Son, behind every and any blind. But Sidney's got my cigarette lighter and Flora my flat, why those cheapskates, I'll never forgive them for that. Easy son, that's what you were like before you got up here. But Sidney's playing my gramophone and Flora's taken my Ming horse. Son, next time leave nothing behind and you'll feel no remorse.

Well, Maker, what do we do now. Son, it's time for a swim and workout in the gym and after a good scrub I'll take you to a nightclub. But Maker I can't see how we so readily agree, this is even better than it was down there and it's free. Son, look me in the eye and see what you see. Whoa, Maker, you're me.

PHYLLIS McGINLEY

Phyllis McGinley (1905-1978) received the Pulitzer Prize for poetry in 1961 for Times Three: Selected Verse from Three Decades; *she was the first writer of light verse to win that award. She spent her childhood on a Colorado ranch and then went through high school and college in Ogden, Utah. She studied at the University of Southern California but returned to graduate from the University of Utah and to teach school for a year in Ogden. In 1928 she moved to New Rochelle, New York, where she taught school for four years, then moved to Manhattan and turned to free-lance writing. After her marriage in 1937, she lived in the New York suburb of Larchmont and later in Weston, Connecticut.*

Her first book of poetry was On the Contrary *(1934); others, besides* Times Three, *include* A Pocketful of Wry *(1940),* A Short Walk from the Station *(1951),* The Love Letters of Phyllis McGinley *(1954), and* Wonders and Surprises *(1968). Her prose works include* Saint Watching *(1969), the autobiographical* Sixpence in Her Shoe *(1964), children's books, and* The Province of the Heart *(1959), a collection of essays from which we have taken "Suburbia, of Thee I Sing." She wrote it, she said, in response to John Marquand, who had been "wittily naming and then demolishing in print the village where I lived and shopped for grapefruit and attended library meetings and weeded dandelions and composed my poems. I felt I knew that village better than he, and that it was not at all the dreary stronghold of mediocrity which he pictured, but a lively, interesting, and desirable dwelling-place. I felt it ought to be defended."*

Suburbia, of Thee I Sing

Twenty miles east of New York City as the New Haven Railroad flies sits a village I shall call Spruce Manor. The Boston Post Road, there, for the length of two blocks, becomes Main Street, and on one side of that thundering thoroughfare are the grocery stores and the drug stores and the Village

Spa where teen-agers gather of an afternoon to drink their Cokes and speak their curious confidences. There one finds the shoe repairers and the dry cleaners and the second-hand stores which sell "antiques," and the stationery stores which dispense comic books to ten-year-olds and greeting cards and lending-library masterpieces to their mothers. On the opposite side stand the bank, the fire house, the public library. The rest of this town of perhaps five or six thousand people lies to the south and is bounded largely by Long Island Sound, curving protectively on three borders. The movie theater (dedicated to the showing of second-run, single-feature pictures) and the grade schools lie north, beyond the Post Road, and that is a source of worry to Spruce Manorites. They are always a little uneasy about the children, crossing, perhaps, before the lights are safely green. However, two excellent policemen—Mr. Crowley and Mr. Lang—station themselves at the intersections four times a day, and so far there have been no accidents.

Spruce Manor in the spring and summer and fall is a pretty town, full of gardens and old elms. (There are few spruces but the village council is considering planting some on the station plaza, out of sheer patriotism.) In the winter, the houses reveal themselves as comfortable, well kept, architecturally insignificant. Then one can see the town for what it is and has been since it left off being farm and woodland some sixty years ago—the epitome of Suburbia, not the country and certainly not the city. It is a commuter's town, the living center of a web which unrolls each morning as the men swing aboard the locals, and contracts again in the evening when they return. By day, with even the children pent in schools, it is a village of women. They trundle mobile baskets at the A & P, they sit under driers at the hairdressers, they sweep their porches and set out bulbs and stitch up slipcovers. Only on week ends does it become heterogeneous and lively, the parking places difficult to find.

Spruce Manor has no country club of its own, though devoted golfers have their choice of two or three not far away. It does have a small yacht club and a beach which can be used by anyone who rents or owns a house here. The village supports a little park with playground equipment and a counselor, where children, unattended by parents, can spend summer days if they have no more pressing engagements.

It is a town not wholly without traditions. Residents will point out the two-hundred-year-old Manor house, now a minor museum; and in the autumn they line the streets on a scheduled evening to watch the volunteer firemen parade. That is a fine occasion, with so many heads of households marching in their red blouses and white gloves, some with flaming helmets, some swinging lanterns, most of them genially out of step. There is a bigger parade on Memorial Day, with more marchers than watchers and with the Catholic priest, the rabbi, and the Protestant ministers each delivering a short prayer when the paraders gather near the war memorial. On the whole, however, outside of contributing generously to the Community Chest, Manorites are not addicted to municipal get-togethers.

No one is very poor here and not many families rich enough to be awesome. In fact, there is not much to distinguish Spruce Manor from any other of a thousand suburbs outside of New York City or San Francisco or Detroit or Chicago or even Stockholm, for that matter. Except for one thing. For some reason, Spruce Manor has become a sort of symbol to writers and reporters familiar only with its name or trivial aspects. It has become a symbol of all that is middle-class in the worst sense, of settled-downness or rootlessness, according to what the writer is trying to prove; of smug and prosperous mediocrity—or even, in more lurid novels, of lechery at the country club and Sunday-morning hangovers.

To condemn Suburbia has long been a literary cliché, anyhow. I have yet to read a book in which the suburban life was pictured as the good life or the commuter as a sympathetic figure. He is nearly as much a stock character as the old stage Irishman: the man who "spends his life riding to and from his wife," the eternal Babbitt who knows all about Buicks and nothing about Picasso, whose sanctuary is the club locker room, whose ideas spring ready-made from the illiberal newspapers. His wife plays politics at the P.T.A. and keeps up with the Joneses. Or—if the scene is more gilded and less respect-able—the commuter is the high-powered advertising executive with a sta-tion wagon and an eye for the ladies, his wife a restless baggage given to too many cocktails in the afternoon.

These clichés I challenge. I have lived in the country. I have lived in the city. I have lived in an average Middle Western small town. But for the best fifteen years of my life I have lived in Suburbia, and I like it.

"Compromise!" cried our friends when we came here from an expensive, inconvenient, moderately fashionable tenement in Manhattan. It was the period in our lives when everyone was moving somewhere—farther uptown, farther downtown, across town to Sutton Place, to a half-dozen rural acres in Connecticut or New Jersey or even Vermont. But no one in our rather rarefied little group was thinking of moving to the suburbs except us. They were aghast that we could find anything appealing in the thought of a middle-class house on a middle-class street in a middle-class village full of middle-class people. That we were tired of town and hoped for children, that we couldn't afford both a city apartment and a farm, they put down as feeble excuses. To this day they cannot understand us. You see, they read the books. They even write them.

Compromise? Of course we compromise. But compromise, if not the spice of life, is its solidity. It is what makes nations great and marriages happy and Spruce Manor the pleasant place it is. As for its being middle-class, what is wrong with acknowledging one's roots? And how free we are! Free of the city's noise, of its ubiquitous doormen, of the soot on the window sill and the radio in the next apartment. We have released ourselves from the seasonal hegira to the mountains or the seashore. We have only one address, one house to keep supplied with paring knives and blankets. We are free from the snows that block the countryman's roads in winter and his electricity which always goes off in a thunderstorm. I do not insist that we are typical. There is nothing really typical about any of our friends and neighbors here, and therein lies my point. The true suburbanite needs to conform less than anyone else; much less than the gentleman farmer with his remodeled salt-box or than the determined cliff-dweller with his necessity for living at the right address. In Spruce Manor all addresses are right. And since we are fairly numerous here, we need not fall back on the people nearest us for total companionship. There is not here, as in a small city away from truly urban centers, some particular family whose codes must be ours. And we could not keep up with the Joneses even if we wanted to, for we know many Joneses and they are all quite different people leading the most various lives.

The Albert Joneses spend their week ends sailing, the Bertram Joneses cultivate their delphinium, the Clarence Joneses—Clarence being a handy man with a cello—are enthusiastic about amateur chamber music. The David Joneses dote on bridge, but neither of the Ernest Joneses understands it and they prefer staying home of an evening so that Ernest Jones can carve his witty caricatures out of pieces of old fruit wood. We admire one another's gardens, applaud one another's sailing records; we are too busy to compete. So long as our clapboards are painted and our hedges decently trimmed, we have fulfilled our community obligations. We can live as anonymously as in a city or we can call half the village by their first names.

On our half-acre or three-quarters, we can raise enough tomatoes for our salads and assassinate enough beetles to satisfy the gardening urge. Or we can buy our vegetables at the store and put the whole place to lawn without feeling that we are neglecting our property. We can have privacy and shade and the changing of the seasons and also the Joneses next door from whom to borrow a cup of sugar or a stepladder. Despite the novelists, the shadow of the country club rests lightly on us. Half of us wouldn't be found dead with a golf stick in our hands, and loathe Saturday dances. Few of us expect to be deliriously wealthy or world-famous or divorced. What we do expect is to pay off the mortgage and send our healthy children to good colleges.

For when I refer to life here, I think, of course, of living with children. Spruce Manor without children would be a paradox. The summer waters are full of them, gamboling like dolphins. The lanes are alive with them, the yards overflow with them, they possess the tennis courts and the skating pond and the vacant lots. Their roller skates wear down the asphalt and their bicycles make necessary the twenty-five-mile speed limit. They converse interminably on the telephones and make rich the dentist and the pediatrician. Who claims that a child and a half is the American middle-class average? A nice medium Spruce Manor family runs to four or five, and we count proudly, but not with amazement, the many solid households running to six, seven, eight, nine, even up to twelve. Our houses here are big and not new, most of them, and there is a temptation to fill them up, let the *décor* fall where it may.

Besides, Spruce Manor seems designed by providence and town planning for the happiness of children. Better designed than the city; better, I say defiantly, than the country. Country mothers must be constantly arranging and contriving for their children's leisure time. There is no neighbor child next door for playmate, no school within walking distance. The ponds are dangerous to young swimmers, the woods full of poison ivy, the romantic dirt roads unsuitable for bicycles. An extra acre or two gives a fine sense of possession to an adult; it does not compensate children for the give-and-take of our village, where there is always a contemporary to help swing the skipping rope or put on the catcher's mitt. Where in the country is the Friday-evening dancing class or the Saturday-morning movie (approved by the P.T.A.)? It is the greatest fallacy of all time that children love the country as a year-around plan. Children would take a dusty corner of Washington Square or a city sidewalk, even, in preference to the lonely sermons in stones and books in running brooks which their contemporaries cannot share.

As for the horrors of bringing up progeny in the city, for all its museums and other cultural advantages (so perfectly within reach of suburban families if they feel strongly about it), they were summed up for me one day last winter. The harried mother of one, speaking to me on the telephone just after Christmas, sighed and said, "It's been a really wonderful time for me, as vacations go. Barbara has had an engagement with a child in our apartment house every afternoon this week. I have had to take her almost nowhere." Barbara is eleven. For six of those eleven years, I realized, her mother must have dreaded Christmas vacation, not to mention spring, as a time when Barbara had to be entertained. I thought thankfully of my own daughters, whom I had scarcely seen since school closed, out with their skis and their sleds and their friends, sliding down the roped-off hill half a block away, coming in hungrily for lunch and disappearing again, hearty, amused, and safe—at least as safe as any sled-borne child can be.

Spruce Manor is not Eden, of course. Our taxes are higher than we like, and there is always that 8:02 in the morning to be caught, and we sometimes resent the necessity of rushing from a theater to a train on a weekday evening. But the taxes pay for our really excellent schools and for our garbage collections (so that the pails of orange peels need not stand in the halls overnight as ours did in the city) and for our water supply, which does not give out every dry summer as it frequently does in the country. As for the theaters—they are twenty miles away and we don't get to them more than twice a month. But neither, I think, do many of our friends in town. The 8:02 is rather a pleasant train, too, say the husbands; it gets them to work in thirty-four minutes, and they read the papers restfully on the way.

"But the suburban mind!" cry our diehard friends in Manhattan and Connecticut. "The suburban conversation! The monotony!" They imply that they and I must scintillate or we perish. Let me anatomize Spruce Manor, for them and for the others who envision Suburbia as a congregation of mindless housewives and amoral go-getters.

From my window, now, on a June morning, I have a view. It contains neither solitary hills nor dramatic skyscrapers. But I can see my roses in bloom, and my foxglove, and an arch of trees over the lane. I think comfortably of my friends whose houses line this and other streets rather like it. Not one of them is, so far as I know, doing any of the things that suburban ladies are popularly supposed to be doing. One of them, I happen to know, has gone bowling for her health and figure, but she has already tidied up her house and arranged to be home before the boys return from school. Some, undoubtedly, are ferociously busy in the garden. One lady is on her way to Ellis Island, bearing comfort and gifts to a Polish boy—a seventeen-year-old stowaway who did slave labor in Germany and was liberated by a cousin of hers during the war—who is being held for attempting to attain the land of which her cousin told him. The boy has been on the island for three months. Twice a week she takes this tedious journey, meanwhile besieging courts and immigration authorities on his behalf. This lady has a large house, a part-time maid, and five children.

My friend around the corner is finishing her third novel. She writes daily from nine-thirty until two. After that her son comes back from school and she plunges into maternity; at six she combs her pretty hair, refreshes her lipsick, and is charming to her doctor husband. The village dancing school is run by another neighbor, as it has been for twenty years. She has sent a number of ballerinas on to the theatrical world as well as having shepherded for many a successful season the white-gloved little boys and full-skirted little girls through their first social tasks.

Some of the ladies are no doubt painting their kitchens or a nursery; one of them is painting the portrait, on assignment, of a very distinguished personage. Some of them are nurses' aides and Red Cross workers and supporters of good causes. But all find time to be friends with their families and to meet the 5:32 five nights a week. They read something besides the newest historical novel. Braque is not unidentifiable to most of them, and their conversation is for the most part as agreeable as the tables they set. The tireless bridge players, the gossips, the women bored by their husbands live perhaps in our suburb, too. Let them. Our orbits need not cross.

And what of the husbands, industriously selling bonds or practicing law or editing magazines or looking through microscopes or managing offices in the city? Do they spend their evenings and their week ends in the gaudy bars of 52nd Street? Or are they the perennial householders, their lives a dreary round of taking down screens and mending drains? Well, screens they have always with them, and a man who is good around the house can spend happy hours with the plumbing even on a South Sea island. Some of them cut their own lawns and some of them try to break par and some of them sail their little boats all summer with their families for crew. Some of them are village trustees for nothing a year, and some listen to symphonies, and some think Steve Allen ought to be President. There is a scientist who plays wonderful bebop, and an insurance salesman who has bought a big old house nearby and with his own hands is gradually tearing it apart and reshaping it nearer to his heart's desire. Some of them are passionate hedge-clippers, and some read Plutarch for fun. But I do not know many—though there may be such—who either kiss their neighbors' wives behind doors or whose idea of sprightly talk is to tell you the plot of an old movie.

It is June, now, as I have said. This afternoon my daughters will come home from school with a crowd of their peers at their heels. They will eat up the cookies and drink up the ginger ale and go down for a swim at the beach if the water is warm enough, that beach which is only three blocks away and open to all Spruce Manor. They will go unattended by me, since they have been swimming since they were four, and besides there are life guards and no big waves. (Even our piece of ocean is a compromise.) Presently it will be time for us to climb into our very old Studebaker—we are not car-proud in Spruce Manor—and meet the 5:32. That evening expedition is not vitally necessary, for a bus runs straight down our principal avenue from the station to the shore, and it meets all trains. But it is an event we enjoy. There is something delightfully ritualistic about the moment when the train pulls in and the men swing off, with the less sophisticated children running squealing to meet them. The women move over from the driver's seat, surrender the keys, and receive an absent-minded kiss. It is the sort of picture that wakes John Marquand screaming from his sleep. But, deluded people that we are, we do not realize how mediocre it all seems. We will eat our undistinguished meal, probably without even a cocktail to enliven it. We will drink our coffee at the table, not carry it into the living room; if a husband changes for dinner here it is into old and spotty trousers and more comfortable shoes. The children will then go through the regular childhood routine—complain about their homework, grumble about going to bed, and finally accomplish both ordeals. Perhaps later the Gerard Joneses will drop in. We will talk a great deal of unimportant chatter and compare notes on food prices; we will also discuss the headlines and disagree. (Some of us in the Manor are Republicans, some are Democrats, a few lean plainly leftward. There are probably anti-Semites and anti-Catholics and even anti-Americans. Most of us are merely anti-antis.) We will all have one highball and the Joneses will leave early. Tomorrow and tomorrow and tomorrow the pattern will be repeated. This is Suburbia.

But I think that some day people will look back on our little interval here, on our Spruce Manor way of life, as we now look back on the Currier and Ives kind of living, with nostalgia and respect. In a world of terrible extremes, it will stand out as the safe, important medium.

Suburbia, of thee I sing!

JOAN DIDION

A native Californian, Joan Didion was born in Sacramento in 1934 and educated at the University of California, Berkeley. She received Vogue's *Prix de Paris in 1956, the year of her graduation, and in 1963 was awarded the Bread Loaf Fellowship in fiction. A frequent contributor of articles and reviews to the* Saturday Evening Post, *to* Mademoiselle, *and to other magazines, she has been associate feature editor of* Vogue *and has taught creative writing at Berkeley. Her books include three novels:* Run River *(1963);* Play It as It Lays *(1970), for which she also wrote the screenplay; and* A Book of Common Prayer *(1975). She was coauthor with her husband, John Gregory Dunne, of the screenplay for* A Star Is Born *(1976). Highly regarded as a reportorial essayist, she has written two collections of essays:* Slouching Toward Bethlehem *(1968), from which we reprint the selection below, and* The White Album *(1979).*

Some Dreamers of the Golden Dream

This is a story about love and death in the golden land, and begins with the country. The San Bernardino Valley lies only an hour east of Los Angeles by the San Bernardino Freeway but is in certain ways an alien place: not the coastal California of the subtropical twilights and the soft westerlies off the Pacific but a harsher California, haunted by the Mojave just beyond the mountains, devastated by the hot dry Santa Ana wind that comes down through the passes at 100 miles an hour and whines through the eucalyptus windbreaks and works on the nerves. October is the bad month for the wind, the month when breathing is difficult and the hills blaze up spontaneously. There has been no rain since April. Every voice seems a scream. It is the season of suicide and divorce and prickly dread, wherever the wind blows.

The Mormons settled this ominous country, and then they abandoned it, but by the time they left the first orange tree had been planted and for the next hundred years the San Bernardino Valley would draw a kind of people who imagined they might live among the talismanic fruit and prosper in the dry air, people who brought with them Midwestern ways of building and cooking and praying and who tried to graft those ways upon the land. The graft took in curious ways. This is the California where it is possible to live and die without ever eating an artichoke, without ever meeting a Catholic or a Jew. This is the California where it is easy to Dial-A-Devotion, but hard to buy a book. This is the country in which a belief in the literal interpretation of Genesis has slipped imperceptibly into a belief in the literal interpretation of *Double Indemnity*, the country of the teased hair and the Capris and the girls for whom all life's promise comes down to a waltz-length white wedding dress and the birth of a Kimberly or a Sherry or a Debbi and a Tijuana divorce and a return to hairdressers' school. "We were just crazy kids," they say without regret, and look to the future. The future always looks good in the golden land, because no one remembers the past. Here is where the hot wind blows and the old ways do not seem relevant, where the divorce rate is double the national average and where one person in every thirty-eight lives in a trailer. Here is the last stop for all those who come from somewhere else, for all those who drifted away from the cold and the past and the old ways. Here is where they are trying to find a new life style, trying to find it in the only places they know to look: the movies and the newspapers. The case of Lucille Marie Maxwell Miller is a tabloid monument to that new life style.

Imagine Banyan Street first, because Banyan is where it happened. The way to Banyan is to drive west from San Bernardino out Foothill Boulevard, Route 66: past the Santa Fe switching yards, the Forty Winks Motel. Past the motel that is nineteen stucco tepees: "SLEEP IN A WIGWAM—GET MORE FOR YOUR WAMPUM." Past Fontana Drag City and the Fontana Church of the Nazarene and the Pit Stop A Go-Go; past Kaiser Steel, through Cucamonga, out to the Kapu Kai Restaurant-Bar and Coffee Shop, at the corner of Route 66 and Carnelian Avenue. Up Carnelian Avenue from the Kapu Kai, which means "Forbidden Seas," the subdivision flags whip in the harsh

wind. "HALF-ACRE RANCHES! SNACK BARS! TRAVERTINE ENTRIES! $95 DOWN."
It is the trail of an intention gone haywire, the flotsam of the New California. But after a while the signs thin out on Carnelian Avenue, and the
houses are no longer the bright pastels of the Springtime Home owners but
the faded bungalows of the people who grow a few grapes and keep a few
chickens out here, and then the hill gets steeper and the road climbs and
even the bungalows are few, and here—desolate, roughly surfaced, lined
with eucalyptus and lemon groves—is Banyan Street.

Like so much of this country, Banyan suggests something curious and
unnatural. The lemon groves are sunken, down a three- or four-foot retaining wall, so that one looks directly into their dense foliage, too lush, unset-
tlingly glossy, the greenery of nightmare; the fallen eucalyptus bark is too
dusty, a place for snakes to breed. The stones look not like natural stones but
like the rubble of some unmentioned upheaval. There are smudge pots, and
a closed cistern. To one side of Banyan there is the flat valley, and to the
other the San Bernardino Mountains, a dark mass looming too high, too
fast, nine, ten, eleven thousand feet, right there above the lemon groves. At
midnight on Banyan Street there is no light at all, and no sound except the
wind in the eucalyptus and a muffled barking of dogs. There may be a
kennel somewhere, or the dogs may be coyotes.

Banyan Street was the route Lucille Miller took home from the twenty-
four-hour Mayfair Market on the night of October 7, 1964, a night when
the moon was dark and the wind was blowing and she was out of milk, and
Banyan Street was where, at about 12:20 A.M., her 1964 Volkswagen came
to a sudden stop, caught fire, and began to burn. For an hour and fifteen
minutes Lucille Miller ran up and down Banyan calling for help, but no
cars passed and no help came. At three o'clock that morning, when the fire
had been put out and the California Highway Patrol officers were completing their report, Lucille Miller was still sobbing and incoherent, for her
husband had been asleep in the Volkswagen. "What will I tell the children,
when there's nothing left, nothing left in the casket," she cried to the friend
called to comfort her. "How can I tell them there's nothing left?"

In fact there was something left, and a week later it lay in the Draper
Mortuary Chapel in a closed bronze coffin blanketed with pink carnations.
Some 200 mourners heard Elder Robert E. Denton of the Seventh-Day
Adventist Church of Ontario speak of "the temper of fury that has broken
out among us." For Gordon Miller, he said, there would be "no more death,
no more heartaches, no more misunderstandings." Elder Ansel Bristol mentioned the "peculiar" grief of the hour. Elder Fred Jensen asked "what shall
it profit a man, if he shall gain the whole world, and lose his own soul?" A
light rain fell, a blessing in a dry season, and a female vocalist sang "Safe in
the Arms of Jesus." A tape recording of the service was made for the widow,
who was being held without bail in the San Bernardino County Jail on a
charge of first-degree murder.

Of course she came from somewhere else, came off the prairie in search of
something she had seen in a movie or heard on the radio, for this is a

Southern California story. She was born on January 17, 1930, in Winnipeg, Manitoba, the only child of Gordon and Lily Maxwell, both schoolteachers and both dedicated to the Seventh-Day Adventist Church, whose members observe the Sabbath on Saturday, believe in an apocalyptic Second Coming, have a strong missionary tendency, and, if they are strict, do not smoke, drink, eat meat, use makeup, or wear jewelry, including wedding rings. By the time Lucille Maxwell enrolled at Walla Walla College in College Place, Washington, the Adventist school where her parents then taught, she was an eighteen-year-old possessed of unremarkable good looks and remarkable high spirits. "Lucille wanted to see the world," her father would say in retrospect, "and I guess she found out."

The high spirits did not seem to lend themselves to an extended course of study at Walla Walla College, and in the spring of 1949 Lucille Maxwell met and married Gordon ("Cork") Miller, a twenty-four-year-old graduate of Walla Walla and of the university of Oregon dental school, then stationed at Fort Lewis as a medical officer. "Maybe you could say it was love at first sight," Mr. Maxwell recalls. "Before they were ever formally introduced, he sent Lucille a dozen and a half roses with a card that said even if she didn't come out on a date with him, he hoped she'd find the roses pretty anyway." The Maxwells remember their daughter as a "radiant" bride.

Unhappy marriages so resemble one another that we do not need to know too much about the course of this one. There may or may not have been trouble on Guam, where Cork and Lucille Miller lived while he finished his Army duty. There may or may not have been problems in the small Oregon town where he first set up private practice. There appears to have been some disappointment about their move to California: Cork Miller had told friends that he wanted to become a doctor, that he was unhappy as a dentist and planned to enter the Seventh-Day Adventist College of Medical Evangelists at Loma Linda, a few miles south of San Bernardino. Instead he bought a dental practice in the west end of San Bernardino County, and the family settled there, in a modest house on the kind of street where there are always tricycles and revolving credit and dreams about bigger houses, better streets. That was 1957. By the summer of 1964 they had achieved the bigger house on the better street and the familiar accouterments of a family on its way up: the $30,000 a year, the three children for the Christmas card, the picture window, the family room, the newspaper photographs that showed "Mrs. Gordon Miller, Ontario Heart Fund Chairman. . . ." They were paying the familiar price for it. And they had reached the familiar season of divorce.

It might have been anyone's bad summer, anyone's siege of heat and nerves and migraine and money worries, but this one began particularly early and particularly badly. On April 24 an old friend, Elaine Hayton, died suddenly; Lucille Miller had seen her only the night before. During the month of May, Cork Miller was hospitalized briefly with a bleeding ulcer, and his usual reserve deepened into depression. He told his accountant that he was "sick of looking at open mouths," and threatened suicide. By July 8, the conventional tensions of love and money had reached the conventional impasse in the new house on the acre lot of 8488 Bella Vista, and Lucille Miller filed for divorce. Within a month, however, the Millers seemed reconciled. They saw a marriage counselor. They talked about a fourth child. It seemed that the marriage had reached the traditional truce, the point at which so many resign themselves to cutting both their losses and their hopes.

But the Millers' season of trouble was not to end that easily. October 7 began as a commonplace enough day, one of those days that sets the teeth on edge with its tedium, its small frustrations. The temperature reached 102° in San Bernardino that afternoon, and the Miller children were home from school because of Teachers' Institute. There was ironing to be dropped off. There was a trip to pick up a prescription for Nembutal, a trip to a self-service dry cleaner. In the early evening, an unpleasant accident with the Volkswagen: Cork Miller hit and killed a German shepherd, and afterward said that his head felt "like it had a Mack truck on it." It was something he often said. As of that evening Cork Miller was $63,479 in debt, including the $29,637 mortgage on the new house, a debt load which seemed oppressive to him. He was a man who wore his responsibilities uneasily, and complained of migraine headaches almost constantly.

He ate alone that night, from a TV tray in the living room. Later the Millers watched John Forsythe and Senta Berger in *See How They Run*, and when the movie ended, about eleven, Cork Miller suggested that they go out for milk. He wanted some hot chocolate. He took a blanket and pillow from the couch and climbed into the passenger seat of the Volkswagen. Lucille Miller remembers reaching over to lock his door as she backed down the driveway. By the time she left the Mayfair Market, and long before they reached Banyan Street, Cork Miller appeared to be asleep.

There is some confusion in Lucille Miller's mind about what happened between 12:30 A.M., when the fire broke out, and 1:50 A.M., when it was reported. She says that she was driving east on Banyan Street at about 35 m.p.h. when she felt the Volkswagen pull sharply to the right. The next thing she knew the car was on the embankment, quite near the edge of the retaining wall, and flames were shooting up behind her. She does not remember jumping out. She does remember prying up a stone with which she broke the window next to her husband, and then scrambling down the retaining wall to try to find a stick. "I don't know how I was going to push him out," she says. "I just thought if I had a stick. I'd push him out." She could not, and after a while she ran to the intersection of Banyan and Carnelian Avenue. There are no houses at that corner, and almost no traffic. After one car had passed without stopping. Lucille Miller ran back down Banyan toward the burning Volkswagen. She did not stop, but she slowed down, and in the flames she could see her husband. He was, she said, "just black."

At the first house up Sapphire Avenue, half a mile from the Volkswagen, Lucille Miller finally found help. There Mrs. Robert Swenson called the sheriff, and then, at Lucille Miller's request, she called Harold Lance, the Millers' lawyer and their close friend. When Harold Lance arrived he took Lucille Miller home to his wife, Joan. Twice Harold Lance and Lucille

Miller returned to Banyan Street and talked to the Highway Patrol officers. A third time Harold Lance returned alone, and when he came back he said to Lucille Miller, "O.K. . . . you don't talk any more."

When Lucille Miller was arrested the next afternoon, Sandy Slagle was with her. Sandy Slagle was the intense, relentlessly loyal medical student who used to baby-sit for the Millers, and had been living as a member of the family since she graduated from high school in 1959. The Millers took her away from a difficult home situation, and she thinks of Lucille Miller not only as "more or less a mother or a sister" but as "the most wonderful character" she has ever known. On the night of the accident, Sandy Slagle was in her dormitory at Loma Linda University, but Lucille Miller called her early in the morning and asked her to come home. The doctor was there when Sandy Slagle arrived, giving Lucille Miller an injection of Nembutal. "She was crying as she was going under," Sandy Slagle recalls. "Over and over she'd say, 'Sandy, all the hours I spent trying to save him and now what are they trying to *do* to me?' "

At 1:30 that afternoon, Sergeant William Paterson and Detectives Charles Callahan and Joseph Karr of the Central Homicide Division arrived at 8488 Bella Vista. "One of them appeared at the bedroom door," Sandy Slagle remembers, "and said to Lucille, 'You've got ten minutes to get dressed or we'll take you as you are.' She was in her nightgown, you know, so I tried to get her dressed."

Sandy Slagle tells the story now as if by rote, and her eyes do not waver. "So I had her panties and bra on her and they opened the door again, so I got some Capris on her, you know, and a scarf." Her voice drops. "And then they just took her."

The arrest took place just twelve hours after the first report that there had been an accident on Banyan Street, a rapidity which would later prompt Lucille Miller's attorney to say that the entire case was an instance of trying to justify a reckless arrest. Actually what first caused the detectives who arrived on Banyan Street toward dawn that morning to give the accident more than routine attention were certain apparent physical inconsistencies. While Lucille Miller had said that she was driving about 35 m.p.h. when the car swerved to a stop, an examination of the cooling Volkswagen showed that it was in low gear, and that the parking rather than the driving lights were on. The front wheels, moreover, did not seem to be in exactly the position that Lucille Miller's description of the accident would suggest, and the right rear wheel was dug in deep, as if it had been spun in place. It seemed curious to the detectives, too, that a sudden stop from 35 m.p.h.— the same jolt which was presumed to have knocked over a gasoline can in the back seat and somehow started the fire—should have left two milk cartons upright on the back floorboard, and the remains of a Polaroid camera box lying apparently undisturbed on the back seat.

No one, however, could be expected to give a precise account of what did and did not happen in a moment of terror, and none of these inconsistencies seemed in themselves incontrovertible evidence of criminal intent. But they did interest the Sheriff's Office, as did Gordon Miller's apparent unconsciousness at the time of the accident, and the length of time it had taken Lucille Miller to get help. Something, moreover, struck the investigators as wrong about Harold Lance's attitude when he came back to Banyan Street the third time and found the investigation by no means over. "The way Lance was acting," the prosecuting attorney said later, "they thought maybe they'd hit a nerve."

And so it was that on the morning of October 8, even before the doctor had come to give Lucille Miller an injection to calm her, the San Bernardino County Sheriff's Office was trying to construct another version of what might have happened between 12:30 and 1:50 A.M. The hypothesis they would eventually present was based on the somewhat tortuous premise that Lucille Miller had undertaken a plan which failed: a plan to stop the car on the lonely road, spread gasoline over her presumably drugged husband, and, with a stick on the accelerator, gently "walk" the Volkswagen over the embankment, where it would tumble four feet down the retaining wall into the lemon grove and almost certainly explode. If this happened, Lucille Miller might then have somehow negotiated the two miles up Carnelian to Bella Vista in time to be home when the accident was discovered. This plan went awry, according to the Sheriff's Office hypothesis, when the car would not go over the rise of the embankment. Lucille Miller might have panicked then—after she had killed the engine the third or fourth time, say, out there on the dark road with the gasoline already spread and the dogs baying and the wind blowing and the unspeakable apprehension that a pair of headlights would suddenly light up Banyan Street and expose her there—and set the fire herself.

Although this version accounted for some of the physical evidence—the car in low because it had been started from a dead stop, the parking lights on because she could not do what needed doing without some light, a rear wheel spun in repeated attempts to get the car over the embankment, the milk cartons upright because there had been no sudden stop—it did not seem on its own any more or less credible than Lucille Miller's own story. Moreover, some of the physical evidence did seem to support her story: a nail in a front tire, a nine-pound rock found in the car, presumably the one with which she had broken the window in an attempt to save her husband. Within a few days an autopsy had established that Gordon Miller was alive when he burned, which did not particularly help the State's case, and that he had enough Nembutal and Sandoptal in his blood to put the average person to sleep, which did: on the other hand Gordon Miller habitually took both Nembutal and Fiorinal (a common headache prescription which contains Sandoptal), and had been ill besides.

It was a spotty case, and to make it work at all the State was going to have to find a motive. There was talk of unhappiness, talk of another man. That kind of motive, during the next few weeks, was what they set out to establish. They set out to find it in accountants' ledgers and double-indemnity clauses and motel registers, set out to determine what might move a woman who believed in all the promises of the middle class—a woman who had been chairman of the Heart Fund and who always knew a reasonable

little dressmaker and who had come out of the bleak wild of prairie fundamentalism to find what she imagined to be the good life—what should drive
such a woman to sit on a street called Bella Vista and look out her new
picture window into the empty California sun and calculate how to burn
her husband alive in a Volkswagen. They found the wedge they wanted
closer at hand than they might have at first expected, for, as testimony
would reveal later at the trial, it seemed that in December of 1963 Lucille
Miller had begun an affair with the husband of one of her friends, a man
whose daughter called her "Auntie Lucille," a man who might have seemed
to have the gift for people and money and the good life that Cork Miller so
noticeably lacked. The man was Arthwell Hayton, a well-known San Bernardino attorney and at one time a member of the district attorney's staff.

In some ways it was the conventional clandestine affair in a place like San
Bernardino, a place where little is bright or graceful, where it is routine to
misplace the future and easy to start looking for it in bed. Over the seven
weeks that it would take to try Lucille Miller for murder, Assistant District
Attorney Don A. Turner and defense attorney Edward P. Foley would
between them unfold a curiously predictable story. There were the falsified
motel registrations. There were the lunch dates, the afternoon drives in
Arthwell Hayton's red Cadillac convertible. There were the interminable
discussions of the wronged partners. There were the confidantes ("I knew
everything," Sandy Slagle would insist fiercely later. "I knew every time,
places, everything") and there were the words remembered from bad magazine stories ("Don't kiss me, it will trigger things," Lucille Miller remembered telling Arthwell Hayton in the parking lot of Harold's Club in Fontana after lunch one day) and there were the notes, the sweet exchanges:
"Hi Sweetie Pie! You are my cup of tea!! Happy Birthday—you don't look
a day over 29!! Your baby, Arthwell."

And, toward the end, there was the acrimony. It was April 24, 1964,
when Arthwell Hayton's wife, Elaine, died suddenly, and nothing good
happened after that. Arthwell Hayton had taken his cruiser, *Captain's Lady*,
over to Catalina that weekend; he called home at nine o'clock Friday night,
but did not talk to his wife because Lucille Miller answered the telephone
and said that Elaine was showering. The next morning the Haytons' daughter found her mother in bed, dead. The newspapers reported the death as
accidental, perhaps the result of an allergy to hair spray. When Arthwell
Hayton flew home from Catalina that weekend, Lucille Miller met him at
the airport, but the finish had already been written.

It was in the breakup that the affair ceased to be in the conventional
mode and began to resemble instead the novels of James M. Cain, the
movies of the late 1930's, all the dreams in which violence and threats and
blackmail are made to seem commonplaces of middle-class life. What was
most startling about the case that the State of California was preparing
against Lucille Miller was something that had nothing to do with law at all,
something that never appeared in the eight-column afternoon headlines but
was always there between them: the revelation that the dream was teaching

the dreamers how to live. Here is Lucille Miller talking to her lover some-time in the early summer of 1964, after he had indicated that, on the advice of his minister, he did not intend to see her any more: "First, I'm going to go to that dear pastor of yours and tell him a few things. . . . When I do tell him that, you won't be in the Redlands Church any more. . . . Look, Sonny Boy, if you think your reputation is going to be ruined, your life won't be worth two cents." Here is Arthwell Hayton, to Lucille Miller: "I'll go to Sheriff Frank Bland and tell him some things that I know about you until you'll wish you'd never heard of Arthwell Hayton." For an affair between a Seventh-Day Adventist dentist's wife and a Seventh-Day Adventist per-sonal-injury lawyer, it seems a curious kind of dialogue.

"Boy, I could get that little boy coming and going," Lucille Miller later confided to Erwin Sprengle, a Riverside contractor who was a business part-ner of Arthwell Hayton's and a friend to both the lovers. (Friend or no, on this occasion he happened to have an induction coil attached to his tele-phone in order to tape Lucille Miller's call.) "And he hasn't got one thing on me that he can prove. I mean, I've got concrete—he has nothing con-crete." In the same taped conversation with Erwin Sprengle, Lucille Miller mentioned a tape that she herself had surreptitiously made, months before, in Arthwell Hayton's car.

"I said to him, I said 'Arthwell, I just feel like I'm being used.' . . . He started sucking his thumb and he said 'I love you. . . . This isn't something that happened yesterday. I'd marry you tomorrow if I could. I don't love Elaine.' He'd love to hear that played back, wouldn't he?"

"Yeah," drawled Sprengle's voice on the tape. "That would be just a little incriminating, wouldn't it?"

"Just a *little* incriminating," Lucille Miller agreed. "It really *is*."

Later on the tape, Sprengle asked where Cork Miller was.

"He took the children down to the church."

"You didn't go?"

"No."

"You're naughty."

It was all, moreover, in the name of "love"; everyone involved placed a magical faith in the efficacy of the very word. There was the significance that Lucille Miller saw in Arthwell's saying that he "loved" her, that he did not "love" Elaine. There was Arthwell insisting, later, at the trial, that he had never said it, that he may have "whispered sweet nothings in her ear" (as her defense hinted that he had whispered in many ears), but he did not remember bestowing upon her the special seal, saying the word, declaring "love." There was the summer evening when Lucille Miller and Sandy Slagle followed Arthwell Hayton down to his new boat in its mooring at Newport Beach and untied the lines with Arthwell aboard, Arthwell and a girl with whom he later testified he was drinking hot chocolate and watch-ing television. "I did that on purpose," Lucille Miller told Erwin Sprengle later, "to save myself from letting my heart do something crazy."

January 11, 1965, was a bright warm day in Southern California, the kind of day when Catalina floats on the Pacific horizon and the air smells of orange blossoms and it is a long way from the bleak and difficult East, a long way from the cold, a long way from the past. A woman in Hollywood staged an all-night sit-in on the hood of her car to prevent repossession by a finance company. A seventy-year-old pensioner drove his station wagon at five miles an hour past three Gardena poker parlors and emptied three pistols and a twelve-gauge shotgun through their windows, wounding twenty-nine people. "Many young women became prostitutes just to have enough money to play cards," he explained in a note. Mrs. Nick Adams said that she was "not surprised" to hear her husband announce his divorce plans on the Les Crane Show, and, farther north, a sixteen-year-old jumped off the Golden Gate Bridge and lived.

And, in the San Bernardino County Courthouse, the Miller trial opened. The crowds were so bad that the glass courtroom doors were shattered in the crush, and from then on identification disks were issued to the first forty-three spectators in line. The line began forming at 6 A.M., and college girls camped at the courthouse all night, with stores of graham crackers and No-Cal.

All they were doing was picking a jury, those first few days, but the sensational nature of the case had already suggested itself. Early in December there had been an abortive first trial, a trial at which no evidence was ever presented because on the day the jury was seated the San Bernardino *Sun-Telegram* ran an "inside" story quoting Assistant District Attorney Don Turner, the prosecutor, as saying, "We are looking into the circumstances of Mrs. Hayton's death. In view of the current trial concerning the death of Dr. Miller, I do not feel I should comment on Mrs. Hayton's death." It seemed that there had been barbiturates in Elaine Hayton's blood, and there had seemed some irregularity about the way she was dressed on that morning when she was found under the covers, dead. Any doubts about the death at the time, however, had never gotten as far as the Sheriff's Office. "I guess somebody didn't want to rock the boat," Turner said later. "These were prominent people."

Although all of that had not been in the *Sun-Telegram*'s story, an immediate mistrial had been declared. Almost as immediately, there had been another development: Arthwell Hayton had asked newspapermen to an 11 A.M. Sunday morning press conference in his office. There had been television cameras, and flash bulbs popping. "As you gentlemen may know," Hayton had said, striking a note of stiff bonhomie, "there are very often women who become amorous toward their doctor or lawyer. This does not mean on the physician's or lawyer's part that there is any romance toward the patient or client."

"Would you deny that you were having an affair with Mrs. Miller?" a reporter had asked.

"I would deny that there was any romance on my part whatsoever."

It was a distinction he would maintain through all the wearing weeks to come.

So they had come to see Arthwell, these crowds who now milled beneath the dusty palms outside the courthouse, and they had also come to see Lucille, who appeared as a slight, intermittently pretty woman, already pale from lack of sun, a woman who would turn thirty-five before the trial was over and whose tendency toward haggardness was beginning to show, a meticulous woman who insisted, against her lawyer's advice, on coming to court with her hair piled high and lacquered. "I would've been happy if she'd come in with it hanging loose, but Lucille wouldn't do that," her lawyer said. He was Edward P. Foley, a small, emotional Irish Catholic who several times wept in the courtroom. "She has a great honesty, this woman," he added, "but this honesty about her appearance always worked against her."

By the time the trial opened, Lucille Miller's appearance included maternity clothes, for an official examination on December 18 had revealed that she was then three and a half months pregnant, a fact which made picking a jury even more difficult than usual, for Turner was asking the death penalty. "It's unfortunate but there it is," he would say of the pregnancy to each juror in turn, and finally twelve were seated, seven of them women, the youngest forty-one, an assembly of the very peers—housewives, a machinist, a truck driver, a grocery-store manager, a filing clerk—above whom Lucille Miller had wanted so badly to rise.

That was the sin, more than the adultery, which tended to reinforce the one for which she was being tried. It was implicit in both the defense and the prosecution that Lucille Miller was an erring woman, a woman who perhaps wanted too much. But to the prosecution she was not merely a woman who would want a new house and want to go to parties and run up high telephone bills ($1,152 in ten months), but a woman who would go so far as to murder her husband for his $80,000 in insurance, making it appear an accident in order to collect another $40,000 in double indemnity and straight accident policies. To Turner she was a woman who did not want simply her freedom and a reasonable alimony (she could have had that, the defense contended, by going through with her divorce suit), but wanted everything, a woman motivated by "love and greed." She was a "manipulator." She was a "user of people."

To Edward Foley, on the other hand, she was an impulsive woman who "couldn't control her foolish little heart." Where Turner skirted the pregnancy, Foley dwelt upon it, even calling the dead man's mother down from Washington to testify that her son had told her they were going to have another baby because Lucille felt that it would "do much to weld our home again in the pleasant relations that we used to have." Where the prosecution saw a "calculator," the defense saw a "blabbermouth," and in fact Lucille Miller did emerge as an ingenuous conversationalist. Just as, before her husband's death, she had confided in her friends about her love affair, so she chatted about it after his death, with the arresting sergeant. "Of course Cork lived with it for years, you know," her voice was heard to tell Sergeant Paterson on a tape made the morning after her arrest. "After Elaine died, he pushed the panic button one night and just asked me right out, and that, I think, was when he really—the first time he really faced it." When the

sergeant asked why she had agreed to talk to him, against the specific instructions of her lawyers, Lucille Miller said airily, "Oh, I've always been
basically quite an honest person. . . . I mean I can put a hat in the cupboard
and say it cost ten dollars less, but basically I've always kind of just lived my
life the way I wanted to, and if you don't like it you can take off."

The prosecution hinted at men other than Arthwell, and even, over
Foley's objections, managed to name one. The defense called Miller suicidal. The prosecution produced experts who said that the Volkswagen fire
could not have been accidental. Foley produced witnesses who said that it
could have been. Lucille's father, now a junior-high-school teacher in Oregon, quoted Isaiah to reporters: "*Every tongue that shall rise against thee in
judgment thou shalt condemn.*" "Lucille did wrong, her affair," her mother said
judiciously. "With her it was love. But with some I guess it's just passion."
There was Debbie, the Millers' fourteen-year-old, testifying in a steady
voice about how she and her mother had gone to a supermarket to buy the
gasoline can the week before the accident. There was Sandy Slagle, in the
courtroom every day, declaring that on at least one occasion Lucille Miller
had prevented her husband not only from committing suicide but from
committing suicide in such a way that it would appear an accident and
ensure the double-indemnity payment. There was Wenche Berg, the pretty
twenty-seven-year-old Norwegian governess to Arthwell Hayton's children,
testifying that Arthwell had instructed her not to allow Lucille Miller to see
or talk to the children.

Two months dragged by, and the headlines never stopped. Southern
California's crime reporters were headquartered in San Bernardino for the
duration: Howard Hertel from the *Times*, Jim Bennett and Eddy Jo Bernal
from the *Herald-Examiner*. Two months in which the Miller trial was pushed
off the *Examiner*'s front page only by the Academy Award nominations and
Stan Laurel's death. And finally, on March 2, after Turner had reiterated
that it was a case of "love and greed," and Foley had protested that his
client was being tried for adultery, the case went to the jury.

They brought in the verdict, guilty of murder in the first degree, at 4:50
P.M. on March 5. "She didn't do it," Debbie Miller cried, jumping up from
the spectators' section. "She didn't *do* it." Sandy Slagle collapsed in her seat
and began to scream. "Sandy, for God's sake please *don't*," Lucille Miller
said in a voice that carried across the courtroom, and Sandy Slagle was
momentarily subdued. But as the jurors left the courtroom she screamed
again: "You're murderers. . . . Every last one of you is a *murderer*." Sheriff's
deputies moved in then, each wearing a string tie that read "1965 SHERIFF's
RODEO," and Lucille Miller's father, the sad-faced junior-high-school
teacher who believed in the word of Christ and the dangers of wanting to see
the world, blew her a kiss off his fingertips.

The California Institution for Women at Frontera, where Lucille Miller
is now, lies down where Euclid Avenue turns into country road, not too
many miles from where she once lived and shopped and organized the
Heart Fund Ball. Cattle graze across the road, and Rainbirds sprinkle the

alfalfa. Frontera has a softball field and tennis courts, and looks as if it might be a California junior college, except that the trees are not yet high enough to conceal the concertina wire around the top of the Cyclone fence. On visitors' day there are big cars in the parking area, big Buicks and Pontiacs that belong to grandparents and sisters and fathers (not many of them belong to husbands), and some of them have bumper stickers that say "SUPPORT YOUR LOCAL POLICE."

A lot of California murderesses live here, a lot of girls who somehow misunderstood the promise. Don Turner put Sandra Garner here (and her husband in the gas chamber at San Quentin) after the 1959 desert killings known to crime reporters as "the soda-pop murders." Carole Tregoff is here, and has been ever since she was convicted of conspiring to murder Dr. Finch's wife in West Covina, which is not too far from San Bernardino. Carole Tregoff is in fact a nurse's aide in the prison hospital, and might have attended Lucille Miller had her baby been born at Frontera; Lucille Miller chose instead to have it outside, and paid for the guard who stood outside the delivery room in St. Bernardine's Hospital. Debbie Miller came to take the baby home from the hospital, in a white dress with pink ribbons, and Debbie was allowed to choose a name. She named the baby Kimi Kai. The children live with Harold and Joan Lance now, because Lucille Miller will probably spend ten years at Frontera. Don Turner waived his original request for the death penalty (it was generally agreed that he had demanded it only, in Edward Foley's words, "to get anybody with the slightest trace of human kindness in their veins off the jury"), and settled for life imprisonment with the possibility of parole. Lucille Miller does not like it at Frontera, and has had trouble adjusting. "She's going to have to learn humility," Turner says. "She's going to have to use her ability to charm, to manipulate."

The new house is empty now, the house on the street with the sign that says

PRIVATE ROAD

BELLA VISTA

DEAD END

The Millers never did get it landscaped, and weeds grow up around the fieldstone siding. The television aerial has toppled on the roof, and a trash can is stuffed with the debris of family life: a cheap suitcase, a child's game called "Lie Detector." There is a sign on what would have been the lawn, and the sign reads "ESTATE SALE." Edward Foley is trying to get Lucille Miller's case appealed, but there have been delays. "A trial always comes down to a matter of sympathy," Foley says wearily now. "I couldn't create sympathy for her." Everyone is a little weary now, weary and resigned, everyone except Sandy Slagle, whose bitterness is still raw. She lives in an apartment near the medical school in Loma Linda, and studies reports of the case in *True Police Cases* and *Official Detective Stories*. "I'd much rather we not talk about the Hayton business too much," she tells visitors, and she keeps a tape recorder running. "I'd rather talk about Lucille and what a wonderful person she is and how her rights were violated." Harold Lance does not talk to visitors at all. "We don't want to give away what we can sell," he explains pleasantly; an attempt was made to sell Lucille Miller's personal story to *Life*, but *Life* did not want to buy it. In the district attorney's offices they are prosecuting other murders now, and do not see why the Miller trial attracted so much attention. "It wasn't a very interesting murder as murders go," Don Turner says laconically. Elaine Hayton's death is no longer under investigation. "We know everything we want to know," Turner says.

Arthwell Hayton's office is directly below Edward Foley's. Some people around San Bernardino say that Arthwell Hayton suffered; others say that he did not suffer at all. Perhaps he did not, for time past is not believed to have any bearing upon time present or future, out in the golden land where every day the world is born anew. In any case, on October 17, 1965, Arthwell Hayton married again, married his children's pretty governness, Wenche Berg, at a service in the Chapel of the Roses at a retirement village near Riverside. Later the newlyweds were feted at a reception for seventy-five in the dining room of Rose Garden Village. The bridegroom was in black tie, with a white carnation in his buttonhole. The bride wore a long white *peau de soie* dress and carried a shower bouquet of sweetheart roses with stephanotis streamers. A coronet of seed pearls held her illusion veil.

[1966]

E. F. SCHUMACHER

E. F. Schumacher (1911-1977), economist and writer, was born in Germany. He studied abroad in the early 1930s, including a stay at Columbia University, but in 1937 he left Germany permanently for England, where he lived the rest of his life. During World War II, he was interned and required to work on farms in Britain for a short period, but he was soon released and worked with Lord Beveridge, who is credited with the theoretical framework for Britain's welfare state. After the war, Schumacher advised British authorities in postwar Germany. He was economic adviser to Britain's National Coal Board (1950-1970) and director of a company that pioneered common ownership and workers' control. His books—all on economic policy and planning—include Roots of Economic Growth *(1962);* Small Is Beautiful *(1973), a best seller that was translated into fifteen languages; and* A Guide for the Perplexed *(1977). The article reprinted below appeared in a book of essays edited by Dom Moraes,* Voices for Life: Reflections on the Human Condition *(1975).*

A Culture of Poverty

Schon in der Kindheit hört' ich es mit Beben:
Nur wer im Wohlstand lebt, lebt angenehm.
(Even as a child I felt terror-struck when I heard it said that to live an agreeable life you have got to be rich.)
                                                        —BERTOLT BRECHT

Only the rich can have a good life—this is the daunting message that has been drummed into the ears of all mankind during the last half-century or so. It is the implicit doctrine of "development," and the growth of income serves as the very criterion of progress. Everyone, it is held, has not only the right but the duty to become rich, and this applies to societies even more stringently than to individuals. The most succinct and most relevant indicator of a country's status in the world is thought to be *average income per head*, while the prime object of admiration is not the level already attained but the current *rate of growth*.

It follows logically—or so it seems—that the greatest obstacle to progress is a growth of population: It frustrates, diminishes, offsets what the growth of gross national product would otherwise achieve. What is the point of, let us say, doubling the GNP over a period, if population is also allowed to double during the same time? It would mean running faster merely to stand still; *average income per head* would remain stationary, and there would be no advance at all toward the cherished goal of universal affluence.

In the light of this received doctrine the well-nigh unanimous prediction of the demographers—that world population, barring unforeseen catastrophes, will double during the next thirty years—is taken as an intolerable threat. What other prospect is this than one of limitless frustration?

Some mathematical enthusiasts are still content to project the economic "growth curves" of the last thirty years for another thirty or even fifty years to "prove" that all mankind can become immensely rich within a generation or two. Our only danger, they suggest, is to succumb at this glorious hour in the history of progress to a "failure of nerve." They presuppose the existence of limitless resources in a finite world, an equally limitless capacity of living nature to cope with pollution, and the omnipotence of science and social engineering.

The sooner we stop living in the Cloud-Cuckoo-Land of such fanciful projections and presuppositions the better it will be, and this applies to the people of the rich countries just as much as to those of the poor. *It would apply even if all population growth stopped entirely forthwith.* The modern assumption that "only the rich can have a good life" springs from a crudely materialistic philosophy that contradicts the universal tradition of mankind. The material *needs* of man are limited and in fact quite modest, even though his material *wants* may know no bounds. Man does not live by bread alone, and no increase in his *wants* above his needs can give him the "good life." Christianity teaches that man must seek *first* "the kingdom of God, and his righteousness" and that all the other things—the material things to cover his needs—will then be "added unto" him. The experience of the modern world suggests that this teaching carries not only a promise but also a threat, namely, that "unless he seeks first the kingdom of God, those material things, which he unquestionably also needs, will cease to be available to him."

Our task, however, is to bring such insights, supported, as I said, by the universal tradition of mankind, down to the level of everyday economic reality. To do so, we must study, both theoretically and in practice, the possibilities of "a culture of poverty."

To make our meaning clear, let us state right away that there are degrees of poverty that may be totally inimical to any kind of culture in the ordinarily accepted sense. They are essentially different from poverty and deserve a separate name; the term that offers itself is "misery." We may say that poverty prevails when people have enough to keep body and soul together but little to spare, whereas in misery they cannot keep body and soul together, and even the soul suffers deprivation. Some thirteen years ago when I began seriously to grope for answers to these perplexing questions, I wrote this in *Roots of Economic Growth*:

> All peoples—with exceptions that merely prove the rule—have always known how to help themselves, they have always *discovered a pattern of living which fitted their peculiar natural surroundings*. Societies and cultures have collapsed when they deserted their own pattern and fell into decadence, but even then, unless devastated by war, the people normally continued to provide for themselves, with something to spare for higher things. Why not now, in so many parts of the world? I am not speaking of ordinary poverty, but of actual and acute misery; not of the poor, who according to the universal tradition of mankind are in a special way blessed, but of the miserable and degraded ones who, by the same tradition, should not exist at all and should be helped by all. Poverty may have been the rule in the past, but misery was not. Poor peasants and artisans have existed from time immemorial: but miserable and destitute villages in their thousands and urban pavement dwellers in their hundreds of thousands—not in wartime or as an aftermath of war, but in the midst of peace and as a seemingly permanent feature—that is a monstrous and scandalous thing which is altogether abnormal in the history of mankind. We cannot be satisfied with the snap answer that this is due to population pressure. Since every mouth that comes into the world is also endowed with a pair of hands, population pressure could serve as an explanation only if it meant an absolute shortage of land—and although that situation may arise in the future, it decidedly has not arrived today (a few islands excepted). It cannot be argued that population increase as such must produce increasing poverty, because the additional pairs of hands could not be endowed with the capital they needed to help themselves. Millions of people have started without capital and have shown that a pair of hands can provide not only the income but also the durable goods, i.e., capital, or civilized existence. So the question stands and demands an answer. What has gone wrong? Why cannot these people help themselves?

The answer, I suggest, lies in the abandonment of their indigenous culture of poverty, which means not only that they lost true culture but also that their poverty, in all too many cases, has turned into misery.

A culture of poverty such as mankind has known in innumerable variants before the industrial age is based on one fundamental distinction—which may have been made consciously or instinctively, it does not matter—the distinction between the "ephemeral" and the "eternal." All religions, of course, deal with this distinction, suggesting that the ephemeral is relatively unreal and only the eternal is real. On the material plane we deal with goods and services, and the same distinction applies: All goods and services can be arranged, as it were, on a scale that extends from the ephemeral to the eternal. Needless to say, neither of these terms may be taken in an absolute sense (because there is nothing absolute on the material plane), although there may well be something absolute in the maker's *intention*: He may see his product as something to be *used up*, that is to say, to be destroyed in the act of consumption, or as something to be used or enjoyed as a permanent asset, ideally forever.

The extremes are easily recognized. An article of consumption, like a loaf of bread, is *intended* to be *used up*, while a work of art, like the Mona Lisa, is *intended* to be there forever. Transport services to take a tourist on holiday are intended to be used up and therefore ephemeral, while a bridge across the river is intended to be a permanent facility. Entertainment is intended to be ephemeral; education (in the fullest sense) is intended to be eternal.

Between the extremes of the ephemeral and the eternal, there extends a vast range of goods and services with regard to which the producer may exercise a certain degree of choice: He may be producing with the intention of supplying something relatively ephemeral or something relatively eternal. A publisher, for instance, may produce a book with the intention that it should be purchased, read, and treasured by countless generations or his intention may be that it should be purchased, read, and thrown away as quickly as possible.

Ephemeral goods are—to use the language of business—"depreciating assets" and have to be "written off." Eternal goods, on the other hand, are never "depreciated" but "maintained." (You don't "depreciate" the Taj Mahal; you try to maintain its splendor for all time.)

Ephemeral goods are subject to the economic calculus. Their only value lies in being used up, and it is necessary to ensure that their *cost* of production does not exceed the *benefit* derived from destroying them. But eternal goods are not intended for destruction; there is no occasion for an economic calculus, because the benefit—the product of annual value and time—is infinite and therefore incalculable.

Once we recognize the validity of the distinction between the ephemeral and the eternal, we are able to distinguish, in principle, between two different types of "standards of living." Two societies may have the same volume of production and the same *income per head of population*, but the *quality of life* or life-style may show fundamental and incomparable differences: the one placing its main emphasis on ephemeral satisfactions and the other devoting itself primarily to the creation of eternal values. In the former there may be opulent living in terms of ephemeral goods and starvation in terms of eternal goods—eating, drinking, and wallowing in entertainment, in sordid, ugly, mean, and unhealthy surroundings—while in the latter there may be frugal living in terms of ephemeral goods and opulence in terms of eternal goods—modest, simple, and healthy consumption in a noble setting. In terms of conventional economic accounting they are both equally developed—which merely goes to show that the purely quantitative approach misses the point.

The study of these two models can surely teach us a great deal. It is clear, however, that the question "Which of the two is better?" reaches far beyond the economic calculus, since quality cannot be calculated.

No one, I suppose, would wish to deny that the life-style of modern industrial society is one that places primary emphasis on ephemeral satisfactions and is characterized by a gross neglect of eternal goods. Under certain immanent compulsions, moreover, modern industrial society is engaged in a process of what might be called ever-increasing ephemeralization; that is to say, goods and services that by their very nature belong to the eternal side are being produced as if their purpose were ephemeral. The economic calculus is applied everywhere, even at the cost of skimping and paring on goods that should last forever. At the same time purely ephemeral goods are produced to standards of refinement, elaboration, and luxury, as if they were meant to serve eternal purposes and to last for all time.

Nor, I suppose, would anyone wish to deny that many preindustrial societies have been able to create superlative cultures by placing their emphasis in the exactly opposite way. The greatest part of the modern world's cultural heritage stems from these societies.

The affluent societies of today make such exorbitant demands on the world's resources, create ecological dangers of such intensity, and produce such a high level of neurosis among their populations that they cannot possibly serve as a model to be imitated by those two-thirds or three-quarters of mankind who are conventionally considered underdeveloped or developing. The *failure of modern affluence*—which seems obvious enough, although it is by no means freely admitted by people of a purely materialistic outlook—cannot be attributed to affluence as such but is directly due to mistaken priorities (the cause of which cannot be discussed here): a gross overemphasis on the ephemeral and a brutal undervaluation of the eternal. Not surprisingly, no amount of indulgence on the ephemeral side can compensate for starvation on the eternal side.

In the light of these considerations, it is not difficult to understand the meaning and feasibility of a culture of poverty. It would be based on the insight that the real needs of man are limited and must be met, but that his wants tend to be unlimited, cannot be met, and must be resisted with the utmost determination. Only by a reduction of wants to needs can resources for genuine progress be freed. The required resources cannot be found from foreign aid; they cannot be mobilized via the technology of the affluent society that is immensely capital-intensive and labor-saving and is dependent on an elaborate infrastructure that is itself enormously expensive. Uncritical technology transfer from the rich societies to the poor cannot but transfer into poor societies a life-style that, placing primary emphasis on ephemeral satisfactions, may suit the taste of small, rich minorities but condemns the great, poor majority to increasing misery.

The resources for genuine progress can be found only by a life-style that emphasizes frugal living in terms of ephemeral goods. Only such a life-style can create (or maintain and develop) an ever-increasing supply of eternal goods.

Frugal living in terms of ephemeral goods means a dogged adherence to simplicity, a conscious avoidance of any unnecessary elaborations, and a magnanimous rejection of luxury—puritanism, if you like—on the ephemeral side. This makes it possible to enjoy a high standard of living on the eternal side, as a compensation and reward. Luxury and refinement have their proper place and function but only with eternal, not with ephemeral, goods. This is the essence of a culture of poverty.

One further point has to be added: The ultimate resource of any society is its labor power, which is infinitely creative. When the primary emphasis is on ephemeral goods, there is an automatic preference for mass production, and there can be no doubt that mass production is more congenial to machines than it is to men. The result is the progressive elimination of the human factor from the productive process. For a poor society, this means that its ultimate resource cannot be properly used; its creativity remains largely untapped. This is why Gandhi, with unerring instinct, insisted that "it is not mass production but only production by the masses that can do the trick." A society that places its primary emphasis on eternal goods will automatically prefer production by the masses to mass production, because such goods, intended to last, must fit the precise conditions of their place; they cannot be standardized. This brings the whole human being back into the productive process, and it then emerges that even ephemeral goods (without which human existence is obviously impossible) are far more efficient and economical when a proper fit has been ensured by the human factor.

All the above does not claim to be more than an assembly of a few preliminary indications. I entertain the hope that, in view of increasing threats to the very survival of culture—and even life itself—there will be an upsurge of serious study of the possibilities of a culture of poverty. We might find that we have nothing to lose and a world to gain.

URSULA LE GUIN

Ursula Le Guin is best known as a science-fiction writer, but she also has published essays, children's books, and "straight" fiction, and her audience now includes an increasing number of readers who are not science-fiction fans. She was born in Berkeley, California, in 1929, attended Radcliffe College (A.B., 1951) and Columbia University

(A.M., 1952), and then married. She is the mother of three children. She has taught— writing workshops and French—and she writes steadily. Her many books include The Left Hand of Darkness *(1969), which won both a Hugo Award and the Science Fiction of America Nebula Award;* The Tombs of Atuan *(1971), which received the Newberry Silver Medal;* The Farthest Shore *(1972), winner of a National Book Award and a Hugo Award; and* The Dispossessed *(1974), winner of the Nebula Award. More recent work includes* Orsinian Tales *(1976), a collection of short stories;* Malafrena *(1979), a "straight" novel set in fantasy Orsinia;* Very Far Away from Anywhere Else *(1976), a children's story; and* The Language of the Night: Essays on Fantasy and Science Fiction *(1979). We take the story reprinted below from a collection of Hugo Award winners of 1974, edited by Isaac Asimov.*

The Ones Who Walk Away from Omelas

With a clamor of bells that set the swallows soaring, the Festival of Summer came to the city Omelas, bright-towered by the sea. The rigging of the boats in harbor sparkled with flags. In the streets between houses with red roofs and painted walls, between old moss-grown gardens and under avenues of trees, past great parks and public buildings, processions moved. Some were decorous: old people in long stiff robes of mauve and gray, grave master workmen, quiet, merry women carrying their babies and chatting as they walked. In other streets the music beat faster, a shimmering of gong and tambourine, and the people went dancing, the procession was a dance. Children dodged in and out, their high calls rising like the swallows' crossing flights over the music and the singing. All the processions wound toward the north side of the city, where on the great watermeadow called the Green Fields boys and girls, naked in the bright air, with mudstained feet and ankles and long, lithe arms, exercised their restive horses before the race. The horses wore no gear at all but a halter without bit. Their manes were braided with streamers of silver, gold, and green. They blew out their nostrils and pranced and boasted to one another; they were vastly excited, the horse being the only animal who has adopted our ceremonies as his own. Far off to the north and west the mountains stood up half-encircling Omelas on her bay. The air of morning was so clear that the snow still crowning the Eighteen Peaks burned with white-gold fire across the miles of sunlit air, under the dark blue of the sky. There was just enough wind to make the banners that marked the race course snap and flutter now and then. In the silence of the broad green meadows one could hear the music winding through the city streets, farther and nearer and ever approaching, a cheerful faint sweetness of the air that from time to time trembled and gathered together and broke out into the great joyous clanging of the bells.

Joyous! How is one to tell about joy? How describe the citizens of Omelas?

They were not simple folk, you see, though they were happy. But we do not say the words of cheer much any more. All smiles have become archaic. Given a description such as this one tends to make certain assumptions. Given a description such as this one tends to look next for the King, mounted on a splendid stallion and surrounded by his noble knights, or perhaps in a golden litter borne by great-muscled slaves. But there was no king. They did not use swords, or keep slaves. They were not barbarians. I do not know the rules and laws of their society, but I suspect that they were singularly few. As they did without monarchy and slavery, so they also got on without the stock exchange, the advertisement, the secret police, and the bomb. Yet I repeat that these were not simple folk, not dulcet shepherds, noble savages, bland utopians. They were not less complex than we. The trouble is that we have a bad habit, encouraged by pedants and sophisticates, of considering happiness as something rather stupid. Only pain is intellectual, only evil interesting. This is the treason of the artist: a refusal to admit the banality of evil and the terrible boredom of pain. If you can't lick 'em, join 'em. If it hurts, repeat it. But to praise despair is to condemn delight, to embrace violence is to lose hold of everything else. We have almost lost hold; we can no longer describe a happy man, nor make any celebration of joy. How can I tell you about the people of Omelas? They were not naive and happy children—though their children were, in fact, happy. They were mature, intelligent, passionate adults whose lives were not wretched. O miracle! But I wish I could describe it better. I wish I could convince you. Omelas sounds in my words like a city in a fairytale, long ago and far away, once upon a time. Perhaps it would be best if you imagined it as your own fancy bids, assuming it will rise to the occasion, for certainly I cannot suit you all. For instance, how about technology? I think that there would be no cars or helicopters in and above the streets; this follows from the fact that the people of Omelas are happy people. Happiness is based on a just discrimination of what is necessary, what is neither necessary nor destructive, and what is destructive. In the middle category, however—that of the unnecessary but undestructive, that of comfort, luxury, exuberance, etc.—they could perfectly well have central heating, subway trains, washing machines, and all kinds of marvelous devices not yet invented here, floating lightsources, fuelless power, a cure for the common cold. Or they could have none of that: it doesn't matter. As you like it. I incline to think that people from towns up and down the coast have been coming in to Omelas during the last days before the Festival on very fast little trains and doubledecked trams, and that the train station of Omelas is actually the handsomest building in town, though plainer than the magnificent Farmers Market. But even granted trains, I fear that Omelas so far strikes some of you as goody-goody. Smiles, bells, parades, horses, bleh. If so, please add an orgy. If an orgy would help, don't hesitate. Let us not, however, have temples from which issue beautiful nude priests and priestesses already half in ecstasy and ready to copulate with whosoever, man or woman, lover or stranger, desires union with the deep godhead of the blood, although that was my first idea. But really it would be better not to have any temples in Omelas—at least, not manned temples. Religion yes, clergy no. Surely the beautiful nudes can just wander about, offering themselves like divine soufflés to the hunger of the needy and the rapture of the flesh. Let them join the processions. Let tambourines be struck above the copulations, and the glory of desire be proclaimed upon the gongs, and (a not unimportant point) let the offspring of these delightful rituals be beloved and looked after by all. One thing I know there is none of in Omelas is guilt. But what else should there be? I thought at first there were no drugs, but that is puritanical. For those who like it, the faint insistent sweetness of *drooz* may perfume the ways of the city, *drooz* which first brings a great lightness and brilliance to the mind and limbs, and then after some hours a dreamy languor, and wonderful visions at last of the very arcana and inmost secrets of the Universe, as well as exciting the pleasure of sex beyond all belief; and it is not habit-forming. For more modest tastes I think there ought to be beer. What else, what else belongs in the joyous city? The sense of victory, surely, the celebration of courage. But as we did without clergy, let us do without soldiers. The joy built upon successful slaughter is not the right kind of joy; it will not do; it is fearful and it is trivial. A boundless and generous contentment, a magnanimous triumph felt not against some outer enemy but in communion with the finest and fairest in the souls of all men everywhere and the splendor of the world's summer: this is what swells the hearts of the people of Omelas, and the victory they celebrate is that of life. I really don't think many of them need to take *drooz*.

Most of the processions have reached the Green Fields by now. A marvelous smell of cooking goes forth from the red and blue tents of the provisioners. The faces of small children are amiably sticky; in the benign gray beard of a man a couple of crumbs of rich pastry are entangled. The youths and girls have mounted their horses and are beginning to group around the starting line of the course. An old woman, small, fat, and laughing, is passing out flowers from a basket, and tall young men wear her flowers in their shining hair. A child of nine or ten sits at the edge of the crowd, alone, playing on a wooden flute. People pause to listen, and they smile, but they do not speak to him, for he never ceases playing and never sees them, his dark eyes wholly rapt in the sweet, thin magic of the tune.

He finishes, and slowly lowers his hands holding the wooden flute.

As if that little private silence were the signal, all at once a trumpet sounds from the pavilion near the starting line: imperious, melancholy, piercing. The horses rear on their slender legs, and some of them neigh in answer. Sober-faced, the young riders stroke the horses' necks and soothe them, whispering, "Quiet, quiet, there my beauty, my hope . . ." They begin to form in rank along the starting line. The crowds along the race course are like a field of grass and flowers in the wind. The Festival of Summer has begun.

Do you believe? Do you accept the festival, the city, the joy? No? Then let me describe one more thing.

In a basement under one of the beautiful buildings of Omelas, or perhaps in the cellar of one of its spacious private homes, there is a room. It has one locked door, and no window. A little light seeps in dustily between cracks in the boards, secondhand from a cobwebbed window somewhere across the cellar. In one corner of the little room a couple of mops, with stiff, clotted, foul-smelling heads, stand near a rusty bucket. The floor is dirt, a little damp to the touch, as cellar dirt usually is. The room is about three paces long and two wide: a mere broom closet or disused toolroom. In the room a child is sitting. It might be a boy or a girl. It looks about six, but actually is nearly ten. It is feebleminded. Perhaps it was born defective, or perhaps it has become imbecile through fear, malnutrition, and neglect. It picks its nose and occasionally fumbles vaguely with its toes or genitals, as it sits hunched in the corner farthest from the bucket and the two mops. It is afraid of the mops. It finds them horrible. It shuts its eyes, but it knows the mops are still standing there; and the door is locked; and nobody will come. The door is always locked, and nobody ever comes, except that sometimes—the child has no understanding of time or interval—sometimes the door rattles terribly and opens, and a person, or several people, are there. One of them may come in and kick the child to make it stand up. The others never come close, but peer in at it with frightened, disgusted eyes. The food bowl and the water jug are hastily filled, the door is locked, the eyes disappear. The people at the door never say anything, but the child, who has not always lived in the toolroom, and can remember sunlight and its mother's voice, sometimes speaks, "I will be good," it says. "Please let me out. I will be good!" They never answer. The child used to scream for help at night, and cry a good deal, but now it only makes a kind of whining, "eh-haa, eh-haa," and it speaks less and less often. It is so thin there are no calves to its legs; its belly protrudes; it lives on a half-bowl of cornmeal and grease a day. It is naked. Its buttocks and thighs are a mass of festered sores, as it sits in its own excrement continually.

They all know it is there, all the people of Omelas. Some of them have come to see it, others are content merely to know it is there. They all know that it has to be there. Some of them understand why, and some do not, but they all understand that their happiness, the beauty of their city, the tenderness of their friendships, the health of their children, the wisdom of their scholars, the skill of their makers, even the abundance of their harvest and the kindly weathers of their skies, depend wholly on this child's abominable misery.

This is usually explained to children when they are between eight and twelve, whenever they seem capable of understanding; and most of those who come to see the child are young people, though often enough an adult comes, or comes back, to see the child. No matter how well the matter has been explained to them, these young spectators are always shocked and sickened at the sight. They feel disgust, which they had thought themselves superior to. They feel anger, outrage, impotence, despite all the explanations. They would like to do something for the child. But there is nothing they can do. If the child were brought up into the sunlight out of that vile place, if it were cleaned and fed and comforted, that would be a good thing, indeed; but if it were done, in that day and hour all the prosperity and beauty and delight of Omelas would wither and be destroyed. Those are the terms. To exchange all the goodness and grace of every life in Omelas for that single, small improvement: to throw away the happiness of thousands for the chance of the happiness of one: that would be to let guilt within the walls indeed.

The terms are strict and absolute; there may not even be a kind word spoken to the child.

Often the young people go home in tears, or in a tearless rage, when they have seen the child and faced this terrible paradox. They may brood over it for weeks or years. But as time goes on they begin to realize that even if the child could be released, it would not get much good of its freedom: a vague pleasure of warmth and food, no doubt, but little more. It is too degraded and imbecile to know any real joy. It has been afraid too long ever to be free of fear. Its habits are too uncouth for it to respond to humane treatment. Indeed after so long it would probably be wretched without walls about it to protect it, and darkness for its eyes, and its own excrement to sit in. Their tears at the bitter injustice dry when they begin to perceive the terrible justice of reality, and to accept it. Yet it is their tears and anger, the trying of their generosity and the acceptance of their helplessness, which are per-haps the true source of the splendor of their lives. Theirs is no vapid, irre-sponsible happiness. They know that they, like the child, are not free. They know compassion. It is the existence of the child, and their knowledge of its existence, that makes possible the nobility of their architecture, the poign-ancy of their music, the profundity of their science. It is because of the child that they are so gentle with children. They know that if the wretched one were not there sniveling in the dark, the other one, the flute player, could make no joyful music as the young riders line up in their beauty for the race in the sunlight of the first morning of summer.

Now do you believe in them? Are they not more credible? But there is one more thing to tell, and this is quite incredible.

At times one of the adolescent girls or boys who go to see the child does not go home to weep or rage, does not, in fact, go home at all. Sometimes also a man or woman much older falls silent for a day or two, and then leaves home. These people go out into the street, and walk down the street alone. They keep walking, and walk straight out of the city of Omelas, through the beautiful gates. They keep walking across the farmlands of Omelas. Each one goes alone, youth or girl, man or woman. Night falls; the traveler must pass down village streets, between the houses with yellow-lit windows, and on out into the darkness of the fields. Each alone, they go west or north, toward the mountains. They go on. They leave Omelas, they walk ahead into the darkness, and they do not come back. The place they go toward is a place even less imaginable to most of us than the city of happi-ness. I cannot describe it at all. It is possible that it does not exist. But they seem to know where they are going, the ones who walk away from Omelas.

ON THE MEANING OF WORK

ERICH FROMM

Erich Fromm, born in Germany in 1900, studied sociology and psychology at Heidelberg, Frankfurt, and Munich and received his Ph.D. from Heidelberg in 1922. He then trained in psychoanalysis at Munich and at the Psychoanalytic Institute in Berlin. In 1934 he settled in the United States and eventually became an American citizen. He became Professor of Psychiatry at New York University in 1962, has lectured at Columbia, was for a long time on the faculty of Bennington College, and from 1951 to 1977 taught psychoanalysis at the National University of Mexico. His particular interest is the application of psychoanalytic theory to the problems of culture and society, and he has published a number of widely read books in this area. Among them are Escape from Freedom *(1941),* The Sane Society *(1955),* Zen Buddhism and Psychoanalysis *(1960),* You Shall Be as Gods: A Radical Interpretation of the Old Testament and Its Tradition *(1966),* The Well-Being of Man and Society: Essays on a Humanist Psychology *(1978), and* The Revolution of Hope: Toward a Humanized Technology *(1968). The present selection is a self-contained part of Chapter 5 of* The Sane Society.

Work in an Alienated Society

What becomes the meaning of *work* in an alienated society?

We have already made some brief comments about this question in the general discussion of alienation. But since this problem is of the utmost importance, not only for the understanding of present-day society, but also for any attempt to create a saner society, I want to deal with the nature of work separately and more extensively in the following pages.

Unless man exploits others, he has to work in order to live. However primitive and simple his method of work may be, by the very fact of production, he has risen above the animal kingdom; rightly has he been defined as "the animal that produces." But work is not only an inescapable necessity for man. Work is also his liberator from nature, his creator as a social and independent being. *In the process of work, that is, the molding and changing of nature outside of himself, man molds and changes himself.* He emerges from nature by mastering her; he develops his powers of cooperation, of reason, his sense of beauty. He separates himself from nature, from the original unity with her, but at the same time unites himself with her again as her master and builder. The more his work develops, the more his individuality develops. In molding nature and re-creating her, he learns to make use of his powers, increasing his skill and creativeness. Whether we think of the beautiful paintings in the caves of Southern France, the ornaments on weapons among primitive people, the statues and temples of Greece, the cathedrals of the Middle Ages, the chairs and tables made by skilled craftsmen, or the cultivation of flowers, trees or corn by peasants—all are expressions of the creative transformation of nature by man's reason and skill.

In Western history, craftsmanship, especially as it developed in the thirteenth and fourteenth centuries, constitutes one of the peaks in the evolution of creative work. Work was not only a useful activity, but one which carried with it a profound satisfaction. The main features of craftsmanship have been very lucidly expressed by C. W. Mills. "There is no ulterior motive in work other than the product being made and the processes of its creation. The details of daily work are meaningful because they are not detached in the worker's mind from the product of the work. The worker is free to control his own working action. The craftsman is thus able to learn from his work; and to use and develop his capacities and skills in its prosecution. There is no split of work and play, or work and culture. The craftsman's way of livelihood determines and infuses his entire mode of living."[1]

With the collapse of the medieval structure, and the beginning of the modern mode of production, the meaning and function of work changed fundamentally, especially in the Protestant countries. Man, being afraid of his newly won freedom, was obsessed by the need to subdue his doubts and fears by developing a feverish activity. The outcome of this activity, success or failure, decided his salvation, indicating whether he was among the saved or the lost souls. *Work, instead of being an activity satisfying in itself and pleasureable, became a duty and an obsession.* The more it was possible to gain riches by work, the more it became a pure means to the aim of wealth and success. Work became, in Max Weber's terms, the chief factor in a system of "innerworldly asceticism," an answer to man's sense of aloneness and isolation.

However, work in this sense existed only for the upper and middle classes, those who could amass some capital and employ the work of others. For the vast majority of those who had only their physical energy to sell, work became nothing but forced labor. The worker in the eighteenth or nineteenth century who had to work sixteen hours if he did not want to starve was not doing it because he served the Lord in this way, nor because his success would show that he was among the "chosen" ones, but because he was forced to sell his energy to those who had the means of exploiting it. The first centuries of the modern era find the meaning of work divided into that of *duty* among the middle class, and that of *forced labor* among those without property.

The religious attitude toward work as a duty, which was still so prevalent in the nineteenth century, has been changing considerably in the last decades. Modern man does not know what to do with himself, how to spend his lifetime meaningfully, and he is driven to work in order to avoid an unbearable boredom. But work has ceased to be a moral and religious obligation in the sense of the middle-class attitude of the eighteenth and nineteenth centuries. Something new has emerged. Ever-increasing production, the drive to make bigger and better things, have become aims in themselves, new

---

[1] C. W. Mills, *White Collar*, Oxford University Press, New York, 1951, p. 220.

ideals. Work has become alienated from the working person.

What happens to the industrial worker? He spends his best energy for seven or eight hours a day in producing "something." He needs his work in order to make a living, but his role is essentially a passive one. He fulfills a small isolated function in a complicated and highly organized process of production, and is never confronted with "his" product as a whole, at least not as a producer, but only as a consumer, provided he has the money to buy "his" product in a store. He is concerned neither with the whole product in its physical aspects nor with its wider economic and social aspects. He is put in a certain place, has to carry out a certain task, but does not participate in the organization or management of the work. He is not interested, nor does he know why one produces this, instead of another commodity—what relation it has to the needs of society as a whole. The shoes, the cars, the electric bulbs, are produced by "the enterprise," using the machines. He is a part of the machine, rather than its master as an active agent. The machine, instead of being in his service to do work for him which once had to be performed by sheer physical energy, has become his master. Instead of the machine being the substitute for human energy, man has become a substitute for the machine. *His work can be defined as the performance of acts which cannot yet be performed by machines.*

Work is a means of getting money, not in itself a meaningful human activity. P. Drucker, observing workers in the automobile industry, expresses this idea very succinctly: "For the great majority of automobile workers, the only meaning of the job is in the pay check, not in anything connected with the work or the product. Work appears as something unnatural, a disagreeable, meaningless and stultifying condition of getting the pay check, devoid of dignity as well as of importance. No wonder that this puts a premium on slovenly work, on slow-downs, and on other tricks to get the same pay check with less work. No wonder that this results in an unhappy and discontented worker—because a pay check is not enough to base one's self-respect on."[2]

This relationship of the worker to his work is an outcome of the whole social organization of which he is a part. Being "employed,"[3] he is not an active agent, has no responsibility except the proper performance of the isolated piece of work he is doing, and has little interest except the one of bringing home enough money to support himself and his family. Nothing more is expected of him, or wanted from him. He is part of the equipment hired by capital, and his role and function are determined by this quality of being a piece of equipment. In recent decades, increasing attention has been paid to the psychology of the worker, and to his attitude toward his work, to the "human problem of industry"; but this very formulation is indicative of the underlying attitude; there is a human being spending most of his lifetime at work, and what should be discussed is the *"industrial problem of human beings,"* rather than *"the human problem of industry."*

Most investigations in the field of industrial psychology are concerned

---

[2] Cf. Peter F. Drucker, *Concept of the Corporation*, The John Day Company, New York, 1946, p. 179.
[3] The English "employed" like the German *angestellt* are terms which refer to things rather than to human beings.

with the question of how the productivity of the individual worker can be increased, and how he can be made to work with less friction; psychology has lent its services to "human engineering," an attempt to treat the worker and employee like a machine which runs better when it is well oiled. While Taylor was primarily concerned with a better organization of the technical use of the worker's physical powers, most industrial psychologists are mainly concerned with the manipulation of the worker's psyche. The underlying idea can be formulated like this: if he works better when he is happy, then let us make him happy, secure, satisfied, or anything else, provided it raises his output and diminishes friction. In the name of "human relations," the worker is treated with all devices which suit a completely alienated person; even happiness and human values are recommended in the interest of better relations with the public. Thus, for instance, according to *Time* magazine, one of the best-known American psychiatrists said to a group of fifteen hundred Supermarket executives: "It's going to be an increased satisfaction to our customers if we are happy. . . . It is going to pay off in cold dollars and cents to management, if we could put some of these general principles of values, human relationships, really into practice." One speaks of "human relations" and one means the most in-human relations, those between alienated automatons; one speaks of happiness and means the perfect routinization which has driven out the last doubt and all spontaneity.

The alienated and profoundly unsatisfactory character of work results in two reactions: one, the ideal of complete *laziness*; the other a deep-seated, though often unconscious hostility toward work and everything and everybody connected with it.

It is not difficult to recognize the widespread longing for the state of complete laziness and passivity. Our advertising appeals to it even more than to sex. There are, of course, many useful and labor saving gadgets. But this usefulness often serves only as a rationalization for the appeal to complete passivity and receptivity. A package of breakfast cereal is being advertised as *"new—easier to eat."* An electric toaster is advertised with these words: " . . . the most distinctly different toaster in the world! Everything is done *for* you with this new toaster. You need not even bother to lower the bread. Power-action, through a unique electric motor, *gently takes the bread right out of your fingers!"* How many courses in languages, or other subjects are announced with the slogan "effortless learning, no more of the old drudgery." Everybody knows the picture of the elderly couple in the advertisement of a life-insurance company, who have retired at the age of sixty, and spend their life in the complete bliss of having nothing to do except just travel.

Radio and television exhibit another element of this yearning for laziness: the idea of "push-button power"; by pushing a button, or turning a knob on my machine, I have the power to produce music, speeches, ball games, and on the television set, to command events of the world to appear before my eyes. The pleasure of driving cars certainly rests partly upon this same satisfaction of the wish for push-button power. By the effortless pushing of a button, a powerful machine is set in motion; little skill and effort is needed to make the driver feel that he is the ruler of space.

But there is far more serious and deep-seated reaction to the meaninglessness and boredom of work. It is a hostility toward work which is much less conscious than our craving for laziness and inactivity. Many a businessman feels himself the prisoner of his business and the commodities he sells; he has a feeling of fraudulency about his product and a secret contempt for it. He hates his customers, who force him to put up a show in order to sell. He hates his competitors because they are a threat; his employees as well as his superiors, because he is in a constant competitive fight with them. Most important of all, he hates himself, because he sees his life passing by, without making any sense beyond the momentary intoxication of success. Of course, this hate and contempt for others and for oneself, and for the very things one produces, is mainly unconscious, and only occasionally comes up to awareness in a fleeting thought, which is sufficiently disturbing to be set aside as quickly as possible.

STUDS TERKEL

Studs Terkel is perhaps best known for his interviews and oral histories, recording the feelings and thoughts of "ordinary" people who are rarely heard. His tool is a portable tape recorder, a tool, he says, that can be used or misused. Hidden, it can be a means of blackmail or an instrument of the police state. In the open, "on the steps of a public housing project, in a frame bungalow, in a furnished apartment, in a parked car," it can capture the thoughts of the uncelebrated and "carry away valuables beyond price." He has published these valuables in three different books: Division Street: America *(1966), interviews with people from different groups and classes in Chicago;* Hard Times: An Oral History of the Great Depression *(1970), interviews with one hundred Americans who survived the Great Depression; and* Working: People Talk About What They Do All Day and How They Feel About What They Do *(1974), which is the source of the three selections below. His latest book is* Talking to Myself: A Memoir of My Times *(1977).*

Terkel's background probably helped him develop his ability to talk with many kinds of people and his interest in what they have to say. He was born Louis Terkel in New York in 1912; his family moved to Chicago when he was eleven. His father was a tailor; his mother took over a hotel for blue-collar workers, mechanics, and craftsmen, men he knew as he was growing up. He later changed his first name to Studs, after Studs Lonigan, from James T. Farrell's novels about the Chicago proletarian Irish. After high school he went to Crane Junior College, then graduated from the University of Chicago (Ph.D., 1932). He went on to law school (J.D., 1934) but failed his first bar examination and never practiced. Instead, he has been a radio and stage actor, a radio writer, a jazz columnist, and a disc jockey. In recent years he has developed the interview style—what he calls "guerilla journalism"—into the provocative studies of American culture mentioned above.

Carl Murray Bates, Mason

We're in a tavern no more than thirty yards from the banks of the Ohio. Toward the far side of the river, Alcoa smokestacks belch forth: an uneasy coupling of a bucolic past and an industrial present. The waters are polluted, yet the jobs out there offer the townspeople their daily bread.

He is fifty-seven years old. He's a stonemason who has pursued his craft since he was seventeen. None of his three sons is in his trade.

As far as I know, masonry is older than carpentry, which goes clear back to Bible times. Stonemason goes back way *before* Bible time: the pyramids of Egypt, things of that sort. Anybody that starts to build anything, stone, rock, or brick, starts on the northeast corner. Because when they built King Solomon's Temple, they started on the northeast corner. To this day, you look at your courthouses, your big public buildings, you look at the cornerstone, when it was created, what year, it will be on the northeast corner. If I was gonna build a septic tank, I would start on the northeast corner. (Laughs.) Superstition, I suppose.

With stone we build just about anything. Stone is the oldest and best building material that ever was. Stone was being used even by the cavemen that put it together with mud. They built out of stone before they even used logs. He got him a cave, he built stone across the front. And he learned to use dirt, mud, to make the stones lay there without sliding around—which was the beginnings of mortar, which we still call mud. The Romans used mortar that's almost as good as we have today.

Everyone hears these things, they just don't remember 'em. But me being in the profession, when I hear something in that line, I remember it. Stone's my business. I, oh, sometimes talk to architects and engineers that have made a study and I pick up the stuff here and there.

Every piece of stone you pick up is different, the grain's a little different and this and that. It'll split one way and break the other. You pick up your stone and look at it and make an educated guess. It's a pretty good day layin' stone or brick. Not tiring. Anything you like to do isn't tiresome. It's hard work; stone is heavy. At the same time, you get interested in what you're doing and you usually fight the clock the other way. You're not lookin' for quittin'. You're wondering you haven't got enough done and it's almost quittin' time. (Laughs.) I ask the hod carrier what time it is and he says two thirty. I say, "Oh, my Lord, I was gonna get a whole lot more than this."

I pretty well work by myself. On houses, usually just one works. I've got the hod carrier there, but most of the time I talk to myself, "I'll get my hammer and I'll knock the chip off there." (Laughs.) A good hod carrier is half your day. He won't work as hard as a poor one. He knows what to do and make every move count makin' the mortar. It has to be so much water, so much sand. His skill is to see that you don't run out of anything. The hod carrier, he's above the laborer. He has a certain amount of prestige.

I think a laborer feels that he's the low man. Not so much that he works with his hands, it's that he's at the bottom of the scale. He always wants to get up to a skilled trade. Of course he'd make more money. The main thing is the common laborer—even the word *common* laborer—just sounds so common, he's at the bottom. Many that works with his hands takes pride in his work.

I get a lot of phone calls when I get home: how about showin' me how and I'll do it myself; I always wind up doin' it for 'em. (Laughs.) So I take a lot of pride in it and I do get, oh, I'd say, a lot of praise or whatever you want to call it. I don't suppose anybody, however much he's recognized, wouldn't like to be recognized a little more. I think I'm pretty well recognized.

One of my sons is an accountant and the other two are bankers. They're mathematicians, I suppose you'd call 'em that. Air-conditioned offices and all that. They always look at the house I build. They stop by and see me when I'm workin'. Always want me to come down and fix somethin' on their house, too. (Laughs.) They don't buy a house that I don't have to look at it first. Oh sure, I've got to crawl under it and look on the roof, you know. . . .

I can't seem to think of any young masons. So many of 'em before, the man lays stone and his son follows his footsteps. Right now the only one of these sons I can think of is about forty, fifty years old.

I started back in the Depression times when there wasn't any apprenticeships. You just go out and if you could hold your job, that's it. I was just a kid then. Now I worked real hard and carried all the blocks I could. Then I'd get my trowel and I'd lay one or two. The second day the boss told me: I think you could lay enough blocks to earn your wages. So I guess I had only one day of apprenticeship. Usually it takes about three years of being a hod carrier to start. And it takes another ten or fifteen years to learn the skill.

I admired the men that we had at that time that were stonemasons. They knew their trade. So naturally I tried to pattern after them. There's been very little change in the work. Stone is still stone, mortar is still the same as it was fifty years ago. The style of stone has changed a little. We use a lot more, we call it golf. A stone as big as a baseball up to as big as a basketball. Just round balls and whatnot. We just fit 'em in the wall that way.

Automation has tried to get in the bricklayer. Set 'em with a crane. I've seen several put up that way. But you've always got in-between the windows and this and that. It just doesn't seem to pan out. We do have a power saw. We do have an electric power mix to mix the mortar, but the rest of it's done by hand as it always was.

In the old days they all seemed to want it cut out and smoothed. It's harder now because you have no way to use your tools. You have no way to use a string, you have no way to use a level or a plumb. You just have to look at it because it's so rough and many irregularities. You have to just back up and look at it.

All construction, there's always a certain amount of injuries. A scaffold will break and so on. But practically no real danger. All I ever did do was work on houses, so we don't get up very high—maybe two stories. Very seldom that any more. Most of 'em are one story. And so many of 'em use stone for a trim. They may go up four, five feet and then paneling or something. There's a lot of skinned fingers or you hit your finger with a hammer. Practically all stone is worked with hammers and chisels. I wouldn't call it dangerous at all.

Stone's my life. I daydream all the time, most times it's on stone. Oh, I'm gonna build me a stone cabin down on the Green River. I'm gonna build stone cabinets in the kitchen. That stone door's gonna be awful heavy and I don't know how to attach the hinges. I've got to figure out how to make a stone roof. That's the kind of thing. All my dreams, it seems like it's got to have a piece of rock mixed in it.

If I got some problem that's bothering me, I'll actually wake up in the night and think of it. I'll sit at the table and get a pencil and paper and go over it, makin' marks on paper or drawin' or however . . . this way or that way. Now I've got to work this and I've only got so much. Or they decided they want it that way when you already got it fixed this way. Anyone hates tearing his work down. It's all the same price but you still don't like to do it.

These fireplaces, you've got to figure how they'll throw out heat, the way you curve the fireboxes inside. You have to draw a line so they reflect heat. But if you throw out too much of a curve, you'll have them smoke. People in these fine houses don't want a puff of smoke coming out of the house.

The architect draws the picture and the plans, and the draftsman and the engineer, they help him. They figure the strength and so on. But when it comes to actually makin' the curves and doin' the work, you've got to do it with your hands. It comes right back to your hands.

When you get into stone, you're gettin' away from the prefabs, you're gettin' into the better homes. Usually at this day and age they'll start into sixty to seventy thousand and run up to about half a million. We've got one goin' now that's mighty close, three or four hundred thousand. That type of house is what we build.

The lumber is not near as good as it used to be. We have better fabricating material, such as plywood and sheet rock and things of that sort, but the lumber itself is definitely inferior. Thirty, forty years ago a house was almost entirely made of lumber, wood floors . . . Now they have vinyl, they have carpet, everything, and so on. The framework wood is getting to be of very poor quality.

But stone is still stone and the bricks are actually more uniform than they used to be. Originally they took a clay bank . . . I know a church been built that way. Went right on location, dug a hole in the ground and formed bricks with their hands. They made the bricks that built the building on the spot.

Now we've got modern kilns, modern heat, the temperature don't vary. They got better bricks now than they used to have. We've got machines that make brick, so they're made true. Where they used to, they were pretty rough. I'm buildin' a big fireplace now out of old brick. They run wide, long, and it's a headache. I've been two weeks on that one fireplace.

The toughest job I ever done was this house, a hundred years plus. The lady wanted one room left just that way. And this doorway had to be closed. It had deteriorated and weathered for over a hundred years. The bricks was made out of broken pieces, none of 'em were straight. If you lay 'em crooked, it gets awful hard right there. You spend a lifetime tryin' to learn to lay bricks straight. And it took a half-day to measure with a spoon, to try to get the mortar to match. I'd have so much dirt, so much soot, so much lime, so when I got the recipe right I could make it in bigger quantity. Then I made it with a coffee cup. Half a cup of this, half a cup of that . . . I even used soot out of a chimney and sweepin's off the floor. I was two days layin' up a little doorway, mixin' the mortar and all. The boss told the lady it couldn't be done. I said, "Give me the time, I believe I can do it." I defy you to find where that door is right now. That's the best job I ever done.

There's not a house in this country that I haven't built that I don't look at every time I go by. (Laughs.) I can set here now and actually in my mind see so many that you wouldn't believe. If there's one stone in there crooked, I know where it's at and I'll never forget it. Maybe thirty years, I'll know a place where I should have took that stone out and redone it but I didn't. I still notice it. The people who live there might not notice it, but I notice it. I never pass that house that I don't think of it. I've got one house in mind right now. (Laughs.) That's the work of my hands. 'Cause you see, stone, you don't prepaint it, you don't camouflage it. It's there, just like I left it forty years ago.

I can't imagine a job where you go home and maybe go by a year later and you don't know what you've done. My work, I can see what I did the first day I started. All my work is set right out there in the open and I can look at it as I go by. It's something I can see the rest of my life. Forty years ago, the first blocks I ever laid in my life, when I was seventeen years old. I never go through Eureka—a little town down there on the river—that I don't look thataway. It's always there.

Immortality as far as we're concerned. Nothin' in this world lasts forever, but did you know that stone—Bedford limestone, they claim—deteriorates one-sixteenth of an inch every hundred years? And it's around four or five inches for a house. So that's gettin' awful close. (Laughs.)

Nora Watson, Editor

Jobs are not big enough for people. It's not just the assembly line worker whose job is too small for his spirit, you know? A job like mine, if you really put your spirit into it, you would sabotage immediately. You don't dare. So you absent your spirit from it. My mind has been so divorced from my job, except as a source of income, it's really absurd.

As I work in the business world, I am more and more shocked. You throw yourself into things because you feel that important questions—self-discipline, goals, a meaning of your life—are carried out in your *work*. You invest a job with a lot of values that the society doesn't allow you to put into a job. You find yourself like a pacemaker that's gone crazy or something. You want it to be a million things that it's not and you want to give it a million parts of yourself that nobody else wants there. So you end up wrecking the curve or else settling down and conforming. I'm really in a funny place right now. I'm so calm about what I'm doing and what's coming . . .

She is twenty-eight. She is a staff writer for an institution publishing health care literature. Previously she had worked as an editor for a corporation publishing national magazines.

She came from a small mountain town in western Pennsylvania. "My father was a preacher. I didn't like what he was doing, but it was his vocation. That was the good part of it. It wasn't just: go to work in the morning and punch a time clock. It was a profession of himself. I expected work to be like that. All my life, I planned to be a teacher. It wasn't until late in college, my senior year, that I realized what the public school system was like. A little town in the mountains is one thing . . .

"My father, to my mind, is a weird person, but whatever he is, he is. Being a preacher was so important to him he would call it the Call of the Lord. He was willing to make his family live in very poor conditions. He was willing to strain his relationship to my mother, not to mention his children. He put us through an awful lot of things, including just bare survival, in order to stay being a preacher. His evenings, his weekends, and his days, he was out calling on people. Going out with healing oil and anointing the sick, listening to their troubles. The fact that he didn't do the same for his family is another thing. But he saw himself as the core resource in the community—at a great price to himself. He really believed that was what he was supposed to be doing. It was his life.

Most of the night he wouldn't go to bed. He'd pull out sermons by Wesley or Spurgeon or somebody, and he'd sit down until he fell asleep, maybe at three o'clock in the morning. Reading sermons. He just never stopped. (Laughs.)

I paper the walls of my office with posters and bring in flowers, bring in an FM radio, bring down my favorite ceramic lamp. I'm the only person in the whole damn building with a desk facing the window instead of the door. I just turn myself around from all that I can. I ration my time so that I'll spend two hours working for the Institution and the rest of the time I'll browse. (Laughs.)

I function better if they leave me alone more. My boss will come in and say, "I know you're overloaded, but would you mind getting this done, it's urgent. I need it in three weeks." I can do it in two hours. So I put it on the back burner and produce it on time. When I first went there, I came in early and stayed late. I read everything I could on the subject at hand. I would work a project to the wall and get it really done right, and then ask for more. I found out I was wrecking the curve, I was out of line.

The people, just as capable as I and just as ready to produce, had realized it was pointless, and had cut back. Everyone, consciously or unconsciously, was rationing his time. Playing cards at lunch time for three hours, going sun bathing, or less obvious ways of blowing it. I realized: Okay, the road to ruin is doing a good job. The amazing, absurd thing was that once I decided to stop doing a good job, people recognized a kind of authority in me. Now I'm just moving ahead like blazes.

I have my own office. I have a secretary. If I want a book case, I get a book case. If I want a file, I get a file. If I want to stay home, I stay home. If I want to go shopping, I go shopping. This is the first comfortable job I've ever had in my life and it is absolutely despicable.

I've been a waitress and done secretarial work. I knew, in those cases, I wasn't going to work at near capacity. It's one thing to work to your limits as a waitress because you end up with a bad back. It's another thing to work to your limits doing writing and editing because you end up with a sharper mind. It's a joy. Here, of all places, where I had expected to put the energy and enthusiasm and the gifts that I may have to work—it isn't happening. They expect less than you can offer. Token labor. What writing you do is writing to order. When I go for a job interview—I must leave this place!— I say, "Sure, I can bring you samples, but the ones I'm proud of are the ones the Institution never published."

It's so demeaning to be there and not be challenged. It's humiliation, because I feel I'm being forced into doing something I would never do of my own free will—which is simply waste itself. It's really not a Puritan hang-up. It's not that I want to be persecuted. It's simply that I know I'm vegetating and being paid to do exactly that. It's possible for me to sit here and read my books. But then you walk out with no sense of satisfaction, with no sense of legitimacy! I'm being had. Somebody has bought the right to you for eight hours a day. The manner in which they use you is completely at their discretion. You know what I mean?

I feel like I'm being pimped for and it's not my style. The level of bitterness in this department is stunning. They take days off quite a bit. They don't show up. They don't even call in. They've adjusted a lot better than I have. They see the Institution as a free ride as long as it lasts. I don't want to be party to it, so I've gone my own way. It's like being on welfare. Not that that's a shameful thing. It's the surprise of this enforced idleness. It makes you feel not at home with yourself. I'm furious. It's a feeling that I will not be humiliated. I will not be dis-used.

For all that was bad about my father's vocation, he showed me it was possible to fuse your life to your work. His home was also his work. A parish is no different from an office, because it's the whole countryside. There's nothing I would enjoy more than a job that was so meaningful to me that I brought it home.

The people I work with are not buffoons. I think they're part of a culture, like me, who've been sold on a dum-dum idea of human nature. It's frightening. I've made the best compromise available. If I were free, economically free, I would go back to school. It galls me that in our culture we have to pay for the privilege of learning.

A guy was in the office next to mine. He's sixty-two and he's done. He came to the Institution in the forties. He saw the scene and said, "Yes, I'll play drone to you. I'll do all the piddley things you want. I won't upset the apple cart by suggesting anything else." With a change of regimes in our department, somebody came across him and said, "Gee, he hasn't contributed anything here. His mind is set in old attitudes. So we'll throw him out." They fired him unceremoniously, with no pension, no severance pay, no nothing. Just out on your ear, sixty-two. He gets back zero from having invested so many years playing the game.

The drone has his nose to the content of the job. The politicker has his nose to the style. And the politicker is what I think our society values. The politicker, when it's apparent he's a winner, is helped. Everyone who has a stake in being on the side of the winner gives him a boost. The minute I finally realized the way to exist at the Institution—for the short time I'll be here—was not to break my back but to use it for my own ends, I was a winner.

Granted, there were choices this guy could have made initially. He might have decided on a more independent way of life. But there were all sorts of forces keeping him from that decision. The Depression, for one thing. You took the job, whatever the terms were. It was a straight negotiation. The drone would get his dole. The Institution broke the contract. He was fired for being dull, which is what he was hired to be.

I resist strongly the mystique of youth that says these kids are gonna come up with the answers. One good thing a lot of the kids are doing, though, is not getting themselves tied up to artificial responsibilities. That includes marriage, which some may or may not call an artificial responsibility. I have chosen to stay unmarried, to not get encumbered with husband and children. But the guy with three kids and a mortgage doesn't have many choices. He wouldn't be able to work two days a week instead of five.

I'm coming to a less moralistic attitude toward work. I know very few people who feel secure with their right just to be—or comfortable. Just you being you and me being me with my mini-talents may be enough. Maybe just making a career of being and finding out what that's about is enough. I don't think I have a calling—at this moment—except to be me. But nobody pays you for being you, so I'm at the Institution—for the moment . . .

When you ask most people who they are, they define themselves by their jobs. "I'm a doctor." "I'm a radio announcer." "I'm a carpenter." If somebody asks me, I say, "I'm Nora Watson." At certain points in time I do things for a living. Right now I'm working for the Institution. But not for long. I'd be lying to you if I told you I wasn't scared.

I have a few options. Given the market, I'm going to take the best job I can find. I really tried to play the game by the rules, and I think it's a hundred percent unadulterated bullshit. So I'm not likely to go back downtown and say, "Here I am. I'm very good, hire me."

You recognize yourself as a marginal person. As a person who can give only minimal assent to anything that is going on in this society: "I'm glad the electricity works." That's about it. What you have to find is your own niche that will allow you to keep feeding and clothing and sheltering your-self without getting downtown. (Laughs.) Because that's death. That's really where death is.

Mike Lefevre, Steelworker

> *Who built the seven towers of Thebes?*
> *The books are filled with the names of kings.*
> *Was it kings who hauled the craggy blocks of stone?* . . .
> *In the evening when the Chinese wall was finished*
> *Where did the masons go?* . . .
>
> —Bertolt Brecht

It is a two-flat dwelling, somewhere in Cicero, on the outskirts of Chicago. He is thirty-seven. He works in a steel mill. On occasion, his wife Carol works as a waitress in a neighborhood restaurant; otherwise, she is at home, caring for their two small children, a girl and a boy.

At the time of my first visit, a sculpted statuette of Mother and Child was on the floor, head severed from body. He laughed softly as he indicated his three-year-old daughter: "She Doctor Spock'd it."

I'm a dying breed. A laborer. Strictly muscle work . . . pick it up, put it down, pick it up, put it down. We handle between forty and fifty thousand pounds of steel a day. (Laughs.) I know this is hard to believe—from four hundred pounds to three- and four-pound pieces. It's dying.

You can't take pride any more. You remember when a guy could point to a house he built, how many logs he stacked. He built it and he was proud of it. I don't really think I could be proud if a contractor built a home for me. I would be tempted to get in there and kick the carpenter in the ass (laughs), and take the saw away from him. 'Cause I would have to be part of it, you know.

It's hard to take pride in a bridge you're never gonna cross, in a door you're never gonna open. You're mass-producing things and you never see the end result of it. (Muses.) I worked for a trucker one time. And I got this tiny satisfaction when I loaded a truck. At least I could see the truck depart loaded. In a steel mill, forget it. You don't see where nothing goes.

I got chewed out by my foreman once. He said, "Mike, you're a good worker but you have a bad attitude." My attitude is that I don't get excited about my job. I do my work but I don't say whoopee-doo. The day I get excited about my job is the day I go to a head shrinker. How are you gonna get excited about pullin' steel? How are you gonna get excited when you're tired and want to sit down?

It's not just the work. Somebody built the pyramids. Somebody's going to build something. Pyramids, Empire State Building—these things just don't happen. There's hard work behind it. I would like to see a building, say, the

Empire State, I would like to see on one side of it a foot-wide strip from top to bottom with the name of every bricklayer, the name of every electrician, with all the names. So when a guy walked by, he could take his son and say. "See, that's me over there on the forty-fifth floor. I put the steel beam in." Picasso can point to a painting. What can I point to? A writer can point to a book. Everybody should have something to point to.

It's the not-recognition by other people. To say a woman is *just* a housewife is degrading right? Okay. *Just* a housewife. It's also degrading to say *just* a laborer. The difference is that a man goes out and maybe gets smashed.

When I was single, I could quit, just split. I wandered all over the country. You worked just enough to get a poke, money in your pocket. Now I'm married and I got two kids . . . (trails off). I worked on a truck dock one time and I was single. The foreman came over and he grabbed my shoulder, kind of gave me a shove. I punched him and knocked him off the dock. I said, "Leave me alone. I'm doing my work, just stay away from me, just don't give me the with-the-hands business."

Hell, if you whip a damn mule he might kick you. Stay out of my way, that's all. Working is bad enough, don't bug me. I would rather work my ass off for eight hours a day with nobody watching me than five minutes with a guy watching me. Who you gonna sock? You can't sock General Motors, you can't sock anybody in Washington, you can't sock a system.

A mule, an old mule, that's the way I feel. Oh yeah. See. (Shows black and blue marks on arms and legs, burns.) You know what I heard from more than one guy at work? "If my kid wants to work in a factory, I am going to kick the hell out of him." I want my kid to be an effete snob. Yeah, mm-hmm. (Laughs.) I want him to be able to quote Walt Whitman, to be proud of it.

If you can't improve yourself, you improve your posterity. Otherwise life isn't worth nothing. You might as well go back to the cave and stay there. I'm sure the first caveman who went over the hill to see what was on the other side—I don't think he went there wholly out of curiosity. He went there because he wanted to get his son out of the cave. Just the same way I want to send my kid to college.

I work so damn hard and want to come home and sit down and lay around. *But I gotta get it out.* I want to be able to turn around to somebody and say, "Hey, fuck you." You know? (Laughs.) The guy sitting next to me on the bus too. 'Cause all day I wanted to tell my foreman to go fuck himself, but I can't.

So I find a guy in a tavern. To tell him that. And he tells me too. I've been in brawls. He's punching me and I'm punching him, because we actually want to punch somebody else. The most that'll happen is the bartender will bar us from the tavern. But at work, you lose your job.

This one foreman I've got, he's a kid. He's a college graduate. He thinks he's better than everybody else. He was chewing me out and I was saying, "Yeah, yeah, yeah." He said, "What do you mean, yeah, yeah, yeah. Yes, *sir*." I told him, "Who the hell are you, Hitler? What is this *"Yes, sir"* bullshit? I came here to work, I didn't come here to crawl. There's a fuckin' difference." One word led to another and I lost.

I got broke down to a lower grade and lost twenty-five cents an hour, which is a hell of a lot. It amounts to about ten dollars a week. He came over—after breaking me down. The guy comes over and smiles at me. I blew up. He didn't know it, but he was about two seconds and two feet away from a hospital. I said, "Stay the fuck away from me." He was just about to say something and was pointing his finger. I just reached my hand up and just grabbed his finger and I just put it back in his pocket. He walked away. I grabbed his finger because I'm married. If I'd a been single, I'd a grabbed his head. That's the difference.

You're doing this manual labor and you know that technology can do it. (Laughs.) Let's face it, a machine can do the work of a man; otherwise they wouldn't have space probes. Why can we send a rocket ship that's un-manned and yet send a man in a steel mill to do a mule's work?

Automation? Depends how it's applied. It frightens me if it puts me out on the street. It doesn't frighten me if it shortens my work week. You read that little thing: what are you going to do when this computer replaces you? Blow up computers. (Laughs.) Really. Blow up computers. I'll be god-damned if a computer is gonna eat before I do! I want milk for my kids and beer for me. Machines can either liberate man or enslave 'im, because they're pretty neutral. It's man who has the bias to put the thing one place or another.

If I had a twenty-hour workweek, I'd get to know my kids better, my wife better. Some kid invited me to go on a college campus. On a Saturday. It was summertime. Hell, if I have a choice of taking my wife and kids to a picnic or going to a college campus, it's gonna be the picnic. But if I worked a twenty-hour week, I could go do both. Don't you think with that extra twenty hours people could really expand? Who's to say? There are some people in factories just by force of circumstance. I'm just like the colored people. Potential Einsteins don't have to be white. They could be in cotton fields, they could be in factories.

The twenty-hour week is a possibility today. The intellectuals, they al-ways say there are potential Lord Byrons, Walt Whitmans, Roosevelts, Pi-cassos working in construction or steel mills or factories. But I don't think they believe it. I think what they're afraid of is the potential Hitlers and Stalins that are there too. The people in power fear the leisure man. Not just the United States. Russia's the same way.

What do you think would happen in this country if, for one year, they experimented and gave everybody a twenty-hour week? How do they know that the guy who digs Wallace today doesn't try to resurrect Hitler tomor-row? Or the guy who is mildly disturbed at pollution doesn't decide to go to General Motors and shit on the guy's desk? You can become a fanatic if you had the time. The whole thing is time. That is, I think, one reason rich kids tend to be fanatic about politics: they have time. Time, that's the important thing.

It isn't that the average working guy is dumb. He's tired, that's all. I picked up a book on chess one time. That thing laid in the drawer for two or three weeks, you're too tired. During the weekends you want to take your kids out. You don't want to sit there and the kid comes up: "Daddy, can I go to the park?" You got your nose in a book? Forget it.

I know a guy fifty-seven years old. Know what he tells me? "Mike, I'm old and tired *all* the time." The first thing happens at work: when the arms start moving, the brain stops. I punch in about ten minutes to seven in the morning. I say hello to a couple of guys I like, I kid around with them. One guy says good morning to you and you say good morning. To another guy you say fuck you. The guy you say fuck you to is your friend.

I put on my hard hat, change into my safety shoes, put on my safety glasses, go to the bonderizer. It's the thing I work on. They rake the metal, they wash it, they dip it in a paint solution, and we take it off. Put it on, take it off, put it on, take it off, put it on, take it off . . .

I say hello to everybody but my boss. At seven it starts. My arms get tired about the first half-hour. After that, they don't get tired any more until maybe the last half-hour at the end of the day. I work from seven to three thirty. My arms are tired at seven thirty and they're tired at three o'clock. I hope to God I never get broke in, because I always want my arms to be tired at seven thirty and three o'clock. (Laughs.) 'Cause that's when I know that there's a beginning and there's an end. That I'm not brainwashed. In between, I don't even try to think.

If I were to put you in front of a dock and I pulled up a skid in front of you with fifty hundred-pound sacks of potatoes and there are fifty more skids just like it, and this is what you're gonna do all day, what would you think about—potatoes? Unless a guy's a nut, he never thinks about work or talks about it. Maybe about baseball or about getting drunk the other night or he got laid or he didn't get laid. I'd say one out of a hundred will actually get excited about work.

Why is it that the communists always say they're for the workingman, and as soon as they set up a country, you got guys singing to tractors? They're singing about how they love the factory. That's where I couldn't buy communism. It's the intellectuals' utopia, not mine. I cannot picture myself singing to a tractor, I just can't. (Laughs.) Or singing to steel. (Sing-songs.) Oh whoop-dee-doo, I'm at the bonderizer, oh how I love this heavy steel. No thanks. Never happen.

Oh yeah, I daydream. I fantasize about a sexy blonde in Miami who's got my union dues. (Laughs.) I think of the head of the union the way I think of the head of my company. Living it up. I think of February in Miami. Warm weather, a place to lay in. When I hear a college kid say, "I'm oppressed," I don't believe him. You know what I'd like to do for one year? Live like a college kid. Just for one year. I'd love to. Wow! (Whispers.) Wow! Sports car! Marijuana! (Laughs.) Wild, sexy broads. I'd love that, hell yes, I would.

Somebody has to do this work. If my kid ever goes to college, I just want him to have a little respect, to realize that his dad is one of those somebodies. This is why even on—(muses) yeah, I guess, sure—on the black thing . . . (Sighs heavily.) I can't really hate the colored fella that's working with me all day. The black intellectual I got no respect for. The white intellectual I got no use for. I got no use for the black militant who's gonna scream three hundred years of slavery to me while I'm busting my ass. You know what I mean? (Laughs.) I have one answer for that guy: go see Rockefeller. See Harriman. Don't bother me. We're in the same cotton field. So just don't bug me. (Laughs.)

After work I usually stop off at a tavern. Cold beer. Cold beer right away. When I was single, I used to go into hillbilly bars, get in a lot of brawls. Just to explode. I got a thing on my arm here (indicates scar). I got slapped with a bicycle chain. Oh, wow! (Softly) Mmm. I'm getting older. (Laughs.) I don't explode as much. You might say I'm broken in. (Quickly) No, I'll never be broken in. (Sighs.) When you get a little older, you exchange the words. When you're younger, you exchange the blows.

When I get home, I argue with my wife a little bit. Turn on TV, get mad at the news. (Laughs.) I don't even watch the news that much. I watch Jackie Gleason. I look for any alternative to the ten o'clock news. I don't want to go to bed angry. Don't hit a man with anything heavy at five o'clock. He just can't be bothered. This is his time to relax. The heaviest thing he wants is what his wife has to tell him.

When I come home, know what I do for the first twenty minutes? Fake it. I put on a smile. I got a kid three years old. Sometimes she says, "Daddy, where've you been?" I say, "Work." I could have told her I'd been in Disneyland. What's work to a three-year-old kid? If I feel bad, I can't take it out on the kids. Kids are born innocent of everything but birth. You can't take it out on your wife either. This is why you go to a tavern. You want to release it there rather than do it at home. What does an actor do when he's got a bad movie? I got a bad movie every day.

I don't even need the alarm clock to get up in the morning. I can go out drinking all night, fall asleep at four, and bam! I'm up at six—no matter what I do. (Laughs.) It's a pseudo-death, more or less. Your whole system is paralyzed and you give all the appearance of death. It's an ingrown clock. It's a thing you just get used to. The hours differ. It depends. Sometimes my wife wants to do something crazy like play five hundred rummy or put a puzzle together. It could be midnight, could be ten o'clock, could be nine thirty.

What do you do weekends?

Drink beer, read a book. See that one? *Violence in America*. It's one of them studies from Washington. One of them committees they're always appointing. A thing like that I read on a weekend. But during the weekdays, gee . . . I just thought about it. I don't do that much reading from Monday through Friday. Unless it's a horny book. I'll read it at work and go home and do my homework. (Laughs.) That's what the guys at the plant call it—homework. (Laughs.) Sometimes my wife works on Saturday and I drink beer at the tavern.

I went out drinking with one guy, oh, a long time ago. A college boy. He was working where I work now. Always preaching to me about how you need violence to change the system and all that garbage. We went into a hillbilly joint. Some guy there, I didn't know him from Adam, he said, "You think you're smart." I said, "What's your pleasure?" (Laughs.) He said, "My pleasure's to kick your ass." I told him I really can't be bothered." He said, "What're you, chicken?" I said, "No, I just don't want to be bothered." He came over and said something to me again. I said, "I don't beat women, drunks, or fools. Now leave me alone."

The guy called his brother over. This college boy that was with me, he came nudging my arm, "Mike, let's get out of here." I said, "What are you worried about?" (Laughs.) This isn't unusual. People will bug you. You fend it off as much as you can with your mouth and when you can't, you punch the guy out.

It was close to closing time and we stayed. We could have left, but when you go into a place to have a beer and a guy challenges you—if you expect to go in that place again, you don't leave. If you have to fight the guy, you fight.

I got just outside the door and one of these guys jumped on me and grabbed me around the neck. I grabbed his arm and flung him against the wall. I grabbed him here (indicates throat), and jiggled his head against the wall quite a few times. He kind of slid down a little bit. This guy who said he was his brother took a swing at me with a garrison belt. He just missed and hit the wall. I'm looking around for my junior Stalin (laughs), who loves violence and everything. He's gone. Split. (Laughs.) Next day I see him at work. I couldn't get mad at him, he's a baby.

He saw a book in my back pocket one time and he was amazed. He walked up to me and he said, "You read?" I said, "What do you mean, I read?" He said, "All these dummies read the sports pages around here. What are you doing with a book?" I got pissed off at the kid right away. I said, "What do you mean, all these dummies? Don't knock a man who's paying somebody else's way through college." He was a nineteen-year-old effete snob.

Yet you want your kid to be an effete snob?

Yes. I want my kid to look at me and say, "Dad, you're a nice guy, but you're a fuckin' dummy." Hell yes, I want my kid to tell me that he's not gonna be like me . . .

If I were hiring people to work, I'd try naturally to pay them a decent wage. I'd try to find out their first names, their last names, keep the company as small as possible, so I could personalize the whole thing. All I would ask a man is a handshake, see you in the morning. No applications, nothing. I wouldn't be interested in the guy's past. Nobody ever checks the pedigree on a mule, do they? But they do on a man. Can you picture walking up to a mule and saying. "I'd like to know who his granddaddy was?"

I'd like to run a combination bookstore and tavern. (Laughs.) I would like to have a place where college kids came and a steelworker could sit down and talk. Where a workingman could not be ashamed of Walt Whitman and where a college professor could not be ashamed that he painted his house over the weekend.

If a carpenter built a cabin for poets, I think the least the poets owe the carpenter is just three or four one-liners on the wall. A little plaque: Though we labor with our minds, this place we can relax in was built by someone who can work with his hands. And his work is as noble as ours. I think the poet owes something to the guy who builds the cabin for him.

I don't think of Monday. You know what I'm thinking about on Sunday night? Next Sunday. If you work real hard, you think of a perpetual vacation. Not perpetual sleep . . . What do I think of on a Sunday night? Lord, I wish the fuck I could do something else for a living.

I don't know who the guy is who said there is nothing sweeter than an unfinished symphony. Like an unfinished painting and an unfinished poem. If he creates this thing one day—let's say, Michelangelo's Sistine Chapel. It took him a long time to do this, this beautiful work of art. But what if he had to create this Sistine Chapel a thousand times a year? Don't you think that would even dull Michelangelo's mind? Or if da Vinci had to draw his anatomical charts thirty, forty, fifty, sixty, eighty, ninety, a hundred times a day? Don't you think that would even bore da Vinci?

Way back, you spoke of the guys who built the pyramids, not the pharaohs, the unknowns. You put yourself in their category?

Yes. I want my signature on 'em, too. Sometimes, out of pure meanness, when I make something, I put a little dent in it. I like to do something to make it really unique. Hit it with a hammer. I deliberately fuck it up to see if it'll get by, just so I can say I did it. It could be anything. Let me put it this way: I think God invented the dodo bird so when we get up there we could tell Him, "Don't you ever make mistakes?" and He'd say, "Sure, look." (Laughs.) I'd like to make my imprint. My dodo bird. A mistake, *mine*. Let's say the whole building is nothing but red bricks. I'd like to have just the black one or the white one or the purple one. Deliberately fuck up.

This is gonna sound square, but my kid is my imprint. He's my freedom. There's a line in one of Hemingway's books. I think it's from *For Whom the Bell Tolls*. They're behind the enemy lines, somewhere in Spain, and she's pregnant. She wants to stay with him. He tells her no. He says, "if you die, I die," knowing he's gonna die. But if you go, I go. Know what I mean? The mystics call it the brass bowl. Continuum. You know what I mean? This is why I work. Every time I see a young guy walk by with a shirt and tie and dressed up real sharp, I'm lookin' at my kid, you know? That's it.

RICHARD SELZER

Richard Selzer is a general surgeon who also teaches at the Yale University Medical School. Born in New York in 1928 (his father a family doctor), he attended Union

College in Schenectady (B.S., 1948) and Albany Medical College (M.D., 1953), and he has done postdoctoral study at Yale. He is also a writer of short stories and essays, which have appeared in such magazines as Harper's, Mademoiselle, *and* Redbook. *In 1975 he received the National Magazine Award from the Columbia University School of Journalism for essays published in* Esquire. *He has published a book of short stories,* Rituals of Surgery *(1974), and two collections of essays:* Mortal Lessons *(1977), from which we reprint the selection below, and* Confessions of a Knife *(1979).*

The Exact Location of the Soul

Someone asked me why a surgeon would write. Why, when the shelves are already too full? They sag under the deadweight of books. To add a single adverb is to risk exceeding the strength of the boards. A surgeon should abstain. A surgeon, whose fingers are more at home in the steamy gullies of the body than they are tapping the dry keys of a typewriter. A surgeon, who feels the slow slide of intestines against the back of his hand and is no more alarmed than were a family of snakes taking their comfort from such an indolent rubbing. A surgeon, who palms the human heart as though it were some captured bird.

Why should he write? Is it vanity that urges him? There is glory enough in the knife. Is it for money? One can make too much money. No. It is to search for some meaning in the ritual of surgery, which is at once murderous, painful, healing, and full of love. It is a devilish hard thing to transmit—to find, even. Perhaps if one were to cut out a heart, a lobe of the liver, a single convolution of the brain, and paste it to a page, it would speak with more eloquence than all the words of Balzac. Such a piece would need no literary style, no mass of erudition or history, but in its very shape and feel would tell all the frailty and strength, the despair and nobility of man. What? Publish a heart? A little piece of bone? Preposterous. Still I fear that is what it may require to reveal the truth that lies hidden in the body. Not all the undressings of Rabelais, Chekhov, or even William Carlos Williams have wrested it free, although God knows each one of those doctors made a heroic assault upon it.

I have come to believe that it is the flesh alone that counts. The rest is that with which we distract ourselves when we are not hungry or cold, in pain or ecstasy. In the recesses of the body I search for the philosophers' stone. I know it is there, hidden in the deepest, dampest cul-de-sac. It awaits discovery. To find it would be like the harnessing of fire. It would illuminate the world. Such a quest is not without pain. Who can gaze on so much misery and feel no hurt? Emerson has written that the poet is the only true doctor. I believe him, for the poet, lacking the impediment of speech with which the rest of us are afflicted, gazes, records, diagnoses, and prophesies.

I invited a young diabetic woman to the operating room to amputate her leg. She could not see the great shaggy black ulcer upon her foot and ankle that threatened to encroach upon the rest of her body, for she was blind as well. There upon her foot was a Mississippi Delta brimming with corruption, sending its raw tributaries down between her toes. Gone were all the little web spaces that when fresh and whole are such a delight to loving men. She could not see her wound, but she could feel it. There is no pain like that of the bloodless limb turned rotten and festering. There is neither unguent nor anodyne to kill such a pain yet leave intact the body.

For over a year I trimmed away the putrid flesh, cleansed, anointed, and dressed the foot, staving off, delaying. Three times each week, in her darkness, she sat upon my table, rocking back and forth, holding her extended leg by the thigh, gripping it as though it were a rocket that must be steadied lest it explode and scatter her toes about the room. And I would cut away a bit here, a bit there, of the swollen blue leather that was her tissue.

At last we gave up, she and I. We could no longer run ahead of the gangrene. We had not the legs for it. There must be an amputation in order that she might live—and I as well. It was to heal us both that I must take up knife and saw, and cut the leg off. And when I could feel it drop from her body to the table, see the blessed *space* appear between her and that leg, I too would be well.

Now it is the day of the operation. I stand by while the anesthetist administers the drugs, watch as the tense familiar body relaxes into narcosis. I turn then to uncover the leg. There, upon her kneecap, she has drawn, blindly, upside down for me to see, a face; just a circle with two ears, two eyes, a nose, and a smiling upturned mouth. Under it she has printed SMILE, DOCTOR. Minutes later I listen to the sound of the saw, until a little crack at the end tells me it is done.

So, I have learned that man is not ugly, but that he is Beauty itself. There is no other his equal. Are we not all dying, none faster or more slowly than any other? I have become receptive to the possibilities of love (for it is love, this thing that happens in the operating room), and each day I wait, trembling in the busy air. Perhaps today it will come. Perhaps today I will find it, take part in it, this love that blooms in the stoniest desert.

All through literature the doctor is portrayed as a figure of fun. Shaw was splenetic about him; Molière delighted in pricking his pompous medicine men, and well they deserved it. The doctor is ripe for caricature. But I believe that the truly great writing about doctors has not yet been done. I think it must be done *by* a doctor, one who is through with the love affair with his technique, who recognizes that he has played Narcissus, raining kisses on a mirror, and who now, out of the impacted masses of his guilt, has expanded into self-doubt, and finally into the high state of wonderment. Perhaps he will be a nonbeliever who, after a lifetime of grand gestures and mighty deeds, comes upon the knowledge that he has done no more than meddle in the lives of his fellows, and that he has done at least as much harm as good. Yet he may continue to pretend, at least, that there is nothing to fear, that death will not come, so long as people depend on his authority. Later, after his patients have left, he may closet himself in his darkened office, sweating and afraid.

There is a story by Unamuno in which a priest, living in a small Spanish village, is adored by all the people for his piety, kindness, and the majesty with which he celebrates the Mass each Sunday. To them he is already a saint. It is a foregone conclusion, and they speak of him as Saint Immanuel. He helps them with their plowing and planting, tends them when they are sick, confesses them, comforts them in death, and every Sunday, in his rich, thrilling voice, transports them to paradise with his chanting. The fact is that Don Immanuel is not so much a saint as a martyr. Long ago his own faith left him. He is an atheist, a good man doomed to suffer the life of a hypocrite, pretending to a faith he does not have. As he raises the chalice of wine, his hands tremble, and a cold sweat pours from him. He cannot stop for he knows that the people need this of him, that their need is greater than his sacrifice. Still . . . still . . . could it be that Don Immanuel's whole life is a kind of prayer, a paean to God?

A writing doctor would treat men and women with equal reverence, for what is the "liberation" of either sex to him who knows the diagrams, the inner geographies of each? I love the solid heft of men as much as I adore the heated capaciousness of women—women in whose penetralia is found the repository of existence. I would have them glory in that. Women are physics and chemistry. They are matter. It is their bodies that tell of the frailty of men. Men have not their cellular, enzymatic wisdom. Man is albuminoid, proteinaceous, laked pearl; woman is yolky, ovoid, rich. Both are exuberant bloody growths. I would use the defects and deformities of each for my sacred purpose of writing, for I know that it is the marred and scarred and faulty that are subject to grace. I would seek the soul in the facts of animal economy and profligacy. Yes, it is the exact location of the soul that I am after. The smell of it is in my nostrils. I have caught glimpses of it in the body diseased. If only I could tell it. Is there no mathematical equation that can guide me? So much pain and pus equals so much truth? It is elusive as the whippoorwill that one hears calling incessantly from out the night window, but which, nesting as it does low in the brush, no one sees. No one but the poet, for he sees what no one else can. He was born with the eye for it.

Once I thought I had it: Ten o'clock one night, the end room off a long corridor in a college infirmary, my last patient of the day, degree of exhaustion suitable for the appearance of a vision, some manifestation. The patient is a young man recently returned from Guatemala, from the excavation of Mayan ruins. His left upper arm wears a gauze dressing which, when removed, reveals a clean punched-out hole the size of a dime. The tissues about the opening are swollen and tense. A thin brownish fluid lips the edge, and now and then a lazy drop of the overflow spills down the arm. An abscess, inadequately drained. I will enlarge the opening to allow better egress of the pus. Nurse, will you get me a scalpel and some . . .?

What happens next is enough to lay Francis Drake avomit in his cabin. No explorer ever stared in wilder surmise than I into that crater from which there now emerges a narrow gray head whose sole distinguishing feature is a pair of black pincers. The head sits atop a longish flexible neck arching now this way, now that, testing the air. Alternately it folds back upon itself, then advances in new boldness. And all the while, with dreadful rhythmicity, the unspeakable pincers open and close. Abscess? Pus? Never. Here is the lair of a beast at whose malignant purpose I could but guess. A Mayan devil, I think, that would soon burst free to fly about the room, with horrid blanket-wings and iridescent scales, raking, pinching, injecting God knows what acid juice. And even now the irony does not escape me, the irony of my patient as excavator excavated.

With all the ritual deliberation of a high priest I advance a surgical clamp toward the hole. The surgeon's heart is become a bat hanging upside down from his rib cage. The rim achieved—now thrust—and the ratchets of the clamp close upon the empty air. The devil has retracted. Evil mocking laughter bangs back and forth in the brain. More stealth. Lying in wait. One must skulk. Minutes pass, perhaps an hour. . . . A faint disturbance in the lake, and once again the thing upraises, farther and farther, hovering. Acrouch, strung, the surgeon is one with his instrument; there is no longer any boundary between its metal and his flesh. They are joined in a single perfect tool of extirpation. It is just for this that he was born. Now—thrust—and clamp—and *yes*. Got him!

Transmitted to the fingers comes the wild thrashing of the creature. Pinned and wriggling, he is mine. I hear the dry brittle scream of the dragon, and a hatred seizes me, but such a detestation as would make of Iago a drooling sucktit. It is the demented hatred of the victor for the vanquished, the warden for his prisoner. It is the hatred of fear. Within the jaws of my hemostat is the whole of the evil of the world, the dark concentrate itself, and I shall kill it. For mankind. And, in so doing, will open the way into a thousand years of perfect peace. Here is Surgeon as Savior indeed.

Tight grip now . . . steady, relentless pull. How it scrabbles to keep its tentacle-hold. With an abrupt moist plop the extraction is complete. There, writhing in the teeth of the clamp, is a dirty gray body, the size and shape of an English walnut. He is hung everywhere with tiny black hooklets. Quickly . . . into the specimen jar of saline . . . the lid screwed tight. Crazily he swims round and round, wiping his slimy head against the glass, then slowly sinks to the bottom, the mass of hooks in frantic agonal wave.

"You are going to be all right," I say to my patient. "We are *all* going to be all right from now on."

The next day I take the jar to the medical school. "That's the larva of the botfly," says a pathologist. "The fly usually bites a cow and deposits its eggs beneath the skin. There, the egg develops into the larval form which, when ready, burrows its way to the outside through the hide and falls to the ground. In time it matures into a full-grown botfly. This one happened to bite a man. It was about to come out on its own, and, of course, it would have died."

The words *imposter, sorehead, servant of Satan* spring to my lips. But now he has been joined by other scientists. They nod in agreement. I gaze from one gray eminence to another, and know the mallet-blow of glory pulverized. I tried to save the world, but it didn't work out.

No, it is not the surgeon who is God's darling. He is the victim of vanity. It is the poet who heals with his words, stanches the flow of blood, stills the rattling breath, applies poultice to the scalded flesh.

Did you ask me why a surgeon writes? I think it is because I wish to be a doctor.

Culture and Race

$\mathbf{A}$MERICA is a country of immigrants. In coming we dislocated the people we found here, the American Indians or Native Americans who now, sadly enough, seem to be suffering some of the traditional problems of the immigrant. Immigrant Americans came from very different circumstances and for very different reasons. They came as religious enthusiasts, as bonded servants, as speculators; some came in preference to imprisonment, others because they felt crowded or restless or hopeful. The slave trade brought many by force; for them America was the prison. In the nineteenth century, immigrants came to escape the Irish potato famine, the Russian pogrom, or equally harsh conditions of poverty and deprivation in other lands, or they came to earn money to support those who stayed behind. World War II brought one wave of political refugees, recent turmoil in Southeast Asia brings others. Some come in large groups, others as lone individuals.

For the immigrants, the country often offered a mixture of hope, economic struggle and exploitation, and of suspicion from those already here. It almost always confronted the newcomers with a need to create a new identity. With regard to this process, the assimilationist favors the melting pot: leave cultural origins behind; mix and blend cultural diversity into a homogeneous Americanism. The pluralist, on the other hand, sees cultural diversity as a source not of division but of strength, and would hope to protect it as the pattern most typically American. Each cultural group, and each new immigrant, needs to reconcile these contradictory feelings and pulls. Every reader, indeed, can consider his or her own cultural heritage in the light of these concepts.

The first four pieces and the two poems in this section all deal with personal and unique experiences, yet each also inevitably reflects the cultural heritage of the writer. And each adds a voice describing "what it was really like."

325

In the next four selections we see that looking close at what it is or was like reveals puzzlement, conflict, or struggle, a felt need to make choices that often seem impossible to make. The story by Isaac Singer shows the wide gulf between generations that no longer understand each other. Peter Berger's story—a fiction put together from true experiences—locates the dilemma within one person, Manuela, who is forced to choose between two very different cultures, courses of action, moralities. Richard Rodriguez faces the choice between cultures within himself: "I am the son of Mexican-American parents who speak a blend of Spanish and English, but who read neither language easily. I am about to receive a Ph.D. in English Renaissance literature. What sort of life," he asks, "what tensions, feelings, conflict—connect these two sentences?" James McPherson struggles toward a new definition of an "American" as one who, conscious of America's complexity, can live in and with the contradictions of such cultural diversity.

The last four pieces focus more explicitly on issues that arise from racial experiences and struggles. Margaret Mead takes on the whole debate about race and intelligence by showing how immigrant groups historically have been classified racially, and challenging the very concept of race as it is used to argue intelligence. Robert Coles shows us our own biases, both as outsiders and insiders; he wants us to become more aware of how we stereotype those who are not of the same race, ethnic group, or class. The final two pieces raise issues from a more personal perspective. Rodriguez's personal narrative leads us to consider the controversy surrounding affirmative action. Finally, the classic essay by James Baldwin interweaves event and insight, private understanding and general idea, choices made and choices to be made; he shows us how personal experience and personal struggle connect to our most profound public issues.

SOME PERSONAL EXPERIENCES

Jeanne Wakatsuki Houston and James D. Houston

Jeanne Wakatsuki Houston was born in Inglewood, California, in 1935, but in April 1942, when she was seven years old, her family was removed by Executive Order 9066 to Japanese internment camp; she lived there until October 1945, when she was eleven. She later studied sociology and journalism at San Jose State College, where she met her husband, James D. Houston; he is a writer who has published many novels, short stories, and essays. They now live in Santa Cruz, California, where James Houston also is a lecturer of writing at the University of California.

Together they wrote Farewell to Manzanar *(1973), a book that records Ms. Houston's experiences during internment. "It had taken me 25 years," she writes, "to reach the point where I could talk openly about Manzanar." When contemplating writing the book, the Houstons were told the issue was dead, but the "issue," they agreed, was not what they wanted to write about: "Everyone knows an injustice was done." Writing about daily life in the camp, says Jeanne Houston, "has been a way of coming to terms with the impact these years have had on my entire life." In April 1972, "thirty years almost to the day" after her original internment, she, her husband, and her children visited the camp, where nothing remained except the gatehouse, the elms, the high-school auditorium (now a Los Angeles Power and Water District maintenance depot), and the graveyard. Soon thereafter, they wrote and published the book. We reprint Chapter 12 here. "Shikata ga nai" (p. 328) means "It can't be helped."*

Manzanar, USA

In Spanish, Manzanar means "apple orchard." Great stretches of Owens Valley were once green with orchards and alfalfa fields. It has been a desert ever since its water started flowing south into Los Angeles, sometime during the twenties. But a few rows of untended pear and apple trees were still growing there when the camp opened, where a shallow water table had kept them alive. In the spring of 1943 we moved to block 28, right up next to one of the old pear orchards. That's where we stayed until the end of the war, and those trees stand in my memory for the turning of our life in camp, from the outrageous to the tolerable.

Papa pruned and cared for the nearest trees. Late that summer we picked the fruit green and stored it in a root cellar he had dug under our new barracks. At night the wind through the leaves would sound like the surf had sounded in Ocean Park, and while drifting off to sleep I could almost imagine we were still living by the beach.

Mama had set up this move. Block 28 was also close to the camp hospital. For the most part, people lived there who had to have easy access to it. Mama's connection was her job as dietician. A whole half of one barracks had fallen empty when another family relocated. Mama hustled us in there almost before they'd snapped their suitcases shut.

For all the pain it caused, the loyalty oath finally did speed up the relocation program. One result was a gradual easing of the congestion in the barracks. A shrewd househunter like Mama could set things up fairly comfortably—by Manzanar standards—if she kept her eyes open. But you had to move fast. As soon as the word got around that so-and-so had been cleared to leave, there would be a kind of tribal restlessness, a nervous rise in the level of neighborhood gossip as wives jockeyed for position to see who would get the empty cubicles.

In Block 28 we doubled our living space—four rooms for the twelve of us. Ray and Woody walled them with sheetrock. We had ceilings this time, and linoleum floors of solid maroon. You had three colors to choose from— maroon, black, and forest green—and there was plenty of it around by this time. Some families would vie with one another for the most elegant floor designs, obtaining a roll of each color from the supply shed, cutting it into diamonds, squares, or triangles, shining it with heating oil, then leaving their doors open so that passers-by could admire the handiwork.

Papa brought his still with him when we moved. He set it up behind the door, where he continued to brew his own sake and brandy. He wasn't drinking as much now, though. He spent a lot of time outdoors. Like many of the older Issei men, he didn't take a regular job in camp. He puttered. He had been working hard for thirty years and, bad as it was for him in some ways, camp did allow him time to dabble with hobbies he would never have found time for otherwise.

Once the first year's turmoil cooled down, the authorities started letting us outside the wire for recreation. Papa used to hike along the creeks that channeled down from the base of the Sierras. He brought back chunks of driftwood, and he would pass long hours sitting on the steps carving myrtle limbs into benches, table legs, and lamps, filling our rooms with bits of gnarled, polished furniture.

He hauled stones in off the desert and built a small rock garden outside our doorway, with succulents and a patch of moss. Near it he laid flat steppingstones leading to the stairs.

He also painted watercolors. Until this time I had not known he could paint. He loved to sketch the mountains. If anything made that country habitable it was the mountains themselves, purple when the sun dropped and so sharply etched in the morning light the granite dazzled almost more than the bright snow lacing it. The nearest peaks rose ten thousand feet higher than the valley floor, with Whitney, the highest, just off to the south. They were important for all of us, but especially for the Issei. Whitney reminded Papa of Fujiyama, that is, it gave him the same kind of spiritual sustenance. The tremendous beauty of those peaks was inspirational, as so many natural forms are to the Japanese (the rocks outside our doorway could be those mountains in miniature). They also represented those forces in nature, those powerful and inevitable forces that cannot be resisted, reminding a man that sometimes he must simply endure that which cannot be changed.

Subdued, resigned, Papa's life—all our lives—took on a pattern that would hold for the duration of the war. Public shows of resentment pretty much spent themselves over the loyalty oath crises. *Shikata ga nai* again became the motto, but under altered circumstances. What had to be endured was the climate, the confinement, the steady crumbling away of family life. But the camp itself had been made livable. The government provided for our physical needs. My parents and older brothers and sisters, like most of the internees, accepted their lot and did what they could to make the best of a bad situation. "We're here," Woody would say. "We're here, and there's no use moaning about it forever."

Gardens had sprung up everywhere, in the firebreaks, between the rows of barracks—rock gardens, vegetable gardens, cactus and flower gardens. People who lived in Owens Valley during the war still remember the flowers and lush greenery they could see from the highway as they drove past the main gate. The soil around Manzanar is alluvial and very rich. With water siphoned off from the Los Angeles-bound aqueduct, a large farm was under cultivation just outside the camp, providing the mess halls with lettuce, corn, tomatoes, eggplant, string beans, horseradish, and cucumbers. Near Block 28 some of the men who had been professional gardeners built a small park, with mossy nooks, ponds, waterfalls, and curved wooden bridges. Sometimes in the evenings we could walk down the raked gravel paths. You could face away from the barracks, look past a tiny rapids toward the darkening mountains, and for a while not be a prisoner at all. You could hang suspended in some odd, almost lovely land you could not escape from yet almost didn't want to leave.

As the months at Manzanar turned to years, it became a world unto itself, with its own logic and familiar ways. In time, staying there seemed far simpler than moving once again to another, unknown place. It was as if the war were forgotten, our reason for being there forgotten. The present, the little bit of busywork you had right in front of you, became the most urgent thing. In such a narrowed world, in order to survive, you learn to contain your rage and your despair, and you try to re-create, as well as you can, your normality, some sense of things continuing. The fact that America had accused us, or excluded us, or imprisoned us, or whatever it might be called, did not change the kind of world we wanted. Most of us were born in this country; we had no other models. Those parks and gardens lent it an oriental character, but in most ways it was a totally equipped American small town, complete with schools, churches, Boy Scouts, beauty parlors, neighborhood gossip, fire and police departments, glee clubs, softball leagues, Abbott and Costello movies, tennis courts, and traveling shows. (I still remember an Indian who turned up one Saturday billing himself as a Sioux chief, wearing bear claws and head feathers. In the firebreak he sang songs and danced his tribal dances while hundreds of us watched.)

In our family, while Papa puttered, Mama made daily rounds to the mess halls, helping young mothers with their feeding, planning diets for the various ailments people suffered from. She wore a bright yellow, longbilled sun hat she had made herself and always kept stiffly starched. Afternoons I would see her coming from blocks away, heading home, her tiny figure warped by heat waves and that bonnet a yellow flower wavering in the glare.

In their disagreement over serving the country, Woody and Papa had struck a kind of compromise. Papa talked him out of volunteering; Woody waited for the army to induct him. Meanwhile he clerked in the co-op general store. Kiyo, nearly thirteen by this time, looked forward to the heavy winds. They moved the sand around and uncovered obsidian arrowheads he could sell to old men in camp for fifty cents apiece. Ray, a few years older, played in the six-man touch football league, sometimes against Caucasian teams who would come in from Lone Pine or Independence. My sister Lillian was in high school and singing with a hillbilly band called The Sierra Stars—jeans, cowboy hats, two guitars, and a tub bass. And my oldest brother, Bill, led a dance band called The Jive Bombers—brass and rhythm, with cardboard fold-out music stands lettered J. B. Dances were held every weekend in one of the recreation halls. Bill played trumpet and took vocals on Glenn Miller arrangements of such tunes as *In the Mood, String of Pearls,* and *Don't Fence Me In.* He didn't sing *Don't Fence Me In* out of protest, as if trying quietly to mock the authorities. It just happened to be a hit song one year, and they all wanted to be an up-to-date American swing band. They would blast it out into recreation barracks full of bobbysoxed, jitterbugging couples:

> Oh, give me land, lots of land
> Under starry skies above,
> Don't fence me in.
> Let me ride through the wide
> Open country that I love . . .

Pictures of the band, in their bow ties and jackets, appeared in the high school yearbook for 1943-1944, along with pictures of just about everything else in camp that year. It was called *Our World.* In its pages you see school kids with armloads of books, wearing cardigan sweaters and walking past rows of tarpapered shacks. You see chubby girl yell leaders, pompons flying as they leap with glee. You read about the school play, called *Growing Pains* ". . . the story of a typical American home, in this case that of the McIn-tyres. They see their boy and girl tossed into the normal awkward growing up stage, but can offer little assistance or direction in their turbulent course . . ." with Shoji Katayama as George McIntyre, Takudo Ando as Terry McIntyre, and Mrs. McIntyre played by Kazuko Nagai.

All the class pictures are in there, from the seventh grade through twelfth, with individual head shots of seniors, their names followed by the names of the high schools they would have graduated from on the outside: Theodore Roosevelt, Thomas Jefferson, Herbert Hoover, Sacred Heart. You see pretty girls on bicycles, chicken yards full of fat pullets, patients back-tilted in dental chairs, lines of laundry, and finally, two large blowups, the first of a high tower with a searchlight, against a Sierra backdrop, the next a two-page endsheet showing a wide path that curves among rows of elm trees. White stones border the path. Two dogs are following an old woman in gardening clothes as she strolls along. She is in the middle distance, small beneath the trees, beneath the snowy peaks. It is winter. All the elms are bare. The scene is both stark and comforting. This path leads toward one edge of camp, but the wire is out of sight, or out of focus. The tiny woman seems very much at ease. She and her tiny dogs seem almost swallowed by the landscape, or floating in it.

MAXINE HONG KINGSTON

Maxine Hong Kingston was born in Stockton, California, in 1940 and earned her bachelor's degree from the University of California in 1962. She has taught a wide variety of students in various places, first as a high-school teacher of English and mathematics in Hayward, California. She later taught English, language arts, and English as a second language in a high school, a drop-in school, and a business college in Hawaii, and has been Visiting Associate Professor of English at the University of Hawaii. She is also a writer and once said, "I have no idea how people who don't write endure their lives." Her stories and articles have appeared in many publications, including Ms., New West, *and the* New York Times. *In 1976 she won the general nonfiction award from the National Book Critics Circle for* The Woman Warrior: Memoirs of a Girlhood Among Ghosts. *A new collection of short pieces will be published in 1980 as* China Men. *It will include the sketch we print here.*

"How Are You?"
"I Am Fine, Thank You. And You?"

With no map sense, I took a trip by myself to San Francisco Chinatown and got lost in the Big City. Wandering in a place very different from Stockton's brown and gray Chinatown, I suddenly heard my own real aunt call my name. We screamed at each other the way our villagers do, hugged, held hands. "Have you had your rice yet?" we shouted. "I have. I have had my rice." "Me too. I've eaten too," letting the whole strange street know we had eaten, and me becoming part of the street, abruptly not a tourist, the street mine to shout in, not to worry if my accent be different. She introduced me to the group of women she'd been talking to. "This is my own actual niece," she said in a way that they would understand that I was not just somebody she called a niece out of politeness but a blood niece. "Hello, Aunt. Hello, Aunt," I said, but mumbling mumbling because there are different kinds of aunts depending on whether they're older or younger than one's mother, and both addresses familiar. And they'd tease also for being too distant, for calling them Lady or Mademoiselle, affectations. Some people feel insulted at young, low-rank titles, but there are also Americanized women who don't like being older, and me not good at ages anyway, and some not wanting to be roped into your family, and some not liking to be excluded. "Who is this?" the women asked, one of them pointing at me with her chin, the way Chinese people point, the other with her rolled up newspaper. This talking about me in the third person, this pointing at me—I shoved the resentment down my throat; they do not mean disdain—or they *do* mean disdain, but it's their proper way of treating young people—mustn't dislike them for it. "This is my real niece come to visit me," my aunt said, as if I had planned to run into her all along. "Come see my new apartment," she said to me, turned around and entered the doorway near which we were standing.

We went up the stairs, flight after flight. I followed her along a hallway like a tunnel. But her apartment need not be dismal, I told myself; these doors could open into surprisingly large, bright, airy apartments with shag carpets. "Our apartment is very small," she warned, her voice leading the way. "Not like a regular house. Not like your mother's big house." So she noticed space; I thought perhaps people from Hong Kong didn't need room, that Chinese people preferred small spaces.

When she opened the door, it just missed the sofa and didn't open up all the way because of a table. Stuff was stored along the walls on shelves above the furniture, which had things on top and underneath. I fitted myself in among the storage. "Cake?" asked my aunt. "Pie? Chuck-who-lick? Le-mun?" She went into the one-person kitchen. There wasn't room in the space between the sink and the stove for me to help. I sat on the sofa, which could open into a bed.

"Small, isn't it?" she said. "Please have some cake."

"I just ate," I said, which was true.

She got herself some chocolate cake and lemon pie and sat next to me. "I saw those hoppies they tell about in the newspaper," she said. "Some of them talked to me. 'Spare change?' That's what they say. 'Spare change?' I memorized it." She held out her hand to show their ways. " 'Spare change?' What does 'spare change' mean?" "They're asking if you have extra mon-ey." "Oh-h, I see," she said laughing. " 'Spare change?' How witty." She was silly compared to my mother; she giggled and talked about inconse-quentials. "Condo?" she asked. "Cottage cheese? Football? Foosball?"

"Are you working?" I asked because it was odd that she was home in the middle of a weekday. "Is it your day off?"

"No. I'm not working anymore."

"What happened to your hotel job? Didn't you have a hotel job? As a maid?" I said "maid" in English, not knowing the Chinese word except for "slave." If she didn't know the word, she wouldn't hear it anyway. Lan-guages are like that.

"I've been fired," she said.

"Oh, no. But why?"

"I've been very sick. High blood pressure," she said. "And I got dizzy working. I had to clean sixteen rooms in eight hours. I was too sick to work that fast." Something I liked about this aunt was her use of exact numbers. "Ten thousand rooms per second," my mother would have said; "Uncount-able. Infinite." I did some math while she talked: half an hour per unit, including bathrooms. "People leave the rooms very messy," she said, "and I kept coughing from the ashes in the ashtrays. I was efficient until I fell sick. Once I was out for six weeks, but when I came back, the head housekeeper said I was doing a good job, and he kept me on." She said the name of the hotel; it was one of the famous ones. I had thought from the dirty work and low pay it was some flop house in Chinatown. She'd given us miniature soaps whenever she came to visit. "The head housekeeper said I was an excellent worker." My mother was the same way, caring tremendously how her employer praised her, never in so much trouble as when a boss repri-manded her, never so proud as when a forelady said she was picking cleanly or fast. ("Folaydee"; " "chup-bo"—trouble; "bossu"; "day offu"—more Chinese American words.) "He said I speak English very well." She was proud of that compliment; I thought it was an insult, but it was too much trouble to try to explain to her why. When white demons said, "You speak

English very well," I muttered, "It's my language too." The Japanese kids, who were always ahead of us socially, said the way to answer is, "Thank you. So do you."

"What do you do all day long now that you aren't cleaning hotel rooms?"

"The days go by very slowly. You know, in these difficult times in the Big City mothers can't leave their children alone. The kidnappers are getting two thousand dollars per child. And whoever reports a missing child to the FBI gets turned over to Immigration. So I posted ads, and one in the newspaper too, that I wanted to mind children, but I haven't gotten any customers. When the mothers see the apartment, they say No." Of course. No place to run, no yard, no trees. "I could mind four or five children," she said. "I'd make as much money as cleaning the hotel. They don't want me to watch their children because I can't speak English. My own son doesn't talk to me," she said. "What's nutrition?"

"It has to do with food and what people ought to eat to keep healthy."

"You mean like cooking? He's going to college to learn how to cook?"

"Well, no. It's planning menus for big companies, like schools and hospitals and the army. They study food to see how it works. It's the science of food," but I did not feel that I was giving an adequate explanation, the only word for "science" I knew was a synonym or derivative of "magic," something like "alchemy."

"You speak Chinese very well," she said. But I could talk to her. Some people dry up each other's language.

JERRE MANGIONE

Jerre Mangione was born in Rochester, New York, in 1909, the son of Italian immigrants Giuseppina Polizzi Mangione and Gaspare Mangione, the latter a housepainter and paperhanger. He attended Syracuse University, where he received his B.A. in 1931, and immediately began to work for Time *as a staff writer; later he was a book editor, a coordinating editor for the Federal Writers Project, a public relations and information specialist for branches of the United States government, and a writer for advertising and public relations firms. In 1961 he joined the faculty of the University of Pennsylvania, where he has been Director of Freshman Composition, Director of the Creative Writing Program, and Professor of English.*

Mangione is a prolific writer, both of fiction and nonfiction, and a frequent contributor to magazines. "I write to please myself," he says. "Whether it is a book of fiction or nonfiction, I write each one as though it were going to be my last." His first, Mount Allegro *(1943), is a fictionalized account of Italian immigrants; we print the opening chapter below.*

In 1965 Mangione visited Sicily and worked for six months with the Sicilian writer Danilo Dolci in the struggle against political corruption, apathy, and Mafia rule. He then wrote A Passion for Sicilians *(1968), republished in 1972 as* The World Around

Danilo Dolci. *Other recent work includes* Night Search *(1965),* America Is Also Italian *(1969),* The Dream and the Deal: Federal Writers Project 1936–43 *(1972), and* An Ethnic at Large: A Memoir of America in the Thirties and Forties *(1978).*

When I Grow Up . . .

'When I grow up I want to be an American,' Giustina said. We looked at our sister; it was something none of us had ever said.

'Me too,' Maria echoed.

'Aw, you don't even know what an American is,' Joe scoffed.

'I do so,' Giustina said.

It was more than the rest of us knew.

'We're Americans right now,' I said. 'Miss Zimmerman says if you're born here you're an American.'

'Aw, she's nuts,' Joe said. He had no use for most teachers. 'We're Italians. If y' don't believe me ask Pop.'

But my father wasn't very helpful. 'Your children will be *Americani*. But you, my son, are half-and-half. Now stop asking me questions. You should know those things from going to school. What do you learn in school, anyway?'

The world, my teacher insisted, was made up of all the colored spots on a globe. One of the purple spots was America, even though America wasn't purple when you looked at it. The orange spot was Italy. Never having been there, that wasn't so hard to believe. You never used this globe as a ball, even after Rosario Alfano gave you one as a birthday present. You just spun it, while some near-by grownup told you that Columbus discovered the world to be round.

You pretended to believe that because it was hard to argue with grownups and be polite at the same time, but you told yourself that any grownup who swallowed that must be nuts. It was confusing when your own father said it because you liked to think he was right about everything; but when your Uncle Sarafino said it, the uncle from Boston who promised to give you a dollar for eating some hot peppers raw, and then refused to give you the money, you were sure he was nuts and the world wasn't round.

Then one day one of your new teachers looked at you brightly and said you were Italian because your last name was Amoroso and that too was puzzling. You talked it over with some of the boys in the gang.

First with Tony Long, who was the leader. Tony said his father changed his name when he came to America because he got tired of spelling it out for a lot of dopes who didn't know how to spell. I showed Tony my globe and he pointed to a red spot on it and said that was where his mother and father came from. That's all he knew about it. Tony couldn't speak Polish and his mother hardly knew any American. He looked angry when she spoke to him in Polish in front of the other kids.

Then there was Abe Rappaport, who went to a synagogue every Saturday. Abe wore glasses and knew a lot. He said his parents came from Russia and pointed to a big gob of blue on the globe. It was close to Poland but Abe looked more like me than he did like Tony, who had blond hair. Abe was one of those who like to read and argue. We spent a whole day once asking each other, 'How do you know I ain't God?' until the other guys said we were crazy.

The other boys in the gang claimed they were Americans even though their parents didn't know how to speak American well. When I showed them my globe and asked them to point to the country where their parents came from, they said they didn't know. They didn't care either.

I showed my globe to a guy who belonged to another gang. His name was Robert Di Nella and he had blond hair and blue eyes like Tony Long. None of us liked him because he was always trying to boss us around, and we called him the Kaiser. He pointed to Italy on the globe, even though his mother didn't speak Italian the way mine did. Then he pointed to a tiny orange splash at the end of the Italian boot and called me a lousy *Siciliano*. I hit him on the jaw and, because he was taller and bigger, ran to safety with the globe tucked under my arm like a football.

This incident marked the beginning of a long and violent feud with the Kaiser. He ambushed me at every possible opportunity and preceded each attack by calling me a Sicilian. From the way he hissed the word at me, I soon realized that while being a Sicilian was a special distinction, it probably was not one that called for cheers and congratulations.

The Kaiser must have been descended from a Medici. He was a talented fiend and would lie in wait for me on Sunday mornings just as I was coming out of church. With my soul just whitewashed for the week, he could hardly have picked a better time to bully me. There I stood, without any of my gang around, hopelessly overflowing with peace and the religious ecstasy I had achieved by singing in tune with the rest of the choir boys.

As I saw the Kaiser waiting, his face ugly with a leer, the forces of good and evil would come to grips within me and before the good could be completely crushed, the Kaiser had already spat out his insults. In a lot behind the church, where we staged our battles, my conscience would make one last futile effort to persuade me to turn the other cheek, but by that time the Kaiser, quite unhampered by a conscience, had already landed the first blow and forced me to retaliate.

From anyone else the name *Siciliano* might not have been so insulting. From the Kaiser it rankled and assumed diabolical meaning, especially when he followed it up with such invectives as 'blackmailer' and 'murderer.' For a time the boys in the gang used this propaganda against my brother and me whenever they became angry with us. As a result, Joe and I, who were usually at war with each other, began coming to one another's rescue when one of us was defending the honor of Sicilians and getting the worst of it.

By such teamwork we usually won our fights. But we soon learned that the odds were hopelessly against us. There were grownup Robert Di Nellas all around who were too big for us. There were also the newspapers, which delighted in featuring murder stories involving persons with foreign names. My father would read these accounts carefully, anxious to determine, first of all, if the killer was an Italian; if so, whether he hailed from Sicily. 'It is bad enough for an Italian to commit a murder, but it is far worse when a Sicilian does,' he would say.

In the event the murderer turned out to be Sicilian, my father would solemnly announce that the criminal undoubtedly came from Carrapipi, a small town in Sicily which—according to my relatives—produced nothing but a population of potential thieves, blackmailers, and murderers. Few of them had ever seen Carrapipi, but the unpleasant experiences they had had with some of its natives were enough to convince them that all Sicilians in the United States found guilty of serious crimes were born in Carrapipi.

My relatives developed a beautiful legend to substantiate this idea. The villain of the piece was a judge in Carrapipi who, in his zeal to save the state the expense of maintaining dangerous criminals in jail for many years, would send them to the United States instead of prison. His tactic was to pronounce a heavy sentence on finding a criminal guilty, and then inform him that a boat was leaving Palermo in a few days for New York. He would then blandly suggest that if the prisoner was found in Italy after the boat left, his sentence would be doubled.

'Naturally,' my Uncle Nino explained whenever he told the story, 'most of the criminals preferred to catch the boat. Going to America, where the streets were said to be lined with gold, certainly seemed more pleasant to them than spending their lives in jail. That pig of a judge, however patriotic his motives were, is undoubtedly to blame for the miserable reputation we Sicilians have in this unhappy land.'

To call anyone *Carrapipanu*, whether or not he actually came from that town, was to insult him, for the name symbolized nearly everything that was villainous or ungracious. One of the most frequent charges made was that a native of Carrapipi could not even speak the Sicilian dialect properly. Instead of saying 'Please come in,' for instance, he would snarl the words—his tongue was likely to be as crooked as his soul—so that the invitation sounded like 'Please do not come in.'

For a long time I believed everything my relatives said about Carrapipi and imagined the town to be an island cut off from civilization and inhabited wholly by desperate characters whose chief ambition was to get to Rochester and prey on the Sicilians there. Joe and I went so far as to draw up careful plans for invading the place with powerful slingshots and rescuing our favorite movie queen from the clutches of the natives. It was a shock to discover a few years later that Carrapipi was a very short distance away from Girgenti, the city where most of my relatives were born, and that the people of Carrapipi considered the natives of Girgenti responsible for the bad reputation Sicilians had here. They had no legend to support their theory, but a nasty little couplet instead which they delighted in repeating every time Girgenti was mentioned:

Girgenti
Mal'agente

My feud with the Kaiser might have died a natural death if I had been able to disregard his name-calling, but already the thought that *Siciliano* implied something sinister had become implanted in me by dozens of small incidents and casual remarks.

Even before the Kaiser came along, my father had indicated that there might be some doubt about the good standing of Sicilians, by being on the defensive about them and by forbidding Joe and me to carry knives because of the unpleasant association they had in the public mind with Sicilians. He enforced this rule so thoroughly that we eventually came to accept it as though it were a self-imposed one. And although it prevented us from joining the Boy Scouts, it gave us great satisfaction to tell non-Sicilians who wanted to borrow a knife from us that we never carried one.

My father's edict came on the heels of an episode in our lives which was of such an unpleasant nature that Joe and I were ready to do anything, even accept his ruling, to prevent him from brooding over it too much. The incident involved Donna Maricchia, our Sicilian washerwoman, and her son, Angelo, and it had the effect of making my father worry as to whether or not knifing was a peculiarly Sicilian expedient which had been inherited by his sons from some vicious ancestor he did not know about.

Donna Maricchia probably weighed less than ninety pounds, but she was an excellent washerwoman who attacked dirty clothes with the fury of a hellcat. Constantly angry with her husband or some of her eight children, she seemed to hoard her anger during the week, so that she could release it in a torrent of complaints and curses on the day she washed for us. With each curse she would give the clothes she held in her fists a savage twist, as though she actually had her husband or one of her children in her grasp. The electric washing machine, which eventually supplanted her, was less noisy and not so dramatic.

Joe and I were her best audience because my mother was too busy making certain that Donna Maricchia did her work properly to care what she was saying. When it came to housework, my mother trusted no one, and stubbornly held to the notion that only she could make things clean. Donna Maricchia, who was almost stone deaf, politely pretended to understand my mother's elaborate instructions and then proceeded to do things her own way.

Donna Maricchia had grown up in a town that was only three or four miles from Realmonte, my mother's home town, but her pronunciation was harsher, and her stream of talk more rapid. Her deafness caused her to speak of the most casual matters in a roaring tone of voice. She was always mourning the death of some relative, here or abroad, and never wore anything but black. Joe and I, under the recent influence of some of Grimm's grimmer fairy tales, called her the Witch, and she figured in some of our more remarkable nightmares.

We were less afraid of her son Angelo. He accompanied his mother on all her washing expeditions because she did not trust him out of her sight. Angelo was chubby and a few years older than either of us. Although he would not permit us to play games with him at first, he taught us how to smoke and what to look for in girls and, of course, generally regarded us with contempt because, compared to him, we were such amateurs in worldly matters.

For a long time we hero-worshiped Angelo; then one day we saw his mother give him a wonderful whipping. Her slaps and his yelling could be heard in the next block. Since we had never been accorded such treatment by our parents, it made us feel quite superior to him. From then on, his attitude toward us improved, and it wasn't long before we were playing games with him on a footing that might have been regarded as equal if you didn't know how clever he was at cheating.

One Wednesday when Donna Maricchia had come to do the weekly wash, we quarreled fiercely with Angelo because we caught him trying to cheat us in a very obvious manner. One threat led to another, and in a few minutes we were pummeling Angelo. As we tried to hold him down and extract from him the promise to 'give up,' he squirmed away and ran to a near-by rock pile. Picking up a large stone, he hurled it at Joe. It struck him just above the eye, making a deep gash which bled immediately and profusely. For a horrible moment I thought he had lost his eye, and I let out a screech that frightened Joe into screaming louder than ever. The screams were even heard by Donna Maricchia, who came running from the kitchen dripping with soapsuds. When she saw the blood, she threw up her hands in despair and sprinted toward Joe, invoking the names of her favorite saints as she ran.

Joe mistook her despair for violence and ran around her into the kitchen, where he locked the door. My mother was the only one who kept her head. She caught him in her arms and led him to the sink. As she washed and bandaged the wound, she talked to him quietly and soothingly until he stopped crying. But though the bleeding and tears had stopped, his feelings toward Angelo had developed to a state of determined violence.

'Mother,' he said in a deadly calm voice, 'please give me the kitchen knife. I'm going to get even with Angelo.' The seriousness with which he made this unusual request, and the hate in his eyes, shocked my poor mother into tears. She seldom cried; when she did, she usually tried to hide her tears from us. Her unrestrained sobbing scared both of us, and we felt we had committed some terrible crime. Joe's mood changed completely and, as he begged her to stop crying, he himself burst into tears again. It was more than I could bear and I joined in too. When Donna Maricchia saw us through the kitchen window, the tears were running down both sides of her nose, and she was begging admittance, and forgiveness for her son. Angelo was nowhere in sight.

That evening there was a family council and it was decided that Donna Maricchia was never to bring Angelo with her again if she wanted to continue washing clothes for us.

The discussion centering around Joe's request for the kitchen knife presented problems that were more difficult to solve. My father gave us both a long lecture on the absurdity of seeking revenge, and blamed us as much as Angelo for the fight. That was to be expected, for he was always threatening to punish us if we got into fights and got the worst of them. He never carried out his threat, but if we came home with stories of fights we had lost, it was useless to expect any sympathy from him.

In this instance we could see that this fight worried him more than the others. First he wanted to know from Joe where he got the idea of knifing anyone. We were both too scared to attempt any explanation. Worried that we might be acquiring criminal habits from sources about which he did not know, my father persisted with his fiery cross-examination. Because I was the elder, I got the brunt of it, despite my protests that I was not the one who had asked for the knife. There was no relenting on my father's part. He was determined to get to the source of Joe's homicidal rage, but he was even more determined to learn why he had chosen a knife as the weapon. I think he would have felt much better if Joe had asked my mother for a revolver instead.

All through the questioning, Joe preserved the most golden of silences, while I sweated under the glare of my father's eyes. After a while I became panicky and threw caution to the winds. I said the first thing that came to my mind.

'What he was really looking for was a hatchet,' I said brightly. My father frowned and looked interested. My brother gave me a look that meant he would try to beat me up the first chance he got.

My mother said, 'What in the world do you mean?'

I didn't really know, but I found myself saying: 'Well, our teacher told us that Washington used a hatchet to cut down a tree. But we don't have one. I mean we don't have a hatchet. I guess we have plenty of trees,' I finished lamely.

This was all my father wanted to know. Unacquainted with either the cherry tree legend or its beautiful moral, he went into an oratorical rampage and delivered a blistering tirade against the American educational system, polishing it off with his inevitable conclusion that our teachers were 'making pigs' of us. We knew no manners, we had no tact, and now, by the holy God and the sainted Devil, we were being taught to revenge ourselves on people we didn't like by scalping them with hatchets.

Porca miseria! What kind of system was that, pray tell him? And why should he pay taxes for American school-teachers who were no better than murdering savages? Etc., etc. Under the fury of his castigation it would have been futile to talk to him about the father of our country. When he had exhausted himself and his repertoire of blasphemies, we all withdrew in respectful silence, quite convinced that school was a bad place for us. But the next morning my mother was screaming at us to get out of bed at once if we didn't want to be late again.

The incident had far-reaching consequences. It left Joe with a permanent scar over his eye, and it provided my father with a deep concern for the criminal tendencies of his sons as well as a new and lurid justification of his contempt for American schools. And, thanks to my mother's perspicacity, it deprived us of the joy of thrilling to the serial movie we used to follow on Saturday afternoons.

Dissatisfied with my father's analysis of the affair, my mother quizzed me further on the hatchet story. She was obviously relieved to learn that my father had misinterpreted it, and was thoroughly charmed with the full account of Washington and the cherry tree. Then she asked me what movies we had been seeing lately. I had barely begun to warm up to some of the exciting weekly episodes in the life of our favorite hero when she interrupted me, in the very middle of a scene where the hero has his back to the wall and the crooks are creeping up to him with knives in their teeth, and announced that we were not to attend the movies any longer on Saturday afternoons. Hereafter, if we must go to the movies it would be on Friday after supper in the company of my Uncle Luigi, who was a habitual movie-goer.

Life without our Saturday afternoon serial seemed rather dull to us for a while, but we soon began to find the adventures of Theda Bara, Mary Pickford, and William S. Hart just as alluring. I think my mother would have been disconcerted to know that there were just as many characters in those movies who won their arguments by the use of knives.

N. SCOTT MOMADAY

N. Scott Momaday was born in Oklahoma in 1934. He studied at New Mexico University (A.B., 1958), at Stanford University (Creative Writing Fellow, 1959; M.A., 1960; Ph.D., 1963), and then taught English at the University of California (Santa Barbara and Berkeley) and at Stanford. In 1974 he joined the faculty of New Mexico University. While teaching, Momaday has all along written and published. He has edited two books, The Complete Poems of Frederick Goddard Tuckerman *(1965) and* American Indian Authors *(1972). He also has written a book for juveniles,* Owl in the Cedar Tree *(1965); a novel,* House Made of Dawn *(1968), for which he won the 1969 Pulitzer Prize; and* The Journey of Tai-Me, Kiowa Indian Tales *(1968), which was revised and published as* The Way to Rainy Mountain *(1969). It records a journey of memory and myth, his actual journey by car following the ancient migration route of the Kiowa Indians from the mountains of Yellowstone, the lost Eden of the Kiowa, to Rainy Mountain in Oklahoma. The Introduction is reprinted here. Other work includes two books of poems,* Angle of Geese and Other Poems *(1963) and* The Gourd Dancer *(1976), and an autobiographical memoir,* The Names *(1978).*

Introduction to
The Way to Rainy Mountain

A single knoll rises out of the plain in Oklahoma, north and west of the Wichita Range. For my people, the Kiowas, it is an old landmark, and they gave it the name Rainy Mountain. The hardest weather in the world is there. Winter brings blizzards, hot tornadic winds arise in the spring, and in summer the prairie is an anvil's edge. The grass turns brittle and brown, and it cracks beneath your feet. There are green belts along the rivers and creeks, linear groves of hickory and pecan, willow and witch hazel. At a distance in July or August the steaming foliage seems almost to writhe in fire. Great green and yellow grasshoppers are everywhere in the tall grass, popping up like corn to sting the flesh, and tortoises crawl about on the red earth, going nowhere in the plenty of time. Loneliness is an aspect of the land. All things in the plain are isolate; there is no confusion of objects in the eye, but *one* hill or *one* tree or *one* man. To look upon that landscape in the early morning, with the sun at your back, is to lose the sense of proportion. Your imagination comes to life, and this, you think, is where Creation was begun.

I returned to Rainy Mountain in July. My grandmother had died in the spring, and I wanted to be at her grave. She had lived to be very old and at last infirm. Her only living daughter was with her when she died, and I was told that in death her face was that of a child.

I like to think of her as a child. When she was born, the Kiowas were living the last great moment of their history. For more than a hundred years they had controlled the open range from the Smoky Hill River to the Red, from the headwaters of the Canadian to the fork of the Arkansas and Cimarron. In alliance with the Comanches, they had ruled the whole of the southern Plains. War was their sacred business, and they were among the finest horsemen the world has ever known. But warfare for the Kiowas was preeminently a matter of disposition rather than of survival, and they never understood the grim, unrelenting advance of the U.S. Cavalry. When at last, divided and ill-provisioned, they were driven onto the Staked Plains in the cold rains of autumn, they fell into panic. In Palo Duro Canyon they abandoned their crucial stores to pillage and had nothing then but their lives. In order to save themselves, they surrendered to the soldiers at Fort Sill and were imprisoned in the old stone corral that now stands as a military museum. My grandmother was spared the humiliation of those high gray walls by eight or ten years, but she must have known from birth the affliction of defeat, the dark brooding of old warriors.

Her name was Aho, and she belonged to the last culture to evolve in North America. Her forebears came down from the high country in western Montana nearly three centuries ago. They were a mountain people, a mysterious tribe of hunters whose language has never been positively classified in any major group. In the late seventeenth century they began a long migration to the south and east. It was a journey toward the dawn, and it led to a golden age. Along the way the Kiowas were befriended by the Crows, who gave them the culture and religion of the Plains. They acquired horses, and their ancient nomadic spirit was suddenly free of the ground. They acquired Tai-me, the sacred Sun Dance doll, from that moment the object and symbol of their worship, and so shared in the divinity of the sun. Not least, they acquired the sense of destiny, therefore courage and pride. When they entered upon the southern Plains they had been transformed.

No longer were they slaves to the simple necessity of survival; they were a lordly and dangerous society of fighters and thieves, hunters and priests of the sun. According to their origin myth, they entered the world through a hollow log. From one point of view, their migration was the fruit of an old prophecy, for indeed they emerged from a sunless world.

Although my grandmother lived out her long life in the shadow of Rainy Mountain, the immense landscape of the continental interior lay like memory in her blood. She could tell of the Crows, whom she had never seen, and of the Black Hills, where she had never been. I wanted to see in reality what she had seen more perfectly in the mind's eye, and traveled fifteen hundred miles to begin my pilgrimage.

Yellowstone, it seemed to me, was the top of the world, a region of deep lakes and dark timber, canyons and waterfalls. But, beautiful as it is, one might have the sense of confinement there. The skyline in all directions is close at hand, the high wall of the woods and deep cleavages of shade. There is a perfect freedom in the mountains, but it belongs to the eagle and the elk, the badger and the bear. The Kiowas reckoned their stature by the distance they could see, and they were bent and blind in the wilderness.

Descending eastward, the highland meadows are a stairway to the plain. In July the inland slope of the Rockies is luxuriant with flax and buckwheat, stonecrop and larkspur. The earth unfolds and the limit of the land recedes. Clusters of trees, and animals grazing far in the distance, cause the vision to reach away and wonder to build upon the mind. The sun follows a longer course in the day, and the sky is immense beyond all comparison. The great billowing clouds that sail upon it are shadows that move upon the grain like water, dividing light. Farther down, in the land of the Crows and Blackfeet, the plain is yellow. Sweet clover takes hold of the hills and bends upon itself to cover and seal the soil. There the Kiowas paused on their way; they had come to the place where they must change their lives. The sun is at home on the plains. Precisely there does it have the certain character of a god. When the Kiowas came to the land of the Crows, they could see the dark lees of the hills at dawn across the Bighorn River, the profusion of light on the grain shelves, the oldest deity ranging after the solstices. Not yet would they veer southward to the caldron of the land that lay below; they must wean their blood from the northern winter and hold the mountains a while longer in their view. They bore Tai-me in procession to the east.

A dark mist lay over the Black Hills, and the land was like iron. At the top of a ridge I caught sight of Devil's Tower upthrust against the gray sky as if in the birth of time the core of the earth had broken through its crust and the motion of the world was begun. There are things in nature that engender an awful quiet in the heart of man; Devil's Tower is one of them. Two centuries ago, because they could not do otherwise, the Kiowas made a legend at the base of the rock. My grandmother said:

Eight children were there at play, seven sisters and their brother. Suddenly the boy was struck dumb; he trembled and began to run upon his hands and feet. His fingers became claws, and his body was covered with fur. Directly there was a bear where the boy had been.

The sisters were terrified; they ran, and the bear after them. They came to the stump of a great tree, and the tree spoke to them. It bade them climb upon it, and as they did so it began to rise into the air. The bear came to kill them, but they were just beyond its reach. It reared against the tree and scored the bark all around with its claws. The seven sisters were borne into the sky, and they became the stars of the Big Dipper.

From that moment, and so long as the legend lives, the Kiowas have kinsmen in the night sky. Whatever they were in the mountains, they could be no more. However tenuous their well-being, however much they had suffered and would suffer again, they had found a way out of the wilderness.

My grandmother had a reverence for the sun, a holy regard that now is all but gone out of mankind. There was a wariness in her, and an ancient awe. She was a Christian in her later years, but she had come a long way about, and she never forgot her birthright. As a child she had been to the Sun Dances; she had taken part in those annual rites, and by them she had learned the restoration of her people in the presence of Tai-me. She was about seven when the last Kiowa Sun Dance was held in 1887 on the Washita River above Rainy Mountain Creek. The buffalo were gone. In order to consummate the ancient sacrifice—to impale the head of a buffalo upon the medicine tree—a delegation of old men journeyed into Texas, there to beg and barter for an animal from the Goodnight herd. She was ten when the Kiowas came together for the last time as a living Sun Dance culture. They could find no buffalo; they had to hang an old hide from the sacred tree. Before the dance could begin, a company of soldiers rode out from Fort Sill under orders to disperse the tribe. Forbidden without cause the essential act of their faith, having seen the wild herds slaughtered and left to rot upon the ground, the Kiowas backed away forever from the medicine tree. That was July 20, 1890, at the great bend of the Washita. My grandmother was there. Without bitterness, and for as long as she lived, she bore a vision of deicide.

Now that I can have her only in memory, I see my grandmother in the several postures that were peculiar to her: standing at the wood stove on a winter morning and turning meat in a great iron skillet; sitting at the south window, bent above her beadwork, and afterwards, when her vision failed, looking down for a long time into the fold of her hands; going out upon a cane, very slowly as she did when the weight of age came upon her; praying. I remember her most often at prayer. She made long, rambling prayers out of suffering and hope, having seen many things. I was never sure that I had the right to hear, so exclusive were they of all mere custom and company. The last time I saw her she prayed standing by the side of her bed at night, naked to the waist, the light of a kerosene lamp moving upon her dark skin. Her long, black hair, always drawn and braided in the day, lay upon her shoulders and against her breasts like a shawl. I do not speak Kiowa, and I never understood her prayers, but there was something inherently sad in the sound, some merest hesitation upon the syllables of sorrow. She began in a high and descending pitch, exhausting her breath to silence; then again and again—and always the same intensity of effort, of something that is, and is not, like urgency in the human voice. Transported so in the dancing light among the shadows of her room, she seemed beyond the reach of time. But that was illusion; I think I knew then that I should not see her again.

Houses are like sentinels in the plain, old keepers of the weather watch. There, in a very little while, wood takes on the appearance of great age. All colors wear soon away in the wind and rain, and then the wood is burned gray and the grain appears and the nails turn red with rust. The window-panes are black and opaque; you imagine there is nothing within, and indeed there are many ghosts, bones given up to the land. They stand here and there against the sky, and you approach them for a longer time than you expect. They belong in the distance; it is their domain.

Once there was a lot of sound in my grandmother's house, a lot of coming and going, feasting and talk. The summers there were full of excitement and reunion. The Kiowas are a summer people; they abide the cold and keep to themselves, but when the season turns and the land becomes warm and vital they cannot hold still; an old love of going returns upon them. The aged visitors who came to my grandmother's house when I was a child were made of lean and leather, and they bore themselves upright. They wore great black hats and bright ample shirts that shook in the wind. They rubbed fat upon their hair and wound their braids with strips of colored cloth. Some of them painted their faces and carried the scars of old and cherished enmities. They were an old council of warlords, come to remind and be reminded of who they were. Their wives and daughters served them well. The women might indulge themselves; gossip was at once the mark and compensation of their servitude. They made loud and elaborate talk among themselves, full of jest and gesture, fright and false alarm. They went abroad in fringed and flowered shawls, bright beadwork and German silver. They were at home in the kitchen, and they prepared meals that were banquets.

There were frequent prayer meetings, and great nocturnal feasts. When I was a child I played with my cousins outside, where the lamplight fell upon the ground and the singing of the old people rose up around us and carried away into the darkness. There were a lot of good things to eat, a lot of laughter and surprise. And afterwards, when the quiet returned, I lay down with my grandmother and could hear the frogs away by the river and feel the motion of the air.

Now there is a funeral silence in the rooms, the endless wake of some final word. The walls have closed in upon my grandmother's house. When I returned to it in mourning, I saw for the first time in my life how small it was. It was late at night, and there was a white moon, nearly full. I sat for a long time on the stone steps by the kitchen door. From there I could see out across the land; I could see the long row of trees by the creek, the low light upon the rolling plains, and the stars of the Big Dipper. Once I looked at the moon and caught sight of a strange thing. A cricket had perched upon the handrail, only a few inches away from me. My line of vision was such that the creature filled the moon like a fossil. It had gone there, I thought, to live and die, for there, of all places, was its small definition made whole and eternal. A warm wind rose up and purled like the longing within me.

The next morning I awoke at dawn and went out on the dirt road to Rainy Mountain. It was already hot, and the grasshoppers began to fill the air. Still, it was early in the morning, and the birds sang out of the shadows. The long yellow grass on the mountain shone in the bright light, and a scissortail hied above the land. There, where it ought to be, at the end of a long and legendary way, was my grandmother's grave. Here and there on the dark stones were ancestral names. Looking back once, I saw the mountain and came away.

MARGARET ATWOOD

1939–

First Neighbours

The people I live among, unforgivingly
previous to me, grudging
the way I breathe their
property, the air,
speaking a twisted dialect to my differently-
shaped ears

though I tried to adapt

(the girl in a red tattered
petticoat, who jeered at me for my burned bread

Go back where you came from

I tightened my lips; knew that England
was now unreachable, had sunk down into the sea
without ever teaching me about washtubs)

got used to being
a minor invalid, expected to make
inept remarks,
futile and spastic gestures

(asked the Indian
about the squat thing on a stick
drying by the fire: Is that a toad?
Annoyed, he said No no,
deer liver, very good)

Finally I grew a chapped tarpaulin
skin; I negotiated the drizzle
of strange meaning, set it
down to just the latitude:
something to be endured
but not surprised by.

Inaccurate. The forest can still trick me:
one afternoon while I was drawing
birds, a malignant face
flickered over my shoulder;
the branches quivered.

    Resolve: to be both tentative and hard to startle
    (though clumsiness and
    fright are inevitable)

    in this area where my damaged
    knowing of the language means
    prediction is forever impossible

ROBERT HAYDEN

1913 —

Aunt Jemima of the Ocean Waves

I

Enacting someone's notion of themselves
(and me), The One And Only Aunt Jemima
and Kokimo The Dixie Dancing Fool
do a bally for the freak show.

I watch a moment, then move on,
pondering the logic that makes them
(and me) confederates
of The Spider Girl, The Snake-skinned Man . . .

Poor devils have to live somehow.

I cross the boardwalk to the beach,
lie in the sand and gaze beyond
the clutter at the sea.

II

Trouble you for a light?
I turn as Aunt Jemima settles down

beside me, her blue-rinsed hair
without the red bandanna now.

I hold the lighter to her cigarette.
Much obliged. Unmindful (perhaps)
of my embarrassment, she looks
at me and smiles: You sure

do favor a friend I used to have.
Guess that's why I bothered you
for a light. So much like him that I—
She pauses, watching white horses rush

to the shore. Way them big old waves
come slamming whopping in,
sometimes it's like they mean to smash
this no-good world to hell.

    Well, it could happen. A book I read—
Crossed that very ocean years ago.
London, Paris, Rome,
Constantinople too—I've seen them all.

Back when they billed me everywhere
as the Sepia High Stepper.
Crowned heads applauded me.
Years before your time. Years and years.

I wore me plenty diamonds then,
and counts or dukes or whatever they were
would fill my dressing room
with the costliest flowers. But of course

there was this one you resemble so.
Get me? The sweetest gentleman.
Dead before his time. Killed in the war
to save the world for another war.

High-stepping days for me
were over after that. Still I'm not one
to let grief idle me for long.
I went out with a mental act—

mind-reading—Mysteria From
The Mystic East—veils and beads
and telling suckers how to get
stolen rings and sweethearts back.

One night he was standing by my bed,
seen him plain as I see you,
and warned me without a single word:
Baby, quit playing with spiritual stuff.

So here I am, so here I am,
fake mammy to God's mistakes.
And that's the beauty part,
I mean, ain't that the beauty part.

She laughs, but I do not, knowing what
her laughter shields. And mocks.
I light another cigarette for her.
She smokes, not saying any more.

Scream of children in the surf,
adagios of sun and flashing foam,
the sexual glitter, oppressive fun. . . .
An antique etching comes to mind.

"The Sable Venus" naked on
a baroque Cellini shell—voluptuous
imago floating in the wake
of slave-ships on fantastic seas.

Jemima sighs, Reckon I'd best
be getting back. I help her up.
Don't you take no wooden nickels, hear?
Tin dimes neither. So long, pàl.

ON HAVING TO CHOOSE

ISAAC BASHEVIS SINGER

Isaac Bashevis Singer, who won the Nobel Prize for literature in 1978, is the most popular living Yiddish writer and is also becoming one of the most popular living American writers. He has been a steady contributor to the Yiddish Jewish Daily Forward *since he arrived in New York City in 1935, and in recent years he also has become a frequent contributor to* The New Yorker. *He still writes in Yiddish, his childhood language ("A writer has to write in his own language or not at all"), but by now he is almost always involved in the translation of his own work ("I do not exaggerate when I say that English has become my 'second original language' ").*

Singer was born in Poland in 1904, the grandson of two rabbis, the son of a Hasidic scholar. He himself received a traditional Jewish education and for a while studied at a rabbinical seminary, but he began to doubt "not the power of God, but all the traditions and dogmas." As a result he disappointed family expectations and instead followed the example of his older brother to become a secular writer. He took a job as proofreader for a Yiddish literary journal in Warsaw. By 1926 Singer began to publish stories and reviews. Then in 1935 he followed his brother to New York City, where he still lives, on the upper West Side of Manhattan.

Success came with the English translation of his 1945 novel, The Family Moskat. *Other novels include the two-volume* The Manor *(1967) and* Shosha *(1978), but he is best known for his short stories. Collections include* Gimpel the Fool *(1957),* The Spinoza of Market Street *(1957),* The Seance *(1968), and* Passions *(1976). In* My Father's Court *(1966),* A Day of Pleasure: Stories of a Boy Growing Up in Warsaw *(1969), and* A Little Boy in Search of God; Mysticism in a Personal Light *(1976) are mainly autobiographical. Singer has also written children's stories, and in 1973 he made his playwriting debut with an adaptation of* The Manor, *produced by the Yale Repertory Theater.*

But primarily Singer is an old-fashioned storyteller. Many of his stories, set in the shtetls and ghettos of prewar Poland, draw heavily on Jewish legend and folklore and are peopled with witches and ghosts and demons. An increasing number now deal with life in the United States and are set in contemporary New York. "Because I have now lived in this country longer than in Poland," he says, "I have developed roots here too." "The Son from America," which we reprint below, tells of an encounter between these two cultures. It first appeared in The New Yorker *and was later reprinted in the short-story collection* A Crown of Feathers *(1970), for which he won the National Book Award. The translation is by the author and Dorothea Straus.*

The Son from America

The village of Lentshin was tiny—a sandy marketplace where the peasants of the area met once a week. It was surrounded by little huts with thatched roofs or shingles green with moss. The chimneys looked like pots. Between the huts there were fields, where the owners planted vegetables or pastured their goats.

In the smallest of these huts lived old Berl, a man in his eighties, and his wife, who was called Berlcha (wife of Berl). Old Berl was one of the Jews who had been driven from their villages in Russia and had settled in Poland. In Lentshin, they mocked the mistakes he made while praying aloud. He spoke with a sharp "r." He was short, broad-shouldered, and had a small white beard, and summer and winter he wore a sheepskin hat, a padded cotton jacket, and stout boots. He walked slowly, shuffling his feet. He had a half acre of field, a cow, a goat, and chickens.

The couple had a son, Samuel, who had gone to America forty years ago. It was said in Lentshin that he became a millionaire there. Every month, the Lentshin letter carrier brought old Berl a money order and a letter that no one could read because many of the words were English. How much money Samuel sent his parents remained a secret. Three times a year, Berl and his wife went on foot to Zakroczym and cashed the money orders there. But they never seemed to use the money. What for? The garden, the cow, and the goat provided most of their needs. Besides, Berlcha sold chickens and eggs, and from these there was enough to buy flour for bread.

No one cared to know where Berl kept the money that his son sent him. There were no thieves in Lentshin. The hut consisted of one room, which contained all their belongings: the table, the shelf for meat, the shelf for milk foods, the two beds, and the clay oven. Sometimes the chickens roosted in the woodshed and sometimes, when it was cold, in a coop near the oven. The goat, too, found shelter inside when the weather was bad. The more prosperous villagers had kerosene lamps, but Berl and his wife did not believe in newfangled gadgets. What was wrong with a wick in a dish of oil? Only for the Sabbath would Berlcha buy three tallow candles at the store. In summer, the couple got up at sunrise and retired with the chickens. In the long winter evenings, Berlcha spun flax at her spinning wheel and Berl sat beside her in the silence of those who enjoy their rest.

Once in a while when Berl came home from the synagogue after evening prayers, he brought news to his wife. In Warsaw there were strikers who demanded that the czar abdicate. A heretic by the name of Dr. Herzl had come up with the idea that Jews should settle again in Palestine. Berlcha listened and shook her bonneted head. Her face was yellowish and wrinkled like a cabbage leaf. There were bluish sacks under her eyes. She was half deaf. Berl had to repeat each word he said to her. She would say, "The things that happen in the big cities!"

Here in Lentshin nothing happened except usual events: a cow gave birth to a calf, a young couple had a circumcision party, or a girl was born and there was no party. Occasionally, someone died. Lentshin had no cemetery, and the corpse had to be taken to Zakroczym. Actually, Lentshin had become a village with few young people. The young men left for Zakroczym, for Nowy Dwor, for Warsaw, and sometimes for the United States. Like Samuel's, their letters were illegible, the Yiddish mixed with the languages of the countries where they were now living. They sent photographs in which the men wore top hats and the women fancy dresses like squiresses.

Berl and Berlcha also received such photographs. But their eyes were failing and neither he nor she had glasses. They could barely make out the pictures. Samuel had sons and daughters with Gentile names—and grandchildren who had married and had their own offspring. Their names were so strange that Berl and Berlcha could never remember them. But what difference do names make? America was far, far away on the other side of the ocean, at the edge of the world. A Talmud teacher who came to Lentshin had said that Americans walk with their heads down and their feet up. Berl and Berlcha could not grasp this. How was it possible? But since the teacher said so it must be true. Berlcha pondered for some time and then she said, "One can get accustomed to everything."

And so it remained. From too much thinking—God forbid—one may lose one's wits.

One Friday morning, when Berlcha was kneading the dough for the Sabbath loaves, the door opened and a nobleman entered. He was so tall that he had to bend down to get through the door. He wore a beaver hat and a cloak bordered with fur. He was followed by Chazkel, the coachman from Zakroczym, who carried two leather valises with brass locks. In astonishment Berlcha raised her eyes.

The nobleman looked around and said to the coachman in Yiddish, "Here it is." He took out a silver ruble and paid him. The coachman tried to hand him change but he said, "You can go now."

When the coachman closed the door, the nobleman said, "Mother, it's me, your son Samuel—Sam."

Berlcha heard the words and her legs grew numb. Her hands, to which pieces of dough were sticking, lost their power. The nobleman hugged her, kissed her forehead, both her cheeks. Berlcha began to cackle like a hen, "My son!" At that moment Berl came in from the woodshed, his arms piled with logs. The goat followed him. When he saw a nobleman kissing his wife, Berl dropped the wood and exclaimed, "What is this?"

The nobleman let go of Berlcha and embraced Berl. "Father!"

For a long time Berl was unable to utter a sound. He wanted to recite holy words that he had read in the Yiddish Bible, but he could remember nothing. Then he asked, "Are you Samuel?"

"Yes, Father, I am Samuel."

"Well, peace be with you." Berl grasped his son's hand. He was still not sure that he was not being fooled. Samuel wasn't as tall and heavy as this man, but then Berl reminded himself that Samuel was only fifteen years old when he had left home. He must have grown in that faraway country. Berl asked, "Why didn't you let us know you were coming?"

"Didn't you receive my cable?" Samuel asked.

Berl did not know what a cable was.

Berlcha had scraped the dough from her hands and enfolded her son. He kissed her again and asked, "Mother, didn't you receive a cable?"

"What? If I lived to see this, I am happy to die," Berlcha said, amazed by her own words. Berl, too, was amazed. These were just the words he would have said earlier if he had been able to remember. After a while Berl came to himself and said, "Pescha, you will have to make a double Sabbath pudding in addition to the stew."

It was years since Berl had called Berlcha by her given name. When he wanted to address her, he would say, "Listen," or "Say." It is the young or those from the big cities who call a wife by her name. Only now did Berlcha begin to cry. Yellow tears ran from her eyes, and everything became dim. Then she called out, "It's Friday—I have to prepare for the Sabbath." Yes, she had to knead the dough and braid the loaves. With such a guest, she had to make a larger Sabbath stew. The winter day is short and she must hurry.

Her son understood what was worrying her, because he said, "Mother, I will help you."

Berlcha wanted to laugh, but a choked sob came out. "What are you saying? God forbid."

The nobleman took off his cloak and jacket and remained in his vest, on which hung a solid-gold watch chain. He rolled up his sleeves and came to the trough. "Mother, I was a baker for many years in New York," he said, and he began to knead the dough.

"What! You are my darling son who will say Kaddish for me." She wept raspingly. Her strength left her, and she slumped onto the bed.

Berl said, "Women will always be women." And he went to the shed to get more wood. The goat sat down near the oven; she gazed with surprise at this strange man—his height and his bizarre clothes.

The neighbors had heard the good news that Berl's son had arrived from America and they came to greet him. The women began to help Berlcha prepare for the Sabbath. Some laughed, some cried. The room was full of people, as at a wedding. They asked Berl's son, "What is new in America?" And Berl's son answered, "America is all right."

"Do Jews make a living?"

"One eats white bread there on weekdays."

"Do they remain Jews?"

"I am not a Gentile."

After Berlcha blessed the candles, father and son went to the little synagogue across the street. A new snow had fallen. The son took large steps, but Berl warned him, "Slow down."

In the synagogue the Jews recited "Let Us Exult" and "Come, My Groom." All the time, the snow outside kept falling. After prayers, when Berl and Samuel left the Holy Place, the village was unrecognizable. Everything was covered in snow. One could see only the contours of the roofs and the candles in the windows. Samuel said, "Nothing has changed here."

Berlcha had prepared gefilte fish, chicken soup with rice, meat, carrot stew. Berl recited the benediction over a glass of ritual wine. The family ate and drank, and when it grew quiet for a while one could hear the chirping of the house cricket. The son talked a lot, but Berl and Berlcha understood little. His Yiddish was different and contained foreign words.

After the final blessing Samuel asked, "Father, what did you do with all the money I sent you?"

Berl raised his white brows. "It's here."

"Didn't you put it in a bank?"

"There is no bank in Lentshin."

"Where do you keep it?"

Berl hesitated. "One is not allowed to touch money on the Sabbath, but I will show you." He crouched beside the bed and began to shove something heavy. A boot appeared. Its top was stuffed with straw. Berl removed the straw and the son saw that the boot was full of gold coins. He lifted it.

"Father, this is a treasure!" he called out.

"Well."

"Why didn't you spend it?"

"On what? Thank God, we have everything."

"Why didn't you travel somewhere?"

"Where to? This is our home."

The son asked one question after the other, but Berl's answer was always the same: they wanted for nothing. The garden, the cow, the goat, the chickens provided them with all they needed. The son said, "If thieves knew about this, your lives wouldn't be safe."

"There are no thieves here."

"What will happen to the money?"

"You take it."

Slowly, Berl and Berlcha grew accustomed to their son and his American Yiddish. Berlcha could hear him better now. She even recognized his voice. He was saying, "Perhaps we should build a larger synagogue."

"The synagogue is big enough," Berl replied.

"Perhaps a home for old people."

"No one sleeps in the street."

The next day after the Sabbath meal was eaten, a Gentile from Zakroczym brought a paper—it was the cable. Berl and Berlcha lay down for a nap. They soon began to snore. The goat, too, dozed off. The son put on his cloak and his hat and went for a walk. He strode with his long legs across the marketplace. He stretched out a hand and touched a roof. He wanted to smoke a cigar, but he remembered it was forbidden on the Sabbath. He had a desire to talk to someone, but it seemed that the whole of Lentshin was asleep. He entered the synagogue. An old man was sitting there, reciting psalms. Samuel asked, "Are you praying?"

"What else is there to do when one gets old?"

"Do you make a living?"

The old man did not understand the meaning of these words. He smiled, showing his empty gums, and then he said, "If God gives health, one keeps on living."

Samuel returned home. Dusk had fallen. Berl went to the synagogue for the evening prayers and the son remained with his mother. The room was filled with shadows.

Berlcha began to recite in a solemn singsong, "God of Abraham, Isaac, and Jacob, defend the poor people of Israel and Thy name. The Holy Sabbath is departing; the welcome week is coming to us. Let it be one of health, wealth and good deeds."

"Mother, you don't need to pray for wealth," Samuel said. "You are wealthy already."

Berlcha did not hear—or pretended not to. Her face had turned into a cluster of shadows.

In the twilight Samuel put his hand into his jacket pocket and touched his passport, his checkbook, his letters of credit. He had come here with big plans. He had a valise filled with presents for his parents. He wanted to bestow gifts on the village. He brought not only his own money but funds from the Lentshin Society in New York, which had organized a ball for the benefit of the village. But this village in the hinterland needed nothing. From the synagogue one could hear hoarse chanting. The cricket, silent all day, started again its chirping. Berlcha began to sway and utter holy rhymes inherited from mothers and grandmothers:

Thy holy sheep
In mercy keep,

In Torah and good deeds;
Provide for all their needs,
Shoes, clothes, and bread
And the Messiah's tread.

PETER BERGER

Peter Berger is a sociologist who is particularly interested in Third World development and political ethics. A naturalized American citizen, he was born in Vienna in 1929 but educated in the United States; he attended Wagner College (B.A., 1949), the New School for Social Research (M.A., 1950; Ph.D., 1954), the Lutheran Theological Seminary in Philadelphia, and Yale Divinity School. In 1954 he began teaching, and since 1966 he has been Professor of Sociology at Brooklyn College. He has written many articles and books, including Rumor of Angels: Modern Society and the Rediscovery of the Supernatural *(1969),* Religion in a Revolutionary Society *(1974),* Protocol of a Damnation: A Novel *(1975), and* Facing Up to Modernity: Excursions in Sociology, Politics and Religion *(1977).*

Pyramids of Sacrifice: Political Ethics and Social Change *(1975) deals with two topics that, he says in the Preface, "are intertwined throughout. One is Third World development. The other is political ethics as applied to social change. . . . No humanly acceptable discussion of the anguishing problems of the world's poverty can avoid ethical considerations. And no political ethics worthy of the name can avoid the centrally important case of the Third World." The book includes several narrative chapters, one of which we reprint below.*

A Tale of Two Moralities

Manuela keeps dreaming about the village.[1] She does not think about it very much in the daytime. Even when she thinks about Mexico, it is not usually about the village. In any case, during the day it is the brash, gleaming reality of California that dominates, its loud demand for full attention pushing into the background the old images and feelings. It is at night that the village comes back, reclaiming its power over Manuela. It is then as if she had never left it—or, worse, as if she must inevitably return to it.

It is often very hot in the village, though at night one may freeze. The earth is dry. Time moves very slowly, as the white clouds move through the brightly blue sky over the brown and arid hills. Time moves slowly in the faces of the people, too, and the faces too are brown and arid. Even the faces of the very young seem to hold old memories. The children do not smile

---

[1] Manuela's story is fiction, made up as a composite from several true stories. Manuela does not exist. But many Manuelas do exist, not only in Mexico but all over the Third World. Their moral dilemma must be understood if one is to understand "development."

easily. The day is measured by the halting motion of shadows over houses and trees. The years are mostly measured by calamities. The past is powerfully present, although there are few words for it. No one in the village speaks an Indian language, though everyone has Indian blood. Can the blood speak, without words? Do the dead speak from the earth? Somewhere in this blue sky and in these brown hills there are very old presences, more threatening than consoling. Some years ago the schoolteacher dug up some Indian artifacts and wanted to take them to the city, to sell them to a museum. Calamity struck at once, all over the village. The dead do not want to be disturbed, and they are dangerous.

The village is distant. Distant from what? Distant from everything, but most importantly distant from the places where time moves quickly and purposefully. There is no paved road, no telephone, no electricity. Even the schoolteacher only comes on two days of the week. He has two other villages to take care of, and he lives somewhere else. To get to the nearest bus station one rides on a donkey for three hours over footpaths of trampled dirt. Time and distance determine the world of the village, in fact and in Manuela's dreams. If she were to put it in one sentence, this world, she would have to say: It is very far away, and life there moves very slowly. On the maps the village is in the state of Guerrero, in a very specific location between Mexico City and the Pacific Ocean. In Manuela's dreams the village is located in the center of her self, deep down inside rather than out there somewhere.

Manuela was born in the village twenty-two years ago. Her mother died shortly afterward. Her father, already married to another woman with seven legitimate children, never acknowledged Manuela. Indeed, he has never spoken with her. She was raised by one of her mother's brothers, a man without land and much of the time without work, with a large family of his own that he barely managed to support. There was never any question about the family obligation to take care of Manuela; the only question at the time, lengthily discussed by her grandfather and the three uncles still living in the area, was which of the three would take the baby in. But this obligation did not greatly exceed supplying the bare necessities of life. There was never the slightest doubt about Manuela's status in her uncle's household as the unwanted bastard who took the food out of the mouths of her more deserving cousins—and she was told so in no uncertain terms on many occasions. If there was little food, she would be the hungriest. If there was hard work, she would be the one to do it. This does not mean that she received no affection. She was a very pretty, winsome child, and often people were kind to her. But she always knew that affection and kindness were not her right, were given to her gratuitously—and, by the same token, could be gratuitously taken away again. As a child Manuela wished for someone who would love her all the time, reliably, "officially." However, she was only dimly unhappy in her uncle's household, since she knew nothing else. She was often hungry, sometimes beaten. She did not have shoes until her tenth birthday, when her grandfather made her a present of a pair. This was also the first occasion when she went outside the village, accompanying her grandfather on a visit to the doctor in the nearest town.

Her grandfather and one of her uncles in the village were *ejidatários*, belonging to the minority that owned parcels of land under the village *ejido* (agricultural cooperative). Most of the time the uncle with whom she stayed worked on this land, too, though he would hire himself out for work elsewhere when there was an opportunity. When she was not working in the house or taking care of her little cousins, Manuela also worked in the fields or with the animals belonging to her family. After her tenth birthday she sometimes worked for outsiders, but she was expected to turn over the money she received for this. Sometimes she succeeded in keeping a few coins for herself, though she knew that she would be beaten if found out. She was allowed to go to school and, being very bright, she learned to read and write well. It was her brightness that attracted her grandfather, who was amused by her and took a liking to her (much to the annoyance of her cousins).

"Bad blood will show." "You will come to no good end, like your mother." Manuela must have heard this hundreds of times during her childhood. The prophecy was fulfilled when she was fifteen and made pregnant by the secretary of the *ejido*, one of the most affluent farmers in the village. When her condition could no longer be concealed, there was a terrible scene and her uncle threw her out of the house. Her grandfather, after slapping her a couple of times rather mildly, gave her the address of an aunt in Acapulco and enough money to pay her busfare there. It was thus that she left the village.

Manuela marveled at Acapulco and its astonishing sights, but, needless to say, she lived there in a world far removed from that experienced by the tourists. Her aunt, a gentle widow with two children and a maid's job in one of the big hotels, took Manuela in very warmly (at least in part because she could use some help in the house). Manuela's baby was born there, a healthy boy whom she named Roberto. Not much later Manuela also started to work outside the house.

A Mexican *campesino*, when he migrates, normally follows an itinerary taken before him by relatives and *compadres*. When he arrives, the latter provide an often intricate network of contacts that are indispensable for his adjustment to the new situation. They will often provide initial housing, they can give information and advice, and, perhaps most important, they serve as an informal labor exchange. Such a network awaited Manuela in Acapulco. In addition to the aunt she was staying with, there were two more aunts and an uncle with their respective families, including some twelve cousins of all ages. This family system, of course, was transposed to the city from the village, but it took on a quite different character in the new context. Freed from the oppressive constraints of village life, the system, on the whole, was more benign. Manuela experienced it as such. Several of her cousins took turns taking care of little Roberto when Manuela started to work. Her aunt's "fiancé" (a somewhat euphemistic term), who was head clerk in the linen supply department of the hotel, found Manuela a job in his department. The uncle, through a *compadre* who was head waiter in another hotel, helped her get a job there as a waitress. It was this uncle, incidentally, who had gone further than any other member of the Acapulco clan, at least for a brief time. An intelligent and aggressive man, he worked himself up in the municipal sanitation department to the rank of inspector. Through a coup, the details of which were shrouded in mystery but which were safely assumed to involve illegality of heroic proportions, Uncle Pepe amassed the equivalent of about one thousand U.S. dollars in a few months' time, a staggering sum in this ambience. With this money he set out for Mexico City, ostensibly to look into a business proposition. In fact he checked into one of the capital's finest hotels, made the rounds of nightclubs and luxury brothels, and returned penniless but not overly unhappy a month later. The clan has viewed him with considerable awe ever since.

Manuela now had a fairly steady cash income, modest to be sure, but enough to keep going. This does not mean, however, that she could keep all of it for herself and her child. The family system operated as a social insurance agency as well as a labor exchange, and there was never a shortage of claimants. An aunt required an operation. An older cousin set up business as a mechanic and needed some capital to start off. Another cousin was arrested and a substantial *mordida* was required to bribe his way out of jail. And then there were always new calamities back in the village, requiring emergency transfers of money back there. Not least among them was the chronic calamity of grandfather's kidney ailment, which consumed large quantities of family funds in expensive and generally futile medical treatments.

Sometimes, at the hotel, Manuela did baby-sitting for tourists with children. It was thus that she met the couple from California. They stayed in Acapulco for a whole month, and soon Manuela took care of their little girl almost daily. When they left the woman asked Manuela whether she wanted a job as a maid in the States. "Yes," replied Manuela at once, without thinking. The arrangements were made quickly. Roberto was put up with a cousin. Uncle Pepe, through two trusted intermediaries, arranged for Manuela to cross the border illegally. Within a month she arrived at the couple's address in California.

And now she has been here for over a year. California was even more astonishing than Acapulco had been when she first left the village, but now she had more time to explore this new world. She learned English in a short time, and, in the company of a Cuban girl who worked for a neighbor, she started forays into the American universe, in ever-wider circles from her employers' house. She even took bus trips to Hollywood and San Francisco. For the first time in her life she slept in a room all by herself. And, despite her regular payments for Roberto's keep, she started to save money and put it in a bank account. Most important, she started to think about her life in a new way, systematically. "What will become of you when you go back?" asked the American woman one day. Manuela did not know then, but she started to think. Carmelita, the Cuban girl, discussed the matter with her many times—in exchange for equal attention paid to her own planning exercises. Eventually, one project won out over all the alternatives: Manuela would return to go to commercial school, to become a bilingual secretary. She even started a typing course in California. But she would not return to Acapulco. She knew that, to succeed, she would have to remove herself from the family there. She would go to Mexico City, first alone, and then she would send for Roberto.

This last decision was made gradually. It was the letters that did it. Manuela, some months before, had mentioned the amount of money she had saved (a very large amount, by her standards, and enough to keep her and Roberto afloat for the duration of the commercial course). Then the letters started coming from just about everyone in the Acapulco clan. Most of the contents were family gossip, inquiries about Manuela's life in the States, and long expressions of affectionate feelings. There were frequent reminders not to forget her relatives, who took such good care of Roberto. Only gradually did the economic infrastructure emerge from all this: There was to be a *fiesta* at the wedding of a cousin, and could Manuela make a small contribution. The cousin who had been in jail was still to be tried, and there were lawyer's expenses. Uncle Pepe was onto the most promising business opportunity of his "long and distinguished career in financial activities" (his own words), and just three hundred American dollars would make it possible for him to avail himself of this never-to-recur opportunity—needless to say, Manuela would be a full partner upon her return. Finally, there was even a very formal letter from grandfather, all the way from the village, containing an appeal for funds to pay for a trip to the capital so as to take advantage of a new treatment that a famous doctor had developed there. It took a while for Manuela to grasp that every dollar of her savings had already been mentally spent by her relatives.

The choice before Manuela now is sharp and crystal-clear: She must return to Mexico—because she wants to, because of Roberto, and because the American authorities would send her back there sooner or later anyway. She can then return to the welcoming bosom of the family system, surrender her savings, and return to her previous way of life. Or she can carry through her plan in the face of family opposition. The choice is not only between two courses of action but between two moralities. The first course is dictated by the morality of collective solidarity, the second by the morality of personal autonomy and advancement. Each morality condemns the other—as uncaring selfishness in the former case, as irresponsible disregard of her own potential and the welfare of her son in the latter. Poor Manuela's conscience is divided; by now she is capable of feeling its pangs either way.

She is in America, not in Mexico, and the new morality gets more support from her immediate surroundings. Carmelita is all for the plan, and so are most of the Spanish-speaking girls with whom Manuela has been going out. Only one, another Mexican, expressed doubt: "I don't know. Your grandfather is ill, and your uncle helped you a lot in the past. Can you just forget them? I think that one must always help one's relatives." Manuela once talked about the matter with the American woman. "Nonsense," said the latter, "you should go ahead with your plan. You owe it to yourself and to your son." So this is what Manuela intends to do, very soon now. But she is not at ease with the decision. Every time another letter arrives from Mexico, she hesitates before opening it, and she fortifies herself against the appeals she knows to be there.

Each decision, as dictated by the respective morality, has predictable consequences: If Manuela follows the old morality, she will, in all likelihood, never raise herself or her son above the level she achieved in Acapulco—not quite at the bottom of the social scale, but not very far above it. If, on the other hand, she decides in accordance with the new morality (new for her, that is), she has at least a chance of making it up one important step on that scale. Her son will benefit from this, but probably no other of her relatives will. To take that step she must, literally, hack off all those hands that would hold her back. It is a grim choice indeed.

What will Manuela do?

She will probably at least start out on her plan. Perhaps she will succeed. But once she is back in Mexico, the tentacles of the old solidarity will be more powerful. They will pull more strongly. It will be harder to escape that other village, the village of the mind within herself. The outcome of the struggle will decide whether the village will be Manuela's past or also her future. Outside observers should think very carefully indeed before they take sides in this contest.

RICHARD RODRIGUEZ

Richard Rodriguez was born in San Francisco in 1944. He attended Catholic primary and secondary schools and then went to Stanford University on a scholarship. He earned a B.A. in English in 1967, went on to receive an M.A. in philosophy from Columbia University in 1969, then studied at the Warburg Institute in London and in the doctoral program in English literature at the University of California, Berkeley. His experiences in school as a "scholarship boy" and as a "minority student" who must straddle two worlds have led him to several reflective autobiographical essays, including "The Achievement of Desire: Personal Reflection on Learning 'Basics' " (College English, *November 1978*) *and "Going Home Again, The New American Scholarship Boy"* (American Scholar, *Winter 1974-75*), *of which we reprint the first part. Rodriguez has withdrawn from doctoral studies and is now a free-lance writer. His first book,* Toward Words, *on life as experienced in language, will be published shortly.*

from *Going Home Again: The New American Scholarship Boy*

At each step, with every graduation from one level of education to the next, the refrain from bystanders was strangely the same: "Your parents must be so proud of you." I suppose that my parents were proud, although I suspect, too, that they felt more than pride alone as they watched me advance through my education. They seemed to know that my education was separating us from one another, making it difficult to resume familiar intimacies. Mixed with the instincts of parental pride, a certain hurt also communicated itself—too private ever to be adequately expressed in words, but real nonetheless.

The autobiographical facts pertinent to this essay are simply stated in two sentences, though they exist in somewhat awkward juxtaposition to each other. I am the son of Mexican-American parents, who speak a blend of Spanish and English, but who read neither language easily. I am about to receive a Ph.D. in English Renaissance literature. What sort of life—what tensions, feelings, conflicts—connects these two sentences? I look back and remember my life from the time I was seven or eight years old as one of constant movement away from a Spanish-speaking folk culture toward the world of the English-language classroom. As the years passed, I felt myself becoming less like my parents and less comfortable with the assumption of visiting relatives that I was still the Spanish-speaking child they remembered. By the time I began college, visits home became suffused with silent embarrassment: there seemed so little to share, however strong the ties of our affection. My parents would tell me what happened in their lives or in the lives of relatives; I would respond with news of my own. Polite questions would follow. Our conversations came to seem more like interviews.

A few months ago, my dissertation nearly complete, I came upon my father looking through my bookcase. He quietly fingered the volumes of Milton's tracts and Augustine's theology with that combination of reverence and distrust those who are not literate sometimes show for the written word. Silently, I watched him from the door of the room. However much he would have insisted that he was "proud" of his son for being able to master the texts, I knew, if pressed further, he would have admitted to complicated feelings about my success. When he looked across the room and suddenly saw me, his body tightened slightly with surprise, then we both smiled.

For many years I kept my uneasiness about becoming a success in education to myself. I did so in part because I wanted to avoid vague feelings that, if considered carefully, I would have no way of dealing with; and in part because I felt that no one else shared my reaction to the opportunity provided by education. When I began to rehearse my story of cultural dislocation publicly, however, I found many listeners willing to admit to similar feelings from their own pasts. Equally impressive was the fact that many among those I spoke with were *not* from nonwhite racial groups, which made me realize that one can grow up to enter the culture of the academy and find it a "foreign" culture for a variety of reasons, ranging from economic status to religious heritage. But why, I next wondered, was it that, though there were so many of us who came from childhood cultures alien to the academy's, we voiced our uneasiness to one another and to ourselves so infrequently? Why did it take *me* so long to acknowledge publicly the cultural costs I had paid to earn a Ph.D. in Renaissance English literature?

Why, more precisely, am I writing these words only now when my connection to my past barely survives except as nostalgic memory?

Looking back, a person risks losing hold of the present while being confounded by the past. For the child who moves to an academic culture from a culture that dramatically lacks academic traditions, looking back can jeopardize the certainty he has about the desirability of this new academic culture. Richard Hoggart's description, in *The Uses of Literacy*, of the cultural pressures on such a student, whom Hoggart calls the "scholarship boy," helps make the point. The scholarship boy must give nearly unquestioning allegiance to academic culture, Hoggart argues, if he is to succeed at all, so different is the milieu of the classroom from the culture he leaves behind. For a time, the scholarship boy may try to balance his loyalty between his concretely experienced family life and the more abstract mental life of the classroom. In the end, though, he must choose between the two worlds: if he intends to succeed as a student, he must, literally and figuratively, separate himself from his family, with its gregarious life, and find a quiet place to be alone with his thoughts.

After a while, the kind of allegiance the young student might once have given his parents is transferred to the teacher, the new parent. Now without the support of the old ties and certainties of the family, he almost mechanically acquires the assumptions, practices, and style of the classroom milieu. For the loss he might otherwise feel, the scholarship boy substitutes an enormous enthusiasm for nearly everything having to do with school.

How readily I read my own past into the portrait of Hoggart's scholarship boy. Coming from a home in which mostly Spanish was spoken, for example, I had to decide to forget Spanish when I began my education. To succeed in the classroom, I needed psychologically to sever my ties with Spanish. Spanish represented an alternate culture as well as another language—and the basis of my deepest sense of relationship to my family. Although I recently taught myself to read Spanish, the language that I see on the printed page is not quite the language I heard in my youth. That other Spanish, the spoken Spanish of my family, I remember with nostalgia and guilt: guilt because I cannot explain to aunts and uncles why I do not answer their questions any longer in their own idiomatic language. Nor was I able to explain to teachers in graduate school, who regularly expected me to read and speak Spanish with ease, why my very ability to reach graduate school as a student of English literature in the first place required me to loosen my attachments to a language I spoke years earlier. Yet, having lost the ability to speak Spanish, I never forgot it so totally that I could not understand it. Hearing Spanish spoken on the street reminded me of the community I once felt a part of, and still cared deeply about. I never forgot Spanish so thoroughly, in other words, as to move outside the range of its nostalgic pull.

Such moments of guilt and nostalgia were, however, just that—momentary. They punctuated the history of my otherwise successful progress from *barrio* to classroom. Perhaps they even encouraged it. Whenever I felt my determination to succeed wavering, I tightened my hold on the conventions of academic life.

Spanish was one aspect of the problem, my parents another. They could raise deeper, more persistent doubts. They offered encouragement to my brothers and me in our work, but they also spoke, only half jokingly, about the way education was putting "big ideas" into our heads. When we would come home, for example, and challenge assumptions we earlier believed, they would be forced to defend their beliefs (which, given our new verbal skills, they did increasingly less well) or, more frequently, to submit to our logic with the disclaimer, "It's what we were taught in our time to believe. . . ." More important, after we began to leave home for college, they voiced regret about how "changed" we had become, how much further away from one another we had grown. They partly yearned for a return to the time before education assumed their children's primary loyalty. This yearning was renewed each time they saw their nieces and nephews (none of whom continued their education beyond high school, all of whom continued to speak fluent Spanish) living according to the conventions and assumptions of their parents' culture. If I was already troubled by the time I graduated from high school by that refrain of congratulations ("Your parents must be so proud. . . ."), I realize now how much more difficult and complicated was my progress into academic life for my parents, as they saw the cultural foundation of their family erode, than it was for me.

Yet my parents were willing to pay the price of alienation and continued to encourage me to become a scholarship boy because they perceived, as others of the lower classes had before them, the relation between education and social mobility. Lacking the former themselves made them acutely aware of its necessity as prerequisite for the latter. They sent their children off to school in the hopes of their acquiring something "better" beyond education. Notice the assumption here that education is something of a tool or license—a means to an end, which has been the traditional way the lower or working classes have viewed the value of education in the past. That education might alter children in more basic ways than providing them with skills, certificates of proficiency, and even upward mobility, may come as a surprise for some, but the financial cost is usually tolerated.

JAMES ALAN McPHERSON

James Alan McPherson was born in Savannah, Georgia, in 1943. He attended Morgan State College (B.A., 1965), Harvard Law School (LL.B., 1968), and then went on to the University of Iowa, where he received a Master of Fine Arts degree in 1969. He recalls some of his experiences during those years in the essay we reprint here. He has had many jobs—waiter, janitor, research assistant—has taught at the University of Iowa and the University of California at Santa Cruz, and since 1978 has been Associate Professor of English at the University of Virginia. He is also a contributing editor of the Atlantic.

McPherson is probably best known as a writer of short stories. He has received numerous awards, and his stories have been selected for inclusion in O. Henry Prize Stories *and* Best American Short Stories. *He has published two collections,* Hue and Cry *(1969) and* Elbow Room *(1977), for which he won the Pulitzer Prize. The essay we reprint below, adapted from a speech delivered at Chautauqua, first appeared in the* Atlantic *1978.*

On Becoming an American Writer

In 1974, during the last months of the Nixon Administration, I lived in San Francisco, California. My public reason for leaving the East and going there was that my wife had been admitted to the San Francisco Medical Center School of Nursing, but my private reason for going was that San Francisco would be a very good place for working and for walking. Actually, during that time San Francisco was not that pleasant a place. We lived in a section of the city called the Sunset District, but it rained almost every day. During the late spring Patricia Hearst helped to rob a bank a few blocks from our apartment, a psychopath called "the Zebra Killer" was terrorizing the city, and the mayor seemed about to declare martial law. Periodically the FBI would come to my apartment with pictures of the suspected bank robbers. Agents came several times, until it began to dawn on me that they had become slightly interested in why, of all the people in a working-class neighborhood, I alone sat at home every day. They never asked any questions on this point, and I never volunteered that I was trying to keep my sanity by working very hard on a book dealing with the relationship between folklore and technology in nineteenth-century America.

In the late fall of the same year a friend came out from the East to give a talk in Sacramento. I drove there to meet him, and then drove him back to San Francisco. This was an older black man, one whom I respect a great deal, but during our drive an argument developed between us. His major worry was the recession, but eventually his focus shifted to people in my age group and our failures. There were a great many of these, and he listed them point by point. He said, while we drove through a gloomy evening rain. "When the smoke clears and you start counting, I'll bet you won't find that many more black doctors, lawyers, accountants, engineers, dentists. . . ." The list went on. He remonstrated a bit more, and said, "White people are very generous. When they start a thing they usually finish it. But after all this chaos, imagine how mad and tired they must be. Back in the fifties, when this thing started, they must have known anything could happen. They must have said, 'Well, we'd better settle in and hold on tight. Here come the niggers.' " During the eighteen months I spent in San Francisco, this was the only personal encounter that really made me mad.

In recent years I have realized that my friend, whom I now respect even more, was speaking from the perspective of a tactician. He viewed the situation in strict bread-and-butter terms: a commitment had been made to redefine the meaning of democracy in this country, certain opportunities had been provided, and people like him were watching to see what would be made of those opportunities and the freedom they provided. From his point of view, it was simply a matter of fulfilling a contractual obligation: taking full advantage of the educational opportunities that had been offered to achieve middle-class status in one of the professions. But from my point of view, one that I never shared with him, it was not that simple. Perhaps it was because of the differences in our generations and experiences. Or perhaps it was because each new generation, of black people at least, has to redefine itself even while it attempts to grasp the new opportunities, explore the new freedom. I can speak for no one but myself, yet maybe in trying to preserve the uniqueness of my experience, as I tried to do in *Elbow Room*, I can begin to set the record straight for my friend, for myself, and for the sake of the record itself.

In 1954, when *Brown* v. *Board of Education* was decided, I was eleven years old. I lived in a lower-class black community in Savannah, Georgia, attended segregated public schools, and knew no white people socially. I can't remember thinking of this last fact as a disadvantage, but I do know that early on I was being conditioned to believe that I was not *supposed* to know any white people on social terms. In our town the children of the black middle class were expected to aspire to certain traditional occupations; the children of the poor were expected not to cause too much trouble.

There was in those days a very subtle, but real, social distinction based on gradations of color, and I can remember the additional strain under which darker-skinned poor people lived. But there was also a great deal of optimism, shared by all levels of the black community. Besides a certain reverence for the benign intentions of the federal government, there was a belief in the idea of progress, nourished, I think now, by the determination of older people not to pass on to the next generation too many stories about racial conflict, their own frustrations and failures. They censored a great deal. It was as if they had made basic and binding agreements with themselves, or with their ancestors, that for the consideration represented by their silence on certain points they expected to receive, from either Providence or a munificent federal government, some future service or remuneration, the form of which would be left to the beneficiaries of their silence. Lawyers would call this a contract with a condition precedent. And maybe because they did tell us less than they knew, many of us were less informed than we might have been. On the other hand, because of this same silence many of us remained free enough of the influence of negative stories to take chances, be ridiculous, perhaps even try to form our own positive stories out of whatever our own experiences provided. Though ours was a limited world, it was one rich in possibilities for the future.

If I had to account for my life from segregated Savannah to this place and point in time, I would probably have to say that the contract would be no bad metaphor. I am reminded of Sir Henry Maine's observation that the progress of society is from status to contract. Although he was writing about the development of English common law, the reverse of his generalization is most applicable to my situation: I am the beneficiary of a number of contracts, most of them between the federal government and the institutions of society, intended to provide people like me with a certain status.

I recall that in 1960, for example, something called the National Defense Student Loan Program went into effect, and I found out that by my agreeing to repay a loan plus some little interest, the federal government would back my enrollment in a small Negro college in Georgia. When I was a freshman at that college, disagreement over a seniority clause between the Hotel & Restaurant Employees and Bartenders Union and the Great Northern Railway Company, in St. Paul, Minnesota, caused management to begin recruiting temporary summer help. Before I was nineteen I was encouraged to move from a segregated Negro college in the South and through that very beautiful part of the country that lies between Chicago and the Pacific Northwest. That year—1962—the World's Fair was in Seattle, and it was a magnificently diverse panorama for a young man to see. Almost every nation on earth was represented in some way, and at the center of the fair was the Space Needle. The theme of the United States exhibit, as I recall, was drawn from Whitman's *Leaves of Grass*: "Conquering, holding, daring, venturing as we go the unknown ways."

When I returned to the South, in the midst of all the civil rights activity, I saw a poster advertising a creative-writing contest sponsored by *Reader's Digest* and the United Negro College Fund. To enter the contest I had to learn to write and type. The first story I wrote was lost (and very badly typed); but the second, written in 1965, although also badly typed, was awarded first prize by Edward Weeks and his staff at *The Atlantic Monthly*. That same year I was offered the opportunity to enter Harvard Law School. During my second year at law school, a third-year man named Dave Marston (who was in a contest with Attorney General Griffin Bell earlier this year) offered me, through a very conservative white fellow student from Texas, the opportunity to take over his old job as a janitor in one of the apartment buildings in Cambridge. There I had the solitude, and the encouragement, to begin writing seriously. Offering my services in that building was probably the best contract I ever made.

I have not recalled all the above to sing my own praises or to evoke the black American version of the Horatio Alger myth. I have recited these facts as a way of indicating the haphazard nature of events during that ten-year period. I am the product of a contractual process. To put it simply, the 1960s were a crazy time. Opportunities seemed to materialize out of thin air; and if you were lucky, if you were in the right place at the right time, certain contractual benefits just naturally accrued. You were assured of a certain status; you could become a doctor, a lawyer, a dentist, an accountant, an engineer. Achieving these things was easy, if you applied yourself.

But a very hard price was extracted. It seems to me now, from the perspective provided by age and distance, that certain institutional forces, acting impersonally, threw together black peasants and white aristocrats, people who operated on the plane of the intellect and people who valued the perspective of the folk. There were people who were frightened, threatened, and felt inferior; there were light-skinned people who called themselves "black" and darker-skinned people who could remember when this term had been used negatively; there were idealists and opportunists, people who seemed to want to be exploited and people who delighted in exploiting them. Old identities were thrown off, of necessity, but there were not many new ones of a positive nature to be assumed. People from backgrounds like my own, those from the South, while content with the new opportunities, found themselves trying to make sense of the growing diversity of friendships, of their increasing familiarity with the various political areas of the country, of the obvious differences between their values and those of their parents. We *were* becoming doctors, lawyers, dentists, engineers; but at the same time our experiences forced us to begin thinking of ourselves in new and different ways. We never wanted to be "white," but we never wanted to be "black" either. And back during that period there was the feeling that we could be whatever we wanted. But, we discovered, unless we joined a group, subscribed to some ideology, accepted some provisional identity, there was no contractual process for defining and stabilizing what it was we wanted to be. We also found that this was an individual problem, and in order to confront it one had to go inside one's self.

Now I want to return to my personal experience, to one of the contracts that took me from segregated Savannah to the Seattle World's Fair. There were many things about my earlier experiences that I liked and wanted to preserve, despite the fact that these things took place in a context of segregation; and there were a great many things I liked about the vision of all those nations interacting at the World's Fair. But the two seemed to belong to separate realities, to represent two different world views. Similarly, there were some things I liked about many of the dining-car waiters with whom I worked, and some things I liked about people like Dave Marston whom I met in law school. Some of these people and their values were called "black" and some were called "white," and I learned very quickly that all of us tend to wall ourselves off from experiences different from our own by assigning to these terms greater significance than they should have. Moreover, I found that trying to maintain friendships with, say, a politically conservative white Texan, a liberal-to-radical classmate of Scottish-Italian background, my oldest black friends, and even members of my own family introduced psychological contradictions that became tense and painful as the political climate shifted. There were no contracts covering such friendships and such feelings, and in order to keep the friends and maintain the feelings I had to force myself to find a basis other than race on which such contradictory urgings could be synthesized. I discovered that I had to find, first of all, an identity as a writer, and then I had to express what I knew or felt in such a way that I could make something whole out of a necessarily fragmented experience.

While in San Francisco, I saw in the image of the nineteenth-century American locomotive a possible cultural symbol that could represent my folk origins and their values, as well as the values of all the people I had seen at the World's Fair. During that same time, unconsciously, I was also beginning to see that the American language, in its flexibility and variety of idioms, could at least approximate some of the contradictory feelings that had resulted from my experience. Once again, I could not find any contractual guarantee that this would be the most appropriate and rewarding way to hold myself, and my experience, together. I think now there are no such contracts.

I quoted earlier a generalization by Sir Henry Maine to the effect that human society is a matter of movement from status to contract. Actually, I have never read Sir Henry Maine. I lifted his statement from a book by a man named Henry Allen Moe—a great book called *The Power of Freedom*. In that book, in an essay entitled "The Future of Liberal Arts Education," Moe goes on to say that a next step, one that goes beyond contract, is now necessary, but that no one seems to know what that next step should be. Certain trends suggest that it may well be a reversion to status. But if this happens it will be a tragedy of major proportions, because most of the people in the world are waiting for some nation, some people, to provide the model for the next step. And somehow I felt, while writing the last stories in *Elbow Room*, that the condition precedent the old folks in my hometown wanted in exchange for their censoring was not just status of a conventional kind. I want to think that after having waited so long, after having seen so much, they must have at least expected some new stories that would no longer have to be censored to come out of our experience. I felt that if anything, the long experience of segregation could be looked on as a period of preparation for a next step. Those of us who are black and who have had to defend our humanity should be obliged to continue defending it, on higher and higher levels—not of power, which is a kind of tragic trap, but on higher levels of consciousness.

All of this is being said in retrospect, and I am quite aware that I am rationalizing many complex and contradictory feelings. Nevertheless, I do know that early on, during my second year of law school, I became conscious of a model of identity that might help me transcend, at least in my thinking, a provisional or racial identity. In a class in American constitutional law taught by Paul Freund, I began to play with the idea that the Fourteenth Amendment was not just a legislative instrument devised to give former slaves legal equality with other Americans. Looking at the slow but steady way in which the basic guarantees of the Bill of Rights had, through judicial interpretation, been incorporated into the clauses of that amendment, I began to see the outlines of a new identity.

You will recall that the first line of Section 1 of the Fourteenth Amendment makes an all-inclusive definition of citizenship: "All persons born or naturalized in the United States and subject to the jurisdiction thereof, are citizens of the United States. . . ." The rights guaranteed to such a citizen had themselves traveled from the provinces to the World's Fair: from the trial and error of early Anglo-Saxon folk rituals to the rights of freemen established by the Magna Carta, to their slow incorporation into early American colonial charters, and from these charters (especially George Mason's Virginia Declaration of Rights) into the U.S. Constitution as its first ten amendments. Indeed, these same rights had served as the basis for the Charter of the United Nations. I saw that through the protean uses made of the Fourteenth Amendment, in the gradual elaboration of basic rights to be protected by federal authority, an outline of something much more complex than "black" and "white" had been begun.

It was many years before I was to go to the Library of Congress and read the brief of the lawyer-novelist Albion W. Tourgée in the famous case *Plessy* v. *Ferguson*. Argued in 1896 before the United States Supreme Court, Tourgée's brief was the first meaningful attempt to breathe life into the amendment. I will quote here part of his brief, which is a very beautiful piece of literature:

> This provision of Section 1 of the Fourteenth Amendment *creates a new* citizenship of the United States embracing *new* rights, privileges and immunities, derivable in a *new* manner, controlled by *new* authority, having a *new* scope and extent, depending on national authority for its existence and looking to national power for its preservation.

Although Tourgée lost the argument before the Supreme Court, his model of citizenship—and it is not a racial one—is still the most radical idea to come out of American constitutional law. He provided the outline, the clothing, if you will, for a new level of status. What he was proposing in 1896, I think, was that each United States citizen would attempt to approximate the ideals of the nation, be on at least conversant terms with all its diversity, carry the mainstream of the culture inside himself. As an American, by trying to wear these clothes he would be a synthesis of high and low, black and white, city and country, provincial and universal. If he could live with these contradictions, he would be simply a representative American.

This was the model I was aiming for in my book of stories. It can be achieved with or without intermarriage, but it will cost a great many mistakes and a lot of pain. It is, finally, a product of culture and not of race. And achieving it will require that one be conscious of America's culture and the complexity of all its people. As I tried to point out, such a perspective would provide a minefield of delicious ironies. Why, for example, should black Americans raised in Southern culture *not* find that some of their responses are geared to country music? How else, except in terms of cultural diversity, am I to account for the white friend in Boston who taught me much of what I know of black American music? Or the white friend in Virginia who, besides developing a homegrown aesthetic he calls "crackertude," knows more about black American folklore than most black people? Or the possibility that many black people in Los Angeles have been just as much influenced by Hollywood's "star system" of the forties and fifties as they have been by society's response to the color of their skins? I wrote about people like these in *Elbow Room* because they interested me, and because they help support my belief that most of us are products of much more complex cultural influences than we suppose.

What I have said above will make little sense until certain contradictions in the nation's background are faced up to, until personal identities are allowed to partake of the complexity of the country's history as well as of its culture. Last year, a very imaginative black comedian named Richard Pryor appeared briefly on national television in his own show. He offended a great many people, and his show was canceled after only a few weeks. But I remember one episode that may emphasize my own group's confusion about its historical experience. This was a satiric takeoff on the popular television movie *Roots*, and Pryor played an African tribal historian who was selling trinkets and impromptu history to black American tourists. One tourist, a middle-class man, approached the tribal historian and said, "I want you to tell me who my great-great-granddaddy was." The African handed him a picture. The black American looked at it and said, "But that's a *white* man!" The tribal historian said, "That's right." Then the tourist said, "Well, I want you to tell me where I'm from." The tribal historian looked hard at him and said, "You're from Cleveland, nigger." I think I was trying very hard in my book to say the same thing, but not just to black people.

Today I am not the lawyer my friend in San Francisco thought I should be, but this is the record I wanted to present to him that rainy evening back in 1974. It may illustrate why the terms of my acceptance of society's offer had to be modified. I am now a writer, a person who has to learn to live with contradictions, frustrations, and doubts. Still, I have another quote that sustains me, this one from a book called *The Tragic Sense of Life*, by a Spanish philosopher named Miguel de Unamuno. In a chapter called "Don Quixote Today," Unamuno asks, "How is it that among the words the English have borrowed from our language there is to be found this word *desperado*?" And he answers himself: "It is despair, and despair alone, that begets heroic hope, absurd hope, mad hope."

I believe that the United States is complex enough to induce that sort of despair that begets heroic hope. I believe that if one can experience its diversity, touch a variety of its people, laugh at its craziness, distill wisdom from its tragedies, and attempt to synthesize all this inside oneself without going crazy, one will have earned the right to call oneself "citizen of the United States," even though one is not quite a lawyer, doctor, engineer, or accountant. If nothing else, one will have learned a few new stories and, most important, one will have begun on that necessary movement from contract to the next step, from province to the World's Fair, from a hopeless person to a desperado. I wrote about my first uncertain steps in this direction in *Elbow Room* because I have benefited from all the contracts, I have exhausted all the contracts, and at present it is the only new direction I know.

SOME ISSUES

MARGARET MEAD

The following is a chapter from Margaret Mead and Rhoda Metraux's A Way of Seeing. *For further information, see page 218.*

Race and Intelligence

In the sharply accelerating struggle of black Americans finally to achieve full, unequivocal membership in our national society, the schools are storm centers, as they have been so often in the past. Americans believe education is the key to opportunity for the individual and to progress for the nation. Inevitably, schools and the kind of education at all levels open to disadvantaged groups, especially young black Americans, are a focal point in the struggle for the recognition of diversity that is shaking the country.

The present conflict is not unique. It has its counterparts elsewhere in the world; in our own country it marks the culmination of a long series of struggles to make our ancestral diversity a source of national strength. It is the mixture of hope and despair, the bitter intransigence and the new assertiveness of young militants, that gives us a sense of uniqueness at this stage. In spite of the sound and fury, however, I think we are moving toward new, viable solutions.

But the outcome is by no means assured. We still can stumble and fail to reach the goal of creating a truly open society. The principal stumbling block is the belief, shared by many people, that Negro Americans constitute a race.

Recently an attempt has been made—one of many, past and present —to establish the claim that Negro Americans, as a race, are less intelligent than white (or other) Americans. This latest effort is set forth in a long technical article by Arthur H. Jensen, "How Much Can We Boost IQ and Scholastic Achievement?" published in the *Harvard Educational Review.* Although nominally the discussion concerns the question of the heritability of intelligence within whole groups, the fact that Negro Americans are the focus of the discussion of race differences indicates just what is at issue. The contention is that the consistently lower scores achieved by Negro Americans on tests designed to measure IQ and the impermanent effects of very short-term educational "enrichment" programs (for example, the recent Head Start projects) indicate that, as a race, they are less intelligent than other Americans.

If the conclusions were correct, it would mean that Negroes were genetically less well equipped than others to benefit from the kinds of education and training, developed in Western civilization, that open the full range of occupations to members of our own or any other contemporary society. It would mean also that the barriers of ancient prejudice that are being broken down, and not only in our country, would be replaced by new barriers apparently supported by science, and the key to opportunity would be snatched away.

But the arguments are specious. They are based on the false premise that Negro Americans represent a "race."

There are new facets to the arguments as they are presented now. But the *kind* of argument, based on the false premise of race, is an old, familiar one in the struggle to incorporate in our society (or to close the doors to) many different ethnic groups. It is illuminating to recall what happened in the past.

In the decades between 1870 and 1920, millions of immigrants surged across the country and crowded into the ghettos of our growing cities, displacing earlier comers—the Irish, the Germans and others—who were already making their way. These immigrants differed from most older Americans (as well as from one another) in appearance, language, traditions and customary behavior. Those who came, for example, from southern Europe—Italians, Greeks, Spaniards, Portuguese—and from eastern and central Europe—Poles, Russians, Ukrainians—were popularly believed to belong to different unassimilable "races."

Faced with the presence of these masses of newcomers, so many of whom were poor, illiterate and unskilled, pessimists in this country declared that with few exceptions they would always remain at the bottom of the economic and social ladder and that they would soon drag the whole country down to their low level. When intelligence tests were invented, early in the twentieth century, these provided the pessimists with new arguments. Test results showed that, comparatively, the school-age children of many immigrant groups obtained lower IQ scores than other American children. These results were interpreted as proof of the inferior intelligence of these "racial" groups.

But there were also the optimists—educators, classroom teachers, settlement workers and others, including leaders within the immigrant groups. They got down to the hard, practical task of turning the children of immigrants into Americans through education. Less directly, the adults also were transformed as children brought the new language and new ways into their homes. Some forged ahead rapidly in the schools; these belonged to ethnic groups, such as eastern European Jews, in whose traditions learning and scholarship were honored. Others, whose older way of life had cut them off from learning, gained far less from schools and tried other routes.

There were also, among the optimists, some who thought that knowledge of the backgrounds of the newer ethnic groups and of the adaptations they were making could advance the process of integration. This was my mother's hope, for example, when she made the first field study of an Italian community, in Hammonton, New Jersey.

Later, in the 1920's, when I was a student, I returned to the same community to study the relationship of speaking Italian or English in the home to children's test achievement. What I found was that the home language was related to the IQ levels attained; the scores of those speaking Italian were lower. Though all the children came from a similar background, such factors as lack of knowledge of English, lack of experience with the settings of American life and lack of motivation to do well on the tests depressed the IQ scores of the Italian-speaking group; in the English-speaking group better knowledge of the language, more familiarity with American ways of living and a greater expectation that test-taking was rewarding tended to remove inhibitions so that these children could more readily draw on their actual, individual potential.

Insights based on more accurate knowledge played a part, over a period of time, in breaking down the prejudices incorporated in popular, mistaken beliefs about ethnic groups as "races." The integration into American life of the children and grandchildren of immigrants and their achievements have made us realize how ridiculous the predictions of the pessimists were. Today we take pride in the multiplicity of ethnic traditions on which we have drawn in our culture.

Yet many Americans still hold unyieldingly to unscientific folk beliefs about race. The only thing that changes is their application. Now as in the past these mistaken ideas serve to rationalize doubts, failures to bring about assimilation and, for some, a wish to live in the past. It is clear that in every generation we must re-educate ourselves to understand the facts.

There can be no doubt that the components of intelligence, like all genetically determined traits, are inherited by the individual not from a group but from his direct ancestors—two parents, four grandparents, eight great-grandparents, and so on. In a very small population that has lived isolated from other groups for many generations, resemblances are numerous, for the range of traits that are heritable (genetically based) is relatively limited. Through marriage within the group over a long period of time everyone comes to share (though in different ways) much the same ancestry and so also (in a great variety of combinations) the potentialities of the original ancestral group. One famous modern example of a population of this kind is that of the Pitcairn Islanders in Polynesia, all of whom are descendants of two English mutineers from the *Bounty* and eleven Tahitian women who accompanied them to the island in 1790.

In contrast, in a large population the range of individual differences is very great, because of the number and diversity of ancestral lines. Yet even after a long period of isolation, the number of traits peculiar to that group is likely to be extremely small. What chiefly distinguishes two large, relatively stable populations from each other is not particular traits, but differences in the statistical distribution of traits (as, for example, the number of persons who belong to the A, AB or O blood group), which are present in both of these groups as well as in many other human populations. It is this intricate statistical patterning as it occurs in different populations to which biologists and population geneticists are referring in the technical use of the term "race."

By this scientific criterion Negro Americans are not a race at all. They form a group not by racial but by social designation: they are those individuals who have any visible African traits or, lacking these, are known or believed to have some African ancestry. They vary from individuals who may have thirty-one white ancestors and one ancestor who was African in origin, to some who have American Indian as well as African and white ancestors, and to the very few persons who, on the basis of superficial appearance, may be wholly African in descent. By inheritance they are an extraordinarily diversified group; their categorization as members of one group is entirely arbitrary.

This arbitrary social designation in the United States has carried—and in most cases still carries—a terrible burden of discrimination that has the most potent influences on health, length of life, education, economic and social opportunity and freedom of choice. The designation does not change substantially with a black American's economic circumstances or social class. Its deeply punitive effects are part of the experience that shapes the expectations of all black Americans, including what education can offer them.

The fact that, considered as a group, Negro school children, compared with their white (or other) peers, do less well on intelligence tests or tests of achievement is the definitive measure of the complex and multiple pressures to which they are continually subjected as a social group. In special circumstances of trust or hope, the inhibitions depressing their potential may lift somewhat; in circumstances of despair, the inhibitions may weigh more heavily than usual. The fact that, over time, individual Negro children's test scores tend to be consistent does not necessarily mean that we know what their potential is. It means that their feelings of denigration are fixed; all we know is what use they can make of available potential.

The newly burgeoning aspirations of black Americans and the drive for black autonomy can mean that those who have suffered most from the combination of white indifference, lack of knowledge and limited social vision can act, not only out of anger, but also with a new sense of dignity and inner strength. But I believe that the effectiveness of action will depend on our determination to bring our thinking up to date, so that we cannot be misled by the assertions of provincial, naïve or bigoted experts nor even welcome the drive for black autonomy for the wrong reasons.

I would like to think that schools and colleges and universities, where so many contenders in this and other conflicts meet, will be able to carry the major responsibility for creating a community of all Americans. For however inadequate, neglected or downright bad particular schools and school systems may be, our American belief in the value of education carries with it a kind of idealism that finds expression in responsible action and concrete results.

But there is also the danger that an overemphasis on education as the instrument of change may blind us to the necessary involvement of the whole community in bringing about change. Education *alone*, no matter how carefully planned and sustained, cannot change people's destinies. Education can only implement what the members of a society are carrying out in their way of life. It is in our communities that social denigration of black Americans must end; we must broaden our conception of what is involved in community—the community of all Americans.

For it was not the schools, or the schools alone, that made it possible for the children of immigrants in the past to become part of the mainstream of American life; it is not the schools alone that have failed in the task of helping disadvantaged black American children to realize their potential. It is the state of our beliefs, individually and collectively, on which the creation of an open society depends, and this in turn depends, I am convinced, on the matching of belief and reality through scientific knowledge.

[September 1969]

ROBERT COLES

Robert Coles is a psychiatrist concerned with problems of poverty and discrimination. He was born in New England in 1929, attended Harvard, received a medical degree at Columbia, and then trained in child psychiatry, following the direction pointed by Anna Freud and Erik Erikson. After completing his residency, he became head of an air-force neuropsychiatric hospital in Biloxi, Mississippi. In 1961 he returned to the South to study the psychiatric aspects of school desegregation. His work with both children and adults is vividly described in Children of Crisis: A Study of Courage and Fear *(1967), the first volume of an award-winning series. The next two volumes,* Migrants, Sharecroppers, Mountaineers *(1971) and* The South Goes North *(1971), tell of his work with migrant and tenant-farm children, and with northern city and ghetto children; both were awarded a Pulitzer Prize. The final volumes in the series are* Eskimos, Chicanos, Indians *(1978) and* Privileged Ones: The Well-Off and the Rich in America *(1978).*

Coles is a prolific writer of magazine articles, reviews, and books, including Still Hungry in America *(1969); the intellectual biography* Erik H. Erikson, The Growth of His Work *(1970); the conversations with Daniel Berrigan when underground* Geography of Faith *(1971); and together with his wife, Jane Halowell Coles,* Women of Crisis: Lives of Struggle and Hope *(1978). All his work is characterized by the need and struggle to understand the lives of others and his awareness of just how difficult that is, how we must constantly be on guard against our own preconceptions, our own jargon, and all the other ways in which we keep ourselves from seeing and knowing. The article we print here, based on a Phi Beta Kappa address given at Harvard University in 1975, first appeared in* Harvard Magazine, *September 1975.*

Boston and the South

Until recently, a Bostonian who went South and involved him- or herself in that region's vexing racial issues had to be prepared for a number of strong and by no means consistent responses: quick resentment, plaintive self-justification, a certain awe and envy, a touch of shame or humiliation, and, not least, a measure of curiosity.

Best known of these responses is resentment: who is this outsider, one in an apparently endless series, to speak so surely and insistently about people and circumstances that ought to require careful, on-the-spot inquiry rather than immediate, unqualified comments, usually of the scornful kind?

But even the staunchest defenders of the Southern status quo had to contend with slavery and later, segregation. Angry attacks on meddlesome "outsiders" or "agitators" from within, endless salutes to a way of life that had obvious virtues, clever recitals from selected passages in the Bible or from various historians, biologists, social essayists—none of those psychological and intellectual maneuvers could quite shake off an everpresent reality: one group of human beings was terribly at the mercy of the economic and political power of another group. So, even amid the most truculent and uninhibited defenses of Southern customs, one might often be taken aback by the candor of the speaker, and, occasionally, by the scarcely concealed moral torment demonstrated—or denied at great emotional cost.

A lawyer who is a prominent member of the Mississippi White Citizens' Council could talk this way to a Bostonian in 1960, when any possibility of integration in the Delta seemed far off: "I'd die to defend our life here. I've been up North, but I'm always glad to get back—the sooner the better. I wish people would leave us alone. We get all this advice from Yankees. What do they know about the true situation down here? They come up with their cheap advice, but we have to live with each other, the colored and the white, and it's not easy. We're two different races, and you'll never be able to get around that. I believe in being fair; I don't want to be mean to anyone, no matter the race of the person. Sometimes I'll see some of our poor colored folks standing outside their cabins, or on the street in town, half-drunk, and I could cry for them. I speak to our ancestors: why did you ever bring them over here in the first place?"

In fact, the man's wife points out, his particular ancestors weren't responsible for bringing any blacks over here. His father worked as a teller in a bank—a great step upward for him. His grandfather was a tenant farmer, not unlike the kind James Agee described in *Let Us Now Praise Famous Men*—hard-working, self-reliant, obstinate and reticent one minute, generous and thoughtful the next, and, above all, desperately vulnerable and poor. And before the grandfather there were others, a long line of impoverished yeomen who came to Mississippi—at one time part of the "West"—from Pennsylvania, as a matter of fact. By that time, no more slaves were being brought into this country. Nor has anyone in the man's family, at any time, owned slaves or even employed blacks, apart from the black woman who helps his wife three days a week. Yet, he talks as if he and his kin, going back over the generations, were personally responsible for an entire social and economic system. A region's history and traditions have been taken over by this person, lock, stock, and barrel—made into an important element of the individual's self-appraisal.

At the same time there is implicit, and occasionally explicit, dissent from those traditions. The man is not blind to suffering or injustice; rather, he is inclined to notice them out of the corner of his eye, while at the same time venting his rage at outsiders, who have arrived with the avowed purpose of making him look longer and harder at the world he, as a lawyer, feels very much a part of. Soon enough, therefore, he goes on the offensive, as have many other Southerners in the course of this century and the one before it. He forgets his own perceptions, denies himself the capacity for even-handed social observation, allows himself to defend a status quo he only partially wants to uphold and goes after the Yankees even more strenuously than he has done in the quotation above. *They* are responsible for the trouble his beloved region has had to endure; *they* are arrogant, self-centered, interfering, and, most of all, thoroughly ignorant, thoroughly insensitive, for all their traditional credentials and their claim to compassion. Meanwhile, his own vision and good judgment, his social acuity and his power to transcend his own "background" and self-interest, are all temporarily forsaken. A man who never wanted to join an organization like the White Citizens' Council becomes a member, mouths its defensive pieties, even, upon occasion, rants ignorantly, though he always would stop short of advocating "violence."

As for the outsiders he and others railed against, they seemed to have few doubts or qualms. Their cause was just, their ideals high, their willingness to put themselves on the line—even to the point of risking their lives—quite obvious. In the early 1960s they were mostly young men and women, often college students. As the civil-rights movement reached what some consider its climax—the Mississippi Summer Project of 1964—the number of white, Northern, middle-class students increased enormously, to the point that some Southern activists, both black and white, with an outlook and experience vastly different from the Northerners', began to feel the world closing in. On the one hand, there were segregationists, unyielding and hateful; on the other hand, rather well-to-do, urbane, bright, analytical, and articulate "friends," who had a way of intimidating as well as puzzling a person born on a Georgia farm or in an Alabama small town, and reared in the quiet, self-effacing, relaxed tradition that Ralph Ellison has insisted belongs to the black man's as well as the white man's South.

Eventually there would be an explosion. And while its racial aspects have been correctly stressed and discussed, there were other grounds for friction, rising distrust, and, in the end, outright antagonism. A black youth, on leave from Miles College in Birmingham, Alabama, to take part in the activities of the Student Non-Violent Coordinating Committee (SNCC) would observe in 1965: "I've had it with these Northern students. They come down here to help us get free of the segregationists, but they become the new bossmen! Talk, talk—they're full of talk. They have an *idea* about everything. They're full of themselves: I've never met people who think they're so much better than everyone else. They almost make you feel on the side of the enemy! I watched some students from the North talking to a white lady in the post office. She's worked there a long time, and she may be a segregationist, but she's polite to us [blacks] when we go buy stamps or envelopes.

There were three students there, one from Massachusetts and two from New York. They were rude to her. They kept throwing arguments at her. They wouldn't let her go. And the way they talked about Alabama and the South—well, *I'm* from Alabama and the South! My older brother, he's a janitor, and he never went to college and he didn't finish high school. I brought those three home, and my brother listened to them. Later he told me, 'listen here, you'd better send them back where they come from. They're not the ones to help us down here!' "

There was more, much more; and it would be hard for any sociologist or psychiatrist, let alone an ordinary, interested, sensible human being, to disentangle the themes that kept coming up, one after the other, in the course of that youth's remarks and those of many others like him. Racial suspicions and doubts mingled freely with class-connected envies and resentments. All the attitudes that were (and still are, at least in rural and small-town Alabama) distinctively Southern kept company with other attitudes, ones that belonged, after all, to anyone who regards even a medium-sized city like Birmingham—never mind Boston or New York—as a strange, difficult, and confusing place to live. The young man, who would go on to become an attorney in a southern Alabama town, fell back repeatedly and without qualification on his brother's remarks: the Northern students ought to go home, and if they are intent on helping the black cause, they ought to do their work right in their own back yards, and maybe on their front lawns, too. One can all too easily go slumming by day in the big cities of the North, and retire at night to a pleasant suburban town or a well-protected upper-middle-class enclave within a city.

In no time, it seemed, the civil-rights movement—or at least one phase of it—had given way to other social and political struggles. Northern students, and teachers, too, were in significant numbers protesting against our military policy in Vietnam. The South was left changed, unquestionably, through the work of those students. But the long haul of social and political progress—the bargaining, the voting, the pressures, arrangements, threats and promises—would be the work of Southerners, black and white, to the point that, for all its continuing inequities (a large number of poor, both black and white), the South can now claim that in certain respects the goals of the civil-rights movement have been more realized in, say, Auburn, Alabama, or Greenville, Mississippi, than in Boston, Massachusetts.

Certainly the schools are better integrated in many towns of the rural South than in our large Northern cities. And that integration has not always meant large-scale residential shifts—white flight to avoid federal court orders. The South is not now, any more than it ever was (despite its various apologists, some of them Northern), a place where black and white people "really" know one another and "really" get along well. Slavery, and then segregation, prompted all kinds of social deceptions, an elaborate network of bluff, guile, pretense. Yet, one heard strange defenses, or at least partial defenses, of the South, even from militant blacks, so angered had they become by the condescension (and plain ignorance) of their Yankee visitors and allies. "Up North there's a lot of lip service to integration, but blacks and whites stay clear of each other. Up North white liberals talk big—about other people's problems down South. Well, down here blacks and whites grow up knowing each other and living side by side. They're not equal. They're completely unequal legally and socially and economically and politically. We're a caste. But there's a lot of contact; we know how to talk with each other and we've *lived* with each other—slept with each other, worked together. It's been a rotten, exploitative system, but we're not cut off personally from the whites. Up North, they hardly ever lay eyes on each other, black and white people."

Those words were spoken by a black youth in 1964, at a tense, strife-ridden meeting of SNCC, when in fact the organization was becoming torn apart by various tensions, most of them racial but a number generated by the differences in background and assumptions between Northern activists and those who were born and had lived all their lives in the South. Perhaps even *he* was romanticizing the South a bit; it is hard for many not to—including, certainly, black people, who in anger, disgust, and outrage have gladly left the region for a city like Chicago or Detroit, only to begin to wonder, later on, whether one set of awful disadvantages has not been exchanged for a handful of empty promises. There is, accordingly, an increasing return of blacks to the South—still quite small, but not without significance. And anyone who lives in the region knows that many black people who return to visit kin lament as well as boast: "I'm doing fine—or I was; I had a good job up there, until I lost it. I never could have gotten that good a job down here. No, sir. Up there, if you leave the white man alone, he'll leave you alone. When times are good, they're much better up there than here, jobwise, moneywise. There's no sheriff on your back, either. But now we have a black sheriff down here, and we have a lot of our family that didn't leave. And we always missed our life here. We had to go, but we would have stayed if we could have found work and not be always fearing the white man and what he might do. My sister, she never left. She just couldn't tear herself away. I wrote her and I wrote her from Detroit, but no, she wouldn't go along with me. And now I figure it this way: she's not so well off, and I've lost my job, and it's no good being a black man or black woman in this country."

An observation, the last one, that transcends all regional distinctions in its applicability; so one had best not use a man's—or a people's—disenchantment with one experience (up North) as a clever means of blurring still prevalent exploitation, bias, social exclusion, and economic injustice in the South. But when all the demurrers have been made, one is left with the day's news—and a spectacle it is, these days. And if that news includes, within recent memory, Dr. King's grim experience in Cicero, Illinois, the terrible riots in or near Cleveland, New York City, Los Angeles, as well as serious school-integration difficulties in cities like Denver, San Francisco, Detroit, or Philadelphia, then surely it has been especially ironic that Boston, in the middle of 1975, enjoys the reputation nationally as the most seriously, and some would say the most intractably, troubled city of them all. It is a place where mobs have once again (evoking the nightmares of Little Rock, Clinton, Tennessee, and New Orleans) confronted and endangered black children, whose parents have desperately wanted for them, in a word, *out*: an escape from overcrowded, inadequate schools and, more broadly from the mean, brutish, utterly unpromising life of the ghetto, where (it must be stated again and again, especially today) from a third to a half of black youths are unable to find any work, no matter how hard they try.

Boston, where abolitionist periodicals were published and where antislavery societies regularly met in the nineteenth century, the city whose metropolitan area includes Harvard and a number of other important and respected universities. Boston, still known all over the country as a cultured, refined place, the home of first-rate museums, a fine symphony orchestra, an active theater life, an interesting art and dance world, a good newspaper or two, a progressive business climate, and, not least, a tradition of support for liberal political leaders from both national parties. And Boston, the capital of Massachusetts, the only state to turn its back, in 1972, on Richard Nixon and—one has to mention—the city that was home, or temporary home (by virtue of affiliation with a college or university), for a large number of the civil-rights activists who went South in the 1960s.

But the point is not to savor an irony, delicious though it may be to some of the South's white people, and maybe not a few of its blacks. The point is to try to understand not only Boston's historical and continuing relationship to the South (moralistic, scolding preacher, military invader, stern and punitive conqueror, economic exploiter) but to the various immigrants who came to New England in the nineteenth and twentieth centuries. And it is important to ask *which* Boston did the preaching to the South, or profited economically from money invested in Southern utilities, or from the rates set for interstate railroad transport.

The white Southerner quoted above has his opposite up North in Boston—a man from South Boston who also has irrational racial fears but is as anxious to disown a regional heritage as the man from Mississippi is to claim one uncritically. I showed a factory worker from South Boston—Irish, married, and the father of five children, the oldest of whom attends South Boston High School—various letters I had received from Southern friends, gently but firmly and appropriately pointing out the resemblance of Boston's present school-desegregation struggle to the worst episodes the South went through. He managed no wry, philosophical smile, demonstrated no tolerant, good-humored acceptance of history's mysterious ways. Instead, he pointed out to me some historical facts, reminded me of Boston's past and present in a manner that cannot be dismissed as merely polemical. He was being a shrewd social scientist, and, too, I later realized, he had a grasp of historical ironies, ambiguities, inconsistencies, and complexities utterly worthy of that ultimate term of sanction in the university: scholarly.

"What part of Boston are those Southern pals of yours referring to?" After giving me a second to mull over an answer to his question, he began to give me an answer—and a lesson or two. "Not the Boston I grew up in. We weren't the ones who waved our fingers at the South before the Civil War, and went down there to fight, and came back proud of ourselves. My ancestors were half starving to death in Ireland at that time, or getting ready to come over here. And when they did come here, they were treated like scum, as everybody knows. Even ten years ago, we weren't the ones who were sending our kids South to join the civil-rights movement. Those were college kids—from Harvard and places like that. I graduated from South Boston High School, and there was a time that I thought my children would graduate from there, and my grandchildren, though I don't know about that now. And I'll tell you, the kids from Southie don't go to Harvard and don't go South to fight for the colored people, and don't try to protest against their own government by calling it every name in the book and glorifying the dictatorships we're opposed to. The kids from Southie have to work during high school, and they try to get jobs, if they can, as soon as they graduate— if they do. Some just drop out. We're poor here, a lot of us. This is no suburb. This is no Beacon Hill or Back Bay. This is no Brattle Street, off Harvard Square.

"My brother works for the telephone company. He moved out of here. He's lucky. He lives in Watertown. They're working people out there, too— but a little better off. But even the people where he lives haven't the money to keep up with their bills, and to buy a good future for their kids. My brother says the people near Harvard—the professors and doctors and lawyers and fat-cat businessmen—their kids, a lot of them, don't go to Cambridge public schools. They go to fancy private schools and they have nice summer homes and all the rest. Well, who has the money to afford those private schools? Not us. And if we even mention trying to form our own private schools here in South Boston, then they tell us we're trying to 'evade the federal court order' and we're 'racists.' But if rich people send their children to private school, they're not trying to 'evade' anything. Or anybody, like us people here! Oh, no! They're just trying to give their children the 'best education possible,' that's what my brother hears them say—and he's no professor, but he can listen with his ears and he can figure out what he hears. Sometimes you wonder if some of those people who teach in the universities haven't lost all touch with the rest of the people of this country."

He stops. He apologizes for a strongly stated, emotional outburst, for his unqualified generalizations. In a touching moment of self-criticism (and how many of "us," so comfortable and well-educated in comparison with him, are taught to look skeptically at our own assumptions and beliefs?) he acknowledges blind spots, inadequacies, personal failures. He declares himself poorly educated. He admits that he has "never known any colored people, only seen them in the street." He admits that he and others he knows "probably have a prejudice against the colored." He admits that "if the world were a better world, people wouldn't be prejudiced." He also admits, quite candidly, that he is afraid—quite afraid, indeed. He is afraid that he will lose the only savings he has, the value of his small house; he is

afraid that his neighborhood will lose whatever intactness it has; he is afraid
of strangers, of the crime and chaos they will (to his mind) bring with them.
He is not about to deny the considerable delinquency and other violence
that his neighborhood already possesses; it is, as he reminds his listener, "a
place where the people, they're barely getting by—and a lot not even that."
There certainly may be more violence, he allows, in South Boston, especially these days, than one finds in upper-middle-class suburbs.

But a moment later he decides to change his mind. He remembers what
he has read and heard about those suburbs, what his brother has seen in the
course of doing his work: drugs, aimless youth, wanton destructiveness, arrogant self-centeredness, and , not least, plenty of prejudices and provinciali-
ties—maybe not of the kind he owns up to, but enough of them, as he puts
it, "for the people who look down at us, as if we're so awful, to deserve being
called hypocrites." And in a last, pointed thrust, he asks his visitor a question. He prefaces it with yet another self-effacing acknowledgment: he never
went to college, nor will his children. But he can't help wondering about the
abolitionists, and about those like them today: "I'll bet a lot of the people
from Boston who were against slavery a long time ago, I'll bet they didn't
get so worked up about the way people in the factories around Boston were
being treated. Did the people who were against slavery worry about what
was going on right under their eyes? Was it easier for them to shout about
something going on a thousand or two thousand miles away?"

Thus does a white Northerner become, at least for a moment, a white
Southerner. He can with justice, at certain moments, be taken up on his
own, self-acknowledged limitations and inadequacies, his outright intolerance. He need not be romanticized—the noble, proletarian worker. But he
also ought not to be regarded as mere putty in the hands of various rightist
politicians or demagogues, who have nothing to offer him and others like
him but the futile and self-destructive satisfaction of bigotry. As a number of
social observers and union organizers have wisely reminded us (the idiotic
caricatures of television's evening-time soap operas notwithstanding), the
blue-collar workers of places like South Boston did better by George Mc-
Govern in 1972 than many of our suburbs did, despite the objections a large
number of those same workers may have had to the kind of campaign Mr.
McGovern waged (he carried South Boston's wards). If white and black
poor people all over the country are indeed one day turned into political
enemies—that is, if the fears and frustrations and suspicions and antago-
nisms of both races are consolidated into two forces—then the South really
will have bequeathed us the worst aspect of its long, sad, and continuing
racial struggle.

Meanwhile, it may be of interest to some of us Northern middle-class
intellectuals to ask ourselves a few of the questions that the factory worker
suggested directly or by implication. If there is racism in Mississippi and
Alabama and South Boston and Cicero, Illinois—as there most assuredly
is—what is to be said about those parts of our country where well-to-do,
well-educated people live? Are they free of racism, of snobbery, condescen-

sion, arrogance, vanity? Or are their blemishes, if not serious character flaws, hidden by the cozy power of money and privilege and only revealed in more fashionable attitudes, in the wholesale scorn, for instance, that recently went into words like "pig" or "fascist," or in the blanket denunciation of *all* white Southerners, which was, finally, seen by many Southern blacks as an ignorant form of self-satisfaction? And what about those Boston abolitionists—were they indeed all worked up against the South's injustices, but unwilling to move north and west to Massachusetts factory cities like Lowell, Lawrence, Haverhill, or into the heart of Boston's slums, in order to see how thousands of immigrants, including young children, were working from dawn to dusk for a pittance, victims of a severe, unrelenting economic slavery? Weren't some of those abolitionists rather complacent about the fate of the Irish masses (whose condition in Boston Oscar Handlin has so powerfully portrayed in *The Uprooted*)? These abolitionists were not *political* Know-Nothings, but rather, at least some, prominent educated people who found Boston's poor Irish, and later its Italians and Jews, "ignorant" or "rude" or "vulgar."

And for those of us who live near or work in and deeply respect Harvard University for the heritage of ideas it has offered this nation, there are other questions. Do we find it easier to extend our sympathies and generosity (of money, volunteer activity, practical knowledge) to people thousands of miles away than to look around the corner at the working people of Cambridge and Boston? A question like that touches upon vexing issues, and one hopes they do not lend themselves to easy, smug, self-protective answers—the familiar dichotomy of "us" against "them" that each of us is quite capable of falling back upon. They are issues that have to do with race and class *both*, with the power of tradition to remain stubbornly close to us, influencing at every turn our loyalties and sympathies, our sense of who deserves whatever compassion we can muster and who deserves the scorn or contempt that none of us is entirely without. The black people of Boston or Cambridge, like their kinfolk in the South, need friends whose sympathy and activist commitment is not purchased at the price of the worst expressions of noblesse oblige: a disdain for those of their own race who are "lower" socially and economically, accompanied by a hard-to-believe readiness to mobilize friendship or "understanding" for almost any black person anywhere, no matter his or her faults, vices, wrongdoing. (No wonder Chicago's brilliant, forceful, outrageously candid black leader, Jesse Jackson, among others, is getting tired of what he has described as the endless "patronization of black people at the hands of upper-middle-class liberal intelligentsia.")

The white people of Boston, not to mention its suburbs, and, of course, the South—indeed, people of all races—could do worse than look at themselves as intently as the factory worker quoted earlier sometimes (and *only* sometimes) manages to do. Maybe we can—if only for a moment—also manage the same luminous good judgment about our various situations that some of our best social observers have succeeded in demonstrating, from James Agee in the rural South of the 1930s to Paul Cowan in the Boston, Queens, New York, and West Virginia of the 1970s. After all, both Agee and Cowan learned from others—ordinary people who, it turned out, had a lot of valuable and sensible things to say. Agee and Cowan listened to those people, turned their thoughts and reflections back on themselves, and thereby examined their own assumptions; in so doing, they got an extraordinary education for themselves.

But maybe it is the novelist who is best equipped by temperament, sensibility, and craft to do that kind of job for him- or herself and the rest of us—to show us our conceits and deceits, our pretensions and self-deceptions, as well as our decent, honorable strivings (the two sides of us so often inseparable). The so-called "rednecks" of the South, its yeomen farmers and hard-pressed working people, have been unforgettably evoked by Flannery O'Connor in her hard, tough, shrewd, unnerving stories, both unforgiving yet redemptive in their effect. It is not hard to transpose some of her stories North to South Boston, for all their obvious localism. In working-class neighborhoods near our Northern cities one finds the same driven, embattled souls whose malice and small, daily triumphs—the two often unnervingly linked—she was so wonderful at portraying.

I wonder, though, whether her likes will one day grace the lives of those of us, reasonably well-to-do and proudly well-educated, who have it in our power to call others names they may well deserve—reactionaries, racists, Babbitts, and on and on—while reserving for ourselves immunity from sarcasm, condemnation, and the subtle and not so subtle assaults that "analysis" and "theoretical models" can visit upon people in the name of "science" or "objectivity" or "research" (certainly including the kind, like mine, that is called "participant observation"). No doubt about it, Flannery O'Connor could be mercilessly disdainful of Northern intellectuals, whom she singled out repeatedly and, it can justifiably be maintained, with wrongheaded prejudice. In her company during the past half-century one finds others—James Agee, George Orwell, Walker Percy, George Bernanos, Simone Weil, and even, for all her Catholic modesty and piety, Dorothy Day—intellectuals or social activists of strongly reformist political sympathies who have felt it necessary to turn on the narrowness of their own kind. Such a tendency can indeed provoke danger, can be needlessly self-lacerating, grossly unjust, and can become an unfortunate part of a long anti-intellectual tradition in this and other nations. But, given the degree of self-importance and self-righteousness around us these days, and their hurtful potential, one can hardly regard the danger of overly scrupulous self-examination among the intellectuals as one of the serious threats that now stand in our way.

RICHARD RODRIGUEZ

This essay first appeared in California Monthly, *March 1978. For further information about the author, see page 359.*

None of This Is Fair

My plan to become a professor of English—my ambition during long years in college at Stanford, then in graduate school at Columbia and Berkeley—was complicated by feelings of embarrassment and guilt. So many times I would see other Mexican-Americans and know we were alike only in race. And yet, simply because our race was the same, I was, during the last years of my schooling, the beneficiary of their situation. Affirmative Action programs had made it all possible. The disadvantages of others permitted my promotion; the absence of many Mexican-Americans from academic life allowed my designation as a "minority student."

For me opportunities had been extravagant. There were fellowships, summer research grants, and teaching assistantships. After only two years in graduate school, I was offered teaching jobs by several colleges. Invitations to Washington conferences arrived and I had the chance to travel abroad as a "Mexican-American representative." The benefits were often, however, too gaudy to please. In three published essays, in conversations with teachers, in letters to politicians and at conferences, I worried the issue of Affirmative Action. Often I proposed contradictory opinions. Though consistent was the admission that—because of an early, excellent education—I was no longer a principal victim of racism or any other social oppression. I said that but still I continued to indicate on applications for financial aid that I was a Hispanic-American. It didn't really occur to me to say anything else, or to leave the question unanswered.

Thus I complied with and encouraged the odd bureaucratic logic of Affirmative Action. I let government officials treat the disadvantaged condition of many Mexican-Americans with my advancement. Each fall my presence was noted by Health, Education, and Welfare department statisticians. As I pursued advanced literary studies and learned the skill of reading Spenser and Wordsworth and Empson, I would hear myself numbered among the culturally disadvantaged. Still, silent, I didn't object.

But the irony cut deep. And guilt would not be evaded by averting my glance when I confronted a face like my own in a crowd. By late 1975, nearing the completion of my graduate studies at Berkeley, I was so wary of the benefits of Affirmative Action that I feared my inevitable success as an applicant for a teaching position. The months of fall—traditionally that time of academic job-searching—passed without my applying to a single school. When one of my professors chanced to learn this in late November, he was astonished, then furious. He yelled at me: Did I think that because I was a minority student jobs would just come looking for me? What was I thinking? Did I realize that he and several other faculty members had already written letters on my behalf? Was I going to start acting like some other minority students he had known? They struggled for success and then, when it was almost within reach, grew strangely afraid and let it pass. Was that it? Was I determined to fail?

I did not respond to his questions. I didn't want to admit to him, and thus to myself, the reason I delayed.

I merely agreed to write to several schools. (In my letter I wrote: "I cannot claim to represent disadvantaged Mexican-Americans. The very fact that I am in a position to apply for this job should make that clear.") After two or three days, there were telegrams and phone calls, invitations to interviews, then airplane trips. A blur of faces and the murmur of their soft questions. And, over someone's shoulder, the sight of campus buildings shadowing pictures I had seen years before when I leafed through Ivy League catalogues with great expectations. At the end of each visit, interviewers would smile and wonder if I had any questions. A few times I quietly wondered what advantage my race had given me over other applicants. But that was an impossible question for them to answer without embarrassing me. Quickly, several persons insisted that my ethnic identity had given me no more than a "foot inside the door"; at most, I had a "slight edge" over other applicants. "We just looked at your dossier with extra care and we like what we saw. There was never any question of having to alter our standards. You can be certain of that."

In the early part of January, offers arrived on stiffly elegant stationery. Most schools promised terms appropriate for any new assistant professor. A few made matters worse—and almost more tempting—by offering more: the use of university housing; an unusually large starting salary; a reduced teaching schedule. As the stack of letters mounted, my hesitation increased. I started calling department chairmen to ask for another week, then 10 more days—"more time to reach a decision"—to avoid the decision I would need to make.

At school, meantime, some students hadn't received a single job offer. One man, probably the best student in the department, did not even get a request for his dossier. He and I met outside a classroom one day and he asked about my opportunities. He seemed happy for me. Faculty members beamed. They said they had expected it. "After all, not many schools are going to pass up getting a Chicano with a Ph.D. in Renaissance literature," somebody said laughing. Friends wanted to know which of the offers I was going to accept. But I couldn't make up my mind. February came and I was running out of time and excuses. (One chairman guessed my delay was a bargaining ploy and increased his offer with each of my calls.) I had to promise a decision by the 10th; the 12th at the very latest.

On the 18th of February, late in the afternoon, I was in the office I shared with several other teaching assistants. Another graduate student was sitting across the room at his desk. When I got up to leave, he looked over to say in an uneventful voice that he had some big news. He had finally decided to accept a position at a faraway university. It was not a job he especially wanted, he admitted. But he had to take it because there hadn't been any other offers. He felt trapped, and depressed, since his job would separate him from his young daughter.

I tried to encourage him by remarking that he was lucky at least to have found a job. So many others hadn't been able to get anything. But before I finished speaking I realized that I had said the wrong thing. And I anticipated his next question.

"What are your plans?" he wanted to know. "Is it true you've gotten an offer from Yale?"

I said that it was. "Only, I still haven't made up my mind."

He stared at me as I put on my jacket. And smiling, then unsmiling, he asked if I knew that he too had written to Yale. In his case, however, no one had bothered to acknowledge his letter with even a postcard. What did I think of that?

He gave me no time to answer.

"Damn!" he said sharply and his chair rasped the floor as he pushed himself back. Suddenly, it was to *me* that he was complaining. "It's just not right, Richard. None of this is fair. You've done some good work, but so have I. I'll bet our records are just about equal. But when we look for jobs this year, it's a different story. You get all of the breaks."

To evade his criticism, I wanted to side with him. I was about to admit the injustice of Affirmative Action. But he went on, his voice hard with accusation. "It's all very simple this year. You're a Chicano. And I am a Jew. That's the only real difference between us."

His words stung me: there was nothing he was telling me that I didn't know. I had admitted everything already. But to hear someone else say these things, and in such an accusing tone, was suddenly hard to take. In a deceptively calm voice, I responded that he had simplified the whole issue. The phrases came like bubbles to the tip of my tongue: "new blood"; "the importance of cultural diversity"; "the goal of racial integration." These were all the arguments I had proposed several years ago—and had long since abandoned. Of course the offers were unjustifiable. I knew that. All I was saying amounted to a frantic self-defense. I tried to find an end to a sentence. My voice faltered to a stop.

"Yeah, sure," he said. "I've heard all that before. Nothing you say really changes the fact that Affirmative Action is unfair. You see that, don't you? There isn't any way for me to compete with you. Once there were quotas to keep my parents out of certain schools; now there are quotas to get you in and the effect on me is the same as it was for them."

I listened to every word he spoke. But my mind was really on something else. I knew at that moment that I would reject all of the offers. I stood there silently surprised by what an easy conclusion it was. Having prepared for so many years to teach, having trained myself to do nothing else, I had hesitated out of practical fear. But now that it was made, the decision came with relief. I immediately knew I had made the right choice.

My colleague continued talking and I realized that he was simply right. Affirmative Action programs *are* unfair to white students. But as I listened to him assert his rights, I thought of the seriously disadvantaged. How different they were from white, middle-class students who come armed with the testimony of their grades and aptitude scores and self-confidence to complain about the unequal treatment they now receive. I listen to them. I do not want to be careless about what they say. Their rights are important to protect. But inevitably when I hear them or their lawyers, I think about the most seriously disadvantaged, not simply Mexican-Americans, but of all those who do not ever imagine themselves going to college or becoming doctors: white, black, brown. Always poor. Silent. They are not plaintiffs before the court or against the misdirection of Affirmative Action. They lack the confidence (my confidence!) to assume their right to a good education. They lack the confidence and skills a good primary and secondary education provides and which are prerequisites for informed public life. They remain silent.

The debate drones on and surrounds them in stillness. They are distant, faraway figures like the boys I have seen peering down from freeway overpasses in some other part of town.

JAMES BALDWIN

James Baldwin was born in Harlem in 1924, the oldest of nine children, and graduated from DeWitt Clinton High School, where he was editor of the literary magazine. After the death of his father in 1943 he lived in Greenwich Village, working by day as handyman, office boy, or factory worker, and writing at night. A Rosenwald Fellowship received in 1948 enabled him to go to Paris, where he wrote his first two novels, Go Tell It on the Mountain *(1953) and* Giovanni's Room *(1956), and the essays published as* Notes of a Native Son *(1955). The piece that gives the collection its name, reprinted below, is an autobiographical masterpiece.*

In 1957 Baldwin returned to America and since then has continued his literary career with novels, plays, and essays. Baldwin has won many awards, among them a Guggenheim Fellowship (1954), a Partisan Review *Fellowship (1956), and The National Institute for Arts and Letters Award (1956).* Nobody Knows My Name, *a collection of essays, was selected as one of the outstanding books of 1961 by The American Library Association.* The Fire Next Time *(1963)—two searing articles, or letters, on the relationship between black and white Americans—secures Baldwin's lasting reputation both as essayist and as commentator on American culture. Later writings include the plays* Blues for Mr. Charlie *(1964) and* Paul Robeson *(1978); the novels* Tell Me How Long the Train's Been Gone *(1968),* If Beale Street Could Talk *(1974), and* Just Above My Head *(1979); an autobiographical polemic,* No Name in the Street *(1972); and an essay,* The Devil Finds Work *(1976).*

Notes of a Native Son

On the 29th of July, in 1943, my father died. On the same day, a few hours later, his last child was born. Over a month before this, while all our energies were concentrated in waiting for these events, there had been, in Detroit, one of the bloodiest race riots of the century. A few hours after my father's funeral, while he lay in state in the undertaker's chapel, a race riot broke out in Harlem. On the morning of the 3rd of August, we drove my father to the graveyard through a wilderness of smashed plate glass.

The day of my father's funeral had also been my nineteenth birthday. As we drove him to the graveyard, the spoils of injustice, anarchy, discontent, and hatred were all around us. It seemed to me that God himself had devised, to mark my father's end, the most sustained and brutally dissonant of codas. And it seemed to me, too, that the violence which rose all about us as my father left the world had been devised as a corrective for the pride of his eldest son. I had declined to believe in that apocalypse which had been central to my father's vision; very well, life seemed to be saying, here is something that will certainly pass for an apocalypse until the real thing comes along. I had inclined to be contemptuous of my father for the conditions of his life, for the conditions of our lives. When his life had ended I began to wonder about that life and also, in a new way, to be apprehensive about my own.

I had not known my father very well. We had got on badly, partly because we shared, in our different fashions, the vice of stubborn pride. When he was dead I realized that I had hardly ever spoken to him. When he had been dead a long time I began to wish I had. It seems to be typical of life in America, where opportunities, real and fancied, are thicker than anywhere else on the globe, that the second generation has no time to talk to the first. No one, including my father, seems to have known exactly how old he was, but his mother had been born during slavery. He was of the first generation of free men. He, along with thousands of other Negroes, came North after 1919 and I was part of that generation which had never seen the landscape of what Negroes sometimes call the Old Country.

He had been born in New Orleans and had been a quite young man there during the time that Louis Armstrong, a boy, was running errands for the dives and honky-tonks of what was always presented to me as one of the most wicked of cities—to this day, whenever I think of New Orleans, I also helplessly think of Sodom and Gomorrah. My father never mentioned Louis Armstrong, except to forbid us to play his records; but there was a picture of him on our wall for a long time. One of my father's strong-willed female relatives had placed it there and forbade my father to take it down. He never did, but he eventually maneuvered her out of the house and when, some years later, she was in trouble and near death, he refused to do anything to help her.

He was, I think, very handsome. I gather this from photographs and from my own memories of him, dressed in his Sunday best and on his way to preach a sermon somewhere, when I was little. Handsome, proud, and ingrown, "like a toe-nail," somebody said. But he looked to me, as I grew older, like pictures I had seen of African tribal chieftains: he really should have been naked, with war-paint on and barbaric mementos, standing among spears. He could be chilling in the pulpit and indescribably cruel in his personal life and he was certainly the most bitter man I have ever met; yet it must be said that there was something else in him, buried in him, which lent him his tremendous power and, even, a rather crushing charm. It had something to do with his blackness, I think—he was very black—with his blackness and his beauty, and with the fact that he knew that he was black but did not know that he was beautiful. He claimed to be proud of his blackness but it had also been the cause of much humiliation and it had fixed bleak boundaries to his life. He was not a young man when we were growing up and he had already suffered many kinds of ruin; in his outrageously demanding and protective way he loved his children, who were black like him and menaced, like him; and all these things sometimes showed in his face when he tried, never to my knowledge with any success, to establish contact with any of us. When he took one of his children on his knee to play, the child always became fretful and began to cry; when he tried to help one of us with our homework the absolutely unabating tension which emanated from him caused our minds and our tongues to become paralyzed, so that he, scarcely knowing why, flew into a rage and the child, not knowing why, was punished. If it ever entered his head to bring a surprise home for his children, it was, almost unfailingly, the wrong surprise and even the big watermelons he often brought home on his back in the summertime led to the most appalling scenes. I do not remember, in all those years, that one of his children was ever glad to see him come home. From what I was able to gather of his early life, it seemed that this inability to establish contact with other people had always marked him and had been one of the things which had driven him out of New Orleans. There was something in him, therefore, groping and tentative, which was never expressed and which was buried with him. One saw it most clearly when he was facing new people and hoping to impress them. But he never did, not for long. We went from church to smaller and more improbable church, he found himself in less and less demand as a minister, and by the time he died none of his friends had come to see him for a long time. He had lived and died in an intolerable bitterness of spirit and it frightened me, as we drove him to the graveyard through those unquiet, ruined streets, to see how powerful and overflowing this bitterness could be and to realize that this bitterness now was mine.

When he died I had been away from home for a little over a year. In that year I had had time to become aware of the meaning of all my father's bitter warnings, had discovered the secret of his proudly pursed lips and rigid carriage: I had discovered the weight of white people in the world. I saw that this had been for my ancestors and now would be for me an awful thing to live with and that the bitterness which had helped to kill my father could also kill me.

He had been ill a long time—in the mind, as we now realized, reliving instances of his fantastic intransigence in the new light of his affliction and endeavoring to feel a sorrow for him which never, quite, came true. We had not known that he was being eaten up by paranoia, and the discovery that his cruelty, to our bodies and our minds, had been one of the symptoms of his illness was not, then, enough to enable us to forgive him. The younger children felt, quite simply, relief that he would not be coming home anymore. My mother's observation that it was he, after all, who had kept them alive all these years meant nothing because the problems of keeping children alive are not real for children. The older children felt, with my father gone, that they could invite their friends to the house without fear that their friends would be insulted or, as had sometimes happened with me, being told that their friends were in league with the devil and intended to rob our family of everything we owned. (I didn't fail to wonder, and it made me hate him, what on earth we owned that anybody would want.)

His illness was beyond all hope of healing before anyone realized that he was ill. He had always been so strange and had lived, like a prophet, in such unimaginably close communion with the Lord that his long silences which were punctuated by moans and hallelujahs and snatches of old songs while he sat at the living-room window never seemed odd to us. It was not until he refused to eat because, he said, his family was trying to poison him that my mother was forced to accept as a fact what had, until then, been only an unwilling suspicion. When he was committed, it was discovered that he had tuberculosis and, as it turned out, the disease of his mind allowed the disease of his body to destroy him. For the doctors could not force him to eat, either, and, though he was fed intravenously, it was clear from the beginning that there was no hope for him.

In my mind's eye I could see him, sitting at the window, locked up in his terrors; hating and fearing every living soul including his children who had betrayed him, too, by reaching towards the world which had despised him. There were nine of us. I began to wonder what it could have felt like for such a man to have had nine children whom he could barely feed. He used to make little jokes about our poverty, which never, of course, seemed very funny to us; they could not have seemed very funny to him, either, or else our all too feeble response to them would never have caused such rages. He spent great energy and achieved, to our chagrin, no small amount of success in keeping us away from the people who surrounded us, people who had all-night rent parties to which we listened when we should have been sleeping, people who cursed and drank and flashed razor blades on Lenox Avenue. He could not understand why, if they had so much energy to spare, they could not use it to make their lives better. He treated almost everybody on our block with a most uncharitable asperity and neither they, nor, of course, their children were slow to reciprocate.

The only white people who came to our house were welfare workers and bill collectors. It was almost always my mother who dealt with them, for my father's temper, which was at the mercy of his pride, was never to be trusted. It was clear that he felt their very presence in his home to be a violation: this was conveyed by his carriage, almost ludicrously stiff, and by his voice, harsh and vindictively polite. When I was around nine or ten I wrote a play which was directed by a young, white schoolteacher, a woman, who then took an interest in me, and gave me books to read and, in order to corroborate my theatrical bent, decided to take me to see what she somewhat tactlessly referred to as "real" plays. Theater-going was forbidden in our house, but, with the really cruel intuitiveness of a child, I suspected that the color of this woman's skin would carry the day for me. When, at school, she suggested taking me to the theater, I did not, as I might have done if she had been a Negro, find a way of discouraging her, but agreed that she should pick me up at my house one evening. I then, very cleverly, left all the rest to my mother, who suggested to my father, as I knew she would, that it would not be very nice to let such a kind woman make the trip for nothing. Also, since it was a schoolteacher, I imagine that my mother countered the idea of sin with the idea of "education," which word, even with my father, carried a kind of bitter weight.

Before the teacher came my father took me aside to ask *why* she was coming, what *interest* she could possibly have in our house, in a boy like me. I said I didn't know but I, too, suggested that it had something to do with education. And I understood that my father was waiting for me to say something—I didn't quite know what; perhaps that I wanted his protection against this teacher and her "education." I said none of these things and the teacher came and we went out. It was clear, during the brief interview in our living room, that my father was agreeing very much against his will and that he would have refused permission if he had dared. The fact that he did not dare caused me to despise him: I had no way of knowing that he was facing in that living room a wholly unprecedented and frightening situation.

Later, when my father had been laid off from his job, this woman became very important to us. She was really a very sweet and generous woman and went to a great deal of trouble to be of help to us, particularly during one awful winter. My mother called her by the highest name she knew: she said she was a "christian." My father could scarcely disagree but during the four or five years of our relatively close association he never trusted her and was always trying to surprise in her open, Midwestern face the genuine, cunningly hidden, and hideous motivation. In later years, particularly when it began to be clear that this "education" of mine was going to lead me to perdition, he became more explicit and warned me that my white friends in high school were not really my friends and that I would see, when I was older, how white people would do anything to keep a Negro down. Some of them could be nice, he admitted, but none of them were to be trusted and most of them were not even nice. The best thing was to have as little to do with them as possible. I did not feel this way and I was certain, in my innocence, that I never would.

But the year which preceded my father's death had made a great change in my life. I had been living in New Jersey, working in defense plants, working and living among southerners, white and black. I knew about the south, of course, and about how southerners treated Negroes and how they expected them to behave, but it had never entered my mind that anyone would look at me and expect *me* to behave that way. I learned in New Jersey that to be a Negro meant, precisely, that one was never looked at but was simply at the mercy of the reflexes the color of one's skin caused in other people. I acted in New Jersey as I had always acted, that is as though I thought a great deal of myself—I had to *act* that way—with results that were, simply, unbelievable. I had scarcely arrived before I had earned the enmity, which was extraordinarily ingenious, of all my superiors and nearly all my co-workers. In the beginning, to make matters worse, I simply did not know what was happening. I did not know what I had done, and I shortly began to wonder what *anyone* could possiby do, to bring about such unanimous, active, and unbearably vocal hostility. I knew about jim-crow but I had never experienced it. I went to the same self-service restaurant three times and stood with all the Princeton boys before the counter, waiting for a hamburger and coffee; it was always an extraordinarily long time before anything was set before me; but it was not until the fourth visit that I learned that, in fact, nothing had ever been set before me: I had simply picked something up. Negroes were not served there, I was told, and they had been waiting for me to realize that I was always the only Negro present. Once I was told this, I determined to go there all the time. But now they were ready for me and, though some dreadful scenes were subsequently enacted in that restaurant, I never ate there again.

It was the same story all over New Jersey, in bars, bowling alleys, diners, places to live. I was always being forced to leave, silently, or with mutual imprecations. I very shortly became notorious and children giggled behind me when I passed and their elders whispered or shouted—they really believed that I was mad. And it did begin to work on my mind, of course; I began to be afraid to go anywhere and to compensate for this I went to places to which I really should not have gone and where, God knows, I had no desire to be. My reputation in town naturally enhanced my reputation at work and my working day became one long series of acrobatics designed to keep me out of trouble. I cannot say that these acrobatics succeeded. It began to seem that the machinery of the organization I worked for was turning over, day and night, with but one aim: to eject me. I was fired once, and contrived, with the aid of a friend from New York, to get back on the payroll; was fired again, and bounced back again. It took a while to fire me for the third time, but the third time took. There were no loopholes anywhere. There was not even any way of getting back inside the gates.

That year in New Jersey lives in my mind as though it were the year during which, having an unsuspected predilection for it, I first contracted some dread, chronic disease, the unfailing symptom of which is a kind of blind fever, a pounding in the skull and fire in the bowels. Once this disease is contracted, one can never be really carefree again, for the fever, without an instant's warning, can recur at any moment. It can wreck more important things than race relations. There is not a Negro alive who does not have this rage in his blood—one has the choice, merely, of living with it consciously or surrendering to it. As for me, this fever has recurred in me, and does, and will until the day I die.

My last night in New Jersey, a white friend from New York took me to the nearest big town, Trenton, to go to the movies and have a few drinks. As it turned out, he also saved me from, at the very least, a violent whipping. Almost every detail of that night stands out very clearly in my memory. I even remember the name of the movie we saw because its title impressed me as being so patly ironical. It was a movie about the German occupation of France, starring Maureen O'Hara and Charles Laughton and called *This Land Is Mine*. I remember the name of the diner we walked into when the movie ended: it was the "American Diner." When we walked in the coun-terman asked what we wanted and I remember answering with the casual sharpness which had become my habit: "We want a hamburger and a cup of coffee, what do you think we want?" I do not know why, after a year of such rebuffs, I so completely failed to anticipate his answer, which was, of course, "We don't serve Negroes here." This reply failed to discompose me, at least for the moment. I made some sardonic comment about the name of the diner and we walked out into the streets.

This was the time of what was called the "brown-out," when the lights in all American cities were very dim. When we re-entered the streets some-thing happened to me which had the force of an optical illusion, or a night-mare. The streets were very crowded and I was facing north. People were moving in every direction but it seemed to me, in that instant, that all of the people I could see, and many more than that, were moving toward me, against me, and that everyone was white. I remember how their faces gleamed. And I felt, like a physical sensation, a *click* at the nape of my neck as though some interior string connecting my head to my body had been cut. I began to walk. I heard my friend call after me, but I ignored him. Heaven only knows what was going on in his mind, but he had the good sense not to touch me—I don't know what would have happened if he had—and to keep me in sight. I don't know what was going on in my mind, either; I certainly had no conscious plan. I wanted to do something to crush these white faces, which were crushing me. I walked for perhaps a block or two until I came to an enormous, glittering, and fashionable restaurant in which I knew not even the intercession of the Virgin would cause me to be served. I pushed through the doors and took the first vacant seat I saw, at a table for two, and waited.

I do not know how long I waited and I rather wonder, until today, what I could possibly have looked like. Whatever I looked like, I frightened the waitress who shortly appeared, and the moment she appeared all of my fury flowed towards her. I hated her for her white face, and for her great, as-tounded, frightened eyes. I felt that if she found a black man so frightening I would make her fright worth-while.

She did not ask me what I wanted, but repeated, as though she had learned it somewhere, "We don't serve Negroes here." She did not say it with the blunt, derisive hostility to which I had grown so accustomed, but, rather, with a note of apology in her voice, and fear. This made me colder and more murderous than ever. I felt I had to do something with my hands. I wanted her to come close enough for me to get her neck between my hands.

So I pretended not to have understood her, hoping to draw her closer. And she did step a very short step closer, with her pencil poised incongru-ously over her pad, and repeated the formula: ". . . don't serve Negroes here."

Somehow, with the repetition of that phrase, which was already ringing in my head like a thousand bells of a nightmare, I realized that she would never come any closer and that I would have to strike from a distance.

There was nothing on the table but an ordinary watermug half full of water, and I picked this up and hurled it with all my strength at her. She ducked and it missed her and shattered against the mirror behind the bar. And, with that sound, my frozen blood abruptly thawed, I returned from wherever I had been, I *saw*, for the first time, the restaurant, the people with their mouths open, already, as it seemed to me, rising as one man, and I realized what I had done, and where I was, and I was frightened. I rose and began running for the door. A round, potbellied man grabbed me by the nape of the neck just as I reached the doors and began to beat me about the face. I kicked him and got loose and ran into the streets. My friend whispered, *"Run!"* and I ran.

My friend stayed outside the restaurant long enough to misdirect my pursuers and the police, who arrived, he told me, at once. I do not know what I said to him when he came to my room that night. I could not have said much. I felt, in the oddest, most awful way, that I had somehow betrayed him. I lived it over and over and over again, the way one relives an automobile accident after it has happened and one finds oneself alone and safe. I could not get over two facts, both equally difficult for the imagination to grasp, and one was that I could have been murdered. But the other was that I had been ready to commit murder. I saw nothing very clearly but I did see this: that my life, my *real* life, was in danger, and not from anything other people might do but from the hatred I carried in my own heart.

[II]

I had returned home around the second week in June—in great haste because it seemed that my father's death and my mother's confinement were both but a matter of hours. In the case of my mother, it soon became clear that she had simply made a miscalculation. This had always been her tendency and I don't believe that a single one of us arrived in the world, or has since arrived anywhere else, on time. But none of us dawdled so intolerably about the business of being born as did my baby sister. We sometimes amused ourselves, during those endless, stifling weeks, by picturing the baby sitting within in the safe, warm dark, bitterly regretting the necessity of becoming a part of our chaos and stubbornly putting it off as long as possible. I understood her perfectly and congratulated her on showing such good sense so soon. Death, however, sat as purposefully at my father's bedside as life stirred within my mother's womb and it was harder to understand why he so lingered in that long shadow. It seemed that he had bent, and for a long time, too, all of his energies towards dying. Now death was ready for him but my father held back.

All of Harlem, indeed, seemed to be infected by waiting. I had never before known it to be so violently still. Racial tensions throughout this country were exacerbated during the early years of the war, partly because the labor market brought together hundreds of thousands of ill-prepared people and partly because Negro soldiers, regardless of where they were born, received their military training in the south. What happened in defense plants and army camps had repercussions, naturally, in every Negro ghetto. The

situation in Harlem had grown bad enough for clergymen, policemen, educators, politicians, and social workers to assert in one breath that there was
no "crime wave" and to offer, in the very next breath, suggestions as how to
combat it. These suggestions always seemed to involve playgrounds, despite
the fact that racial skirmishes were occurring in the playgrounds, too. Playground or not, crime wave or not, the Harlem police force had been augmented in March, and the unrest grew—perhaps, in fact, partly as a result
of the ghetto's instinctive hatred of policemen. Perhaps the most revealing
news item, out of the steady parade of reports of muggings, stabbings, shoot-
ings, assaults, gang wars, and accusations of police brutality, is the item
concerning six Negro girls who set upon a white girl in the subway because,
as they all too accurately put it, she was stepping on their toes. Indeed she
was, all over the nation.

I had never before been so aware of policemen, on foot, on horseback, on
corners, everywhere, always two by two. Nor had I ever been so aware of
small knots of people. They were on stoops and on corners and in doorways,
and what was striking about them, I think, was that they did not seem to be
talking. Never, when I passed these groups, did the usual sound of a curse or
a laugh ring out and neither did there seem to be any hum of gossip. There
was certainly, on the other hand, occurring between them communication
extraordinarily intense. Another thing that was striking was the unexpected
diversity of the people who made up these groups. Usually, for example, one
would see a group of sharpies standing on the street corner, jiving the passing chicks; or a group of older men, usually, for some reason, in the vicinity
of a barber shop, discussing baseball scores, or the numbers, or making
rather chilling observations about women they had known. Women, in a
general way, tended to be seen less often together—unless they were church
women, or very young girls, or prostitutes met together for an unprofessional
instant. But that summer I saw the strangest combinations: large, respectable, churchly matrons standing on the stoops or the corners with their hair
tied up, together with a girl in sleazy satin whose face bore the marks of gin
and the razor, or heavy-set, abrupt, no-nonsense older men, in company
with the most disreputable and fanatical "race" men, or these same "race"
men with the sharpies, or these sharpies with the churchly women. Seventh
Day Adventists and Methodists and Spiritualists seemed to be hobnobbing
with Holyrollers and they were all, alike, entangled with the most flagrant
disbelievers; something heavy in their stance seemed to indicate that they
had all, incredibly, seen a common vision, and on each face there seemed to
be the same strange, bitter shadow.

The churchly women and the matter-of-fact, no-nonsense men had children in the Army. The sleazy girls they talked to had lovers there, the
sharpies and the "race" men had friends and brothers there. It would have
demanded an unquestioning patriotism, happily as uncommon in this country as it is undesirable, for these people not to have been disturbed by the
bitter letters they received, by the newspaper stories they read, not to have
been enraged by the posters, then to be found all over New York, which
described the Japanese as "yellow-bellied Japs." It was only the "race"

men, to be sure, who spoke ceaselessly of being revenged—how this vengeance was to be exacted was not clear—for the indignities and dangers suffered by Negro boys in uniform; but everybody felt a directionless, hopeless bitterness, as well as that panic which can scarcely be suppressed when one knows that a human being one loves is beyond one's reach, and in danger. This helplessness and this gnawing uneasiness does something, at length, to even the toughest mind. Perhaps the best way to sum all this up is to say that the people I knew felt, mainly, a peculiar kind of relief when they knew that their boys were being shipped out of the south, to do battle overseas. It was, perhaps, like feeling that the most dangerous part of a dangerous journey had been passed and that now, even if death should come, it would come with honor and without the complicity of their countrymen. Such a death would be, in short, a fact with which one could hope to live.

It was on the 28th of July, which I believe was a Wednesday, that I visited my father for the first time during his illness and for the last time in his life. The moment I saw him I knew why I had put off this visit so long. I had told my mother that I did not want to see him because I hated him. But this was not true. It was only that I *had* hated him and I wanted to hold on to this hatred. I did not want to look at him as a ruin: it was not a ruin I had hated. I imagine that one of the reasons people cling to their hates so stubbornly is because they sense, once hate is gone, that they will be forced to deal with pain.

We traveled out to him, his older sister and myself, to what seemed to be the very end of a very Long Island. It was hot and dusty and we wrangled, my aunt and I, all the way out, over the fact that I had recently begun to smoke and, as she said, to give myself airs. But I knew that she wrangled with me because she could not bear to face the fact of her brother's dying. Neither could I endure the reality of her despair, her unstated bafflement as to what had happened to her brother's life, and her own. So we wrangled and I smoked and from time to time she fell into a heavy reverie. Covertly, I watched her face, which was the face of an old woman; it had fallen in, the eyes were sunken and lightless; soon she would be dying too.

In my childhood—it had not been so long ago—I had thought her beautiful. She had been quick-witted and quick-moving and very generous with all the children and each of her visits had been an event. At one time one of my brothers and myself had thought of running away to live with her. Now she could no longer produce out of her handbag some unexpected and yet familiar delight. She made me feel pity and revulsion and fear. It was awful to realize that she no longer caused me to feel affection. The closer we came to the hospital the more querulous she became and at the same time, naturally, grew more dependent on me. Between pity and guilt and fear I began to feel that there was another me trapped in my skull like a jack-in-the-box who might escape my control at any moment and fill the air with screaming.

She began to cry the moment we entered the room and she saw him lying there, all shriveled and still, like a little black monkey. The great, gleaming apparatus which fed him and would have compelled him to be still even if he had been able to move brought to mind, not beneficence, but torture; the tubes entering his arm made me think of pictures I had seen when a child, of Gulliver, tied down by the pygmies on that island. My aunt wept and wept, there was a whistling sound in my father's throat; nothing was said; he could not speak. I wanted to take his hand, to say something. But I do not know what I could have said, even if he could have heard me. He was not really in that room with us, he had at last really embarked on his journey; and though my aunt told me that he said he was going to meet Jesus, I did not hear anything except that whistling in his throat. The doctor came back and we left, into that unbearable train again, and home. In the morning came the telegram saying that he was dead. Then the house was suddenly full of relatives, friends, hysteria, and confusion and I quickly left my mother and the children to the care of those impressive women, who, in Negro communities at least, automatically appear at times of bereavement armed with lotions, proverbs, and patience, and an ability to cook. I went downtown. By the time I returned, later the same day, my mother had been carried to the hospital and the baby had been born.

[III]

For my father's funeral I had nothing black to wear and this posed a nagging problem all day long. It was one of those problems, simple, or impossible of solution, to which the mind insanely clings in order to avoid the mind's real trouble. I spent most of the day at the downtown apartment of a girl I knew, celebrating my birthday with whiskey and wondering what to wear that night. When planning a birthday celebration one naturally does not expect that it will be up against competition from a funeral and this girl had anticipated taking me out that night, for a big dinner and a night club afterwards. Sometime during the course of that long day we decided that we would go out anyway, when my father's funeral service was over. I imagine *I* decided it, since, as the funeral hour approached, it became clearer and clearer to me that I would not know what to do with myself when it was over. The girl, stifling her very lively concern as to the possible effects of the whiskey on one of my father's chief mourners, concentrated on being conciliatory and practically helpful. She found a black shirt for me somewhere and ironed it and, dressed in the darkest pants and jacket I owned, and slightly drunk, I made my way to my father's funeral.

The chapel was full, but not packed, and very quiet. There were, mainly, my father's relatives, and his children, and here and there I saw faces I had not seen since childhood, the faces of my father's one-time friends. They were very dark and solemn now, seeming somehow to suggest that they had known all along that something like this would happen. Chief among the mourners was my aunt, who had quarreled with my father all his life; by which I do not mean to suggest that her mourning was insincere or that she had not loved him. I suppose that she was one of the few people in the world who had, and their incessant quarreling proved precisely the strength of the tie that bound them. The only other person in the world, as far as I knew, whose relationship to my father rivaled my aunt's in depth was my mother, who was not there.

It seemed to me, of course, that it was a very long funeral. But it was, if anything, a rather shorter funeral than most, nor, since there were no overwhelming, uncontrollable expressions of grief, could it be called—if I dare to use the word—successful. The minister who preached my father's funeral sermon was one of the few my father had still been seeing as he neared his end. He presented to us in his sermon a man whom none of us had ever seen—a man thoughtful, patient, and forbearing, a Christian inspiration to all who knew him, and a model for his children. And no doubt the children, in their disturbed and guilty state, were almost ready to believe this; he had been remote enough to be anything and, anyway, the shock of the incontrovertible, that it was really our father lying up there in that casket, prepared the mind for anything. His sister moaned and this grief-stricken moaning was taken for corroboration. The other faces held a dark, noncommittal thoughtfulness. This was not the man they had known, but they had scarcely expected to be confronted with *him*; this was, in a sense deeper than question of fact, the man they had not known, and the man they had not known may have been the real one. The real man, whoever he had been, had suffered and now he was dead: this was all that was sure and all that mattered now. Every man in the chapel hoped that when his hour came he, too, would be eulogized, which is to say forgiven, and that all of his lapses, greeds, errors, and strayings from the truth would be invested with coherence and looked upon with charity. This was perhaps the last thing human beings could give each other and it was what they demanded, after all, of the Lord. Only the Lord saw the midnight tears, only He was present when one of His children, moaning and wringing hands, paced up and down the room. When one slapped one's child in anger the recoil in the heart reverberated through heaven and became part of the pain of the universe. And when the children were hungry and sullen and distrustful and one watched them, daily, growing wilder, and further away, and running headlong into danger, it was the Lord who knew what the charged heart endured as the strap was laid to the backside; the Lord alone knew what one *would* have said if one had had, like the Lord, the gift of the living word. It was the Lord who knew of the impossibility every parent in the room faced: how to prepare the child for the day when the child would be despised and how to *create* in the child—by what means?—a stronger antidote to this poison than one had found for oneself. The avenues, side streets, bars, billiard halls, hospitals, police stations, and even the playgrounds of Harlem—not to mention the houses of correction, the jails, and the morgue—testified to the potency of the poison while remaining silent as to the efficacy of whatever antidote, irresistibly raising the question of whether or not such an antidote existed; raising, which was worse, the question of whether or not an antidote was desirable; perhaps poison should be fought with poison. With these several schisms in the mind and with more terrors in the heart than could be named, it was better not to judge the man who had gone down under an impossible burden. It was better to remember: *Thou knowest this man's fall; but thou knowest not his wrassling.*

While the preacher talked and I watched the children—years of changing their diapers, scrubbing them, slapping them, taking them to school, and scolding them had had the perhaps inevitable result of making me love them, though I am not sure I knew this then—my mind was busily breaking out with a rash of disconnected impressions. Snatches of popular songs, indecent jokes, bits of books I had read, movie sequences, faces, voices, political issues—I thought I was going mad; all these impressions suspended, as it were, in the solution of the faint nausea produced in me by the heat and liquor. For a moment I had the impression that my alcoholic breath, inefficiently disguised with chewing gum, filled the entire chapel. Then someone began singing one of my father's favorite songs and, abruptly, I was with him, sitting on his knee, in the hot, enormous, crowded church which was the first church we attended. It was the Abyssinia Baptist Church on 138th Street. We had not gone there long. With this image, a host of others came. I had forgotten, in the rage of my growing up, how proud my father had been of me when I was little. Apparently, I had had a voice and my father had liked to show me off before the members of the church. I had forgotten what he had looked like when he was pleased but now I remembered that he had always been grinning with pleasure when my solos ended. I even remembered certain expressions on his face when he teased my mother—had he loved her? I would never know. And when had it all begun to change? For now it seemed that he had not always been cruel. I remembered being taken for a haircut and scraping my knee on the footrest of the barber's chair and I remembered my father's face as he soothed my crying and applied the stinging iodine. Then I remembered our fights, fights which had been of the worst possible kind because my technique had been silence.

I remembered the one time in all our life together when we had really spoken to each other.

It was on a Sunday and it must have been shortly before I left home. We were walking, just the two of us, in our usual silence, to or from church. I was in high school and had been doing a lot of writing and I was, at about this time, the editor of the high school magazine. But I had also been a Young Minister and had been preaching from the pulpit. Lately, I had been taking fewer engagements and preached as rarely as possible. It was said in the church, quite truthfully, that I was "cooling off."

My father asked me abruptly, "You'd rather write than preach, wouldn't you?"

I was astonished at his question—because it was a real question. I answered, "Yes."

That was all we said. It was awful to remember that that was all we had *ever* said.

The casket now was opened and the mourners were being led up the aisle to look for the last time on the deceased. The assumption was that the family was too overcome with grief to be allowed to make this journey alone and I watched while my aunt was led to the casket and, muffled in black, and shaking, led back to her seat. I disapproved of forcing the children to look on their dead father, considering that the shock of his death, or, more truthfully, the shock of death as a reality, was already a little more than a child could bear, but my judgment in this matter had been overruled and there they were, bewildered and frightened and very small, being led, one by one, to the casket. But there is also something very gallant about children at such moments. It has something to do with their silence and gravity and with the fact that one cannot help them. Their legs, somehow, seemed *exposed*, so that it is at once incredible and terribly clear that their legs are all they have to hold them up.

I had not wanted to go to the casket myself and I certainly had not wished to be led there, but there was no way of avoiding either of these forms. One of the deacons led me up and I looked on my father's face. I cannot say that it looked like him at all. His blackness had been equivocated by powder and there was no suggestion in that casket of what his power had or could have been. He was simply an old man dead, and it was hard to believe that he had ever given anyone either joy or pain. Yet, his life filled that room. Further up the avenue his wife was holding his newborn child. Life and death so close together, and love and hatred, and right and wrong, said something to me which I did not want to hear concerning man, concerning the life of man.

After the funeral, while I was downtown desperately celebrating my birthday, a Negro soldier, in the lobby of the Hotel Braddock, got into a fight with a white policeman over a Negro girl. Negro girls, white policemen, in or out of uniform, and Negro males—in or out of uniform—were part of the furniture of the lobby of the Hotel Braddock and this was certainly not the first time such an incident had occurred. It was destined, however, to receive an unprecedented publicity, for the fight between the policeman and the soldier ended with the shooting of the soldier. Rumor, flowing immediately to the streets outside, stated the soldier had been shot in the back, an instantaneous and revealing invention, and that the soldier had died protecting a Negro woman. The facts were somewhat different—for example, the soldier had not been shot in the back, and was not dead, and the girl seems to have been as dubious a symbol of womanhood as her white counterpart in Georgia usually is, but no one was interested in the facts. They preferred the invention because this invention expressed and corroborated their hates and fears so perfectly. It is just as well to remember that people are always doing this. Perhaps many of those legends, including Christianity, to which the world clings began their conquest of the world with just some such concerted surrender to distortion. The effect, in Harlem, of this particular legend was like the effect of a lit match in a tin of gasoline. The mob gathered before the doors of the Hotel Braddock simply began to swell and to spread in every direction, and Harlem exploded.

The mob did not cross the ghetto lines. It would have been easy, for example, to have gone over Morningside Park on the west side or to have crossed the Grand Central railroad tracks at 125th Street on the east side, to wreak havoc in the white neighborhoods. The mob seems to have been mainly interested in something more potent and real than the white face, that is, in white power, and the principal damage done during the riot of the summer of 1943 was to white business establishments in Harlem. It might have been a far bloodier story, of course, if, at the hour the riot began, these establishments had still been open. From the Hotel Braddock the mob fanned out, east and west along 125th Street, and for the entire length of Lenox, Seventh, and Eighth avenues. Along each of these avenues, and along each major side street—116th, 125th, 135th, and so on—bars, stores, pawnshops, restaurants, even little luncheonettes had been smashed open and entered and looted—looted, it might be added, with more haste than efficiency. The shelves really looked as though a bomb had struck them. Cans of beans and soup and dog food, along with toilet paper, corn flakes, sardines and milk tumbled every which way, and abandoned cash registers and cases of beer leaned crazily out of the splintered windows and were strewn along the avenues. Sheets, blankets, and clothing of every description formed a kind of path, as though people had dropped them while running. I truly had not realized that Harlem *had* so many stores until I saw them all smashed open; the first time the word *wealth* ever entered my mind in relation to Harlem was when I saw it scattered in the streets. But one's first, incongruous impression of plenty was countered immediately by an impression of waste. None of this was doing anybody any good. It would have been better to have left the plate glass as it had been and the goods lying in the stores.

It would have been better, but it would also have been intolerable, for Harlem had needed something to smash. To smash something is the ghetto's chronic need. Most of the time it is the members of the ghetto who smash each other, and themselves. But as long as the ghetto walls are standing there will always come a moment when these outlets do not work. That summer, for example, it was not enough to get into a fight on Lenox Avenue, or curse out one's cronies in the barber shops. If ever, indeed, the violence which fills Harlem's churches, pool halls, and bars erupts outward in a more direct fashion, Harlem and its citizens are likely to vanish in an apocalyptic flood. That this is not likely to happen is due to a great many reasons, most hidden and powerful among them the Negro's real relation to the white American. This relation prohibits, simply, anything as uncomplicated and satisfactory as pure hatred. In order really to hate white people, one has to blot so much out of the mind—and the heart—that this hatred itself becomes an exhausting and self-destructive pose. But this does not mean, on the other hand, that love comes easily: the white world is too powerful, too complacent, too ready with gratuitous humiliation, and, above all, too ignorant and too innocent for that. One is absolutely forced to make perpetual qualifications and one's own reactions are always canceling each other out. It is this, really, which has driven so many people mad, both white and black. One is always in the position of having to decide between amputation and gangrene. Amputation is swift but time may prove that the amputation was not necessary—or one may delay the amputation too long.

Gangrene is slow, but it is impossible to be sure that one is reading one's symptoms right. The idea of going through life as a cripple is more than one can bear, and equally unbearable is the risk of swelling up slowly, in agony, with poison. And the trouble, finally, is that the risks are real even if the choices do not exist.

"But as for me and my house," my father had said, "we will serve the Lord." I wondered, as we drove him to his resting place, what this line had meant for him. I had heard him preach it many times. I had preached it once myself, proudly giving it an interpretation different from my father's. Now the whole thing came back to me, as though my father and I were on our way to Sunday school and I were memorizing the golden text: *And if it seem evil unto you to serve the Lord, choose you this day whom you will serve; whether the gods which your fathers served that were on the other side of the flood, or the gods of the Amorites, in whose land ye dwell: but as for me and my house, we will serve the Lord.* I suspected in these familiar lines a meaning which had never been there for me before. All of my father's texts and songs, which I had decided were meaningless, were arranged before me at his death like empty bottles, waiting to hold the meaning which life would give them for me. This was his legacy: nothing is ever escaped. That bleakly memorable morning I hated the unbelievable streets and the Negroes and whites who had, equally, made them that way. But I knew that it was folly, as my father would have said, this bitterness was folly. It was necessary to hold on to the things that mattered. The dead man mattered, the new life mattered; blackness and whiteness did not matter; to believe that they did was to acquiesce in one's own destruction. Hatred, which could destroy so much, never failed to destroy the man who hated and this was an immutable law.

It began to seem that one would have to hold in the mind forever two ideas which seemed to be in opposition. The first idea was acceptance, the acceptance, totally without rancor, of life as it is, and men as they are: in the light of this idea, it goes without saying that injustice is a commonplace. But this did not mean that one could be complacent, for the second idea was of equal power: that one must never, in one's own life, accept these injustices as commonplace but must fight them with all one's strength. This fight begins, however, in the heart and it now had been laid to my charge to keep my own heart free of hatred and despair. This intimation made my heart heavy and, now that my father was irrecoverable, I wished that he had been beside me so that I could have searched his face for the answers which only the future would give me now.

On Women and Men

"WOMEN'S liberation" is one of the great topics of our time. Although there are comparatively few of us who have not heard of it, and there are more and more people who believe, in general, that it is a "good thing," the issues for most of us are neither clear nor settled. One of the most difficult and interesting issues has to do with the barriers that still prevent women from enjoying equal status with men. While many people are in favor of "equality" for women, and feel that the barriers are coming down with appropriate legislation, many also fail to realize that some of the barriers are invisible, presenting a problem that cannot be corrected by laws, but must be worked out in the consciousness of each individual, whether woman or man.

We print first a piece by Virginia Woolf that memorably and wittily casts doubt on any notions of an inherent difference of talent between men and women, and helps us imagine what a supremely talented woman might have been up against before women's liberation. The next three essays turn to the "invisible barriers." Brigid Brophy argues that social pressure has taken the place of laws in restricting the freedom of women. Judith Wells and Matina Horner show, the one from personal experience and the other from field research, how many of the socially created barriers become internalized in women, who, by adopting certain roles or fearing certain judgments, enforce these social taboos within themselves.

The next three essays deal with the roles of wives and husbands. Judy Syfers and Esther Vilar differ violently and, we hope, interestingly on which partner is more the victim, which the more favored. But we must keep in mind that these and most other contemporary discussions of "women's roles" are devoted predominantly to the problems of middle-class, white, American or Western European women; comparatively little has been said of how the problems change with differences of racial, social, economic, and historical **403**

background. In general, women who live in poverty and under racial discrimination have problems that may overshadow traditional sexism. The
essay by Merle Hodge cogently describes one such instance from Caribbean
culture, where the relationship between women and their men is heavily
overshadowed by the dark history of the region.

Real changes in the roles of women, of course, involve changes in the roles of
men; lately there has been a growing consciousness of the imprisonment of
men in stereotyped roles of their own, and an increasing sense among men of
the emotional cost of the traditional American ideal of masculinity. Harold
Rosenberg, writing in the 1960s, already senses something theatrical and
defensive, something weak, in the traditional pose of the he-man. Marc
Feigen Fasteau specifically examines what that pose costs in terms of men's
capacity for friendship.

The section closes with Gloria Steinem's account of two versions of sexuality
as forms of expression, the one based on equality and shared pleasure, the
other on inequality, dominance, and pain. Ms. Steinem implies a view of
the sexes that is also implicit in Brigid Brophy's closing paragraphs, and that
may well signal a new phase in feminist thinking: When we are liberated,
when we are free, let us be equal.

BARRIERS, VISIBLE AND INVISIBLE

VIRGINIA WOOLF

*Virginia Woolf (1882-1941) was the daughter of a prominent English scholar and
critic, Sir Leslie Stephen, and was educated mainly in her father's library and from
extensive travels. In 1917, she and her husband, Leonard Woolf, began printing on a
hand press their own writings and those of other (then obscure) authors like Katherine
Mansfield, T. S. Eliot, and E. M. Forster. This was the beginning of the celebrated
Hogarth Press and center of the so-called "Bloomsbury Group" of intellectuals and
writers. Virginia Woolf is particularly noted for her novels, among which we mention*
Mrs. Dalloway *(1925),* To the Lighthouse *(1927),* Orlando *(1928), and* The
Waves *(1931) as a few of the best. They are considered important experiments in
novelistic form: she disregards ordinary factual description of characters and action, concentrating instead on psychological penetration and on variations in temporal perspective
and rhythm. She also wrote many reviews and essays, on art and literature, and on the
problems of social and economic reform. Her literary essays were collected in* The
Common Reader *(1925; second series, 1932),* The Death of the Moth *(1942),*
The Moment and Other Essays *(1947), and* Three Guineas *(1938).*

*A Room of One's Own (1929), a seminal feminist piece, is a long essay in which she
uses metaphor and history to show the relative status of women in twentieth-century
English society. From it we have taken the selection printed below.*

Shakespeare's Sister

. . . I thought of that old gentleman, who is dead now, but was a bishop, I think, who declared that it was impossible for any woman, past, present, or to come, to have the genius of Shakespeare. He wrote to the papers about it. He also told a lady who applied to him for information that cats do not as a matter of fact go to heaven, though they have, he added, souls of a sort. How much thinking those old gentlemen used to save one! How the borders of ignorance shrank back at their approach! Cats do not go to heaven. Women cannot write the plays of Shakespeare.

Be that as it may, I could not help thinking, as I looked at the works of Shakespeare on the shelf, that the bishop was right at least in this; it would have been impossible, completely and entirely, for any woman to have written the plays of Shakespeare in the age of Shakespeare. Let me imagine, since facts are so hard to come by, what would have happened had Shakespeare had a wonderfully gifted sister, called Judith, let us say. Shakespeare himself went, very probably—his mother was an heiress—to the grammar school, where he may have learnt Latin—Ovid, Virgil and Horace—and the elements of grammar and logic. He was, it is well known, a wild boy who poached rabbits, perhaps shot a deer, and had, rather sooner than he should have done, to marry a woman in the neighbourhood, who bore him a child rather quicker than was right. That escapade sent him to seek his fortune in London. He had, it seemed, a taste for the theatre; he began by holding horses at the stage door. Very soon he got work in the theatre, became a successful actor, and lived at the hub of the universe, meeting everybody, knowing everybody, practising his art on the boards, exercising his wits in the streets, and even getting access to the palace of the queen. Meanwhile his extraordinarily gifted sister, let us suppose, remained at home. She was as adventurous, as imaginative, as agog to see the world as he was. But she was not sent to school. She had no chance of learning grammar and logic, let alone of reading Horace and Virgil. She picked up a book now and then, one of her brother's perhaps, and read a few pages. But then her parents came in and told her to mend the stockings or mind the stew and not moon about with books and papers. They would have spoken sharply but kindly, for they were substantial people who knew the conditions of life for a woman and loved their daughter—indeed, more likely than not she was the apple of her father's eye. Perhaps she scribbled some pages up in an apple loft on the sly, but was careful to hide them or set fire to them. Soon, however, before she was out of her teens, she was to be betrothed to the son of a neighbouring wool-stapler. She cried out that marriage was hateful to her, and for that she was severely beaten by her father. Then he ceased to scold her. He begged her instead not to hurt him, not to shame him in this matter of her marriage. He would give her a chain of beads or a fine petticoat, he said; and there were tears in his eyes. How could she disobey him? How could she break his heart? The force of her own gift alone drove her to it. She made up a small parcel of her belongings, let herself down by a rope one summer's night and took the road to London. She was not seventeen. The birds that sang in the hedge were not more musical than she was. She had the quickest fancy, a gift like her brother's, for the tune of words. Like him, she had a taste for the theatre. She stood at the stage door; she wanted to act, she said. Men laughed in her face. The manager—a fat, loose-lipped man—guffawed. He bellowed something about poodles dancing and women acting—no woman, he said, could possibly be an actress. He hinted—you can imagine what. She could get no training in her craft. Could she even seek her dinner in a tavern or roam the streets at midnight? Yet her genius was for fiction and lusted to feed abundantly upon the lives of men and women and the study of their ways. At last—for she was very young, oddly like Shakespeare the poet in her face, with the same grey eyes and rounded brows—at last Nick Greene the actor-manager took pity on her; she found herself with child by that gentleman and so—who shall measure the heat and violence of the poet's heart when caught and tangled in a woman's body?—killed herself one winter's night and lies buried at some cross-roads where the omnibuses now stop outside the Elephant and Castle.

BRIGID BROPHY

A prolific and witty writer of essays, articles, novels, short stories, biographies, plays, and criticism, Brigid Brophy was born in London in 1929 and has lived there since. She studied classics at Oxford from 1947 to 1948 but soon turned to free-lance writing and promptly won the Cheltenham Literary Festival prize for a first novel, Hackenfeller's Ape *(1954).*

Ms. Brophy wants her novels to "bring the reader suddenly around a corner to confront incongruity—which may be comic or ironic but is always poetic and is always in Bad Taste." Her recent works are masterpieces of polylingual punning, books to be read aloud or, as she says, sung in operatic style. Her novels include Flesh *(1962),* The Snow Ball *(1964),* In Transit: An Heroi-Cyclic Novel *(1969), and* Palace Without Chairs *(1978). She has written biographical studies of Mozart (1964), Aubrey Beardsley (1968), and Ronald Firbank (1973). Her favorite book of literary criticism is the one she wrote in collaboration with her husband and Charles Osborne—*Fifty Works of English and American Literature We Could Do Without *(1967). She has also written plays for radio and stage and devised a literary talk-show format for British television. Her essay and story collections include* The Adventures of God in His Search for the Black Girl *(1973)—a twist on George Bernard Shaw's* The Adventures of the Black Girl in Her Search for God*—and* Don't Never Forget *(1966), which includes the essay we reprint below. It first appeared in the* Saturday Evening Post, *November 2, 1963, from which we take our text.*

Women Are Prisoners of Their Sex

All right, nobody's disputing it. Women are free. At least, they *look* free. They even feel free. But in reality women in the western, industrialized world today are like the animals in a modern zoo. There are no bars. It appears that cages have been abolished. Yet in practice women are still kept in their place just as firmly as the animals are kept in their enclosures. The barriers which keep them in now are invisible.

It is about 40 years since the pioneer feminists raised such a rumpus by rattling the cage bars that society was at last obliged to pay attention. The result was that the bars were uprooted, the cage thrown open: whereupon the majority of the women who had been held captive decided that they would rather stay inside the cage anyway.

To be more precise, they *thought* they decided; and society, which can with perfect truth point out, "Look, no bars," *thought* it was giving them the choice. There are no laws and very little discrimination to prevent western, industralized women from voting, being voted for or entering the professions. If there are still few women lawyers and engineers, let alone women Presidents of the United States, what are women to conclude except that this is the result either of their own free choice or of something inherent in female nature?

Many of them do draw just this conclusion. They have come back to the old argument of the antifeminists that women are unfit by nature for life outside the cage. And in letting this old wheel come full cycle, women have fallen victim to one of the most insidious and ingenious confidence tricks ever perpetrated.

In point of fact, neither female nature nor women's individual free choice has been put to the test. As American Negroes have discovered, to be officially free is by no means the same as being actually and psychologically free. A society as adept at propaganda as ours has become should know that "persuasion," which means the art of launching myths and artificially inducing inhibitions, is every bit as effective as force of law. No doubt the reason society eventually agreed to abolish its antiwomen laws was that it had become confident of a commanding battery of hidden dissuaders which would do the job just as well. Cage bars are clumsy methods of control, which excite the more rebellious personalities inside to rattle them. Modern society, like the modern zoo, has contrived to get rid of the bars without altering the fact of imprisonment. All the zoo architect needs to do is run a zone of hot or cold air, whichever the animal concerned cannot tolerate, round the cage where the bars used to be. Human animals are not less sensitive to social climate.

The ingenious point about the new-model zoo is that it deceives both sides of the invisible barrier. Not only cannot the animal see how it is imprisoned; the visitor's conscience is relieved of the unkindness of keeping animals shut up. He can say, "Look, no bars round the animals," just as society can say, "Look, no laws restricting women," even while it keeps women rigidly in place by zones of fierce social pressure.

There is, however, one great difference. A woman, being a thinking animal, may actually be more distressed because the bars of her cage cannot be seen. What relieves society's conscience may afflict hers. Unable to perceive what is holding her back, she may accuse herself and her whole sex of craven timidity because women have not jumped at what has the appearance of an offer of freedom. Evidently quite a lot of women have succumbed to guilt of this sort, since in recent years quite an industry has arisen to assuage it. Comforting voices make the air as thick and reassuring as cotton wool while they explain that there is nothing shameful in not wanting a career, that to be intellectually unadventurous is no sin, that taking care of home and family may be personally "fulfilling" for a woman and socially valuable.

This is an argument without a flaw—except that it is addressed exclusively to women. Address it to both sexes and instantly it becomes progressive and humane. As it stands, it is merely antiwoman prejudice revamped.

That many women would be happier not pursuing careers or intellectual adventures is only part of the truth. The whole truth is that many people would be. If society had the clear sight to assure men as well as women that there is no shame in preferring to stay noncompetitively and nonaggressively at home, many masculine neuroses and ulcers would be avoided, and many children would enjoy the benefit of being brought up by a father with a talent for the job of child-rearing instead of a mother with no talent for it but a sense of guilt about the lack.

But society does nothing so sensible. Blindly it goes on insisting on the tradition that men are the ones who go out to work and adventure—an arrangement which simply throws talent away. All homemaking talent born inside male bodies is wasted; and our businesses and governments are staffed largely by people whose aptitude for the work consists solely of their being what is, by tradition, the right sex for it.

The pressures society exerts to drive men out of the house are very nearly as irrational and unjust as those by which it keeps women in. The mistake of the early reformers was to assume that men were emancipated already and that therefore reform need ask only for the emancipation of women. What we ought to do now is go right back to scratch and demand the emancipation of both sexes.

The zones of hot and cold air which society uses to perpetuate its uneconomic and unreasonable state of affairs are the simplest and most effective conceivable. Society is playing on our sexual vanity. Tell a man that he is not a real man, or a woman that she is not 100 percent woman, and you are threatening both with not being attractive to the opposite sex. No one can bear not to be attractive to the opposite sex. That is the climate which the human animal cannot tolerate.

So society has us all at its mercy. It has only to murmur to the man that staying home is a feminine characteristic, and he will be out of the house like a bullet. It has only to suggest to the woman that logic and reason are the exclusive province of the masculine mind, whereas "intuition" and "feeling" are the female forte, and she will throw her physics textbooks out of the window, barricade herself into the house and give herself up to having wishy-washy poetical feelings while she arranges the flowers.

She will, incidentally, take care that her feelings *are* wishy-washy. She has been persuaded that to have cogent feelings, of the kind which really do go into great poems—most of which are by men—would make her an unfeminine woman, a woman who imitates men. In point of fact, she would not be imitating men as such, most of whom have never written a line of great poetry, but poets most of whom so far happen to be men. But the bad logic passes muster with a woman because part of the mythology she has swallowed ingeniously informs her that logic is not her forte.

Should a woman's talent or intelligence be so irrepressible that she insists on producing cogent works of art or water-tight meshes of argument, she will be said to have "a mind like a man's."

What is more, this habit of thought actually contributes to perpetuating a state of affairs where most good minds really do belong to men. It is difficult for a woman to want to be intelligent when she has been told that to be so will make her like a man. She inclines to think an intelligence would be as unbecoming to her as a moustache; and, pathetically, many women have tried in furtive privacy to disembarrass themselves of intellect as though it were facial hair.

Discouraged from growing "a mind like a man's," women are encouraged to have thoughts and feelings of a specifically feminine tone. Women, it is said, have some specifically feminine contribution to make to culture. Unfortunately, as culture had already been shaped and largely built up by men before the invitation was issued, this leaves women little to do. Culture consists of reasoned thought and works of art composed of cogent feelings and imagination. There is only one way to be reasonable, and that is to reason correctly; and the only kind of art which is any good is good art. If women are to eschew reason and artistic imagination in favor of "intuition" and "feeling," it is pretty clear what is meant. "Intuition" is just a polite name for bad reasoning, and "feeling" for bad art.

In reality, the whole idea of a specifically feminine—or, for the matter of that, masculine—contribution to culture is a contradiction of culture. A contribution to culture is not something which could not have been made by the other sex; it is something which could not have been made by any other *person*. The arts are a sphere where women seem to have done well; but really they have done too well—too well for the good of the arts. Rather than women sharing the esteem which ought to belong to artists, art is becoming smeared with femininity. We are approaching a Philistine state of affairs where the arts are something which it is nice for women to take up in their spare time—men having slammed out of the house to get on with society's "serious" business, like making money, running the country and the professions.

In that "serious" sphere it is still rare to encounter a woman. A man sentenced to prison would probably feel his punishment was redoubled by indignity if he were to be sentenced by a woman judge under a law drafted by a woman legislator—and if, on admission, he were to be examined by a woman prison doctor. If such a thing happened every day, it would be no indignity but the natural course of events. It has never been given the chance to become the natural course of events and never will be so long as women remain persuaded it would be unnatural of them to want it.

So brilliantly has society contrived to terrorize women with this threat that certain behavior is unnatural and unwomanly, that it has left them no time to consider—or even sheerly observe—what womanly nature really is. For centuries arrant superstitions were accepted as natural law. The physiological fact that only women can secrete milk for feeding babies was extended into the pure myth that it was women's business to cook for and wait on the entire family. The kitchen became woman's "natural" place because, for the first few months of her baby's life, the nursery really was. To this day a woman may fear she is unfeminine if she can discover in herself no aptitude or liking for cooking. Fright has thrown her into such a muddle that she confuses having no taste for cookery with having no breasts, and conversely assumes that nature has unfailingly endowed the human female with a special handiness with frying pans.

Even psychoanalysis, which in general has been the greatest benefactor of civilization since the wheel, has unwittingly reinforced the terrorization campaign. The trouble was that it brought with it from its origin in medical therapy a criterion of normality instead of rationality. On sheer statistics every pioneer, genius and social reformer, including the first woman who demanded to be let out of the kitchen and into the polling booth, is abnormal, along with every lunatic and eccentric. What distinguishes the genius from the lunatic is that the genius's abnormality is justifiable by reason or aesthetics. If a woman who is irked by confinement to the kitchen merely looks around to see what other women are doing and finds they are accepting their kitchens, she may well conclude that she is abnormal and had better enlist her psychoanalyst's help toward "living with" her kitchen. What she ought to ask is whether it is rational for women to be kept to the kitchen, and whether nature really does insist on that in the way it insists women have breasts.

And in a far-reaching sense to ask that question is much more normal and natural than learning to "live with" the handicap of women's inferior social status. The normal and natural thing for human beings is not to tolerate handicaps but to reform society and to circumvent or supplement nature. We don't learn to live minus a leg; we devise an artificial limb.

That, indeed, is the crux of the matter. Not only are the distinctions we draw between male nature and female nature largely arbitrary and often pure superstition, they are completely beside the point. They ignore the essence of *human* nature. The important question is not whether women are or are not less logical by nature than men, but whether education, effort and the abolition of our illogical social pressures can improve on nature and make them—and, incidentally, men as well—more logical. What distinguishes human from any other animal nature is its ability to be unnatural. Logic and art are not natural or instinctive activities; but our nature includes a propensity to acquire them. It is not natural for the human body to orbit the earth; but the human mind has a natural adventurousness which enables it to invent machines whereby the body can do so.

Civilization consists not necessarily in defying nature but in making it possible for us to do so if we judge it desirable. The higher we can lift our noses from the grindstone of nature, the wider the area we have of choice; and the more choices we have freely made, the more individualized we are. We are at our most civilized when nature does not dictate to us, as it does to animals and peasants, but when we can opt to fall in with it or better it. If modern civilization has invented methods of preparing baby foods and methods of education which make it possible for men to feed babies and for women to think logically, we are betraying civilization itself if we do not set both sexes free to make a free choice.

JUDITH WELLS

Judith Wells was born in 1944, grew up in San Francisco, and got her B.A. in French from Stanford and her Ph.D. in comparative literature from the University of California, Berkeley. Her Ph.D. dissertation was about women and madness in modern literature— madness meaning both anger and insanity. She has helped develop the women's studies program at Berkeley and has taught several courses on women and madness in literature. She has also headed a program at Napa Community College designed to encourage older women to return to school. "Daddy's Girl," her first published work, appeared in Libera, *Winter 1972.*

Daddy's Girl

> *"A little girl, full of innocence and indulgence. And then this madness. . . ."*
> —Ladders to Fire, ANAIS NIN

Nothing is more startling to a Daddy's girl than to find herself in revolt against her Daddies. Because of her intimacy with and desire for approval from her Daddies, she finds it painful to make a clean break with them. "Daddy, daddy, you bastard, I'm through," cries Sylvia Plath in her poem "Daddy"; in spite of the voodoo murder of her Father, Plath is still a little girl murderess who addresses the "Panzer man," "the brute," the "Fascist" of her poem as Daddy. Even her closing words, "I'm through," strangely undercut her patricide—as if she herself dies with her Father—an echo of her death wish in a previous stanza: "At twenty I tried to die/And get back, back, back, to you."

This complicity with "Daddy" has been my own peculiar emotional madness for years. A large part of what I always called my "self" has been invested in the personality of the Daddy's Girl or the Little Girl. The Little Girl is fragile, vulnerable, helpless, bewildered, compliant. She feels she occupies a very tiny amount of both physical and psychological space. In my own dreams this smallness is experienced through seeing myself as a miniature person—a girl who melts down to a face in a postage stamp or a girl whose full size is as small as a person's hands (and thus easily manipulated). The Little Girl is an object, not a subject.

It took me a good deal of hard work in psychotherapy and the Women's Movement to reach any understanding about my own Little Girl. For a long time I maintained a masque of independence; I made myself believe I didn't care what my father and men thought about me. Yet underneath, I based most of my personality on masculine approval. Any criticism from a male brought me a haunting sense of guilt. The least assertion of my own preference or will was stepping over the line; I internalized the reply "You've gone too far" even before I opened my mouth. I was unable to work when my boyfriend was around and felt guilty over surpassing male friends and my father in intellectual achievements; but I also knew I had to accomplish something to get masculine approval. The only activity this ambivalence brought on was diarrhea. Then I became sick and could nurture my vulnerable, fragile self which was, and still is, in effect, my Little Girl.

The Little Girl infects many females because she is nurtured by so much of society as well as by ourselves. She has no age limit:

> She wears sweet little dresses, her tears and caprices are viewed indulgently, her hair is done up carefully, older people are amused at her expressions and coquetries—bodily contacts and agreeable glances protect her against the anguish of solitude. (*The Second Sex*, p. 252)

Although this is Simone de Beauvoir's description of a small girl in childhood, it could well apply to the Little Girl aspect of ourselves, our mothers, and our grandmothers. I was surprised when I realized that some of the gestures of my boss's eight-year-old daughter were not far from my own— her cajoling, indirect expression of what she wanted, her refusal to attempt a simple task without precise, precise instructions. The Little Girl pose is designed to elicit maternal or paternal indulgence—specifically, because the Little Girl is or thinks she is helpless.

Although the Little Girl can inhabit any woman's body, a small woman is particularly susceptible to this syndrome. In her first *Diary*, Anais Nin relates a conversation with her psychiatrist about this sense of vulnerability and helplessness that a small woman experiences:

> My greatest fear is that people will become aware that I am fragile, not a full-blown woman physically, that I am emotionally vulnerable, that I have small breasts like a girl. (p. 86)

My own sense that I am physically slight and fragile has not only bolstered my feelings of helplessness, but it has also contributed to my feeling that I am not quite a grown woman—that creature who is defined by having curves in the right places. The curveless woman easily sees herself as a Little Girl.

Although the Little Girl may be more readily apparent in a woman with a small body, most women experience the Little Girl at times as a psychic state. In Nin's *Children of the Albatross*, Djuna remembers:

She remembered, too, that whenever she became entangled in too great a difficulty she had these swift regressions into her adolescent state. Almost as if in the large world of maturity, when the obstacle loomed too large, she shrank again into the body of the young girl for whom the world had first appeared as a violent and dangerous place, forcing her to retreat, and when she retreated she fell back into smallness. (p. 40)

Djuna experiences a "psychic smallness" which is her inability to affect significantly the world around her—hence, her helplessness.

In the Little Girl, "psychic smallness" is also directly related to her desire for approval from authority figures, especially from Daddies. As a Little Girl, I found that I had based my personality for such a long time on approval from authority figures that *they* were my personality. I experienced "psychic smallness" because I had never defined who I was or what I wanted in life; my only sense of identity stemmed from Daddy's approval.

The real tragedy of the Little Girl, then, is her inability to define herself in her own terms, select her own goals, and feel her life has significance *without* Daddy's support. The Little Girl turns over the responsibility for her own life to her Daddies (real fathers, boyfriends, husbands, professors, psychiatrists) and sits devotedly, if a bit uneasily, at their feet. Unfortunately, society sanctions this pose of the Child-Woman, especially in its sexual images and stereotypes.

In the Magic Theater's recent production of *Miles Gloriosus*, two poles of stereotyped female sexuality are portrayed: the Vixen-Whore in black wasp waist corset and tights, and the Baby Doll in pink pajamas, with freckles on her nose and ribbons in her hair. Although the Baby Doll is parody in this play, many girls are schooled in this image of coyness, flirtation, and "innocent" sexuality which they carry over into adult life. The Little Girl clothes syndrome, which periodically runs rampant through fashion as it has recently, supports this image: the mod "little dresses," the clingy pastel tee shirts with patterns from babyhood, the overall and romper outfits—all designed to make females resemble innocent little girls yet still be sexually appealing. Roger Vadim exploited this combination of innocence and sexuality to the hilt in his presentation of Brigitte Bardot to moviegoers. In Simone de Beauvoir's book, *Brigitte Bardot and the Lolita Syndrome*, the author relates:

> He [Vadim] painted her as naive to the point of absurdity. According to him, at the age of eighteen she thought that mice laid eggs. (p. 13)

De Beauvoir comments on Bardot's roles in "And God Created Woman" and "Love Is My Profession":

> BB is a lost, pathetic child who needs a guide and protector. This cliché has proved its worth. It flatters masculine vanity. . . . (p. 15)

The child-woman poses no threat to the male ego—hence her appeal. De Beauvoir notes the particular charm of the child-woman to the American male:

> . . . he feels a certain antipathy to the 'real woman.' He regards her as an antagonist, a praying mantis, a tyrant. He abandons himself eagerly to the charms of the 'nymph' in whom the formidable figure of the wife and 'Mom' is not yet apparent. (p. 23)

Although I hardly possess the "nymph" looks of Bardot, my own appearance and Little Girl personality have encouraged me to maintain this child-woman sexual role. When I was younger, this child role came easily; but with increased sexual experience, the role became harder and harder to maintain. I can't kid myself anymore. I know my own sexual desires, but the child-woman in me still makes me embarrassed when I want to be sexually aggressive or state my desires straight out. I know many women share this problem—this embarrassment over wanting to be a subject, not an object in sexual activity. And the male attitude doesn't help much; for even though "The Sexual Revolution's Here," a woman is discouraged subtly (a male's slightly chilly response to her phone call) and not so subtly (his impotence when she asks him to bed) when she is sexually aggressive.

As a Little Girl I have spent a good deal of my life adjusting to just such masculine requirements, adapting myself to gain their approval. Finally, I felt pain—the intense frustration of being confined by my own compliancy. I understand all too well the statement of the man I work for (who designed an educational program to improve the self-image of Blacks) about the accommodation attitudes of Blacks. I have substituted *woman* for *man* in the quote and *her* for *him:*

> Let us assume I am standing with my foot on the neck of a *woman* who is lying on the ground; I am wearing a hobnail boot. I say to *her,* "Your role is simply different from mine, not worse; you are horizontal and I am vertical." And then I say to *her,* "Your role has certain advantages over mine; you do not have to worry about falling down. Furthermore, you are developing a very interesting adaptive behavior. You are learning to breathe with my foot on your neck." (*Teaching and Testing the Disadvantaged,* William Johntz)

Interestingly enough, the sado-masochistic imagery of this passage exactly fits sexual politics. The victim is made to feel she is lucky she doesn't have the "burdens" of the victor. The victim's final adaptive behavior is what the Little Girl and, in actuality, any woman, has done all her life. She has learned to breathe with a foot on her neck until she finally explodes in frustration and cries out with Sylvia Plath, "You do not do, you do not do/Any more, black shoe. . . ."

It would be great if the Little Girl could join the Women's Movement and instantly become a self-sufficient woman. I have found that my Little Girl personality is not shed so easily, and that my rebellion against my Daddies has its own peculiar Little Girl cyclic rhythm: compliancy towards a man—simmering hate—explosion of outrage—anxiety over having stepped over the line—fear of reprisal—compliancy towards a man—and the cycle begins again. Because the Little Girl has suffocated her own desires so completely in favor of her Daddies, her potential for rage is volcanic once she questions the belief that "Father knows best." Yet for myself and probably for most Little Girls, each explosion is followed less by a sense of triumph than by anxiety and fear of reprisal. Since the Little Girl's only previous sense of identity stemmed from approval from her Daddies, cutting these figures out of her life will seem like cutting out the core of herself. At first, "destruction" of Daddy seems like self-destruction. This anxiety over self-destruction in the elimination of her source of identity brings on the Little Girl's helplessness. She is then a weak, vulnerable, compliant child again, fearing Daddy's reprisal.

Even if she finally rebels against her Daddies, the Little Girl will remain caught in this circle of anger and compliancy until she learns to stop loving and nurturing the Little Girl in herself. If I had to select the most important moment in my several years of psychotherapy, it would be the moment I realized who loved the Little Girl in me most. I was astonished to find it was myself. I was finally able to objectify my Little Girl enough to see her as separate from another part of me. I experienced myself caressing and cherishing that Little Girl as I had loved my dolls many years ago—the same kind of love I desperately wanted to experience when I was a real little girl. Perhaps, above everything else, this desperation for love kept me locked into my first childhood attempts to gain approval from adults. And when, as a real little girl, I realized that the "adult world" was governed mainly by male figures, I began to base my worth on how much love and approval I could get from my Daddies. The Little Girl pose stuck.

I am coming to realize more and more that I no longer receive much approval for the Little Girl role; it's an illusion I maintain which has little basis in my own daily life. As a friend of mine in graduate school put it, "I'm thirty years old. I look like a grown woman. If I start to do the Little Girl bit with my professors, they look at me funny." The Little Girl role has a few benefits but enormous drawbacks: a stifling of one's intelligence and creativity, a confining sexual role, an arresting of growth of one's personality. When I experienced myself cherishing my Little Girl doll self, I flashed on a picture I had drawn when I was ten years old to illustrate a poem I had read called "The long ago, far away doll." I drew a doll in a sea chest; she was dressed in a lovely yellow fancy dress, and her cheeks were rouged; but her eyes stared into space, and she looked like a dead person. The Little Girl aspect of any woman keeps her like this doll—repressed, inactive, dead.

The Little Girl has no place to grow but up. It is true that if she does choose to continue her growth, she may not receive some of the masculine approval she received in the past. As I stated previously, certain men like a Little Girl because she is less threatening to the masculine ego. Too, the growing Little Girl must risk the disapproval of her real father—often the man who clings the most tenaciously to the idea of his daughter as a perpetual girl child. She may be regarded as a rebel or even a bitch. Yet there will be others, both women and men, who will approve of her—not for feminine fluff, but for her real talents and developing personality. More important, she will gain self-respect from presenting her *own self* to the world, and this self-respect will be worth much more than the approval she received as a crippled Little Girl.

I read someplace in my many psychological readings, when I was trying to pinpoint my "problems," about a young girl in an African society. In her early teens, she was listless, lacked confidence, and was fearful of males and masculine authority. Her tribe used a mode of transvestitism to exorcise her fears. She dressed up in the male military costume of the former colonial power of the area and began to dance in this costume. After the ceremony, the girl's confidence increased enormously, she no longer feared men, and she eventually developed into a mature, self-reliant woman. The girl in this story acts out symbolically what the Little Girl must learn to do for herself: incorporate the authority, which she objectifies outside of herself, into her own person. She must develop a sense of her *own personal authority* and hence, *self-approval*. When the Little Girl develops this sense of self-approval, she will no longer be a Little Girl, but a mature woman—a full, complete human being. With this new sense of personal authority, she can look back on her "rebellious" struggles as Anais Nin does:

> Very often I would say I rebelled against this or that. Much later it occurred to me to question this statement. Instead of rebellion could it be that I was merely asserting my own belief? (*Diary* III, p. xiii)

And I answer with Nin: YES.

MATINA HORNER

Matina Horner was born in 1933 to Greek parents, who decided to stay in the United States after the outbreak of World War II. She received her bachelor's degree from Bryn Mawr College in 1961 and then attended the University of Michigan, where in 1968 she received her doctorate in psychology with some of the research she writes about in the present essay. The research appeared in Psychology Today *in November 1969, headed by a quotation from Balzac: "A woman who is guided by the head and not by the heart is a social pestilence: she has all the defects of a passionate and affectionate woman with none of her compensations: she is without pity, without love, without virtue, without sex."*

Besides being an authority on motivation and achievement in women, Dr. Horner has studied ability grouping in schools, the impact of internalized sex and race role stereotypes, and factors that foster the development of curiosity. She has been on the Harvard faculty since 1969 in the Department of Social Relations, and in 1972 she became President of Radcliffe College, which is integrated as a coeducational institution with Harvard.

Fail: Bright Women

Consider Phil, a bright young college sophomore. He has always done well in school, he is in the honors program, he has wanted to be a doctor as long as he can remember. We ask him to tell us a story based on one clue: *"After first-term finals, John finds himself at the top of his medical school class."* Phil writes:

> John is a conscientious young man who worked hard. He is pleased with himself. John has always wanted to go into medicine and is very dedicated . . . John continues working hard and eventually graduates at the top of his class.

Now consider Monica, another honors student. She too has always done well and she too has visions of a flourishing career. We give her the same clue, but with "Anne" as the successful student—*after first-term finals, Anne finds herself at the top of her medical school class.* Instead of identifying with Anne's triumph, Monica tells a bizarre tale:

> Anne starts proclaiming her surprise and joy. Her fellow classmates are so disgusted with her behavior that they jump on her in a body and beat her. She is maimed for life.

Next we ask Monica and Phil to work on a series of achievement tests by themselves. Monica scores higher than Phil. Finally we get them together, competing against each other on the same kind of tests. Phil performs magnificently, but Monica dissolves into a bundle of nerves.

The glaring contrast between the two stories and the dramatic changes in performance in competitive situations illustrate important differences between men and women in reacting to achievement.

In 1953, David McClelland, John Atkinson and colleagues published the first major work on the "achievement motive." Through the use of the Thematic Apperception Test (TAT), they were able to isolate the psychological characteristic of a *need to achieve.* This seemed to be an internalized standard of excellence, motivating the individual to do well in any achievement-oriented situation involving intelligence and leadership ability. Subsequent investigators studied innumerable facets of achievement motivation: how it is instilled in children, how it is expressed, how it relates to social class, even how it is connected to the rise and fall of civilizations. The result of all this research is an impressive and a theoretically consistent body of data about the achievement motive—in men.

Women, however, are conspicuously absent from almost all of the studies. In the few cases where the ladies were included, the results were contradictory or confusing. So women were eventually left out altogether. The predominantly male researchers apparently decided, as Freud had before them, that the only way to understand woman was to turn to the poets. Atkinson's 1958 book, *Motives in Fantasy, Action and Society,* is an 800-page compilation of all of the theories and facts on achievement motivation in men. Women got a footnote, reflecting the state of the science.

To help remedy this lopsided state of affairs, I undertook to explore the basis for sex differences in achievement motivation. But where to begin?

My first clue came from the one consistent finding on the women: they get higher test-anxiety scores than do the men. Eleanor Maccoby has suggested that the girl who is motivated to achieve is defying conventions of what girls "should" do. As a result, the intellectual woman pays a price in anxiety. Margaret Mead concurs, noting that intense intellectual striving can be viewed as "competitively aggressive behavior." And of course Freud thought that the whole essence of femininity lay in repressing aggressiveness (and hence intellectuality).

Thus consciously or unconsciously the girl equates intellectual achievement with loss of femininity. A bright woman is caught in a double bind. In testing and other achievement-oriented situations she worries not only about failure, but also about success. If she fails, she is not living up to her own standards of performance; if she succeeds, she is not living up to societal expectations about the female role. Men in our society do not experience this kind of ambivalence, because they are not only permitted but actively encouraged to do well.

For women, then, the desire to achieve is often contaminated by what I call the *motive to avoid success*. I define it as the fear that success in competitive achievement situations will lead to negative consequences, such as unpopularity and loss of femininity. This motive, like the achievement motive itself, is a stable disposition within the person, acquired early in life along with other sex-role standards. When fear of success conflicts with a desire to be successful, the result is an inhibition of achievement motivation.

I began my study with several hypotheses about the motive to avoid success:

1) Of course, it would be far more characteristic of women than of men.

2) It would be more characteristic of women who are capable of success and who are career-oriented than of women not so motivated. Women who are not seeking success should not, after all, be threatened by it.

3) I anticipated that the anxiety over success would be greater in competitive situations (when one's intellectual performance is evaluated against someone else's) than in noncompetitive ones (when one works alone). The aggressive, masculine aspects of achievement striving are certainly more pronounced in competitive settings, particularly when the opponent is male. Women's anxiety should therefore be greatest when they compete with men.

I administered the standard TAT achievement motivation measures to a sample of 90 girls and 88 boys, all undergraduates at the University of Michigan. In addition, I asked each to tell a story based on the clue described before: *After first-term finals, John (Anne) finds himself (herself) at the top of his (her) medical school class.* The girls wrote about Anne, the boys about John.

Their stories were scored for "motive to avoid success" if they expressed any negative imagery that reflected concern about doing well. Generally, such imagery fell into three categories:

1) The most frequent Anne story reflected strong fears of social rejection

as a result of success. The girls in this group showed anxiety about becoming unpopular, unmarriageable and lonely.

> Anne is an acne-faced bookworm. She runs to the bulletin board and finds she's at the top. As usual she smarts off. A chorus of groans is the rest of the class's reply. . . . She studies 12 hours a day, and lives at home to save money. "Well it certainly paid off. All the Friday and Saturday nights without dates, fun—I'll be the best woman doctor alive." And yet a twinge of sadness comes thru—she wonders what she really has . . .

> Although Anne is happy with her success she fears what will happen to her social life. The male med. students don't seem to think very highly of a female who has beaten them in their field . . . She will be a proud and successful but alas a very *lonely* doctor.

> Anne doesn't want to be number one in her class . . . she feels she shouldn't rank so high because of social reasons. She drops down to ninth in the class and then marries the boy who graduates number one.

> Anne is pretty darn proud of herself, but everyone hates and envies her.

2) Girls in the second category were less concerned with issues of social approval or disapproval; they were more worried about definitions of womanhood. Their stories expressed guilt and despair over success, and doubts about their femininity or normality.

> Unfortunately Anne no longer feels so certain that she really wants to be a doctor. She is worried about herself and wonders if perhaps she isn't normal . . . Anne decides not to continue with her medical work but to take courses that have a deeper personal meaning for her.

> Anne feels guilty . . . She will finally have a nervous breakdown and quit medical school and marry a successful young doctor.

> Anne is pleased. She had worked extraordinarily hard and her grades showed it. "It is not enough," Anne thinks. "I am not happy." She didn't even want to be a doctor. She is not sure what she wants. Anne says to hell with the whole business and goes into social work—not hardly as glamorous, prestigious or lucrative; but she is happy.

3) The third group of stories did not even try to confront the ambivalence about doing well. Girls in this category simply denied the possibility that any mere woman could be so successful. Some of them completely changed the content of the clue, or distorted it, or refused to believe it, or absolved Anne of responsibility for her success. These stories were remarkable for their psychological ingenuity:

Anne is a *code name* for a nonexistent person created by a group of med. students. They take turns writing exams for Anne . . .

Anne is really happy she's on top, though *Tom is higher than she*—though that's as it should be . . . Anne doesn't mind Tom winning.

Anne is talking to her counselor. Counselor says she will make a fine *nurse*.

It was *luck* that Anne came out on top because she didn't want to go to medical school anyway.

Fifty-nine girls—over 65 per cent—told stories that fell into one or another of the above categories. But only eight boys, fewer than 10 per cent, showed evidence of the motive to avoid success. (These differences are significant at better than the .0005 level.) In fact, sometimes I think that most of the young men in the sample were incipient Horatio Algers. They expressed unequivocal delight at John's success (clearly John had worked hard for it), and projected a grand and glorious future for him. There was none of the hostility, bitterness and ambivalence that the girls felt for Anne. In short, the differences between male and female stories based on essentially the same clue were enormous.

Two of the stories are particularly revealing examples of this male-female contrast. The girls insisted that Anne give up her career for marriage:

Anne has a boyfriend, Carl, in the same class and they are quite serious . . . She wants him to be scholastically higher than she is. Anne will deliberately lower her academic standing the next term, while she does all she subtly can to help Carl. His grades come up and Anne soon drops out of medical school. They marry and he goes on in school while she raises their family.

But of course the boys would ask John to do no such thing:

John has worked very hard and his long hours of study have paid off . . . He is thinking about his girl, Cheri, whom he will marry at the end of med. school. He realizes he can give her all the things she desires after he becomes established. He will go on in med. school and be successful in the long run.

Success inhibits social life for the girls; it enhances social life for the boys.

Earlier I suggested that the motive to avoid success is especially aroused in competitive situations. In the second part of this study I wanted to see whether the aggressive overtones of competition against men scared the girls away. Would competition raise their anxiety about success and thus lower their performance?

First I put all of the students together in a large competitive group, and gave them a series of achievement tests (verbal and arithmetic). I then assigned them randomly to one of three other experimental conditions. One-third worked on a similar set of tests, each in competition with a member of the same sex. One-third competed against a member of the opposite sex. The last third worked by themselves, a non-competitive condition.

Ability is an important factor in achievement motivation research. If you want to compare two persons on the strength of their *motivation* to succeed, how do you know that any differences in performance are not due to initial differences in *ability* to succeed? One way of avoiding this problem is to use each subject as his own control; that is, the performance of an individual working alone can be compared with his score in competition. Ability thus remains constant; any change in score must be due to motivational factors. This control over ability was, of course, possible only for the last third of my subjects: the 30 girls and 30 boys who had worked alone *and* in the large group competition. I decided to look at their scores first.

Performance changed dramatically over the two situations. A large number of the men did far better when they were in competition than when they worked alone. For the women the reverse was true. Fewer than one-third of the women, but more than two-thirds of the men, got significantly higher scores in competition.

When we looked at just the girls in terms of the motive to avoid success, the comparisons were even more striking. As predicted, the students who felt ambivalent or anxious about doing well turned in their best scores when they worked by themselves. Seventy-seven percent of the girls who feared success did better alone than in competition. Women who were low on the motive, however, behaved more like the men: 93 per cent of them got higher scores in competition. (Results significant at the .005.)

Female Fear of Success & Performance

	perform better working alone	perform better in competition
high fear of success	13	4
low fear of success	1	12

As a final test of motivational differences, I asked the students to indicate on a scale from 1 to 100 "How important was it for you to do well in this situation?" The high-fear-of-success girls said that it was much more important for them to do well when they worked alone than when they worked in either kind of competition. For the low-fear girls, such differences were not statistically significant. Their test scores were higher in competition, as we saw, and they thought that it was important to succeed no matter what the setting. And in all experimental conditions—working alone, or in competition against males or females—high-fear women consistently lagged behind their fearless comrades on the importance of doing well.

The findings suggest that most women will fully explore their intellectual potential only when they do not need to compete—and least of all when they are competing with men. This was most true of women with a strong anxiety about success. Unfortunately, these are often the same women who could be very successful if they were free from that anxiety. The girls in my sample who feared success also tended to have high intellectual ability and histories of academic success. (It is interesting to note that all but two of these girls were majoring in the humanities and in spite of very high grade points aspired to traditional female careers: housewife, mother, nurse, schoolteacher. Girls who did not fear success, however, were aspiring to graduate degrees and careers in such scientific areas as math, physics and chemistry.)

We can see from this small study that achievement motivation in women is much more complex than the same drive in men. Most men do not find many inhibiting forces in their path if they are able and motivated to succeed. As a result, they are not threatened by competition; in fact, surpassing an opponent is a source of pride and enhanced masculinity.

If a woman sets out to do well, however, she bumps into a number of obstacles. She learns that it really isn't ladylike to be too intellectual. She is warned that men will treat her with distrustful tolerance at best, and outright prejudice at worst, if she pursues a career. She learns the truth of Samuel Johnson's comment, "A man is in general better pleased when he has a good dinner upon his table, than when his wife talks Greek." So she doesn't learn Greek, and the motive to avoid success is born.

In recent years many legal and educational barriers to female achievement have been removed; but it is clear that a psychological barrier remains. The motive to avoid success has an all-too-important influence on the intellectual and professional lives of women in our society. But perhaps there is cause for optimism. Monica may have seen Anne maimed for life, but a few of the girls forecast a happier future for our medical student. Said one:

> Anne is quite a lady—not only is she tops academically, but she is liked and admired by her fellow students—quite a trick in a man-dominated field. She is brilliant—but she is also a woman. She will continue to be at or near the top. And . . . always a lady.

WIVES AND HUSBANDS

JUDY SYFERS

Judy Syfers, who was born in San Francisco in 1937, describes herself as "middle-aged, middle-class, and still married." She feels that the problems of American wives "stem from a social system which places primary value on profits rather than on people's needs.

As long as we continue to tolerate the system, we will continue to be exploited as workers and as wives." Ms. Syfers received her B.F.A. in painting from the University of Iowa in 1960. She wanted to go on for a higher degree that would enable her to paint and to teach in a university, but her (male) teachers advised that the best she could hope for as a woman was teaching in high school with a secondary-education credential. Her reaction was to drop school, get married, and have two children. Thus the present piece, which appeared in the Spring 1972 preview issue of Ms, *arises from real experience.*

Ms. Syfers lives in San Francisco, continues to write for such causes as the United Farm Workers, and is editing a pair of diaries—one that she kept during a six-week visit to Cuba in 1973, the other kept by her husband who stayed behind to take care of the house, two girls, and his job.

I Want a Wife

I belong to that classification of people known as wives. I am A Wife. And, not altogether incidentally, I am a mother.

Not too long ago a male friend of mine appeared on the scene fresh from a recent divorce. He had one child, who is, of course, with his ex-wife. He is looking for another wife. As I thought about him while I was ironing one evening, it suddenly occurred to me that I, too, would like to have a wife. Why do I want a wife?

I would like to go back to school so that I can become economically independent, support myself, and, if need be, support those dependent upon me. I want a wife who will work and send me to school. And while I am going to school I want a wife to take care of my children. I want a wife to keep track of the children's doctor and dentist appointments. And to keep track of mine, too. I want a wife to make sure my children eat properly and are kept clean. I want a wife who will wash the children's clothes and keep them mended. I want a wife who is a good nurturant attendant to my children, who arranges for their schooling, makes sure that they have an adequate social life with their peers, takes them to the park, the zoo, etc. I want a wife who takes care of the children when they are sick, a wife who arranges to be around when the children need special care, because, of course, I cannot miss classes at school. My wife must arrange to lose time at work and not lose the job. It may mean a small cut in my wife's income from time to time, but I guess I can tolerate that. Needless to say, my wife will arrange and pay for the care of the children while my wife is working.

I want a wife who will take care of *my* physical needs. I want a wife who will keep my house clean. A wife who will pick up after me. I want a wife who will keep my clothes clean, ironed, mended, replaced when need be, and who will see to it that my personal things are kept in their proper place so that I can find what I need the minute I need it. I want a wife who cooks the meals, a wife who is a *good* cook. I want a wife who will plan the menus, do the necessary grocery shopping, prepare the meals, serve them pleasantly, and then do the cleaning up while I do my studying. I want a wife who will care for me when I am sick and sympathize with my pain and loss of time from school. I want a wife to go along when our family takes a vacation so that someone can continue to care for me and my children when I need a rest and change of scene.

I want a wife who will not bother me with rambling complaints about a wife's duties. But I want a wife who will listen to me when I feel the need to explain a rather difficult point I have come across in my course of studies. And I want a wife who will type my papers for me when I have written them.

I want a wife who will take care of the details of my social life. When my wife and I are invited out by friends, I want a wife who will take care of the babysitting arrangements. When I meet people at school that I like and want to entertain, I want a wife who will have the house clean, will prepare a special meal, serve it to me and my friends, and not interrupt when I talk about the things that interest me and my friends. I want a wife who will have arranged that the children are fed and ready for bed before my guests arrive so that the children do not bother us. I want a wife who takes care of the needs of my guests so that they feel comfortable, who makes sure that they have an ashtray, that they are passed the hors d'oeuvres, that they are offered a second helping of the food, that their wine glasses are replenished when necessary, that their coffee is served to them as they like it. And I want a wife who knows that sometimes I need a night out by myself.

I want a wife who is sensitive to my sexual needs, a wife who makes love passionately and eagerly when I feel like it, a wife who makes sure that I am satisfied. And, of course, I want a wife who will not demand sexual attention when I am not in the mood for it. I want a wife who assumes the complete responsibility for birth control, because I do not want more children. I want a wife who will remain sexually faithful to me so that I do not have to clutter up my intellectual life with jealousies. And I want a wife who understands that *my* sexual needs may entail more than strict adherence to monogamy. I must, after all, be able to relate to people as fully as possible.

If, by chance, I find another person more suitable as a wife than the wife I already have, I want the liberty to replace my present wife with another one. Naturally, I will expect a fresh, new life; my wife will take the children and be solely responsible for them so that I am left free.

When I am through with school and have a job, I want my wife to quit working and remain at home so that my wife can more fully and completely take care of a wife's duties.

My God, who *wouldn't* want a wife?

ESTHER VILAR

Esther Vilar was born of German parents in 1935 in Buenos Aires, Argentina; she grew up there and received a medical degree from the University of Buenos Aires. She now lives

*in Munich, Germany, where she practiced as a physician from 1960 to 1961 but has since
worked as a free-lance writer. She was married for two years to a German writer and has
a son.*

Der dressierte Mann (1971; trans. The Manipulated Man, *1973), from which
we reprint a chapter below, is Esther Vilar's fourth book and first success. It has been
translated into twenty-one languages and has sold over half a million copies. Its thesis is
clear: A man is a human being who works; a woman is a human being who does not.
Woman manipulates man in the way Pavlov conditioned his dogs. She says that she
"wrote the book very quickly, much of it in the United States where I spent about a year
in all, gathering material that convinced me American men are the most manipulated of
all by their women. . . . Ever since Simone de Beauvoir and* The Second Sex *it has
been popular to say women are suppressed by men, but I never saw any signs of it."*

What Is Woman?

A woman, as we have already said, is, in contrast to a man, a human being
who does not work. One might leave it at that, for there isn't much more to
say about her, were the basic concept of "human being" not so general and
inexact in embracing both "man" and "woman."

Life offers the human being two choices: animal existence—a lower order
of life—and spiritual existence. In general, a woman will choose the former
and opt for physical well-being, a place to breed, and an opportunity to
indulge unhindered in her breeding habits.

At birth, men and women have the same intellectual potential; there is
no primary difference in intelligence between the sexes. It is also a fact that
potential left to stagnate will atrophy. Women do not use their mental
capacity: they deliberately let it disintegrate. After a few years of sporadic
training, they revert to a state of irreversible mental torpor.

Why do women not make use of their intellectual potential? For the
simple reason that they do not need to. It is not essential for their survival.
Theoretically it is possible for a beautiful woman to have less intelligence
than a chimpanzee and still be considered an acceptable member of society.

By the age of twelve at the latest, most women have decided to become
prostitutes. Or, to put it another way, they have planned a future for themselves which consists of choosing a man and letting him do all the work. In
return for his support, they are prepared to let him make use of their vagina
at certain given moments. The minute a woman has made this decision she
ceases to develop her mind. She may, of course, go on to obtain various
degrees and diplomas. These increase her market value in the eyes of men,
for men believe that a woman who can recite things by heart must also *know
and understand* them. But any real possibility of communication between the
sexes ceases at this point. Their paths are divided forever.

One of man's worst mistakes, and one he makes over and over again, is to
assume that woman is his equal, that is, a human being of equal mental and
emotional capacity. A man may observe his wife, listen to her, judge her

feelings by her reactions, but in all this he is judging her only by outward symptoms, for he is using his *own* scale of values.

He knows what *he* would say, think, and do if he were in her shoes. When he looks at her depressing ways of doing things, he assumes there must be something that prevents her from doing what he himself would have done in her position. This is natural, as he considers himself the measure of all things—and rightly so—if humans define themselves as being capable of abstract thought.

When a man sees a woman spending hours cooking, washing dishes, and cleaning, it never occurs to him that such jobs probably make her quite happy since they are exactly at her mental level. Instead he assumes that this drudgery prevents her from doing all those things which he himself considers worthwhile and desirable. Therefore, he invents automatic dishwashers, vacuum cleaners, and precooked foods to make her life easier and to allow her to lead the dream life he himself longs for.

But he will be disappointed: rarely using the time she has gained to take an active interest in history, politics, or astrophysics, woman bakes cakes, irons underclothes, and make ruffles and frills for blouses or, if she is especially enterprising, covers her bathroom with flower decals. It is natural, therefore, that man assumes such things to be the essential ingredients of *gracious living*. This idea must have been instilled by woman, as he himself really doesn't mind if his cakes are store-bought, his underpants unironed, or his bathroom devoid of flowery patterns. He invents cake mixes to liberate her from drudgery, automatic irons and toilet-paper holders already covered with flower patterns to make gracious living easier to attain—and still women take no interest in serious literature, politics, or the conquest of the universe. For her, this newfound leisure comes at just the right moment. At last she can take an interest in *herself:* since a longing after intellectual achievements is alien to her, she concentrates on her external appearance.

Yet even this occupation is acceptable to man. He really loves his wife and wants her happiness more than anything in the world. Therefore, he produces nonsmear lipstick, waterproof mascara, home permanents, no-iron frilly blouses, and throwaway underwear—always with the same aim in view. In the end, he hopes, this being whose needs seem to him so much more sensitive, so much more refined, will gain freedom—freedom to achieve in *her* life the ideal state which is *his* dream: to live the life of a *free* man.

Then he sits back and waits. Finally, as woman does not come to him of her own free will, he tries to tempt her into his world. He offers her coeducation, so that she is accustomed to his way of life from childhood. With all sorts of excuses, he gets her to attend his universities and initiates her into the mysteries of his own discoveries, hoping to awaken her interest in the wonders of life. He gives her access to the very last male strongholds, thereby relinquishing traditions sacred to him by encouraging her to make use of her right to vote in the hope that she will change the systems of government he has managed to think up so laboriously, according to her own ideas. Possibly he even hopes that she will be able to create peace in the world—for, in his opinion, women are a pacifist influence.

In all this he is so determined and pigheaded that he fails to see what a fool he is making of himself—ridiculous by his own standards, not those of women, who have absolutely no sense of humor.

No, women do not laugh at men. At most they get irritated. The old institutions of house and home are not yet so obviously outdated and derelict that they can't justify relinquishing all their intellectual pursuits and renouncing all their claims to better jobs. One does wonder, however, what will happen when housework is still further mechanized, when there are *enough* good nursery schools nearby, or when—as must occur before long— men discover that children themselves are not essential.

If only man would stop for one moment in his heedless rush toward progress and think about this state of affairs, he would inevitably realize that his efforts to give woman a sense of mental stimulation have been totally in vain. It is true that woman gets progressively more elegant, more well-groomed, more "cultured," but her demands on life will always be material, never intellectual.

Has she ever made use of the mental processes he teaches at his universities to develop her own theories? Does she do independent research in the institutes he has thrown open to her? Someday it will dawn on man that woman does not read the wonderful books with which he has filled his libraries. And though she may well admire his marvelous works of art in museums, she herself will rarely create, only copy. Even the plays and films, visual exhortations to woman on her own level to liberate herself, are judged only by their entertainment value. They will never be a first step to revolution.

When a man, believing woman his equal, realizes the futility of her way of life, he naturally tends to think that it must be *his* fault, that *he* must be suppressing *her*. But in our time women are no longer subject to the will of men. Quite the contrary. They have been given every opportunity to win their independence and if, after all this time, they have not liberated themselves and thrown off their shackles, we can only arrive at one conclusion: there are no shackles to throw off.

It is true that men love women, but they also despise them. Anyone who gets up in the morning fresh and ready to conquer new worlds (with infrequent success, admittedly, because he has to earn a living) is bound to despise someone who simply isn't interested in such pursuits. Contempt may even be one of the main reasons for his efforts to further the mental development of a woman. He feels ashamed of her and assumes that she, too, must be ashamed of herself. So, being a gentleman, he tries to help.

Men seem incapable of realizing that women entirely lack ambition, desire for knowledge, and need to prove themselves, all things which, to him, are a matter of course. They allow men to live in a world apart because they do not want to join them. Why should they? The sort of independence men have means nothing to women, because women don't feel dependent. They are not even embarrassed by the intellectual superiority of men because they have no ambition in that direction.

There is one great advantage which women have over men: *they have a choice*—a choice between the life of a man and the life of a dimwitted, parasitic luxury item. There are too few women who would not select the latter. Men do not have this choice.

If women really felt oppressed by men, they would have developed hate and fear for them, as the oppressed always do, but women do not fear men, much less hate them. If they really felt humiliated by men's mental superiority, they would have used every means in their power to change the situation. If women really felt unfree, surely, at such a favorable time in their history, they would have broken free of the oppressors.

In Switzerland, one of the most highly developed countries of the world, where until recently women were not allowed to vote, in a certain canton, it is reported, the majority of women were against introducing the vote for women. The Swiss men were shattered, for they saw in this unworthy attitude yet another proof of centuries of male oppression.

How very wrong they were! Women feel anything but oppressed by men. On the contrary, one of the many depressing truths about the relationship between the sexes is simply that man hardly exists in a woman's world: Man is not even powerful enough to revolt against. Woman's dependence on him is only material, of a "physical" nature, something like a tourist's dependence on an airline, a café proprietor's on his espresso machine, a car's on gasoline, a television set's on electric current. Such dependencies hardly involve agonizing.

Ibsen, who suffered from the same misapprehensions as other men, meant his *Doll's House* to be a kind of manifesto for the freedom of women. The première in 1880 certainly shocked *men*, and they determined to fight harder to improve women's position.

For women themselves, however, the struggle for emancipation as usual took shape in a change of style: for a while they delighted in their often-laughed-at masquerade as suffragettes.

Later on, the philosophy of Sartre made a similarly profound impression on women. As proof that they understood it completely, they let their hair grow down to their waists and wore black pullovers and trousers.

Even the teachings of the Chinese Communist leader Mao Tse-tung were a success—the Mao look lasted a whole season.

MERLE HODGE

Merle Hodge, a teacher and writer, was born on the Caribbean island of Trinidad in 1944. She went to primary and secondary school there, then left to study French at the University of London. She traveled in Europe, lived in Senegal and Gambia, and in April

1970 published her first novel, Crick Crack, Monkey. *In 1970 she returned to Trinidad. For two years she taught French, West Indian literature, and English at a government secondary school, then became a lecturer in French Caribbean and French African literature at the University of the West Indies, Kingston, Jamaica. The present essay appeared in the collection* Is Massa Day Dead? Black Moods in the Caribbean, *edited by Orde Coombs (1974).*

The Shadow of the Whip

The man-woman relationship is nowhere a straightforward, uncomplicated one—it is always perhaps the most vulnerable, the most brittle of human relationships. And in the Caribbean this relationship had been adversely affected by certain factors of our historical development, notably, I think, by the legacy of violence and disruption with which our society has never adequately come to terms.

Caribbean society was born out of brutality, destructiveness, rape; the destruction of the Amerindian peoples, the assault on Africa, the forced uprooting and enslavement of the African; the gun, the whip, the authority of force. Yet the Caribbean area today is not particularly noted for any large-scale, organized violence. Caribbean governments sit securely and complacently, with or without popular support.

But the violence of our history has not evaporated. It is still there. It is there in the relations between adult and child, between black and white, between man and woman. It has been internalized, it has seeped down into our personal lives. Drastic brutality—physical and verbal—upon children is an accepted part of child rearing in the Caribbean. "Gavin," threatens Laura of *Miguel Street* to one of her children, "Gavin, if you don't come here this minute, I make you fart fire, you hear." And C. L. R. James in his novel *Minty Alley* describes a hair-raising scene of violence upon a child which contains not an inch of exaggeration.

Our capacity for verbal violence is limitless. Teasing and heckling are taken to lengths which would shock in another society. For example, we award nicknames on the basis of hopeless physical deformities—"Hop-and-Drop," for example, for a polio victim who walks with a pathetic limp. Our expressions of abuse would fill catalogues. Quarreling is a national pastime—quarrels are spectacular: a great deal of energy and artistry are applied to body movements, the ingenuity of insults, the graphic recitation of the antagonist's crimes; a good quarrel will provide a morning's dramatic diversion for a whole neighborhood, for quarrels often emerge onto the street as if in search of an adequate stage.

And the fact that a physical fight between a man and a woman—or more accurately, a woman-beating—may erupt into the open air and rage for hours without any serious alarm on the part of onlookers for the safety of the woman, without attracting the intervention of the law, is a strong comment on our attitudes:

> Never never put yu mouth
> In husband-and-wife business.

runs the refrain of one calypso, a word of warning to the sentimental, to those who may be naïve enough to think that a woman minds being beaten by her man. It is the message of many a calypso. Another song recounts with mock disapproval a public "licking." The thinly veiled sexual imagery is a stock device of calypso, but here it illustrates effectively the idea of violence being part and parcel of the normal relations between man and woman: a policeman who would intervene is rebuffed by none other than the "victim" of the licking:

> Constable have a care
> This is my man licking me here
> And if he feel to lick me
> He could lick me,
> Dammit, don't interfere.

Of course, calypsonians are mainly men, and men are largely responsible for perpetuating the myth of women thriving on violence from their men:

> Every now and then cuff them down,
> They'll love you long and they'll love you strong.
> Black-up their eye
> Bruise-up their knee
> And they will love you eternally.

The idea is not far removed from the maxim coined in the era of slavery: "Battre un nègre, c'est le nourrir"—a beating is food to a nigger.

But of course, violence in its narrowest definition, namely, physical violence, is only a visible manifestation of a wider disruption, a basic breakdown of respect. For violence to women includes the whole range of mental cruelty which is part and parcel of women's experiences in the Caribbean.

Every now and then our attention is drawn to this existing situation when a woman, known to her neighbors as a devoted, hard-working, self-sacrificing mother, of no particular wickedness, appears trembling and speechless before a judge for having killed her man.

And the familiar, almost humdrum details roll out again—a history of intolerable ill-treatment by the man both upon her and upon her children: neglect, desertion, humiliation, tyranny, unreasonableness, lack of consideration . . . the last straw falls and the woman runs at him with a kitchen knife.

It would seem that the precedents of this case stretch far enough back into our history to have entered our folklore—there is the folk song about Betsy Thomas who killed her husband stone cold dead in the market and had no doubt that she would be absolved of crime:

> I ain't kill nobody but me husband.

In fact, our society implicitly acknowledges the permanent situation out of which husband killings arise, in the leniency the court generally affords to a woman who has been driven to this act. Of course, killing your man is an extreme measure, but, again, it is a crisis which is but the visible tip of the iceberg or, to bring our imagery home, the eruption of a volcano that all along has been silently cooking.

The black man in the role of Dispenser of Violence is very likely a descendant of the white slave-overseer asserting an almost bottomless authority over the whipped. But there is one fundamental difference, for whereas the overseer beat and tortured his victim because he had power over him, the black man ill-treating his woman is expressing his desire for power, is betraying a dire insecurity vis-à-vis the female.

In the Caribbean the "war of the sexes" takes on a very special character. It is not a straight fight between handicapped Woman on the one hand and omnipotent Man on the other. From the very beginning of West Indian history the black woman has had a *de facto* "equality" thrust upon her—the equality of cattle in a herd. We became "equal" from the moment African men and women were bundled together onto galleys, men and women clamped to the floor alongside each other for the horrifying middle passage. A slave was a slave—male or female—a head of livestock, a unit of the power that drove the plantation. The women worked equally hard out in the fields with the men, were equally subject to torture and brutality. The black woman in the Caribbean has never been a delicate flower locked away in a glass case and "protected" from responsibility. Of course, the African woman in Africa is no delicate flower either, wielding a tremendous physical force in her daily chores of pounding, planting, etc., all the while carrying around her latest child upon her back.

From the very beginning of our history on this side of the Atlantic, woman has been mobilized in the society's work force. But there was, of course, some division of labor or functions, and this is where the male-female trouble began.

In the first place, the whole humiliation of slavery meant an utter devaluation of the manhood of the race; the male was powerless to carry out his traditional role of protector of the tribe, he was unable to defend either himself or his women and children from capture and transportation, from daily mishandling. His manhood was reduced to his brawn for the labor he could do for his master and to his reproductive function.

And the function of fatherhood was limited to fertilizing the female. Gone was the status of head of the family, for there was no family, no living in a unit with wife and children. A man might not even know who his children were, and at any rate they did not belong to him in any sense; he was unable to provide for them—their owner performed the function of provider. The black man had no authority over his children, but the woman did. The children's mothers, or female child-rearers, were responsible for the upbringing of the race. Women became mother and father to the race.

And it is this concentration of moral authority in the person of the woman that has influenced relations between men and women of African descent in the Caribbean. For today the average Afro-West Indian is still reared more or less singlehandedly by a mother, or aunt, or big sister, or god-mother—the men have still not returned to the functions of fatherhood. Fathers are either physically absent—the prevalent pattern of concubinage and male mobility results in a man not necessarily staying put in one household until the children he has deposited there have grown up—or, even when the father is present in the home, his part in the bringing up of the children is a limited one. His role is not clearly defined and not binding. One of the roles he may play is that of Punisher, administering beatings at the request of the mother; but the strongest influence in the home is usually female.

The society may be called a matriarchal one—many of our ancestors were in fact brought from West African societies which were matriarchal in structure, although there this by no means implied an abdication of responsibility on the part of the males. But this meant that our women had precedents of matriarchy upon which to draw in the new situation of male defection.

The Caribbean, and indeed black America on the whole, has produced the new black matriarch, the strong female figure who is responsible not only for the propagation of the race but by whose strength our humanity has been preserved.

Most Afro-West Indians have grown up "fatherless" in one way or another, most have been reared under almost exclusive female influence. So in the society moral authority is female, an authority that may sometimes be harsh and driven to extremes by the situation of stress in which a Caribbean mother often finds herself—often ill-feeling against a deserting man is vented upon the children he has left in her lap.

Caribbean writing teems with the strong woman type. Many of Samuel Selvon's immigrants are our feckless, happy-go-lucky men now and then marshaled into responsibility by brisk, matter-of-fact women. The female figures of James's *Minty Alley*, the dignified, almost statuesque Mrs. Rouse; Maisie the wraith, invincible in any situation. The women of *Miguel Street*, bawling out, battering (as well as being battered by) or working to support their unstable men. And I have discovered that my own book, *Crick Crack, Monkey*, is full of strong woman figures and that men are, like Auntie Beatrice's husband, "either absent or unnoticeable"—even the heroine's succession of "uncles" do not constitute any solid presence. And I had once intended to give the children a grandfather—Ma's husband—but I had conceived of him as an invalid in a rocking chair, ably looked after by Ma!

Caribbean woman has developed a strong moral fiber to compensate for the weakening of the male. Hence the desire of the man to do her down, to put her in her place, to safeguard his manhood threatened by the authority of the female upstart.

The black man in the Caribbean is capable of deep respect for his mother and for older women in general. The worst insult in our language is to curse a man's mother. An "obscenity" flung in the heat of quarrel is, quite simply, "Yu mother!" Authority is female, a man will have instinctive qualms about disrespecting his mother or, by extension, her contemporaries, but he will take his revenge on the black female by seeking to degrade women within reach of his disrespect.

Young men at a loose end (usually unemployed—the devaluation of black manhood is perpetuated in economic frustration) will position themselves on a culvert, at a street corner, on a pavement, and vie with each other in the ingenuity of their comments to embarrass women going by. The embarrassment of woman is part of the national ethos, stemming, I am convinced, from a deep-seated resentment against the strength of women.

In Trinidad the calypsonian, the folk poet, is assured of heartfelt, howling approval when he devotes his talent to the degradation of woman:

> Clarabelle,
> She could chase the Devil from Hell
> With the kind of way she does smell
> Anytime she pass yu could tell.

Our folk poet is rarely given to flattering and extolling the qualities of womanhood—woman and her sexual attributes are almost only a stock dirty joke in his repertoire. And the calypsonian mirrors collective attitudes—he is the product of his society and sings to please his audience.

There has, however, been one major development in our contemporary history which promises to have a salutary effect upon relations between black men and women in the Caribbean. This is the advent of black power ideology.

An important element of the history of male-female relations in the Caribbean has been the imposition of European standards of physical beauty— the tendency of the man to measure the desirability of women by these standards, and the corresponding struggle of black women to alter their appearance as far as possible in the direction of European requirements for beauty but of course still falling short of these requirements. A large part of male disrespect for the black woman was an expression of his dissatisfaction with her, "inferior" as she was to the accepted white ideal of womanhood.

This bred a great deal of destructive dishonesty, a canker eating away at the roots of our self-respect. For these attitudes were especially destructive as they were to a large extent disavowed or even entirely subconscious. A man would vehemently deny that he could be the victim of this mesmerism. His cousin, yes, damn fool who went to England to study and could find nothing else to get married to but a white woman—but *he* would never be found putting milk in his coffee, unthinkable, *he* had a healthy attitude toward these white people.

It was indeed a difficult burden to bear—his very deep-seated resentment of whitedom and this hopeless involvement with them.

Today's ideology has begun to liberate us from this particular dishonesty. It has forced into the open, and at popular level (a success not achieved by the literary movements of the first half of the century), the discussion of our polarization toward whiteness, and it has effectively set about revising our concepts of physical beauty. The progressive abolition of hair-straightening in the Caribbean is a momentous revolution. It is part of the revaluation of the black woman.

And the revaluation of black womanhood inevitably also implies a restoration of black manhood, when the black man no longer forcibly evaluates his women by the standards of a man who once held the whip over him. It is one stage of his liberation from the whip hand.

And it is only when our lives cease to be governed by the shadow of the whip that we can begin to heal the grave disruption of relations between men and women that we have suffered in the Caribbean.

TOWARD MEN'S LIBERATION

HAROLD ROSENBERG

Harold Rosenberg was one of America's two or three most celebrated twentieth-century art critics. He was born in New York, in 1906, attended City College, then took a law degree at St. Lawrence University. He started out as an avant-garde intellectual and poet, but his main interest soon became art. All his life he remained in intimate contact with the New York art world, generally siding with the artists and against the establishment of art dealers, museum directors, and critics. He did much lecturing, taught at the University of Chicago, was a consultant to the Advertising Council and art critic for The New Yorker *from 1967 until his death in 1979. Collections of his essays appeared as* The Tradition of the New *(1959);* The Anxious Object *(1964);* Artworks and Packages *(1969); and* The De-definition of Art: Action Art to Pop to Earthworks *(1972), which responds gloomily to what Rosenberg took to be a vogue for art that had no real meaning. The present essay, first published in the November 1967 issue of* Vogue, *is reprinted from a volume of his selected essays entitled* Discovering the Present *(1973). (In the essay Rosenberg quotes a poem by Cummings that has a tantalizingly obscure third line. Our guess is that it is a comically distorted version, in baby talk, of "Dust thou art, to dust returnest.")*

Masculinity: Style and Cult

Societies of the past have admired different personifications of the manly virtues: the warrior, the patriarch, the sage; the lover, the seducer; Zeus the Thunderer, Jehovah the Lawgiver.

In America, masculinity is associated primarily with the outdoors, and with such outdoor trades as cattledriving, railroading, whaling, and trucking. The outdoor type is presumed to possess masculine character traits: toughness, resourcefulness, love of being alone, fraternity with animals, and attractiveness to women and the urge to abandon them. To the man of the open spaces is also attributed the ultimate mark of manliness, the readiness to die.

From the outdoors America derives the boots, lumber jackets and shirts, sailor's caps, pipes, and guns that are its paraphernalia of masculinity. Oddly enough, in the United States, military and police uniforms do not confer masculinity, as they do among Cossacks and Hussars. One can as readily imagine women in our army uniform as men. To prove that he was all man, General Patton had to augment his battle costume with a pearl-handled revolver. (It is true, however, that he wrote poetry and may have felt the need to overcome this handicap.)

As to hair, masculinity is ambivalent. Long hair belongs to the style of frontier scouts and trappers, the most male of men. Yet "longhairs" is the name applied to intellectuals, a breed always suspected of sexual inauthenticity. Beards used to be a material evidence of maleness; today they are as frequently an appurtenance of masquerade.

In the last century the outdoors represented genuine hazards. It took self-reliance, identifiable with masculinity (though the pioneer mother had it, too), to venture very far from the farm or town.

Today there are still risky occupations—piloting spaceships, handling nuclear substances—but these trades have become increasingly technical and depersonalized. As for the rugged outdoors, it is used chiefly for sports; and a vacation at a ranch or ski lodge, or shooting lions in Kenya, is about as hazardous as a trip to the Riviera.

The outdoors, representing once-hostile nature, has been transformed into a stage set. Masculinity in the American sense has thus lost its locale and, perhaps, its reason for being. On the neon-lighted lonesome prairie, masculinity is a matter of certain traditional costume details: the cowboy hat, jeans, and guitar. It has become clear that the traditional traits of the man's man (and the ladies' man) can be put on, too. One *plays* manliness, with or without dark goggles.

Big-game hunters, mountain climbers, horsemen, and other representative male types are actors in a charade of nostalgia. Old masculine pursuits, like baseball or wrestling, when carried on at night under the glare of fluorescent tubes, come to resemble spectacles on television and wind up in the living room. In the epoch of the picture window, outdoors and indoors have lost their separateness.

In modern mass societies the uniforms of all kinds of cults compete with one another. Masculinity is one of these cults, and to create an impression the practitioner of maleness must stand out in a crowd. Persons with other interests are not disposed to make an issue of their sex. Only psychiatrists and sociologists complain that boys and girls today look alike and are often mistaken for each other. Even tough adolescents, like members of big-city gangs, don't mind if their girls wear the same shirts and jeans as the men. All are more concerned with identifying themselves as outsiders than as males and females.

Masculinity today is a myth that has turned into a comedy. A ten-gallon hat still seems to bestow upon its wearer the old male attributes of taciturnity, resourcefulness, courage, and love of solitude. At the same time, the virility of the cowboy and the truck driver, like that of the iceman of yesterday, is a joke that everyone sees through.

A person uncertain of his sexual identity dresses up in boots, bandanna, and riding breeches not so much to fool the public as to parade his ambiguity. Those who have gone over the line may advertise their desires for male company by wearing a beard in addition to sheepskins. Women can be masculine too, of course, in the degree necessary to make them irresistible to feminine men.

Hemingway, who constantly kept the issue of masculinity alive in his writings, flaunted both the look of the outdoor man and his presumed character qualities of daring, self-detachment, contempt for the over-civilized, and eagerness to court death.

Hemingway's he-man performance was, among other things, a means of combatting the American stereotype of the writer as a sissy. In the United States, the artist and man of ideas have always lived under the threat of having their masculinity impugned. Richard Hofstadter, in his *Anti-Intellectualism in American Life*, lists a dozen instances in which the "stigma of effeminacy" was branded upon intellectuals by political bullies, ranging from Tammany Hall leaders in the nineteenth century, who attacked reformers as "political hermaphrodites," to Communist Party hacks in the 1930s, who denounced independent writers as "scented whores." Evidently, it has always been possible to convince the common man that his intellectual superiors fall short of him in manliness.

To the overhanging charge of being contaminated by a ladylike occupation, Hemingway responded by injecting the romance of masculinity into the making of literature. At least as far as he was concerned, the sexual legitimacy of the male writer was to be put beyond question. Besides lining up with traditional outdoor types, such as bullfighters and deep-sea fishermen, Hemingway's strategy included identification with the new activist male image of the Depression decade: the leather-jacketed revolutionist allied with the peasant and factory worker. One might say that each of his novels originated in a new choice of male makeup.

Unfortunately, demonstrating his manhood was not enough for Hemingway. He found it necessary to challenge the masculinity of other writers. Like Theodore Roosevelt earlier in the century, he became an instance of the intellectual who slanders intellectuals generally, in the hope of putting himself right with the regular guys. During the Spanish Civil War he forgot himself to the extent of sneering publicly at Leon Trotsky for remaining at his typewriter in Mexico, implying that the former chief of the Red Army lacked the manliness to go to Spain and fight. He, himself, of course, went to Spain to write. In *For Whom the Bell Tolls* he identified himself with the dynamiter Jordan who also shook the earth by his love feats in a sleeping bag.

Thirty years ago not all of Hemingway's contemporaries were convinced that he had established his masculinity through displaying an appetite for violence, sex, and death. In *no thanks*, E. E. Cummings translated Hemingway's romance of maleness back into the daydreams of boyhood:

> "what does little Ernest croon
> in his death at afternoon?
> (kow dow r 2 bul retoinis
> wus de woids uf lil Oinis"

To Cummings, Hemingway's heroics were not only childish ("lil Oinis") but feminine ("kow dow r").

The post-Hemingway he-man has labored under the handicap of a masculinity that is generally recognized to be a masquerade. The adventurer living dangerously has disintegrated into the tongue-in-cheek élan of James Bond. Neither at work nor at home is maleness any longer endowed with glamour or privilege. The cosmonaut is less a birdman than a specialist minding his signals and dials. The father who has entered into a diapering partnership with his wife has nothing in common with the patriarch. To the public of Norman Mailer (more male?) the outdoor rig (Mailer in sea captain's cap on the jacket of *Advertisements for Myself*) and chronicles of supersex are suspect, both psychologically and as playing to the gallery. It is no secret that a Bogartean toughness with women may represent the opposite of male self-confidence.

The mass media exploit the ambiguity of the male role and the sexual sophistication that goes with the increasing awareness of it. In male comedy teams, one of the partners almost invariably plays the "wife," confident that the audience will know when to smirk. Analysts of mass culture speak of the decline of the American male and of the "masculinity crisis" as topics capable of arousing libidinous responses. The public is given the image of luscious females starving in vain for the attention of men, and of men who, egged on and deprived by frigid seductresses, end by falling into each other's arms.

Masculinity-building is urged, a theme which the media are not slow to adapt for their own purposes. Masculinity is the alfalfa peddled in Marlboro Country. It is the essence of worn leather laced with campfire smoke that provides the aroma of the man of distinction. It also comes in powder form, none genuine without the Shaggy Dog on the wrapping.

To those who resent the fact that their pretension to masculinity is not taken seriously, one means is available for gaining respect: violence. The victim of rape is not inclined to question the virility of her assailant.

The relation between masculinity that has been put into doubt and violence reveals itself most clearly in the recent history of the Civil Rights movement. The black has derived from white America the lesson that physical force is the mark of manhood. White society is "the Man," whose insignia of power are the club, the whip, the bloodhounds. The presence of the Man impeaches the masculinity of the young black and demands that he prove himself. He becomes full grown when he resolves to fight the Man. To confront the Man, the black militant has resurrected the figure of the radical activist of the thirties, the model of Hemingway's he-man, honor-bound to risk his life in physical combat.

An article in the *New York Times Magazine* on the Black Panthers is illustrated by photographs of its two leaders. Both wear the traditional leather jackets and berets of the Left fighters of thirty years ago—these could be photographs of two Lincoln Brigade volunteers. A statement by one of the Panthers touches the philosophical essence of the romantic conception of masculinity: to be a man one must dare to die. "The ghetto black," said Bobby Seale, "isn't afraid to stand up to the cops, because he already lives with violence. He expects to die any day."

In our culture all human attributes tend to be over-defined and become a basis of self-consciousness. The behavioral sciences collaborate with the mass media in making a man anxious about his sex status; both then provide him with models of aggressiveness by which to correct his deficiencies. Yet the present uneasiness about masculinity, coupled with theatrical devices for attaining it, may be more harmful than any actual curtailment of manliness discovered by researchers and editorialists. The real damage may lie in the remedy rather than the ailment, since the desire to have one's masculinity acknowledged may lead, as we have seen, to absurd postures and acts of force. It is hard to believe that Americans would be worse off by becoming more gentle. Nor that mildness in manners and social relations would make them less manly. In the real world nothing is altogether what it is. True maleness is never without its vein of femininity. The Greeks understood this and made it the theme of their tales of sexual metamorphosis, the remarkable account of Hercules, of all men, taking on temporarily the character of a woman and wearing women's clothes. Total masculinity is an ideal of the frustrated, not a fact of biology. With the cult of masculinity put aside, maleness might have a better chance to develop in the United States.

MARC FEIGEN FASTEAU

Marc Feigen Fasteau was born in Washington, D.C., in 1942. He was educated at Harvard College, Georgetown University, and Harvard Law School, where he was an editor of the Law Review. *While in Washington, he worked as an assistant in foreign affairs to Senator Mike Mansfield and as a staff member of the Joint Economic Committee of Congress. He served as a research fellow at the Kennedy Institute of Politics before joining a New York law firm. Since 1974, Fasteau and his wife, feminist attorney Brenda Feigen Fasteau, have been practicing law in partnership. Both in his work and in his writing he has been actively engaged in the breaking of sexual stereotypes. The* Male Machine (1974), *from which we reprint a chapter below, is his first book. An article, "The High Price of Macho," appeared in* Psychology Today, *September 1975.*

Friendships Among Men

There is a long-standing myth in our society that the great friendships are between men. Forged through shared experience, male friendship is portrayed as the most unselfish, if not the highest form, of human relationship. The more traditionally masculine the shared experience from which it springs, the stronger and more profound the friendship is supposed to be. Going to war, weathering crises together at school or work, playing on the same athletic team, are some of the classic experiences out of which friendships between men are believed to grow.

By and large, men do prefer the company of other men, not only in their structured time but in the time they fill with optional, nonobligatory activity. They prefer to play games, drink, and talk, as well as work and fight together. Yet something is missing. Despite the time men spend together, their contact rarely goes beyond the external, a limitation which tends to make their friendships shallow and unsatisfying.

My own childhood memories are of doing things with my friends—playing games or sports, building walkie-talkies, going camping. Other people and my relationships to them were never legitimate subjects for attention. If someone liked me, it was an opaque, mysterious occurrence that bore no analysis. When I was slighted, I felt hurt. But relationships with people just happened. I certainly had feelings about my friends, but I can't remember a single instance of trying consciously to sort them out until I was well into college.

For most men this kind of shying away from the personal continues into adult life. In conversations with each other, we hardly ever use ourselves as reference points. We talk about almost everything except how we ourselves are affected by people and events. Everything is discussed as though it were taking place out there somewhere, as though we had no more felt response to it than to the weather. Topics that can be treated in this detached, objective way become conversational mainstays. The few subjects which are fundamentally personal are shaped into discussions of abstract general questions. Even in an exchange about their reactions to liberated women—a topic of intensely personal interest—the tendency will be to talk in general, theoretical terms. Work, at least its objective aspects, is always a safe subject. Men also spend an incredible amount of time rehashing the great public issues of the day. Until early 1973, Vietnam was the work-horse topic. Then came Watergate. It doesn't seem to matter that we've all had a hundred similar conversations. We plunge in for another round, trying to come up with a new angle as much to impress the others with what we know as to keep from being bored stiff.

Games play a central role in situations organized by men. I remember a weekend some years ago at the country house of a law-school classmate as a blur of softball, football, croquet, poker, and a dice-and-board game called Combat, with swimming thrown in on the side. As soon as one game ended, another began. Taken one at a time, these "activities" were fun, but the impression was inescapable that the host, and most of his guests, would do anything to stave off a lull in which they would be together without some impersonal focus for their attention. A snapshot of almost any men's club would show the same thing, ninety percent of the men engaged in some activity—ranging from backgammon to watching the tube—other than, or at least as an aid to, conversation.[1]

My composite memory of evenings spent with a friend at college and later when we shared an apartment in Washington is of conversations punctuated by silences during which we would internally pass over any personal or emotional thoughts which had arisen and come back to the permitted track. When I couldn't get my mind off personal matters, I said very little. Talks with my father have always had the same tone. Respect for privacy was the rationale for our diffidence. His questions to me about how things were going at school or at work were asked as discreetly as he would have asked a friend about someone's commitment to a hospital for the criminally in-sane. Our conversations, when they touched these matters at all, to say nothing of more sensitive matters, would veer quickly back to safe topics of general interest.

In our popular literature, the archetypal male hero embodying this per-sonal muteness is the cowboy. The classic mold for the character was set in 1902 by Owen Wister's novel *The Virginian* where the author spelled out, with an explicitness that was never again necessary, the characteristics of his protagonist. Here's how it goes when two close friends the Virginian hasn't seen in some time take him out for a drink:

> All of them had seen rough days together, and they felt guilty with emotion.
> "It's hot weather," said Wiggin.
> "Hotter in Box Elder," said McLean. "My kid has started teething."
> Words ran dry again. They shifted their positions, looked in their glasses, read the labels on the bottles. They dropped a word now and then to the proprietor about his trade, and his ornaments.[2]

One of the Virginian's duties is to assist at the hanging of an old friend as a horse thief. Afterward, for the first time in the book, he is visibly upset. The narrator puts his arm around the hero's shoulders and describes the Virgin-ian's reaction:

> I had the sense to keep silent, and presently he shook my hand, not looking at me as he did so. He was always very shy of demonstration.[3]

And, for explanation of such reticence, "As all men know, he also knew that many things should be done in this world in silence, and that talking about them is a mistake."[4]

---

[1] Women may use games as a reason for getting together—bridge clubs, for example. But the show is more for the rest of the world—to indicate that they are doing *something*—and the games themselves are not the only means of communication.
[2] Owen Wister, *The Virginian* ([Macmillan: 1902] Grosset & Dunlap ed.: 1929), pp. 397-98.
[3] *Ibid.*, p. 343.
[4] *Ibid.*, p. 373.

There are exceptions, but they only prove the rule.

One is the drunken confidence: "Bob, ole boy, I gotta tell ya—being divorced isn't so hot. . . . [and see, I'm too drunk to be held responsible for blurting it out]." Here, drink becomes an excuse for exchanging confidences and a device for periodically loosening the restraint against expressing a need for sympathy and support from other men—which may explain its importance as a male ritual.[5] Marijuana fills a similar need.

Another exception is talking to a stranger—who may be either someone the speaker doesn't know or someone who isn't in the same social or business world. (Several black friends told me that they have been on the receiving end of personal confidences from white acquaintances that they were sure had not been shared with white friends.) In either case, men are willing to talk about themselves only to other men with whom they do not have to compete or whom they will not have to confront socially later.

Finally, there is the way men depend on women to facilitate certain conversations. The women in a mixed group are usually the ones who make the first personal reference, about themselves or others present. The men can then join in without having the onus for initiating a discussion of "personalities." Collectively, the men can "blame" the conversation on the women. They can also feel in these conversations that since they are talking "to" the women instead of "to" the men, they can be excused for deviating from the masculine norm. When the women leave, the tone and subject invariably shift away from the personal.

The effect of these constraints is to make it extraordinarily difficult for men to really get to know each other. A psychotherapist who has conducted a lengthy series of encounter groups for men summed it up:

> With saddening regularity [the members of these groups] described how much they wanted to have closer, more satisfying relationships with other men: "I'd settle for having one really close man friend. I supposedly have some close men friends now. We play golf or go for a drink. We complain about our jobs and our wives. I care about them and they care about me. We even have some physical contact—I mean we may even give a hug on a big occasion. But it's not enough."[6]

The sources of this stifling ban on self-disclosure, the reasons why men hide from each other, lie in the taboos and imperatives of the masculine stereotype.

To begin with, men are supposed to be functional, to spend their time working or otherwise solving or thinking about how to solve problems. Personal reaction, how one feels about something, is considered dysfunctional, at best an irrelevant distraction from the expected objectivity. Only weak

---

[5]Lionel Tiger, *Men in Groups* (Random House: 1969), p. 185.
[6]Don Clark, "Homosexual Encounter in All-Male Groups," in L. Solomon and B. Berzon (eds.), *New Perspectives on Encounter Groups* (Jossey-Bass: 1972), pp. 376-77. See also Alan Booth, "Sex and Social Participation," *American Sociological Review*, Vol. 37 (April 1972), p. 183, an empirical study showing that, contrary to Lionel Tiger's much publicized assertion (*Men in Groups*), women form stronger and closer friendship bonds with each other than men do.

men, and women, talk about—i.e., "give in," to their feelings. "I group my friends in two ways," said a business executive:

> those who have made it and don't complain and those who haven't made it. And only the latter spend time talking to their wives about their problems and how bad their boss is and all that. The ones who concentrate more on communicating . . . are those who have realized that they aren't going to make it and therefore they have changed the focus of attention.[7]

In a world which tells men they have to choose between expressiveness and manly strength, this characterization may be accurate. Most of the men who talk personally to other men *are* those whose problems have gotten the best of them, who simply can't help it. Men not driven to despair don't talk about themselves, so the idea that self-disclosure and expressiveness are associated with problems and weakness becomes a self-fulfilling prophecy.

Obsessive competitiveness also limits the range of communication in male friendships. Competition is the principal mode by which men relate to each other—at one level because they don't know how else to make contact, but more basically because it is the way to demonstrate, to themselves and others, the key masculine qualities of unwavering toughness and the ability to dominate and control. The result is that they inject competition into situations which don't call for it.

In conversations, you must show that you know more about the subject than the other man, or at least as much as he does. For example, I have often engaged in a contest that could be called My Theory Tops Yours, disguised as a serious exchange of ideas. The proof that it wasn't serious was that I was willing to participate even when I was sure that the participants, including myself, had nothing fresh to say. Convincing the other person— victory—is the main objective, with control of the floor an important tactic. Men tend to lecture at each other, insist that the discussion follow their train of thought, and are often unwilling to listen.[8] As one member of a men's rap group said,

> When I was talking I used to feel that I had to be driving to a point, that it had to be rational and organized, that I had to persuade at all times, rather than exchange thoughts and ideas.[9]

Even in casual conversation some men hold back unless they are absolutely sure of what they are saying. They don't want to have to change a position once they have taken it. It's "just like a woman" to change your mind, and, more important, it is inconsistent with the approved masculine posture of total independence.

---

[7]Fernando Bartolomé, "Executives as Human Beings," *Harvard Business Review*, Vol. 50 (November-December 1972), p. 64.

[8]The contrast with women on this point is striking. Casual observation will confirm that women's conversations move more quickly, with fewer long speeches and more frequent changes of speaker.

[9]*Boston Globe*, March 12, 1972, p. B-1.

Competition was at the heart of one of my closest friendships, now defunct. There was a good deal of mutual liking and respect. We went out of our way to spend time with each other and wanted to work together. We both had "prospects" as "bright young men" and the same "liberal but tough" point of view. We recognized this about each other, and this recognition was the basis of our respect and of our sense of equality. That we saw each other as equals was important—our friendship was confirmed by the reflection of one in the other. But our constant and all-encompassing competition made this equality precarious and fragile. One way or another, everything counted in the measuring process. We fought out our tennis matches as though our lives depended on it. At poker, the two of us would often play on for hours after the others had left. These *mano a mano* poker marathons seem in retrospect especially revealing of the competitiveness of the relationship: playing for small stakes, the essence of the game is in outwitting, psychologically beating down the other player—the other skills involved are negligible. Winning is the only pleasure, one that evaporates quickly, a truth that struck me in inchoate form every time our game broke up at four a.m. and I walked out the door with my five-dollar winnings, a headache, and a sense of time wasted. Still, I did the same thing the next time. It was what we did together, and somehow it counted. Losing at tennis could be balanced by winning at poker; at another level, his moving up in the federal government by my getting on the *Harvard Law Review*.

This competitiveness feeds the most basic obstacle to openness between men, the inability to admit to being vulnerable. Real men, we learn early, are not supposed to have doubts, hopes and ambitions which may not be realized, things they don't (or even especially do) like about themselves, fears and disappointments. Such feelings and concerns, of course, are part of everyone's inner life, but a man must keep quiet about them. If others know how you really feel you can be hurt, and that in itself is incompatible with manhood. The inhibiting effect of this imperative is not limited to disclosures of major personal problems. Often men do not share even ordinary uncertainties and half-formulated plans of daily life with their friends. And when they do, they are careful to suggest that they already know how to proceed—that they are not really asking for help or understanding but simply for particular bits of information. Either way, any doubts they have are presented as external, carefully characterized as having to do with the issue as distinct from the speaker. They are especially guarded about expressing concern or asking a question that would invite personal comment. It is almost impossible for men to simply exchange thoughts about matters involving them personally in a comfortable, non-crisis atmosphere. If a friend tells you of his concern that he and a colleague are always disagreeing, for example, he is likely to quickly supply his own explanation—something like "different professional backgrounds." The effect is to rule out observations or suggestions that do not fit within this already reconnoitered protective structure. You don't suggest, even if you believe it is true, that in fact the disagreements arise because he presents his ideas in a way which tends to provoke a hostile reaction. It would catch him off guard; it would be something he hadn't already thought of and accepted about himself and, for that reason, no matter how constructive and well-intentioned you might be, it would put you in control for the moment. He doesn't want that; he is afraid of losing your respect. So, sensing he feels that way, because you would yourself, you say something else. There is no real give-and-take.

It is hard for men to get angry at each other honestly. Anger between friends often means that one has hurt the other. Since the straightforward expression of anger in these situations involves an admission of vulnerability, it is safer to stew silently or find an "objective" excuse for retaliation. Either way, trust is not fully restored.

Men even try not to let it show when they feel good. We may report the reasons for our happiness, if they have to do with concrete accomplishments, but we try to do it with a straight face, as if to say, "Here's what happened, but it hasn't affected my grown-up unemotional equilibrium, and I am not asking for any kind of response." Happiness is a precarious, "childish" feeling, easy to shoot down. Others may find the event that triggers it trivial or incomprehensible, or even threatening to their own self-esteem—in the sense that if one man is up, another man is down. So we tend not to take the risk of expressing it.

What is particularly difficult for men is seeking or accepting help from friends. I, for one, learned early that dependence was unacceptable. When I was eight, I went to a summer camp I disliked. My parents visited me in the middle of the summer and, when it was time for them to leave, I wanted to go with them. They refused, and I yelled and screamed and was miserably unhappy for the rest of the day. That evening an older camper comforted me, sitting by my bed as I cried, patting me on the back soothingly and saying whatever it is that one says at times like that. He was in some way clumsy or funny-looking, and a few days later I joined a group of kids in cruelly making fun of him, an act which upset me, when I thought about it, for years. I can only explain it in terms of my feeling, as early as the age of eight, that by needing and accepting his help and comfort I had compromised myself, and took it out on him.

"You can't express dependence when you feel it," a corporate executive said, "because it's a kind of absolute. If you are loyal 90% of the time and disloyal 10%, would you be considered loyal? Well, the same happens with independence: you are either dependent or independent; you can't be both."[10] "Feelings of dependence," another explained, "are identified with weakness or 'untoughness' and our culture doesn't accept those things in men."[11] The result is that we either go it alone or "act out certain games or rituals to provoke the desired reaction in the other and have our needs satisfied without having to ask for anything."[12]

Somewhat less obviously, the expression of affection also runs into emotional barriers growing out of the masculine stereotype. When I was in college, I was suddenly quite moved while attending a friend's wedding.

---

[10]Bartolomé, *op. cit.*, p. 65.
[11]*Ibid.*, p. 64.
[12]*Ibid.*, p. 66.

The surge of feeling made me uncomfortable and self-conscious. There was nothing inherently difficult or, apart from the fact of being moved by a moment of tenderness, "unmasculine" about my reaction. I just did not know how to deal with or communicate what I felt. "I consider myself a sentimentalist," one man said, "and I think I am quite able to express my feelings. But the other day my wife described a friend of mine to some people as my best friend and I felt embarrassed when I heard her say it."[13]

A major source of these inhibitions is the fear of being, or being thought, homosexual. Nothing is more frightening to a heterosexual man in our society. It threatens, at one stroke, to take away every vestige of his claim to a masculine identity—something like knocking out the foundations of a building—and to expose him to the ostracism, ranging from polite tolerance to violent revulsion, of his friends and colleagues. A man can be labeled as homosexual not just because of overt sexual acts but because of almost any sign of behavior which does not fit the masculine stereotype. The touching of another man, other than shaking hands or, under emotional stress, an arm around the shoulder, is taboo. Women may kiss each other when they meet; men are uncomfortable when hugged even by close friends.[14] Onlookers might misinterpret what they saw, and, more important, what would we think of ourselves if we felt a twinge of sensual pleasure from the embrace.

Direct verbal expressions of affection or tenderness are also something that only homosexuals and women engage in. Between "real" men affection has to be disguised in gruff, "you old son-of-a-bitch" style. Paradoxically, in some instances, terms of endearment between men can be used as a ritual badge of manhood, dangerous medicine safe only for the strong. The flirting with homosexuality that characterizes the initiation rites of many fraternities and men's clubs serves this purpose. Claude Brown wrote about black life in New York City in the 1950s:

> The term ["baby"] had a hip ring to it. . . . It was like saying, "Man, look at me. I've got masculinity to spare. . . . I can say 'baby' to another cat and he can say 'baby' to me, and we can say it with strength in our voices." If you could say it, this meant that you really had to be sure of yourself, sure of your masculinity.[15]

Fear of homosexuality does more than inhibit the physical display of affection. One of the major recurring themes in the men's groups led by psychotherapist Don Clark was:

> "A large segment of my feelings about other men are unknown or distorted because I am afraid they might have something to do with homosexuality. Now I'm lonely for other men and don't know how to find what I want with them."

---
[13] *Ibid.*, p. 64.
[14] *Ibid.*, p. 65.
[15] Claude Brown, *Manchild in the Promised Land* ([Macmillan: 1965] Signet ed.: 1965), p. 171.

As Clark observes, "The spectre of homosexuality seems to be the dragon at the gateway to self-awareness, understanding, and acceptance of male-male needs. If a man tries to pretend the dragon is not there by turning a blind eye to erotic feelings for all other males, he also blinds himself to the rich variety of feelings that are related."[16]

The few situations in which men do acknowledge strong feelings of affection and dependence toward other men are exceptions which prove the rule. With "cop couples," for example, or combat soldier "buddies," intimacy and dependence are forced on the men by their work—they have to ride in the patrol car or be in the same foxhole with somebody—and the jobs themselves have such highly masculine images that the men can get away with behavior that would be suspect under any other conditions.

Futhermore, even these combat-buddy relations, when looked at closely, turn out not to be particularly intimate or personal. Margaret Mead has written:

> During the last war English observers were confused by the apparent contradiction between American soldiers' emphasis on the buddy, so grievously exemplified in the break-downs that followed a buddy's death, and the results of detailed inquiry which showed how transitory these buddy relationships were. It was found that men actually accepted their buddies as derivatives from their outfit, and from accidents of association, rather than because of any special personality characteristics capable of ripening into friendship.[17]

One effect of the fear of appearing to be homosexual is to reinforce the practice that two men rarely get together alone without a reason. I once called a friend to suggest that we have dinner together. "O.K.," he said. "What's up?" I felt uncomfortable telling him that I just wanted to talk, that there was no other reason for the invitation.

Men get together to conduct business, to drink, to play games and sports, to re-establish contact after long absences, to participate in heterosexual social occasions—circumstances in which neither person is responsible for actually wanting to see the other. Men are particularly comfortable seeing each other in groups. The group situation defuses any possible assumptions about the intensity of feeling between particular men and provides the safety of numbers—"All the guys are here." It makes personal communication, which requires a level of trust and mutual understanding not generally shared by all members of a group, more difficult and offers an excuse for avoiding this dangerous territory. And it provides what is most sought after in men's friendships: mutual reassurance of masculinity.

Needless to say, the observations in this chapter did not spring full-blown from my head. The process started when I began to understand that, at least with Brenda, a more open, less self-protective relationship was possible.

---

[16]Clark, *op. cit.*, p. 378.
[17]Margaret Mead, *Male and Female* ([William Morrow: 1949] Mentor ed.: 1949), p. 214.

At first, I perceived my situation as completely personal. The changes I was trying to effect in myself had to do, I thought, only with Brenda and me, and could be generalized, if at all, only to other close relationships between men and women. But, as Brenda came to be deeply involved in the women's movement, I began to see, usually at one remove but sometimes directly, the level of intimacy that women, especially women active in the movement, shared with each other. The contrast between this and the friendships I had with men was striking. I started listening to men's conversations, including my own, and gradually the basic outlines of the pattern described here began to emerge. I heard from women that the men they knew had very few really close male friends; since then I have heard the same thing from men themselves. It was, I realized, my own experience as well. It wasn't that I didn't know a lot of men, or that I was not on friendly terms with them. Rather, I gradually became dissatisfied with the impersonality of these friendships.

Of course, some constraints on self-disclosure do make sense. Privacy is something you give up selectively and gradually to people you like and trust, and who are capable of understanding—instant, indiscriminate intimacy is nearly always formularized, without real content and impact. Nor does self-disclosure as a kind of compartmentalized rest-and-recreation period work: "Well, John, let me tell you about myself. . . ."

Having said all this, it is nonetheless true that men have carried the practice of emotional restraint to the point of paralysis. For me, at least, the ritual affirmations of membership in the fraternity of men that one gets from participation in "masculine" activities do nothing to assuage the feeling of being essentially alone; they have become a poor substitute for being known by and knowing other people. But the positive content of what will replace the old-style friendship is only beginning to take shape. I am learning, though, that when I am able to articulate my feelings as they arise in the context of my friendships, I often find that they are shared by others. Bringing them out into the open clears the air; avoiding them, even unconsciously, is stultifying. I have found also that I am not as fragile as I once thought. The imagined hazards of showing oneself to be human, and thus vulnerable, to one's friends tend not to materialize when actually put to the test. But being oneself is an art, an art sensitive to variations in the receptivity of others as well as to one's own inner life. It is still, for me, something to be mastered, to be tried out and practiced.

ON SEXUALITY

GLORIA STEINEM

Gloria Steinem, whose grandmother was president of a women's suffrage group, is one of America's best-known feminists. Born in 1934, she graduated from Smith College in

1956, studied in India for two years, then turned to a career in research and journalism. She wrote for television and for political campaigns, did magazine articles, and wrote a column for New York *magazine. She is reported to have become active in the women's movement when, in 1968, she attended a Redstocking meeting to get material for a* New York *column. She was a leader in the Women's Strike for Equality in 1970, helped found the National Women's Political Caucus in 1971, and in 1972* Ms *magazine, of which she remains editor. An exceptionally effective press agent for women, Ms. Steinem has continued to be an important organizer for women's causes and an influential thinker about sex roles. In 1977 she was a Fellow of the Woodrow Wilson International Center for Scholars. The essay we present below was published in* Ms, *November 1978.*

Erotica and Pornography: A Clear and Present Difference

Human beings are the only animals that experience the same sex drive at times when we can—and cannot—conceive.

Just as we developed uniquely human capacities for language, planning, memory, and invention along our evolutionary path, we also developed sexuality as a form of expression; a way of communicating that is separable from our need for sex as a way of perpetuating ourselves. For humans alone, sexuality can be and often is primarily a way of bonding, of giving and receiving pleasure, bridging differentness, discovering sameness, and communicating emotion.

We developed this and other human gifts through our ability to change our environment, adapt physically, and in the long run, to affect our own evolution. But as an emotional result of this spiraling path away from other animals, we seem to alternate between periods of exploring our unique abilities to forge new boundaries, and feelings of loneliness in the unknown that we ourselves have created; a fear that sometimes sends us back to the comfort of the animal world by encouraging us to exaggerate our sameness.

The separation of "play" from "work," for instance, is a problem only in the human world. So is the difference between art and nature, or an intellectual accomplishment and a physical one. As a result, we celebrate play, art, and invention as leaps into the unknown; but any imbalance can send us back to nostalgia for our primate past and the conviction that the basics of work, nature, and physical labor are somehow more worthwhile or even moral.

In the same way, we have explored our sexuality as separable from conception: a pleasurable, empathetic bridge to strangers of the same species. We have even invented contraception—a skill that has probably existed in some form since our ancestors figured out the process of birth—in order to extend this uniquely human difference. Yet we also have times of atavistic suspicion that sex is not complete—or even legal or intended-by-god—if it cannot end in conception.

No wonder the concepts of "erotica" and "pornography" can be so crucially different, and yet so confused. Both assume that sexuality can be separated from conception, and therefore can be used to carry a personal message. That's a major reason why, even in our current culture, both may be called equally "shocking" or legally "obscene," a word whose Latin derivative means "dirty, containing filth." This gross condemnation of all sexuality that isn't harnessed to childbirth and marriage has been increased by the current backlash against women's progress. Out of fear that the whole patriarchal structure might be upset if women really had the autonomous power to decide our reproductive futures (that is, if we controlled the most basic means of production), right-wing groups are not only denouncing prochoice abortion literature as "pornographic," but are trying to stop the sending of all contraceptive information through the mails by invoking obscenity laws. In fact, Phyllis Schlafly recently denounced the entire Women's Movement as "obscene."

Not surprisingly, this religious, visceral backlash has a secular, intellectual counterpart that relies heavily on applying the "natural" behavior of the animal world to humans. That is questionable in itself, but these Lionel Tiger-ish studies make their political purpose even more clear in the particular animals they select and the habits they choose to emphasize.[1] The message is that females should accept their "destiny" of being sexually dependent and devote themselves to bearing and rearing their young.

Defending against such reaction in turn leads to another temptation: to merely reverse the terms, and declare that *all* nonprocreative sex is good. In fact, however, this human activity can be as constructive or destructive, moral or immoral, as any other. Sex as communication can send messages as different as life and death; even the origins of "erotica" and "pornography" reflect that fact. After all, "erotica" is rooted in *eros* or passionate love, and thus in the idea of positive choice, free will, the yearning for a particular person. (Interestingly, the definition of erotica leaves open the question of gender.) "Pornography" begins with a root meaning "prostitution" or "female captives," thus letting us know that the subject is not mutual love, or love at all, but domination and violence against women. (Though, of course, homosexual pornography may imitate this violence by putting a man in the "feminine" role of victim.) It ends with a root meaning "writing about" or "description of " which puts still more distance between subject and object, and replaces a spontaneous yearning for closeness with objectification and a voyeur.

The difference is clear in the words. It becomes even more so by example.

Look at any photo or film of people making love; really making love. The images may be diverse, but there is usually a sensuality and touch and warmth, an acceptance of bodies and nerve endings. There is always a spontaneous sense of people who are there because they *want* to be, out of shared pleasure.

Now look at any depiction of sex in which there is clear force, or an

---

[1]See "The Law of the Jungle (Revised)," by Cynthia Moss, *Ms.*, January 1978.

unequal power that spells coercion. It may be very blatant, with weapons of torture or bondage, wounds and bruises, some clear humiliation, or an adult's sexual power being used over a child. It may be much more subtle: a physical attitude of conqueror and victim, the use of race or class difference to imply the same thing, perhaps a very unequal nudity, with one person exposed and vulnerable while the other is clothed. In either case, there is no sense of equal choice or equal power.

The first is erotic: a mutually pleasurable, sexual expression between people who have enough power to be there by positive choice. It may or may not strike a sense-memory in the viewer, or be creative enough to make the unknown seem real; but it doesn't require us to identify with a conqueror or a victim. It is truly sensuous, and may give us a contagion of pleasure.

The second is pornographic: its message is violence, dominance, and conquest. It is sex being used to reinforce some inequality, or to create one, or to tell us the lie that pain and humiliation (ours or someone else's) are really the same as pleasure. If we are to feel anything, we must identify with conqueror or victim. That means we can only experience pleasure through the adoption of some degree of sadism or masochism. It also means that we may feel diminished by the role of conqueror, or enraged, humiliated, and vengeful by sharing identity with the victim.

Perhaps one could simply say that erotica is about sexuality, but pornography is about power and sex-as-weapon—in the same way we have come to understand that rape is about violence, and not really about sexuality at all.

Yes, it's true that there are women who have been forced by violent families and dominating men to confuse love with pain; so much so that they have become masochists. (A fact that in no way excuses those who administer such pain.) But the truth is that, for most women—and for men with enough humanity to imagine themselves into the predicament of women—true pornography could serve as aversion therapy for sex.

Of course, there will always be personal differences about what is and is not erotic, and there may be cultural differences for a long time to come. Many women feel that sex makes them vulnerable and therefore may continue to need more sense of personal connection and safety before allowing any erotic feelings. We now find competence and expertise erotic in men, but that may pass as we develop those qualities in ourselves. Men, on the other hand, may continue to feel less vulnerable, and therefore more open to such potential danger as sex with strangers. As some men replace the need for submission from childlike women with the pleasure of cooperation from equals, they may find a partner's competence to be erotic, too.

Such group changes plus individual differences will continue to be reflected in sexual love between people of the same gender, as well as between women and men. The point is not to dictate sameness, but to discover ourselves and each other through sexuality that is an exploring, pleasurable, empathetic part of our lives; a human sexuality that is unchained both from unwanted pregnancies and from violence.

But that is a hope, not a reality. At the moment, fear of change is increasing both the indiscriminate repression of all nonprocreative sex in the religious and "conservative" male world, and the pornographic vengeance against women's sexuality in the secular world of "liberal" or "radical" men. It's almost futuristic to debate what is and is not truly erotic, when many women are again being forced into compulsory motherhood, and the number of pornographic murders, tortures, and woman-hating images are on the increase in both popular culture and real life.

It's a familiar division: wife or whore, "good" woman who is constantly vulnerable to pregnancy or "bad" woman who is unprotected from violence. *Both* roles would be upset if we were to control our own sexuality. And that's exactly what we must do.

In spite of all our atavistic suspicions and training for the "natural" role of motherhood, we took up the complicated battle for reproductive freedom. Our bodies had borne the health burden of endless births and poor abortions, and we had a greater motive for separating sexuality and conception.

Now we have to take up the equally complex burden of explaining that all nonprocreative sex is *not* alike. We have a motive: our right to a uniquely human sexuality, and sometimes even to survival. As it is, our bodies have too rarely been enough our own to develop erotica in our own lives, much less in art and literature. And our bodies have too often been the objects of pornography and the woman-hating, violent practice that it preaches. Consider also our spirits that break a little each time we see ourselves in chains or full labial display for the conquering male viewer, bruised or on our knees, screaming a real or pretended pain to delight the sadist, pretending to enjoy what we don't enjoy, to be blind to the images of our sisters that really haunt us—humiliated often enough ourselves by the truly obscene idea that sex and the domination of women must be combined.

Sexuality *is* human, free, separate—and so are we.

But until we untangle the lethal confusion of sex with violence, there will be more pornography and less erotica. There will be little murders in our beds—and very little love.

Mass Culture
and
Mass Media

In the essay that begins this section, Alexis de Tocqueville, writing a century and a half ago, makes a clear distinction between "aristocratic" and "democratic" societies and between the kind of arts (by which he means arts and also crafts) each tends to produce. In fixed, aristocratic societies, he says, only the aristocratic class can afford the arts, and members of that class develop a sort of hereditary taste for high quality, which artisans and artists try to satisfy out of pride in their craft. Under democracy, with its loss of stable ranks, class, and privileges, the number of possible consumers increases, but "the merit of each production is diminished." Since de Tocqueville's time, the forces accompanying the "democratization" of the arts have continued powerfully to work, creating what many today call a "mass culture."

The term *mass culture* can mean at least two different, interrelated things. It can mean something like "popular culture," the art, music, literature, and entertainment of most people, as contrasted to the old "elite" culture of the aristocracy. Hannah Arendt and others have argued, indeed, that most people in mass society neither have nor want "culture" in the aristocratic sense; all they want for their vacant time is entertainment, which in a commercial civilization like ours is offered by specialized industries and consumed just like any other product. *Mass culture* can also mean something a little more broad and anthropological: a culture made up of large masses of people who have lost their separate, local, tribal, or folk cultures, and who now share the same customs, attitudes, and values.

John Simon mainly addresses himself to the issue of popular culture versus elite culture, coming down strongly for the view that the elitist culture is the only one of value; the rest is vulgarity. The remaining essays come to grips more with mass culture in the second sense, and with the immense dangers and benefits created in such a culture by the presence of the means of mass communication—the mass media—which not only pervade our culture but have massively helped to create it in both senses.

Television, with its enormous audiences and its predominant commercialism, is perhaps the most controversial of the media. William Lee Miller's balanced assessment is followed by the more negative judgments of Jerry Mander and Henry Fairlie, whose particular focus is on television news. Daniel Boorstin and Aldous Huxley present contrasting views of the threat to democracy by advertising.

If mass entertainment gives the public what it wants, it also gives that public an image of itself. Michael Roberts looks closely at the way we use spectator sports as an expression of our (sometimes unsocial) impulses. Andrew Griffin finds an insight into our culture even in monster movies and creature movies. Joyce Carol Oates' frightening story evokes, among other things, the pervasive power of popular music for American adolescent culture.

HIGH CULTURE AND POPULAR CULTURE

ALEXIS de TOCQUEVILLE

This is Chapter 11, volume 2, of Democracy in America. *For information on the author and his writings, see page 241.*

In What Spirit the Americans Cultivate the Arts

It would be to waste the time of my readers and my own if I strove to demonstrate how the general mediocrity of fortunes, the absence of superfluous wealth, the universal desire for comfort, and the constant efforts by which everyone attempts to procure it make the taste for the useful predominate over the love of the beautiful in the heart of man. Democratic nations, among whom all these things exist, will therefore cultivate the arts that serve to render life easy in preference to those whose object is to adorn it. They will habitually prefer the useful to the beautiful, and they will require that the beautiful should be useful.

But I propose to go further, and, after having pointed out this first feature, to sketch several others.

It commonly happens that in the ages of privilege the practice of almost all the arts becomes a privilege, and that every profession is a separate sphere of action, into which it is not allowable for everyone to enter. Even when productive industry is free, the fixed character that belongs to aristocratic nations gradually segregates all the persons who practice the same art till they form a distinct class, always composed of the same families, whose members are all known to each other and among whom a public opinion of their own and a species of corporate pride soon spring up. In a class or guild of this kind each artisan has not only his fortune to make, but his reputation to preserve. He is not exclusively swayed by his own interest or even by that of his customer, but by that of the body to which he belongs; and the interest of that body is that each artisan should produce the best possible workmanship. In aristocratic ages the object of the arts is therefore to manufacture as well as possible, not with the greatest speed or at the lowest cost.

When, on the contrary, every profession is open to all, when a multitude of persons are constantly embracing and abandoning it, and when its several members are strangers, indifferent to and because of their numbers hardly seen by each other, the social tie is destroyed, and each workman, standing alone, endeavors simply to gain the most money at the least cost. The will of the customer is then his only limit. But at the same time a corresponding change takes place in the customer also. In countries in which riches as well as power are concentrated and retained in the hands of a few, the use of the greater part of this world's goods belongs to a small number of individuals, who are always the same. Necessity, public opinion, or moderate desires exclude all others from the enjoyment of them. As this aristocratic class remains fixed at the pinnacle of greatness on which it stands, without diminution or increase, it is always acted upon by the same wants and affected by them in the same manner. The men of whom it is composed naturally derive from their superior and hereditary position a taste for what is extremely well made and lasting. This affects the general way of thinking of the nation in relation to the arts. It often occurs among such a people that even the peasant will rather go without the objects he covets than procure them in a state of imperfection. In aristocracies, then, the handicraftsmen work for only a limited number of fastidious customers; the profit they hope to make depends principally on the perfection of their workmanship.

Such is no longer the case when, all privileges being abolished, ranks are intermingled and men are forever rising or sinking in the social scale. Among a democratic people a number of citizens always exists whose patrimony is divided and decreasing. They have contracted, under more prosperous circumstances, certain wants, which remain after the means of satisfying such wants are gone; and they are anxiously looking out for some surreptitious method of providing for them. On the other hand, there is always in democracies a large number of men whose fortune is on the increase, but whose desires grow much faster than their fortunes, and who gloat upon the gifts of wealth in anticipation, long before they have means to obtain them. Such men are eager to find some short cut to these gratifications, already almost within their reach. From the combination of these two causes the result is that in democracies there is always a multitude of persons whose wants are above their means and who are very willing to take up with imperfect satisfaction rather than abandon the object of their desires altogether.

The artisan readily understands these passions, for he himself partakes in them. In an aristocracy he would seek to sell his workmanship at a high price to the few; he now conceives that the more expeditious way of getting rich is to sell them at a low price to all. But there are only two ways of lowering the price of commodities. The first is to discover some better, shorter, and more ingenious method of producing them; the second is to manufacture a larger quantity of goods, nearly similar, but of less value. Among a democratic population all the intellectual faculties of the workman are directed to these two objects: he strives to invent methods that may enable him not only to work better, but more quickly and more cheaply; or if he cannot succeed in that, to diminish the intrinsic quality of the thing he makes, without rendering it wholly unfit for the use for which it is intended. When none but the wealthy had watches, they were almost all very good ones; few are now made that are worth much, but everybody has one in his pocket. Thus the democratic principle not only tends to direct the human mind to the useful arts, but it induces the artisan to produce with great rapidity many imperfect commodities, and the consumer to content himself with these commodities.

Not that in democracies the arts are incapable, in case of need, of producing wonders. This may occasionally be so if customers appear who are ready to pay for time and trouble. In this rivalry of every kind of industry, in the midst of this immense competition and these countless experiments, some excellent workmen are formed who reach the utmost limits of their craft. But they rarely have an opportunity of showing what they can do; they are scrupulously sparing of their powers; they remain in a state of accomplished mediocrity, which judges itself, and, though well able to shoot beyond the mark before it, aims only at what it hits. In aristocracies, on the contrary, workmen always do all they can; and when they stop, it is because they have reached the limit of their art.

When I arrive in a country where I find some of the finest productions of the arts, I learn from this fact nothing of the social condition or of the political constitution of the country. But if I perceive that the productions of the arts are generally of an inferior quality, very abundant, and very cheap, I am convinced that among the people where this occurs privilege is on the decline and that ranks are beginning to intermingle and will soon become one.

The handicraftsmen of democratic ages not only endeavor to bring their useful productions within the reach of the whole community, but strive to give to all their commodities attractive qualities that they do not in reality possess. In the confusion of all ranks everyone hopes to appear what he is not, and makes great exertions to succeed in this object. This sentiment, indeed, which is only too natural to the heart of man, does not originate in the democratic principle; but that principle applies it to material objects. The hypocrisy of virtue is of every age, but the hypocrisy of luxury belongs more particularly to the ages of democracy.

To satisfy these new cravings of human vanity the arts have recourse to every species of imposture; and these devices sometimes go so far as to defeat their own purpose. Imitation diamonds are now made which may be easily mistaken for real ones; as soon as the art of fabricating false diamonds becomes so perfect that they cannot be distinguished from real ones, it is probable that both will be abandoned and become mere pebbles again.

This leads me to speak of those arts which are called, by way of distinction, the fine arts. I do not believe that it is a necessary effect of a democratic social condition and of democratic institutions to diminish the number of those who cultivate the fine arts, but these causes exert a powerful influence on the manner in which these arts are cultivated. Many of those who had already contracted a taste for the fine arts are impoverished; on the other hand, many of those who are not yet rich begin to conceive that taste, at least by imitation; the number of consumers increases, but opulent and fastidious consumers become more scarce. Something analogous to what I have already pointed out in the useful arts then takes place in the fine arts; the productions of artists are more numerous, but the merit of each production is diminished. No longer able to soar to what is great, they cultivate what is pretty and elegant, and appearance is more attended to than reality.

In aristocracies a few great pictures are produced; in democratic countries a vast number of insignificant ones. In the former, statues are raised of bronze; in the latter, they are modeled in plaster.

When I arrived for the first time at New York, by that part of the Atlantic Ocean which is called the East River, I was surprised to perceive along the shore, at some distance from the city, a number of little palaces of white marble, several of which were of classic architecture. When I went the next day to inspect more closely one which had particularly attracted my notice, I found that its walls were of whitewashed brick, and its columns of painted wood. All the edifices that I had admired the night before were of the same kind.

The social condition and the institutions of democracy impart, moreover, certain peculiar tendencies to all the imitative arts, which it is easy to point out. They frequently withdraw them from the delineation of the soul to fix them exclusively on that of the body, and they substitute the representation of motion and sensation for that of sentiment and thought; in a word, they put the real in the place of the ideal.

I doubt whether Raphael studied the minute intricacies of the mechanism of the human body as thoroughly as the draftsmen of our own time. He did not attach the same importance as they do to rigorous accuracy on this point because he aspired to surpass nature. He sought to make of man something which should be superior to man and to embellish beauty itself. David and his pupils, on the contrary, were as good anatomists as they were painters. They wonderfully depicted the models that they had before their eyes, but they rarely imagined anything beyond them; they followed nature with fidelity, while Raphael sought for something better than nature. They have left us an exact portraiture of man, but he discloses in his works a glimpse of the Divinity.

This remark as to the manner of treating a subject is no less applicable to its choice. The painters of the Renaissance generally sought far above themselves, and away from their own time, for mighty subjects, which left to their imagination an unbounded range. Our painters often employ their talents in the exact imitation of the details of private life, which they have always before their eyes; and they are forever copying trivial objects, the originals of which are only too abundant in nature.

JOHN SIMON

John Simon, an acerbic American critic of literature, the theater, the cinema, and the visual arts, claims to have "written for everything, from encyclopedias to record jackets." He was born in Yugoslavia in 1925 and still speaks both Serbo-Croatian and Hungarian. He attended school in Yugoslavia, England, and, after his family came to America during World War II, in New York. He went to Harvard (B.A., M.A., Ph.D.) and taught literature and humanities at several colleges while completing his 732-page doctoral thesis on the European prose poem.

Simon then left teaching to work as an associate editor for the Mid-Century Book Society, where he worked under W. H. Auden, Jacques Barzun, and Lionel Trilling. He wrote art criticism and book reviews, and took the job of drama critic for the Hudson Review. *He also wrote film criticism for the* New Leader *and eventually became drama critic for* New York *magazine.* Acid Test, *a collection of his criticism, was published in 1963; subsequent volumes include* Private Screenings, *which he edited with Richard Schickel (1967);* Movies into Film: Film Criticism 1967-1970 *(1971);* Uneasy Stages: A Chronicle of the New York Theater 1963-1973 *(1976); and* Singularities: Essays on the Theater 1964-1974 *(1976). Simon is also a contributing editor of* Esquire, *for which he writes a column entitled "The Language."*

As a critic, Simon adheres to three tenets: "to write on as many different subjects as I decently can"; "to try to make a critique something written as carefully as a story or poem"; "to remain absolutely independent in my criticism." His defense of elitism, reprinted here from the December 1978 Atlantic, *demonstrates these critical principles.*

In Defense of Elitism

As the Carter Administration takes over the reins of culture, the two horses in the cultural team, the National Endowment for the Arts and the National Endowment for the Humanities, have been rearing up more restive than ever. They are being goaded in contradictory directions: are subsidies from tax money to go toward more popular forms of art and culture, spread around the country more or less evenly, or are we going to uphold standards of high art and individual excellence, wherever they occur?

I shall try to enlist you in the struggle to give elitism a good name. If I believe anything, it is this: there can be neither true culture nor true art without elitism. And yet "elitism" is a word that seems to get dirtier every day in the mouths of Americans, and may already be beyond the ministrations of our most miraculous detergents.

What does this dirty word actually mean? It comes from "elite," obviously, which means the elect, deriving from the Latin *eligere*, to elect, wherefrom, through the Old French feminine past participle *élité* (elected), we get the modern French and English nouns. The elite, then, are the elected or elect, and elitism is belief in the superior wisdom or ability of such a group. On the face of it, this sounds quite democratic—elected government and all that—but it is not, and, sensing this, populism, the more maniacal form of democracy, is the bitter enemy of elitism. The point is that in culture and the arts it is not, as (at least theoretically) in government, the people who do the electing. Who, then, are the members of the cultural-artistic elite, how do we recognize them, what are their aims, and who are their enemies?

There is one part—and one part only—of this process of election that is quite democratic: the cultural elite come from all layers of society, wherever talent mysteriously springs up, wherever intellect inexplicably manifests itself, wherever taste and the cogent advocacy of taste occur. The son of a Pennsylvania coal miner, the daughter of an immigrant Brooklyn peddler, the child of ghetto blacks, may become a member of that elite. The trouble is that it is not possible to define them wholly satisfactorily, just as it is impossible to give a foolproof definition of, say, poetry. Recently, Professor Charles Kadushin, in his book *The American Intellectual Elite*, tried to establish the quiddity of that elite by statistical means, but, even though he included me on his list of the seventy top intellectuals of 1970, I had to review unfavorably both the list and the book that grew up around it; they were as tenuous and assailable as a list of the ten best movies of the year, or of all time, as it is periodically and otiosely compiled.

The difficulty is that any systematic method of defining or delimiting an elite is always arbitrary. Whereas one knows in a general way that, for example, Eric Bentley and Robert Brustein are part of the elite in dramatic criticism even as Clive Barnes and Brendan Gill are not, there is always room for discussion in these matters. It is easy enough to demonstrate that Judith Viorst, Erica Jong, and Ntozake Shange do not belong to the poetic elite (though the latter two would claim it), but what does one do with borderline cases? For instance, is *Porgy and Bess* an opera, and therefore elite, or a musical, and therefore "popular"? There is, I suspect, an honorable middle ground—much smaller than people think, to be sure—where elite and popular tastes converge.

We must, however, be on guard against that inverse snobbism at work among intellectuals, which (often mixed in with a certain trendiness) prompts an elite critic such as Richard Poirier to hail the Beatles and Bette Midler as comparable to high (i.e., elite) art. Of course, when pressed, Poirier and his kind will go into some extremely fancy footwork about what "comparable to" (or whatever similar phrase they may have used) actually means: not really "identical," it seems; more like "analogous"—but what, then, is *that*? And once you start opening the floodgates even a crack, the next thing, inevitably, is a deluge.

Tentatively, very tentatively, I offer the following description of what constitutes an elitist, eight aspects of elitism on which all members of the elite might well agree. All, that is, who are not afflicted with the Poirier syndrome, which may also be termed *nostalgie de la boue*, or "yearning for the gutter" (literally, "mud"), as it is usually Englished. Herewith my eight points.

1) *Art and culture are not easy.* All elitists would concur that the art and culture that matter are not easily sellable to the people at large. They are not nearly so simple to digest as popularizations and vulgarizations, but they should, of course, be made available to all. However, great efforts and expenditures to bribe and cajole the public into culture are a waste. The various National Endowments and foundations that swoon with ecstasy because of the thousands of people they were able to coax into viewing a traveling show of Khmer art are usually felicitating themselves prematurely; what matters is how much the viewers got from the show, and on this there are no figures available.

2) *No art is as good as the highest form of it.* Arthur Miller is less good than Samuel Beckett; Norman Rockwell is no Andrew Wyeth, and Wyeth is no Paul Klee; Robert Aldrich is less than Robert Altman, who is less than Ingmar Bergman; folk dancing is not up to ballet; and so on. There is a hierarchy in the arts, and thus in culture; a critic such as Edmund Wilson or Susan Sontag is unmatched by a John Ciardi or a Marya Mannes—and first things must be allowed to come first. This is not to say that art or culture must be of the highest order to be of interest and value; nevertheless, priorities exist, and it is the apex of the pyramid that matters most.

Unlike in nature, where the root feeds the plant, in art, the pinnacle makes possible the base. Drama did not begin with a lot of hacks gradually evolving into Aeschylus and Sophocles; the novel did not start with a slew of James Micheners and Leon Urises building up to Dickens and Joyce. Richardson, Fielding, Sterne, and Smollett started things on a pretty high level; it is they who made the Jacqueline Susanns possible, not the other way around. Public funds for the dissemination of culture are necessary, but unless the most difficult and demanding creations on the individual level are subsidized, no amount of grants to public television to put on *The Adams Chronicles* will prevent culture and art from withering away or becoming debased, which is the same thing.

3) *The elitist is usually hated, ignored, or unrecognized by the vast majority.* This has always been so. Shaw put it well in his preface to *Saint Joan*: "It is not easy for mental giants who neither hate nor intend to injure their fellows to

realize that nevertheless their fellows hate mental giants and would like to destroy them, not only enviously because the juxtaposition of a superior wounds their vanity, but quite humbly and honestly because it frightens them."

4) *There is no democracy in culture and the arts.* In other words, the *vox populi* is usually worth nothing. With rare exceptions, the artists and cultural voices that caught the public's fancy did not survive. For the occasional genius recognized in his lifetime, such as Dickens, there are always scores who are ridiculed if they are noticed at all. This does not mean that critics or cultural gurus have not been able to sell good art to the public on occasion— though not necessarily getting understanding along with the lip service.

Especially in the fine arts, much that is garbage has been sold by so-called pundits to an uncultivated public grown rich enough to afford art patronage. I fully believe that nine tenths of what passes for great painting and sculpture today will be deservedly forgotten in time to come. And when I deplore public taste, I do not mean just Nevada; I mean the supposedly civilized opera-goers right here in New York, who will crowd into every performance of *Andrea Chénier* and *La Gioconda* but leave a good many empty seats for any performance of *Wozzeck*. And speaking of Dickens, that perennial example of public good taste, wasn't he outsold in his day by one Martin Tupper?

5) *There is no such thing as "popular" art.* Long ago, when unnamed artists functioned as dedicated artisans throughout the world, Anonymous, who was a man or a woman of the people, created genuine works of art. Today, the commercialized, mass-produced pop-art industry has so permeated the people as to destroy their individual creativity. Pop music—rock, folk, country-and-western, or whatever—has nothing to do with art. In fact, a person who can tell one rock group from another usually neither knows nor cares about music. In 1960, in his essay "Masscult & Midcult," Dwight Macdonald wrote: "Today, in the United States, the demands of the audience, which has changed from a small body of connoisseurs into a large body of ignoramuses, have become the chief criteria of success." Success, it must be stressed, is no sign of belonging to the cultural elite; but neither, necessarily, is failure.

6) *A member of the elite is one so recognized by other members.* Unfortunately, this criterion is of very limited use, because there is so much cliquishness and trendiness even among the elite—or what passes for them—that discrimination is obfuscated by gamesmanship.

7) *The elite are skeptical about the artistic and cultural sensations of the day.* "Unless he bites the hand that feeds him, the writer cannot live; and this those who would prefer him dead (so they can erect statues of him) can never understand." So wrote Leslie Fiedler, perceptively, before he himself defected to pop culture and started perceiving important truths in soap operas. Or, to quote Macdonald again, this time from the collection *Discriminations* (1974), "I've always specialized in negative criticism—literary, political, cinematic, cultural—because I found so few contemporary products about which I could be 'constructive' without hating myself in the morning." The elitist is

not unmoved by art of the simplest kind; the trouble is that this is almost rarer than the more complex sort. But he does not find a pearl in every oyster, a chicken in every potboiler, as most writers for the popular press unfailingly do.

8) *For the elitist, there is voluptuousness in the processes of discrimination and ratiocination.* He reflects on and distinguishes between true and false cultural values as naturally as he breathes, and with much greater delight than in breathing.

These, as nearly as I can pinpoint them, are the hallmarks of the elite and the values for which they stand. You may think elitism and members of the elite odious—and some, like some populists, certainly are—but if you let them die out, it will mean, as surely as starving the brain of oxygen causes death, your participation in the murder of culture and the arts.

ON TELEVISION

WILLIAM LEE MILLER

William Lee Miller is a student of American culture, a writer, and an educator. He was born in 1926 and educated at Nebraska (A.B., 1947) and Yale (Ph.D., 1958). He was on the staff of The Reporter *from 1955 to 1958, has taught at Yale and Smith, and was once a radio-television-movie critic for a small magazine. Since 1969 he has been a professor of political science and religious studies at Indiana University, where he is also the director of the Poynter Center, devoted to studies of contemporary American issues with special reference to the media. He has written several books:* Piety Along the Potomac *(1964);* The Fifteenth Ward and the Great Society *(1966), an account of his experience as a New Haven alderman;* Of Thee, Nevertheless, I Sing: An Essay on American Values *(1976); and* Yankee from Georgia: The Emergence of Jimmy Carter *(1978). "Television Power and American Values" was presented as a paper at a 1978 Rockefeller Foundation Conference and was printed in* The Search for a Value Consensus *(Rockefeller Foundation Working Papers, September 1978).*

Television Power and American Values

I am as old as radio; our oldest child is as old as television. She and her younger siblings have a hard time imagining a world, a home, an evening, in which there is no television. It is even a little hard for me to remember life before television. Stephen Leacock wrote that he had long years of experience in the bank field—as a depositor. I have an analogous experience in the television field, from watching Milton Berle to watching "Saturday Night Live"; from finding a bar with a TV set in Chicago to watching

Murrow's program on Joseph McCarthy to taping Walter Cronkite's interview with Miss Lillian.

The interpretation of American television at the most general level is like that of other "advances" of modern technology, the so-called "progress" since the Industrial Revolution. These advances are accompanied by enormous costs and dangers. And of course the full effect is not that of one invention alone but of the complex whole; television is inextricably interwoven with the rest of modern technological society.

But television, like modern technological society, is not the total monster that some, partly in reaction to the opposite view, see it to be: writers like Jacques Ellul, agrarian romantics, returners to the soil. With all of the costs, these developments in industrial productivity, in transportation, and in communication represent net gains in the life of the broad populace. Modern technology, particularly television, has values that are peculiarly difficult for the articulate to appreciate and dangers that are peculiarly difficult for the general public to perceive.

As to the articulate classes, we dictate our denunciations of "impersonal," "dehumanizing" modern technology onto transcribing machines; they are typed on electric typewriters; they are "published" by the earliest of the decisive technological advances, the printing press; they are transmitted (to the allegedly alienated public) by modern means of transportation and communication. We will discuss our books denouncing television on television talk shows, if any one will invite us to appear on them. Jacques Ellul's excoriation of technology is available in paperback in small Midwestern cities; to bring about that result requires a whole series of uses of the technology the book denounces.

More important, the daily life of the ordinary man is concretely improved in mundane ways. People in what used to be called the underdeveloped countries are busily striving to attain what literati in the advanced nations busily denounce. Television shares to some extent, ambiguously, in that mundane improvement in the daily life of millions that is more obvious in other technological advances—central heating, motor cars, penicillin, modern plumbing, the telephone. These are not what poets sing about, but they are what people latch onto. The justification of mass television is not, first of all, the occasional "good" program but just the addition to the life of the ordinary person of another, more complete and accessible and varied source of entertainment and information than had hitherto been available. Proposition: Life is more *interesting* for the elderly poor, for people living alone, for patients in hospitals (you walk down the corridor and quickly learn what is on all three networks), for residents of Gnaw Bone, Indiana, and Skyline, Wyoming, for working class and poor people, the forest of TV aerials over whose homes the critics used to deplore—life is more interesting for the broad public, and especially for the poorer, and more remote, the disabled, disconnected, and disadvantaged, than it was before the advent of television. I was struck by this aside in Kenneth Tynan's article on Johnny Carson in *The New Yorker*: "Between April and September, the numbers dip, but this reflects a seasonal pattern by which all TV shows are affected. A top NBC executive explained to me, with heartless candor, 'People who can afford vacations go away in the summer. It's only the poor people who watch us all the year round.' "

I wasn't poor, but I never saw Hank Luisetti shoot a jump shot nor did I know what Art Tatum looked like, much as I admired them, in my culturally deprived youth before television. My son has seen Julius Erving, Walt Frazier, and Bill Walton of the NBA on CBS. The defense rests.

Neither unambiguous progress nor monster, television is not "neutral" either. Television, like technology generally, is not *simply* an instrument or tool which extends human powers, to be used according to one's choice for good or for evil. The giant levers of modernity have a particularly powerful shape—each one, and the collection of all of them. Taken together, they make the simultaneous centripetal and centrifugal forces that Mannheim described: great new centers of power (30 Rock, hard rock, Black Rock, Fred Silverman) combined with wider and wider "mass democratization" (99 percent of households with a set; 78 percent color sets; 46 percent more than one set; on an "average" Sunday night—the biggest night—97 million viewers; on other nights, 80 million, 30 million and more watching the same program; 104 million watching Super Bowl XII; 111 million watching Nixon's resignation; 75 million watching at least part of the Carter-Ford debates).

As the automobile eliminated the Sunday-night church service and the use of the parlor for courting and helped to create the suburb, so television will have its own string of *unintended* side effects in the shaping of a social order. Television, like technology, is neither an unequivocal good nor an unequivocal evil, nor yet simply neutral, but an enormously powerful phenomenon with quite particular traits, about which the society needs to make conscious social decisions, recognizing the mammoth dangers and kinds of damage those traits can represent.

Television is a condition of our present social life, irreversible; it is an aspect of the perennial human struggle to live together well, which struggle never ends. Obviously, it was an enormous mistake that this potent instrument was allowed simply to grow out of radio and given over therefore to commercial control. It did not require the sponsorship of Maxwell House coffee or the billion-dollar annual revenues for three commercial networks in order for life to be a little more interesting in Gnaw Bone.

The first of the evident traits of American TV, upon which the others rest, acquired with stunning rapidity in my adult lifetime, is the pervasiveness, ubiquity, inescapability that the figures I cited above indicate. There's no hiding place down here. A friend of mine, disturbed that his son recited television commercials, banished the set from his house. He wrote an article about the impact of television on our values which drew a large response and was reprinted in the *Reader's Digest*—with, interestingly, the paragraph condemning advertising omitted. He mentioned in the article the TV-less condition of his home, and when he appeared on radio discussion programs incredulous interviewers asked how his children could survive without a television set—how they could learn about President Nixon standing by the China Wall, an event of the time, for example. He calmly explained that there were perfectly good photographs of the President looking at the China Wall on the front page of *The New York Times*, which ought to suffice.

But his wife had to cope with the children's compulsion to go next door to watch "Sesame Street" and other programs that are not "Sesame Street." And this man sometimes simply couldn't follow the politics that he needed to follow without a television set. I had the same experience in a futile effort at abstemiousness during a year in California in 1960–61: No television set, I said. The children would have to get along without one. Then came the Nixon-Kennedy debates, and it was Daddy who went out and rather sheepishly brought home a used set. So with my television-criticizing friend, in whose den a TV set now gives out its nightly dose of distorted values.

Even if you don't have one, or even if, as the television people are always saying you can do, you turn off the knob or never turn it on, still you live in a society in which everybody else has a set and everybody else has it turned on. (I remember nightly walks in Princeton, early in the TV days, in which we passed house after dark house in which we would be startled to see the blue-white glimmerings of a TV set.) Man is a social animal. If you don't know who Starsky and Hutch or who Laverne and Shirley are—with some nimble footwork I do not—your children do, your students do, your coworkers do, *Time* magazine does, and you will. I will.

I read in an article while I was preparing to write these paragraphs that there are two actors who play parts called "Pride" and "Price" in advertisements for the A&P, and that they are better known than was John F. Kennedy. They are asked for their autographs, and dutifully sign "Pride" and "Price." I had never heard of them, but in the end I found out about them. And so will you, whether your sets are on or not. The numbers for television are so huge, crossing all lines of society, and the time spent is so great—six and half hours a day on the average, eight hours in households with children—as to make television an unavoidable given condition whether we like it or not.

It sets conditions for other institutions. The current President was careful to schedule his State of the Union message on an evening that would avoid competition with, or the supplanting of, the aforesaid Starsky and Hutch; the two previous Presidents were careful to avoid interference with telecast sporting events; television critics enjoy telling about the Milton Berle Effect from the early days, the Senator Montoya Effect during the telecast of the Ervin Committee hearings in 1973, each of which effects has to do with abrupt changes in water pressure in major cities at certain moments (during Berle's program at the commercials). These are but symbols, of course, of deeper effects and displacements. A pair of book publishers talk to their new author and look him over carefully in order to assess not his book but his presence for the purpose of TV talk shows, by which books are sold.

Television not only takes over as the primary celebrity-maker, but also accelerates the celebrity focus in the society. The star system of Hollywood is augmented and made even emptier. Here's Roone Arledge explaining the superiority of boxing to football for television purposes (it will surprise many, no doubt, to learn that pro football is not regarded as the apex, or nadir, of television). "Boxing is great television," Arledge says. "It has all the elements of every kind of television that fascinates people. The small ring—not a big playing space like a baseball diamond. The primitive, simple act of it, so easy to understand.

"And then there is the fact that in boxing you have people who are not only not in the kind of big, anonymous uniforms that football players wear, but in fact their bodies, their faces, almost everything about them is visible, and right there in your living room. You get to know them as people. You fight with them, you get in close.

"It's made for television."

As with sports, so with politics, and life: you get in close, it's made for television. TV seeks the simple set with a single person, in a conflict, dramatized, not the complex arrangement with many people, in the undramatic, unresolved continuity of living.

My interpretation of television has been built around these four quotations:

Walter Lippmann: "The larger the number of people the simpler the communication must be."

A television executive: "There's no highbrow in the lowbrow, but there's a little lowbrow in everybody."

Fred Friendly in *Due to Circumstances Beyond Our Control*: "Because television can make so much money doing its worst, it cannot afford to do its best."

Lippmann again: TV attempts to "attract the attention without engaging the mind."

It seeks the focus of the eyeballs, this bubble gum for the eyes, without requiring intellectual effort. When the point is to get the largest possible number—*huge* numbers—then the point is also to make it as *easy* as possible, as *catchy* as possible, as *riskless* as possible, because every element of difficulty, of controversy, of risk causes a certain drop-off in the huge percentage of the population one tries to catch.

Friendly, of course—to go back to his quotation—was recounting his experience with CBS's famous rerun of "I Love Lucy" during the Fulbright Committee hearings on Vietnam. Friendly wrote: "If we had to interrupt the program for a news bulletin, deletion of a commercial should be the last resort. The standard procedure was to sacrifice the plot, not revenue."

Those quotations represent the obvious defining characteristics of American commercial television: enormous numbers of viewers, attracted for the purpose of marketing products, at a great profit, under fiercely competitive conditions. This last of course is very important: what counts is the share of total viewers one takes away from the opposition. If Fred Silverman can raise NBC's Nielsen ratings one point, it will be worth twenty-five million dollars to the network.

There is, therefore, an enormous struggle for that audience, a high-powered, expensive, market-researched effort to find the ways to get and to keep the prime-time audience. One measures one's work not by external standards, but by Nielsen ratings in competition with the others. An American television program can be watched by twenty million people and judged a *failure*. From this underlying economic imperative—this "cost per thousand" battle of billion-dollar empires—comes the stereotypes, simplicities, and formulae of the programs, the "Beverly Hillbillies" and the program about the talking horse. "They make no drafts on thought, conscience, or truth."

The industry defends itself by an appeal to democracy and to free enterprise. But American television fits the moral ideal of neither.

The industry is oligopolistic at the Sixth Avenue top, and oligopolistic with a federal license at the local level—the FCC license to print money. Think with what fierce resistance the industry—the alleged free enterprisers—has fought the possibilities for free entry or wider competition: pay TV, cable TV, public TV as a genuine fourth network. As has been known to happen elsewhere, it's "free" enterprise only for those who have already captured a powerful position.

As to "democracy"—the industry uses the prestige of enormous numbers, of majorities, of the common people, to embarrass democratic critics: if millions of ordinary folk like it, who are you, you highbrow, to say it's lousy? The alternative (it is regularly said) is an "elite" imposing *their* tastes, or the government imposing its will. But obviously those aren't the only alternatives, as the network battles to retain their power attest.

And the numbers they so desperately assemble do not make their enterprise in any meaningful sense "democratic." Democratic counting of heads assumes that the heads have been used for judgment and thought. The action of voting is intended to be a conscious, deliberate act, guided by some notion of the social good, and sometimes it is that. The *theory* matters. It imputes to the voter deliberate, rational choice and even choice that considers the common good. Go to a swearing-in of naturalized citizens to see what democratic *voting* means. Nobody pretends that turning on the knob of a television set is such an act. Counting the number of knobs turned is no democratic procedure. It has no heritage of interpretation to accompany it; it has no legal status nor any political philosophy justifying it. If large numbers of people gather to watch a gory accident or gawk at a man standing on the ledge of a high building, such gatherings do not have any of the moral authority of properly assembled majorities in a democracy. A television audience is not a conscious public but a peculiar kind of crowd—almost the sedentary, separated, quiescent equivalent of a mob, because it has been assembled by deliberate calculations about, and manipulations of, its emotions and nonrational drives.

In each of us there are many different attributes, impulses and capacities, at many levels—higher, lower, and in between. We do gaze at gory accidents, bright lights, pretty girls, freaks, oddities. But doing that in large numbers is making no political judgment and has no moral authority.

But this new instrument does have power—not only the power represented by those numbers, but also the power inherent in the medium. It does more for the recipient with less effort on his or her part. Radio required a use of the imagination to picture Fibber McGee's closet. Television will show you. Visual radio adds sight to the sound of radio; adds movement to the still pictures of photography; adds the transmission of an event as it happens to film. (Aldous Huxley pictured a future means of communication that added the sense of touch and smell, and there were jokes in the early days of TV especially about the latter. Henry Morgan said he'd hate to follow an animal act.) TV adds accessibility to the cinema; the viewer does not need to leave home to get himself to the Bluebird Theatre. Each one of these additions is an increase in communication power. Each is correspondingly a decrease in the demands put upon the recipient.

A professor of comparative literature, arguing against colleagues hostile to television because they think it encourages "passivity" on the part of viewers, wrote "surely watching television is no more passive than reading a novel. Television can stimulate thought," he went on, "as easily as a painting in a museum, or music in a concert hall, or a film in a theatre." His comment stimulated thought on my part, and the thought is that he is wrong. A novel requires the ability to absorb the meaning of a printed page and to create in one's own mind images that the words are intended to convey: there is Wuthering Heights, here is Heathcliff. Television provides the sight and sound of all that for you, with Heathcliff looking all wrong. The experience in the immediate moment of communication at least is more passive on the part of the recipient, with more power in the instruments of the communicator. Richard Hoggart's fine book, *The Uses of Literacy*, weaves into its careful examination of the impact of mass culture on folk culture de Tocqueville's phrase about a morally empty "democracy" that "silently unbends the springs of action."

Let me make comparisons between commercial television and three other institutions which it has in part supplanted and which it resembles in its culture-shaping: church, school, newspaper. They are "secondary" institutions that pump their stuff into individuals, face-to-face groups, families, circles of friends, and hence into the culture.

Each of these others has in some way a *content* antecedent to its effort to reach the people, which content has some authority, places some limit, and makes some claims. Churches have their messages out of the religious traditions. The schools have subject matter that is to be taught even though students do not understand it or do not want to learn it. Newspapers have a norm besides that of making money—to present news and opinion.

Commercial television has no such *given*. The great difference between television and these others is that they have a *content* antecedent to their seeking an audience; TV does not.

The overriding claim on American commercial television is the delivery of audiences to advertisers for the sale of products, in order to make money. Churches, schools, and newspapers have a dual claim—both of the content of which they are the bearers and at the same time of the public to which they should bring it. But television seeks a public with nothing but avarice in its heart. When the industry people say, defensively, "We give the public what it wants," one makes two replies. The first is, no, you don't; the public wants what it gets. You entice and habituate, for your purposes—you do control it, despite your effort to deny your responsibility. The other reply is more damning. You give the public what it "wants"? Yes, you do, in a sense, and that is your self-condemnation.

Each of the other three institutions I have mentioned has its traditional vocation, with established norms. The priesthood is an authoritative, indelible office, even to the point of being valid independent of the character of the priest; as we know from the novels of Graham Greene, a sacrament is valid even if the celebrant is a bad priest; a mass is valid even if no congregations participate in or understand it. The priest stands in an apostolic succession that is authoritative prior to any characteristics, behavior, attitudes, or votes of believers (or nonbelievers). Though other religious traditions do not have as sharply defined an authority as the Roman Catholic Church, they have some priest, preacher, rabbi, whose calling is defined by norms out of a tradition not dependent on the passing daily crowd. The teacher has an obligation to subject matter, and a heritage "bequeathed of Socrates," as a teacher of mine used to say. Obviously, good teachers have to listen, to pay attention to the student's state of mind and receptivity, but teachers have a *dual* responsibility, to the integrity of the subject as well as to the mind of the student.

Though the newsperson has no such longevity of tradition, nor such clarity of professional definition, as the priest and the teacher, he has nevertheless developed an ethic that does make its claims upon him—factual reporting of the news—as many current cases attest.

Commercial TV has no norms, no tradition, no established vocation with its disciplines. Perhaps it should be compared not to the high institutions listed above but to popular entertainment—to the circuses that went with the bread, to the music hall, to the movies. Even with such comparisons, there are significant differences. These activities at their higher levels developed their inclination toward art—that is, toward fulfilling aesthetic criteria within the limits of popular appeal. In commercial television, the aesthetic possibilities are stunted because the prime principle is not just sufficient popular appeal to keep the show going but the delivery of the attention of the immense mob of isolated viewers to the sellers of products. In other words, the mixture of box office and broad acclaim that is the test of popular entertainment—the Music Hall, say, or movies—is not quite the determining criterion of commercial TV. That criterion is "cost-per-thousand"—the attention of huge multitudes of viewers when a commercial is shown. The entertainment is not the substance of the transaction but an instrument of the real transaction. And so the irony that some commercials have aesthetic possibilities the programs—the game shows and sit-coms—don't. As Les Brown wrote: "In day-to-day commerce, television is not so much interested in the business of communications as in the business of delivering people to advertisers. People are the merchandise, not the shows. The shows are merely the bait."

The content of programs is a by-product of this central purpose, and is therefore less likely to take on an artistic life of its own and is under more severe constraints in doing so. It is an artifact manufactured by a collective to respond to market research. Charlie Chaplin didn't work that way.

Now come some of the exceptions and qualifications. I don't want to mention the "many good things" on commercial TV—actually "Eleanor and Franklin" shows are few, measured by the hours and hours of telecasting. (Public television, with MacNeil/Lehrer and BBC series, is of course another matter.) I want instead to make one small point and discuss one exception.

It isn't quite true that TV seeks the *lowest* common denominator, as people often say. It does not deliberately seek or reflect the *worst* shared interests, but rather the widest; in the books, they talk now about the "least objectionable program": the program that won't make viewers, who are already watching television, switch to another channel. Least objectionableness is different from lowest, however uninteresting the distinction may be to the serious critic of the higher arts. There is a benchmark or minimum allowable effect in mass television that has its own modest worth. It isn't our absolute *worst* you see there. Blacks, though still stereotyped and carefully subordinated, are in better shape in American television commercials than in American white attitudes and American life. Or in movies in the thirties, full of Stepin Fetchit. TV marks a minimum achievement.

Now the last and most important point: news and public affairs. Here is a division of TV that *does* recognize a moral obligation, however inadequately it fulfills it.

I chaired a meeting at which a professor of cultural subjects at MIT defended the recent "docu-dramas," like ABC's "Washington: Behind Closed Doors," and Fred Friendly strongly protested. To the MIT professor, it did not matter whether presentations—"stories"—involving actual historical figures were or were not accurate. For Friendly, *accurate* presentation of the news, of *factual* reality, is an overriding norm.

Whatever the limitations of the American press, there is a traditional obligation to truthful presentation of factual material, including unpleasant material—some news the public does not want to hear. Television taken as a whole has no such obligation. The news divisions within television have fought uphill against the tendency of the institution of which they are a part—uphill as Friendly's own experience would indicate. The development of "happy talk" news and the use of market consultants to shape TV news programs is a further indication of the underlying current. Ron Powers tells in his book *The Newscasters* the terrible story of happy talk and market consultants beginning to carry the day, on behalf of the upstart competitor ABC, against the older normative content of journalism.

In 1952, I made my way to a Denver hotel where sellers of TV sets had set up several sets on which the general public could watch the two conventions (a marked contrast in the constituencies for Ike-GOP and for the Democrats). In the spring of 1953, we all watched the Army-McCarthy hearings, later Frank Costello's hands in the Kefauver hearings; in 1956, the two Betty Furness programs (i.e., the two conventions). There is a lot wrong with TV's coverage of conventions, campaigns, and elections, greatly due to those characteristics already stated; yet it is in the coverage of public events that television justifies itself (justifies itself because it fulfills a genuine external norm). On the great occasions, it is appropriate that we gather as one people to watch, to participate in, the same event—perhaps most powerfully to this day in the assassination and funeral of John F. Kennedy. We saw President Kennedy inaugurated, with Robert Frost's difficulty reading his poem and Cardinal Cushing's endless prayer. We saw Martin Luther King's "I Have a Dream" speech at the Lincoln Memorial and Lyndon Johnson, saying that we shall overcome. I called my daughter to come and watch, in March 1967, because of a suggestion that something important was coming in another Johnson speech. The Chicago convention? Well, the whole world is watching. My son has not only seen Kareem Abdul-Jabbar; he has also seen Senator Ervin, Sam Dash, Haldeman-Ehrlichman, and the House Judiciary Committee. With the tall ships of the Bicentennial, TV carried a national public ritual of another kind. The service to the common good of all that sharing in public life justifies a lot of quiz shows.

JERRY MANDER

Born in 1936 and educated at Wharton (B.S. in economics, 1958) and Columbia (M.S. in international economics, 1959), Jerry Mander was the president of the innovative advertising agency of Freeman, Mander and Gossage by the time he was twenty-nine. He left the agency in 1972, however, to serve as founding director of Public Interest Communications, America's first nonprofit advertising agency; he is also one of the founding directors of Friends of the Earth.

In 1974 Mander gave up his advertising career to write his book Four Arguments for the Elimination of Television. *In the following version of his four arguments (from the January 1978 issue of* Mother Jones *magazine), Mander shows that television cannot convey complex messages and that the medium best communicates images of products—that is, advertising. Believing that advertising "exists only to purvey what people don't need" and "to homogenize people and culture," he proposes that we give up television, a form of mass technology controlled by fewer and fewer people, in order to gain some control over our lives. He owns a television set, but he has trained his children to be "aware watchers" and limits their viewing to five hours a week.*

Mander has also written (with Howard Gossage and George Dippel) The Great International Paper Airplane Book *(1967), and he is working now on a book on mass technology, which will be published by the Sierra Club.*

TV's Capture of the Mind

I was once asked to give advice on publicity to some traditional Hopi elders, who were fighting a strip mine on their reservation at Black Mesa, Arizona. Black Mesa was sacred ground to the traditional Hopis. To rip it open and remove its contents was a violation of the Hopis' most ancient religious tenets.

The problem at Black Mesa was typical of what has happened on many American Indian reservations. The traditional Hopis had always refused to deal with the Bureau of Indian Affairs, which functions as overlord on all reservations, and so they had been pushed aside. In their stead, the Bureau had created a tribal council composed mainly of Indians who no longer lived on the reservation. The tribal council members were not really even Hopis anymore; they were Mormons. Most had moved to Salt Lake City, had businesses there and returned to the reservation only for their council meetings. They agreed with the BIA that their job was to sell off Indian resources and land at the best possible price, thereby helping Indian people turn into Americans more quickly. The sale of strip-mine rights to a coal company was part of this process.

The traditional "government" that had preceded the tribal council was not really a government at all. It was a kind of informal grouping of religious leaders from the dozens of independent clans that together formed the Hopis. They did not sit in a hierarchical arrangement over the rest of the Hopis; they functioned more as teachers or as guides to their religious conceptions.

The religion itself was based on what we would now think of as ecological laws of balance. The land was alive, the source of life. To rip it up and ship away its contents was so outrageous as to be unthinkable. To the Mormon-American Hopis, however, strip mines were indeed thinkable.

Eventually the traditionals realized that while they were ignoring the BIA and the tribal council, the land was being destroyed and the religion with it. The elders decided to fight. To fight they needed to learn white legal systems, white tactics and white means of manipulating the media. To learn these, they had to restructure their minds and conceptions. And so, to fight the enemy, the traditional Hopis began the process of self-destroying what remained of their own Indian-ness.

At some point television news discovered the struggle. Network crews were flown out from Hollywood. They shot images of the deserts, images of the 50-foot cranes, images of the older men and women standing picturesquely near their kivas. Following the network news guidelines for "good television," they sought a "balanced report." They interviewed members of the Bureau of Indian Affairs, members of the tribal council and representatives of the coal company, all of whom discussed the issues in terms of contracts, rights, jobs and energy.

These opinions were juxtaposed with shots of some of the elderly Hopis, standing in the desert, speaking of the Great Spirit being represented in all things.

The news people added some footage of Hopi sacred dances and some images of the Hopis' most spiritual place, the kiva. The elders limited how far the reporters could go into their religion. It is against the Hopi religion for ceremonies and "power objects" to be photographed. The elders felt that to photograph these things "steals their aura." They also felt that exposing their ceremonies to people who have not been trained to understand them—a process that takes Hopi apprentices many years—would undermine the meaning of the ceremonies.

A week later, I watched the report on television. It got four minutes on the evening news. It was an earnest report. The reporters revealed that their sympathies lay with the traditionals, but they had created—as they had no choice but to do—a formula story: Progress vs. Tradition. Forty million Americans obtained their first, and perhaps only, views of the Hopi people in the form of images of cranes juxtaposed with Indians in suits and ties, responsible government officials concerned about jobs, and a lot of old savage-looking types in funny clothes, talking about a religion that says that to dig up the land is dangerous for the survival of every creature on the planet. These 40 million people also saw a white, modishly dressed TV newsman explain the crosscurrents in the struggle and plaintively ask whether something of an earlier culture couldn't be permitted to remain. "From Black Mesa, Arizona, this is John Doe reporting." This was followed by a commercial for Pacific Gas and Electric on the growing energy crisis and the need to tap all energy resources. The next story on the news was about a bank robbery.

I turned off the television set and wondered what effect this story had had on viewers. Did it help the Hopis? Would any good come from it?

It was certain that the old people had not come through as well as the businessmen, the government officials and the reporter's objective, practical analysis. The old people just seemed tragic and a little silly, if poignant. They were attempting to convey something subtle, complex, foreign and ancient through a medium that didn't seem able to handle any of those things, one that is better suited to objective data, conflict and fast, packaged information.

I wondered, if I had been shooting that story myself for the evening news, could I have done a better job of it? Would I have been able to explain to white America that to care about what was going on down there they would have to care about the Hopi perception of reality, the Hopi mind and its integration with natural forces? Viewers would have to care about the landscape, the spaces, the time, the wind, the color, the feel of the land and the sacred places and things. How could I have conveyed something through the medium so that anyone would have cared, when everyone was sitting at home in darkened living rooms, watching television? It was time travel that needed to be conveyed. How could I have carried a viewer from home through time and space to another reality that can only make sense if experienced directly? I decided that my report would have been no better than this Hollywood crew's had been. In fact, theirs was probably as good as could have been done within the limits of the medium. But in the end, the

Hopis were hurt, not helped. Their struggle was revealed, perhaps, but they themselves were further fixed into the model of artifact. The medium could not be stretched to encompass their message.

On the other hand, what if I had four minutes, or even one minute, to convey the essence of a product? A car? A stereo set? A vacuum cleaner? Could I accomplish that efficiently? I certainly could. A product is a lot easier to get across on television than a desert or a cultural mind-set. Understanding Indian ways enough to care about them requires understanding a variety of dimensions of nuance and philosophy.

You don't need any of that to understand a product. If you are attempting to convey the essence of a product, you do not have problems of subtlety, detail, time and space, historical context or organic form. Products are inherently communicable on television because of their static quality, their sharp, clear, highly visible lines, and because they carry no informational meaning beyond what they themselves are. They contain no life at all and are therefore not capable of dimension. Nothing works better in telecommunication than images of products. Might television itself have no higher purpose?

Try a little experiment. Please go look into a mirror. As you gaze at yourself, try to get a sense of what is lost between the mirror image of you and *you*.

You might ask someone to join you facing the mirror. If so, you will surely feel that other person's presence as you stand there. But in the reflection, this feeling will be lost. You will be left with only the image, possibly an expressive one, but only an image. What is missing from the reflection is life, or essence.

Finally, place an object in front of the mirror: a hair dryer, a chair, a vacuum cleaner, a comb. What is lost? I won't say nothing is lost in the reflection; a mirror image does slightly alter the dimension and the color of an object. But life has not dropped out, because the object did not have any life in it. Nothing emanates from it.

More information is lost in the reflection of a living thing than of an object. In the living creature, there is something that can be experienced only in person, no matter how vivid the attempt at visual reproduction. The inanimate object, on the other hand, has only its form. This can be reflected, if not perfectly, at least very well in the mirror image.

What applies to a mirror applies even more to a photograph or a film, and still more to a television reproduction.

The great German art critic Walter Benjamin said that *all* technical reproduction (he was writing of still photography and film; television was not yet in use), of art, of nature and of human beings, deletes what he called "aura." The art object, once separated from its source in time and place, loses the powers invested in it. Nature loses its depth and complexity of sound and smell and texture. The human being, with image separated from body, loses humanness itself. Benjamin describes the plight of a film actor who has the job of conveying himself or herself through machinery that is predisposed not to allow such a conveyance: "For the first time [the actor] has to operate with his whole living person, yet foregoing [his] aura. For aura is tied to his presence; there can be no replica of it."

Mechanical reproduction is the great equalizer. When you reproduce any image of anything that formerly had aura (or life), the effect is to separate the image from the aura, leaving only the image. At this point, the image is neutral; it has no greater inherent power than commodities do.

Products have no life to begin with; neither did they have any aura that attached to some original artistic or religious use at a certain place and time. They are all duplications of each other, like the 50th copy of a photograph. So products lose virtually nothing when their images are reproduced mechanically or electronically, while original art objects lose their contextual meaning, and human beings and other living creatures lose virtually everything that qualifies as meaningful. Humans become image shells, containing nothing inside, no better or worse, more or less meaningful than the product images that interrupt them every few minutes.

By the simple process of having their images removed from immediate experience and passed through a machine, human beings lose the attributes that differentiate us from objects. Products thereby obtain a kind of equality with these aura-amputated living creatures shown on television. These factors, among many others, conspire to make television an inherently more efficient and effective medium for advertising than for conveying any information in which life force exists: human feeling, human interaction, natural environment or ways of thinking and being.

Advertisers, however, are not satisfied with equality. Leaving their products in their natural deadness would not instill any desire to buy. And so the advertising person goes a step further by constructing drama around the product, investing it with an *apparent* life. Since a product has no inherent drama, techniques are used to dramatize and enliven the product. Cuts, edits, zooms, cartoons and other effects seem to add an artificial life force to the product. These technical events make it possible for products to surpass in power the images of the creatures whose aura has been separated from them.

So television can accomplish something that in real life would be impossible: making products more "alive" than people.

Television is watched in darkened rooms. Some people leave on small lights, or daylight filters in, but it is a requirement of television viewing that the set be the brightest image in the environment or it cannot be seen well.

To increase the effect, background sounds are dimmed out. Viewers try to eliminate household noises. The point, of course, is to further the focus on the television set. Awareness of the outer environment gets in the way.

Many people watch television alone a substantial amount of the time. This eliminates yet another aspect of outer awareness. Even while watching with others, a premium is placed upon quiet. Talking interferes with attention to the set. So other people are dimmed out like the light, the sounds and the rest of the world.

Overall, while we are watching television, our bodies are in a quieter condition over a longer period of time than in any other of life's non-sleeping experiences. This is true even for the eyes, which are widely presumed to be active during television viewing. In fact, the eyes move *less* while watching television than in any other experience of daily life. This is particularly so if you sit at a distance from the set or if your set is small. In such cases you take in the entire image without scanning. Even with huge television screens, the eyes do not move as much as they do when seeing a movie, where the very size of the theater screen requires eye and even head movement.

While you are watching television, in addition to the non-movement of the eyeball, there is a parallel freezing of the focusing mechanism. The eye remains at a fixed distance from the object observed for a longer period of time than in any other human experience.

Ordinarily, the process of focusing, defocusing and refocusing engages the eye nonstop all day long, even during sleeping and dreaming. But while you are watching television, no matter what is happening on the screen, however far away the action of the story is supposed to be inside the set, the set itself remains at a fixed distance and requires only an infinitesimal change in focus. As we shall see, the result is to flatten all information into one dimension and to put the viewer in a condition akin to unconscious staring.

Furthermore, when you are watching television and believe you are looking at pictures, you are actually looking at the phosphorescent glow of three hundred thousand tiny dots. There is no picture there.

These dots seem to be lit constantly, but in fact they are not. All the dots go off thirty times per second, creating what is called the flicker effect of television, which is similar to strobe or ordinary fluorescent light.

For many years conventional wisdom held that since this flickering happens at a rate beyond the so-called flicker-fusion rate of the human eye, we do not consciously note it, and we presumably are not affected by it. However, recent discoveries about the biological effects of very minor stimuli by W. Ross Adey and others, and the growing incidence of a medical condition called television epilepsy among those particularly sensitive to flicker, have shown that whether we consciously note the flicker or not, our bodies react to it.

A second factor is that, even when the dots go "on," not all of them are lit simultaneously. Which dots are on determines the picture. In a sense, the television screen is like a newspaper photograph or the images on a film, which are also composed of dots, except that the television dots are lighted one at a time according to a scanning system that starts behind the screen. Proceeding along a line from the upper-left-hand portion of your screen across the top to the right, the scan essentially lights some dots and not others, depending upon the image to be conveyed. Then the scan goes down another line, starts at the left again and goes across to the right, and so on.

What you perceive as a picture is actually an image that never exists in any given moment but rather is constructed over time. Your perception of it as an image depends upon your brain's ability to gather in all the lit dots, collect the image they make on your retina in sequence and form a picture. The picture itself, however, never existed. Unlike ordinary life, in which whatever you see actually exists outside you before you let it in through your eyes, a television image gains its existence *only* once you've put it together inside your head.

As you watch television you do not "see" any of this fancy construction work happening. It is taking place at a rate faster than the nerve pathways between your retina and the portion of your brain that "sees" can process them. You can only see things that happen within a range of speeds. This is because four million years of human evolution developed our eyes to process only the data that was concretely useful. Until this generation, there was no need to see anything that moved at electronic speed. Everything that we humans can actually do anything about moves slowly enough for us to see.

One friend of mine put the problem this way: "The images seem to pass right through *me*; they go way inside, past my consciousness into a deeper level of my mind, as if they were dreams." From what we know of how the images are formed, this statement is uncannily accurate.

Given the way the retina collects impressions emanating from dots, the picture is formed only after it is well inside your brain. The image doesn't exist in the world and so cannot be observed as you would observe another person, or a car or a fight. The images pass through your eyes in a dematerialized form, invisible. They are reconstituted only after they are already inside your head.

This quality of nonexistence, at least in concrete worldly form, disqualifies this image information from being subject to conscious processes: thinking, discernment, analysis. You may think about the sound but not the images.

Television viewing may then qualify as a kind of wakeful dreaming, except that it's a stranger's dream, from a far-away place, and it plays against the screen of your mind.

The stillness the eyes require while watching the small television screen is another contributor to this problem of feeling by-passed by images proceeding merrily into our unconscious minds. There are hundreds of studies to show that eye movement and thinking are directly connected. The act of seeking information with the eyes requires and also *causes* the seeker/viewer to be alert, active, not passively accepting whatever comes. There are corollary studies that show that when the eyes are not moving, staring zombie-like, thinking is diminished.

Consider, by contrast, the act of keeping a journal or diary. Recording a dream or the events or feelings of the day is an act of transferring internal information from the unconscious mind, where it is stored, into the conscious mind, where you can think about it. In this way you can see patterns, develop better understanding and perhaps stimulate personal change.

Once you have described a dream to a friend, or written it down in a journal, you have literally moved it out of one mental territory, where it was inaccessible, into another territory (consciousness), where it is accessible. At that point you can think about it.

The same is true with a review of the day's activities. At the end of the day, most of us feel it has been a blur of activity. If you review it, however, either out loud to a friend or in writing, the day takes on patterns that you would otherwise miss. The events become concrete, available to your conscious mind.

Entire cultures are based on this process of transferring information from the unconscious to the conscious mind. The most widely studied are the Senoi people of Malaysia, who begin each day by describing the details of their dreams to each other. The Balinese do this unconscious-conscious transfer process via shadow theater, in which people's behavior is "played back" so it can be consciously noted and discussed. Other cultures talk a lot, describing the details of life's intimate experiences all day long. Describing the details helps one "see" them and understand them.

In some ways, reading a book is an interactive process, similar to conversation or writing in journals. Unlike images, words that you read do *not* pour into you. The reader, not the book, sets the pace. All people read at different speeds and rhythms. When you are reading you have the choice of re-reading, stopping to think or underlining. All of these acts further conscious awareness of the material being read. You effectively create the information you wish to place in your mind.

We all have had the experience of reading a paragraph only to realize that we've not absorbed any of it. This requires going over the paragraph a second time, deliberately giving it conscious effort. It is *only* with conscious effort and direct participation at one's own speed that words gain any meaning.

Images require nothing of the sort. They only require that your eyes be open. The images enter you and are recorded in memory whether you think about them or not. They pour into you like fluid into a container, one following the next. You are the container. The television is the pourer.

In the end, the viewer is little more than a vessel of reception, and television itself is less a communications or educational medium, as we have wanted to think of it, than an instrument that plants images in the unconscious realms of the mind. We become affixed to the changing images, but, as it is impossible to do anything about them as they enter us, we merely give ourselves over to them. It is total involvement on the one hand (complete immersion in the image stream) and total unconscious detachment on the other hand—no cognition, no discernment, no notations upon the experience one is having.

While researching this, I came across a fascinating study of television completed in 1975 by a team of researchers headed by psychologists Merrelyn and Fred Emery of the Australian National University at Canberra. It caused a sensation in Australia, where TV viewing is less widespread than here, but was barely noted in America.

The Emerys say the evidence shows that human beings "habituate" to repetitive light-stimuli (flickering light, dot patterns, limited eye move-ment). If habituation occurs, then the brain has essentially decided that there is nothing of interest going on—at least nothing that anything can be done about—and virtually quits processing the information that goes in. In particular, they report, the left-brain "common integrative area" goes into a kind of holding pattern. "Viewing is at the conscious level of somnambu-lism," they assert.

The right half of the brain, which deals with more subjective cognitive processes—dream images, fantasy, intuition—continues to receive the televi-sion images. But, because the bridge between the right and left brains has been effectively shattered, all cross-processing—the making conscious of the unconscious data, so that the information is useable—is eliminated. The information goes in, but it cannot be easily recalled or thought about.

The Emerys report at length on one study that measured brainwave activity during television viewing. It established that, no matter what the program is, human brainwave activity enters a "characteristic" pattern. The response is to the medium, rather than to any of its content. Once the set goes on, the brain waves slow down until a preponderance of alpha and delta brain waves becomes the habitual pattern. The longer the set is on, the slower the brainwave activity.

The Emerys explain that slow, synchronous brainwave activity is ordinarily associated with "lack of eye movement, fixation, lack of defini-tion, idleness, inactivity, overall body inertness." They quote from A.R. Luria, who writes in *The Psychophysiology of the Frontal Lobes*: "No organized thought is possible in these phasic states, and selective associations are re-placed by nonselective association, deprived of their purposeful character."

The Emerys' findings support the idea that television information enters unfiltered and whole, directly into the memory banks, but it is not available for conscious analysis, understanding or learning. Television is an instru-ment of sleep teaching.

Most Americans will argue that technology is neutral, that any technol-ogy is merely a benign instrument, a tool, and, depending upon the hands into which it falls, it may be used one way or another. There is nothing that prevents a technology from being used well or badly, nothing intrinsic in the technology itself that can predetermine its use, its control or its effects upon individual lives or political forms.

Television is merely a window or a conduit, the argument goes, through which any perception or reality may pass. It therefore has the potential to be enlightening to people who watch it and is potentially useful to demo-cratic processes. These assumptions about TV, as about other technologies, are wrong.

If you accept the principle of an army—a collection of military technol-ogies and people to run them—all gathered together for the purpose of fighting, overpowering, killing and winning, then it is obvious that the su-pervisors of armies will be the sort of people who desire to fight, overpower, kill and win and who are also good at these assignments: generals. The fact of generals, then, is predictable by the creation of armies. The kinds of generals are also predetermined. Humanistic, loving, pacifistic generals are extremely rare. It is useless to advocate that we have more of them.

If you accept the existence of automobiles, you also accept the existence of roads laid upon the landscape, oil to run the cars and huge institutions to find the oil, pump it and distribute it. In addition you accept a speeded-up lifestyle and movement through the terrain at speeds that make it impossible to pay attention to whatever is growing there. Humans who use cars sit in fixed positions for long hours following a narrow strip of gray pavement, with eyes fixed forward, engaged in the task of driving. Slowly they evolve into car-people. McLuhan told us that cars "extended" the human feet, but he put it the wrong way. They *replaced* them.

If you accept nuclear power plants, you also accept a techno-scientific-industrial-military elite. Without these people in charge, you could not have nuclear power. You and I getting together with a few friends could not build such a plant, nor could we handle or store the radioactive waste products that remain dangerous to life for thousands of years. The wastes, in turn, determine that *future* societies will have to maintain a technological capacity to deal with the problem and the military capability to protect the wastes.

In all of these instances, the basic form of the technology determines the way it will be used, who will use it and to what ends.

And so it is with television. Far from being "neutral," TV is a narrow channel through which much perception and information may not pass. Dozens of technical limitations define the boundaries of the medium's content. Some information can be conveyed totally on television, some in only a very distorted way; but most knowledge useful to human understanding of the complexities of existence cannot be conveyed.

Not accidentally, the kinds and forms of information that *can* pass through fit the interests of the handful of corporations that dominate TV. For them, television is an instrument of psychic colonization, funnelling human awareness into a hard-edged reality based upon saleable products. That television serves that reality was obvious to those corporations soon after TV's invention. It should have been obvious to us as well.

Beyond the way it filters information, we have seen that the TV signal itself produces a hypnotic-addictive effect in viewers. The way the image is processed in the brain suppresses creative thought. In many ways, TV is akin to sense deprivation, leaving a viewer totally passive, lost within implanted images.

When these effects of television and many others—above all, the inherently centralized nature of its technology—are considered together, we see that an entire nation of human beings is being redesigned and unified to fit in with the passive, anomic, commodity-based economy, the civilization of freeways, skyscrapers, suburbs and supermarkets that is today's dominant form of social organization. There is an ideology in TV's technology itself. To speak of television as "neutral" and therefore subject to change is as absurd as speaking of the reform of a technology such as guns.

HENRY FAIRLIE

Henry Fairlie (born 1924) has written, as he says, "on both sides of the Atlantic."
Educated at London's Highgate School and Oxford, from which he received a B.A. in
1945, he wrote for the London Observer *and was the main political editorial writer for*
the London Times *until he resigned in 1954 to free-lance in England and America. In*
a political column in The Spectator *in 1955, he was the first person to use the term*
Establishment *in the sense now used (a distinction triumphantly confirmed by the New*
Supplement of the Oxford English Dictionary*). Fairlie has also written for* Punch
and the New Statesman, *and he has been foreign correspondent for the* Daily Mail.
While still in England, Fairlie did reporting for several television documentaries but
stopped because, as he explained in an article in Encounter, *television is an "idiot box,"*
and "if you've seen it on television, it didn't happen."

He has lived in the United States since 1966, writing for the New York Times
Magazine, The New Yorker, *and* Life, *among others; he now contributes regularly*
to the New Republic *and has a biweekly column in the* Washington Post. *His books*
include The Life of Politics *(1968);* The Kennedy Promise *(1973);* The
Spoiled Child of the Western World: The Miscarriage of the American Idea
in Our Time *(1976); and, published in 1978, two books expanded from essays,* The
Parties *and* The Seven Deadly Sins Today. *The essay we reprint here first ap-*
peared in Horizon, *Spring 1967.*

Can You Believe Your Eyes?

None of us has ever seen Alexander the Great emerging from his tent. If
there had been television in his day and we could look at the tape, would we
know him any better, as we think we now know a John F. Kennedy or a
Lyndon B. Johnson when we see them, on television news, emerging from a
convention?

None of us has ever heard Julius Caesar speak. But if there had been
radio in his day and we could listen to the recording, would we know him
any better, as we think we know something important about Franklin D.
Roosevelt from his fireside chats?

The answer is far from clear. Of all historical evidence, the public presence of voice or of physical appearance is the most revealing but can also be
the most misleading. Yet the problem of historical evidence is raised every
night on television news, when we are asked to accept what we see and hear
as genuine. It is raised especially by the two most important television news
programs in the United States: Huntley-Brinkley on NBC, and Walter
Cronkite on CBS. Millions of people have to decide not so much whether
they can believe what they are told but whether they can believe what they
see flickering in front of them.

"The evidence of their own eyes": but that is precisely what is not available to them. What *is* available is the evidence, first, of the camera, making
its own selection, dictating its own terms; and it is the evidence, then, of the

small screen—still the best description of television—which in turn dictates to the camera. Can television, by its nature, ever tell the truth?

Amid all the pretentiousness of his theorizing, Marshall McLuhan is right to this extent: the medium is the message. Television does not merely create news. That is an old business, practiced for generations by newspapers. Television creates its own events, something even the most imaginative newspaper reporter cannot do. The newspaperman can only create words, and however powerful they may be, words do not *happen* over the breakfast table as television *happens* in a living room. Thomas W. Moore, ABC's president, came very near to the point when he said: "It is difficult to retain one's perspective when, without leaving the security of our living rooms, we become witness to such startling events as the assassination of an assassin, or a war in progress."

It is because television *happens* in this way that people begin to think that the small excerpts from life which they see on the screen in their living rooms are more "real" than the life which they experience around them. There is a vital margin of difference between saying, "Did you see the report in *The New York Times* of the massacres in the Congo?" and saying, "Did you see the massacres in the Congo on television last night?" The first remark implies only that one has seen a report (which may conflict with a report from another source). The second implies that one has seen the event itself. However carefully television is used, it cannot avoid this deception.

It is doubtful whether it is ever easy—sometimes whether it is ever possible—for a newspaper or television reporter to report an event. He can report incidents, and it is the nature of incidents that they can, and do, happen in isolation. But the true meaning of an event depends on all of its known and unknown causes, on all of the known and unknown incidents that contribute to it, and in the process, cease to be isolated, and on all of its known and unknown repercussions. The whole of an incident can easily be described; the whole of an event may escape even the historian.

If this is a difficulty that confronts the newspaper reporter from day to day, it is one that the television reporter can rarely overcome. For the newspaper reporter possesses a flexibility that the television reporter does not have. He has flexibility because he can move without the paraphernalia and encumbrance of a camera or a camera crew. He has flexibility because he can reach where the camera cannot reach: the camera can never go "off the record."

The newspaperman has flexibility, above all, because words are flexible and the length of a story is flexible: the one able to qualify, even in the shortest parenthetical expression; the other capable of imposing its own perspective. But however carefully chosen the words of a television reporter, they can never properly qualify a spectacular picture; and however discriminating the apportionment of stories in a television program, they are in length too nearly the same.

Incidents are usually in the open; the whole of an event, often obscure and private. Not only is the core of television the public and the spectacular, but there is an important sense in which television has a vested interest in disaster. From the point of view of a good story, both newspapers and television prefer covering a major strike to negotiations which prevent a strike. But it is possible for the newspaper reporter to make negotiations almost as exciting a story as a strike itself: by word of mouth, he can collect a picture of the comings and goings which are the essence of negotiation and, by his words in print, vividly describe them. But what can television do with negotiations? It can only show pictures of people arriving at a building and people leaving it. However colorful they may be—and the modern business executive is not normally colorful—this does not make exciting viewing.

Violence is the stuff of television, and the question of how to deal with it is the most important one confronting the medium.

To be sure, the same question confronts newspapers; but the impact of violence—whether a boxing match, a riot, or a massacre—is much greater in a moving picture than in a still picture or in descriptive prose. Violence is movement—the raising of an arm, the smashing of it on someone's head—and movement is what television cannot help emphasizing.

In covering violent situations, three distinct characteristics of television conspire to intensify both its special problems and the special temptations to which it is exposed. There is, first, the limitation of time. A lead news story in a paper such as *The New York Times* may take twenty minutes to read; in a popular newspaper or a tabloid, as many as ten. There simply is not this time available in television news. In the reporting of all news, this means concentration to the point of distortion. In the reporting of violence, it means concentration on the violent incident to the exclusion of the whole event.

An outstanding example of such distortion was the police attack on civil rights marchers at the Selma, Alabama, bridge in March, 1965. I was not present myself. But I do not know one reporter who was present, and whose opinion I trust, who does not point out that there was first a prolonged period during which police and demonstrators faced each other, without violence, in an atmosphere of unbearable tension, and who does not agree that the tension had to break in the form of police action.

Television news—except in special features and documentaries—did not, and could not, show this preliminary encounter. Three minutes of film is an extended sequence in a news program, and the time is best filled with action, not inaction. On the other hand, a single phrase in a newspaper story, placed correctly, where it carries weight, can put even an extended description of violence in perspective.

The point of such perspective is not to excuse any eventual police brutality, but to explain it. Without this explanation, whether implicit or explicit, one begins to think that brutality is automatic, that the police will always behave in such a manner; demonstrators begin to think that they can, and should, goad the police; and the police begin to think, since restraint is so frail anyhow, they may as well give way to exasperation from the start.

There is, secondly, television's tendency to produce self-generating news. The problem arose most notably during the disturbances in Watts; but it has arisen, again and again, whenever there have been similar disturbances in other cities. However spontaneous the original outbreak of violence, an external provocation is added once it has occurred. That provocation is the presence of television cameras in the middle of the trouble spots.

This is especially true on the night after the original outbreak. Then, as dusk gathers, television cameramen and reporters move into the streets looking—literally looking—for trouble, and the crowds begin to play up to them. Their presence is very different from the presence of newspaper reporters, who either roam around, hardly distinguishable, or lounge in bars until they hear that action has broken out somewhere down the block. Television, merely by its presence, helps to create incidents and then itself remains part of the happening. There is no doubt that this participation occurred after the first night in Watts, and that it occurred again last summer in Chicago.

But in order to create on the screen the impression of continuing disturbance, of continuing riots, television needs only one incident. One spectacular incident of violence can occupy a two-minute sequence in a news program just as impressively as a series of incidents. Much of the Watts film is a classic example of this: showing that it needs only one defiant boy and only one hot-headed policeman to suggest that a neighborhood is aflame.

In this connection it seems worth pointing out that a newspaper reporter's dishonesty—or imagination—can be a great deal less dangerous and provocative than a television reporter's. The newspaper reporter, after all, need only create—or exaggerate—a story in his own mind. But the television reporter must create—or exaggerate—it in actuality: he must make it a happening.

Finally, in this matter of violence, there is the size of the screen: the limitations which it imposes, the temptations it offers. At the end of last summer, television news showed some alarming pictures of white men and women in the Chicago suburb of Cicero screaming abuse at some Negro marchers. Their hating faces—a dozen of them, perhaps—filled the screen. They looked as if they were a representative example of a much larger crowd. But anyone who was there knows that these particular whites were only a small part of the crowds in the streets; and that the crowds themselves were only a small part of the total white population of Cicero. To this vital extent, television that night distorted badly.

What all this amounts to is not only that people sitting in their homes begin to think that all police are brutal, that all demonstrators are violent, that all disturbances are riots, that all crowds are aggressive; the fact that they usually go through each day without either meeting or themselves displaying violence becomes less real to them than the violence on the small screen.

Anyone who has appeared regularly on television knows that complete strangers think they have actually met him. They smile or nod at him in the street or across bars; they approach him and shake his hand; they even ask him to drop in when next he is around their way, as if they really believe that he has been in their homes. It is this imaginary "real" presence of television in people's living rooms which is the background to the whole problem. Surely much of the feeling of living in a condition of perpetual crisis, and the agitation arising from it, comes from a sense of being a witness to a world which is more actual than the routine world in which one lives.

Television can create, not only events out of incidents, but movements and people. The television news coverage of the Meredith march across Mississippi, during the couple of days when I accompanied it myself, constantly appalled me. It was near the beginning of the march, when it had barely gotten organized, and when the numbers were few and the individuals composing the numbers were anything but impressive.

All the familiar hazards of television reporting were displayed. A straggling column—it was at the time little more—could be made on the small screen to look like an army. When the cameras were rolling, the marchers pulled themselves together and played the role expected of them. The several civil rights leaders strode in line abreast, at the head of their enthusiastic followers.

The real story of the Meredith march was not this unified demonstration at all, but the fact that it produced the deeply significant clash between different factions of the civil rights movement over "black power." Newspapers felt their way to this story and were, by the end, reporting it fully. It was a story which, for the most part, was taking place in private meetings where the cameras could not reach. But then when television at last caught on to the fact of "black power," it inevitably exaggerated and distorted it. Film is expensive. Getting film ready for a news program is a hurried job. The result is that in reporting any speech the television reporter and cameraman make an automatic, almost involuntary, selection. They wait for the mention of a phrase like "black power," and on go the lights and the film rolls.

But, given the length of the usual sequence in a news program, that is all. The impact is far greater than that of any selection made by newspapers. By constant reiteration on the small screen day after day, the slogan of "black power" was elevated into a movement. It was suddenly there. It had suddenly happened. "Black power" switched the cameras on, and in turn the cameras switched the movement on. It was a classic case of self-generating news.

Stokely Carmichael, of the Student Nonviolent Co-ordinating Committee, could not have emerged so rapidly as a national figure without television. (SNCC is a master at using television.) But he is not the only example of television's ability to create—or destroy—people. No one, I think, questions that Governor Ronald Reagan is the creature of the television cameras, just as previously Actor Ronald Reagan was the creature of the movie cameras. John Morgan, one of the British Broadcasting Corporation's most experienced television reporters, returned from the California gubernatorial campaign last fall, amazed at Reagan's professionalism in the television studio, and the use that he made of it to dictate camera angles and even the moments for close-ups.

Much of the poor impression that President Johnson has often made is the direct result of his comparatively poor television "image." The close-up, especially, can distort in the crudest way and make what is simply unprepossessing actually repellent. In fact, in considering the impact of the closeup, one can notice the vital difference between television and the movies; between what is legitimate in the cinema and illegitimate in a living room.

Movies are intended to be, and are taken to be, larger than life. Sitting in the theatre, one does not imagine that what one is seeing is real. The closeup in the movies, therefore, is a legitimate *and understood* distortion. But a distortion it is. We never do see anyone in real life as close in as the camera can go, except in one position and in one activity: when making love. There is no reason why President Johnson, or any other public figure, should have to pass this private test in public. Moreover, not only does the close-up bring one ridiculously close to a face, it shows it in isolation. It removes the general bearing; it removes the whole man.

Perhaps the most striking demonstration of the power of television to create personalities is one that most people will think also demonstrates its power for good. For a comparatively short time three men seemed to bestride the world: John F. Kennedy, Pope John XXIII, and Nikita Khrushchev. Their impact, all over the world, was quite out of proportion to the length of time any of them held office. In a few years they had made as great an impression as Queen Victoria had in sixty years. This was the work of television.

Television news is new, and we have not yet got the measure of it. Its hazards are numerous: some of them are inherent in the nature of the medium, and are likely to be permanent. Others are more technical and, with technical advances, may be removed.

Camera crews are costly, and costly to move about; this automatically imposes a preselection of news far more rigorous than it is in a newspaper. Film costs impose a second automatic selection. Time on the screen is expensive, and this imposes a final selection. Again and again, when I have been making news films with a camera crew, I have wanted to utter over the pictures, "It was not like this at all."

However paradoxical it may seem, the only immediate answer to most of the problems of television news lies not in pictures but in words. Given the powerful impact of the pictures, the words covering them must provide the corrective. Most television reporting just describes the pictures, and by doing so, reinforces them. But the object of words in television news should be to distract from the pictures, to say: "It was not quite so. This was not the whole story." Pictures simplify; the object of words should be to supply qualification and complication. Pictures involve; the object of words should be to detach the viewer, to remind him that he is not seeing an event, only an impression of one.

The manner of delivery—especially of the "anchor" men in the studio— is as important as the substance of the words themselves. There is something very professional and very engaging about the television manners of Chet Huntley and David Brinkley and Walter Cronkite. All of them, in dissimilar ways, cultivate a deadpan approach. In Huntley, it is made to suggest a judicial impartiality; in Brinkley, an ironical detachment; in Cronkite, an unfailing common sense. Each of them by his manner reinforces the impact of the pictures over which he is speaking, suggesting that they can be taken at their face value.

Only now and then, when Brinkley's irony is allowed to break loose into that overnourished flicker of a smile, is the value of the pictures ever questioned. The vital role of the television reporter or commentator is to make watching as difficult as reading, to invite the viewer to make comparisons and judgments from his own experience so that he never reacts by assuming that he is seeing actual life.

That television news can do some things remarkably well, especially in full-length features and documentaries, that those involved in making television programs are conscientious and skillful, does not touch the main problem. Television news holds a mirror up to the world in a way that newspapers never can; and the world is beginning to believe that it can recognize itself in it. Life is not made up of dramatic incidents—not even the life of a nation. It is made up of slowly evolving events and processes, which newspapers, by a score of different forms of emphasis, can reasonably attempt to explore from day to day.

But television news jerks from incident to incident. For the real world of patient and familiar arrangements, it substitutes an unreal world of constant activity, and the effect is already apparent in the way in which the world behaves. It is almost impossible, these days, to consider any problem or any event except as a crisis; and, by this very way of looking at it, it in fact becomes a crisis.

Television, by its emphasis on movement and activity, by its appetite for incident, has become by far the most potent instrument in creating this overexcited atmosphere, this barely recognizable world. The medium, to this very important extent, has become the message; and the message is perpetual stimulation, perpetual agitation, perpetual change. The world it creates is a world which is never still.

Many of our unnecessary anxieties about the way in which we live, about the fearful things that may happen to us, might be allayed if television news began, now and then, to say: "It has been a dull day. But we have collected some rather interesting pictures for you, of no particular significance." Television news has a deep responsibility to try to be dull, from time to time, and let the world go to sleep.

The Language of Advertising

DANIEL BOORSTIN

Daniel Boorstin, historian, educator, and Pulitzer Prize-winning author, was born in 1914, grew up in Tulsa, and received his B.A. summa cum laude from Harvard in 1934. A Rhodes Scholar, he attended Balliol College at Oxford and read law at the Inner

Temple in London, becoming one of the few Americans qualified to plead cases in English courts. Boorstin returned to the United States to teach at Harvard and attend Yale Law School (J.S.D., 1940), and he was admitted to the Massachusetts bar in 1942. After working briefly in Washington administering the Lend-Lease Program and teaching at Swarthmore for two years, he joined the faculty of the University of Chicago in 1944, where he is the Preston and Sterling Morton Distinguished Service Professor of History. Boorstin has served on a number of commissions and boards, was director of the Smithsonian Institution's National Museum of History and Technology (1969-1973), became Librarian of Congress in 1975, and has received many honors and awards for his work.

The Americans, *his* magnum opus, *has earned a number of prizes. The first volume,* The Colonial Experience *(1958), won the 1959 Bancroft Prize for books in American history, diplomacy, and international relations; the second,* The National Experience *(1973), was awarded the 1974 Pulitzer Prize, as well as the Dexter Prize. He has written many other books on history and the law, including* The Genius of American Politics *(1953) and the two-volume* Landmark History of the American People *(1968 and 1970). In* The Image; or, What Happened to the American Dream *(1962), he maintains that the mass media create "pseudo-events," so that contemporary Americans live in a world of self-created illusions.*

The following essay first appeared in his Democracy and Its Discontents *(1974) and was featured in the bicentennial issue of* Advertising Age, *the advertising industry's magazine.*

The Rhetoric of Democracy

Advertising, of course, has been part of the mainstream of American civilization, although you might not know it if you read the most respectable surveys of American history. It has been one of the enticements to the settlement of this New World, it has been a producer of the peopling of the United States, and in its modern form, in its world-wide reach, it has been one of our most characteristic products.

Never was there a more outrageous or more unscrupulous or more ill-informed advertising campaign than that by which the promoters for the American colonies brought settlers here. Brochures published in England in the seventeenth century, some even earlier, were full of hopeful overstatements, half-truths, and downright lies, along with some facts which nowadays surely would be the basis for a restraining order from the Federal Trade Commission. Gold and silver, fountains of youth, plenty of fish, venison without limit, all these were promised, and of course some of them were found. It would be interesting to speculate on how long it might have taken to settle this continent if there had not been such promotion by enterprising advertisers. How has American civilization been shaped by the fact that there was a kind of natural selection here of those people who were willing to believe advertising?

Advertising has taken the lead in promising and exploiting the new. This was a new world, and one of the advertisements for it appears on the dollar bill on the Great Seal of the United States, which reads *novus ordo seclorum*, one of the most effective advertising slogans to come out of this country. "A new order of the centuries"—belief in novelty and in the desirability of opening novelty to everybody has been important in our lives throughout our history and especially in this century. Again and again advertising has been an agency for inducing Americans to try anything and everything— from the continent itself to a new brand of soap. As one of the more literate and poetic of the advertising copywriters, James Kenneth Frazier, a Cornell graduate, wrote in 1900 in "The Doctor's Lament":

> This lean M.D. is Dr. Brown
> Who fares but ill in Spotless Town.
> The town is so confounded clean,
> It is no wonder he is lean,
> He's lost all patients now, you know,
> Because they use *Sapolio*.

The same literary talent that once was used to retail Sapolio was later used to induce people to try the Edsel or the Mustang, to experiment with Lifebuoy or Body-All, to drink Pepsi-Cola or Royal Crown Cola, or to shave with a Trac II razor.

And as expansion and novelty have become essential to our economy, advertising has played an ever-larger role: in the settling of the continent, in the expansion of the economy, and in the building of an American standard of living. Advertising has expressed the optimism, the hyperbole, and the sense of community, the sense of reaching which has been so important a feature of our civilization.

Here I wish to explore the significance of advertising, not as a force in the economy or in shaping an American standard of living, but rather as a touchstone of the ways in which we Americans have learned about all sorts of things.

The problems of advertising are of course not peculiar to advertising, for they are just one aspect of the problems of democracy. They reflect the rise of what I have called Consumption Communities and Statistical Communities, and many of the special problems of advertising have arisen from our continuously energetic effort to give everybody everything.

If we consider democracy not just as a political system, but as a set of institutions which do aim to make everything available to everybody, it would not be an overstatement to describe advertising as the characteristic rhetoric of democracy. One of the tendencies of democracy, which Plato and other antidemocrats warned against a long time ago, was the danger that rhetoric would displace or at least overshadow epistemology; that is, *the temptation to allow the problem of persuasion to overshadow the problem of knowledge.* Democratic societies tend to become more concerned with what people believe than with what is true, to become more concerned with credibility than with truth. All these problems become accentuated in a large-scale democracy like ours, which possesses all the apparatus of modern industry. And the problems are accentuated still further by universal literacy, by instantaneous communication, and by the daily plague of words and images.

In the early days it was common for advertising men to define advertisements as a kind of news. The best admen, like the best journalists, were supposed to be those who were able to make their news the most interesting and readable. This was natural enough, since the verb to "advertise" originally meant, intransitively, to take note or to consider. For a person to "advertise" meant originally, in the fourteenth and fifteenth centuries, to reflect on something, to think about something. Then it came to mean, transitively, to call the attention of another to something, to give him notice, to notify, admonish, warn or inform in a formal or impressive manner. And then, by the sixteenth century, it came to mean: to give notice of anything, to make generally known. It was not until the late eighteenth century that the word "advertising" in English came to have a specifically "advertising" connotation as we might say today, and not until the late nineteenth century that it began to have a specifically commercial connotation. By 1879 someone was saying, "Don't advertise unless you have something worth advertising." But even into the present century, newspapers continue to call themselves by the title "Advertiser"—for example, the Boston *Daily Advertiser*, which was a newspaper of long tradition and one of the most dignified papers in Boston until William Randolph Hearst took it over in 1917. Newspapers carried "Advertiser" on their mastheads, not because they sold advertisements but because they brought news.

Now, the main role of advertising in American civilization came increasingly to be that of persuading and appealing rather than that of educating and informing. By 1921, for instance, one of the more popular textbooks, Blanchard's *Essentials of Advertising*, began: "Anything employed to influence people favorably is advertising. The mission of advertising is to persuade men and women to act in a way that will be of advantage to the advertiser." This development—in a country where a shared, a rising, and a democratized standard of living was the national pride and the national hallmark— meant that advertising had become the rhetoric of democracy.

What, then, were some of the main features of modern American advertising—if we consider it as a form of rhetoric? First, and perhaps most obvious, is *repetition*. It is hard for us to realize that the use of repetition in advertising is not an ancient device but a modern one, which actually did not come into common use in American journalism until just past the middle of the nineteenth century.

The development of what came to be called "iteration copy" was a result of a struggle by a courageous man of letters and advertising pioneer, Robert Bonner, who bought the old New York *Merchant's Ledger* in 1851 and turned it into a popular journal. He then had the temerity to try to change the ways of James Gordon Bennett, who of course was one of the most successful of the American newspaper pioneers, and who was both a sensationalist and at the same time an extremely stuffy man when it came to things that he did not consider to be news. Bonner was determined to use advertisements in Bennett's wide-circulating New York *Herald* to sell his own literary product, but he found it difficult to persuade Bennett to allow him to use any but agate type in his advertising. (Agate was the smallest type used by newspapers in that day, only barely legible to the naked eye.) Bennett would not allow advertisers to use larger type, nor would he allow them to use illustrations except stock cuts, because he thought it was undignified. He said, too, that to allow a variation in the format of ads would be undemocratic. He insisted that all advertisers use the same size type so that no one would be allowed to prevail over another simply by presenting his message in a larger, more clever, or more attention-getting form.

Finally Bonner managed to overcome Bennett's rigidity by leasing whole pages of the paper and using the tiny agate type to form larger letters across the top of the page. In this way he produced a message such as "Bring home the New York Ledger tonight." His were unimaginative messages, and when repeated all across the page they technically did not violate Bennett's agate rule. But they opened a new era and presaged a new freedom for advertisers in their use of the newspaper page. Iteration copy—the practice of presenting prosaic content in ingenious, repetitive form—became common, and nowadays of course is commonplace.

A second characteristic of American advertising which is not unrelated to this is the development of *an advertising style*. We have histories of most other kinds of style—including the style of many unread writers who are remembered today only because they have been forgotten—but we have very few accounts of the history of advertising style, which of course is one of the most important forms of our language and one of the most widely influential.

The development of advertising style was the convergence of several very respectable American traditions. One of these was the tradition of the "plain style," which the Puritans made so much of and which accounts for so much of the strength of the Puritan literature. The "plain style" was of course much influenced by the Bible and found its way into the rhetoric of American writers and speakers of great power like Abraham Lincoln. When advertising began to be self-conscious in the early years of this century, the pioneers urged copywriters not to be too clever, and especially not to be fancy. One of the pioneers of the advertising copywriters, John Powers, said, for example, "The commonplace is the proper level for writing in business; where the first virtue is plainness, 'fine writing' is not only intellectual, it is offensive." George P. Rowell, another advertising pioneer, said, "You must write your advertisement to catch damned fools—not college professors." He was a very tactful person. And he added, "And you'll catch just as many college professors as you will of any other sort." In the 1920's, when advertising was beginning to come into its own, Claude Hopkins, whose name is known to all in the trade, said, "Brilliant writing has no place in advertising. A unique style takes attention from the subject. Any apparent effort to sell creates corresponding resistance. . . . One should be natural and simple. His language should not be conspicuous. In fishing for buyers, as in fishing for bass, one should not reveal the hook." So there developed a characteristic advertising style in which plainness, the phrase that anyone could understand, was a distinguishing mark.

At the same time, the American advertising style drew on another, and what might seem an antithetic, tradition—the tradition of hyperbole and tall talk, the language of Davy Crockett and Mike Fink. While advertising could think of itself as 99.44 percent pure, it used the language of "Toronado" and "Cutlass." As I listen to the radio in Washington, I hear a celebration of heroic qualities which would make the characteristics of Mike Fink and Davy Crockett pale, only to discover at the end of the paean that what I have been hearing is a description of the Ford dealers in the District of Columbia neighborhood. And along with the folk tradition of hyperbole and tall talk comes the rhythm of folk music. We hear that Pepsi-Cola hits the spot, that it's for the young generation—and we hear other products celebrated in music which we cannot forget and sometimes don't want to remember.

There grew somehow out of all these contradictory tendencies—combining the commonsense language of the "plain style," and the fantasy language of "tall talk"—an advertising style. This characteristic way of talking about things was especially designed to reach and catch the millions. It created a whole new world of myth. A myth, the dictionary tells us, is a notion based more on tradition or convenience than on facts; it is a received idea. Myth is not just fantasy and not just fact but exists in a limbo, in the world of the "Will to Believe," which William James has written about so eloquently and so perceptively. This is the world of the neither true nor false—of the statement that 60 percent of the physicians who expressed a choice said that our brand of aspirin would be more effective in curing a simple headache than any other leading brand.

That kind of statement exists in a penumbra. I would call this the "advertising penumbra." It is not untrue, and yet, in its connotation it is not exactly true.

Now, there is still another characteristic of advertising so obvious that we are inclined perhaps to overlook it. I call that *ubiquity*. Advertising abhors a vacuum and we discover new vacuums every day. The parable, of course, is the story of the man who thought of putting the advertisement on the other side of the cigarette package. Until then, that was wasted space and a society which aims at a democratic standard of living, at extending the benefits of consumption and all sorts of things and services to everybody, must miss no chances to reach people. The highway billboard and other outdoor advertising, bus and streetcar and subway advertising, and skywriting, radio and TV commercials—all these are of course obvious evidence that advertising abhors a vacuum.

We might reverse the old mousetrap slogan and say that anyone who can devise another place to put another mousetrap to catch a consumer will find people beating a path to his door. "Avoiding advertising will become a little harder next January," the *Wall Street Journal* reported on May 17, 1973, "when a Studio City, California, company launches a venture called Store Vision. Its product is a system of billboards that move on a track across supermarket ceilings. Some 650 supermarkets so far are set to have the system." All of which helps us understand the observation attributed to a French man of letters during his recent visit to Times Square. "What a beautiful place, if only one could not read!" Everywhere is a place to be filled, as we discover in a recent *Publishers Weekly* description of one advertising program: "The $1.95 paperback edition of Dr. Thomas A. Harris' million-copy best seller 'I'm O.K., You're O.K.' is in for full-scale promotion in July by its publisher, Avon Books. Plans range from bumper stickers to airplane streamers, from planes flying above Fire Island, the Hamptons and Malibu. In addition, the $100,000 promotion budget calls for 200,000 bookmarks, plus brochures, buttons, lipcards, floor and counter displays, and advertising in magazines and TV."

The ubiquity of advertising is of course just another effect of our uninhibited efforts to use all the media to get all sorts of information to everybody everywhere. Since the places to be filled are everywhere, the amount of advertising is not determined by the *needs* of advertising, but by the *opportunities* for advertising which become unlimited.

But the most effective advertising, in an energetic, novelty-ridden society like ours, tends to be "self-liquidating." To create a cliché you must offer something which everybody accepts. The most successful advertising therefore self-destructs because it becomes cliché. Examples of this are found in the tendency for copyrighted names of trademarks to enter the vernacular— for the proper names of products which have been made familiar by costly advertising to become common nouns, and so to apply to anybody's products. Kodak becomes a synonym for camera, Kleenex a synonym for facial tissue, when both begin with a small k, and Xerox (now, too, with a small x) is used to describe all processes of copying, and so on. These are prototypes of the problem. If you are successful enough, then you will defeat your purpose in the long run—by making the name and the message so familiar that people won't notice them, and then people will cease to distinguish your product from everybody else's.

In a sense, of course, as we will see, the whole of American civilization is an example. When this was a "new" world, if people succeeded in building a civilization here, the New World would survive and would reach the time—in our age—when it would cease to be new. And now we have the oldest written Constitution in use in the world. This is only a parable of which there are many more examples.

The advertising man who is successful in marketing any particular product, then—in our high-technology, well-to-do democratic society, which aims to get everything to everybody—is apt to be diluting the demand for his particular product in the very act of satisfying it. But luckily for him, he is at the very same time creating a fresh demand for his services as advertiser.

And as a consequence, there is yet another role which is assigned to

American advertising. This is what I call "erasure." Insofar as advertising is competitive or innovation is widespread, erasure is required in order to persuade consumers that this year's model is superior to last year's. In fact, we consumers learn that we might be risking our lives if we go out on the highway with those very devices that were last year's lifesavers but without whatever special kind of brakes or wipers or seat belt is on this year's model. This is what I mean by "erasure"—and we see it on our advertising pages or our television screen every day. We read in the *New York Times* (May 20, 1973), for example, that "For the price of something small and ugly, you can drive something small and beautiful"—an advertisement for the Fiat 250 Spider. Or another, perhaps more subtle example is the advertisement for shirts under a picture of Oliver Drab: "Oliver Drab. A name to remember in fine designer shirts? No kidding. . . . Because you pay extra money for Oliver Drab. And for all the other superstars of the fashion world. Golden Vee [the name of the brand that is advertised] does not have a designer's label. But we do have designers. . . . By keeping their names *off* our label and simply saying Golden Vee, we can afford to sell our $7 to $12 shirts for just $7 to $12, which should make Golden Vee a name to remember. Golden Vee, you only pay for the shirt."

Having mentioned two special characteristics—the self-liquidating tendency and the need for erasure—which arise from the dynamism of the American economy, I would like to try to place advertising in a larger perspective. The special role of advertising in our life gives a clue to a pervasive oddity in American civilization. A leading feature of past cultures, as anthropologists have explained, is the tendency to distinguish between "high" culture and "low" culture—between the culture of the literate and the learned on the one hand and that of the populace on the other. In other words, between the language of literature and the language of the vernacular. Some of the most useful statements of this distinction have been made by social scientists at the University of Chicago—first by the late Robert Redfield in his several pioneering books on peasant society, and then by Milton Singer in his remarkable study of Indian civilization, *When a Great Tradition Modernizes* (1972). This distinction between the great tradition and the little tradition, between the high culture and the folk culture, has begun to become a commonplace of modern anthropology.

Some of the obvious features of advertising in modern America offer us an opportunity to note the significance or insignificance of that distinction for us. Elsewhere I have tried to point out some of the peculiarities of the American attitude toward the *high* culture. There is something distinctive about the place of thought in American life, which I think is not quite what it has been in certain Old World cultures.

But what about distinctive American attitudes to *popular* culture? What is our analogue to the folk culture of other peoples? Advertising gives us some clues—to a characteristically American democratic folk culture. Folk culture is a name for the culture which ordinary people everywhere lean on. It is not the writings of Dante and Chaucer and Shakespeare and Milton, the teachings of Machiavelli and Descartes, Locke or Marx. It is, rather, the pattern of slogans, local traditions, tales, songs, dances, and ditties. And of course holiday observances. Popular culture in other civilizations has been for the most part both an area of continuity with the past, a way in which people reach back into the past and out to their community, and at the same time an area of local variations. An area of individual and amateur expression in which a person has his own way of saying, or notes his mother's way of saying or singing, or his own way of dancing, his own view of folk wisdom and the cliché.

And here is an interesting point of contrast. In other societies outside the United States, it is the *high* culture that has generally been an area of centralized, organized control. In Western Europe, for example, universities and churches have tended to be closely allied to the government. The institutions of higher learning have had a relatively limited access to the people as a whole. This was inevitable, of course, in most parts of the world, because there were so few universities. In England, for example, there were only two universities until the early nineteenth century. And there was central control over the printed matter that was used in universities or in the liturgy. The government tended to be close to the high culture, and that was easy because the high culture itself was so centralized and because literacy was relatively limited.

In our society, however, we seem to have turned all of this around. Our high culture is one of the least centralized areas of our culture. And our universities express the atomistic, diffused, chaotic, and individualistic aspect of our life. We have in this country more than twenty-five hundred colleges and universities, institutions of so-called higher learning. We have a vast population in these institutions, somewhere over seven million students.

But when we turn to our popular culture, what do we find? We find that in our nation of Consumption Communities and emphasis on Gross National Product (GNP) and growth rates, advertising has become the heart of the folk culture and even its very prototype. And as we have seen, American advertising shows many characteristics of the folk culture of other societies: repetition, a plain style, hyperbole and tall talk, folk verse, and folk music. Folk culture, wherever it has flourished, has tended to thrive in a limbo between fact and fantasy, and of course, depending on the spoken word and the oral tradition, it spreads easily and tends to be ubiquitous. These are all familiar characteristics of folk culture and they are ways of describing our folk culture, but how do the expressions of our peculiar folk culture come to *us*?

They no longer sprout from the earth, from the village, from the farm, or even from the neighborhood or the city. They come to us primarily from enormous centralized self-consciously *creative* (an overused word, for the overuse of which advertising agencies are in no small part responsible) organizations. They come from advertising agencies, from networks of newspapers, radio, and television, from outdoor-advertising agencies, from the copywriters for ads in the largest-circulation magazines, and so on. These "creators" of folk culture—or pseudo-folk culture—aim at the widest intelligibility and charm and appeal.

But in the United States, we must recall, the advertising folk culture (like all advertising) is also confronted with the problems of self-liquidation and erasure. These are by-products of the expansive, energetic character of our economy. And they, too, distinguish American folk culture from folk cultures elsewhere.

Our folk culture is distinguished from others by being discontinuous, ephemeral, and self-destructive. Where does this leave the common citizen? All of us are qualified to answer.

In our society, then, those who cannot lean on the world of learning, on the high culture of the classics, on the elaborated wisdom of the books, have a new problem. The University of Chicago, for example, in the 1930's and 1940's was the center of a quest for a "common discourse." The champions of that quest, which became a kind of crusade, believed that such a discourse could be found through familiarity with the classics of great literature—and especially of Western European literature. I think they were misled; such works were not, nor are they apt to become, the common discourse of our society. Most people, even in a democracy, and a rich democracy like ours, live in a world of popular culture, our special kind of popular culture.

The characteristic folk culture of our society is a creature of advertising, and in a sense it *is* advertising. But advertising, our own popular culture, is harder to make into a source of continuity than the received wisdom and commonsense slogans and catchy songs of the vivid vernacular. The popular culture of advertising attenuates and is always dissolving before our very eyes. Among the charms, challenges, and tribulations of modern life, we must count this peculiar fluidity, this ephemeral character of that very kind of culture on which other peoples have been able to lean, the kind of culture to which they have looked for the continuity of their traditions, for their ties with the past and with the future.

We are perhaps the first people in history to have a centrally organized mass-produced folk culture. Our kind of popular culture is here today and gone tomorrow—or the day after tomorrow. Or whenever the next semiannual model appears. And insofar as folk culture becomes advertising, and advertising becomes centralized, it becomes a way of depriving people of their opportunities for individual and small-community expression. Our technology and our economy and our democratic ideals have all helped make that possible. Here we have a new test of the problem that is at least as old as Heraclitus—an everyday test of man's ability to find continuity in his experience. And here democratic man has a new opportunity to accommodate himself, if he can, to the unknown.

ALDOUS HUXLEY

This is Chapter 6 of Huxley's Brave New World Revisited *(1958). For information on the author and his writings, see page 44.*

The Arts of Selling

The survival of democracy depends on the ability of large numbers of people to make realistic choices in the light of adequate information. A dictatorship, on the other hand, maintains itself by censoring or distorting the facts, and by appealing, not to reason, nor to enlightened self-interest, but to passion and prejudice, to the powerful "hidden forces," as Hitler called them, present in the unconscious depths of every human mind.

In the West, democratic principles are proclaimed and many able and conscientious publicists do their best to supply electors with adequate information and to persuade them, by rational argument, to make realistic choices in the light of that information. All this is greatly to the good. But unfortunately propaganda in the Western democracies, above all in America, has two faces and a divided personality. In charge of the editorial department there is often a democratic Dr. Jekyll—a propagandist who would be very happy to prove that John Dewey had been right about the ability of human nature to respond to truth and reason. But this worthy man controls only a part of the machinery of mass communication. In charge of advertising we find an anti-democratic, because antirational, Mr. Hyde—or rather a Dr. Hyde, for Hyde is now a Ph.D. in psychology and has a master's degree as well in the social sciences. This Dr. Hyde would be very unhappy indeed if everybody always lived up to John Dewey's faith in human nature. Truth and reason are Jekyll's affair, not his. Hyde is a motivation analyst, and his business is to study human weaknesses and failings, to investigate those unconscious desires and fears by which so much of men's conscious thinking and overt doing is determined. And he does this, not in the spirit of the moralist who would like to make people better, or of the physician who would like to improve their health, but simply in order to find out the best way to take advantage of their ignorance and to exploit their irrationality for the pecuniary benefit of his employers. But after all, it may be argued, "capitalism is dead, consumerism is king"—and consumerism requires the services of expert salesmen versed in all the arts (including the more insidious arts) of persuasion. Under a free enterprise system commercial propaganda by any and every means is absolutely indispensable. But the indispensable is not necessarily the desirable. What is demonstrably good in the sphere of economics may be far from good for men and women as voters or even as human beings. An earlier, more moralistic generation would have been profoundly shocked by the bland cynicism of the motivation analysts. Today we read a book like Mr. Vance Packard's *The Hidden Persuaders*, and are more amused than horrified, more resigned than indignant. Given Freud, given Behaviorism, given the mass producer's chronically desperate need for mass consumption, this is the sort of thing that is only to be expected. But what, we may ask, is the sort of thing that is to be expected in the future? Are Hyde's activities compatible in the long run with Jekyll's? Can a campaign in favor of rationality be successful in the teeth of another and even more vigorous campaign in favor of irrationality? These are questions which, for the moment, I shall not attempt to answer, but shall leave hanging, so to speak, as a backdrop to our discussion of the methods of mass persuasion in a technologically advanced democratic society.

The task of the commercial propagandist in a democracy is in some ways easier and in some ways more difficult than that of a political propagandist employed by an established dictator or a dictator in the making. It is easier inasmuch as almost everyone starts out with a prejudice in favor of beer, cigarettes and iceboxes, whereas almost nobody starts out with a prejudice in favor of tyrants. It is more difficult inasmuch as the commercial propagandist is not permitted, by the rules of his particular game, to appeal to the more savage instincts of his public. The advertiser of dairy products would dearly love to tell his readers and listeners that all their troubles are caused by the machinations of a gang of godless international margarine manufacturers, and that it is their patriotic duty to march out and burn the oppressors' factories. This sort of thing, however, is ruled out, and he must be content with a milder approach. But the mild approach is less exciting than the approach through verbal or physical violence. In the long run, anger and hatred are self-defeating emotions. But in the short run they pay high dividends in the form of psychological and even (since they release large quantities of adrenalin and noradrenalin) physiological satisfaction. People may start out with an initial prejudice against tyrants; but when tyrants or would-be tyrants treat them to adrenalin-releasing propaganda about the wickedness of their enemies—particularly of enemies weak enough to be persecuted—they are ready to follow him with enthusiasm. In his speeches Hitler kept repeating such words as "hatred," "force," "ruthless," "crush," "smash"; and he would accompany these violent words with even more violent gestures. He would yell, he would scream, his veins would swell, his face would turn purple. Strong emotion (as every actor and dramatist knows) is in the highest degree contagious. Infected by the malignant frenzy of the orator, the audience would groan and sob and scream in an orgy of uninhibited passion. And these orgies were so enjoyable that most of those who had experienced them eagerly came back for more. Almost all of us long for peace and freedom; but very few of us have much enthusiasm for the thoughts, feelings and actions that make for peace and freedom. Conversely almost nobody wants war or tyranny; but a great many people find an intense pleasure in the thoughts, feelings and actions that make for war and tyranny. These thoughts, feelings and actions are too dangerous to be exploited for commercial purposes. Accepting this handicap, the advertising man must do the best he can with the less intoxicating emotions, the quieter forms of irrationality.

Effective rational propaganda becomes possible only when there is a clear understanding, on the part of all concerned, of the nature of symbols and of their relations to the things and events symbolized. Irrational propaganda depends for its effectiveness on a general failure to understand the nature of symbols. Simple-minded people tend to equate the symbol with what it stands for, to attribute to things and events some of the qualities expressed by the words in terms of which the propagandist has chosen, for his own purposes, to talk about them. Consider a simple example. Most cosmetics are made of lanolin, which is a mixture of purified wool fat and water beaten up into an emulsion. This emulsion has many valuable properties: it penetrates the skin, it does not become rancid, it is mildly antiseptic and so forth. But the commercial propagandists do not speak about the genuine virtues of the emulsion. They give it some picturesquely voluptuous name, talk ecstatically and misleadingly about feminine beauty and show pictures of gorgeous blondes nourishing their tissues with skin food. "The cosmetic manufacturers," one of their number has written, "are not selling lanolin, they are selling hope." For this hope, this fraudulent implication of a promise that they will be transfigured, women will pay ten or twenty times the value of the emulsion which the propagandists have so skilfully related, by means of misleading symbols, to a deep-seated and almost universal feminine wish—the wish to be more attractive to members of the opposite sex. The principles underlying this kind of propaganda are extremely simple. Find some common desire, some widespread unconscious fear or anxiety; think out some way to relate this wish or fear to the product you have to sell; then build a bridge of verbal or pictorial symbols over which your customer can pass from fact to compensatory dream, and from the dream to the illusion that your product, when purchased, will make the dream come true. "We no longer buy oranges, we buy vitality. We do not buy just an auto, we buy prestige." And so with all the rest. In toothpaste, for example, we buy, not a mere cleanser and antiseptic, but release from the fear of being sexually repulsive. In vodka and whisky we are not buying a protoplasmic poison which, in small doses, may depress the nervous system in a psychologically valuable way; we are buying friendliness and good fellowship, the warmth of Dingley Dell and the brilliance of the Mermaid Tavern. With our laxatives we buy the health of a Greek god, the radiance of one of Diana's nymphs. With the monthly best seller we acquire culture, the envy of our less literate neighbors and the respect of the sophisticated. In every case the motivation analyst has found some deep-seated wish or fear, whose energy can be used to move the consumer to part with cash and so, indirectly, to turn the wheels of industry. Stored in the minds and bodies of countless individuals, this potential energy is released by, and transmitted along, a line of symbols carefully laid out so as to bypass rationality and obscure the real issue.

Sometimes the symbols take effect by being disproportionately impressive, haunting and fascinating in their own right. Of this kind are the rites and pomps of religion. These "beauties of holiness" strengthen faith where it already exists and, where there is no faith, contribute to conversion. Appealing, as they do, only to the aesthetic sense, they guarantee neither the truth nor the ethical value of the doctrines with which they have been, quite arbitrarily, associated. As a matter of plain historical fact, the beauties of holiness have often been matched and indeed surpassed by the beauties of unholiness. Under Hitler, for example, the yearly Nuremberg rallies were masterpieces of ritual and theatrical art. "I had spent six years in St. Petersburg before the war in the best days of the old Russian ballet," writes Sir

Nevile Henderson, the British ambassador to Hitler's Germany, "but for grandiose beauty I have never seen any ballet to compare with the Nuremberg rally." One thinks of Keats—"beauty is truth, truth beauty." Alas, the identity exists only on some ultimate, supramundane level. On the levels of politics and theology, beauty is perfectly compatible with nonsense and tyranny. Which is very fortunate; for if beauty were incompatible with nonsense and tyranny, there would be precious little art in the world. The masterpieces of painting, sculpture and architecture were produced as religious or political propaganda, for the greater glory of a god, a government or a priesthood. But most kings and priests have been despotic and all religions have been riddled with superstition. Genius has been the servant of tyranny and art has advertised the merits of the local cult. Time, as it passes, separates the good art from the bad metaphysics. Can we learn to make this separation, not after the event, but while it is actually taking place? That is the question.

In commercial propaganda the principle of the disproportionately fascinating symbol is clearly understood. Every propagandist has his Art Department, and attempts are constantly being made to beautify the billboards with striking posters, the advertising pages of magazines with lively drawings and photographs. There are no masterpieces; for masterpieces appeal only to a limited audience, and the commercial propagandist is out to captivate the majority. For him, the ideal is a moderate excellence. Those who like this not too good, but sufficiently striking, art may be expected to like the products with which it has been associated and for which it symbolically stands.

Another disproportionately fascinating symbol is the Singing Commercial. Singing Commercials are a recent invention; but the Singing Theological and the Singing Devotional—the hymn and the psalm—are as old as religion itself. Singing Militaries, or marching songs, are coeval with war, and Singing Patriotics, the precursors of our national anthems, were doubtless used to promote group solidarity, to emphasize the distinction between "us" and "them," by the wandering bands of paleolithic hunters and food gatherers. To most people music is intrinsically attractive. Moreover, melodies tend to ingrain themselves in the listener's mind. A tune will haunt the memory during the whole of a lifetime. Here, for example, is a quite uninteresting statement or value judgment. As it stands nobody will pay attention to it. But now set the words to a catchy and easily remembered tune. Immediately they become words of power. Moreover, the words will tend automatically to repeat themselves every time the melody is heard or spontaneously remembered. Orpheus has entered into an alliance with Pavlov—the power of sound with the conditioned reflex. For the commercial propagandist, as for his colleagues in the fields of politics and religion, music possesses yet another advantage. Nonsense which it would be shameful for a reasonable being to write, speak or hear spoken can be sung or listened to by that same rational being with pleasure and even with a kind of intellectual conviction. Can we learn to separate the pleasure of singing or of listening to song from the all too human tendency to believe in the propaganda which the song is putting over? That again is the question.

Thanks to compulsory education and the rotary press, the propagandist has been able, for many years past, to convey his messages to virtually every adult in every civilized country. Today, thanks to radio and television, he is in the happy position of being able to communicate even with unschooled adults and not yet literate children.

Children, as might be expected, are highly susceptible to propaganda. They are ignorant of the world and its ways, and therefore completely unsuspecting. Their critical faculties are undeveloped. The youngest of them have not yet reached the age of reason and the older ones lack the experience on which their new-found rationality can effectively work. In Europe, conscripts used to be playfully referred to as "cannon fodder." Their little brothers and sisters have now become radio fodder and television fodder. In my childhood we were taught to sing nursery rhymes and, in pious households, hymns. Today the little ones warble the Singing Commercials. Which is better—"Rheingold is my beer, the dry beer," or "Hey diddle-diddle, the cat and the fiddle"? "Abide with me" or "You'll wonder where the yellow went, when you brush your teeth with Pepsodent"? Who knows?

"I don't say that children should be forced to harass their parents into buying products they've seen advertised on television, but at the same time I cannot close my eyes to the fact that it's being done every day." So writes the star of one of the many programs beamed to a juvenile audience. "Children," he adds, "are living, talking records of what we tell them every day." And in due course these living, talking records of television commercials will grow up, earn money and buy the products of industry. "Think," writes Mr. Clyde Miller ecstatically, "think of what it can mean to your firm in profits if you can condition a million or ten million children, who will grow up into adults trained to buy your product, as soldiers are trained in advance when they hear the trigger words, Forward March!" Yes, just think of it! And at the same time remember that the dictators and the would-be dictators have been thinking about this sort of thing for years, and that millions, tens of millions, hundreds of millions of children are in process of growing up to buy the local despot's ideological product and, like well-trained soldiers, to respond with appropriate behavior to the trigger words implanted in those young minds by the despot's propagandists.

Self-government is in inverse ratio to numbers. The larger the constituency, the less the value of any particular vote. When he is merely one of millions, the individual elector feels himself to be impotent, a negligible quantity. The candidates he has voted into office are far away, at the top of the pyramid of power. Theoretically they are the servants of the people; but in fact it is the servants who give orders and the people, far off at the base of the great pyramid, who must obey. Increasing population and advancing technology have resulted in an increase in the number and complexity of organizations, an increase in the amount of power concentrated in the hands of officials and a corresponding decrease in the amount of control exercised by electors, coupled with a decrease in the public's regard for democratic procedures. Already weakened by the vast impersonal forces at work in the modern world, democratic institutions are now being undermined from within by the politicians and their propagandists.

Human beings act in a great variety of irrational ways, but all of them seem to be capable, if given a fair chance, of making a reasonable choice in the light of available evidence. Democratic institutions can be made to work only if all concerned do their best to impart knowledge and to encourage rationality. But today, in the world's most powerful democracy, the politicians and their propagandists prefer to make nonsense of democratic procedures by appealing almost exclusively to the ignorance and irrationality of the electors. "Both parties," we were told in 1956 by the editor of a leading business journal, "will merchandize their candidates and issues by the same methods that business has developed to sell goods. These include scientific selection of appeals and planned repetition. . . . Radio spot announcements and ads will repeat phrases with a planned intensity. Billboards will push slogans of proven power. . . . Candidates need, in addition to rich voices and good diction, to be able to look 'sincerely' at the TV camera."

The political merchandisers appeal only to the weaknesses of voters, never to their potential strength. They make no attempt to educate the masses into becoming fit for self-government; they are content merely to manipulate and exploit them. For this purpose all the resources of psychology and the social sciences are mobilized and set to work. Carefully selected samples of the electorate are given "interviews in depth." These interviews in depth reveal the unconscious fears and wishes most prevalent in a given society at the time of an election. Phrases and images aimed at allaying or, if necessary, enhancing these fears, at satisfying these wishes, at least symbolically, are then chosen by the experts, tried out on readers and audiences, changed or improved in the light of the information thus obtained. After which the political campaign is ready for the mass communicators. All that is now needed is money and a candidate who can be coached to look "sincere." Under the new dispensation, political principles and plans for specific action have come to lose most of their importance. The personality of the candidate and the way he is projected by the advertising experts are the things that really matter.

In one way or another, as vigorous he-man or kindly father, the candidate must be glamorous. He must also be an entertainer who never bores his audience. Inured to television and radio, that audience is accustomed to being distracted and does not like to be asked to concentrate or make a prolonged intellectual effort. All speeches by the entertainer-candidate must therefore be short and snappy. The great issues of the day must be dealt with in five minutes at the most—and preferably (since the audience will be eager to pass on to something a little livelier than inflation or the H-bomb) in sixty seconds flat. The nature of oratory is such that there has always been a tendency among politicians and clergymen to oversimplify complex issues. From a pulpit or a platform even the most conscientious of speakers finds it very difficult to tell the whole truth. The methods now being used to merchandise the political candidate as though he were a deodorant positively guarantee the electorate against ever hearing the truth about anything.

IMAGES OF OURSELVES

MICHAEL ROBERTS

Michael Roberts is a staff writer for Time-Life Books. Born in Providence, Rhode Island, in 1945, he received his B.A. in 1967 from American University in Washington, D.C. He has been a trackman and calltaker for the New York Daily Racing Form *(from 1970 to 1972), the author of a horse-racing column, "Roberts on Racing," for the* Washington Daily News *(1972), and a sports columnist ("Mike Roberts") for the* Washington Star *(from 1972 to 1975). In 1974 he won the Front Page Award of the Washington-Baltimore Newspaper Guild for two series, one on sports and drugs, the other on truth in sportscasting.*

Roberts also contributes to The New Republic; *the following essay appeared in its sixtieth anniversary supplement on American culture, November 23, 1974. His essay graphically illustrates what he discovered as a sports columnist for the* Washington Star: *"how many people were living life vicariously through athletes and judging their own worth on the outcome of games played by others." He had developed this idea in his 1976 book* Fans! How We Go Crazy Over Sports.

The Vicarious Heroism of the Sports Spectator

In the fall of 1973 a man in Colorado attempted suicide by shooting himself in the head. The note he left alluded to the Denver Broncos, a professional football team that had just fumbled seven times in the course of a drubbing by the Chicago Bears. "I have been a Broncos fan since the Broncos were first organized," the note said, "and I can't stand their fumbling any more."

Poor marksmanship was all that averted a human sacrifice to the football gods. But the act itself—fumbled, appropriately, as it was—could be regarded (if only by persons relatively indifferent to the teams of the National Football League) as the *reductio ad absurdum* of the widely approved and encouraged tendency of spectators to get involved emotionally.

Not that it was the most absurd of all possible absurdities. There are time-honored precedents elsewhere in the world. In Latin America, for example, murders and suicides stemming from soccer scores are commonplace. Observers groping for explanations are usually inclined to attribute such behavior to the reputedly volatile temperament of the average Latin. The validity of such a claim must be left to the ethnologists to decide, but one needn't be an expert of any kind to discern one significant distinction: soccer, at its top levels, is conducted on an international scale, and in many cases the vexation that touches off violence against self or others is generated by wounded feelings of national pride. It's harder to comprehend a death occasioned by frustration over the inefficiency of a privately owned, profit-making business that, strictly for commercial purposes, calls itself by the name of the city in which it is located.

Here a bit of historical review is in order. Whatever their scope, strong feelings of kinship between doer and watcher find their earliest antecedents on the playing fields of ancient cultures. The Greeks, fine sporting fellows that they were, celebrated individual competition, the development of the whole man for his own benefit. With their Olympic Games, however, they also gave rise to the practice of grouping lads together to compete in the names of their respective hometowns. (As Western civilization advanced, the Romans broke away from the team-representation idea in favor, again, of contests in which the participant played on behalf of himself—particularly contact sports involving armed men or a man and an aggressive beast. There were exceptions—occasionally church groups were asked to assemble teams for these events.)

Hence the notion that athletic glory could be shared in by the neighbors of the glorious athlete, or team, gained early acceptance and has survived, largely unexamined, to the present. When the poet reminisces to his athlete, dying young, about "That time you won your town the race," there seems no need to explain what, precisely, the town has done to be deserving.

Thus endures the foundation stone of nearly every variety of spectator sport now flourishing: the linking of the participant's destiny with the fan's, in terms of a common city, nation, race, religion or institution of higher learning. In short the whole system depends on *granfalloonery*, a Kurt Vonnegut word, to express "a proud and meaningless association of human beings."

But these are persistent, consequential (economically) forms of *granfalloonery*, and fascinated observers have striven to unravel their mysteries. One scholar finds the direct antecedents of the 19th century's town-versus-town baseball games in the older custom of town-versus-town melees. "Most of the games . . . ended up in brawls," folklorist Tristram P. Coffin writes, going on to suggest that the games represented "semi-civilized replacements for village-to-village wars. And this is an aspect of the game that has never left it." (Interestingly the word "donnybrook" has its origin in the Irish brawls of this sort.) For evidence Coffin refers to the American League pennant race of 1967, when work virtually came to a standstill in four large American cities so that everyone could pay attention to baseball. "During the final two games, when Boston amazingly defeated Minnesota to win it all, a number of classes were suspended at such an unlikely place as Wellesley College so that girls who barely knew where Carl Yastrzemski would run after hitting the ball could take rapt part in this modern village-to-village crisis."

Significant also is the fact that the object of attention was no son of the Boston soil. The Red Sox had imported Yastrzemski from Long Island, and nearly all his teammates from distant regions of the country as well as a few other places in the Western Hemisphere; in fact in modern times the appearance of a local boy on a professional or college roster is the exception, not the rule, and is usually the random accident of a player draft or a recruiter's good fortune. This is a far cry from the old days when the town team was rounded up in town and its immediate environs, or when the young bucks who happened to be enrolled together at Princeton threw down a football challenge to their counterparts at Rutgers. But the evolution toward universal use of mercenaries has never affected the phenomenon of spectator identification.

The seasonal, predictable crises of sport remain as provincial in flavor as ever. One reason this is so is instant naturalization of athletic citizens (those of indisputable worthiness, of course), a process long since rendered unremarkable by fans of pro and college teams. It takes effect with a startling fluidity and is just as easily reversible. A notable recent case is that of Moses Malone, a teenaged basketball whiz who was transformed from savior of the University of Maryland to traitor in the time it took him to decide to skip college, going instead directly from high school into the pro game. Malone now resides in Salt Lake City, where—as he had been in College Park, Maryland—he has been graciously adopted by the natives, pending proof that he'll be as useful an acquisition as the Utah Stars expect him to be.

In the matter of taking the immigrant athlete unto the local bosom, in fact, spectators tend to take a more practical approach than the players themselves do. Some football players of domestic origin make no effort to hide their resentment of foreign-born field-goal kickers (whose soccer-bred skill has enabled them to dominate the field). Fans, on the other hand, invariably look at it this way: in the case of anyone who is consistently accurate from 40 yards out, prejudices will cheerfully be waived. On occasion such tolerant impulses have even been known to transcend racial hatreds, although in certain regions conflicting emotions are accommodated through the recognition of artificially distinct categories, namely "their niggers" and "our colored boys."

This specialized tolerance is explained simply enough. For the most part the spectator's stake in the proceedings is the gratification that comes from identifying with success. Whoever can provide such vicarious joy needs no other justification as a human being. The capacity of one man's actions to buttress the self-esteem of another is demonstrably a potent force—a force that has been exploited whenever possible by the entrepreneurs of sports events. In this regard the promoters of prizefighting have been more meticulous than anyone else. They are virtuosos of the ethnic sell, profiting even now from pitches that have scarcely grown more subtle since the "Golden Age of Sport." Granted, it may have been a while since anyone has instructed the public that Joe Louis, the former heavyweight champion, was "a credit to his race." But in places like New York it is still considered sound salesmanship to promote a California-born contestant as "Irish Jerry

Quarry," with a liberal sprinkling of shamrocks on the posters, and to introduce another boxer as "The Jewish Bomber."

It's a reliable, if hoary, approach, appealing as it does to the inflammable sensitivities of the various branches of the human family—particularly those individuals who can feel themselves ennobled by someone else's left hook. And in much the same manner, the self-image of an entire city can be manipulated, lowered to despair or raised to giddy heights according to the capabilities of athletes-for-hire. When the Philadelphia Flyers won the championship of the National Hockey League last spring, the reaction of the populace—encouraged all the way by the local and national press—suggested that nothing in the city's past, not even the canonized epithets of W. C. Fields, had done such violence to the collective psyche of Philadelphia as the monotonously regular inferiority of its professional sports franchises. Once the Stanley Cup had been secured, publications started falling over one another in their haste to congratulate the city on, as *Time* put it, "the tangible proof that Philadelphia is at long last a winner." The curious logic of spectator sport: what was tangible, precisely speaking, was the Stanley Cup, a large, hideous piece of metalwork worth less than $100, which came into the possession of the Flyers' management for a year. The players had won that. They also had won bonuses and probably salary increases. The owners of the franchise had won extra revenue from the playoff games and a more salable product than ever for next season. What had Philadelphia— the civic entity—won? That's an elusive, metaphysical question. But for sure, millions of residents were being counseled to think more highly of themselves for the Flyers' accomplishments.

At least, given the cover of big-city anonymity, they had a choice. There are places in this country, medium to small college towns primarily, where it is a serious social liability to dissociate oneself from the ups and downs and everyday existence of the football team. According to a sociologist whose findings were reported in *New Times*, people who live in Columbus, Ohio, are "not free" to admit indifference to the Ohio State football team. Nonenthusiasts who dwell in Columbus are categorized by normal folk as "freaks." Respondents to a poll overwhelmingly listed the Buckeyes as their most frequent topic of conversation and also ventured that a sound, working knowledge of the team's activities was a *sine qua non* for doing business with fellow townsmen. Most subjects agreed, furthermore, that a lack of interest in the team could be termed "downright unpatriotic."

To say nothing of the mood on campuses themselves in such cities, where over the decades student bodies and faculties have been conditioned to a notion that long ago gained respectability in American academic life: athletic teams are what give an institution its sense of worth and unity, its verve, its feeling that life is worth living. Yet historians are firm on the point that colleges and universities predated intercollegiate athletics. To those who hold dear the school-spirit ideal, it must be sad to reflect on the gloomy aimlessness that presumably palled college life in those long-ago days before the football weekend was conceived. On the other hand it must be comforting to realize that it can never be that way again.

The academic world simply couldn't afford a relapse. Year by year, in fact, the pace intensifies in the all-out competition to seduce the best brawn available in the grant-in-aid market; to field the finest teams money and flattery can put together. Assistance comes from many quarters—from governors, senators, legendary coaches, even pretty girls recruited specifically for the purpose. It costs, but experience has proved it a prudent—if not imperative—investment, because endowments at a staggering number of institutions have been found to be dependent largely upon won-lost records. The outcome of last year's game against an arch-rival can be pivotal too. After all an alumnus can't be expected to be proud of a loser, and an alumnus who is not proud is not, statistics show, much of a contributor.

Obviously vicarious triumphs are not the only rewards alumni-patrons look forward to. For many there is that keenly anticipated weekend each year when many of society's conventions are temporarily suspended. Then, the old grad, along with the undergrad, can indulge in conduct that might be regarded as indecorous in other settings. Behavior such as assault and battery and indecent exposure are considered quite correct under the etiquette prevailing at, say, the Texas-Oklahoma football game.

In the final analysis this may be college sport's most significant service to its followers, more valuable even than the fomenting of campus chauvinism. For the public seems to need a permissible outlet for certain barbaric impulses. Sport provides that outlet, on an ever-expanding scale. Control of sporting crowds has lately become recognized as a new specialty in the armed-guard business. The Burns Security Institute reports that fan behavior nationwide has been growing markedly worse, with regard to such particulars as drinking, gambling, profanity and missile-throwing.

Paradoxically most fans are believed to harbor a highly exploitable reverence for the performers upon whom they shower such vulgarity. The commercial implications are staggering. Anyone who dared produce a razor blade commercial without an athlete would be branded a heretic. Jocks have repeatedly been employed to sell everything from bubble gum to politicians. An administrator in charge of fund-raising at a major metropolitan hospital some years ago still marvels at the results of an inspired campaign of television commercials. They were testimonials from pro hockey players: "I got my knee bashed in, and this place fixed me up real good." Contributions from the public ultimately rose from $250,000 annually to more than four million dollars.

For some time sports figures have also performed a parallel job as counselors to the public on moral, social and political issues. Hence it was altogether fitting in the days just before Richard Nixon threw in the towel that the coach of the professional football team in Washington should go on record: "I don't think he should resign . . . That's the type of determination and leadership and doggedness you have to have in a President."

No vote of confidence could have been less unpredictable. In his astuteness as an interpreter of public tastes, Nixon had been cultivating the athletic community for years. (President Ford, a quick study, immediately adopted his predecessor's compulsive habit of phoning big-time sports winners right after their victories.) If Kennedy had been trying to establish Camelot, Nixon was going for something a little more familiar—a Columbus, Ohio, perhaps, or a Green Bay, Wisconsin. And during the glory days of his administration it was observed time and again that no private citizen in Washington, no congressional figure, no cabinet member save possibly John Mitchell, had as frequent access to the White House as George Allen, coach of the Washington Redskins.

ANDREW GRIFFIN

Andrew Griffin was born in Portland, Oregon, in 1939 and was educated at Harvard University (B.A., 1960; Ph.D., 1969). Since 1967 he has been on the English faculty of the University of California at Berkeley; he teaches courses ranging from freshman composition to graduate seminars, and at present also serves as assistant dean of the College of Letters and Science. His enthusiasm for monster movies dates back to the Blue Mouse Theater in Portland, where he first watched and thought about the genre he writes about here. The article first appeared in the Winter 1979 issue of University Publishing.

Sympathy for the Werewolf

> Have pity on the Werewolf,
> Have sympathy;
> For the Werewolf may be someone
> Just like you and me.
>
> Have pity on the Werewolf,
> Not fear—not hate;
> For the Werewolf may be someone
> That you've known of late.
>
> *The Moray Eel Meets the Holy Modal Rounders*

The fact is that we do feel pity for the Werewolf, along with the fear and hate. Monsters frighten us, as they do their movie victims, especially at first sight; but at some point in the course of every classic monster movie we begin to feel sorry for them and, forgetting their victims, to fear for them.

In short, we sympathize; we take the monster's side, at least some of the time, and almost always at the end. When it is finally dispatched we feel a great deal of relief, to be sure, but at the same time much sincere regret and guilt. The relief is in any case not the sort of feeling that comes with the simple lifting of a threat; it is the easing of the pressure of our unconscious identification with this dreadful and dangerous being on the screen, whom we have come to see as in some way "just like you and me." It is this identification that makes us regret the loss of the monster, without whom the world is a poorer place, somehow incomplete. And we have to feel guilty for conniving in its death. The mob of villagers with their torches, the old doctor with his stake seem to be acting for us, yet we are shocked by their brutality, remembering the monster's moments of tenderness.

" 'Twas Beauty killed the Beast!" intones Carl Denham, King Kong's captor, always the impresario, dictating tomorrow's headlines to the waiting reporters. But we know better. 'Twasn't Beauty at all but something uncompromising in the human world, a failure of that sympathy for the Werewolf that we have been developing there in our seats—a failure on the part of Denham and his crew, the Army Air Force, and of course civilization itself, represented as usual by images of the metropolis with its skyscrapers and machines. Not that we imagine King Kong could have been saved! We know he can't survive, let alone rule, in New York City. But recognizing this, as the movie forces us to do, we have to reexamine our own relations to the city, "our" world. A part of ourselves clearly belongs to his world: not to Manhattan Island but to Skull Island, where Kong is King indeed.

It is obvious what part of ourselves that is. The classic movie monster (excepting Frankenstein's) is all instinct and energy and appetite, especially the latter: so simple and primitive that, for him, love and hate are almost the same thing. Monster movies are, of course, sexually explicit and sexually aggressive; they might almost be said to be about rape. And yet, they remain somehow innocent and presexual—because, I think, the monster is incorrigibly *oral*, seeking to incorporate both what it desires and what it wants to destroy, approaching the world in general through the mouth. Dracula, a fastidious aristocrat, nips and sips; the Wolfman, howling with lust, tears out your throat; King Kong's mighty jaws are capable of masticating and swallowing you whole (at one point he chews up a native). Even the movies' Mr. Hyde, who bites no one to death, has a dandy set of teeth, strong and crude, bared by his habitual lip-twitching simian grin.

Surely we are not like that! But we have been—have been all mouth, that is, and have wanted to eat the world—and the movies insist that we still are. Both *The Wolfman* and *Dr. Jekyll and Mr. Hyde* depend on the cinematic trick by which a man becomes a monster before our very eyes: Hyde *is* Jekyll, or a piece of him, and the Wolfman is Lon Chaney Jr., in many ways an improvement. Dracula's kiss may bring about the same transformation: Mina the good and true struggles *not* to become that narrow but intense "Miss Hyde" within who loves the kiss and would long to return it. King Kong can best be understood, I think, not as Fay Wray's giant lover but as her sexual desire made outward and visible . . . and just as big as she has feared it would be if she ever gave in to it. She has been toying with temptation ever since the first frames of the movie, which show a famished Fay reaching almost experimentally toward an apple in a sidewalk grocery window; on shipboard she flirts with the "Aw, shucks" officer and, at Denham's direction, *acts* the emotion she is soon to experience. When at last Kong takes her in his enormous hand she is literally "in the grip of passion." Her fear now is, quite naturally, that she will be "swallowed up" by this immense feeling, her identity—like Mina Harker's or Lon Chaney's or Dr. Jekyll's—lost in it. But the feeling is still her own, of course: summoned out of the darkness of her inexperience as surely as Kong is called out of the jungle by the annual rituals, brought to the gates of consciousness roaring, demanding to be acknowledged, to have his due.

This is what monsters are, this is what monster movies do: they reacquaint us with our own forgotten or forbidden selves, inviting us to recognize and, in imagination, deal with them. They keep alive in us a large and tolerant idea of the human—large enough anyway to include what seems at first inhuman, alien. The fact that monster movies invariably end in another repression makes less difference than one might think at first. For one thing, the viewer always knows the nature of his own silent participation, there in the dark; to watch the movie at all is to accept some responsibility for violence done and passions expressed. Probably, too, this demonstration that outrageous feelings and dangerous appetites *can* be mastered or handled, though at some cost, tends to reassure us, making us not less but more open to our own impulses in the future, soothing exaggerated fears about loss of control and loss of identity.

But the fifties changed all this. The classic monster movie is a product of the thirties; sequels and variations dominate the forties. With the coming of the Cold War, however, monsters all but disappear, to be replaced by Creatures from this, Beasts from that, and things too fierce to mention. There are exceptions. *Forbidden Planet* (1956) is a monster movie in science fiction clothing, featuring no less than the Freudian Id itself on a rampage: Walter Pidgeon's unconscious desires, objectified and magnified enormously through the power of alien technology. The first of the Creatures has a lot of monster in him too. *The Creature from the Black Lagoon* (1954) comes from the dawn of time, roused by scientists incautiously probing its habitat; the plot turns on its inarticulate relations with a pretty girl and, in *Revenge of the Creature* (1955), its rage against mankind and his cities. The Creature is, nevertheless, not a monster. It is, like all its numerous progeny, much farther down the evolutionary scale than the ape-, wolf-, and bat-people of the monster movies (a mammalian genre)—closer to the dinosaurs against whom, in fact, King Kong is really leagued with Fay Wray and ourselves. Though it shadows or mirrors us in important ways (notably its desire for the virgin, stylishly expressed in underwater sequences), it is always clear that it is *not* one of us, nor a part of ourselves, but profoundly alien—almost as alien as the Martians that attack earth in *War of the Worlds* (also 1954).

Sympathy for the Creature is by no means impossible, though it would seem to argue a fair degree of alienation or self-loathing to recognize oneself behind those rubber gills. Sympathy with still lower forms of life is out of the question, and it is these low life forms that came to dominate the screen. Hordes, swarms, blobs and slimes, giant insects, sentient plants—these were

our bogeys then, images of the fifties' paranoid fear of dangers wholly external and coldly implacable, inexorably encroaching, endangering life-as-we-
know-it. It seems reasonable to hold the politics of the period responsible.
Certainly the fifties taught us that there was an Enemy pressing against our
borders, subverting our institutions, godless and ruthless, to be met with
total war. The politics of the day, like the movies, simplified and dehumanized the world, denying relationship, shifting responsibility. Where the monster movies of the thirties showed us similarity in difference, the menace
movies of the fifties presented only unlikeness and danger. They told us to
look to our weapons, draw the wagons into a circle and stay awake. Their
central image is the small community under siege: not (as in *King Kong*) the
monster in the city's midst, but almost the reverse—the city surrounded by
monsters or, more precisely, by nameless and terrible "things." It is no
accident that these films are often set in the desert or the arctic (not to
mention imaginary lands still more inhospitable): environments that themselves express the pure inhuman otherness felt to lie just a step beyond the
circle of the human, a circle now unnaturally, defensively and anxiously
contracted.

What this meant for life in the fifties I needn't say. For the movies it
meant the end of an era and a genre. Without the play of ambivalent
feelings, uneasy alliances made and broken in the course of the film—without the monster, in short—the viewer's experience is impoverished and his
intelligence insulted. If we are only victims, we can only scream—unless, of
course, we laugh. In *Attack of the Giant Shrews*, what appear to be Alsatian
dogs loosely draped with Spanish moss encircle a house in the bayous. Or
take *Night of the Lapis*, with its nocturnes of huge bunnies in a slow-motion
romp through a model of a town—an extraordinary but in no way frightening spectacle. Shrews and rabbits? These movies have vanished even from
late night TV. They can be made and watched only in a world where
absolutely anything might turn on you, a world that doesn't understand
itself or what's outside itself—and doesn't want to understand. No wonder
that the "things" the fifties feared seem to increase and multiply, spreading
and creeping—words that had a special and horrible meaning for this decade (the spread of communism, creeping socialism). No wonder either that
the fifties feared itself, felt some loss of contact with itself. *Mutation* and *mind-
control*, both insidious forms of usurpation or loss of real identity, play as
large a part in the mythology of the decade as do Creatures and Slimes.

The best of the menace movies not only exploit this cultural paranoia,
they expose it too. Don Siegel's *Invasion of the Body Snatchers* (1956), perhaps
the best of the best, shows us an America ironically betrayed by what must
be understood as its own dream of the Good Life. In this deadly little
parable, a species of alien plant beings (pods) silently infiltrates a small
California town, replacing its inhabitants one by one with vegetable simu-
lacra, perfect replicas in every respect—the business of the town continuing,
eerily and very meaningfully, as usual. Siegel must have enjoyed confounding the rigid categories of the fifties and overturning its convictions. In *Body*

Snatchers, conformity is subversion, the suburban is alien—or, as Siegel plainly suggests, terribly alienating. The implication is, of course, that the one big difference between person and pod is no difference at all; we are all already hollow at the core, pretend people. At the end of the movie a frantic Kevin McCarthy, still human but just one step ahead of the pods, screams "You're next!" at the cars that flash past him on the highway. "I think the world is populated by pods," Siegel has said, "and I wanted to show them."

But as this remark itself indicates, Siegel remains true to the fifties formula. The problem, it seems, is still "them," not "us"—even if "them" is your neighborhood automata. The decline of the monster movie and its ethic is best exemplified in a movie actually entitled *Them!* (1954) which opens almost where *Body Snatchers* leaves off. We see a little girl stumbling along a desert road, dirty and disoriented, clutching her doll. What has happened? Where's your mommy and daddy? All the little girl can answer, all her decade ever does answer, is "Them!"

They turn out to be, in this instance, giant ants, grown to their present size through atomic accident, invading the human world in search of (mainly) sugar. They make an effective movie, too, as we follow the desperate search for Their nest, confront Their fierce warriors, and, the battle over, explore Their underground tunnels and chambers, big as a coal mine and much more interesting. The movie ends effectively in the storm drains beneath Los Angeles with the systematic destruction of a second colony (and the rescue of two little boys) by the National Guard.

Needless to say, we feel no sympathy for Them. We might wonder, however, why They don't present more of a problem. For despite Their size, They are fairly easy to handle, no tougher than (say) the Japanese dug in on Tarawa. Gas and flamethrowers do the job. Every monster one can think of, although in most cases not nearly so dangerous to life-as-we-know-it, has been more difficult to deal with. Why don't They give more trouble? And why, after the movie is over, don't we give a damn?

The answer to both questions is that, oddly enough, there is little at stake. Monster movies dramatize a kind of negotiation with ourselves about what we are; somewhere, a little below the level of conscious thought, the monster is proposed, explored, debated, rejected, as we have already seen. But in a movie like *Them!*, or *The Thing*, or *The Beast from 20,000 Fathoms*, there is no such negotiation, only the defense of an idea of what's human that the movie never questions. Nor, finally, is there much to choose between human and alien. The storm drains of Los Angeles are uncannily well-adapted to the purposes of myrmecoid existence; the ants seem as at home under the city as we are in the ant heap that sprawls above them. And the National Guard, in their uniforms, their shiny helmets, especially with their gas masks on: not only are they indistinguishable from each other, they are hard to tell from the ants. One horde sweeps out another, red ants *vs* black. It seems unlikely that the makers of *Them!* meant to draw our attention to these similarities, but there they are. The implication is, as in *Invasion of the Body Snatchers*, that the supplanting of the human, by ant or pod, would scarcely be noticed by the universe at large.

BOB DYLAN

It's All Over Now, Baby Blue (1941-)

You must leave now, take what you need, you think will last.
But whatever you wish to keep, you better grab it fast.
Yonder stands your orphan with his gun,
Crying like a fire in the sun.
Look out the saints are comin' through
And it's all over now, Baby Blue.

The highway is for gamblers, better use your sense.
Take what you have gathered from coincidence.
The empty-handed painter from your streets
Is drawing crazy patterns on your sheets.
This sky, too, is folding under you
And it's all over now, Baby Blue.

All your seasick sailors, they are rowing home.
All your reindeer armies, are all going home.
The lover who just walked out your door
Has taken all his blankets from the floor.
The carpet, too, is moving under you
And it's all over now, Baby Blue.

Leave your stepping stones behind, something calls for you.
Forget the dead you've left, they will not follow you.
The vagabond who's rapping at your door
Is standing in the clothes that you once wore.
Strike another match, go start anew
And it's all over now, Baby Blue.

(1973)

JOYCE CAROL OATES

Joyce Carol Oates was born in Lockport, New York, in 1938 and graduated from Syracuse University in 1960. She received an M.A. in English from the University of Wisconsin the following year, but was turned from further academic training by the persistent success of her short stories, which she had been writing since childhood. Her first collection of stories, By the North Gate *(1963), has been followed by over two dozen more volumes of stories, novels, poems, plays, and essays. Her novel* Them *(1970) won the National Book Award.*

In addition to being a writer, Ms. Oates teaches creative writing and modern literature at the University of Windsor, Canada. Her critical writing includes a volume of essays, The Edge of Impossibility: Tragic Forms in Literature *(1972), and a book on the poetry of D. H. Lawrence,* The Hostile Sun *(1973).*

Ms. Oates' fiction encompasses a great range of styles—from lyricism and fantasy to naturalism—and it often deals with violent and pessimistic themes. In an interview with John Knott and Christopher Reaske (included in their anthology Mirrors*) she said: "So many of my characters are actually based on real people . . . just as most of the plots are 'real' plots, taken from life and fixed up slightly. . . . After hearing for some weeks Dylan's song 'It's All Over Now, Baby Blue,' and after having read about a killer in some Southwestern state, and after having thoughts about the old legends and folk songs of Death and the Maiden, the story ["Where Are You Going, Where Have You Been?"] came to me more or less in a piece. Dylan's song is very beautiful, very disturbing."*

We print the words to the song above. The killer she refers to is Charles Schmid who, according to an account in Life Magazine *(March 4, 1966), "did weird things . . . wore crazy make-up . . . was known at all the joints." He is the prototype for Arnold Friend in the story below. It first appeared in* Epoch, *Fall 1966, and later, dedicated to Bob Dylan, in a collection* The Wheel of Love *(1970).*

Where Are You Going, Where Have You Been?

Her name was Connie. She was fifteen and she had a quick nervous giggling habit of craning her neck to glance into mirrors, or checking other people's faces to make sure her own was all right. Her mother, who noticed everything and knew everything and who hadn't much reason any longer to look at her own face, always scolded Connie about it. "Stop gawking at yourself, who are you? You think you're so pretty?" she would say. Connie would raise her eyebrows at these familiar complaints and look right through her mother, into a shadowy vision of herself as she was right at that moment: she knew she was pretty and that was everything. Her mother had been pretty once too, if you could believe those old snapshots in the album, but now her looks were gone and that was why she was always after Connie.

"Why don't you keep your room clean like your sister? How've you got your hair fixed—what the hell stinks? Hair spray? You don't see your sister using that junk."

Her sister June was twenty-four and still lived at home. She was a secretary in the high school Connie attended, and if that wasn't bad enough—with her in the same building—she was so plain and chunky and steady that Connie had to hear her praised all the time by her mother and her mother's sisters. June did this, June did that, she saved money and helped clean the house and cooked and Connie couldn't do a thing, her mind was all filled with trashy daydreams. Their father was away at work most of the time and when he came home he wanted supper and he read the newspaper at supper and after supper he went to bed. He didn't bother talking much to them, but around his bent head Connie's mother kept picking at her until Connie wished her mother was dead and she herself was dead and it was all over. "She makes me want to throw up sometimes," she complained to her friends. She had a high, breathless, amused voice which made everything she said sound a little forced, whether it was sincere or not.

There was one good thing: June went places with girl friends of hers, girls who were just as plain and steady as she, and so when Connie wanted to do that her mother had no objections. The father of Connie's best girl friend drove the girls the three miles to town and left them off at a shopping plaza, so that they could walk through the stores or go to a movie, and when he came to pick them up again at eleven he never bothered to ask what they had done.

They must have been familiar sights, walking around that shopping plaza in their shorts and flat ballerina slippers that always scuffed the sidewalk, with charm bracelets jingling on their thin wrists; they would lean together to whisper and laugh secretly if someone passed by who amused or interested them. Connie had long dark blond hair that drew anyone's eye to it, and she wore part of it pulled up on her head and puffed out and the rest of it she let fall down her back. She wore a pull-over jersey blouse that looked one way when she was at home and another way when she was away from home. Everything about her had two sides to it, one for home and one for anywhere that was not home: her walk that could be childlike and bobbing, or languid enough to make anyone think she was hearing music in her head, her mouth which was pale and smirking most of the time, but bright and pink on these evenings out, her laugh which was cynical and drawling at home—"Ha, ha, very funny"—but high-pitched and nervous anywhere else, like the jingling of the charms on her bracelet.

Sometimes they did go shopping or to a movie, but sometimes they went across the highway, ducking fast across the busy road, to a drive-in restaurant where older kids hung out. The restaurant was shaped like a big bottle, though squatter than a real bottle, and on its cap was a revolving figure of a grinning boy who held a hamburger aloft. One night in mid-summer they ran across, breathless with daring, and right away someone leaned out a car window and invited them over, but it was just a boy from high school they didn't like. It made them feel good to be able to ignore him. They went up through the maze of parked and cruising cars to the bright-lit, fly-infested restaurant, their faces pleased and expectant as if they were entering a sacred building that loomed out of the night to give them what haven and what blessing they yearned for. They sat at the counter and crossed their legs at the ankles, their thin shoulders rigid with excitement, and listened to the music that made everything so good: the music was always in the background like music at a church service, it was something to depend upon.

A boy named Eddie came in to talk with them. He sat backwards on his stool, turning himself jerkily around in semi-circles and then stopping and turning again, and after awhile he asked Connie if she would like something to eat. She said she did and so she tapped her friend's arm on her way out—

her friend pulled her face up into a brave droll look—and Connie said she would meet her at eleven, across the way. "I just hate to leave her like that," Connie said earnestly, but the boy said that she wouldn't be alone for long. So they went out to his car and on the way Connie couldn't help but let her eyes wander over the windshields and faces all around her, her face gleaming with a joy that had nothing to do with Eddie or even this place; it might have been the music. She drew her shoulders up and sucked in her breath with the pure pleasure of being alive, and just at that moment she happened to glance at a face just a few feet from hers. It was a boy with shaggy black hair, in a convertible jalopy painted gold. He stared at her and then his lips widened into a grin. Connie slit her eyes at him and turned away, but she couldn't help glancing back and there he was still watching her. He wagged a finger and laughed and said, "Gonna get you, baby," and Connie turned away again without Eddie noticing anything.

She spent three hours with him, at the restaurant where they ate hamburgers and drank Cokes in wax cups that were always sweating, and then down an alley a mile or so away, and when he left her off at five to eleven only the movie house was still open at the plaza. Her girl friend was there, talking with a boy. When Connie came up the two girls smiled at each other and Connie said, "How was the movie?" and the girl said, "*You* should know." They rode off with the girl's father, sleepy and pleased, and Connie couldn't help but look at the darkened shopping plaza with its big empty parking lot and its signs that were faded and ghostly now, and over at the drive-in restaurant where cars were still circling tirelessly. She couldn't hear the music at this distance.

Next morning June asked her how the movie was and Connie said, "So-so."

She and that girl and occasionally another girl went out several times a week that way, and the rest of the time Connie spent around the house—it was summer vacation—getting in her mother's way and thinking, dreaming, about the boys she met. But all the boys fell back and dissolved into a single face that was not even a face, but an idea, a feeling, mixed up with the urgent insistent pounding of the music and the humid night air of July. Connie's mother kept dragging her back to the daylight by finding things for her to do or saying, suddenly, "What's this about the Pettinger girl?"

And Connie would say nervously, "Oh, her. That dope." She always drew thick clear lines between herself and such girls, and her mother was simple and kindly enough to believe her. Her mother was so simple, Connie thought, that it was maybe cruel to fool her so much. Her mother went scuffling around the house in old bedroom slippers and complained over the telephone to one sister about the other, then the other called up and the two of them complained about the third one. If June's name was mentioned her mother's tone was approving, and if Connie's name was mentioned it was disapproving. This did not really mean she disliked Connie and actually Connie thought that her mother preferred her to June because she was prettier, but the two of them kept up a pretense of exasperation, a sense that they were tugging and struggling over something of little value to either of them. Sometimes, over coffee, they were almost friends, but something would come up—some vexation that was like a fly buzzing suddenly around their heads—and their faces went hard with contempt.

One Sunday Connie got up at eleven—none of them bothered with church—and washed her hair so that it could dry all day long, in the sun. Her parents and sisters were going to a barbecue at an aunt's house and Connie said no, she wasn't interested, rolling her eyes to let mother know just what she thought of it. "Stay home alone then," her mother said sharply. Connie sat out back in a lawn chair and watched them drive away, her father quiet and bald, hunched around so that he could back the car out, her mother with a look that was still angry and not at all softened through the windshield, and in the back seat poor old June all dressed up as if she didn't know what a barbecue was, with all the running yelling kids and the flies. Connie sat with her eyes closed in the sun, dreaming and dazed with the warmth about her as if this were a kind of love, the caresses of love, and her mind slipped over onto thoughts of the boy she had been with the night before and how nice he had been, how sweet it always was, not the way someone like June would suppose but sweet, gentle, the way it was in movies and promised in songs; and when she opened her eyes she hardly knew where she was, the back yard ran off into weeds and a fence-line of trees and behind it the sky was perfectly blue and still. The asbestos "ranch house" that was now three years old startled her—it looked small. She shook her head as if to get awake.

It was too hot. She went inside the house and turned on the radio to drown out the quiet. She sat on the edge of her bed, barefoot, and listened for an hour and a half to a program called XYZ Sunday Jamboree, record after record of hard, fast, shrieking songs she sang along with, interspersed by exclamations from "Bobby King": "An' look here you girls at Napoleon's—Son and Charley want you to pay real close attention to this song coming up!"

And Connie paid close attention herself, bathed in a glow of slow-pulsed joy that seemed to rise mysteriously out of the music itself and lay languidly about the airless little room, breathed in and breathed out with each gentle rise and fall of her chest.

After a while she heard a car coming up the drive. She sat up at once, startled, because it couldn't be her father so soon. The gravel kept crunching all the way in from the road—the driveway was long—and Connie ran to the window. It was a car she didn't know. It was an open jalopy, painted a bright gold that caught the sunlight opaquely. Her heart began to pound and her fingers snatched at her hair, checking it, and she whispered "Christ, Christ," wondering how bad she looked. The car came to a stop at the side door and the horn sounded four short taps as if this were a signal Connie knew.

She went into the kitchen and approached the door slowly, then hung out the screen door, her bare toes curling down off the step. There were two boys in the car and now she recognized the driver: he had shaggy, shabby black hair that looked crazy as a wig and he was grinning at her.

"I ain't late, am I?" he said.

"Who the hell do you think you are?" Connie said.

"Toldja I'd be out, didn't I?"

"I don't even know who you are."

She spoke sullenly, careful to show no interest or pleasure, and he spoke in a fast bright monotone. Connie looked past him to the other boy, taking her time. He had fair brown hair, with a lock that fell onto his forehead. His sideburns gave him a fierce, embarrassed look, but so far he hadn't even bothered to glance at her. Both boys wore sunglasses. The driver's glasses were metallic and mirrored everything in miniature.

"You wanta come for a ride?" he said.

Connie smirked and let her hair fall loose over one shoulder.

"Don'tcha like my car? New paint job," he said. "Hey."

"What?"

"You're cute."

She pretended to fidget, chasing flies away from the door.

"Don'cha believe me, or what?" he said.

"Look, I don't even know who you are," Connie said in disgust.

"Hey, Ellie's got a radio, see. Mine's broke down." He lifted his friend's arm and showed her the little transistor the boy was holding, and now Connie began to hear the music. It was the same program that was playing inside the house.

"Bobby King?" she said.

"I listen to him all the time. I think he's great."

"He's kind of great," Connie said reluctantly.

"Listen, that guy's *great*. He knows where the action is."

Connie blushed a little, because the glasses made it impossible for her to see just what this boy was looking at. She couldn't decide if she liked him or if he was just a jerk, and so she dawdled in the doorway and wouldn't come down or go back inside. She said, "What's all that stuff painted on your car?"

"Can'tcha read it?" He opened the door very carefully, as if he was afraid it might fall off. He slid out just as carefully, planting his feet firmly on the ground, the tiny metallic world in his glasses slowing down like gelatine hardening and in the midst of it Connie's bright green blouse. "This here is my name, to begin with," he said. ARNOLD FRIEND was written in tar-like black letters on the side, with a drawing of a round grinning face that reminded Connie of a pumpkin, except it wore sunglasses. "I wanta intro-duce myself. I'm Arnold Friend and that's my real name and I'm gonna be your friend, honey, and inside the car's Ellie Oscar, he's kinda shy." Ellie brought his transistor radio up to his shoulder and balanced it there. "Now these numbers are a secret code, honey," Arnold Friend explained. He read off the numbers 33, 19, 17 and raised his eyebrows at her to see what she thought of that, but she didn't think much of it. The left rear fender had been smashed and around it was written, on the gleaming gold background: DONE BY CRAZY WOMAN DRIVER. Connie had to laugh at that. Arnold Friend was pleased at her laughter and looked up at her. "Around the other side's a lot more—you wanta come and see them?"

"No."

"Why not?"

"Why should I?"

"Don'tcha wanta see what's on the car? Don'tcha wanta go for a ride?"

"I don't know."

"Why not?"

"I got things to do."

"Like what?"

"Things."

He laughed as if she had said something funny. He slapped his thighs. He was standing in a strange way, leaning back against the car as if he were balancing himself. He wasn't tall, only an inch or so taller than she would be if she came down to him. Connie liked the way he was dressed, which was the way all of them dressed: tight faded jeans stuffed into black, scuffed boots, a belt that pulled his waist in and showed how lean he was, and a white pull-over shirt that was a little soiled and showed the hard small muscles of his arms and shoulders. He looked as if he probably did hard work, lifting and carrying things. Even his neck looked muscular. And his face was a familiar face, somehow: the jaw and chin and cheeks slightly darkened, because he hadn't shaved for a day or two, and the nose long and hawk-like, sniffing as if she were a treat he was going to gobble up and it was all a joke.

"Connie, you ain't telling the truth. This is your day set aside for a ride with me and you know it," he said, still laughing. The way he straightened and recovered from his fit of laughing showed that it had been all fake.

"How do you know what my name is?" she said suspiciously.

"It's Connie."

"Maybe and maybe not."

"I know my Connie," he said, wagging his finger. Now she remembered him even better, back at the restaurant, and her cheeks warmed at the thought of how she sucked in her breath just at the moment she passed him—how she must have looked to him. And he had remembered her. "Ellie and I come out here especially for you," he said. "Ellie can sit in back. How about it?"

"Where?"

"Where what?"

"Where're we going?"

He looked at her. He took off the sunglasses and she saw how pale the skin around his eyes was, like holes that were not in shadow but instead in light. His eyes were like chips of broken glass that catch the light in an amiable way. He smiled. It was as if the idea of going for a ride somewhere, to some place, was a new idea to him.

"Just for a ride, Connie sweetheart."

"I never said my name was Connie," she said.

"But I know what it is. I know your name and all about you, lots of things," Arnold Friend said. He had not moved yet but stood still leaning back against the side of his jalopy. "I took a special interest in you, such a pretty girl, and found out all about you like I know your parents and sister are gone somewheres and I know where and how long they're going to be gone, and I know who you were with last night, and your best girl friend's name is Betty. Right?"

He spoke in a simple lilting voice, exactly as if he were reciting the words to a song. His smile assured her that everything was fine. In the car Ellie turned up the volume on his radio and did not bother to look around at them.

"Ellie can sit in the back seat," Arnold Friend said. He indicated his friend with a casual jerk of his chin, as if Ellie did not count and she should not bother with him.

"How'd you find out all that stuff?" Connie said.

"Listen: Betty Schultz and Tony Fitch and Jimmy Pettinger and Nancy Pettinger," he said, in a chant. "Raymond Stanley and Bob Hutter—"

"Do you know all those kids?"

"I know everybody."

"Look, you're kidding. You're not from around here."

"Sure."

"But—how come we never saw you before?"

"Sure you saw me before," he said. He looked down at his boots, as if he were a little offended. "You just don't remember."

"I guess I'd remember you," Connie said.

"Yeah?" He looked up at this, beaming. He was pleased. He began to mark time with the music from Ellie's radio, tapping his fists lightly together. Connie looked away from his smile to the car, which was painted so bright it almost hurt her eyes to look at it. She looked at that name, ARNOLD FRIEND. And up at the front fender was an expression that was familiar—MAN THE FLYING SAUCERS. It was an expression kids had used the year before, but didn't use this year. She looked at it for a while as if the words meant something to her that she did not yet know.

"What're you thinking about? Huh?" Arnold Friend demanded. "Not worried about your hair blowing around in the car, are you?"

"No."

"Think I maybe can't drive good?"

"How do I know?"

"You're a hard girl to handle. How come?" he said. "Don't you know I'm your friend? Didn't you see me put my sign in the air when you walked by?"

"What sign?"

"My sign." And he drew an X in the air, leaning out toward her. They were maybe ten feet apart. After his hand fell back to his side the X was still in the air, almost visible. Connie let the screen door close and stood perfectly still inside it, listening to the music from her radio and the boy's blend together. She stared at Arnold Friend. He stood there so stiffly relaxed, pretending to be relaxed, with one hand idly on the door handle as if he were keeping himself up that way and had no intention of ever moving again. She recognized most things about him, the tight jeans that showed his thighs and buttocks and the greasy leather boots and the tight shirt, and even that slippery friendly smile of his, that sleepy dreamy smile that all the boys used to get across ideas they didn't want to put into words. She recognized all this and also the sing-song way he talked, slightly mocking, kidding, but serious and a little melancholy, and she recognized the way he tapped one fist against the other in homage to the perpetual music behind him. But all these things did not come together.

She said suddenly, "Hey, how old are you?"

His smile faded. She could see then that he wasn't a kid, he was much older—thirty, maybe more. At this knowledge her heart began to pound faster.

"That's a crazy thing to ask. Can'tcha see I'm your own age?"

"Like hell you are."

"Or maybe a coupla years older, I'm eighteen."

"Eighteen?" she said doubtfully.

He grinned to reassure her and lines appeared at the corners of his mouth. His teeth were big and white. He grinned so broadly his eyes became slits and she saw how thick the lashes were, thick and black as if painted with a black tar-like material. Then he seemed to become embarrassed, abruptly, and looked over his shoulder at Ellie. "*Him*, he's crazy," he said. "Ain't he a riot, he's a nut, a real character." Ellie was still listening to the music. His sunglasses told nothing about what he was thinking. He wore a bright orange shirt unbuttoned halfway to show his chest, which was a pale, bluish chest and not muscular like Arnold Friend's. His shirt collar was turned up all around and the very tips of the collar pointed out past his chin as if they were protecting him. He was pressing the transistor radio up against his ear and sat there in a kind of daze, right in the sun.

"He's kinda strange," Connie said.

"Hey, she says you're kinda strange! Kinda strange!" Arnold Friend cried. He pounded on the car to get Ellie's attention. Ellie turned for the first time and Connie saw with shock that he wasn't a kid either—he had a fair, hairless face, cheeks reddened slightly as if the veins grew too close to the surface of his skin, the face of a forty-year-old baby. Connie felt a wave of dizziness rise in her at this sight and she stared at him as if waiting for something to change the shock of the moment, make it all right again. Ellie's lips kept shaping words, mumbling along with the words blasting in his ear.

"Maybe you two better go away," Connie said faintly.

"What? How come?" Arnold Friend cried. "We come out here to take you for a ride. It's Sunday." He had the voice of the man on the radio now. It was the same voice, Connie thought. "Don'tcha know it's Sunday all day and honey, no matter who you were with last night today you're with Arnold Friend and don't you forget it!—Maybe you better step out here," he said, and this last was in a different voice. It was a little flatter, as if the heat was finally getting to him.

"No. I got things to do."

"Hey."

"You two better leave."

"We ain't leaving until you come with us."

"Like hell I am—"

"Connie, don't fool around with me. I mean, I mean, don't fool *around*," he said, shaking his head. He laughed incredulously. He placed his sunglasses on top of his head, carefully, as if he were indeed wearing a wig, and brought the stems down behind his ears. Connie stared at him, another wave of dizziness and fear rising in her so that for a moment he wasn't even in focus but was just a blur, standing there against his gold car, and she had the idea that he had driven up the driveway all right but had come from nowhere before that and belonged nowhere and that everything about him and even about the music that was so familiar to her was only half real.

"If my father comes and sees you—"

"He ain't coming. He's at a barbecue."

"How do you know that?"

"Aunt Tillie's. Right now they're—uh—they're drinking. Sitting around," he said vaguely, squinting as if he were staring all the way to town and over to Aunt Tillie's back yard. Then the vision seemed to get clear and he nodded energetically. "Yeah. Sitting around. There's your sister in a blue dress, huh? And high heels, the poor sad bitch—nothing like you, sweetheart! And your mother's helping some fat woman with the corn, they're cleaning the corn—husking the corn—"

"What fat woman?" Connie cried.

"How do I know what fat woman, I don't know every goddam fat woman in the world!" Arnold Friend laughed.

"Oh, that's Mrs. Hornby. . . . Who invited her?" Connie said. She felt a little light-headed. Her breath was coming quickly.

"She's too fat. I don't like them fat. I like them the way you are, honey," he said, smiling sleepily at her. They stared at each other for a while, through the screen door. He said softly, "Now what you're going to do is this: you're going to come out that door. You're going to sit up front with me and Ellie's going to sit in the back, the hell with Ellie, right? This isn't Ellie's date. You're my date. I'm your lover, honey."

"What? You're crazy—"

"Yes, I'm your lover. You don't know what that is but you will," he said. "I know that too. I know all about you. But look: it's real nice and you couldn't ask for nobody better than me, or more polite. I always keep my word. I'll tell you how it is, I'm always nice at first, the first time. I'll hold you so tight you won't think you have to try to get away or pretend anything because you'll know you can't. And I'll come inside you where it's all secret and you'll give in to me and you'll love me—"

"Shut up! You're crazy!" Connie said. She backed away from the door. She put her hands against her ears as if she'd heard something terrible, something not meant for her. "People don't talk like that, you're crazy," she muttered. Her heart was almost too big now for her chest and its pumping made sweat break out all over her. She looked out to see Arnold Friend pause and then take a step toward the porch lurching. He almost fell. But, like a clever drunken man, he managed to catch his balance. He wobbled in his high boots and grabbed hold of one of the porch posts.

"Honey?" he said. "You still listening?"

"Get the hell out of here!"

"Be nice, honey. Listen."

"I'm going to call the police—"

He wobbled again and out of the side of his mouth came a fast spat curse, an aside not meant for her to hear. But even this "Christ!" sounded forced. Then he began to smile again. She watched this smile come, awkward as if he were smiling from inside a mask. His whole face was a mask, she thought wildly, tanned down onto his throat but then running out as if he had plastered make-up on his face but had forgotten about his throat.

"Honey—? Listen, here's how it is. I always tell the truth and I promise you this: I ain't coming in that house after you."

"You better not! I'm going to call the police if you—if you don't—"

"Honey," he said, talking right through her voice, "honey, I'm not coming in there but you are coming out here. You know why?"

She was panting. The kitchen looked like a place she had never seen before, some room she had run inside but which wasn't good enough, wasn't going to help her. The kitchen window had never had a curtain, after three years, and there were dishes in the sink for her to do—probably—and if you ran your hand across the table you'd probably feel something sticky there.

"You listening, honey? Hey?"

"—going to call the police—"

"Soon as you touch the phone I don't need to keep my promise and can come inside. You won't want that."

She rushed forward and tried to lock the door. Her fingers were shaking. "But why lock it," Arnold Friend said gently, talking right into her face. "It's just a screen door. It's just nothing." One of his boots was at a strange angle, as if his foot wasn't in it. It pointed out to the left, bent at the ankle. "I mean, anybody can break through a screen door and glass and wood and iron or anything else if he needs to, anybody at all and specially Arnold Friend. If the place got lit up with a fire honey you'd come runnin out into my arms, right into my arms an safe at home—like you knew I was your lover and'd stopped fooling around. I don't mind a nice shy girl but I don't like no fooling around." Part of those words were spoken with a slight rhythmic lilt, and Connie somehow recognized them—the echo of a song from last year, about a girl rushing into her boy friend's arms and coming home again—

Connie stood barefoot on the linoleum floor, staring at him. "What do you want?" she whispered.

"I want you," he said.

"What?"

"Seen you that night and thought, that's the one, yes sir. I never needed to look any more."

"But my father's coming back. He's coming to get me. I had to wash my hair first--" She spoke in a dry, rapid voice, hardly raising it for him to hear.

"No, your Daddy is not coming and yes, you had to wash your hair and you washed it for me. It's nice and shining and all for me, I thank you, sweetheart," he said, with a mock bow, but again he almost lost his balance. He had to bend and adjust his boots. Evidently his feet did not go all the way down; the boots must have been stuffed with something so that he would seem taller. Connie stared out at him and behind him Ellie in the car, who seemed to be looking off toward Connie's right, into nothing. This Ellie said, pulling the words out of the air one after another as if he were just discovering them, "You want me to pull out the phone?"

"Shut your mouth and keep it shut," Arnold Friend said, his face red from bending over or maybe from embarrassment because Connie had seen his boots. "This ain't none of your business."

"What—what are you doing? What do you want?" Connie said. "If I call the police they'll get you, they'll arrest you—"

"Promise was not to come in unless you touch that phone, and I'll keep that promise," he said. He resumed his erect position and tried to force his shoulders back. He sounded like a hero in a movie, declaring something important. He spoke too loudly and it was as if he were speaking to someone behind Connie. "I ain't made plans for coming in that house where I don't belong but just for you to come out to me, the way you should. Don't you know who I am?"

"You're crazy," she whispered. She backed away from the door but did not want to go into another part of the house, as if this would give him permission to come through the door. "What do you. . . . You're crazy, you . . ."

"Huh? What're you saying, honey?"

Her eyes darted everywhere in the kitchen. She could not remember what it was, this room.

"This is how it is, honey: you come out and we'll drive away, have a nice ride. But if you don't come out we're gonna wait till your people come home and then they're all going to get it."

"You want that telephone pulled out?" Ellie said. He held the radio away from his ear and grimaced, as if without the radio the air was too much for him.

"I toldja shut up, Ellie," Arnold Friend said, "you're deaf, get a hearing aid, right? Fix yourself up. This little girl's no trouble and's gonna be nice to me, so Ellie keep to yourself, this ain't your date—right? Don't hem in on me. Don't hog. Don't crush. Don't bird dog. Don't trail me," he said in a rapid meaningless voice, as if he were running through all the expressions he'd learned but was no longer sure which one of them was in style, then rushing on to new ones, making them up with his eyes closed, "Don't crawl under my fence, don't squeeze in my chipmunk hole, don't sniff my glue, suck my popsicle, keep your own greasy fingers on yourself!" He shaded his eyes and peered in at Connie, who was backed against the kitchen table.

"Don't mind him honey he's just a creep. He's a dope. Right? I'm the boy for you and like I said you come out here nice like a lady and give me your hand, and nobody else gets hurt, I mean, your nice old bald-headed daddy and your mummy and your sister in her high heels. Because listen: why bring them in this?"

"Leave me alone," Connie whispered.

"Hey, you know that old woman down the road, the one with the chickens and stuff—you know her?"

"She's dead!"

"Dead? What? You know her?" Arnold Friend said.

"She's dead—"

"Don't you like her?"

"She's dead—she's—she isn't here any more—"

"But don't you like her, I mean, you got something against her? Some grudge or something?" Then his voice dipped as if he were conscious of a rudeness. He touched the sunglasses perched on top of his head as if to make sure they were still there. "Now you be a good girl."

"What are you going to do?"

"Just two things, or maybe three." Arnold Friend said. "But I promise it won't last long and you'll like me the way you get to like people you're close to. You will. It's all over for you here, so come on out. You don't want your people in any trouble, do you?"

She turned and bumped against a chair or something, hurting her leg, but she ran into the back room and picked up the telephone. Something roared in her ear, a tiny roaring, and she was so sick with fear that she could do nothing but listen to it—the telephone was clammy and very heavy and her fingers groped down to the dial but were too weak to touch it. She began to scream into the phone, into the roaring. She cried out, she cried for her mother, she felt her breath start jerking back and forth in her lungs as if it were something Arnold Friend were stabbing her with again and again with no tenderness. A noisy sorrowful wailing rose all about her and she was locked inside it the way she was locked inside this house.

After a while she could hear again. She was sitting on the floor with her wet back against the wall.

Arnold Friend was saying from the door. "That's a good girl. Put the phone back."

She kicked the phone away from her.

"No, honey. Pick it up. Put it back right."

She picked it up and put it back. The dial tone stopped.

"That's a good girl. Now you come outside."

She was hollow with what had been fear, but what was now just an emptiness. All that screaming had blasted it out of her. She sat, one leg cramped under her, and deep inside her brain was something like a pinpoint of light that kept going and would not let her relax. She thought, I'm not going to see my mother again. She thought, I'm not going to sleep in my bed again. Her bright green blouse was all wet.

Arnold Friend said, in a gentle-loud voice that was like a stage voice,

"The place where you came from ain't there any more, and where you had in mind to go is cancelled out. This place you are now—inside your daddy's house—is nothing but a cardboard box I can knock down any time. You know that and always did know it. You hear me?"

She thought, I have to think. I have to know what to do.

"We'll go out to a nice field, out in the country here where it smells so nice and it's sunny," Arnold Friend said. "I'll have my arms tight around you so you won't need to try to get away and I'll show you what love is like, what it does. The hell with this house! It looks solid all right," he said. He ran a fingernail down the screen and the noise did not make Connie shiver, as it would have the day before. "Now put your hand on your heart, honey. Feel that? That feels solid too but we know better, be nice to me, be sweet like you can because what else is there for a girl like you but to be sweet and pretty and give in?—and get away before her people come back?"

She felt her pounding heart. Her hand seemed to enclose it. She thought for the first time in her life that it was nothing that was hers, that belonged to her, but just a pounding, living thing inside this body that wasn't really hers either.

"You don't want them to get hurt," Arnold Friend went on. "Now get up, honey. Get up all by yourself."

She stood.

"Now turn this way. That's right. Come over here to me.—Ellie, put that away, didn't I tell you? You dope. You miserable creepy dope," Arnold Friend said. His words were not angry but only part of an incantation. The incantation was kindly. "Now come out through the kitchen to me honey and let's see a smile, try it, you're a brave sweet little girl and now they're eating corn and hotdogs cooked to bursting over an outdoor fire, and they don't know one thing about you and never did and honey you're better than them because not a one of them would have done this for you."

Connie felt the linoleum under her feet; it was cool. She brushed her hair back out of her eyes. Arnold Friend let go of the post tentatively and opened his arms for her, his elbows pointing in toward each other and his wrists limp, to show that this was an embarrassed embrace and a little mocking, he didn't want to make her self-conscious.

She put out her hand against the screen. She watched herself push the door slowly open as if she were safe back somewhere in the other doorway, watching this body and this head of long hair moving out into the sunlight where Arnold Friend waited.

"My sweet little blue-eyed girl," he said, in a half-sung sigh that had nothing to do with her brown eyes but was taken up just the same by the vast sunlit reaches of the land behind him and on all sides of him, so much land that Connie had never seen before and did not recognize except to know that she was going to it.

Science, Technology, and Human Values

The successful application of science to our practical problems has been truly described as "one of the miracles of mankind." But no serious writer today can discuss technological progress without misgivings. Most of us, at least, are aware of some of the terrifying losses that seem always to accompany the gains: the atomic balance of terror; the population explosion; the poisoning of our air, water, and soil; the electronic and psychological threat to privacy; the displacement of skilled workers by skilled machines; the recent advances in brain chemistry and genetics that promise even more terrifying danger to human beings.

We place E. B. White's comical science fiction of 1950 first because it not only epitomizes the truth that technological progress is always ambiguous, but it deftly brings into the orbit of our present subject the topic raised in the preceding section—mass culture and mass media—and of course reaches far beyond both.

There follow groups of essays on three of the many urgent problems that follow from the explosion of science and technology. Carl Sagan makes a case for "intelligent machines." He is answered by Joseph Weizenbaum, computer scientist, whose impulse to write arises in part from concern over misinterpretation of his own pioneer work. If Weizenbaum believes that **527** "there are certain tasks that computers ought not be made to do," the philosopher Hubert Dreyfus argues that in fact there are many tasks that computers can never be made to do, that they can never be made intelligent in the human sense at all.

James D. Watson and Ivan Illich take up problems from the realm of bio-medicine. Watson calmly but probingly discusses the consequences "if test-tube conception becomes a common occurrence"; the first such conception had not yet occurred when his essay was written. Illich emphasizes not the technical breakthroughs of medical science but what happens to them administratively afterward. He describes an expanding pyramid of bureaucratic professional control that creates diseases rather than curing them.

The section ends with three modest probings of our problems of pollution, waste, and overconsumption. A *New Yorker* editorial reminds us that "there is no such thing as throwing something 'away.'" Appletree Rodden celebrates the advantages of smallness in our consumer habits. The 1990s science fiction of Isaac Asimov, on what a real fuel shortage might be like, makes us wonder chillingly whether his vision will turn out to be as true as E. B. White's has already become.

TECHNOLOGY, THE MASS MEDIA, AND THE GOOD LIFE

E. B. WHITE

Elwyn Brooks White, born in 1899, graduated from Cornell in 1921 and joined the staff of The New Yorker *in 1926. He regularly wrote its "Notes and Comment" section until 1938 and contributed to the page in the 1940s and 1950s. His sensitive, humorous character and his witty yet natural and exact literary style, along with the congenial talents of James Thurber and of a few others, were in part responsible for the extraordinary reputation of* New Yorker *writing at that time. He contributed a monthly column, entitled "One Man's Meat," to* Harper's *from 1938 to 1943 and resumed writing for* The New Yorker *on a free-lance basis in 1945. Since 1937 he has taken periodic refuge in a Maine farm. He has been awarded honorary degrees from Dartmouth, Maine, Bowdoin, Hamilton, Colby, Yale, and Harvard, the National Institute of Arts and Letters gold medal in 1960 for his contribution to literature, and the Presidential Medal of Freedom in 1963. White has published two excellent children's books,* Stuart Little *(1945) and* Charlotte's Web *(1952), and received the 1970 Laura Ingalls Wilder Award for his "substantial and lasting contribution to literature for children." Among his best-known other books are* Is Sex Necessary?, *written with James Thurber (1929);* Every Day Is Saturday *(1934);* One Man's Meat *(1942);* The Wild Flag *(1946); and* The Elements of Style *(1959), a reverent re-editing of the textbook of his former professor William Strunk, Jr. His* Letters *was published in 1976 and his* Essays *in 1977. The story we present below, taken from* The Second Tree from the Corner *(1954), was first published in* The New Yorker *in February 1950.*

The Morning of the Day They Did It

My purpose is to tell how it happened and to set down a few impressions of that morning while it is fresh in memory. I was in a plane that was in radio communication with the men on the platform. To put the matter briefly, what was intended as a military expedient turned suddenly into a holocaust. The explanation was plain enough to me, for, like millions of others, I was listening to the conversation between the two men and was instantly aware of the quick shift it took. That part is clear. What is not so clear is how I myself survived, but I am beginning to understand that, too. I shall not burden the reader with an explanation, however, as the facts are tedious and implausible. I am now in good health and fair spirits, among friendly people on an inferior planet, at a very great distance from the sun. Even the move from one planet to another has not relieved me of the nagging curse that besets writing men—the feeling that they must produce some sort of record of their times.

The thing happened shortly before twelve noon. I came out of my house on East Harding Boulevard at quarter of eight that morning, swinging my newspaper and feeling pretty good. The March day was mild and spring-like, the warmth and the smells doubly welcome after the rotten weather we'd been having. A gentle wind met me on the Boulevard, frisked me, and went on. A man in a leather cap was loading bedsprings into a van in front of No. 220. I remember that as I walked along I worked my tongue around the roof of my mouth, trying to dislodge a prune skin. (These details have no significance; why write them down?)

A few blocks from home there was a Contakt plane station and I hurried in, caught the 8:10 plane, and was soon aloft. I always hated a jet-assist takeoff right after breakfast, but it was one of the discomforts that went with my job. At ten thousand feet our small plane made contact with the big one, we passengers were transferred, and the big ship went on up to fifty thousand, which was the height television planes flew at. I was a script writer for one of the programs. My tour of duty was supposed to be eight hours.

I should probably explain here that at the period of which I am writing, the last days of the planet earth, telecasting was done from planes circling the stratosphere. This eliminated the coaxial cable, a form of relay that had given endless trouble. Coaxials worked well enough for a while, but eventually they were abandoned, largely because of the extraordinary depredations of earwigs. These insects had developed an alarming resistance to bugspray and were out of control most of the time. Earwigs increased in size and in numbers, and the forceps at the end of their abdomen developed so that they could cut through a steel shell. They seemed to go unerringly for coaxials. Whether the signals carried by the cables had anything to do with it I don't know, but the bugs fed on these things and were enormously stimulated. Not only did they feast on the cables, causing the cables to disintegrate, but they laid eggs in them in unimaginable quantities, and as the eggs hatched the television images suffered greatly, there was more and more flickering on the screen, more and more eyestrain and nervous tension among audiences, and of course a further debasement of taste and intellectual life in general. Finally the coaxials were given up, and after much experimenting by Westinghouse and the Glenn Martin people a satisfactory substitute was found in the high-flying planes. A few of these planes, spotted around the country, handled the whole television load nicely. Known as Stratovideo planes, they were equipped with studios; many programs originated in the air and were transmitted directly, others were beamed to the aircraft from ground stations and then relayed. The planes flew continuously, twenty-four hours a day, were refuelled in air, and dropped down to ten thousand feet every eight hours to meet the Contakt planes and take on new shifts of workers.

I remember that as I walked to my desk in the Stratoship that morning, the nine-o'clock news had just ended and a program called "Author, Please!" was going on, featuring Melonie Babson, a woman who had written a best-seller on the theme of euthanasia, called "Peace of Body." The program was sponsored by a dress-shield company.

I remember, too, that a young doctor had come aboard the plane with the rest of us. He was a newcomer, a fellow named Cathcart, slated to be the physician attached to the ship. He had introduced himself to me in the Contakt plane, had asked the date of my Tri-D shot, and had noted it down in his book. (I shall explain about these shots presently.) This doctor certainly had a brief life in our midst. He had hardly been introduced around and shown his office when our control room got a radio call asking if there was a doctor in the stratosphere above Earthpoint F-plus-6, and requesting medical assistance at the scene of an accident.

F-plus-6 was almost directly below us, so Dr. Cathcart felt he ought to respond, and our control man gave the word and asked for particulars and instructions. It seems there had been a low-altitude collision above F-plus-6 involving two small planes and killing three people. One plane was a Diaheliper, belonging to an aerial diaper service that flew diapers to rural homes by helicopter. The other was one of the familiar government-owned sprayplanes that worked at low altitudes over croplands, truck gardens, and commercial orchards, delivering a heavy mist of the deadly Tri-D solution, the pesticide that had revolutionized agriculture, eliminated the bee from nature, and given us fruits and vegetables of undreamed-of perfection but very high toxicity.

The two planes had tangled and fallen onto the observation tower of a whooping-crane sanctuary, scattering diapers over an area of half a mile and releasing a stream of Tri-D. Cathcart got his medical kit, put on his parachute, and paused a moment to adjust his pressurizer, preparatory to bailing out. Knowing that he wouldn't be back for a while, he asked if anybody around the shop was due for a Tri-D shot that morning, and it turned out that Bill Foley was. So the Doctor told Foley to come along, and explained that he would give him his injection on the way down. Bill threw me a quick look of mock anguish, and started climbing into his gear. This must have been six or seven minutes past nine.

It seems strange that I should feel obliged to explain Tri-D shots. They were a commonplace at this time—as much a part of a person's life as his toothbrush. The correct name for them was Anti-Tri-D, but people soon shortened the name. They were simply injections that everyone had to receive at regular twenty-one-day intervals, to counteract the lethal effect of food, and the notable thing about them was the great importance of the twenty-one-day period. To miss one's Tri-D shot by as much as a couple of hours might mean serious consequences, even death. Almost every day there were deaths reported in the papers from failure to get the injection at the proper time. The whole business was something like insulin control in diabetes. You can easily imagine the work it entailed for doctors in the United States, keeping the entire population protected against death by poisoning.

As Dr. Cathcart and Bill eased themselves out of the plane through the chute exit, I paused briefly and listened to Miss Babson, our author of the day.

"It is a grand privilege," she was saying, "to appear before the television audience this morning and face this distinguished battery of critics, including my old sparring partner, Ralph Armstrong, of the *Herald Tribune*. I suppose after Mr. Armstrong finishes with me I will be a pretty good candidate for euthanasia myself. Ha. But seriously, ladies and gentlemen, I feel that a good book is its own defense."

The authoress had achieved a state of exaltation already. I knew that her book, which she truly believed to be great, had been suggested to her by an agent over a luncheon table and had been written largely by somebody else, whom the publisher had had to bring in to salvage the thing. The final result was a run-of-the-can piece of rubbish easily outselling its nearest competitor.

Miss Babson continued, her exaltation stained with cuteness:

"I have heard my novel criticized on the ground that the theme of euthanasia is too daring, and even that it is anti-Catholic. Well, I can remember, way back in the dark ages, when a lot of things that are accepted as commonplace today were considered daring or absurd. My own father can recall the days when dairy cows were actually bred by natural methods. The farmers of those times felt that the artificial-breeding program developed by our marvellous experiment stations was high-falutin nonsense. Well, we all know what has happened to the dairy industry, with many of our best milch cows giving milk continuously right around the clock, in a steady stream. True, the cows do have to be propped up and held in position in special stanchions and fed intravenously, but I always say it isn't the hubbub that counts, it's the butterfat. And I doubt if even Mr. Armstrong here would want to return to the days when a cow just gave a bucket of milk and then stopped to rest."

Tiring of the literary life, I walked away and looked out a window. Below, near the layer of cumulus, the two chutes were visible. With the help of binoculars I could see Bill manfully trying to slip his chute over next to the Doc, and could see Cathcart fumbling with his needle. Our telecandid man was at another window, filming the thing for the next newscast, as it was a new wrinkle in the Tri-D world to have somebody getting his shot while parachuting.

I had a few chores to do before our program came on, at eleven-five. "Town Meeting of the Upper Air" was the name of it. "Town Meeting" was an unrehearsed show, but I was supposed to brief the guests, distribute copies of whatever prepared scripts there were, explain the cuing, and make everybody happy generally. The program we were readying that morning had had heavy advance billing, and there was tremendous interest in it everywhere, not so much because of the topic ("Will the fear of retaliation stop aggression?") or even the cast of characters, which included Major General Artemus T. Recoil, but because of an incidental stunt we were planning to pull off. We had arranged a radio hookup with the space platform, a gadget the Army had succeeded in establishing six hundred miles up, in the regions of the sky beyond the pull of gravity. The Army, after many years of experimenting with rockets, had not only got the platform established but had sent two fellows there in a Spaceship, and also a liberal supply of the New Weapon.

The whole civilized world had read about this achievement, which swung the balance of power so heavily in our favor, and everyone was aware that the damned platform was wandering around in its own orbit at a dizzy distance from the earth and not subject to gravitational pull. Every kid in America had become an astrophysicist overnight and talked knowingly of exhaust velocities, synergy curves, and Keplerian ellipses. Every subway rider knew that the two men on the platform were breathing oxygen thrown off from big squash vines that they had taken along. The *Reader's Digest* had added to the fun by translating and condensing several German treatises on rockets and space travel, including the great *Wege zur Raumschiffahrt*. But to date, because of security regulations and technical difficulties, there had been no radio-television hookup. Finally we got clearance from Washington, and General Recoil agreed to interview the officers on the platform as part of the "Town Meeting" program. This was big stuff—to hear directly from the Space Platform for Checking Aggression, known pretty generally as the SPCA.

I was keyed up about it myself, but I remember that all that morning in the plane I felt disaffected, and wished I were not a stratovideo man. There were often days like that in the air. The plane, with its queer cargo and its cheap goings on, would suddenly seem unaccountably remote from the world of things I admired. In a physical sense we were never very remote: the plane circled steadily in a fixed circle of about ten miles diameter, and

I was never far from my own home on East Harding Boulevard. I could talk to Ann and the children, if I wished, by radiophone.

In many respects mine was a good job. It paid two hundred and twenty-five dollars a week, of which two hundred and ten was withheld. I should have felt well satisfied. Almost everything in the way of social benefits was provided by the government—medical care, hospitalization, education for the children, accident insurance, fire and theft, old-age retirement, Tri-D shots, vacation expense, amusement and recreation, welfare and well-being, Christmas and good will, rainy-day resource, staples and supplies, beverages and special occasions, baby-sitzfund—it had all been worked out. Any man who kept careful account of his pin money could get along all right, and I guess I should have been happy. Ann never complained much, except about one thing. She found that no matter how we saved and planned, we never could afford to buy flowers. One day, when she was a bit lathered up over household problems, she screamed, "God damn it, I'd rather live danger-ously and have one dozen yellow freesias!" It seemed to prey on her mind.

Anyway, this was one of those oppressive days in the air for me. Some-thing about the plane's undeviating course irritated me; the circle we flew seemed a monstrous excursion to nowhere. The engine noise (we flew at subsonic speed) was an unrelieved whine. Usually I didn't notice the en-gines, but today the ship sounded in my ears every minute, reminding me of a radiotherapy chamber, and there was always the palpable impact of vul-gar miracles—the very nature of television—that made me itchy and fretful.

Appearing with General Recoil on "Town Meeting of the Upper Air" were to be Mrs. Florence Gill, president of the Women's Auxiliary of the Sons of Original Matrons; Amory Buxton, head of the Economics and Withholding Council of the United Nations; and a young man named Tol-lip, representing one of the small, ineffectual groups that advocated world federation. I rounded up this stable of intellects in the reception room, went over the procedure with them, gave the General a drink (which seemed to be what was on his mind), and then ducked out to catch the ten-o'clock news and to have a smoke.

I found Pete Everhardt in the control room. He looked bushed. "Quite a morning, Nuncle," he said. Pete not only had to keep his signal clean on the nine-o'clock show (Melonie Babson was a speaker who liked to range all over the place when she talked) but he had to keep kicking the ball around with the two Army officers on the space platform, for fear he would lose them just as they were due to go on. And on top of that he felt obliged to stay in touch with Dr. Cathcart down below, as a matter of courtesy, and also to pick up incidental stuff for subsequent newscasts.

I sat down and lit a cigarette. In a few moments the day's authoress wound up her remarks and the news started, with the big, tense face of Ed Peterson on the screen dishing it out. Ed was well equipped by nature for newscasting; he had the accents of destiny. When he spread the news, it penetrated in depth. Each event not only seemed fraught with meaning, it seemed fraught with Ed. When he said "I predict . . ." you felt the full flow of his pipeline to God.

To the best of my recollection the ten-o'clock newscast on this awful morning went as follows:

(Announcer) "Good morning. Tepky's Hormone-Enriched Dental Floss brings you Ed Peterson and the news."

(Ed) "Flash! Three persons were killed and two others seriously injured a few minutes ago at Earthpoint F-plus-6 when a government sprayplane collided with a helicopter of the Diaheliper Company. Both pilots were thrown clear. They are at this moment being treated by a doctor released by parachute from Stratovideo Ship 3, from which I am now speaking. The sprayplane crashed into the observation tower of a whooping-crane sanctuary, releasing a deadly mist of Tri-D and instantly killing three wardens who were lounging there watching the love dance of the cranes. Diapers were scattered widely over the area, and these sterile garments proved invaluable to Dr. Herbert L. Cathcart in bandaging the wounds of the injured pilots, Roy T. Bliss and Homer Schenck. [Here followed a newsreel shot showing Cathcart winding a diaper around the head of one of the victims.] You are now at the scene of the disaster," droned Ed. "This is the first time in the history of television that an infant's napkin has appeared in the role of emergency bandage. Another first for American Tel. & Vid.!

"Washington! A Senate committeee, with new facts at its disposal, will reopen the investigation to establish the blame for Pearl Harbor.

"Chicago! Two members of the Department of Sanitation were removed from the payroll today for refusal to take the loyalty oath. Both are members of New Brooms, one of the four hundred thousand organizations on the Attorney General's subversive list.

"Hollywood! It's a boy at the Roscoe Pews. Stay tuned to this channel for a closeup of the Caesarean section during the eleven-o'clock roundup!

"New York! Flash! The Pulitzer Prize in editorial writing has been awarded to Frederick A. Mildly, of the New York *Times*, for his nostalgic editorial 'The Old Pumphandle.'

"Flash! Donations to the Atlantic Community Chest now stand at a little over seven hundred billion dollars. Thanks for a wonderful job of giving—I mean that from my heart.

"New York! The vexing question of whether Greek athletes will be allowed to take part in next year's Olympic Games still deadlocks the Security Council. In a stormy session yesterday the Russian delegate argued that the presence of Greek athletes at the games would be a threat to world peace. Most of the session was devoted to a discussion of whether the question was a procedural matter or a matter of substance.

"Flash! Radio contact with the two United States Army officers on the Space Platform for Checking Aggression, known to millions of listeners as the SPCA, has definitely been established, despite rumors to the contrary. The television audience will hear their voices in a little more than one hour from this very moment. You will *not* see their faces. Stay tuned! This is history, ladies and gentlemen—the first time a human voice freed from the pull of gravity has been heard on earth. The spacemen will be interviewed by Major General Artemus T. Recoil on the well-loved program 'Town Meeting of the Upper Air.'

"I predict: that because of SPCA and the Army's Operation Space, the whole course of human destiny will be abruptly changed, and that the age-old vision of peace is now on the way to becoming a reality."

Ed finished and went into his commercial, which consisted of digging a piece of beef gristle out of his teeth with dental floss.

I rubbed out my cigarette and walked back toward my cell. In the studio next to ours, "The Bee" was on the air, and I paused for a while to watch. "The Bee" was a program sponsored by the Larry Cross Pollination Company, aimed principally at big orchardists and growers—or rather at their wives. It was an interminable mystery-thriller sort of thing, with a character called the Bee, who always wore a green hood with two long black feelers. Standing there in the aisle of the plane, looking into the glass-enclosed studio, I could see the Bee about to strangle a red-haired girl in slinky pajamas. This was America's pollination hour, an old standby, answer to the housewife's dream. The Larry Cross outfit was immensely rich. I think they probably handled better than eighty per cent of all fertilization in the country. Bees, as I have said, had become extinct, thanks to the massive doses of chemicals, and of course this had at first posed a serious agricultural problem, as vast areas were without natural pollination. The answer came when the Larry Cross firm was organized, with the slogan "We Carry the Torch for Nature." The business mushroomed, and branch offices sprang up all over the nation. During blossom time, field crews of highly trained men fanned out and pollinized everything by hand—a huge job and an arduous one. The only honey in the United States was synthetic—a blend of mineral oil and papaya juice. Ann hated it with a morbid passion.

When I reached my studio I found everybody getting ready for the warmup. The Town Crier, in his fusty costume, stood holding his bell by the clapper, while the makeup man touched up his face for him. Mrs. Gill, the S.O.M. representative, sat gazing contemptuously at young Tollip. I had riffled through her script earlier, curious to find out what kind of punch she was going to throw. It was about what I expected. Her last paragraph contained the suggestion that all persons who advocated a revision of the Charter of the United Nations be automatically deprived of their citizenship. "If these well-meaning but misguided persons," ran the script, "with their utopian plans for selling this nation down the river are so anxious to acquire world citizenship, I say let's make it easy for them—let's take away the citizenship they've already got and see how they like it. As a lineal descendant of one of the Sons of Original Matrons, I am sick and tired of these cuckoo notions of one world, which come dangerously close to simple treachery. We've enough to do right here at home without . . ."

And so on. In my mind's ear I could already hear the moderator's salutary and impartial voice saying, "Thank you, Mrs. Florence Gill."

At five past eleven, the Crier rang his bell. "Hear ye! See ye! Town

Meetin' today! Listen to both sides and make up your own minds!" Then George Cahill, the moderator, started the ball rolling.

I glanced at Tollip. He looked as though his stomach were filling up with gas. As the program got under way, my own stomach began to inflate, too, the way it often did a few hours after breakfast. I remember very little of the early minutes of that morning's Town Meeting. I recall that the U.N. man spoke first, then Mrs. Gill, then Tollip (who looked perfectly awful). Finally the moderator introduced General Recoil, whose stomach enjoyed the steadying effects of whiskey and who spoke in a loud, slow, confident voice, turning frequently to smile down on the three other guests.

"We in the Army," began the General, "don't pretend that we know all the answers to these brave and wonderful questions. It is not the Army's business to know whether aggression is going to occur or not. Our business is to put on a good show if it *does* occur. The Army is content to leave to the United Nations and to idealists like Mr. Tollip the troublesome details of political progress. I certainly don't know, ladies and gentlemen, whether the fear of retaliation is going to prevent aggression, but I *do* know that there is no moss growing on we of Operation Space. As for myself, I guess I am what you might call a retaliatin' fool. [Laughter in the upper air.] Our enemy is well aware that we are now in a most unusual position to retaliate. That knowledge on the part of our enemy is, in my humble opinion, a deterrent to aggression. If I didn't believe that, I'd shed this uniform and get into a really well-paid line of work, like professional baseball."

Will this plane never quit circling? (I thought). Will the words never quit going round and round? Is there no end to this noisy carrousel of indigestible ideas? Will no one ever catch the brass ring?

"But essentially," continued the General, "our job is not to deal with the theoretical world of Mr. Tollip, who suggests that we merge in some vast superstate with every Tom, Dick, and Harry, no matter what their color or race or how underprivileged they are, thus pulling down our standard of living to the level of the lowest common denominator. Our job is not to deal with the diplomatic world of Mr. Buxton, who hopes to find a peaceful solution around a conference table. No, the Army must face the world as it is. We know the enemy is strong. In our dumb way, we think it is just horse sense for us to be stronger. And I'm proud, believe me, ladies and gentlemen, proud to be at one end of the interplanetary conversation that is about to take place on this very, *very* historic morning. The achievement of the United States Army in establishing the space platform—which is literally a man-made planet—is unparalleled in military history. We have led the way into space. We have given Old Lady Gravity the slip. We have got there, and we have got there fustest with the mostest. [Applause.]

"I can state without qualification that the New Weapon, in the capable hands of the men stationed on our platform, brings the *entire* globe under our dominion. We can pinpoint any spot, anywhere, and sprinkle it with our particular brand of thunder. Mr. Moderator, I'm ready for this interview if the boys out there in space are ready."

Everyone suspected that there might be a slipup in the proceedings at this point, that the mechanical difficulties might prove insuperable. I glanced at the studio clock. The red sweep hand was within a few jumps of eleven-thirty—the General had managed his timing all right. Cahill's face was tenser than I had ever seen it before. Because of the advance buildup, a collapse at this moment would put him in a nasty hole, even for an old experienced m.c. But at exactly eleven-thirty the interview started, smooth as silk. Cahill picked it up from the General.

"And now, watchers of television everywhere, you will hear a conversation between Major General Artemus T. Recoil, who pioneered Operation Space, and two United States Army officers on the platform—Major James Obblington, formerly of Brooklyn, New York, now of Space, and Lieutenant Noble Trett, formerly of Sioux City, Iowa, now of Space. Go ahead, General Recoil!"

"Come in, Space!" said the General, his tonsils struggling in whiskey's undertow, his eyes bearing down hard on the script. "Can you hear me, Major Obblington and Lieutenant Trett?"

"I hear you," said a voice. "This is Trett." The voice, as I remember it, astonished me because of a certain laconic quality that I had not expected. I believe it astonished everyone. Trett's voice was cool, and he sounded as though he were right in the studio.

"Lieutenant Trett," continued the General, "tell the listeners here on earth, tell us, in your position far out there in free space, do you feel the pull of gravity?"

"No, sir, I don't," answered Trett. In spite of the "sir," Trett sounded curiously listless, almost insubordinate.

"Yet you are perfectly comfortable, sitting there on the platform, with the whole of earth spread out before you like a vast target?"

"Sure I'm comfortable."

The General waited a second, as though expecting amplification, but it failed to come. "Well, ah, how's the weather up there?" he asked heartily.

"There isn't any," said Trett.

"No weather? No weather in space? That's very interesting."

"The hell it is," said Trett. "It's God-damn dull. This place is a dump. Worse than some of the islands in the Pacific."

"Well, I suppose it must get on your nerves a bit. That's all part of the game. Tell us, Lieutenant, what's it like to be actually part of the solar system, with your own private orbit?"

"It's all right, except I'd a damn sight rather get drunk," said Trett.

I looked at Cahill. He was swallowing his spit. General Recoil took a new hold on his script.

"And you say you don't feel the pull of gravity, not even a little?"

"I just told you I didn't feel any pull," said Trett. His voice now had a surly quality.

"Well, ah," continued the General, who was beginning to tremble, "can you describe, briefly, for the television audience—" But it was at this point that Trett, on the platform, seemed to lose interest in talking with General Recoil and started chinning with Major Obblington, his sidekick in space.

At first the three voices clashed and blurred, but the General, on a signal from the moderator, quit talking, and the conversation that ensued between Trett and Obblington was audible and clear. Millions of listeners must have heard the dialogue.

"Hey, Obie," said Trett, "you want to know something else I don't feel the pull of, besides gravity?"

"What?" asked his companion.

"Conscience," said Trett cheerfully. "I don't feel my conscience pulling me around."

"Neither do I," said Obblington. "I ought to feel some pulls but I don't."

"I also don't feel the pull of duty."

"Check," said Obblington.

"And what is even more fantastic, I don't feel the pull of dames."

Cahill made a sign to the General. Stunned and confused by the turn things had taken, Recoil tried to pick up the interview and get it back on the track. "Lieutenant Trett," he commanded, "you will limit your remarks to the—"

Cahill waved him quiet. The next voice was the Major's.

"Jesus, now that you mention it, I don't feel the pull of dames either! Hey, Lieutenant—you suppose gravity has anything to do with sex?"

"God damn if *I* know," replied Trett. "I know I don't *weigh* anything, and when you don't weigh anything, you don't seem to *want* anything."

The studio by this time was paralyzed with attention. The General's face was swollen, his mouth was half open, and he struggled for speech that wouldn't come.

Then Trett's cool, even voice again: "See that continent down there, Obie? That's where old Fatso Recoil lives. You feel drawn toward that continent in any special way?"

"Naa," said Obblington.

"You feel like doing a little shooting, Obie?"

"You're rootin' tootin' I feel like shootin'."

"Then what are we waiting for?"

I am, of course, reconstructing this conversation from memory. I am trying to report it faithfully. When Trett said the words "Then what are we waiting for?" I quit listening and dashed for the phones in the corridor. As I was leaving the studio, I turned for a split second and looked back. The General had partially recovered his power of speech. He was mumbling something to Cahill. I caught the words "phone" and "Defense Department."

The corridor was already jammed. I had only one idea in my head—to speak to Ann. Pete Everhardt pushed past me. He said crisply, "This is it." I nodded. Then I glanced out of a window. High in the east a crazy ribbon of light was spreading upward. Lower down, in a terrible parabola, another streak began burning through. The first blast was felt only slightly in the plane. It must have been at a great distance. It was followed immediately by two more. I saw a piece of wing break up, saw one of the starboard engines shake itself loose from its fastenings and fall. Near the phone booths, the

Bee, still in costume, fumbled awkwardly for a parachute. In the crush one of his feelers brushed my face. I never managed to reach a phone. All sorts of things flashed through my mind. I saw Ann and the children, their heads in diapers. I saw again the man in the leather cap, loading bedsprings. I heard again Pete's words, "This is it," only I seemed to hear them in translation: "Until the whole wide world to nothingness do sink." (How durable the poets are!) As I say, I never managed the phone call. My last memory of the morning is of myriads of bright points of destruction where the Weapon was arriving, each pyre in the characteristic shape of an artichoke. Then a great gash, and the plane tumbling. Then I lost consciousness.

I cannnot say how many minutes or hours after that the earth finally broke up. I do not know. There is, of course, a mild irony in the fact that it was the United States that was responsible. Insofar as it can be said of any country that it had human attributes, the United States was well-meaning. Of that I am convinced. Even I, at this date and at this distance, cannot forget my country's great heart and matchless ingenuity. I can't in honesty say that I believe we were wrong to send the men to the platform—it's just that in any matter involving love, or high explosives, one can never foresee all the factors. Certainly I can't say with any assurance that Tollip's theory was right; it seems hardly likely that anyone who suffered so from stomach gas could have been on the right track. I did feel sympathetic toward some of his ideas, perhaps because I suffered from flatulence myself. Anyway, it was inevitable that it should have been the United States that developed the space platform and the new weapon that made the H-bomb obsolete. It was inevitable that what happened, at last, was conceived in good will.

Those times—those last days of earth! I think about them a lot. A sort of creeping ineptitude had set in. Almost everything in life seemed wrong to me, somehow, as though we were all hustling down a blind alley. Many of my friends seemed mentally confused, emotionally unstable, and I have an idea I seemed the same to them. In the big cities, horns blew before the light changed, and it was clear that motorists no longer had the capacity to endure the restrictions they had placed on their own behavior. When the birds became extinct (all but the whooping crane), I was reasonably sure that human beings were on the way out, too. The cranes survived only because of their dance—which showmen were quick to exploit. (Every sanctuary had its television transmitter, and the love dance became a more popular spectacle than heavyweight prizefighting.) Birds had always been the symbol of freedom. As soon as I realized that they were gone, I felt that the significance had gone from my own affairs. (I was a cranky man, though—I must remember that, too—and am not trying here to suggest anything beyond a rather strong personal sadness at all this.)

Those last days! There were so many religions in conflict, each ready to save the world with its own dogma, each perfectly intolerant of the other. Every day seemed a mere skirmish in the long holy war. It was a time of debauch and conversion. Every week the national picture magazines, as though atoning for past excesses, hid their cheesecake carefully away among four-color reproductions of the saints. Television was the universal peep-show—in homes, schools, churches, bars, stores, everywhere. Children early formed the habit of gaining all their images at second hand, by looking at a screen; they grew up believing that anything perceived directly was vaguely fraudulent. Only what had been touched with electronics was valid and real. I think the decline in the importance of direct images dated from the year television managed to catch an eclipse of the moon. After that, nobody ever looked at the sky, and it was as though the moon had joined the shabby company of buskers. There was really never a moment when a child, or even a man, felt free to look away from the television screen—for fear he might miss the one clue that would explain everything.

In many respects I like the planet I'm on. The people here have no urgencies, no capacity for sustained endeavor, but merely tackle things by fits and starts, leaving undone whatever fails to hold their interest, and so, by witlessness and improvidence, escape many of the errors of accomplishment. I like the apples here better than those on earth. They are often wormy, but with a most wonderful flavor. There is a saying here: "Even a very lazy man can eat around a worm."

But I would be lying if I said I didn't miss that other life, I loved it so.

ARTIFICIAL INTELLIGENCE?

CARL SAGAN

Carl Sagan (born 1934) is a Renaissance man of the scientific age: astronomer, astrophysicist, exobiologist, geneticist, teacher, writer, and humanist. As an undergraduate at the University of Chicago, Sagan earned both a B.A. (1954) and a B.S. (1955), and worked in the laboratory of Nobel Prize-winning geneticist Hermann J. Muller at Indiana University. He returned to the University of Chicago on a National Science Fellowship, completing his M.S. in physics in 1956 and, not yet 26, his Ph.D. in astronomy and astrophysics in 1960.

While doing postdoctoral work at the Institute for Basic Research at Berkeley, he wrote a Science *article (March 24, 1961) analyzing existing data on Venus; in 1967 some of his inferences were borne out by the Soviet Venera IV data. In 1962 he was appointed to the Smithsonian Astrophysical Observatory, and he taught genetics at Stanford, where he worked with Nobel Prize winner Joshua Lederberg on research into the development of life on earth. He then taught astronomy at Harvard until 1968. In the years 1968–1970 Sagan and his colleagues were the first to create amino acids, the building blocks of protein, in the laboratory.*

Since 1968 he has been a professor of astronomy and space sciences at Cornell, where he is also the director of the Laboratory for Planetary Studies. In 1968 he was Oregon's Condon lecturer (an honor previously awarded J. Robert Oppenheimer, among others), and in 1970 he won NASA's Apollo Achievement Award. His theories on Mars (Na-

tional Geographic, *December 1967) were substantiated by the 1971 Mars Mariner data, and in 1972 he received the NASA medal for exceptional scientific achievement. He also worked on the Viking project.*

A prolific writer of professional papers and journal articles, he has been editor of Icarus, *an international journal of astronomy, since 1968. He also writes for the lay audience (in the* Encyclopaedia Britannica *and* Encyclopedia Americana, *among others), and his books include* Intelligent Life in the Universe *(with I. S. Shklovsky, 1966);* The Cosmic Connection *(1973), for which he received the Campbell Award for best science book;* Mars and the Mind of Man *(1973);* Dragons of Eden *(1977); and* Broca's Brain *(1979), from which we reprint Chapter 20.*

In Defense of Robots

Thou com'st in such a questionable shape
　That I will speak to thee . . .
William Shakespeare, Hamlet, Act 1, Scene 4

The word "robot," first introduced by the Czech writer Karel Čapek, is derived from the Slavic root for "worker." But it signifies a machine rather than a human worker. Robots, especially robots in space, have often received derogatory notices in the press. We read that a human being was necessary to make the terminal landing adjustments on Apollo 11, without which the first manned lunar landing would have ended in disaster; that a mobile robot on the Martian surface could never be as clever as astronauts in selecting samples to be returned to Earth-bound geologists; and that machines could never have repaired, as men did, the Skylab sunshade, so vital for the continuance of the Skylab mission.

But all these comparisons turn out, naturally enough, to have been written by humans. I wonder if a small self-congratulatory element, a whiff of human chauvinism, has not crept into these judgments. Just as whites can sometimes detect racism and men can occasionally discern sexism, I wonder whether we cannot here glimpse some comparable affliction of the human spirit—a disease that as yet has no name. The word "anthropocentrism" does not mean quite the same thing. The word "humanism" has been preempted by other and more benign activities of our kind. From the analogy with sexism and racism I suppose the name for this malady is "speciesism"—the prejudice that there are no beings so fine, so capable, so reliable as human beings.

This is a prejudice because it is, at the very least, a prejudgment, a conclusion drawn before all the facts are in. Such comparisons of men and machines in space are comparisons of smart men and dumb machines. We have not asked what sorts of machines could have been built for the $30-or-so billion that the Apollo and Skylab missions cost.

Each human being is a superbly constructed, astonishingly compact, self-ambulatory computer—capable on occasion of independent decision making and real control of his or her environment. And, as the old joke goes, these computers can be constructed by unskilled labor. But there are serious limitations to employing human beings in certain environments. Without a great deal of protection, human beings would be inconvenienced on the ocean floor, the surface of Venus, the deep interior of Jupiter, or even on long space missions. Perhaps the only interesting result of Skylab that could not have been obtained by machines is that human beings in space for a period of months undergo a serious loss of bone calcium and phosphorus—which seems to imply that human beings may be incapacitated under 0 g for missions of six to nine months or longer. But the minimum interplanetary voyages have characteristic times of a year or two. Because we value human beings highly, we are reluctant to send them on very risky missions. If we do send human beings to exotic environments, we must also send along their food, their air, their water, amenities for entertainment and waste recycling, and companions. By comparison, machines require no elaborate life-support systems, no entertainment, no companionship, and we do not yet feel any strong ethical prohibitions against sending machines on one-way, or suicide, missions.

Certainly, for simple missions, machines have proved themselves many times over. Unmanned vehicles have performed the first photography of the whole Earth and of the far side of the Moon; the first landings on the Moon, Mars and Venus; and the first thorough orbital reconnaissance of another planet, in the Mariner 9 and Viking missions to Mars. Here on Earth it is increasingly common for high-technology manufacturing—for example, chemical and pharmaceutical plants—to be performed largely or entirely under computer control. In all these activities machines are able, to some extent, to sense errors, to correct mistakes, to alert human controllers some great distance away about perceived problems.

The powerful abilities of computing machines to do arithmetic—hundreds of millions of times faster than unaided human beings—are legendary. But what about really difficult matters? Can machines in any sense think through a new problem? Can they make discussions of the branched-contingency tree variety which we think of as characteristically human? (That is, I ask Question 1; if the answer is A, I ask Question 2; but if the answer is B, I ask Question 3; and so on.) Some decades ago the English mathematician A. M. Turing described what would be necessary for him to believe in machine intelligence. The condition was simply that he could be in teletype communication with a machine and be unable to tell that it was not a human being. Turing imagined a conversation between a man and a machine of the following quality:

> *Interrogator:* In the first line of your sonnet which reads "Shall I compare thee to a Summer's day," would not "a Spring day" do as well or better?
>
> *Witness:* It wouldn't scan.
>
> *Interrogator:* How about "a Winter's day"? That would scan all right.
>
> *Witness:* Yes, but nobody wants to be compared to a Winter's day.

> *Interrogator:* Would you say Mr. Pickwick reminded you of Christmas?
> *Witness:* In a way.
> *Interrogator:* Yet Christmas is a Winter's day, and I do not think Mr. Pickwick would mind the comparison.
> *Witness:* I don't think you're serious. By a Winter's day one means a typical Winter's day, rather than a special one like Christmas.

No device of this sophistication has yet been built, although I am not sure how many humans would pass Turing's human test. But the amount of effort and money put into artificial intelligence has been quite limited, and there are only about a half-dozen major centers of such activity in the world. One of the more striking results obtained in a very limited universe of discourse—that of children's blocks—has come from the work of Terry Winograd, then at the Massachusetts Institute of Technology. Here is a dialogue between man and machine, the machine having been programmed by Winograd:

> *Q:* What does the box contain?
> *A:* The blue pyramid and the blue box.
> *Q:* How many blocks are not in the box?
> *A:* Four of them.
> *Q:* Is at least one of them narrower than the one which I told you to pick up?
> *A:* Yes, the red cube.
> *Q:* Is there a steeple?
> *A:* Sorry, I don't know the word "steeple."
> *Q:* A steeple is a stack which contains two green cubes and a pyramid, for example.
> *A:* I understand.
> *Q:* Are there any steeples now?
> *A:* No.
> *Q:* Build one.

The machine does. It reaches out its mechanical hand, moves the cubes and builds the structure that has just been described.

> *Q:* When did you pick up the pyramid?
> *A:* While I was stacking up the red cube, the large red block and the large green cube.
> *Q:* Why?
> *A:* To get rid of it.
> *Q:* Why did you clear off that cube?
> *A:* To put it on the large green cube.

As another example, a machine psychiatrist has been developed by Joseph Weizenbaum, also at MIT. This is a much simpler program than Winograd's, since it involves nondirective psychotherapy, which, generally speaking, requires extremely simple-minded computer programs. Here is a striking dialogue between a human being and a computer psychotherapist. (There is certainly a selection effect here. Many other such machine/human psychiatric dialogues are not nearly so striking. But I suppose most human/human psychiatric dialogues are not very striking either.) In this interaction, in order to spell out clearly the respective roles of therapist and patient, the computer therapist types upper case while the patient types lower case:

> men are all alike
> IN WHAT WAY
> they're always bugging us about something or other
> CAN YOU THINK OF A SPECIFIC EXAMPLE
> well, my boy friend made me come here
> YOUR BOY FRIEND MADE YOU COME HERE
> he noticed that i'm depressed much of the time
> I AM SORRY TO HEAR YOU ARE DEPRESSED
> he's right. i am unhappy
> DO YOU THINK COMING HERE WILL HELP YOU NOT TO BE
> UNHAPPY
> i need some help, that much is clear
> WHAT WOULD IT MEAN TO YOU IF YOU GOT SOME HELP
> perhaps i could learn to get along with my mother
> TELL ME MORE ABOUT YOUR FAMILY
> my mother takes care of me
> WHO ELSE IN YOUR FAMILY TAKES CARE OF YOU
> my father
> YOUR FATHER
> you are like my father in some ways
> WHAT RESEMBLANCE DO YOU SEE
> you are not very aggressive, but i don't think you want me to notice that
> WHAT MAKES YOU THINK I AM NOT VERY AGGRESSIVE
> you don't argue with me
> WHY DO YOU THINK I DON'T ARGUE WITH YOU
> you are afraid of me
> DOES IT PLEASE YOU TO BELIEVE I AM AFRAID OF YOU
> it pleases my father to think i am afraid of him
> WHAT ELSE COMES TO MIND WHEN YOU THINK OF YOUR
> FATHER
> bullies
> DOES THAT HAVE ANYTHING TO DO WITH THE FACT THAT
> YOUR BOY FRIEND MADE YOU COME HERE

This astonishing—one is very tempted to say "perceptive"—response from the computer is, of course, preprogrammed. But, then, so are the responses of human psychotherapists. In a time when more and more people in our society seem to be in need of psychiatric counseling, and when time-sharing of computers is widespread, I can even imagine the development of a network of computer psychotherapeutic terminals, something like arrays of large telephone booths, in which, for a few dollars a session, we are able to talk to an attentive, tested and largely nondirective psychotherapist. Ensuring the confidentiality of the psychiatric dialogue is one of several important steps still to be worked out.

Another sign of the intellectual accomplishments of machines is in games. Even exceptionally simple computers—those that can be wired by a bright ten-year-old—can be programmed to play perfect tic-tac-toe. Some computers can play world-class checkers. Chess is of course a much more complicated game than tic-tac-toe or checkers. Here programming a machine to win is more difficult, and novel strategies have been used, including several rather successful attempts to have a computer learn from its own experience in playing previous chess games. Computers can learn, for example, empirically the rule that it is better in the beginning game to control the center of the chessboard than the periphery. The ten best chess players in the world still have nothing to fear from any present computer. But the situation is changing. Recently a computer for the first time did well enough to enter the Minnesota State Chess Open. This may be the first time that a nonhuman has entered a major sporting event on the planet Earth (and I cannot help but wonder if robot golfers and designated hitters may be attempted sometime in the next decade, to say nothing of dolphins in free-style competition.) The computer did not win the Chess Open, but this is the first time one has done well enough to enter such a competition. Chess-playing computers are improving extremely rapidly.

I have heard machines demeaned (often with a just audible sigh of relief) for the fact that chess is an area where human beings are still superior. This reminds me very much of the old joke in which a stranger remarks with wonder on the accomplishments of a checker-playing dog. The dog's owner replies, "Oh, it's not all that remarkable. He loses two games out of three." A machine that plays chess in the middle range of human expertise is a very capable machine; even if there are thousands of better human chess players, there are millions who are worse. To play chess requires strategy, foresight, analytical powers, and the ability to cross-correlate large numbers of variables and to learn from experience. These are excellent qualities in those whose job it is to discover and explore, as well as those who watch the baby and walk the dog.

With this as a more or less representative set of examples of the state of development of machine intelligence, I think it is clear that a major effort over the next decade could produce much more sophisticated examples. This is also the opinion of most of the workers in machine intelligence.

In thinking about this next generation of machine intelligence, it is important to distinguish between self-controlled and remotely controlled robots. A self-controlled robot has its intelligence within it; a remotely controlled robot has its intelligence at some other place, and its successful operation depends upon close communication between its central computer and itself. There are, of course, intermediate cases where the machine may be partly self-activated and partly remotely controlled. It is this mix of remote and *in situ* control that seems to offer the highest efficiency for the near future.

For example, we can imagine a machine designed for the mining of the ocean floor. There are enormous quantities of manganese nodules littering the abyssal depths. They were once thought to have been produced by meteorite infall on Earth, but are now believed to be formed occasionally in vast manganese fountains produced by the internal tectonic activity of the Earth. Many other scarce and industrially valuable minerals are likewise to be found on the deep ocean bottom. We have the capability today to design devices that systematically swim over or crawl upon the ocean floor; that are able to perform spectrometric and other chemical examinations of the surface material; that can automatically radio back to ship or land all findings; and that can mark the locales of especially valuable deposits—for example, by low-frequency radio-homing devices. The radio beacon will then direct great mining machines to the appropriate locales. The present state of the art in deep-sea submersibles and in spacecraft environmental sensors is clearly compatible with the development of such devices. Similar remarks can be made for off-shore oil drilling, for coal and other subterranean mineral mining, and so on. The likely economic returns from such devices would pay not only for their development, but for the entire space program many times over.

When the machines are faced with particularly difficult situations, they can be programmed to recognize that the situations are beyond their abilities and to inquire of human operators—working in safe and pleasant environments—what to do next. The examples just given are of devices that are largely self-controlled. The reverse also is possible, and a great deal of very preliminary work along these lines has been performed in the remote handling of highly radioactive materials in laboratories of the U.S. Department of Energy. Here I imagine a human being who is connected by radio link with a mobile machine. The operator is in Manila, say; the machine in the Mindanao Deep. The operator is attached to an array of electronic relays, which transmits and amplifies his movements to the machine and which can, conversely, carry what the machine finds back to his senses. So when the operator turns his head to the left, the television cameras on the machine turn left, and the operator sees on a great hemispherical television screen around him the scene the machine's searchlights and cameras have revealed. When the operator in Manila takes a few strides forward in his wired suit, the machine in the abyssal depths ambles a few feet forward. When the operator reaches out his hand, the mechanical arm of the machine likewise extends itself; and the precision of the man/machine interaction is such that precise manipulation of material at the ocean bottom by the machine's fingers is possible. With such devices, human beings can enter environments otherwise closed to them forever.

In the exploration of Mars, unmanned vehicles have already soft-landed, and only a little further in the future they will roam about the surface of the Red Planet, as some now do on the Moon. We are not ready for a manned mission to Mars. Some of us are concerned about such missions because of the dangers of carrying terrestrial microbes to Mars, and Martian microbes, if they exist, to Earth, but also because of their enormous expense. The Viking landers deposited on Mars in the summer of 1976 have a very interesting array of sensors and scientific instruments, which are the extension of human senses to an alien environment.

The obvious post-Viking device for Martian exploration, one which takes advantage of the Viking technology, is a Viking Rover in which the equivalent of an entire Viking spacecraft, but with considerably improved science, is put on wheels or tractor treads and permitted to rove slowly over the Martian landscape. But now we come to a new problem, one that is never encountered in machine operation on the Earth's surface. Although Mars is the second closest planet, it is so far from the Earth that the light travel time becomes significant. At a typical relative position of Mars and the Earth, the planet is 20 light-minutes away. Thus, if the spacecraft were confronted with a steep incline, it might send a message of inquiry back to Earth. Forty minutes later the response would arrive saying something like "For heaven's sake, stand dead still." But by then, of course, an unsophisticated machine would have tumbled into the gully. Consequently, any Martian Rover requires slope and roughness sensors. Fortunately, these are readily available and are even seen in some children's toys. When confronted with a precipitous slope or large boulder, the spacecraft would either stop until receiving instructions from the Earth in response to its query (and televised picture of the terrain), or back off and start in another and safer direction.

Much more elaborate contingency decision networks can be built into the onboard computers of spacecraft of the 1980s. For more remote objectives, to be explored further in the future, we can imagine human controllers in orbit around the target planet, or on one of its moons. In the exploration of Jupiter, for example, I can imagine the operators on a small moon outside the fierce Jovian radiation belts, controlling with only a few seconds' delay the responses of a spacecraft floating in the dense Jovian clouds.

Human beings on Earth can also be in such an interaction loop, if they are willing to spend some time on the enterprise. If every decision in Martian exploration must be fed through a human controller on Earth, the Rover can traverse only a few feet an hour. But the lifetimes of such Rovers are so long that a few feet an hour represents a perfectly respectable rate of progress. However, as we imagine expeditions into the farthest reaches of the solar system—and ultimately to the stars—it is clear that self-controlled machine intelligence will assume heavier burdens of responsibility.

In the development of such machines we find a kind of convergent evolution. Viking is, in a curious sense, like some great outsized, clumsily constructed insect. It is not yet ambulatory, and it is certainly incapable of self-reproduction. But it has an exoskeleton, it has a wide range of insectlike sensory organs, and it is about as intelligent as a dragonfly. But Viking has an advantage that insects do not: it can, on occasion, by inquiring of its controllers on Earth, assume the intelligence of a human being—the controllers are able to reprogram the Viking computer on the basis of decisions they make.

As the field of machine intelligence advances and as increasingly distant objects in the solar system become accessible to exploration, we will see the development of increasingly sophisticated onboard computers, slowly climbing the phylogenetic tree from insect intelligence to crocodile intelligence to squirrel intelligence and—in the not very remote future, I think—to dog intelligence. Any flight to the outer solar system must have a computer capable of determining whether it is working properly. There is no possibility of sending to the Earth for a repairman. The machine must be able to sense when it is sick and skillfully doctor its own illnesses. A computer is needed that is able either to fix or replace failed computer, sensor or structural components. Such a computer, which has been called STAR (self-testing and repairing computer), is on the threshold of development. It employs redundant components, as biology does—we have two lungs and two kidneys partly because each is protection against failure of the other. But a computer can be much more redundant than a human being, who has, for example, but one head and one heart.

Because of the weight premium on deep space exploratory ventures, there will be strong pressures for continued miniaturization of intelligent machines. It is clear that remarkable miniaturization has already occurred: vacuum tubes have been replaced by transistors, wired circuits by printed circuit boards, and entire computer systems by silicon-chip microcircuitry. Today a circuit that used to occupy much of a 1930 radio set can be printed on the tip of a pin. If intelligent machines for terrestrial mining and space exploratory applications are pursued, the time cannot be far off when household and other domestic robots will become commercially feasible. Unlike the classical anthropoid robots of science fiction, there is no reason for such machines to look any more human than a vacuum cleaner does. They will be specialized for their functions. But there are many common tasks, ranging from bartending to floor washing, that involve a very limited array of intellectual capabilities, albeit substantial stamina and patience. All-purpose ambulatory household robots, which perform domestic functions as well as a proper nineteenth-century English butler, are probably many decades off. But more specialized machines, each adapted to a specific household function, are probably already on the horizon.

It is possible to imagine many other civic tasks and essential functions of everyday life carried out by intelligent machines. By the early 1970s, garbage collectors in Anchorage, Alaska, and other cities won wage settlements guaranteeing them salaries of about $20,000 per annum. It is possible that the economic pressures alone may make a persuasive case for the development of automated garbage-collecting machines. For the development of domestic and civic robots to be a general civic good, the effective re-employment of those human beings displaced by the robots must, of course, be arranged; but over a human generation that should not be too difficult—particularly if there are enlightened educational reforms. Human beings enjoy learning.

We appear to be on the verge of developing a wide variety of intelligent machines capable of performing tasks too dangerous, too expensive, too onerous or too boring for human beings. The development of such machines is, in my mind, one of the few legitimate "spin-offs" of the space program. The efficient exploitation of energy in agriculture—upon which our survival as a species depends—may even be contingent on the development of such machines. The main obstacle seems to be a very human problem, the quiet feeling that comes stealthily and unbidden, and argues that there is something threatening or "inhuman" about machines performing certain tasks as well as or better than human beings; or a sense of loathing for creatures made of silicon and germanium rather than proteins and nucleic acids. But in many respects our survival as a species depends on our transcending such primitive chauvinisms. In part, our adjustment to intelligent machines is a matter of acclimatization. There are already cardiac pacemakers that can sense the beat of the human heart; only when there is the slightest hint of fibrillation does the pacemaker stimulate the heart. This is a mild but very useful sort of machine intelligence. I cannot imagine the wearer of this device resenting its intelligence. I think in a relatively short period of time there will be a very similar sort of acceptance for much more intelligent and sophisticated machines. There is nothing inhuman about an intelligent machine; it is indeed an expression of those superb intellectual capabilities that only human beings, of all the creatures on our planet, now possess.

JOSEPH WEIZENBAUM

Joseph Weizenbaum is a scientist and engineer who has spent most of his adult life studying artificial intelligence, the structure of computer language, the understanding of natural language by computers, and the social implications of these studies. He was born in Berlin in 1923 but has subsequently become a citizen of the United States. Educated at Wayne University, where he earned his M.S. in 1950, he worked as a systems engineer for General Electric before joining the faculty of the Massachusetts Institute of Technology in 1963. Since 1970 he has been Professor of Computer Science. His major publication that is available to nonspecialists is his book Computer Power and Human Reason *(1976), which, he says, contains two major arguments: "first, that there is a difference between man and machine, and, second, that there are certain tasks which computers* ought not *be made to do, independent of whether computers* can *be made to do them." The book's Introduction is reprinted below.*

Introduction to *Computer Power and Human Reason*

In 1935, Michael Polanyi, then holder of the Chair of Physical Chemistry at the Victoria University of Manchester, England, was suddenly shocked into a confrontation with philosophical questions that have ever since dominated his life. The shock was administered by Nicolai Bukharin, one of the leading theoreticians of the Russian Communist party, who told Polanyi that "under socialism the conception of science pursued for its own sake would disappear, for the interests of scientists would spontaneously turn to the problems of the current Five Year Plan." Polanyi sensed then that "the scientific outlook appeared to have produced a mechanical conception of man and history in which there was no place for science itself." And further that "this conception denied altogether any intrinsic power to thought and thus denied any grounds for claiming freedom of thought."[1]

I don't know how much time Polanyi thought he would devote to developing an argument for a contrary concept of man and history. His very shock testifies to the fact that he was in profound disagreement with Bukharin, therefore that he already conceived of man differently, even if he could not then give explicit form to his concept. It may be that he determined to write a counterargument to Bukharin's position, drawing only on his own experience as a scientist, and to have done with it in short order. As it turned out, however, the confrontation with philosophy triggered by Bukharin's revelation was to demand Polanyi's entire attention from then to the present day.

I recite this bit of history for two reasons. The first is to illustrate that ideas which seem at first glance to be obvious and simple, and which ought therefore to be universally credible once they have been articulated, are sometimes buoys marking out stormy channels in deep intellectual seas. That science is creative, that the creative act in science is equivalent to the creative act in art, that creation springs only from autonomous individuals, is such a simple and, one might think, obvious idea. Yet Polanyi has, as have many others, spent nearly a lifetime exploring the ground in which it is anchored and the turbulent sea of implications which surrounds it.

The second reason I recite this history is that I feel myself to be reliving part of it. My own shock was administered not by any important political figure espousing his philosophy of science, but by some people who insisted on misinterpreting a piece of work I had done. I write this without bitterness and certainly not in a defensive mood. Indeed, the interpretations I have in mind tended, if anything, to overrate what little I had accomplished and certainly its importance. No, I recall that piece of work now only because it seems to me to provide the most parsimonious way of identifying the issues I mean to discuss.

The work was done in the period 1964–1966, and was reported in the computer-science literature in January 1966 and August 1967. To summarize it briefly, I composed a computer program with which one could "converse" in English. The human conversationalist partner would type his portion of the conversation on a typewriter connected to a computer, and the computer, under control of my program, would analyze the message that had so been transmitted to it, compose a response to it in English, and cause the response to be typed on the computer's typewriter.

---

[1]M. Polanyi, *The Tacit Dimension* (New York: Doubleday, Anchor ed., 1967), pp. 3–4.

I chose the name ELIZA for the language analysis program because, like the Eliza of Pygmalion fame, it could be taught to "speak" increasingly well. Because conversations must be about something, that is, because they must take place within some context, the program was constructed in a two-tier arrangement, the first tier consisting of the language analyzer and the second of a script. The script is a set of rules rather like those that might be given to an actor who is to use them to improvise around a certain theme. Thus ELIZA could be given a script to enable it to maintain a conversation about cooking eggs or about managing a bank checking account, and so on. Each specific script thus enabled ELIZA to play a specific conversational role.

For my first experiment, I gave ELIZA a script designed to permit it to play (I should really say parody) the role of a Rogerian psychotherapist engaged in an initial interview with a patient. The Rogerian psychotherapist is relatively easy to imitate because much of his technique consists of drawing his patient out by reflecting the patient's statements back to him. The following conversation between a young lady and ELIZA playing doctor illustrates both the Rogerian technique of encouraging a patient to keep talking and the operation of the computer program ELIZA. The first to "speak" is the young lady. The computer's responses are printed entirely in capitals.[2]

Men are all alike.
IN WHAT WAY
They're always bugging us about something or other.
CAN YOU THINK OF A SPECIFIC EXAMPLE
Well, my boyfriend made me come here.
YOUR BOYFRIEND MADE YOU COME HERE
He says I'm depressed much of the time.
I AM SORRY TO HEAR YOU ARE DEPRESSED
It's true. I am unhappy.
DO YOU THINK COMING HERE WILL HELP YOU NOT TO BE UNHAPPY
I need some help, that much seems certain.
WHAT WOULD IT MEAN TO YOU IF YOU GOT SOME HELP
Perhaps I could learn to get along with my mother.
TELL ME MORE ABOUT YOUR FAMILY
My mother takes care of me.
WHO ELSE IN YOUR FAMILY TAKES CARE OF YOU
My father.
YOUR FATHER
You are like my father in some ways.
WHAT RESEMBLANCE DO YOU SEE
You are not very aggressive but I think you don't want me to notice that.

---

[2]This "conversation" is extracted from J. Weizenbaum, "ELIZA—A Computer Program For the Study of Natural Language Communication Between Man and Machine," *Communications of the Association for Computing Machinery*, vol. 9, no. 1 (January 1965), pp. 36–45.

WHAT MAKES YOU THINK I AM NOT VERY AGGRESSIVE
You don't argue with me.
WHY DO YOU THINK I DON'T ARGUE WITH YOU
You are afraid of me.
DOES IT PLEASE YOU TO BELIEVE I AM AFRAID OF YOU
My father is afraid of everybody.
WHAT ELSE COMES TO MIND WHEN YOU THINK OF YOUR
FATHER
Bullies.
DOES THAT HAVE ANYTHING TO DO WITH THE FACT THAT
YOUR BOYFRIEND MADE YOU COME HERE

DOCTOR, as ELIZA playing psychiatrist came to be known, soon became famous around the Massachusetts Institute of Technology, where it first came into existence, mainly because it was an easy program to demonstrate. Most other programs could not vividly demonstrate the information-processing power of a computer to visitors who did not already have some specialized knowledge, say, of some branch of mathematics. DOCTOR, on the other hand, could be appreciated on some level by anyone. Its power as a demonstration vehicle was further enhanced by the fact that the visitor could actually participate in its operation. Soon copies of DOCTOR, constructed on the basis of my published description of it, began appearing at other institutions in the United States. The program became nationally known and even, in certain circles, a national plaything.

The shocks I experienced as DOCTOR became widely known and "played" were due principally to three distinct events.

1. A number of practicing psychiatrists seriously believed the DOCTOR computer program could grow into a nearly completely automatic form of psychotherapy. Colby *et al.* write, for example,

> "Further work must be done before the program will be ready for clinical use. If the method proves beneficial, then it would provide a therapeutic tool which can be made widely available to mental hospitals and psychiatric centers suffering a shortage of therapists. Because of the time-sharing capabilities of modern and future computers, several hundred patients an hour could be handled by a computer system designed for this purpose. The human therapist, involved in the design and operation of this system, would not be replaced, but would become a much more efficient man since his efforts would no longer be limited to the one-to-one patient-therapist ratio as now exists."[3]*

[3]K. M. Colby, J. B. Watt, and J. P. Gilbert, "A Computer Method of Psychotherapy: Preliminary Communication," *The Journal of Nervous and Mental Disease,* vol. 142, no. 2 (1966), pp. 148–152.
*Nor is Dr. Colby alone in his enthusiasm for computer administered psychotherapy. Dr. Carl Sagan, the astrophysicist, recently commented on ELIZA in *Natural History,* vol. LXXXIV, no. 1 (Jan. 1975), p. 10: "No such computer program is adequate for psychiatric use today, but the same can be remarked about some human psychotherapists. In a period when more and more people in our society seem to be in need of psychiatric counseling, and when time sharing of computers is widespread, I can imagine the development of a network of computer psychotherapeutic terminals, something like arrays of large telephone booths, in which, for a few dollars a session, we would be able to talk with an attentive, tested, and largely non-directive psychotherapist."

I had thought it essential, as a prerequisite to the very possibility that one person might help another learn to cope with his emotional problems, that the helper himself participate in the other's experience of those problems and, in large part by way of his own empathic recognition of them, himself come to understand them. There are undoubtedly many techniques to facilitate the therapist's imaginative projection into the patient's inner life. But that it was possible for even one practicing psychiatrist to advocate that this crucial component of the therapeutic process be entirely supplanted by pure technique—*that* I had not imagined! What must a psychiatrist who makes such a suggestion think he is doing while treating a patient, that he can view the simplest mechanical parody of a single interviewing technique as having captured anything of the essence of a human encounter? Perhaps Colby *et al.* give us the required clue when they write;

> "A human therapist can be viewed as an information processor and decision maker with a set of decision rules which are closely linked to short-range and long-range goals, . . . He is guided in these decisions by rough empiric rules telling him what is appropriate to say and not to say in certain contexts. To incorporate these processes, to the degree possessed by a human therapist, in the program would be a considerable undertaking, but we are attempting to move in this direction."[4]

What can the psychiatrist's image of his patient be when he sees himself, as therapist, not as an engaged human being acting as a healer, but as an information processor following rules, etc.?

Such questions were my awakening to what Polanyi had earlier called a "scientific outlook that appeared to have produced a mechanical conception of man."

2. I was startled to see how quickly and how very deeply people conversing with DOCTOR became emotionally involved with the computer and how unequivocally they anthropomorphized it. Once my secretary, who had watched me work on the program for many months and therefore surely knew it to be merely a computer program, started conversing with it. After only a few interchanges with it, she asked me to leave the room. Another time, I suggested I might rig the system so that I could examine all conversations anyone had had with it, say, overnight. I was promptly bombarded with accusations that what I proposed amounted to spying on people's most intimate thoughts; clear evidence that people were conversing with the computer as if it were a person who could be appropriately and usefully addressed in intimate terms. I knew of course that people form all sorts of emotional bonds to machines, for example, to musical instruments, motorcycles, and cars. And I knew from long experience that the strong emotional ties many programmers have to their computers are often formed after only short exposures to their machines. What I had not realized is that extremely short exposures to a relatively simple computer program could induce powerful delusional thinking in quite normal people. This insight led

---

[4] *Ibid.*

me to attach new importance to questions of the relationship between the individual and the computer, and hence to resolve to think about them.

3. Another widespread, and to me surprising, reaction to the ELIZA program was the spread of a belief that it demonstrated a general solution to the problem of computer understanding of natural language. In my paper, I had tried to say that no general solution to that problem was possible, i.e., that language is understood only in contextual frameworks, that even these can be shared by people to only a limited extent, and that consequently even people are not embodiments of any such general solution. But these conclusions were often ignored. In any case, ELIZA was such a small and simple step. Its contribution was, if any at all, only to vividly underline what many others had long ago discovered, namely, the importance of context to language understanding. The subsequent, much more elegant, and surely more important work of Winograd[5] in computer comprehension of English is currently being misinterpreted just as ELIZA was. This reaction to ELIZA showed me more vividly than anything I had seen hitherto the enormously exaggerated attributions an even well-educated audience is capable of making, even strives to make, to a technology it does not understand. Surely, I thought, decisions made by the general public about emergent technologies depend much more on what that public attributes to such technologies than on what they actually are or can and cannot do. If, as appeared to be the case, the public's attributions are wildly misconceived, then public decisions are bound to be misguided and often wrong. Difficult questions arise out of these observations; what, for example, are the scientist's responsibilities with respect to making his work public? And to whom (or what) is the scientist responsible?

As perceptions of these kinds began to reverberate in me, I thought, as perhaps Polanyi did after his encounter with Bukharin, that the questions and misgivings that had so forcefully presented themselves to me could be disposed of quickly, perhaps in a short, serious article. I did in fact write a paper touching on many points mentioned here.[6] But gradually I began to see that certain quite fundamental questions had infected me more chronically than I had first perceived. I shall probably never be rid of them.

There are as many ways to state these basic questions as there are starting points for coping with them. At bottom they are about nothing less than man's place in the universe. But I am professionally trained only in computer science, which is to say (in all seriousness) that I am extremely poorly educated; I can mount neither the competence, nor the courage, not even the chutzpah, to write on the grand scale actually demanded. I therefore grapple with questions that couple more directly to the concerns I have expressed, and hope that their larger implications will emerge spontaneously.

---

[5] T. Winograd, "Procedures As A Representation For Data In A Computer Program For Understanding Natural Language." Ph.D. dissertation submitted to the Dept. of Mathematics (M.I.T.), August 24, 1970.

[6] J. Weizenbaum, "On the Impact of Computers on Society," *Science*, vol. 176, no. 12 (May, 1972).

I shall thus have to concern myself with the following kinds of questions:

1. What is it about the computer that has brought the view of man as a machine to a new level of plausibility? Clearly there have been other machines that imitated man in various ways, e.g., steam shovels. But not until the invention of the digital computer have there been machines that could perform intellectual functions of even modest scope; i.e., machines that could in any sense be said to be intelligent. Now "artificial intelligence" (AI) is a subdiscipline of computer science. This new field will have to be discussed. Ultimately a line dividing human and machine intelligence must be drawn. If there is no such line, then advocates of computerized psychotherapy may be merely heralds of an age in which man has finally been recognized as nothing but a clock-work. Then the consequences of such a reality would need urgently to be divined and contemplated.

2. The fact that individuals bind themselves with strong emotional ties to machines ought not in itself to be surprising. The instruments man uses become, after all, extensions of his body. Most importantly, man must, in order to operate his instruments skillfully, internalize aspects of them in the form of kinesthetic and perceptual habits. In that sense at least, his instruments become literally part of him and modify him, and thus alter the basis of his affective relationship to himself. One would expect man to cathect more intensely to instruments that couple directly to his own intellectual, cognitive, and emotive functions than to machines that merely extend the power of his muscles. Western man's entire milieu is now pervaded by complex technological extensions of his every functional capacity. Being the enormously adaptive animal he is, man has been able to accept as authentically natural (that is, as given by nature) such technological bases for his relationship to himself, for his identity. Perhaps this helps to explain why he does not question the appropriateness of investing his most private feelings in a computer. But then, such an explanation would also suggest that the computing machine represents merely an extreme extrapolation of a much more general technological usurpation of man's capacity to act as an autonomous agent in giving meaning to his world. It is therefore important to inquire into the wider senses in which man has come to yield his own autonomy to a world viewed as machine.

3. It is perhaps paradoxical that just, when in the deepest sense man has ceased to believe in—let alone to trust—his own autonomy, he has begun to rely on autonomous machines, that is, on machines that operate for long periods of time entirely on the basis of their own internal realities. If his reliance on such machines is to be based on something other than unmitigated despair or blind faith, he must explain to himself what these machines do and even how they do what they do. This requires him to build some conception of their internal "realities." Yet most men don't understand computers to even the slightest degree. So, unless they are capable of very great skepticism (the kind we bring to bear while watching a stage magician), they can explain the computer's intellectual feats only by bringing to

bear the single analogy available to them, that is, their model of their own capacity to think. No wonder, then, that they overshoot the mark; it is truly impossible to imagine a human who could imitate ELIZA, for example, but for whom ELIZA's language abilities were his limit. Again, the computing machine is merely an extreme example of a much more general phenomenon. Even the breadth of connotation intended in the ordinary usage of the word "machine," large as it is, is insufficient to suggest its true generality. For today when we speak of, for example, bureaucracy, or the university, or almost any social or political construct, the image we generate is all too often that of an autonomous machine-like process.

These, then, are the thoughts and questions which have refused to leave me since the deeper significances of the reactions to ELIZA I have described began to become clear to me. Yet I doubt that they could have impressed themselves on me as they did were it not that I was (and am still) deeply involved in a concentrate of technological society as a teacher in the temple of technology that is the Massachusetts Institute of Technology, an institution that proudly boasts of being "polarized around science and technology." There I live and work with colleagues, many of whom trust only modern science to deliver reliable knowledge of the world. I confer with them on research proposals to be made to government agencies, especially to the Department of "Defense." Sometimes I become more than a little frightened as I contemplate what we lead ourselves to propose, as well as the nature of the arguments we construct to support our proposals. Then, too, I am constantly confronted by students, some of whom have already rejected all ways but the scientific to come to know the world, and who seek only a deeper, more dogmatic indoctrination in that faith (although that word is no longer in their vocabulary). Other students suspect that not even the entire collection of machines and instruments at M.I.T. can significantly help give meaning to their lives. They sense the presence of a dilemma in an education polarized around science and technology, an education that implicitly claims to open a privileged access-path to fact, but that cannot tell them how to decide what is to count as fact. Even while they recognize the genuine importance of learning their craft, they rebel at working on projects that appear to address themselves neither to answering interesting questions of fact nor to solving problems in theory.

Such confrontations with my own day-to-day social reality have gradually convinced me that my experience with ELIZA was symptomatic of deeper problems. The time would come, I was sure, when I would no longer be able to participate in research proposal conferences, or honestly respond to my students' need for therapy (yes, that is the correct word), without first attempting to make sense of the picture my own experience with computers had so sharply drawn for me.

Of course, the introduction of computers into our already highly technological society has, as I will try to show, merely reinforced and amplified those antecedent pressures that have driven man to an ever more highly rationalistic view of his society and an ever more mechanistic image of himself. It is therefore important that I construct my discussion of the impact of the computer on man and his society so that it can be seen as a particular kind of encoding of a much larger impact, namely, that on man's role in the face of technologies and techniques he may not be able to understand and control. Conversations around that theme have been going on for a long time. And they have intensified in the last few years.

Certain individuals of quite differing minds, temperaments, interests, and training have—however much they differ among themselves and even disagree on many vital questions—over the years expressed grave concern about the conditions created by the unfettered march of science and technology; among them are Mumford, Arendt, Ellul, Roszak, Comfort, and Boulding. The computer began to be mentioned in such discussions only recently. Now there are signs that a full-scale debate about the computer is developing. The contestants on one side are those who, briefly stated, believe computers can, should, and will do everything, and on the other side those who, like myself, believe there are limits to what computers ought to be put to do.

It may appear at first glance that this is an in-house debate of little consequence except to a small group of computer technicians. But at bottom, no matter how it may be disguised by technological jargon, the question is whether or not every aspect of human thought is reducible to a logical formalism, or, to put it into the modern idiom, whether or not human thought is entirely computable. That question has, in one form or another, engaged thinkers in all ages. Man has always striven for principles that could organize and give sense and meaning to his existence. But before modern science fathered the technologies that reified and concretized its otherwise abstract systems, the systems of thought that defined man's place in the universe were fundamentally juridical. They served to define man's obligations to his fellow men and to nature. The Judaic tradition, for example, rests on the idea of a contractual relationship between God and man. This relationship must and does leave room for autonomy for both God and man, for a contract is an agreement willingly entered into by parties who are free not to agree. Man's autonomy and his corresponding responsibility is a central issue of all religious systems. The spiritual cosmologies engendered by modern science, on the other hand, are infected with the germ of logical necessity. They, except in the hands of the wisest scientists and philosophers, no longer content themselves with explanations of appearances, but claim to say how things actually are and must necessarily be. In short, they convert truth to provability.

As one consequence of this drive to modern science, the question, "What aspects of life are formalizable?" has been transformed from the moral question, "How and in what form may man's obligations and responsibilities be known?" to the question, "Of what technological genus is man a species?" Even some philosophers whose every instinct rebels against the idea that man is entirely comprehensible as a machine have succumbed to this spirit

of the times. Hubert Dreyfus, for example, trains the heavy guns of phenomenology on the computer model of man.[7] But he limits his argument to the
technical question of what computers can and cannot do. I would argue that
if computers could imitate man in every respect—which in fact they cannot—even then it would be appropriate, nay, urgent, to examine the computer in the light of man's perennial need to find his place in the world. The
outcomes of practical matters that are of vital importance to everyone hinge
on how and in what terms the discussion is carried out.

One position I mean to argue appears deceptively obvious: it is simply
that there are important differences between men and machines as thinkers.
I would argue that, however intelligent machines may be made to be, there
are some acts of thought that *ought* to be attempted only by humans. One
socially significant question I thus intend to raise is over the proper place of
computers in the social order. But, as we shall see, the issue transcends
computers in that it must ultimately deal with logicality itself—quite apart
from whether logicality is encoded in computer programs or not.

The lay reader may be forgiven for being more than slightly incredulous
that anyone should maintain that human thought is entirely computable.
But his very incredulity may itself be a sign of how marvelously subtly and
seductively modern science has come to influence man's imaginative construction of reality.

Surely, much of what we today regard as good and useful, as well as much
of what we would call knowledge and wisdom, we owe to science. But
science may also be seen as an addictive drug. Not only has our unbounded
feeding on science caused us to become dependent on it, but, as happens
with many other drugs taken in increasing dosages, science has been gradually converted into a slow-acting poison. Beginning perhaps with Francis
Bacon's misreading of the genuine promise of science, man has been seduced
into wishing and working for the establishment of an age of rationality, but
with his vision of rationality tragically twisted so as to equate it with logicality. Thus have we very nearly come to the point where almost every genuine
human dilemma is seen as a mere paradox, as a merely apparent contradiction that could be untangled by judicious applications of cold logic derived
from a higher standpoint. Even murderous wars have come to be perceived
as mere problems to be solved by hordes of professional problemsolvers. As
Hannah Arendt said about recent makers and executors of policy in the
Pentagon:

> "They were not just intelligent, but prided themselves on being 'rational' . . .
> They were eager to find formulas, preferably expressed in a pseudo-mathe-
> matical language, that would unify the most disparate phenomena with
> which reality presented them; that is, they were eager to discover *laws* by
> which to explain and predict political and historical facts as though they were
> as necessary, and thus as reliable, as the physicists once believed natural

---

[7]Hubert L. Dreyfus, *What Computers Can't Do* (Harper and Row, 1972).

phenomena to be . . . [They] did not *judge;* they calculated. . . . an utterly irrational confidence in the calculability of reality [became] the leitmotif of the decision making."[8]

And so too have nearly all political confrontations, such as those between races and those between the governed and their governors, come to be perceived as mere failures of communication. Such rips in the social fabric can then be systematically repaired by the expert application of the latest information-handling techniques—at least so it is believed. And so the rationality-is-logicality equation, which the very success of science has drugged us into adopting as virtually an axiom, has led us to deny the very existence of human conflict, hence the very possibility of the collision of genuinely incommensurable human interests and of disparate human values, hence the existence of human values themselves.

It may be that human values are illusory, as indeed B. F. Skinner argues. If they are, then it is presumably up to science to demonstrate that fact, as indeed Skinner (as scientist) attempts to do. But then science must itself be an illusory system. For the only certain knowledge science can give us is knowledge of the behavior of formal systems, that is, systems that are games invented by man himself and in which to assert truth is nothing more or less than to assert that, as in a chess game, a particular board position was arrived at by a sequence of legal moves. When science purports to make statements about man's experiences, it bases them on identifications between the primitive (that is, undefined) objects of one of its formalisms, the pieces of one of its games, and some set of human observations. No such sets of correspondences can ever be proved to be correct. At best, they can be falsified, in the sense that formal manipulations of a system's symbols may lead to symbolic configurations which, when read in the light of the set of correspondences in question, yield interpretations contrary to empirically observed phenomena. Hence all empirical science is an elaborate structure built on piles that are anchored, not on bedrock as is commonly supposed, but on the shifting sand of fallible human judgment, conjecture, and intuition. It is not even true, again contrary to common belief, that a single purported counter-instance that, if accepted as genuine would certainly falsify a specific scientific theory, generally leads to the immediate abandonment of that theory. Probably all scientific theories currently accepted by scientists themselves (excepting only those purely formal theories claiming no relation to the empirical world) are today confronted with contradicting evidence of more than negligible weight that, again if fully credited, would logically invalidate them. Such evidence is often explained (that is, explained away) by ascribing it to error of some kind, say, observational error, or by characterizing it as inessential, or by the assumption (that is, the faith) that some yet-to-be-discovered way of dealing with it will some day permit it to be acknowledged but nevertheless incorporated into the scientific theories it was originally thought to contradict. In this way scientists continue to

---

[8]Hannah Arendt, *Crises of the Republic* (Harcourt Brace Jovanovich, Harvest edition, 1972), pp. 11 *et seq.*

rely on already impaired theories and to infer "scientific fact" from them.*

The man in the street surely believes such scientific facts to be as well-established, as well-proven, as his own existence. His certitude is an illusion. Nor is the scientist himself immune to the same illusion. In his praxis, he must, after all, suspend disbelief in order to do or think anything at all. He is rather like a theatergoer, who, in order to participate in and understand what is happening on the stage, must for a time pretend to himself that he is witnessing real events. The scientist must believe his working hypothesis, together with its vast underlying structure of theories and assumptions, even if only for the sake of the argument. Often the "argument" extends over his entire lifetime. Gradually he becomes what he at first merely pretended to be: a true believer. I choose the word "argument" thoughtfully, for scientific demonstrations, even mathematical proofs, are fundamentally acts of persuasion.

Scientific statements can never be certain; they can be only more or less credible. And credibility is a term in individual psychology, i.e., a term that has meaning only with respect to an individual observer. To say that some proposition is credible is, after all, to say that it is believed by an agent who is free not to believe it, that is, by an observer who, after exercising judgment and (possibly) intuition, chooses to accept the proposition as worthy of his believing it. How then can science, which itself surely and ultimately rests on vast arrays of human value judgments, demonstrate that human value judgments are illusory? It cannot do so without forfeiting its own status as the single legitimate path to understanding man and his world.

But no merely logical argument, no matter how cogent or eloquent, can undo this reality: that science has become the sole legitimate form of understanding in the common wisdom. When I say that science has been gradually converted into a slow-acting poison, I mean that the attribution of certainty to scientific knowledge by the common wisdom, an attribution now made so nearly universally that it has become a commonsense dogma, has virtually delegitimatized all other ways of understanding. People viewed the arts, especially literature, as sources of intellectual nourishment and understanding, but today the arts are perceived largely as entertainments. The ancient Greek and Oriental theaters, the Shakespearian stage, the stages peopled by the Ibsens and Chekhovs nearer to our day—these were schools. The curricula they taught were vehicles for understanding the societies they represented. Today, although an occasional Arthur Miller or Edward Albee survives and is permitted to teach on the New York or London stage, the people hunger only for what is represented to them to be scientifically validated knowledge. They seek to satiate themselves at such scientific cafeterias as *Psychology Today*, or on popularized versions of the works of

---

*Thus, Charles Everett writes on the now-discarded phlogiston theory of combustion (in the *Encyclopaedia Britannica*, 11th ed., 1911, vol. VI, p. 34): "The objections of the antiphlogistonists, such as the fact that the calices weigh more than the original metals instead of less as the theory suggests, were answered by postulating that phlogiston was a principle of levity, or even completely ignored as an accident, the change in qualities being regarded as the only matter of importance." Everett lists H. Cavendish and J. Priestley, both great scientists of their time, as adherents to the phlogiston theory.

Masters and Johnson, or on scientology as revealed by L. Ron Hubbard. Belief in the rationality-logicality equation has corroded the prophetic power of language itself. We can count, but we are rapidly forgetting how to say what is worth counting and why.

HUBERT DREYFUS

Hubert Dreyfus is Professor of Philosophy at the University of California, Berkeley. Born in 1929, he received his Ph.D. from Harvard, won Sheldon and Fulbright fellowships for research in Europe, then taught for eight years at the Massachusetts Institute of Technology, where he won prizes for outstanding teaching. The questions of some of his technology students led him to becoming acquainted at firsthand with the most promising experimenters in artificial intelligence. Professor Dreyfus is a specialist in the existentialist-phenomenologist philosophy of such thinkers as Sören Kierkegaard, Edmond Husserl, Martin Heidegger, and Maurice Merleau-Ponty. In light of the phenomenologist conception of mind and understanding, he soon became skeptical of the possibility of artificial intelligence and has attacked the matter in a series of articles and in a book, What Computers Can't Do: A Critique of Artificial Reason *(1972), which has been translated into Japanese, Russian, Portuguese, and Yugoslavian. A second edition appeared in March 1979. The author has kindly revised a portion of its Introduction for inclusion in the present volume.*

Why Computers Can't Be Intelligent

Even the most tough-minded men and women have a sense that, although they are made out of matter, they are not machines; yet lately they are more and more frequently being told, as if it were obvious, that "each human being is a superbly constructed . . . computer"[1] and that computers will eventually behave as intelligently as people do. Some scientists say that computers, like HAL in "*2001*," will be just like people; others claim that intelligent machines will be better than human beings, since they will not suffer from fatigue, emotions, self doubt, and the illusion that they are not machines. Each of these predictions is associated with its own disaster scenario: the emotional computer loses its cool and destroys everyone in its passionate attempt to save the mission; the purely intellectual computer coolly turns society into a rational hell fit only for robots. Since spreading the good news of the imminence of artificial intelligence as well as prophesying inevitable disaster is becoming a new media industry, it is high time to look again at our quiet assurance that we are not computers and that claims that computers can be intelligent must be nonsense.

---

[1] Carl Sagan, "In Defense of Robots"; see above, page 541.

Two of the most popularized computer "successes" which seem to support the notion that scientists are making steady progress toward intelligent machines are Winograd's blocks program (SHRDLU)[2] and the impressive performance of recent chess machines.

When it was first unveiled ten years ago Winograd's program did, indeed, seem a major advance toward intelligent machines. SHRDLU simulates a robot arm which can move a set of variously shaped blocks and allows a person to engage in a dialogue with the computer, asking questions, making statements, and issuing commands about this simple world of movable blocks. Workers in AI (artificial intelligence) did not try to cover up the fact that it was SHRDLU's restricted domain which made apparent understanding possible. They even had a name for Winograd's method of restricting the domain of discourse. He was dealing with a "micro-world." Marvin Minsky and Seymour Papert, co-directors of MIT's "robot project," explain:

> Each model—or "micro-world" as we shall call it—is very schematic; it talks about a fairyland in which things are so simplified that almost every statement about them would be literally false if asserted about the real world.[3]

But they immediately add:

> Nevertheless, we feel that they (the micro-worlds) are so important that we are assigning a large portion of our effort toward developing a collection of these micro-worlds and finding how to use the suggestive and predictive powers of the models without being overcome by their incompatibility with literal truth.

Given the admittedly artificial and arbitrary character of micro-worlds, why did Minsky and Papert think they provide a promising line of research?

To find the answer we must follow Minsky and Papert's perceptive remarks on the understanding of narrative and their less than perceptive conclusions:

> . . . In a familiar fable, the wily Fox tricks the vain Crow into dropping the meat by asking it to sing. The usual test of understanding is the ability of the child to answer questions like: "Did the Fox think the Crow had a lovely voice?" The topic is sometimes classified as "natural language manipulation" or as "deductive logic," etc. These descriptions are badly chosen. For the real problem is not to understand English; it is to *understand* at all. The difficulty in getting a machine to give the right answer does not at all depend on "disam-

---

[2]Terry Winograd, "A Procedural Model of Language Understanding," *Computer Models of Thought and Language*, Roger Schank and Kenneth Colby, eds. (San Francisco: W. H. Freeman Press, 1973). (SHRDLU is an anti-acronym whose letters don't stand for anything. It was picked up by Winograd from *Mad Magazine*, which uses this frequent typesetter's error as the name of mythical monsters and the like.)

[3]Marvin Minsky and Seymour Papert, Draft, July 1970, of a Proposal to ARPA for Research on Artificial Intelligence at M.I.T., 1970-1971, p. 39.

biguating" the words (at least, not in the usual primitive sense of selecting one "meaning" out of a discrete set of "meanings"). And neither does the difficulty lie in the need for unusually powerful logical apparatus. The main problem is that no one has constructed the elements of a body of knowledge about such matters that is adequate for understanding the story. Let us see what is involved.

To begin with, there is never a unique solution to such problems, so we do not ask what the Understander *must* know. But he will surely gain by having the concept of FLATTERY. To provide this knowledge, we imagine a "micro-theory" of flattery—an extendible collection of facts or procedures that describe conditions under which one might expect to find flattery, what forms it takes, what its consequences are, and so on. How complex this theory is depends on what is presupposed. Thus it would be very difficult to describe flattery to our Understander if he (or it) does not already know that statements can be made for purposes other than to convey literally correct, factual information. It would be almost impossibly difficult if he does not even have some concept like PURPOSE or INTENTION.[4]

The surprising move here is the conclusion that there *could* be a circumscribed "micro-theory" of flattery—somehow intelligible apart from the rest of human life—while at the same time the account shows that an understanding of flattery would depend on a further opening out into the understanding of the rest of our everyday world, with its complex purposes and intentions.

What characterizes the period of the early seventies, and makes SHRDLU seem an advance toward general intelligence, is the pseudo-scientific concept of a micro-world—a domain which can be analyzed in isolation.

In our everyday life we are, indeed, involved in various "sub-worlds" such as the world of the theater, of business, or of mathematics, but each of these is a "mode" of our shared everyday world.[5] That is, sub-worlds are not related like isolatable physical systems to larger systems they *compose*; rather, they are local elaborations of a whole which they *presuppose*.

Only recently has the illusion that one can generalize work done in narrowly constrained domains been diagnosed and laid to rest by Winograd himself:

> The AI programs of the late sixties and early seventies are much too literal. They deal with meaning as if it were a structure to be built up of the bricks and mortar provided by the words. . . . This gives them a "brittle" character, able to deal well with tightly specified areas of meaning in an artificially formal conversation. They are correspondingly weak in dealing with natural utterances, full of bits and fragments, continual (unnoticed) metaphor, and reference to much less easily formalizable areas of knowledge.[6]

---

[4]*Ibid.*, pp. 42–44.

[5]This view is worked out by Martin Heidegger in *Being and Time* (New York: Harper & Row, 1962). See especially p. 93 and all of section 18.

[6]Winograd, "Artificial Intelligence and Language Comprehension," in *Artificial Intelligence and Language Comprehension* (Washington, D.C.: National Institute of Education, 1976), p. 17.

While popularizers are still praising SHRDLU, it is now generally acknowledged by serious workers in the field that the micro-world approach to everyday intelligence is a dead end.

Everyday human life turns out to be one interrelated whole, but games are just the sort of totally circumscribed micro-worlds in which computers excel. Thus, while expecting failures in dealing with human language, we should expect game-playing programs to have great success. But we must be on our guard against attributing this success to anything like human intelligence.

Chess, for example, is a perfect micro-world in which relevance is restricted to the narrow domain of the kind of chess piece (pawn, knight, etc.), its color, and the position of the piece on the board. The size, weight and temperature of a piece are never relevant. But while the game's circumscribed character makes a world champion chess program possible in principle, there is a great deal of evidence that human beings play chess quite differently from the way computers do. Indeed, computers do not use long-range strategy, learn from experience, or even remember previous moves.

To understand the difference between human and machine play, we must first understand how a chess program works. A chess program uses situation-to-action rules. A situation is characterized in terms of context-free features: the position and color of each piece on the board. All possible legal moves and the positions which result are then defined in terms of these features. To evaluate and compare positions, rules are provided for calculating scores on attributes such as "material balance" (where a numerical value is assigned to each piece on the board and the total score is computed for each player) or "center control" (where the number of pieces bearing on each centrally located square is counted). Finally, there must be a formula for evaluating alternative positions on the basis of these scores. Using this approach and looking at around 3 million possible positions, CHESS 4.5 recently won the 84th Minnesota Open Tournament, but a chess master generally looks at the results of less than 100 possible moves and yet plays a far better game. How can this be?

It seems that by playing over book games chess masters develop the ability to recognize present positions as similar to positions which occurred in classic games. These previous positions have already been analyzed in terms of their significant aspects. Aspects of a chess position include such overall characteristics as "control of the situation" (the extent to which a player's opponent's moves can be forced by making threatening moves), "cramped-ness of the position" (the amount of freedom of maneuver inherent in both the player's position and the opponent's position), or "overextendedness" (the fact that while the position might be superficially quite strong, one is not in sufficient control of the situation to follow through and, with correct play by the opponent, a massive retreat will be required). The already analyzed remembered positions focus the player's attention on critical areas before he begins to count out specific moves.

The distinction between features and aspects is central here. *Aspects* play a role in an account of human play similar to that of *features* in the computer model, but there is a crucial difference. In the computer model the *situation is* DEFINED IN TERMS OF *the features*, whereas in human play *situational understanding is* PRIOR TO *aspect specification*. For example, the numerical value of a feature such as material balance can be calculated independently of any understanding of the game, whereas an aspect like overextendedness cannot be calculated simply in terms of the position of the pieces, since the same board position can have different aspects depending on its place in the long-range strategy of a game.

No *feature-based* matching of the present position against a stored library of previous positions could account for a master player's ability to use past experience to zero in. It is astronomically unlikely that two positions will ever turn out to be *identical*, so that what has to be compared are *similar* positions. But similarity cannot be defined as having a large number of pieces on identical squares. Two positions which are identical except for one pawn moved to an adjacent square can be totally different, while two positions can be similar although no pieces are on the same square in each. Thus similarity depends on the player's sense of the issues at stake, not merely on the position of the pieces. Seeing two positions as similar is exactly what requires a deep understanding of the game. By thus structuring the current situation in terms of aspects of remembered similar situations the human player is able to avoid the massive counting out required by a computer which can only "recognize" positions characterized in terms of context-free features.

Human intelligence, then, even in games, requires the use of background knowledge; in the everyday world this background knowledge consists of the commonsense understanding of how to do things which we share with other human beings. Recent work in artificial intelligence has been forced to deal directly with this background of everyday practices. Faced with this necessity, researchers have implicitly tried to treat the background as a complex of facts related by rules—sometimes called a "belief system." This assumption that the background of practices can be treated as just another object is the basis of the claim that human beings are just very sophisticated computers. This conviction runs deep in our whole philosophical tradition. Following Martin Heidegger, who is the first to have identified and criticized this view, I will call it the metaphysical assumption.

The obvious question to ask is: Is there any reason besides the persistent difficulties and history of unfulfilled promises in AI for believing that the metaphysical assumption is unjustified? Is there any defense against this subtle version of mechanism? The best argument, I think, is that whenever human behavior is analyzed in terms of facts related by rules, these rules must always contain a *ceteris paribus* condition, that is, they apply "everything else being equal," and what "everything else" and "equal" means in any specific situation can never be fully spelled out. Moreover, this *ceteris paribus* condition is not merely an annoyance which shows that the analysis is not yet complete and might be an "infinite task." Rather the *ceteris paribus* condition points to the background of practices which is the condition of the possibility of all rulelike activity. In explaining our actions we must always sooner or later fall back on our everyday practices and simply say "this is what we do" or "that's what it is to be a human being." Thus in the last analysis all intelligibility and all intelligent behavior must be traced back to our sense of what we *are*, which is something we can never explicitly *know*.

This claim can best be made plausible by means of an example from an MIT story-understanding project. Consider the following story fragment:

> Today was Jack's birthday. Penny and Janet went to the store. They were going to get presents. Janet decided to get a kite. "Don't do that," said Penny. "Jack has a kite. He will make you take *it* back."[7]

The goal is to construct a theory that explains how the reader understands that "*it*" refers to the new kite, not the one Jack already owns. Grammatical tricks (such as assigning the referent of "*it*" to the last mentioned noun) are clearly inadequate, as the result would be to mistakenly understand the last sentence of the story as meaning that Jack will make Janet take back the kite *he already owns*. It is clear that one cannot know "*it*" refers to the new kite without knowledge about the trading habits of our society. One could imagine a different world in which newly bought objects are never returned to the store, but old ones are.

The AI approach dictated by the metaphysical assumption is, of course, to try to make the background practices involved in understanding this story explicit as a set of beliefs. But once games and micro-worlds are left behind, a yawning abyss threatens to swallow up those who try to carry out such a program. As Papert notes:

> . . . The story does not include explicitly all important facts. Look back at the story. Some readers will be surprised to note that the text itself does not state (a) that the presents bought by Penny and Janet were for *Jack*, (b) that the [kite] bought by Janet was intended as a present, and (c) that having an object implies that one does not want another.[8]

Our example turns on the question: How does one store the "facts" mentioned in (c) above about returning presents? To begin with there are perhaps indefinitely many reasons for taking a present back. It may be the wrong size, run on the wrong voltage, be carcinogenic, make too much noise, be considered too childish, too feminine, too masculine, too American, etc. And each of these facts requires further facts to be understood. But we will concentrate on the reason mentioned in (c): that normally, i.e., *everything else being equal*, if one has an object, one does not want another just like it. Of course, this cannot simply be entered as a true proposition. It does not hold for dollar bills, cookies, or marbles. (It is not clear it even holds for kites.) Papert would answer that, of course, once we talk of the norm we must be prepared to deal with exceptions.

---

[7]Ira Goldstein and Seymour Papert, M.I.T. AI Laboratory, AI Memo No. 337 (July 1975, revised March 1976), "Artificial Intelligence, Language and the Study of Knowledge," pp. 29–31.
[8]*Ibid.*, p. 33.

But here the desperate hand-waving begins, for the text need not explicitly mention the exceptions at all. If the gift were marbles or cookies the text surely would not mention that these were exceptions to the general rule that one of a kind is enough. So the data base would have to contain *an account of all possible exceptions* to augment the text—if it even makes sense to think of this as a definite list. Worse, even if one listed all the exceptional cases where one would be glad to possess more than one specimen of a certain type of object, there are situations which allow an exception to this exception: already having one cookie is more than enough if the cookie in question is three feet in diameter; one thousand marbles is more than a normal child can handle. Must we then list the situations which lead one to expect exceptions to the exceptions? But these exceptions too can be overridden in the case of, say, a cookie monster or a marble freak, and so it goes. The computer programmer writing a story-understander must try to list all possibly relevant information, and once that information contains appeals to the *normal* or *typical* there is no way to avoid an endless series of qualifications of qualifications for applying that knowledge to a specific situation.

The only "answer" Papert offers is the metaphysical assumption that the background of everyday life is a set of rigidly defined situations in which the relevant facts are as clear as in a game:

> The fundamental frame assumption is the thesis that . . . [m]ost situations in which people find themselves *have sufficient in common* with previously encountered situations for the salient features to be *pre-analyzed* and stored in a *situation-specific* form.[9]

But this "solution" is untenable for two reasons:

1. Even if the current situation is, indeed, *similar* to a preanalyzed one, we still have the problem of deciding which situation it is similar to. We have already seen that even in games such as chess no two positions are likely to be identical, so a deep understanding of what is going on is required to decide what counts as a similar position in any two games. This should be even more obvious in cases where the problem is to decide which pre-analyzed situation a given real-world situation most resembles: for example, whether a situation where there are well-dressed babies and new toys being presented has more in common with a birthday party or a beauty contest.

2. Even if all our lives *were* lived in identical stereotypical situations, we have just seen that any real-world frame must be described in terms of the normal, and that appeal to the normal necessarily leads to a regress when we try to characterize the conditions which determine the applicability of the norm to a specific case. Only our *general* sense of what is typical can decide here, and *that* background understanding by definition cannot be "situation-specific."

Still, to this dilemma the AI researchers might plausibly respond: "Whatever the background of shared interests, feelings, and practices necessary for understanding specific situations, that knowledge *must* somehow be in the

---

[9] *Ibid.*, pp. 30–31. (My italics.)

human beings who have that understanding. And how else could such knowledge be represented but as some explicit set of facts and beliefs?" Indeed, the kind of computer programming accepted by all workers in AI would require such a data structure, and so would philosophers who hold that all knowledge must be explicitly represented in our minds; but there are two alternatives which, by avoiding the idea that everything we know must be in the form of some explicit description, would avoid contradictions inherent in the information-processing model.

One response, shared by existential phenomenologists such as Maurice Merleau-Ponty[10] and ordinary language philosophers such as Ludwig Wittgenstein, is to say that such "knowledge" of human interests and practices need not be represented at all. As Wittgenstein puts it in *On Certainty*, "Children do not learn that books exist, that armchairs exist, etc., etc.—they learn to fetch books, sit in armchairs, etc., etc."[11] Just as it seems plausible that I can learn to swim by practicing until I develop the necessary patterns of responses which run off automatically without my ever describing my body and muscular movements to myself, so too what I "know" about cultural practices which enables me to recognize and act in specific situations has been gradually acquired through training—against an already meaningful background—although no one ever did or could make explicit what was being learned.

Another possible account would allow a place for representations, at least in special cases where I have to stop and reflect, but such a position would stress that these are usually not explicit descriptions but more like images, by means of which I explore what I *am*, not what I *know*. In this view I don't normally represent to myself that I have desires, or that standing up requires balance, or, to take an example from Schank's pathetic attempt to make explicit a bit of our interpersonal knowledge, that:

> (I)f two people are positively emotionally related, then a negative change in one person's state will cause the other person to develop the goal of causing a positive change in the other's state.[12]

When it is helpful, however, as in understanding a story, I can picture myself in a specific situation and ask myself what I would do or how I would feel—if I were in Jack's place how I would react to being given a second kite—without having to make explicit all that a computer would have to be told to come to a similar conclusion. We thus appeal to *concrete* representation (images or memories) based on our own experience without having to make explicit the strict rules and their spelled out *ceteris paribus* conditions required by *abstract* symbolic descriptions.

Indeed, it is hard to see how the subtle variety of ways things can matter to us could be exhaustively spelled out. We can anticipate and understand

---

[10]Maurice Merleau-Ponty, *Phenomenology of Perception* (London: Routledge and Kegan Paul, 1962).

[11]Ludwig Wittgenstein, *On Certainty* (New York: Harper Torch Book, 1972), p. 62.

[12]Roger Schank and Robert P. Abelson, *Scripts, Plans, Goals and Understanding* (Hillsdale, N.J.: Lawrence Erlbaum Associates, 1970), p. 144.

Jack's reaction because we remember what it feels like to be amused, amazed, incredulous, disappointed, disgruntled, saddened, annoyed, disgusted, upset, angry, furious, outraged, etc., and we recognize the impulses to action associated with these various degrees and kinds of concerns. A computer model would have to be given a description of each shade of feeling as well as each feeling's normal occasion and likely result.

The idea that feelings, memories, and images *must* be the conscious tip of an unconscious explicit description runs up against both *prima facie* evidence and the problem of explicating the *ceteris paribus* conditions. Moreover, this mechanistic assumption is not supported by one shred of scientific evidence from neurophysiology or psychology, or from the past successes of AI, whose repeated failures required appeal to the metaphysical assumption in the first place. When AI workers finally face and analyze their failures, it might well be the metaphysical/mechanistic assumption that they will find they have to reject.

Looking back over the past ten years of AI research, we might say that the basic point which has emerged is that *since intelligence must be situated it cannot be separated from the rest of human life*. The persistent denial of this seemingly obvious point cannot, however, be laid at the door of AI. It starts with Plato's separation of the intellect or rational soul from the body with its skills, emotions, and appetites. Aristotle continued this unlikely dichotomy when he separated the theoretical from the practical, and defined man as a rational animal—as if one could separate man's rationality from his animal needs and desires. If one thinks of the importance of the sensory-motor skills in the development of our ability to recognize and cope with objects, or of the role of needs and desires in structuring all social situations, or finally of the whole cultural background of human self-interpretation involved in our simply knowing how to pick out and use chairs, the idea that we can ignore this know-how while formalizing our intellectual understanding as a complex system of facts and rules is highly implausible.

However incredible, this dubious dichotomy now pervades our thinking about everything including computers. In the *Star Trek* TV series, the episode entitled "The Return of the Archons" tells of a wise statesman named Landru who programmed a computer to run a society. Unfortunately, he could give the computer only his abstract intelligence, not his concrete wisdom, so the computer turned the society into a plannified hell. No one stops to wonder how, without Landru's embodied skills, feelings, and concerns, the computer could understand everyday situations and so run a society at all.

Great artists have always sensed the truth, stubbornly denied by both philosophers and technologists, that, just because man is material in the special way that he is, he can never have the clarity characteristic of a computer. Artists sense that the basis of human understanding cannot be isolated and explicitly understood. In *Moby Dick*, Melville writes of the tattooed savage, Queequeg, who had "written out on his body a complete theory of the heavens and the earth, and a mystical treatise on the art of attaining truth; so that Queequeg in his own proper person was a riddle to unfold; a wondrous work in one volume; but whose mysteries not even himself could read . . ." The monomaniac philosopher Ahab prefigures AI's insistence that all such cultural know-how be made explicit. One morning turning away from surveying Queequeg, Ahab exclaims, "Oh, devilish tantalization of the gods!" Melville is attracted by the philosopher's demand for explicit, settled knowledge but senses the power that the obscure and endlessly reinterpreted traditional wisdom we each embody has to save us from meaninglessness. The mysterious symbols engraved in Queequeg's flesh are carefully copied onto Queequeg's coffin, which, in the end, saves Ishmael from Ahab's disaster. Yeats expresses even more succinctly the poet's appreciation of our incarnate limitations: "I have found what I wanted—to put it in a phrase, I say, 'Man can embody truth, but he cannot know it'."

BIOMEDICINE

JAMES D. WATSON

James D. Watson, a biologist, is one of the discoverers of the double-helical structure of DNA, the substance in the nucleus of cells that transmits genetic data. His work has been called "one of the great biological discoveries of our time" and earned him and his colleagues the Nobel Prize for medicine in 1962. Watson was born in 1928, earned a bachelor of science degree from the University of Chicago in 1947 and a doctorate from Indiana University in 1950. He did a few years' research at Cal Tech, then moved as visitor to the Cavendish Laboratory in Cambridge, England, attracted by the work of Francis Crick on what was then the most important problem in biochemistry. Within two years Watson and Crick had solved it, and uncountable honors followed.

Watson followed, too, with an extraordinary book recounting the discovery. The Double Helix *(1968) is extraordinary because it is no dry, tight-lipped scientific narrative, but tells of the event as Watson saw it happen, with all the peculiarities and human foibles of the principals fully exposed. As the great sociologist of science Robert K. Merton describes the book, Watson "depicts a variety and confusion of motives, in which the objective . . . is intertwined with the tormenting pleasures of competition, contest and reward. Absorption in the scientific problem alternated with periodic idleness, escape, play and girl-watching. . . . I know of nothing quite like it in all the literature about scientists at work." Watson's colleagues were upset by the idea of the book, and tried to prevent its publication. The president of Harvard, where Watson had been on the faculty since 1956, ordered the university's press not to print it. Published finally by Atheneum in New York, it became a best-seller.*

Watson continues to teach at Harvard. His more scholarly book, The Molecular Biology of the Gene, *is considered a classic in its field, and has gone through three editions (1965-1976). The present article appeared in the* Atlantic *for May 1971.*

Moving Toward the Clonal Man

The notion that man might sometime soon be reproduced asexually upsets many people. The main public effect of the remarkable clonal frog produced some ten years ago in Oxford by the zoologist John Gurdon has not been awe of the elegant scientific implication of this frog's existence, but fear that a similar experiment might someday be done with human cells. Until recently, however, this foreboding has seemed more like a science fiction scenario than a real problem which the human race has to live with.

For the embryological development of man does not occur free in the placid environment of a fresh-water pond, in which a frog's eggs normally turn into tadpoles and then into mature frogs. Instead, the crucial steps in human embryology always occur in the highly inaccessible womb of a human female. There the growing fetus enlarges unseen, and effectively out of range of almost any manipulation except that which is deliberately designed to abort its existence. As long as all humans develop in this manner, there is no way to take the various steps necessary to insert an adult diploid nucleus from a pre-existing human into a human egg whose maternal genetic material has previously been removed. Given the continuation of the normal processes of conception and development, the idea that we might have a world populated by people whose genetic material was identical to that of previously existing people can belong only to the domain of the novelist or moviemaker, not to that of pragmatic scientists who must think only about things which can happen.

Today, however, we must face up to the fact that the unexpectedly rapid progress of R. G. Edwards and P. S. Steptoe in working out the conditions for routine test-tube conception of human eggs means that human embryological development need no longer be a process shrouded in secrecy. It can become instead an event wide-open to a variety of experimental manipulations. Already the two scientists have developed many embryos to the eight-cell stage, and a few more into blastocysts, the stage where successful implantation into a human uterus should not be too difficult to achieve. In fact, Edwards and Steptoe hope to accomplish implantation and subsequent growth into a normal baby within the coming year.

The question naturally arises, why should any woman willingly submit to the laparoscopy operation which yields the eggs to be used in test-tube conceptions? There is clearly some danger involved every time Steptoe operates. Nonetheless, he and Edwards believe that the risks are more than counterbalanced by the fact that their research may develop methods which could make their patients able to bear children. All their patients, though having normal menstrual cycles, are infertile, many because they have blocked oviducts which prevent passage of eggs into the uterus. If so, *in vitro* growth of their eggs up to the blastocyst stage may circumvent infertility, thereby allowing normal childbirth. Moreover, since the sex of a blastocyst is easily determined by chromosomal analysis, such women would have the possibility of deciding whether to give birth to a boy or a girl.

Clearly, if Edwards and Steptoe succeed, their success will be followed up in many other places. The number of such infertile women, while small on a relative percentage basis, is likely to be large on an absolute basis. Within the United States there could be 100,000 or so women who would like a similar chance to have their own babies. At the same time, we must anticipate strong, if not hysterical, reactions from many quarters. The certainty that the ready availability of this medical technique will open up the possibility of hiring out unrelated women to carry a given baby to term is bound to outrage many people. For there is absolutely no reason why the blastocyst need be implanted in the same woman from whom the pre-ovulatory eggs were obtained. Many women with anatomical complications which prohibit successful childbearing might be strongly tempted to find a suitable surrogate. And it is easy to imagine that other women who just don't want the discomforts of pregnancy would also seek this very different form of motherhood. Of even greater concern would be the potentialities for misuse by an inhumane totalitarian government.

Some very hard decisions may soon be upon us. It is not obvious, for example, that the vague potential of abhorrent misuse should weigh more strongly than the unhappiness which thousands of married couples feel when they are unable to have their own children. Different societies are likely to view the matter differently, and it would be surprising if all should come to the same conclusion. We must, therefore, assume that techniques for the *in vitro* manipulation of human eggs are likely to become general medical practice, capable of routine performance in many major countries, within some ten to twenty years.

The situation would then be ripe for extensive efforts, either legal or illegal, at human cloning. But for such experiments to be successful, techniques would have to be developed which allow the insertion of adult diploid nuclei into human eggs which previously have had their maternal haploid nucleus removed. At first sight, this task is a very tall order since human eggs are much smaller than those of frogs, the only vertebrates which have so far been cloned. Insertion by micropipettes, the device used in the case of the frog, is always likely to damage human eggs irreversibly. Recently, however, the development of simple techniques for fusing animal cells has raised the strong possibility that further refinements of the cell-fusion method will allow the routine introduction of human diploid nuclei into enucleated human eggs. Activation of such eggs to divide to become blastocysts, followed by implantation into suitable uteri, should lead to the development of healthy fetuses, and subsequent normal-appearing babies.

The growing up to adulthood of these first clonal humans could be a very startling event, a fact already appreciated by many magazine editors, one of whom commissioned a cover with multiple copies of Ringo Starr, another of whom gave us overblown multiple likenesses of the current sex goddess, Raquel Welch. It takes little imagination to perceive that different people will have highly different fantasies, some perhaps imagining the existence of countless people with the features of Picasso or Frank Sinatra or Walt Frazier or Doris Day. And would monarchs like the Shah of Iran, knowing they might never be able to have a normal male heir, consider the possibility of having a son whose genetic constitution would be identical to their own?

Clearly, even more bizarre possibilities can be thought of, and so we might have expected that many biologists, particularly those whose work impinges upon this possibility, would seriously ponder its implication, and begin a dialogue which would educate the world's citizens and offer suggestions which our legislative bodies might consider in framing national science policies. On the whole, however, this has not happened. Though a number of scientific papers devoted to the problem of genetic engineering have casually mentioned that clonal reproduction may someday be with us, the discussion to which I am party has been so vague and devoid of meaningful time estimates as to be virtually soporific.

Does this effective silence imply a conspiracy to keep the general public unaware of a potential threat to their basic ways of life? Could it be motivated by fear that the general reaction will be a further damning of all science, thereby decreasing even more the limited money available for pure research? Or does it merely tell us that most scientists do live such an ivory-tower existence that they are capable of thinking rationally only about pure science, dismissing more practical matters as subjects for the lawyers, students, clergy, and politicians to face up to?

One or both of these possibilities may explain why more scientists have not taken cloning before the public. The main reason, I suspect, is that the prospect to most biologists still looks too remote and chancy—not worthy of immediate attention when other matters, like nuclear-weapon overproliferation and pesticide and auto-exhaust pollution, present society with immediate threats to its orderly continuation. Though scientists as a group form the most future-oriented of all professions, there are few of us who concentrate on events unlikely to become reality within the next decade or two.

To almost all the intellectually most adventurous geneticists, the seemingly distant time when cloning might first occur is more to the point than its far-reaching implication, were it to be practiced seriously. For example, Stanford's celebrated geneticist, Joshua Lederberg, among the first to talk about cloning as a practical matter, now seems bored with further talk, implying that we should channel our limited influence as public citizens to the prevention of the wide-scale, irreversible damage to our genetic material that is now occurring through increasing exposure to man-created mutagenic compounds. To him, serious talk about cloning is essentially crying wolf when a tiger is already inside the walls.

This position, however, fails to allow for what I believe will be a frenetic rush to do experimental manipulation with human eggs once they have become a readily available commodity. And that is what they will be within several years after Edwards-Steptoe methods lead to the birth of the first healthy baby by a previously infertile woman. Isolated human eggs will be found in hundreds of hospitals, and given the fact that Steptoe's laparoscopy technique frequently yields several eggs from a single woman donor, not all of the eggs so obtained, even if they could be cultured to the blastocyst stage, would ever be reimplanted into female bodies. Most of these excess eggs would likely be used for a variety of valid experimental purposes, many, for example, to perfect the Edwards-Steptoe techniques. Others could be devoted to finding methods for curing certain genetic diseases, conceivably through use of cell-fusion methods which now seem to be the correct route to cloning. The temptation to try cloning itself thus will always be close at hand.

No reason, of course, dictates that such cloning experiments need occur. Most of the medical people capable of such experimentation would probably steer clear of any step which looked as though its real purpose were to clone. But it would be shortsighted to assume that everyone would instinctively recoil from such purposes. Some people may sincerely believe the world desperately needs many copies of really exceptional people if we are to fight our way out of the ever-increasing computer-mediated complexity that makes our individual brains so frequently inadequate.

Moreover, given the widespread development of the safe clinical procedures for handling human eggs, cloning experiments would not be prohibitively expensive. They need not be restricted to the super-powers. All smaller countries now possess the resources required for eventual success. Furthermore, there need not exist the coercion of a totalitarian state to provide the surrogate mothers. There already are such widespread divergences regarding the sacredness of the act of human reproduction that the boring meaninglessness of the lives of many women would be sufficient cause for their willingness to participate in such experimentation, be it legal or illegal. Thus, if the matter proceeds in its current nondirected fashion, a human being born of clonal reproduction most likely will appear on the earth within the next twenty to fifty years, and even sooner, if some nation should actively promote the venture.

The first reaction of most people to the arrival of these asexually produced children, I suspect, would be one of despair. The nature of the bond between parents and their children, not to mention everyone's values about the individual's uniqueness, could be changed beyond recognition, and by a science which they never understood but which until recently appeared to provide more good than harm. Certainly to many people, particularly those with strong religious backgrounds, our most sensible course of action would be to de-emphasize all those forms of research which would circumvent the normal sexual reproductive process. If this step were taken, experiments on cell fusion might no longer be supported by federal funds or tax-exempt organizations. Prohibition of such research would most certainly put off the day when diploid nuclei could satisfactorily be inserted into enucleated human eggs. Even more effective would be to take steps quickly to make illegal, or to reaffirm the illegality of, any experimental work with human embryos.

Neither of the prohibitions, however, is likely to take place. In the first place, the cell-fusion technique now offers one of the best avenues for understanding the genetic basis of cancer. Today, all over the world, cancer cells are being fused with normal cells to pinpoint those specific chromosomes responsible for given forms of cancer. In addition, fusion techniques are the basis of many genetic efforts to unravel the biochemistry of diseases like cystic fibrosis or multiple sclerosis. Any attempt now to stop such work using the argument that cloning represents a greater threat than a disease like cancer is likely to be considered irresponsible by virtually anyone able to understand the matter.

Though more people would initially go along with a prohibition of work on human embryos, many may have a change of heart when they ponder the mess which the population explosion poses. The current projections are so horrendous that responsible people are likely to consider the need for more basic embryological facts much more relevant to our self-interest than the not-very-immediate threat of a few clonal men existing some decades ahead. And the potentially militant lobby of infertile couples who see test-tube conception as their only route to the joys of raising children of their own making would carry even more weight. So, scientists like Edwards are likely to get a go-ahead signal even if, almost perversely, the immediate consequences of their "population-money"-supported research will be the production of still more babies.

Complicating any effort at effective legislative guidance is the multiplicity of places where work like Edwards' could occur, thereby making unlikely the possibility that such manipulations would have the same legal (or illegal) status throughout the world. We must assume that if Edwards and Steptoe produce a really workable method for restoring fertility, large numbers of women will search out those places where it is legal (or possible), just as now they search out places where abortions can be easily obtained.

Thus, all nations formulating policies to handle the implications of *in vitro* human embryo experimentation must realize that the problem is essentially an international one. Even if one or more countries should stop such research, their action could effectively be neutralized by the response of a neighboring country. This most disconcerting impotence also holds for the United States. If our congressional representatives, upon learning where the matter now stands, should decide that they want none of it and pass very strict laws against human embryo experimentation, their action would not seriously set back the current scientific and medical momentum which brings us close to the possibility of surrogate mothers, if not human clonal reproduction. This is because the relevant experiments are being done not in the United States, but largely in England. That is partly a matter of chance, but also a consequence of the advanced state of English cell biology, which in certain areas is far more adventurous and imaginative than its American counterpart. There is no American university which has the strength in experimental embryology that Oxford possesses.

We must not assume, however, that today the important decisions lie only before the British government. Very soon we must anticipate that a number of biologists and clinicians of other countries, sensing the potential excitement, will move into this area of science. So even if the current English effort were stifled, similar experimentation could soon begin elsewhere. Thus it appears to me most desirable that as many people as possible be informed about the new ways of human reproduction and their potential consequences, both good and bad.

This is a matter far too important to be left solely in the hands of the scientific and medical communities. The belief that surrogate mothers and clonal babies are inevitable because science always moves forward, an attitude expressed to me recently by a scientific colleague, represents a form of laissez-faire nonsense dismally reminiscent of the creed that American business, if left to itself, will solve everybody's problems. Just as the success of a corporate body in making money need not set the human condition ahead, neither does every scientific advance automatically make our lives more "meaningful." No doubt the person whose experimental skill will eventually bring forth a clonal baby will be given wide notoriety. But the child who grows up knowing that the world wants another Picasso may view his creator in a different light.

I would thus hope that over the next decade wide-reaching discussion would occur, at the informal as well as formal legislative level, about the manifold problems which are bound to arise if test-tube conception becomes a common occurrence. A blanket declaration of the worldwide illegality of human cloning might be one result of a serious effort to ask the world in which direction it wished to move. Admittedly the vast effort, required for even the most limited international arrangement, will turn off some people—those who believe the matter is of marginal importance now, and that it is a red herring designed to take our minds off our callous attitudes toward war, poverty, and racial prejudice. But if we do not think about it now, the possibility of our having a free choice will one day suddenly be gone.

IVAN ILLICH

Ivan Illich is a sort of professional iconoclast, whose book De-Schooling Society *(1971) attracted international attention for the outrageousness of its argument (briefly, that schools do more harm than good) and for the widespread and upsetting suspicion that it might just be true. He has followed it with a similarly upsetting and celebrated attack on the medical profession.*

Illich was born in Vienna in 1926, educated in Florence, Rome, Munich, and Salzburg (Ph.D., 1951), and was ordained a Roman Catholic priest in 1951. He served as assistant pastor in a New York City parish, then as an administrator in the Catholic University of Puerto Rico, and then co-founded the Centro Intercultural de Documentacion in Cuernavaca, Mexico, which has served ever since as the base and headquarters for his spirited attacks on the ills of modern culture. He resigned his priestly functions in 1969.

Some of Illich's other books are Celebration of Awareness *(1970),* Energy and Equity *(1973),* Medical Nemesis *(1974), and* Disabling Professions *(1978). The present essay is the first chapter of his* Tools for Conviviality *(1973).*

Two Watersheds

The year 1913 marks a watershed in the history of modern medicine. Around that year a patient began to have more than a fifty-fifty chance that a graduate of a medical school would provide him with a specifically effective treatment (if, of course, he was suffering from one of the standard diseases recognized by the medical science of the time). Many shamans and herb doctors familiar with local diseases and remedies and trusted by their clients had always had equal or better results.

Since then medicine has gone on to define what constitutes disease and its treatment. The Westernized public learned to demand effective medical practice as defined by the progress of medical science. For the first time in history doctors could measure their efficiency against scales which they themselves had devised. This progress was due to a new perspective of the origins of some ancient scourges; water could be purified and infant mortality lowered; rat control could disarm the plague; treponemas could be made visible under the microscope and Salvarsan could eliminate them with statistically defined risks of poisoning the patient; syphilis could be avoided, or recognized and cured by rather simple procedures; diabetes could be diagnosed and self-treatment with insulin could prolong the life of the patient. Paradoxically, the simpler the tools became, the more the medical profession insisted on a monopoly of their application, the longer became the training demanded before a medicine man was initiated into the legitimate use of the simplest tool, and the more the entire population felt dependent on the doctor. Hygiene turned from being a virtue into a professionally organized ritual at the altar of a science.

Infant mortality was lowered, common forms of infection were prevented or treated, some forms of crisis intervention became quite effective. The spectacular decline in mortality and morbidity was due to changes in sanitation, agriculture, marketing, and general attitudes toward life. But though these changes were sometimes influenced by the attention that engineers paid to new facts discovered by medical science, they could only occasionally be ascribed to the intervention of doctors.

Indirectly, industrialization profited from the new effectiveness attributed to medicine; work attendance was raised, and with it the claim to efficiency on the job. The destructiveness of new tools was hidden from public view by new techniques of providing spectacular treatments for those who fell victims to industrial violence such as the speed of cars, tension on the job, and poisons in the environment.

The sickening side effects of modern medicine became obvious after World War II, but doctors needed time to diagnose drug-resistant microbes or genetic damage caused by prenatal X-rays as new epidemics. The claim made by George Bernard Shaw a generation earlier, that doctors had ceased to be healers and were assuming control over the patient's entire life, could still be regarded as a caricature. Only in the mid-fifties did it become evident that medicine had passed a second watershed and had itself created new kinds of disease.

Foremost among iatrogenic (doctor-induced) diseases was the pretense of doctors that they provided their clients with superior health. First, social planners and doctors became its victims. Soon this epidemic aberration spread to society at large. Then, during the last fifteen years, professional medicine became a major threat to health. Huge amounts of money were spent to stem immeasurable damage caused by medical treatments. The cost of healing was dwarfed by the cost of extending sick life; more people survived longer months with their lives hanging on a plastic tube, imprisoned in iron lungs, or hooked onto kidney machines. New sickness was defined and institutionalized; the cost of enabling people to survive in unhealthy cities and in sickening jobs skyrocketed. The monopoly of the medical profession was extended over an increasing range of everyday occurrences in every man's life.

The exclusion of mothers, aunts, and other nonprofessionals from the care of their pregnant, abnormal, hurt, sick, or dying relatives and friends resulted in new demands for medical services at a much faster rate than the medical establishment could deliver. As the value of *services* rose, it became almost impossible for people to *care*. Simultaneously, more conditions were defined as needing treatment by creating new specializations or paraprofessions to keep the tools under the control of the guild.

At the time of the second watershed, preservation of the sick life of medically dependent people in an unhealthy environment became the principal business of the medical profession. Costly prevention and costly treatment became increasingly the privilege of those individuals who through previous consumption of medical services had established a claim to more of it. Access to specialists, prestige hospitals, and life-machines goes preferentially to those people who live in large cities, where the cost of basic disease prevention, as of water treatment and pollution control, is already exceptionally high. The higher the per capita cost of prevention, the higher, paradoxically, became the per capita cost of treatment. The prior consumption of costly prevention and treatment establishes a claim for even more extraordinary care. Like the modern school system, hospital-based health care fits the principle that those who have will receive even more and those who have not will be taken for the little that they have. In schooling this means that high consumers of education will get postdoctoral grants, while dropouts learn that they have failed. In medicine the same principle assures that suffering will increase with increased medical care; the rich will be given more treatment for iatrogenic diseases and the poor will just suffer from them.

After this second turning point, the unwanted hygienic by-products of medicine began to affect entire populations rather than just individual men. In rich countries medicine began to sustain the middle-aged until they became decrepit and needed more doctors and increasingly complex medical tools. In poor countries, thanks to modern medicine, a larger percentage of children began to survive into adolescence and more women survived more pregnancies. Populations increased beyond the capacities of their environments and the restraints and efficiencies of their cultures to nurture them.

Western doctors abused drugs for the treatment of diseases with which native populations had learned to live. As a result they bred new strains of disease with which modern treatment, natural immunity, and traditional culture could not cope. On a world-wide scale, but particularly in the U.S.A., medical care concentrated on breeding a human stock that was fit only for domesticated life within an increasingly more costly, man-made, scientifically controlled environment. One of the main speakers at the 1970 AMA convention exhorted her pediatric colleagues to consider each new-born baby as a *patient* until the child could be certified as healthy. Hospital-born, formula-fed, antibiotic-stuffed children thus grow into adults who can breathe the air, eat the food, and survive the lifelessness of a modern city, who will breed and raise at almost any cost a generation even more dependent on medicine.

Bureaucratic medicine spread over the entire world. In 1968, after twenty years of Mao's regime, the Medical College of Shanghai had to conclude that it was engaged in the training of "so-called first-rate doctors . . . who ignore five million peasants and serve only minorities in cities. . . . They create large expenses for routine laboratory examinations . . . prescribe huge amounts of antibiotics unnecessarily . . . and in the absence of hospital or laboratory facilities have to limit themselves to explaining the mechanisms of the disease to people for whom they cannot do anything, and to whom this explanation is irrelevant." In China this recognition led to a major institutional inversion. Today, the same college reports that one million health workers have reached acceptable levels of competence. These health workers are laymen who in periods of low agricultural manpower needs have attended short courses, starting with the dissection of pigs, gone on to the performance of routine lab tests, the study of the elements of bacteriology, pathology, clinical medicine, hygiene, and acupuncture, and continued in apprenticeship with doctors or previously trained colleagues. These "barefoot doctors" remain at their work places but are excused occasionally when fellow workers require their assistance. They have responsibility for environmental sanitation, for health education, immunization, first aid, primary medical care, postillness follow-up, as well as for gynecological assistance, birth control, and abortion education. Ten years after the second watershed of Western medicine had been acknowledged, China intends to have one fully competent health worker for every hundred people. China has proved that a sudden inversion of a major institution is possible. It remains to be seen if this deprofessionalization can be sustained against the overweening ideology of unlimited progress and pressures from classical doctors to incorporate their barefoot homonym as part-time professionals on the bottom rung of a medical hierarchy.

In the West during the sixties dissatisfaction with medicine grew in proportion to its cost, reaching the greatest intensity in the U.S.A. Rich foreigners flocked to the medical centers of Boston, Houston, and Denver to seek exotic repair jobs, while the infant mortality of the U.S. poor remained comparable to that in some tropical countries of Africa and Asia. Only the very rich in the United States can now afford what all people in poor countries have: personal attention around the deathbed. An American can now spend in two days of private nursing the median yearly cash income of the world's population.

Instead of exposing the systemic disorder, however, only the symptoms of "sick" medicine are now publicly indicted in the United States. Spokesmen for the poor object to the capitalist prejudices of the AMA and the income of doctors. Community leaders object to the lack of community control over the delivery systems of professional health maintenance or of sick care, believing that laymen on hospital boards can harness professional medics. Black spokesmen object to the concentration of research grants on the types of disease which tend to strike the white, elderly, overfed foundation official who approves them. They ask for research on sickle-cell anemia, which strikes only the black. The general voter hopes that the end of the war in Vietnam will make more funds available for an increase of medical production. This general concern with symptoms, however, distracts attention from the malignant expansion of *institutional* health care which is at the root of the rising costs and demands and the decline in well-being.

The crisis of medicine lies on a much deeper level than its symptoms reveal and is consistent with the present crisis of all industrial institutions. It results from the development of a professional complex supported and exhorted by society to provide increasingly "better" health, and from the willingness of clients to serve as guinea pigs in this vain experiment. People have lost the right to declare themselves sick; society now accepts their claims to sickness only after certification by medical bureaucrats.

It is not strictly necessary to this argument to accept 1913 and 1955 as the two watershed years in order to understand that early in the century medical practice emerged into an era of scientific verification of its results. And later medical science itself became an alibi for the obvious damage caused by the medical professional. At the first watershed the desirable effects of new scientific discoveries were easily measured and verified. Germ-free water reduced infant mortality related to diarrhea, aspirin reduced the pain of rheumatism, and malaria could be controlled by quinine. Some traditional cures were recognized as quackery, but, more importantly, the use of some simple habits and tools spread widely. People began to understand the relationship between health and a balanced diet, fresh air, calisthenics, pure water and soap. New devices ranging from toothbrushes to Band-Aids and condoms became widely available. The positive contribution of modern medicine to individual health during the early part of the twentieth century can hardly be questioned.

But then medicine began to approach the second watershed. Every year medical science reported a new breakthrough. Practitioners of new specialties rehabilitated some individuals suffering from rare diseases. The practice of medicine became centered on the performance of hospital-based staffs. Trust in miracle cures obliterated good sense and traditional wisdom on healing and health care. The irresponsible use of drugs spread from doctors to the general public. The second watershed was approached when the marginal utility of further professionalization declined, at least insofar as it can be expressed in terms of the physical well-being of the largest number of people. The second watershed was superseded when the marginal *dis*utility increased as further monopoly by the medical establishment became an indicator of more suffering for larger numbers of people. After the passage of this second watershed, medicine still claimed continued progress, as measured by the new landmarks doctors set for themselves and then reached: both predictable discoveries and costs. For instance, a few patients survived longer with transplants of various organs. On the other hand, the total social cost exacted by medicine ceased to be measurable in conventional terms. Society can have no quantitative standards by which to add up the negative value of illusion, social control, prolonged suffering, loneliness, genetic deterioration, and frustration produced by medical treatment.

Other industrial institutions have passed through the same two watersheds. This is certainly true for the major social agencies that have been reorganized according to scientific criteria during the last 150 years. Education, the mails, social work, transportation, and even civil engineering have followed this evolution. At first, new knowledge is applied to the solution of a clearly stated problem and scientific measuring sticks are applied to account for the new efficiency. But at a second point, the progress demonstrated in a previous achievement is used as a rationale for the exploitation of society as a whole in the service of a value which is determined and constantly revised by an element of society, by one of its self-certifying professional élites.

In the case of transportation it has taken almost a century to pass from an era served by motorized vehicles to the era in which society has been reduced to virtual enslavement to the car. During the American Civil War steam power on wheels became effective. The new economy in transportation enabled many people to travel by rail at the speed of a royal coach, and to do so with a comfort kings had not dared dream of. Gradually, desirable locomotion was associated and finally identified with high vehicular speeds. But when transportation had passed through its second watershed, vehicles had created more distances than they helped to bridge; more time was used by the entire society for the sake of traffic than was "saved."

It is sufficient to recognize the existence of these two watersheds in order to gain a fresh perspective on our present social crisis. In one decade several major institutions have moved jointly over their second watershed. Schools are losing their claim to be effective tools to provide education; cars have ceased to be effective tools for mass transportation; the assembly line has ceased to be an acceptable mode of production.

The characteristic reaction of the sixties to the growing frustration was further technological and bureaucratic escalation. Self-defeating escalation of power became the core-ritual practiced in highly industrialized nations. In this context the Vietnam war is both revealing and concealing. It makes this ritual visible for the entire world in a narrow theater of war, yet it also distracts attention from the same ritual being played out in many so-called peaceful arenas. The conduct of the war proves that a convivial army limited to bicycle speeds is served by the opponent's escalation of anonymous power. And yet many Americans argue that the resources squandered on the war in the Far East could be used effectively to overwhelm poverty at home. Others are anxious to use the $20 billion the war now costs for increasing international development assistance from its present low of $2 billion. They fail to grasp the underlying institutional structure common to a peaceful war on poverty and a bloody war on dissidence. Both escalate what they are meant to eliminate.

While evidence shows that more of the same leads to utter defeat, nothing less than more and more seems worthwhile in a society infected by the growth mania. The desperate plea is not only for more bombs and more police, more medical examinations and more teachers, but also for more information and research. The editor-in-chief of the *Bulletin of Atomic Scientists* claims that most of our present problems are the result of recently acquired knowledge badly applied, and concludes that the only remedy for the mess created by this information is more of it. It has become fashionable to say that where science and technology have created problems, it is only more scientific understanding and better technology that can carry us past them. The cure for bad management is more management. The cure for specialized research is more costly interdisciplinary research, just as the cure for polluted rivers is more costly nonpolluting detergents. The pooling of stores of information, the building up of a knowledge stock, the attempt to overwhelm present problems by the production of more science is the ultimate attempt to solve a crisis by escalation.

POLLUTION AND CONSUMPTION

THE NEW YORKER

The Wisdom of the Worm

Until quite lately, we had all been used to believing that, generally speaking, it is easier to destroy things than to create them. This rule still holds true for governments, schools, and other institutions of society, but it no longer holds true for a steadily increasing number of our material artifacts. The pollutants that are currently endangering the environment have taught us that in many cases it can be much harder to destroy something than to create it. This lesson was forced home in a particularly striking way by the recent dilemma over how to dispose of several hundred nerve-gas rockets that had been stored for some three years at Defense Department ammunition depots in Alabama and Kentucky. The gap between our talent for manufacturing and our talent for dismantling has rarely been so clearly displayed. Presumably, it took great technological ingenuity to create the rockets, and, as for the gas, we had to turn, after the Second World War, to the files of the Nazi scientists to learn how to make it. When it came to getting rid of the rockets and their gas, however, the cleverest thing the Army could at first think of to do was to encase the rockets in blocks of steel and concrete—a solution that failed to insure against leaks while preventing anyone from getting at the rockets in order to detoxify the gas. Finally, of course, the Army got rid of the gas, the rockets, and their steel-and-concrete cases by the singularly crude method of loading them all onto a ship and sinking it in the ocean off Florida. Spokesmen for the Pentagon have assured us that the dumping will not cause any damage to the ocean environment, but many civilian scientists have argued that it may. The only thing that seems certain is that no one really has any definite information on what its effects will be.

At an earlier stage of the summer's pollution-power-transportation crisis in this city, it was noted here that one difference between the "natural" environment and a man-made environment is that complexity, which is a strength in the natural world, is a weakness in the man-made world. The incident of the nerve-gas rockets suggests some further differences between man's works and nature's. One thing we have all learned recently is that in birth, in life, and in death each species of animal and each species of plant performs innumerable functions that are crucial to the other species and to the environment that supports all species. For example, in "Silent Spring" Rachel Carson wrote of the earthworm, "Of all the larger inhabitants of the soil, probably none is more important than the earthworm. Over three-quarters of a century ago, Charles Darwin published a book titled 'The Formation of Vegetable Mould, Through the Action of Worms, with Observations on Their Habits.' In it he gave the world its first understanding of the fundamental role of earthworms as geologic agents for the transport of soil—a picture of surface rocks being gradually covered by fine soil brought up from below by the worms, in annual amounts running to many tons to the acre in most favorable areas. At the same time, quantities of organic matter contained in leaves and grass (as much as twenty pounds to the square yard in six months) are drawn down into the burrows and incorporated in soil. Darwin's calculations showed that the toil of earthworms might add a layer of soil an inch to an inch and a half thick in a ten-year period. And this is by no means all they do; their burrows aerate the soil, keep it well drained, and aid the penetration of plant roots. The presence of earthworms increases the nitrifying powers of the soil bacteria and decreases putrefaction of the soil. Organic matter is broken down as it passes through the digestive tracts of worms and the soil is enriched by their excretory products." Of course, the plants and the animals are, as far as we can tell, unaware of the multiplicity of services they perform for the environment. The earthworm probably has no conscious intention of enriching the soil as he progresses through the existence charted for him by his instincts. And quite certainly he has no intention of becoming a meal for a robin—another of his crucial roles. It is only man, apparently, who has "intentions" and "purposes." However, as it has turned out, man's purposes—in the area of material production, at least—serve ends that are much narrower than those served unthinkingly by other living things. Usually, man's artifacts are produced with only one end in mind, such as the provision of fuel for engines or of containers for food, and most of what he makes is useful for only a moment or so of its long sojourn in the environment. One inevitable consequence of man's producing things for such narrow ends is the necessity of "throwing away" what he has made when it has served its purpose. In the past, when we threw something "away," we pretty much considered that it had disappeared. But now, because of the ecological crisis, we know that there is no such thing as throwing something "away." There is only throwing it into the sea or into the soil or into the air. And what happens to a milk carton or a gallon of oil or a nerve-gas rocket when it gets there is as much our concern as what these things did when they were sitting in our iceboxes or driving our engines or killing our "enemies." Today, when we consider making something, we must expand our knowledge and concern beyond the moment of its service to us and take responsibility for its entire career on the earth. We must consider the effect it will have on all living things as it travels down our sewers or rises up our chimneys and makes its slow but inevitable circular progress through the chain of life back to our dinner tables or into our lungs. In short, we must learn the unknowing wisdom of the worm.

[From "The Talk of the Town," *The New Yorker*, August 29, 1970]

APPLETREE RODDEN

Appletree Rodden was born in Texas in 1937 and educated at Southwest University (B.S., 1964) and the University of Iowa, where he received a Ph.D. in biochemistry in 1969. He then embarked on a career in both biochemistry and psychiatry, investigating such subjects as the chemistry of the central nervous system and the mechanics of sleep and wakefulness. From 1969 to 1972 he was a bioscience Fellow at Stanford, then a research associate there in psychology and a biochemical consultant in the Linear Accelerator Center. He subsequently left the United States and his scientific career to join the Staatstheater Ballet Company in West Germany. His observation of West German refrigerators doubtless helped impel him to write the present article, which appeared in Harper's *in January 1975.*

Why Smaller Refrigerators Can Preserve the Human Race

Once, long ago, people had special little boxes called refrigerators in which milk, meat, and eggs could be kept cool. The grandchildren of these simple devices are large enough to store whole cows, and they reach temperatures comparable to those at the South Pole. Their operating costs increase each year, and they are so complicated that few home handymen attempt to repair them on their own.

Why has this change in size and complexity occurred in America? It has not taken place in many areas of the technologically advanced world (the average West German refrigerator is about a yard high and less than a yard wide, yet refrigeration technology in Germany is quite advanced). Do we really need (or even want) all that space and cold?

The benefits of a large refrigerator are apparent: a saving of time (one grocery-shopping trip a week instead of several), a saving of money (the ability to buy expensive, perishable items in larger, cheaper quantities), a feeling of security (if the car breaks down or if famine strikes, the refrigerator is well stocked). The costs are there, too, but they are not so obvious.

Cost number one is psychological. Ever since the refrigerator began to grow, food has increasingly become something we buy to store rather than to eat. Few families go to market daily for their daily bread. The manna in the wilderness could be gathered for only one day at a time. The ancient distaste for making food a storage item is echoed by many modern psychiatrists who suggest that such psychosomatic disorders as obesity are often due to the patient's inability to come to terms with the basic transitoriness of life. Research into a relationship between excessive corpulence and the size of one's refrigerator has not been extensive, but we might suspect one to be there.

Another cost is aesthetic. In most of Europe, where grocery marketing is still a part of the daily rhythm, one can buy tomatoes, lettuce, and the like picked on the day of purchase. Many European families have modest refrigerators for storing small items (eggs, milk, butter) for a couple of days, but the concept of buying large quantities of food to store in the refrigerator is not widely accepted. Since fresh produce is easily available in Europe, most people buy it daily.

Which brings to mind another price the large refrigerator has cost us: the friendly neighborhood market. In America, time is money. A large refrigerator means fewer time-consuming trips to the grocery store. One member of a deep-freeze-owning family can do the grocery shopping once or twice a month rather than daily. Since shopping trips are infrequent, most people have been willing to forego the amenities of the little store around the corner in favor of the lower prices found in the supermarket.

If refrigerators weren't so large—that is, if grocery marketing were a daily affair—the "entertainment surcharge" of buying farm-fresh food in a smaller, more intimate setting might carry some weight. But as it is, there is not really that much difference between eggs bought from Farmer Brown's wife and eggs bought from the supermarket which in turn bought them from Eggs Incorporated, a firm operated out of Los Angeles that produces 200,000 eggs a day from chickens that are kept in gigantic warehouses lighted artificially on an eighteen-hour light-and-dark cycle and produce one-and-a-half times as many eggs—a special breed of chickens who die young and insane. Not much difference if you don't mind eating eggs from crazy chickens.

Chalk up Farmer and Mrs. Brown as cost number four of the big refrigerator. The small farmer can't make it in a society dominated by supermarkets and big refrigerators; make way for superfarmers, super yields, and pesticides (cost number five).

Cost number six of the big refrigerator has been the diminution of regional food differences. Of course the homogenization of American fare cannot be blamed solely on the availability of frozen food. Nonetheless, were it not for the trend toward turning regional specialties into frozen dinners, it might still be possible to experience novelty closer to home.

So much for the disadvantages of the big refrigerator. What about the advantages of the small one? First of all, it would help us to "think small," which is what we must learn anyway if the scary predictions of the Club of Rome (*The Limits of Growth*) are true. The advent of smaller refrigerators would set the stage for reversing the "big-thinking" trends brought on with the big refrigerator, and would eventually change our lives.

Ivan Illich makes the point in *Tools for Conviviality* that any tool we use (the automobile, standardized public education, public-health care, the refrigerator) influences the individual, his society, and the relationship between the two. A person's automobile is a part of his identity. The average Volkswagen owner has a variety of characteristics (income, age, occupation) significantly different from those of the average Cadillac owner. American society, with more parking lots than parks, and with gridded streets rather than winding lanes, would be vastly different without the private automobile. Similar conclusions can be drawn about any of the tools we use. They change us. They change our society. Therefore, it behooves us to think well before we decide which tool to use to accomplish a given task. Do we want tools that usurp power unto themselves, the ones called "non-convivial" by Illich?

The telephone, a "convivial tool," has remained under control; it has not impinged itself on society or on the individual. Each year it has become more efficient, and it has not prevented other forms of communication (letter writing, visits). The world might be poorer without the telephone, but it would not be grossly different. Telephones do not pollute, are not status symbols, and interact only slightly (if at all) with one's self-image.

So what about the refrigerator? Or back to the more basic problem to which the refrigerator was a partial answer: what about our supply of food? When did we decide to convert the emotion-laden threat of starvation from a shared community problem (of societal structure: farm-market-home) to a personal one (of storage)? How did we decide to accept a thawed block taken from a supermarket's freezer as a substitute for the voluptuous shapes, smells, and textures of fresh fruits and vegetables obtained from complex individual sources?

The decision for larger refrigerators has been consistent with a change in food-supply routes from highly diversified "trails" (from small farms to neighborhood markets) to uniform, standardized highways (from large farms to centrally located supermarkets). Desirable meals are quick and easy rather than rich and leisurely. Culinary artistry has given way to efficiency, the efficiency of the big refrigerator.

People have a natural propensity for running good things into the ground. Mass production has been a boon to mankind, but its reliance on homogeneity precludes its being a paradigm for all areas of human life. Our forebears and contemporaries have made it possible to mass-produce almost anything. An equally challenging task now lies with us: to choose which things of this world should be mass-produced, and how the standards of mass production should influence other standards we hold dear.

Should houses be mass-produced? Should education? Should food? Which brings us back to refrigerators. How does one decide how large a refrigerator to buy, considering one's life, one's society, and the world, and not simply the question of food storage?

As similar questions are asked about more and more of the things we mass-produce, mass production will become less of a problem and more of a blessing. As cost begins to be measured not only in dollars spent and minutes saved, but in total richness acquired, perhaps smaller refrigerators will again make good sense. A small step backward along some of the roads of "technological progress" might be a large step forward for mankind, and one our age is uniquely qualified to make.

ISAAC ASIMOV

Isaac Asimov is an incredibly prolific author who is one of the best writers on science for the general public and a high priest of science fiction. He was born in the Soviet Union in 1920 and brought by his immigrant parents to New York City three years later. With a photographic memory, a boyhood taste for science fiction, a Ph.D. in biochemistry from Columbia (1948), and an obsessive capacity for work, Asimov early turned from a career in college teaching to the writing of books, which numbered 200 by 1979, not to speak of scores of short stories. Some of his most admired works of science fiction are the novels The Currents of Space *(1952),* The Caves of Steel *(1954), and* The Naked Sun *(1957). On science,* The New Intelligent Man's Guide to Science *(1965) is considered a model of encyclopedic clarity. He has also written popular works on ancient history and on the Bible. No one could have been better qualified to answer the request of the editors of* Time *for a vision of "an energy-poor society that might exist at the end of the 20th century."* Time *pubished it on April 25, 1977. "It is a picture of the worst," said Asimov, "of waste continuing, of oil running out, of nothing in its place, of world population continuing to rise. But then, that could happen, couldn't it?"*

The Nightmare Life Without Fuel

So it's 1997, and it's raining, and you'll have to walk to work again. The subways are crowded, and any given train breaks down one morning out of five. The buses are gone, and on a day like today the bicycles slosh and slide. Besides, you have only a mile and a half to go, and you have boots, raincoat and rain hat. And it's not a very cold rain, so why not?

Lucky you have a job in demolition too. It's steady work. Slow and dirty, but steady. The fading structures of a decaying city are the great mineral mines and hardware shops of the nation. Break them down and re-use the parts. Coal is too difficult to dig up and transport to give us energy in the amounts we need, nuclear fission is judged to be too dangerous, the technical breakthrough toward nuclear fusion that we hoped for never took place, and solar batteries are too expensive to maintain on the earth's surface in sufficient quantity.

Anyone older than ten can remember automobiles. They dwindled. At first the price of gasoline climbed—way up. Finally only the well-to-do drove, and that was too clear an indication that they were filthy rich, so any automobile that dared show itself on a city street was overturned and burned. Rationing was introduced to "equalize sacrifice," but every three months the ration was reduced. The cars just vanished and became part of the metal resource.

There are many advantages, if you want to look for them. Our 1997 newspapers continually point them out. The air is cleaner and there seem to be fewer colds. Against most predictions, the crime rate has dropped. With the police car too expensive (and too easy a target), policemen are back on their beats. More important, the streets are full. Legs are king in the cities of 1997, and people walk everywhere far into the night. Even the parks are full, and there is mutual protection in crowds.

If the weather isn't too cold, people sit out front. If it is hot, the open air is the only air conditioning they get. And at least the street lights still burn. Indoors, electricity is scarce, and few people can afford to keep lights burning after supper.

As for the winter—well, it is inconvenient to be cold, with most of what furnace fuel is allowed hoarded for the dawn; but sweaters are popular indoor wear and showers are not an everyday luxury. Lukewarm sponge baths will do, and if the air is not always very fragrant in the human vicinity, the automobile fumes are gone.

There is some consolation in the city that it is worse in the suburbs. The suburbs were born with the auto, lived with the auto, and are dying with the auto. One way out for the suburbanites is to form associations that assign turns to the procurement and distribution of food. Pushcarts creak from house to house along the posh suburban roads, and every bad snowstorm is a disaster. It isn't easy to hoard enough food to last till the roads are open. There is not much in the way of refrigeration except for the snowbanks, and then the dogs must be fought off.

What energy is left cannot be directed into personal comfort. The nation must survive until new energy sources are found, so it is the railroads and subways that are receiving major attention. The railroads must move the coal that is the immediate hope, and the subways can best move the people.

And then, of course, energy must be conserved for agriculture. The great car factories make trucks and farm machinery almost exclusively. We can huddle together when there is a lack of warmth, fan ourselves should there be no cooling breezes, sleep or make love at such times as there is a lack of light—but nothing will for long ameliorate a lack of food. The American population isn't going up much any more, but the food supply must be kept high even though the prices and difficulty of distribution force each American to eat less. Food is needed for export so that we can pay for some trickle of oil and for other resources.

The rest of the world, of course, is not as lucky as we are. Some cynics say that it is the knowledge of this that helps keep America from despair. They're starving out there, because earth's population has continued to go up. The population on earth is 5.5 billion, and outside the United States and Europe, not more than one in five has enough to eat at any given time.

All the statistics point to a rapidly declining rate of population increase, but that is coming about chiefly through a high infant mortality; the first and most helpless victims of starvation are babies, after their mothers have gone dry. A strong current of American opinion, as reflected in the newspapers (some of which still produce their daily eight pages of bad news), holds that it is just as well. It serves to reduce the population, doesn't it?

Others point out that it's more than just starvation. There are those who manage to survive on barely enough to keep the body working, and that proves to be not enough for the brain. It is estimated that there are now nearly 2 billion people in the world who are alive but who are permanently brain-damaged by undernutrition, and the number is growing year by year. It has already occurred to some that it would be "realistic" to wipe them out quietly and rid the earth of an encumbering menace. The American newspapers of 1997 do not report that this is actually being done anywhere, but some travelers bring back horror tales.

At least the armies are gone—no one can afford to keep those expensive, energy-gobbling monstrosities. Some soldiers in uniform and with rifles are present in almost every still functioning nation, but only the United States and the Soviet Union can maintain a few tanks, planes and ships—which they dare not move for fear of biting into limited fuel reserves.

Energy continues to decline, and machines must be replaced by human muscle and beasts of burden. People are working longer hours and there is less leisure; but then, with electric lighting restricted, television for only three hours a night, movies three evenings a week, new books few and printed in small editions, what is there to do with leisure? Work, sleep and eating are the great trinity of 1997, and only the first two are guaranteed.

Where will it end? It must end in a return to the days before 1800, to the days before the fossil fuels powered a vast machine industry and technology. It must end in subsistence farming and in a world population reduced by starvation, disease and violence to less than a billion.

And what can we do to prevent all this now?

Now? Almost nothing.

If we had started 20 years ago, that might have been another matter. If we had only started 50 years ago, it would have been easy.

Religion and the Need for Meaning

In this section we do not attempt to present a survey of contemporary religious thought, since any such attempt would at best be sketchy and superficial. Instead we focus on the search for meaning in a world reputedly become meaningless. God is dead, philosopher Friedrich Nietzsche proclaimed at the end of the last century, and it seems that the subsequent Western faith in scientific progress and the search for objective truth have been less than fulfilling for many. Spiritual needs remain. These frequently manifest themselves in a quest for meaning, so that to Paul Tillich, for example, "being religious means asking passionately the question of the meaning of our existence and being willing to receive answers, even if the answers hurt." In one way or another, all the writers we present below are concerned with this question.

The predicament is framed by the two poems that introduce the section— Father Hopkins' declaration of faith and Matthew Arnold's cry of doubt and despair. Clarence Darrow and Carl Sagan then speak as agnostics. Darrow, a lawyer writing in 1929, sees a sharp if simple conflict between science and religion. Sagan, a scientist writing fifty years later, sees less of a conflict. He sees "a universe that does not exclude a traditional Western or Eastern God, but that does not require one either," and concludes that "the enterprise of knowledge [also, after all, a way of finding meaning] is consistent with both science and religion."

The next two selections both deal with the loss of the dimension of depth in contemporary life, although from different perspectives. Tillich is a theolo- 591 gian who attempts to discover and define new meanings for religion and for God in our time. Peter Marin speaks more as a social observer, compassionate but concerned. He fears what he calls "the desire for spiritual submission" that leads us to submit to other *persons*. Instead, he recommends "almost anything, done with depth." We conclude the section with two autobiographical statements that simultaneously give personal testimony and assert the reality of God.

GERARD MANLEY HOPKINS
(1844–1889)

God's Grandeur

The world is charged with the grandeur of God.
  It will flame out, like shining from shook foil;
  It gathers to a greatness, like the ooze of oil
Crushed. Why do men then now not reck his rod?
Generations have trod, have trod, have trod;
  And all is seared with trade; bleared, smeared with toil;
  And wears man's smudge and shares man's smell: the soil
Is bare now, nor can foot feel, being shod.

And for all this, nature is never spent;
  There lives the dearest freshness deep down things;
And though the last lights off the black West went
  Oh, morning, at the brown brink eastward, springs—
Because the Holy Ghost over the bent
  World broods with warm breast and with ah! bright wings.

(1877)

MATTHEW ARNOLD
(1822–1888)

Dover Beach

The sea is calm to-night.
The tide is full, the moon lies fair
Upon the straits;—on the French coast the light
Gleams and is gone; the cliffs of England stand
Glimmering and vast, out in the tranquil bay.

Come to the window, sweet is the night-air!
Only, from the long line of spray
Where the sea meets the moon-blanched land,
Listen! you hear the grating roar
Of pebbles which the waves draw back, and fling,
At their return, up the high strand,
Begin, and cease, and then again begin,
With tremulous cadence slow, and bring
The eternal note of sadness in.

Sophocles long ago
Heard it on the Ægean, and it brought
Into his mind the turbid ebb and flow,
Of human misery; we
Find also in the sound a thought,
Hearing it by this distant northern sea.

The Sea of Faith
Was once, too, at the full, and round earth's shore
Lay like the folds of a bright girdle furled.
But now I only hear
Its melancholy, long, withdrawing roar,
Retreating, to the breath
Of the night-wind, down the vast edges drear
And naked shingles of the world.

Ah love, let us be true
To one another! for the world, which seems
To lie before us like a land of dreams,
So various, so beautiful, so new,
Hath really neither joy, nor love, nor light,
Nor certitude, nor peace, nor help for pain;
And we are here as on a darkling plain
Swept with confused alarms of struggle and flight,
Where ignorant armies clash by night.

(1867)

TWO AGNOSTIC VIEWS

CLARENCE DARROW

Clarence Darrow (1857-1938) is probably best known for his distinguished career in criminal law. Born in Ohio, he attended one year of law school at the University of Michigan, spent the next year in an attorney's office, and was admitted to the Ohio bar the following year, at the age of twenty-one. He soon left Ohio for Chicago and became the *most sought-after and controversial criminal lawyer of his time. His most famous cases include the defense of the child-murderers Leopold and Loeb, for whom he won a life sentence instead of the death penalty, and the Scopes Trial in 1925—known as the Monkey Trial—which created a national and international furor. Darrow, an outspoken agnostic, defended John Scopes, a Dayton, Tennessee, science teacher who had taught evolution and thus broken a state law prohibiting "the teaching in public schools of any theories that deny the divine creation of man as taught in the Bible." The prosecuting attorney was William Jennings Bryan, a fundamentalist. Darrow put Bryan on the stand, cross-examined him regarding his fundamentalist beliefs, and won what was considered a triumphant victory, although Scopes was formally convicted and sentenced to a nominal fine of $100. Bryan died five days later. The reader may wish to keep this case in mind when reading the essay we present below, reprinted from* Verdicts Out of Court *(ed. Arthur and Lila Weinberg, 1963). It was originally written in 1929 for a symposium in which Darrow was joined by a rabbi, a Protestant bishop, and a Catholic judge. Among Darrow's other writings are two autobiographical books,* Farmington *(1904) and* The Story of My Life *(1932), and a number of socio-legal works, including* Resist Not Evil *(1904),* Eye for an Eye *(1904), and* Crime: Its Cause and Its Treatment *(1922).*

Why I Am an Agnostic

An agnostic is a doubter. The word is generally applied to those who doubt the verity of accepted religious creeds or faiths. Everyone is an agnostic as to the beliefs or creeds they do not accept. Catholics are agnostics to the Protestant creeds, and the Protestants are agnostic to the Catholic creed. Anyone who thinks is an agnostic about something, otherwise he must believe that he is possessed of all knowledge. And the proper place for such a person is in the madhouse or the home for the feeble-minded. In a popular way, in the western world, an agnostic is one who doubts or disbelieves the main tenets of the Christian faith.

I would say that belief in at least three tenets is necessary to the faith of a Christian: a belief in God, a belief in immortality, and a belief in a supernatural book. Various Christian sects require much more, but it is difficult to imagine that one could be a Christian, under any intelligent meaning of the word, with less. Yet there are some people who claim to be Christians who do not accept the literal interpretation of all the Bible, and who give more credence to some portions of the book than to others.

I am an agnostic as to the question of God. I think that it is impossible for the human mind to believe in an object or thing unless it can form a mental picture of such object or thing. Since man ceased to worship openly an anthropomorphic God and talked vaguely and not intelligently about some force in the universe, higher than man, that is responsible for the existence of man and the universe, he cannot be said to believe in God. One cannot believe in a force excepting as a force that pervades matter and is not an individual entity. To believe in a thing, an image of the thing must be stamped on the mind. If one is asked if he believes in such an animal as a camel, there immediately arises in his mind an image of the camel. This image has come from experience or knowledge of the animal gathered in some way or other. No such image comes, or can come, with the idea of a God who is described as a force.

Man has always speculated upon the origin of the universe, including himself. I feel, with Herbert Spencer, that whether the universe had an origin—and if it had—what the origin is will never be known by man. The Christian says that the universe could not make itself; that there must have been some higher power to call it into being. Christians have been obsessed for many years by Paley's argument that if a person passing through a desert should find a watch and examine its spring, its hands, its case and its crystal, he would at once be satisfied that some intelligent being capable of design had made the watch. No doubt this is true. No civilized man would question that someone made the watch. The reason he would not doubt it is because he is familiar with watches and other appliances made by man. The savage was once unfamiliar with a watch and would have had no idea upon the subject. There are plenty of crystals and rocks of natural formation that are as intricate as a watch, but even to intelligent man they carry no implication that some intelligent power must have made them. They carry no such implication because no one has any knowledge or experience of someone having made these natural objects which everywhere abound.

To say that God made the universe gives us no explanation of the beginning of things. If we are told that God made the universe, the question immediately arises: Who made God? Did he always exist, or was there some power back of that? Did he create matter out of nothing, or is his existence co-extensive with matter? The problem is still there. What is the origin of it all? If, on the other hand, one says that the universe was not made by God, that it always existed, he has the same difficulty to confront. To say that the universe was here last year, or millions of years ago, does not explain its origin. This is still a mystery. As to the question of the origin of things, man can only wonder and doubt and guess.

As to the existence of the soul, all people may either believe or disbelieve. Everyone knows the origin of the human being. They know that it came from a single cell in the body of the mother, and that the cell was one out of ten thousand in the mother's body. Before gestation the cell must have been fertilized by a spermatozoön from the body of the father. This was one out of perhaps a billion spermatozoa that was the capacity of the father. When the cell is fertilized a chemical process begins. The cell divides and multiplies and increases into millions of cells, and finally a child is born. Cells die and are born during the life of the individual until they finally drop apart, and this is death.

If there is a soul, what is it, and where did it come from, and where does it go? Can anyone who is guided by his reason possibly imagine a soul independent of a body, or the place of its residence, or the character of it, or anything concerning it? If man is justified in any belief or disbelief on any subject, he is warranted in the disbelief in a soul. Not one scrap of evidence exists to prove any such impossible thing.

Many Christians base the belief of a soul and God upon the Bible. Strictly speaking, there is no such book. To make the Bible, sixty-six books are bound into one volume. These books were written by many people at different times, and no one knows the time or the identity of any author. Some of the books were written by several authors at various times. These books contain all sorts of contradictory concepts of life and morals and the origin of things. Between the first and the last nearly a thousand years intervened, a longer time than has passed since the discovery of America by Columbus.

When I was a boy the theologians used to assert that the proof of the divine inspiration of the Bible rested on miracles and prophecies. But a miracle means a violation of a natural law, and there can be no proof imagined that could be sufficient to show the violation of a natural law; even though proof seemed to show violation, it would only show that we were not acquainted with all natural laws. One believes in the truthfulness of a man because of his long experience with the man, and because the man has always told a consistent story. But no man has told so consistent a story as nature.

If one should say that the sun did not rise, to use the ordinary expression, on the day before, his hearer would not believe it, even though he had slept all day and knew that his informant was a man of the strictest veracity. He would not believe it because the story is inconsistent with the conduct of the sun in all the ages past.

Primitive and even civilized people have grown so accustomed to believing in miracles that they often attribute the simplest manifestations of nature to agencies of which they know nothing. They do this when the belief is utterly inconsistent with knowledge and logic. They believe in old miracles and new ones. Preachers pray for rain, knowing full well that no such prayer was ever answered. When a politician is sick, they pray for God to cure him, and the politician almost invariably dies. The modern clergyman who prays for rain and for the health of the politician is no more intelligent in this matter than the primitive man who saw a separate miracle in the rising and setting of the sun, in the birth of an individual, in the growth of a plant, in the stroke of lightning, in the flood, in every manifestation of nature and life.

As to prophecies, intelligent writers gave them up long ago. In all prophecies facts are made to suit the prophecy, or the prophecy was made after the facts, or the events have no relation to the prophecy. Weird and strange and unreasonable interpretations are used to explain simple statements, that a prophecy may be claimed.

Can any rational person believe that the Bible is anything but a human document? We now know pretty well where the various books came from, and about when they were written. We know that they were written by human beings who had no knowledge of science, little knowledge of life, and were influenced by the barbarous morality of primitive times, and were grossly ignorant of most things that men know today. For instance, Genesis says that God made the earth, and he made the sun to light the day and the moon to light the night, and in one clause disposes of the stars by saying that "he made the stars also." This was plainly written by someone who had no conception of the stars. Man, by the aid of his telescope, has looked out into the heavens and found stars whose diameter is as great as the distance between the earth and the sun. We now know that the universe is filled with stars and suns and planets and systems. Every new telescope looking further into the heavens only discovers more and more worlds and suns and systems in the endless reaches of space. The men who wrote Genesis believed, of course, that this tiny speck of mud that we call the earth was the center of the universe, the only world in space, and made for man, who was the only being worth considering. These men believed that the stars were only a little way above the earth, and were set in the firmament for man to look at, and for nothing else. Everyone today knows that this conception is not true.

The origin of the human race is not as blind a subject as it once was. Let alone God creating Adam out of hand, from the dust of the earth, does anyone believe that Eve was made from Adam's rib—that the snake walked and spoke in the Garden of Eden—that he tempted Eve to persuade Adam to eat an apple, and that it is on that account that the whole human race was doomed to hell—that for four thousand years there was no chance for any human to be saved, though none of them had anything whatever to do with temptation; and that finally men were saved only through God's son dying for them, and that unless human beings believed this silly, impossible and wicked story they were doomed to hell? Can anyone with intelligence really believe that a child born today should be doomed because the snake tempted Eve and Eve tempted Adam? To believe that is not God-worship; it is devil-worship.

Can anyone call this scheme of creation and damnation moral? It defies every principle of morality, as man conceives morality. Can anyone believe today that the whole world was destroyed by flood, save only Noah and his family and a male and female of each species of animal that entered the Ark? There are almost a million species of insects alone. How did Noah match these up and make sure of getting male and female to reproduce life in the world after the flood had spent its force? And why should all the lower animals have been destroyed? Were they included in the sinning of man? This is a story which could not beguile a fairly bright child of five years of age today.

Do intelligent people believe that the various languages spoken by man on earth came from the confusion of tongues at the Tower of Babel, some four thousand years ago? Human languages were dispersed all over the face of the earth long before that time. Evidences of civilizations are in existence now that were old long before the date claimed for the flood.

Do Christians believe that Joshua made the sun stand still, so that the day could be lengthened, that a battle might be finished? What kind of person wrote that story, and what did he know about astronomy? It is perfectly plain that the author thought that the earth was the center of the universe and stood still in the heavens, and that the sun either went around it or was pulled across its path each day, and that the stopping of the sun would lengthen the day. We know now that had the sun stopped when Joshua commanded it, and had it stood still until now, it would not have lengthened the day. We know that the day is determined by the rotation of the earth upon its axis, and not by the movement of the sun. Everyone knows that this story simply is not true, and not many even pretend to believe the childish fable.

What of the tale of Balaam's ass speaking to him, probably in Hebrew? Is it true, or is it a fable? Many asses have spoken, and doubtless some in Hebrew, but they have not been that breed of asses. Is salvation to depend on a belief in a monstrosity like this?

Above all the rest, would any human being today believe that a child was born without a father? Yet this story was not at all unreasonable in the ancient world; at least three or four miraculous births are recorded in the Bible, including John the Baptist and Samson. Immaculate conceptions were common in the Roman world at the time and at the place where Christianity really had its nativity. Women were taken to the temples to be inoculated of God so that their sons might be heroes, which meant, generally, wholesale butchers. Julius Caesar was a miraculous conception—indeed, they were common all over the world. How many miraculous-birth stories is a Christian now expected to believe?

In the days of the formation of the Christian religion, disease meant the possession of human beings by devils. Christ cured a sick man by casting out the devils, who ran into the swine, and the swine ran into the sea. Is there any question but what that was simply the attitude and belief of a primitive people? Does anyone believe that sickness means the possession of the body by devils, and that the devils must be cast out of the human being that he may be cured? Does anyone believe that a dead person can come to life? The miracles recorded in the Bible are not the only instances of dead men coming to life. All over the world one finds testimony of such miracles; miracles which no person is expected to believe, unless it is his kind of miracle. Still at Lourdes today, and all over the present world, from New York to Los Angeles and up and down the lands, people believe in miraculous occurrences, and even in the return of the dead. Superstition is everywhere prevalent in the world. It has been so from the beginning, and most likely will be so unto the end.

The reasons for agnosticism are abundant and compelling. Fantastic and foolish and impossible consequences are freely claimed for the belief in religion. All the civilization of any period is put down as a result of religion. All the cruelty and error and ignorance of the period has no relation to religion. The truth is that the origin of what we call civilization is not due to religion but to skepticism. So long as men accepted miracles without question, so long as they believed in original sin and the road to salvation, so long as they believed in a hell where man would be kept for eternity on account of Eve, there was no reason whatever for civilization: life was short, and eternity was long, and the business of life was preparation for eternity.

When every event was a miracle, when there was no order or system or law, there was no occasion for studying any subject, or being interested in anything excepting a religion which took care of the soul. As man doubted the primitive conceptions about religion, and no longer accepted the literal, miraculous teachings of ancient books, he set himself to understand nature. We no longer cure disease by casting out devils. Since that time, men have studied the human body, have built hospitals and treated illness in a scientific way. Science is responsible for the building of railroads and bridges, of steamships, of telegraph lines, of cities, towns, large buildings and small, plumbing and sanitation, of the food supply, and the countless thousands of useful things that we now deem necessary to life. Without skepticism and doubt, none of these things could have been given to the world.

The fear of God is not the beginning of wisdom. The fear of God is the death of wisdom. Skepticism and doubt lead to study and investigation, and investigation is the beginning of wisdom.

The modern world is the child of doubt and inquiry, as the ancient world was the child of fear and faith.

CARL SAGAN

This essay, a sermon delivered at Cornell University, is Chapter 23 of Carl Sagan's book Broca's Brain. *For further information about the author, see page 540.*

A Sunday Sermon

Extinguished theologians lie about the cradle of every science as the strangled snakes beside [the cradle] of Hercules.

—T. H. HUXLEY (1860)

We have seen the highest circle of spiraling powers. We have named this circle God. We might have given it any other name we wished: Abyss, Mystery, Absolute Darkness, Absolute Light, Matter, Spirit, Ultimate Hope, Ultimate Despair, Silence.

—NIKOS KAZANTZAKIS (1948)

These days, I often find myself giving scientific talks to popular audiences. Sometimes I am asked to discuss planetary exploration and the nature of the other planets; sometimes, the origin of life or intelligence on Earth; sometimes, the search for life elsewhere; and sometimes, the grand cosmological perspective. Since I have, more or less, heard these talks before, the question period holds my greatest interest. It reveals the attitudes and concerns of people. The most common questions asked are on unidentified flying objects and ancient astronauts—what I believe are thinly disguised religious queries. Almost as common—particularly after a lecture in which I discuss the evolution of life or intelligence—is: "Do you believe in God?" Because the word "God" means many things to many people, I frequently reply by asking what the questioner means by "God." To my surprise, this response is often considered puzzling or unexpected: "Oh, you know, *God*. Everyone knows who God is." Or "Well, kind of a force that is stronger than we are and that exists everywhere in the universe." There are a number of such forces. One of them is called gravity, but it is not often identified with God. And not everyone does know what is meant by "God." The concept covers a wide range of ideas. Some people think of God as an outsized, light-skinned male with a long white beard, sitting on a throne somewhere up there in the sky, busily tallying the fall of every sparrow. Others—for example, Baruch Spinoza and Albert Einstein—considered God to be essentially the sum total of the physical laws which describe the universe. I do not know of any compelling evidence for anthropomorphic patriarchs controlling human destiny from some hidden celestial vantage point, but it would be madness to deny the existence of physical laws. Whether we believe in God depends very much on what we mean by God.

In the history of the world there have been, probably, tens of thousands of different religions. There is a well-intentioned pious belief that they are all fundamentally identical. In terms of an underlying psychological resonance, there may indeed be important similarities at the cores of many religions, but in the details of ritual and doctrine, and the *apologias* considered to be authenticating, the diversity of organized religions is striking. Human religions are mutually exclusive on such fundamental issues as one god versus many; the origin of evil; reincarnation; idolatry; magic and witchcraft; the role of women; dietary proscriptions; rites of passage; ritual sacrifice; direct or mediated access to deities; slavery; intolerance of other religions; and the community of beings to whom special ethical considerations are due. We do no service to religion in general or to any doctrine in particular if we paper over these differences. Instead, I believe we should understand the world views from which differing religions derive and seek to understand what human needs are fulfilled by those differences.

Bertrand Russell once told of being arrested because he peacefully protested Britain's entry into World War I. The jailer asked—then a routine question for new arrivals—Rússell's religion. Russell replied, "Agnostic," which he was asked to spell. The jailer smiled benignly, shook his head and said, "There's many different religions, but I suppose we all worship the same God." Russell commented that the remark cheered him for weeks. And there may not have been much else to cheer him in that prison, although he did manage to write the entire *Introduction to Mathematical Philosophy* and started reading for his work *The Analysis of Mind* within its confines.

Many of the people who ask whether I believe in God are requesting reassurance that their particular belief system, whatever it is, is consistent with modern scientific knowledge. Religion has been scarred in its confrontation with science, and many people—but by no means all—are reluctant to accept a body of theological belief that is too obviously in conflict with what else we know. Apollo 8 accomplished the first manned lunar circumnavigation. In a more or less spontaneous gesture, the Apollo 8 astronauts read from the first verse of the Book of Genesis, in part, I believe, to reassure the taxpayers back in the United States that there were no real inconsistencies between conventional religious outlooks and a manned flight to the Moon. Orthodox Muslims, on the other hand, were outraged after Apollo 11 astronauts accomplished the first manned lunar landing, because the Moon has a special and sacred significance in Islam. In a different religious context, after Yuri Gagarin's first orbital flight, Nikita Khrushchev, the chairman of the Council of Ministers of the USSR, noted that Gagarin had stumbled on no gods or angels up there—that is, Khrushchev reassured his audience that manned orbital flight was not inconsistent with its beliefs.

In the 1950s a Soviet technical journal called *Voprosy Filosofii* (Problems in Philosophy) published an article that argued—very unconvincingly, it seemed to me—that dialectical materialism required there to be life on every planet. Some time later an agonized official rebuttal appeared, decoupling dialectical materialism from exobiology. A clear prediction in an area undergoing vigorous study permits doctrines to be subject to disproof. The last posture a bureaucratic religion wishes to find itself in is vulnerability to disproof, where an experiment can be performed on which the religion stands or falls. And so the fact that life has not been found on the Moon has left the foundations of dialectical materialism unshaken. Doctrines that make no predictions are less compelling than those which make correct predictions; they are in turn more successful than doctrines that make false predictions.

But not always. One prominent American religion confidently predicted that the world would end in 1914. Well, 1914 has come and gone, and—while the events of that year were certainly of some importance—the world does not, at least so far as I can see, seem to have ended. There are at least three responses that an organized religion can make in the face of such a failed and fundamental prophecy. They could have said, "Oh, did we say '1914'? So sorry, we meant '2014.' A slight error in calculation. Hope you weren't inconvenienced in any way." But they did not. They could have said, "Well, the world *would* have ended, except we prayed very hard and interceded with God so He spared the Earth." But they did not. Instead, they did something much more ingenious. They announced that the world *had* in fact ended in 1914, and if the rest of us hadn't noticed, that was our lookout. It is astonishing in the face of such transparent evasions that this religion has any adherents at all. But religions are tough. Either they make no contentions which are subject to disproof or they quickly redesign doctrine after disproof. The fact that religions can be so shamelessly dishonest, so contemptuous of the intelligence of their adherents, and still flourish does not speak very well for the tough-mindedness of the believers. But it does indicate, if a demonstration were needed, that near the core of the religious experience is something remarkably resistant to rational inquiry.

Andrew Dickson White was the intellectual guiding light, founder and first president of Cornell University. He was also the author of an extraordinary book called *The Warfare of Science with Theology in Christendom*, considered so scandalous at the time it was published that his co-author requested his name omitted. White was a man of substantial religious feeling.* But he outlined the long and painful history of erroneous claims which religions had made about the nature of the world, and how, when people directly investigated the nature of the world and discovered it to be different from doctrinal contentions, such people were persecuted and their ideas suppressed. The aged Galileo was threatened by the Catholic hierarchy with torture because he proclaimed the Earth to move. Spinoza was excommunicated by the Jewish hierarchy, and there is hardly an organized religion with a firm body of doctrine which has not at one time or another persecuted people for the crime of open inquiry. Cornell's own devotion to free and non-sectarian inquiry was considered so objectionable in the last quarter of the nineteenth century that ministers advised high school graduates that it was better to receive no college education than to attend so impious an institution. Indeed, this Sage Chapel was constructed in part to placate the pious—although, I am glad to say, it has from time to time made serious efforts at open-minded ecumenicism.

Many of the controversies which White describes are about origins. It used to be believed that every event in the world—the opening of a morning glory, let us say—was due to direct microintervention by the Deity. The flower was unable to open by itself. God had to say, "Hey, flower, open." The application of this idea to human affairs has often had desultory social consequences. For one thing it seems to imply that we are not responsible for our actions. If the play of the world is produced and directed by an omnipotent and omniscient God, does it not follow that every evil that is perpetrated is God's doing? I know this idea is an embarrassment in the West, and attempts to avoid it include the contention that what seems to be evil is really part of the Divine Plan, too complex for us to fathom; or that God chose to cloud his own vision about the causality skein when he set out to make the world. There is nothing utterly impossible about these philosophical rescue attempts, but they do seem to have very much the character of propping up a teetering ontological structure.† In addition, the idea of microintervention in the affairs of the world has been used to support the established social, political and economic conventions. There was, for example, the idea of a "Divine Right of Kings," seriously argued by philosophers such as Thomas Hobbes. If you had revolutionary thoughts directed, let us say, toward George III, you were guilty of blasphemy and impiety, religious crimes, as well as such more commonplace political crimes as treason.

---

*White seems also to have been responsible for the exemplary custom of not awarding honorary doctoral degrees at Cornell University: he was concerned about a potential abuse, that honorary degrees would be traded for financial gifts and bequests. White was a man of strong and courageous ethical standards.

†Many statements about God are confidently made by theologians on grounds that today at least sound specious. Thomas Aquinas claimed to prove that God cannot make another God, or commit suicide, or make a man without a soul, or even make a triangle whose interior angles do not equal 180 degrees. But Bolyai and Lobachevsky were able to accomplish this last feat (on a curved surface) in the nineteenth century, and they were not even approximately gods. It is a curious concept this, of an omnipotent God with a long list of things he is forbidden to do by the fiat of the theologians.

There are many legitimate scientific issues relating to origins and ends: What is the origin of the human species? Where did plants and animals come from? How did life arise? the Earth, the planets, the Sun, the stars? Does the universe have an origin, and if so, what? And finally, a still more fundamental and exotic question, which many scientists would say is essentially untestable and therefore meaningless: Why are the laws of nature the way they are? The idea that a God or gods is necessary to effect one or more of these origins has been under repeated attack over the last few thousand years. Because we know something about phototropism and plant hormones, we can understand the opening of the morning glory independent of divine microintervention. It is the same for the entire skein of causality back to the origin of the universe. As we learn more and more about the universe, there seems less and less for God to do. Aristotle's view was of God as an unmoved prime mover, a *roi fainéant*, a do-nothing king who establishes the universe in the first place and then sits back and watches the intricate, intertwined chains of causality course down through the ages. But this seems abstract and removed from everyday experience. It s a little unsettling and pricks at human conceits.

Humans seem to have a natural abhorrence of an infinite regression of causes, and this distaste is at the root of the most famous and most effective demonstrations of the existence of God by Aristotle and Thomas Aquinas. But these thinkers lived before the infinite series was a mathematical commonplace. If the differential and integral calculus or transfinite arithmetic had been invented in Greece in the fifth century B.C., and not subsequently suppressed, the history of religion in the West might have been very different—or at any rate we would have seen less of the pretension that theological doctrine can be convincingly demonstrated by rational argument to those who reject alleged divine revelation, as Aquinas attempted in the *Summa Contra Gentiles*.

When Newton explained the motion of the planets by the universal theory of gravitation, it no longer was necessary for angels to push and pummel the planets about. When Pierre Simon, the Marquis de Laplace, proposed to explain the origin of the solar system—although not the origin of matter—in terms of physical laws as well, even the necessity for a god involved in the origins of things seemed profoundly challenged. Laplace is said to have presented an edition of his seminal mathematical work *Mécanique céleste* to Napoleon aboard ship in the Mediterranean during the Napoleonic expedition to Egypt, 1798 to 1799. A few days later, so the story goes, Napoleon complained to Laplace that he had found no mention of God in the text.* Laplace's response has been recorded: "Sire, I have no need of that

---

*It is a charming notion that Napoleon actually spent his days aboard ship perusing the highly mathematical *Mécanique céleste*. But he was seriously interested in science and made an earnest attempt to survey the latest findings (see *The Society of Arcueil: A View of French Science at the Time of Napoleon I* by Maurice Crosland, Cambridge, Harvard University Press, 1967). Napoleon did not pretend to read all of the *Mécanique céleste* and wryly wrote to Laplace on another occasion, "The first six months which I can spare will be employed in reading it." But he also remarked, on another of Laplace's books, "Your works contribute to the glory of the nation. The progress and perfection of mathematics are linked closely with the prosperity of the state."

hypothesis." The idea of God as a hypothesis rather than as an obvious truth is by and large a modern idea in the West—although it was certainly discussed seriously and wryly by the Ionian philosophers of 2,400 years ago.

It is often considered that at least the origin of the universe requires a God—indeed, an Aristotelian idea.* This is a point worth looking at in a little more detail. First of all, it is perfectly possible that the universe is infinitely old and therefore requires no Creator. This is consistent with existing knowledge of cosmology, which permits an oscillating universe in which the events since the Big Bang are merely the latest incarnation in an infinite series of creations and destructions of the universe. But secondly, let us consider the idea of a universe created somehow from nothing by God. The question naturally arises—and many ten-year-olds spontaneously think of it before being discouraged by their elders—where does God come from? If we answer that God is infinitely old or present simultaneously in all epochs, we have solved nothing, except perhaps verbally. We have merely postponed by one step coming to grips with the problem. A universe that is infinitely old and a God that is infinitely old are, I think, equally deep mysteries. It is not readily apparent why one should be considered more reliably established than the other. Spinoza might have said that the two possibilities are not really different ideas at all.

I think it is wise, when coming face to face with such profound mysteries, to feel a little humility. The idea that scientists or theologians, with our present still puny understanding of this vast and awesome cosmos, can comprehend the origins of the universe is only a little less silly than the idea that Mesopotamian astronomers of 3,000 years ago—from whom the ancient Hebrews borrowed, during the Babylonian captivity, the cosmological accounts in the first chapter of Genesis—could have understood the origins of the universe. We simply do not know. The Hindu holy book, the Rig Veda (X: 129), has a much more realistic view of the matter:

> Who knows for certain? Who shall here declare it?
> Whence was it born, whence came creation?
> The gods are later than this world's formation;
> Who then can know the origins of the world?
> None knows whence creation arose;
> And whether he has or has not made it;
> He who surveys it from the lofty skies,
> Only he knows—or perhaps he knows not.

But the times we live in are very interesting ones. Questions of origins, including some questions relating to the origin of the universe, may in the next few decades be amenable to experimental inquiry. There is no conceivable answer to the grand cosmological questions which will not resonate

---

*However, from astronomical arguments Aristotle concluded that there were several dozen unmoved prime movers in the universe. Aristotelian arguments for a prime mover would seem to have polytheistic consequences that might be considered dangerous by contemporary Western theologians.

with the religious sensibilities of human beings. But there is a chance that the answers will discomfit a great many bureaucratic and doctrinal religions. The idea of religion as a body of belief, immune to criticism, fixed forever by some founder is, I think, a prescription for the long-term decay of the religion, especially lately. In questions of origins and ends, the religious and scientific sensibilities have much the same objectives. Human beings are built in such a way that we passionately wish to answer these questions—perhaps because of the mystery of our own individual origins. But our contemporary scientific insights, while limited, are much deeper than those of our Babylonian predecessors of 1,000 B.C. Religions unwilling to accommodate to change, both scientific and social, are, I believe, doomed. A body of belief cannot be alive and relevant, vibrant and growing, unless it is responsive to the most serious criticism that can be mustered against it.

The First Amendment to the United States Constitution encourages a diversity of religions but does not prohibit criticism of religion. In fact it protects and encourages criticism of religion. Religions ought to be subject to at least the same degree of skepticism as, for example, contentions about UFO visitations or Velikovskian catastrophism. I think it is healthy for the religions themselves to foster skepticism about the fundamental underpinnings of their evidential bases. There is no question that religion provides a solace and support, a bulwark in time of emotional need, and can serve extremely useful social roles. But it by no means follows that religion should be immune from testing, from critical scrutiny, from skepticism. It is striking how little skeptical discussion of religion there is in the nation that Tom Paine, the author of *The Age of Reason*, helped to found. I hold that belief systems that cannot survive scrutiny are probably not worth having. Those that do survive scrutiny probably have at least important kernels of truth within them.

Religion used to provide a generally accepted understanding of our place in the universe. That surely has been one of the major objectives of myth and legend, philosophy and religion, as long as there have been human beings. But the mutual confrontation of differing religions and of religion with science has eroded those traditional views, at least in the minds of many.* The way to find out about our place in the universe is by examining the universe and by examining ourselves—without preconceptions, with as unbiased a mind as we can muster. We cannot begin with an entirely clean slate, since we arrive at this problem with predispositions of hereditary and

*This subject is rich in irony. Augustine was born in Africa in 354 A.D. and in his early years was a Manichean, an adherent of a dualistic view of the universe in which good and evil are in conflict on roughly equal terms, and which was later condemned as a "heresy" by Christian orthodoxy. The possibility that all was not right with Manicheanism occurred to Augustine when he was studying its astronomy. He discovered that even the leading figures in the faith could not justify its murky astronomical notions. This contradiction between theology and science on matters astronomical was the initial impetus moving him toward Catholicism, the religion of his mother, which in later centuries persecuted scientists such as Galileo for trying to improve our understanding of astronomy. Augustine later became Saint Augustine, one of the major intellectual figures in the history of the Roman Catholic church, and his mother became Saint Monica, after whom a suburb of Los Angeles is named. Bertrand Russell wondered what Augustine's view of the conflict between astronomy and theology would have been had he lived in the time of Galileo.

environmental origin; but, after understanding such built-in biases, is it not possible to pry insights from nature?

Proponents of doctrinal religions—ones in which a particular body of belief is prized and infidels scorned—will be threatened by the courageous pursuit of knowledge. We hear from such people that it may be dangerous to probe too deeply. Many people have inherited their religion like their eye color: they consider it not a thing to think very deeply about, and in any case beyond our control. But those with a set of beliefs they profess to feel deeply about, which they have selected without an unbiased sifting through the facts and the alternatives, will feel uncomfortably challenged by searching questions. Anger at queries about our beliefs is the body's warning signal: here lies unexamined and probably dangerous doctrinal baggage.

Christianus Huygens wrote a remarkable book around 1670 in which bold and prescient speculations were made about the nature of the other planets in the solar system. Huygens was well aware that there were those who held such speculations and his astronomical observations objectionable: "But perhaps they'll say," Huygens mused, "it does not become us to be so curious and inquisitive in these Things which the Supreme Creator seems to have kept for his own Knowledge: For since he has not been pleased to make any farther Discovery or Revelation of them, it seems little better than presumption to make any inquiry into that which he has thought fit to hide. But these Gentlemen must be told," Huygens then thundered, "that they take too much upon themselves when they pretend to appoint how far and no farther Men shall go in their Searches, and to set bounds to other Mens Industry; as if they knew the Marks that God has placed to Knowledge: or as if Men were able to pass those Marks. If our Forefathers had been at this rate scrupulous, we might have been ignorant still of the Magnitude and Figure of the Earth, or that there was such a place as America."

If we look at the universe in the large, we find something astonishing. First of all, we find a universe that is exceptionally beautiful, intricately and subtly constructed. Whether our appreciation of the universe is because we are a part of that universe—whether, no matter how the universe were put together, we would have found it beautiful—is a proposition to which I do not pretend to have an answer. But there is no question that the elegance of the universe is one of its most remarkable properties. At the same time, there is no question that there are cataclysms and catastrophes occurring regularly in the universe and on the most awesome scale. There are, for example, quasar explosions which probably decimate the nuclei of galaxies. It seems likely that every time a quasar explodes, more than a million worlds are obliterated and countless forms of life, some of them intelligent, are utterly destroyed. This is not the traditional benign universe of conventional religiosity in the West, constructed for the benefit of living and especially of human beings. Indeed, the very scale of the universe—more than a hundred billion galaxies, each containing more than a hundred billion stars—speaks to us of the inconsequentiality of human events in the cosmic context. We see a universe simultaneously very beautiful and very violent.

We see a universe that does not exclude a traditional Western or Eastern god, but that does not require one either.

My deeply held belief is that if a god of anything like the traditional sort exists, our curiosity and intelligence are provided by such a god. We would be unappreciative of those gifts (as well as unable to take such a course of action) if we suppressed our passion to explore the universe and ourselves. On the other hand, if such a traditional god does not exist, our curiosity and our intelligence are the essential tools for managing our survival. In either case, the enterprise of knowledge is consistent with both science and religion, and is essential for the welfare of the human species.

In Search of Meaning

PAUL TILLICH

A profound and compassionate thinker and one of the great contemporary theologians, Paul Tillich (1886-1965) was born and educated in Germany and was well on his way to a distinguished academic career when he was dismissed from his post as Professor of Philosophy at the University of Frankfurt because of his outspoken criticism of the Nazi movement. In 1933, at the age of forty-seven, he emigrated to the United States at the invitation of Union Theological Seminary in New York, where he taught until 1954. That year he was appointed to the Divinity School Faculty at Harvard, and in 1962 he was named the first Duween Professor of Theology at the University of Chicago. His books include The Shaking of the Foundations *(1948) and* The New Being *(1955), two volumes of sermons;* The Protestant Era *(1948);* The Courage to Be *(1952);* Dynamics of Faith *(1957); and* Ultimate Concern: Tillich in Dialogue *(ed. D. M. Brown, 1965), based on tape recordings made during a seminar in the spring of 1964.*

Paul Tillich thought of God not as a Being, but as our ultimate concern, the ultimate personal depth and ground of all being. It is this "lost" dimension of depth that he discusses here in an essay first printed in the Saturday Evening Post, *June 14, 1958.*

The Lost Dimension in Religion

Every observer of our Western civilization is aware of the fact that something has happened to religion. It especially strikes the observer of the American scene. Everywhere he finds symptoms of what one has called religious revival, or more modestly, the revival of interest in religion. He finds them in the churches with their rapidly increasing membership. He finds them in the mushroomlike growth of sects. He finds them on college campuses and in the theological faculties of universities. Most conspicuously, he finds them in the tremendous success of men like Billy Graham and Norman Vincent Peale, who attract masses of people Sunday after Sunday, meeting after meeting. The facts cannot be denied, but how should they be interpreted? It is my intention to show that these facts must be seen as expressions of the predicament of Western man in the second half of the twentieth century. But I would even go a step further. I believe that the predicament of man in our period gives us also an important insight into the predicament of man generally—at all times and in all parts of the earth.

There are many analyses of man and society in our time. Most of them show important traits in the picture, but few of them succeed in giving a general key to our present situation. Although it is not easy to find such a key, I shall attempt it and, in so doing, will make an assertion which may be somewhat mystifying at first hearing. The decisive element in the predicament of Western man in our period is his loss of the dimension of depth. Of course, "dimension of depth" is a metaphor. It is taken from the spatial realm and applied to man's spiritual life. What does it mean?

It means that man has lost an answer to the question: What is the meaning of life? Where do we come from, where do we go to? What shall we do, what should we become in the short stretch between birth and death? Such questions are not answered or even asked if the "dimension of depth" is lost. And this is precisely what has happened to man in our period of history. He has lost the courage to ask such questions with an infinite seriousness—as former generations did—and he has lost the courage to receive answers to these questions, wherever they may come from.

I suggest that we call the dimension of depth the religious dimension in man's nature. Being religious means asking passionately the question of the meaning of our existence and being willing to receive answers, even if the answers hurt. Such an idea of religion makes religion universally human, but it certainly differs from what is usually called religion. It does not describe religion as the belief in the existence of gods or one God, and as a set of activities and institutions for the sake of relating oneself to these beings in thought, devotion and obedience. No one can deny that the religions which have appeared in history are religions in this sense. Nevertheless, religion in its innermost nature is more than religion in this narrower sense. It is the state of being concerned about one's own being and being universally.

There are many people who are ultimately concerned in this way who feel far removed, however, from religion in the narrower sense, and therefore from every historical religion. It often happens that such people take the question of the meaning of their life infinitely seriously and reject any historical religion just for this reason. They feel that the concrete religions fail to express their profound concern adequately. They are religious while rejecting the religions. It is this experience which forces us to distinguish the meaning of religion as living in the dimension of depth from particular expressions of one's ultimate concern in the symbols and institutions of a concrete religion. If we now turn to the concrete analysis of the religious situation of our time, it is obvious that our key must be the basic meaning of religion and not any particular religion, not even Christianity. What does this key disclose about the predicament of man in our period?

If we define religion as the state of being grasped by an infinite concern we must say: Man in our time has lost such infinite concern. And the resurgence of religion is nothing but a desperate and mostly futile attempt to regain what has been lost.

How did the dimension of depth become lost? Like any important event, it has many causes, but certainly not the one which one hears often mentioned from ministers' pulpits and evangelists' platforms, namely that a widespread impiety of modern man is responsible. Modern man is neither more pious nor more impious than man in any other period. The loss of the dimension of depth is caused by the relation of man to his world and to himself in our period, the period in which nature is being subjected scientifically and technically to the control of man. In this period, life in the dimension of depth is replaced by life in the horizontal dimension. The driving forces of the industrial society of which we are a part go ahead horizontally and not vertically. In popular terms this is expressed in phrases like "better and better," "bigger and bigger," "more and more." One should not disparage the feeling which lies behind such speech. Man is right in feeling that he is able to know and transform the world he encounters without a foreseeable limit. He can go ahead in all directions without a definite boundary.

A most expressive symbol of this attitude of going ahead in the horizontal dimension is the breaking through of the space which is controlled by the gravitational power of the earth into the world-space. It is interesting that one calls this world-space simply "space" and speaks, for instance, of space travel, as if every trip were not travel into space. Perhaps one feels that the true nature of space has been discovered only through our entering into indefinite world-space. In any case, the predominance of the horizontal dimension over the dimension of depth has been immensely increased by the opening up of the space beyond the space of the earth.

If we now ask what does man do and seek if he goes ahead in the horizontal dimension, the answer is difficult. Sometimes one is inclined to say that the mere movement ahead without an end, the intoxication with speeding forward without limits, is what satisfies him. But this answer is by no means sufficient. For on his way into space and time man changes the world he encounters. And the changes made by him change himself. He transforms everything he encounters into a tool; and in doing so he himself becomes a tool. But if he asks, a tool for what, there is no answer.

One does not need to look far beyond everyone's daily experience in order to find examples to describe this predicament. Indeed our daily life in office and home, in cars and airplanes, at parties and conferences, while reading magazines and watching television, while looking at advertisements and hearing radio, are in themselves continuous examples of a life which has lost the dimension of depth. It runs ahead, every moment is filled with something which must be done or seen or said or planned. But no one can experience depth without stopping and becoming aware of himself. Only if he has moments in which he does not care about what comes next can he experience the meaning of this moment here and now and ask himself about the meaning of his life. As long as the preliminary, transitory concerns are not silenced, no matter how interesting and valuable and important they may be, the voice of the ultimate concern cannot be heard. This is the deepest root of the loss of the dimension of depth in our period—the loss of religion in its basic and universal meaning.

If the dimension of depth is lost, the symbols in which life in this dimension has expressed itself must also disappear. I am speaking of the great symbols of the historical religions in our Western world, of Judaism and Christianity. The reason that the religious symbols became lost is not primarily scientific criticism, but it is a complete misunderstanding of their meaning; and only because of this misunderstanding was scientific critique able, and even justified, in attacking them. The first step toward the non-religion of the Western world was made by religion itself. When it defended its great symbols, not as symbols, but as literal stories, it had already lost the battle. In doing so the theologians (and today many religious laymen) helped to transfer the powerful expressions of the dimension of depth into objects or happenings on the horizontal plane. There the symbols lose their power and meaning and become an easy prey to physical, biological and historical attack.

If the symbol of creation which points to the divine ground of everything is transferred to the horizontal plane, it becomes a story of events in a removed past for which there is no evidence, but which contradicts every piece of scientific evidence. If the symbol of the Fall of Man, which points to the tragic estrangement of man and his world from their true being is transferred to the horizontal plane, it becomes a story of a human couple a few thousand years ago in what is now present-day Iraq. One of the most profound psychological descriptions of the general human predicament becomes an absurdity on the horizontal plane. If the symbols of the Saviour and the salvation through Him which point to the healing power in history and personal life are transferred to the horizontal plane, they become stories of a half-divine being coming from a heavenly place and returning to it. Obviously, in this form, they have no meaning whatsoever for people whose view of the universe is determined by scientific astronomy.

If the idea of God (and the symbols applied to Him) which expresses man's ultimate concern is transferred to the horizontal plane, God becomes a being among others whose existence or nonexistence is a matter of inquiry. Nothing, perhaps, is more symptomatic of the loss of the dimension of depth than the permanent discussion about the existence or nonexistence of God— a discussion in which both sides are equally wrong, because the discussion itself is wrong and possible only after the loss of the dimension of depth.

When in this way man has deprived himself of the dimension of depth and the symbols expressing it, he then becomes a part of the horizontal plane. He loses his self and becomes a thing among things. He becomes an element in the process of manipulated production and manipulated consumption. This is now a matter of public knowledge. We have become aware of the degree to which everyone in our social structure is managed, even if one knows it and even if one belongs himself to the managing group. The influence of the gang mentality on adolescents, of the corporation's demands on the executives, of the conditioning of everyone by public communication, by propaganda and advertising under the guidance of motivation research, et cetera, have all been described in many books and articles.

Under these pressures, man can hardly escape the fate of becoming a thing among the things he produces, a bundle of conditioned reflexes without a free, deciding and responsible self. The immense mechanism, set up by man to produce objects for his use, transforms man himself into an object used by the same mechanism of production and consumption.

But man has not ceased to be man. He resists this fate anxiously, desperately, courageously. He asks the question, for what? And he realizes that there is no answer. He becomes aware of the emptiness which is covered by the continuous movement ahead and the production of means for ends which become means again without an ultimate end. Without knowing what has happened to him, he feels that he has lost the meaning of life, the dimension of depth.

Out of this awareness the religious question arises and religious answers are received or rejected. Therefore, in order to describe the contemporary attitude toward religion, we must first point to the places where the awareness of the predicament of Western man in our period is most sharply expressed. These places are the great art, literature and partly, at least, the philosophy of our time. It is both the subject matter and the style of these creations which show the passionate and often tragic struggle about the meaning of life in a period in which man has lost the dimension of depth. This art, literature, philosophy is not religious in the narrower sense of the word; but it asks the religious question more radically and more profoundly than most directly religious expressions of our time.

It is the religious question which is asked when the novelist describes a man who tries in vain to reach the only place which could solve the problem of his life, or a man who disintegrates under the memory of a guilt which persecutes him, or a man who never had a real self and is pushed by his fate without resistance to death, or a man who experiences a profound disgust of everything he encounters.

It is the religious question which is asked when the poet opens up the horror and the fascination of the demonic regions of his soul, or if he leads us into the deserts and empty places of our being, or if he shows physical and moral mud under the surface of life, or if he sings the song of transitoriness, giving words to the ever-present anxiety of our hearts.

It is the religious question which is asked when the playwright shows the illusion of a life in a ridiculous symbol, or if he lets the emptiness of a life's work end in self-destruction, or if he confronts us with the inescapable bondage to mutual hate and guilt, or if he leads us into the dark cellar of lost hopes and slow disintegration.

It is the religious question which is asked when the painter breaks the visible surface into pieces, then reunites them into a great picture which has little similarity with the world at which we normally look, but which expresses our anxiety and our courage to face reality.

It is the religious question which is asked when the architect, in creating office buildings or churches, removes the trimmings taken over from past styles because they cannot be considered an honest expression of our own period. He prefers the seeming poverty of a purpose-determined style to the deceptive richness of imitated styles of the past. He knows that he gives no final answer, but he does give an honest answer.

The philosophy of our time shows the same hiddenly religious traits. It is divided into two main schools of thought, the analytic and the existentialist. The former tries to analyze logical and linguistic forms which are always used and which underlie all scientific research. One may compare them with the painters who dissolve the natural forms of bodies into cubes, planes and lines; or with those architects who want the structural "bones" of their buildings to be conspicuously visible and not hidden by covering features. This self-restriction produces the almost monastic poverty and seriousness of this philosophy. It is religious—without any contact with religion in its method—by exercising the humility of "learned ignorance."

In contrast to this school the existentialist philosophers have much to say about the problems of human existence. They bring into rational concepts what the writers and poets, the painters and architects, are expressing in their particular material. What they express is the human predicament in time and space, in anxiety and guilt and the feeling of meaninglessness. From Pascal in the seventeenth century to Heidegger and Sartre in our time, philosophers have emphasized the contrast between human dignity and human misery. And by doing so, they have raised the religious question. Some have tried to answer the question they have asked. But if they did so, they turned back to past traditions and offered to our time that which does not fit our time. Is it possible for our time to receive answers which are born out of our time?

Answers given today are in danger of strengthening the present situation and with it the questions to which they are supposed to be the answers. This refers to some of the previously mentioned major representatives of the so-called resurgence of religion, as for instance the evangelist Billy Graham and the counseling and healing minister, Norman Vincent Peale. Against the validity of the answers given by the former, one must say that, in spite of his personal integrity, his propagandistic methods and his primitive theological fundamentalism fall short of what is needed to give an answer to the religious question of our period. In spite of all his seriousness, he does not take the radical questions of our period seriously.

The effect that Norman Peale has on large groups of people is rooted in the fact that he confirms the situation which he is supposed to help overcome. He heals people with the purpose of making them fit again for the demands of the competitive and conformist society in which we are living. He helps them to become adapted to the situation which is characterized by the loss of the dimension of depth. Therefore, his advice is valid on this level; but it is the validity of this level that is the true religious question of our time. And this question he neither raises nor answers.

In many cases the increase of church membership and interest in religious activities does not mean much more than the religious consecration of a state of things in which the religious dimension has been lost. It is the desire to participate in activities which are socially strongly approved and give internal and a certain amount of external security. This is not necessarily bad, but it certainly is not an answer to the religious question of our period.

Is there an answer? There is always an answer, but the answer may not be available to us. We may be too deeply steeped in the predicament out of which the question arises to be able to answer it. To acknowledge this is certainly a better way toward a real answer than to bar the way to it by deceptive answers. And it may be that in this attitude the real answer (within available limits) is given. The real answer to the question of how to regain the dimension of depth is not given by increased church membership or church attendance, nor by conversion or healing experiences. But it is given by the awareness that we have lost the decisive dimension of life, the dimension of depth, and that there is no easy way of getting it back. Such awareness is in itself a state of being grasped by that which is symbolized in the term, dimension of depth. He who realizes that he is separated from the ultimate source of meaning shows by this realization that he is not only separated but also reunited. And this is just our situation. What we need above all—and partly have—is the radical realization of our predicament, without trying to cover it up by secular or religious ideologies. The revival of religious interest would be a creative power in our culture if it would develop into a movement of search for the lost dimension of depth.

This does not mean that the traditional religious symbols should be dismissed. They certainly have lost their meaning in the literalistic form into which they have been distorted, thus producing the critical reaction against them. But they have not lost their genuine meaning, namely, of answering the question which is implied in man's very existence in powerful, revealing and saving symbols. If the resurgence of religion would produce a new understanding of the symbols of the past and their relevance for our situation, instead of premature and deceptive answers, it would become a creative factor in our culture and a saving factor for many who live in estrangement, anxiety and despair. The religious answer has always the character of "in spite of." In spite of the loss of dimension of depth, its power is present, and most present in those who are aware of the loss and are striving to regain it with ultimate seriousness.

PETER MARIN

This essay first appeared in Harper's, *February 1979, as an introduction to journal selections entitled "Tibet in Boulder." For further information about the author, see page 243.*

Spiritual Obedience

A letter came the other day from a good friend of mine, a poet who has always been torn between radical politics and mysticism, and who genuinely aches for the presence of God. A few years ago, astonishing us all, he became a follower of the Guru Maharaj Ji—the smiling, plump young man who heads the Divine Light Mission. Convinced that his guru was in fact God, or at least a manifestation of God, my friend gave his life to him, choosing to become one of his priests, and rapidly rising—because of his brilliance and devotion—to the top of the organization's hierarchy. But last week I received a phone call from my friend, who told me he intended to leave the organization, mainly because, as he said, he could neither "give up the idea of the individual" nor "altogether stop myself from thinking."

Then, a few days later, the letter came, scrawled unevenly on lined yellow paper, in a script more ragged than I remembered, and made somehow poignant by the uneven tone:

> The decision in me to hang it up is the one bright light within me for the time being. Because what is actually the case is that I've lived very much the lifestyle of 1984. Or of Mao's China—or of Hitler's Germany. Imagine for a moment a situation where every single moment of your day is programmed. You begin with exercise, then meditation, then a communal meal. Then the service (the work each member does). As the Director of the House in which I lived and the director of the clinic, it was my job daily to give the requisite pep talks or Satsangs to the staff. You work six days a week, nine to six—then come home to dinner and then go to two hours of spiritual discourse, then meditate. There is no leisure. It is always a group consciousness. You discuss nothing that isn't directly related to "the knowledge." You are censured if you discuss any topics of the world. And, of course, there is always the constant focus on the spiritual leader.
>
> Can you imagine not thinking, not writing, not reading, and no real discussion? Day after day, the rest of your life? That is the norm here.
>
> What is the payoff? *Love.* You are allowed access to a real experience of transcendence. There is a great emotional tie to your fellow devotees and to your Guru—your Guru, being the center stage of everything you do, becomes omnipresent. Everything is ascribed to him. He is positively supernatural after a while. Any normal form of causal thinking breaks down. The ordinary world with its laws and orders is proscribed. It is an "illusion." It is an absolutely foolproof system. Better than Mao, because it delivers a closer-knit cohesiveness than collective criticism and the red book.
>
> Look at me. After a bad relationship, a disintegrated marriage, a long illness, a deep searching for an answer, I was ripe. I was always impulsive anyway. So, I bought in. That feeling of love, of community. The certainty that you are submitting to God incarnate. It creates a wonderfully deep and abiding euphoria which, for some, lasts indefinitely.
>
> To trip away from such a euphoria, back to a world of doubt and criticism, of imperfection—why would anyone reject fascism or communism—in prac-

tice they are the same—once one had experienced the benefits of these systems?

Because there is more to human beings than the desire for love or the wish for problems to go away. There is also the spirit—the reasoning element in man and a sense of morality. My flight now is due out Dec. 5. I am hoping to last that long. I think that with a little luck, I will. If not, I'll call.

Love to you, K

Nothing is simple. A few days later my friend called again, his voice a bit stronger, still anxious to leave, asking me to make his travel arrangements. But this time he began talking about William Buckley, how he liked his work, how he had written to him, gotten a moving letter in return. I could hear, as he talked, the beginning of a new kind of attachment, the hints of a reaction tending toward conservatism, the touch—ever so faint—of a new enthusiasm, a new creed, something new to believe in, to join. Never having been to China, he had once extolled its virtues; now, without seeing it, he denounces its faults. His moods are like the wild swings of a quivering compass needle, with no true pole.

I remember going a few years ago to a lecture in which the speaker, in the name of enlightenment, had advocated total submission to a religious master. The audience, like most contemporary audiences, had been receptive to the idea, or more receptive, rather, than they would have been a while back. Half of them were intrigued by the idea, drawn to it. Total submission. Obedience to a "perfect master." One could hear, inwardly in them, the gathering of breath for a collective sigh of relief. At last, to be set free, to lay down one's burden, to be a child again—not in renewed innocence, but in restored dependence, in *admitted*, undisguised dependence. To be told, again, what to do, and how to do it. . . . The yearning in the audience was so palpable, their need so thick and obvious, that it was impossible not to feel it, impossible not to empathize with it in some way. Why not, after all? Clearly there are truths and kinds of wisdom to which most persons will not come alone; clearly there are in the world authorities in matters of the spirit, seasoned travelers, guides. Somewhere there must be truths other than the disappointing ones we have; somewhere there must be access to a world larger than this one. And if, to get there, we must put aside all arrogance of will and the stubborn ego, why not? Why not admit what we do not know and cannot do and submit to someone who both knows and does, who will teach us if we merely put aside all judgment for the moment and obey with trust and goodwill?

The audience in question was a white and middle-class group, in spiritual need perhaps, but not only in spiritual need. They were also politically frustrated and exhausted, had been harried and bullied into positions of alienation and isolation, had been raised in a variety of systems that taught them simultaneously individual responsibility and high levels of submission to institutional authority. As a result, without adequate or satisfying participation in the *polis*, or the communal or social worlds, the desire for spiritual submission may reveal less of a spiritual yearning and more of a habitual appetite for submission in general. Submission becomes a value and an end in itself, and unless it exists side by side with an insistence upon political power and participation, it becomes a frightening and destructive thing.

There are many things to which a man or woman might submit: to his own work, to the needs of others, to the love of others, to passion, to experience, to the rhythms of nature—the list is endless and includes almost anything men or women might do, for almost anything, done with depth, takes us beyond ourselves and into relation with other things, and that is always a submission, for it is always a joining, a kind of wedding to the world. There is, no doubt, a need for that, for without it we grow exhausted with ourselves, with our wisdom still unspoken, and our needs unmet.

But that general appetite is twisted and used tyrannically when we are asked to submit ourselves unconditionally to other *persons*—whether they wear the masks of the state or of the spirit. In both instances our primary relation is no longer to the world or to others; it is to "the master," and the world or others suffer from that choice, because our relation to them is broken, and with it our sense of possibility. In our attempt to restore to ourselves what is missing, we merely intensify the deprivation rather than diminish it.

THE PERSONAL TESTIMONY

ST. TERESA OF AVILA

St. Teresa (1515-1582) was born in Avila, Spain, and attended a convent school in that town. At eighteen she entered the Carmelite convent of the Incarnation, and, except for severe illnesses, led an unremarkable religious life for many years. Then in 1554, at the age of thirty-nine, she experienced a kind of conversion in the presence of an image of the wounded Christ; from then on she lost every worldly desire and devoted herself to spiritual perfection. She also began to have the ever-deepening mystical experiences, especially of the presence of Christ, that went on all the rest of her life. In the period 1558 to 1560 she had visions that she would later describe in her autobiography, written in colloquial Spanish between 1562 and 1565.

St. Teresa wrote the book at the behest of her confessors, her spiritual directors, in an attempt to make clear the history and quality of her experiences, especially those received in prayer. Her visions were by no means universally accepted by her sisters and superiors; many thought them the work of the devil. Her natural humility led her to accept this possibility and to subject her own mind and spirit to the most rigorous analysis. The result is a remarkable piece of psychological self-examination.

St. Teresa's ideals led her to the founding of a reformed branch of the Carmelites—called the Descalzos, or Barefoots. The last twenty years of her life were spent in establishing its convents and monasteries all over Spain, often against an opposition from inside and outside her Order that severely tested her determination and her great administrative ability. She continued also to write, enlarging and deepening her study of the spiritual life in The Way of Perfection *(about 1565) and* The Interior Castle *(1577).*

The following passages are taken from Chapters 27 and 32 of her autobiography, in the translation of David Lewis (1870; ed. J. J. Burke, 1911).

Visions

I now resume the story of my life. I was in great pain and distress; and many prayers, as I said, were made on my behalf, that our Lord would lead me by another and a safer way; for this, they told me, was so suspicious. The truth is, that though I was praying to God for this, and wished I had a desire for another way, yet, when I saw the progress I was making, I was unable really to desire a change,—though I always prayed for it,—excepting on those occasions when I was extremely cast down by what people said to me, and by the fears with which they filled me.

I felt that I was wholly changed; I could do nothing but put myself in the hands of God: He knew what was expedient for me; let Him do with me according to His will in all things. I saw that by this way I was directed heavenwards, and that formerly I was going down to hell. I could not force myself to desire a change, nor believe that I was under the influence of Satan. Though I was doing all I could to believe the one and to desire the other, it was not in my power to do so. I offered up all my actions, if there should be any good in them, for this end; I had recourse to the Saints for whom I had a devotion, that they might deliver me from the evil one; I made novenas; I commended myself to St. Hilarion, to the Angel St. Michael, to whom I had recently become devout, for this purpose; and many other Saints I importuned, that our Lord might show me the way,—I mean, that they might obtain this for me from His Majesty.

At the end of two years spent in prayer by myself and others for this end, namely, that our Lord would either lead me by another way, or show the truth of this,—for now the locutions of our Lord were extremely frequent,—this happened to me. I was in prayer one day,—it was the feast of the glorious St. Peter,—when I saw Christ close by me, or, to speak more correctly, felt Him; for I saw nothing with my eyes of the body, nothing with the eyes of the soul. He seemed to me to be close beside me; and I saw, too, as I believe, that it was He who was speaking to me. As I was utterly ignorant that such a vision was possible, I was extremely afraid at first, and did nothing but weep; however, when He spoke to me but one word to reassure me, I recovered myself, and was, as usual, calm and comforted, without any fear whatever. Jesus Christ seemed to be by my side continually, and, as the vision was not imaginary, I saw no form; but I had a most distinct feeling that He was always on my right hand, a witness of all I did; and never at any time, if I was but slightly recollected, or not too much distracted, could I be ignorant of His near presence.

I went at once to my confessor, in great distress, to tell him of it. He asked in what form I saw our Lord. I told him I saw no form. He then said: "How did you know that it was Christ?" I replied, that I did not know how I knew it; but I could not help knowing that He was close beside me,—that I saw Him distinctly, and felt His presence,—that the recollectedness of my soul was deeper in the prayer of quiet, and more continuous,—that the effects thereof were very different from what I had hitherto experienced,—and that it was most certain. I could only make comparisons in order to explain myself; and certainly there are no comparisons, in my opinion, by which visions of this kind can be described. Afterwards I learnt from Friar Peter of Alcantara, a holy man of great spirituality,—of whom I shall speak by and by,—and from others of great learning, that this vision was of the highest order, and one with which Satan can least interfere; and therefore there are no words whereby to explain,—at least, none for us women, who know so little: learned men can explain it better.

For if I say that I see Him neither with the eyes of the body, nor with those of the soul,—because it was not an imaginary vision,—how is it that I can understand and maintain that He stands beside me, and be more certain of it than if I saw Him? If it be supposed that it is as if a person were blind, or in the dark, and therefore unable to see another who is close to him, the comparison is not exact. There is a certain likelihood about it, however, but not much, because the other senses tell him who is blind of that presence: he hears the other speak or move, or he touches him; but in these visions there is nothing like this. The darkness is not felt; only He renders Himself present to the soul by a certain knowledge of Himself which is more clear than the sun. I do not mean that we now see either a sun or any brightness, only that there is a light not seen, which illumines the understanding so that the soul may have the fruition of so great a good. This vision brings with it great blessings.

It is not like that presence of God which is frequently felt, particularly by those who have attained to the prayer of union and of quiet, when we seem, at the very commencement of our prayer, to find Him with whom we would converse, and when we seem to feel that He hears us by the effects and the spiritual impressions of great love and faith of which we are then conscious, as well as by the good resolutions, accompanied by sweetness, which we then make. This is a great grace from God; and let him to whom He has given it esteem it much, because it is a very high degree of prayer; but it is not vision. God is understood to be present there by the effects He works in the soul: that is the way His Majesty makes His presence felt; but here, in this vision, it is seen clearly that Jesus Christ is present, the Son of the Virgin. In the prayer of union and of quiet, certain inflowings of the Godhead are present; but in the vision, the Sacred Humanity also, together with them, is pleased to be our visible companion, and to do us good.

My confessor next asked me, who told me it was Jesus Christ. I replied that He often told me so Himself; but, even before He told me so, there was an impression on my understanding that it was He; and before this He used to tell me so, and I saw Him not. If a person whom I had never seen, but of whom I had heard, came to speak to me, and I were blind or in the dark, and told me who he was, I should believe him; but I could not so confidently affirm that he was that person, as I might do if I had seen him. But in this vision I could do so, because so clear a knowledge is impressed on the soul that all doubt seems impossible, though He is not seen. Our Lord wills that this knowledge be so graven on the understanding, that we can no more question His presence than we can question that which we see with our eyes: not so much even; for very often there arises a suspicion that we have imagined things we think we see; but here, though there may be a suspicion in the first instant, there remains a certainty so great, that the doubt has no force whatever. So also is it when God teaches the soul in another way, and speaks to it without speaking, in the way I have described.

There is so much of heaven in this language, that it cannot well be understood on earth, though we may desire ever so much to explain it, if our Lord will not teach it experimentally. Our Lord impresses in the innermost soul that which He wills that soul to understand; and He manifests it there without images or formal words, after the manner of the vision I am speaking of. Consider well this way in which God works, in order that the soul may understand what He means—His great truths and mysteries; for very often what I understand, when our Lord explains to me the vision, which it is His Majesty's pleasure to set before me, is after this manner; and it seems to me that this is a state with which the devil can least interfere, for these reasons; but if these reasons are not good, I must be under a delusion. The vision and the language are matters of such pure spirituality, that there is no turmoil of the faculties, or of the senses, out of which—so it seems to me—the devil can derive any advantage.

It is only at intervals, and for an instant, that this occurs; for generally—so I think—the senses are not taken away, and the faculties are not suspended: they preserve their ordinary state. It is not always so in contemplation; on the contrary, it is very rarely so; but when it is so, I say that we do nothing whatever ourselves: no work of ours is then possible; all that is done is apparently the work of our Lord. It is as if food had been received into the stomach which had not first been eaten, and without our knowing how it entered; but we do know well that it is there, though we know not its nature, nor who it was that placed it there. In this vision, I know who placed it; but I do not know how He did it. I neither saw it, nor felt it; I never had any inclination to desire it, and I never knew before that such a thing was possible.

*   *   *

Some considerable time after our Lord had bestowed upon me the graces I have been describing, and others also of a higher nature, I was one day in prayer when I found myself in a moment, without knowing how, plunged apparently into hell. I understood that it was our Lord's will I should see the place which the devils kept in readiness for me, and which I had deserved by my sins. It was but a moment, but it seems to me impossible I should ever forget it even if I were to live many years.

The entrance seemed to be by a long narrow pass, like a furnace, very low, dark, and close. The ground seemed to be saturated with water, mere mud, exceedingly foul, sending forth pestilential odours, and covered with loathsome vermin. At the end was a hollow place in the wall, like a closet, and in that I saw myself confined. All this was even pleasant to behold in comparison with what I felt there. There is no exaggeration in what I am saying.

But as to what I then felt, I do not know where to begin, if I were to describe it; it is utterly inexplicable. I felt a fire in my soul. I cannot see how it is possible to describe it. My bodily sufferings were unendurable. I have undergone most painful sufferings in this life, and, as the physicians say, the greatest that can be borne, such as the contraction of my sinews when I was paralysed, without speaking of others of different kinds, yea, even those of which I have also spoken, inflicted on me by Satan; yet all these were as nothing in comparison with what I felt then, especially when I saw that there would be no intermission, nor any end to them.

These sufferings were nothing in comparison with the anguish of my soul, a sense of oppression, of stifling, and of pain so keen, accompanied by so hopeless and cruel an infliction, that I know not how to speak of it. If I said that the soul is continually being torn from the body, it would be nothing, for that implies the destruction of life by the hands of another; but here it is the soul itself that is tearing itself in pieces. I cannot describe that inward fire or that despair, surpassing all torments and all pain. I did not see who it was that tormented me, but I felt myself on fire, and torn to pieces, as it seemed to me; and, I repeat it, this inward fire and despair are the greatest torments of all.

Left in that pestilential place, and utterly without the power to hope for comfort, I could neither sit nor lie down: there was no room. I was placed as it were in a hole in the wall; and those walls, terrible to look on of themselves, hemmed me in on every side. I could not breathe. There was no light, but all was thick darkness. I do not understand how it is; though there was no light, yet everything that can give pain by being seen was visible.

Our Lord at that time would not let me see more of hell. Afterwards, I had another most fearful vision, in which I saw the punishment of certain sins. They were most horrible to look at; but, because I felt none of the pain, my terror was not so great. In the former vision, our Lord made me really feel those torments, and that anguish of spirit, just as if I had been suffering them in the body there. I know not how it was, but I understand distinctly that it was a great mercy that our Lord would have me see with mine own eyes the very place from which His compassion saved me. I have listened to people speaking of these things, and I have at other times dwelt on the various torments of hell, though not often, because my soul made no progress by the way of fear; and I have read of the diverse tortures, and how the devils tear the flesh with red-hot pincers. But all is as nothing before this; it is a wholly different matter. In short, the one is a reality, the other a picture; and all burning here in this life is as nothing in comparison with the fire that is there.

I was so terrified by that vision,—and that terror is on me even now while I am writing,—that, though it took place nearly six years ago, the natural warmth of my body is chilled by fear even now when I think of it. And, so, amid all the pain and suffering which I may have had to bear, I remember no time in which I do not think that all we have to suffer in this world is as nothing. It seems to me that we complain without reason. I repeat it, this vision was one of the grandest mercies of our Lord. It has been to me of the greatest service, because it has destroyed my fear of trouble and of the contradiction of the world, and because it has made me strong enough to bear up against them, and to give thanks to our Lord, who has been my Deliverer, as it now seems to me, from such fearful and everlasting pains.

* * *

ST. AUGUSTINE

St. Augustine, Bishop of Hippo, lived during the last years of the Roman Empire and the first years of the dominance of the Christian Church over paganism. Of his writing it was once said, "He lies who says that he has read all of his works." Of 113 books, 218 letters, and over 500 sermons that survive today, many seek to establish the truth of Christian teaching against paganism and Judaism and against the attacks of heretical Christian sects such as the Manicheans, the Donatists, and the Pelagians. In his antiheretical writings Augustine wielded large and permanent influence over the development of ortho-dox Christian doctrine. In addition to works directed against specific heresies, he wrote many works that are still widely enjoyed today. On Christian Doctrine *is a short introduction to reading and interpreting the Bible.* The City of God *(a philosophical approach to the problem of history) is based on the idea that all men are divided into two "cities," or groups of loyalty—one devoted to love of the world and its sins, the other devoted to God and life in heaven. Finally, Augustine's* Confessions *(written between 397 and 400 A.D.), addressed to God, provides a moving account of his spiritual develop-ment from childhood to conversion, at the age of thirty-two, from conscious sinfulness to Christian asceticism.*

Augustine was born in 354 in Thagaste, an agricultural village in North Africa. Since he showed great intellectual promise, his father, a minor official in the local Roman govern-ment, sent him to school in Madauros, a nearby college town, when he was eleven. Remembering his childhood thefts of food and his dishonesty at games, Augustine asks, "Is this boyish innocence? It is not, O Lord, it is not . . . For these are the practises that pass from tutors and teachers, and from nuts and balls and birds, to governors and kings, and to money and estates and slaves." At seventeen he entered school in Carthage, "where a cauldron of shameful loves seethed and sounded about me." Here he joined the Mani-chean sect and took a mistress by whom he had a son when he was eighteen. He acquired at this time a deep interest in philosophy and spent the next thirteen years of his life teaching in Thagaste, Carthage, Rome, and Milan.

After hearing St. Ambrose, Bishop of Milan, preaching in 384, Augustine became gradually convinced that he should convert to Christianity. He was baptized in 387 and returned to Thagaste to establish a religious community. In 391 he traveled to Hippo, a large African port, and was drafted by the Christian congregation to be an assistant to Bishop Valerius. For nearly four decades after the death of Valerius in 396, Augustine as Bishop of Hippo combatted heresies in public and written debates, presided in civil law cases, and was responsible for all the instruction and spiritual care of the church in a large surrounding territory. He died in 430.

In the passages reprinted below, from Book 8 of his Confessions *(trans. F. J. Sheed, 1943), he recalls the day of his conversion.*

Conversion

. . . Now, O Lord, my Helper and my Redeemer, I shall tell and confess to Your name how You delivered me from the chain of that desire of the flesh which held me so bound, and the servitude of worldly things. . . .

On a certain day—Nebridius was away for some reason I cannot recall—there came to Alypius and me at our house one Ponticianus, a fellow countryman of ours, being from Africa, holder of an important post in the emperor's court. There was something or other he wanted of us and we sat down to discuss the matter. As it happened he noticed a book on a gaming table by which we were sitting. He picked it up, opened it, and found that it was the apostle Paul, which surprised him because he had expected that it would be one of the books I wore myself out teaching. Then he smiled a little and looked at me and expressed pleasure but surprise too at having come suddenly upon that book, and only that book, lying before me. For he was a Christian and a devout Christian; he knelt before You in church, O our God, in daily prayer and many times daily. I told him that I had given much care to these writings. Whereupon he began to tell the story of the Egyptian monk Antony, whose name was held in high honour among Your servants, although Alypius and I had never heard it before that time. When he learned this, he was the more intent upon telling the story, anxious to introduce so great a man to men ignorant of him, and very much marvelling at our ignorance. But Alypius and I stood amazed to hear of Your wonderful works, done in the true faith and in the Catholic Church so recently, practically in our own times, and with such numbers of witnesses. All three of us were filled with wonder, we because the deeds we were now hearing were so great, and he because we had never heard them before.

From this story he went on to the great groups in the monasteries, and their ways all redolent of You, and the fertile deserts of the wilderness, of all of which we knew nothing. There was actually a monastery at Milan, outside the city walls. It was full of worthy brethren and under the care of Ambrose. And we had not heard of it. He continued with his discourse and we listened in absolute silence. It chanced that he told how on one occasion he and three of his companions—it was at Treves, when the emperor was at the chariot races in the Circus—had gone one afternoon to walk in the gardens close by the city walls. As it happened they fell into two groups, one of the others staying with him, and the other two likewise walking their own way. But as those other two strolled on they came into a certain house, the dwelling of some servants of Yours, poor in spirit, of whom is the kingdom of God. There they found a small book in which was written the life of Antony. One of them began to read it, marvelled at it, was inflamed by it. While he was actually reading he had begun to think how he might embrace such a life, and give up his worldly employment to serve You alone. For the two men were both state officials. Suddenly the man who was doing the reading was filled with a love of holiness and angry at himself with righteous shame. He looked at his friend and said to him: "Tell me, please, what is the goal of our ambition in all these labours of ours? What are we aiming at? What is our motive in being in the public service? Have we any higher hope at court than to be friends of the emperor? And at that level, is not everything uncertain and full of perils? And how many perils must we meet on the way to this greater peril? And how long before we are there? But if I should choose to be a friend of God, I can become one now." He said this, and all troubled with the pain of the new life coming to birth in him, he turned back his eyes to the book. He read on and was changed inwardly, where You alone could see; and the world dropped away from his mind, as soon appeared outwardly. For while he was reading and his heart thus tossing on its own flood, at length he broke out in heavy weeping, saw the better way and chose it for his own. Being now Your servant he said to his friend, "Now I have broken from that hope we had and have decided to serve God; and I enter upon that service from this hour, in this place. If you have no will to imitate me, at least do not try to dissuade me."

The other replied that he would remain his companion in so great a service for so great a prize. So the two of them, now Your servants, built a spiritual tower at the only cost that is adequate, the cost of leaving all things and following You. Then Ponticianus and the man who had gone walking with him in another part of the garden came looking for them in the same place, and when they found them suggested that they should return home as the day was now declining. But they told their decision and their purpose, and how that will had arisen in them and was now settled in them; and asked them not to try to argue them out of their decision, even if they would not also join them. Ponticianus and his friend, though not changed from their former state, yet wept for themselves, as he told us, and congratulated them in God and commended themselves to their prayers. Then with their own heart trailing in the dust they went off to the palace, while the other two, with their heart fixed upon heaven, remained in the hut. Both these men, as it happened, were betrothed, and when the two women heard of it they likewise dedicated their virginity to You.

This was the story Ponticianus told. But You, Lord, while he was speaking, turned me back towards myself, taking me from behind my own back where I had put myself all the time that I preferred not to see myself. And

You set me there before my own face that I might see how vile I was, how twisted and unclean and spotted and ulcerous. I saw myself and was horrified; but there was no way to flee from myself. If I tried to turn my gaze from myself, there was Ponticianus telling what he was telling; and again You were setting me face to face with myself, forcing me upon my own sight, that I might see my iniquity and loathe it. I had known it, but I had pretended not to see it, had deliberately looked the other way and let it go from my mind.

But this time, the more ardently I approved those two as I heard of their determination to win health for their souls by giving themselves up wholly to Your healing, the more detestable did I find myself in comparison with them. For many years had flowed by—a dozen or more—from the time when I was nineteen and was stirred by the reading of Cicero's Hortensius to the study of wisdom; and here was I still postponing the giving up of this world's happiness to devote myself to the search for that of which not the finding only but the mere seeking is better than to find all the treasures and kingdoms of men, better than all the body's pleasures though they were to be had merely for a nod. But I in my great worthlessness—for it was greater thus early—had begged You for chastity, saying: "Grant me chastity and continence, but not yet." For I was afraid that You would hear my prayer too soon, and too soon would heal me from the disease of lust which I wanted satisfied rather than extinguished. So I had gone wandering in my sacrilegious superstition through the base ways of the Manicheans: not indeed that I was sure they were right but that I preferred them to the Christians, whom I did not inquire about in the spirit of religion but simply opposed through malice.

I had thought that my reason for putting off from day to day the following of You alone to the contempt of earthly hopes was that I did not see any certain goal towards which to direct my course. But now the day was come when I stood naked in my own sight and my conscience accused me: "Why is my voice not heard? Surely you are the man who used to say that you could not cast off vanity's baggage for an uncertain truth. Very well: now the truth is certain, yet you are still carrying the load. Here are men who have been given wings to free their shoulders from the load, though they did not wear themselves out in searching nor spend ten years or more thinking about it."

Thus was I inwardly gnawed at. And I was in the grip of the most horrible and confounding shame, while Ponticianus was telling his story. He finished the tale and the business for which he had come; and he went his way, and I to myself. What did I not say against myself, with what lashes of condemnation did I not scourge my soul to make it follow me now that I wanted to follow You! My soul hung back. It would not follow, yet found no excuse for not following. All its arguments had already been used and refuted. There remained only trembling silence: for it feared as very death the cessation of that habit of which in truth it was dying.

In the midst of that great tumult of my inner dwelling place, the tumult

I had stirred up against my own soul in the chamber of my heart, I turned upon Alypius, wild in look and troubled in mind, crying out: "What is wrong with us? What is this that you heard? The unlearned arise and take heaven by force, and here are we with all our learning, stuck fast in flesh and blood! Is there any shame in following because they have gone before us, would it not be a worse shame not to follow at once?" These words and more of the same sort I uttered, then the violence of my feeling tore me from him while he stood staring at me thunderstruck. For I did not sound like myself. My brow, cheeks, eyes, flush, the pitch of my voice, spoke my mind more powerfully than the words I uttered. There was a garden attached to our lodging, of which we had the use, as indeed we had the whole house: for our host, the master of the house, did not live there. To this garden the storm in my breast somehow brought me, for there no one could intervene in the fierce suit I had brought against myself, until it should reach its issue: though what the issue was to be, You knew, not I: but there I was, going mad on my way to sanity, dying on my way to life, aware how evil I was, unaware that I was to grow better in a little while. So I went off to the garden, and Alypius close on my heels: for it was still privacy for me to have him near, and how could he leave me to myself in that state? We found a seat as far as possible from the house. I was frantic in mind, in a frenzy of indignation at myself for not going over to Your law and Your covenant, O my God, where all my bones cried out that I should be, extolling it to the skies. The way was not by ship or chariot or on foot: it was not as far as I had gone when I went from the house to the place where we sat. For I had but to will to go, in order not merely to go but to arrive; I had only to will to go—but to will powerfully and wholly, not to turn and twist a will half-wounded this way and that, with the part that would rise struggling against the part that would keep to the earth.

Thus I was sick at heart and in torment, accusing myself with a new intensity of bitterness, twisting and turning in my chain in the hope that it might be utterly broken, for what held me was so small a thing! But it still held me. And You stood in the secret places of my soul, O Lord, in the harshness of Your mercy redoubling the scourges of fear and shame lest I should give way again and that small slight tie which remained should not be broken but should grow again to full strength and bind me closer even than before. For I kept saying within myself: "Let it be now, let it be now," and by the mere words I had begun to move towards the resolution. I almost made it, yet I did not quite make it. But I did not fall back into my original state, but as it were stood near to get my breath. And I tried again and I was almost there, and now I could all but touch it and hold it: yet I was not quite there, I did not touch it or hold it. I still shrank from dying unto death and living unto life. The lower condition which had grown habitual was more powerful than the better condition which I had not tried. The nearer the point of time came in which I was to become different, the more it struck me with horror; but it did not force me utterly back nor turn me utterly away, but held me there between the two.

Those trifles of all trifles, and vanities of vanities, my one-time mistresses, held me back, plucking at my garment of flesh and murmuring softly: "Are you sending us away?" And "From this moment shall we not be with you, now or forever?" And "From this moment shall this or that not be allowed you, now or forever?" What were they suggesting to me in the phrase I have written "this or that," what were they suggesting to me, O my God? Do You in your mercy keep from the soul of Your servant the vileness and uncleanness they were suggesting. And now I began to hear them not half so loud; they no longer stood against me face to face, but were softly muttering behind my back and, as I tried to depart, plucking stealthily at me to make me look behind. Yet even that was enough, so hesitating was I, to keep me from snatching myself free, from shaking them off and leaping upwards on the way I was called: for the strong force of habit said to me: "Do you think you can live without them?"

But by this time its voice was growing fainter. In the direction towards which I had turned my face and was quivering in fear of going, I could see the austere beauty of Continence, serene and indeed joyous but not evilly, honourably soliciting me to come to her and not linger, stretching forth loving hands to receive and embrace me, hands full of multitudes of good examples. With her I saw such hosts of young men and maidens, a multitude of youth and of every age, gray widows and women grown old in virginity, and in them all Continence herself, not barren but the fruitful mother of children, her joys, by You, Lord, her Spouse. And she smiled upon me and her smile gave courage as if she were saying: "Can you not do what these men have done, what these women have done? Or could men or women have done such in themselves, and not in the Lord their God? The Lord their God gave me to them. Why do you stand upon yourself and so not stand at all? Cast yourself upon Him and be not afraid; He will not draw away and let you fall. Cast yourself without fear, He will receive you and heal you."

Yet I was still ashamed, for I could still hear the murmuring of those vanities, and I still hung hesitant. And again it was as if she said: "Stop your ears against your unclean members, that they may be mortified. They tell you of delights, but not of such delights as the law of the Lord your God tells." This was the controversy raging in my heart, a controversy about myself against myself. And Alypius stayed by my side and awaited in silence the issue of such agitation as he had never seen in me.

When my most searching scrutiny had drawn up all my vileness from the secret depths of my soul and heaped it in my heart's sight, a mighty storm arose in me, bringing a mighty rain of tears. That I might give way to my tears and lamentations, I rose from Alypius: for it struck me that solitude was more suited to the business of weeping. I went far enough from him to prevent his presence from being an embarrassment to me. So I felt, and he realized it. I suppose I had said something and the sound of my voice was heavy with tears. I arose, but he remained where we had been sitting, still in utter amazement. I flung myself down somehow under a certain fig tree and no longer tried to check my tears, which poured forth from my eyes in a flood, *an acceptable sacrifice to Thee.* And much I said not in these words but to this effect: *"And Thou, O Lord, how long? How long, Lord; wilt Thou be angry forever? Remember not our former iniquities."* For I felt that I was still bound by them. And I continued my miserable complaining: "How long, how long shall I go on saying tomorrow and again tomorrow? Why not now, why not have an end to my uncleanness this very hour?"

Such things I said, weeping in the most bitter sorrow of my heart. And suddenly I heard a voice from some nearby house, a boy's voice or a girl's voice, I do not know: but it was a sort of sing-song, repeated again and again, "Take and read, take and read." I ceased weeping and immediately began to search my mind most carefully as to whether children were accustomed to chant these words in any kind of game, and I could not remember that I had ever heard any such thing. Damming back the flood of my tears I arose, interpreting the incident as quite certainly a divine command to open my book of Scripture and read the passage at which I should open. For it was part of what I had been told about Antony, that from the Gospel which he happened to be reading he had felt that he was being admonished as though what he read was spoken directly to himself: *Go, sell what thou hast and give to the poor and thou shalt have treasure in heaven; and come follow Me.* By this experience he had been in that instant converted to You. So I was moved to return to the place where Alypius was sitting, for I had put down the Apostle's book there when I arose. I snatched it up, opened it and in silence read the passage upon which my eyes first fell: *Not in rioting and drunkenness, not in chambering and impurities, not in contention and envy, but put ye on the Lord Jesus Christ and make not provision for the flesh in its concupiscences.* [Romans xiii, 13.] I had no wish to read further, and no need. For in that instant, with the very ending of the sentence, it was as though a light of utter confidence shone in all my heart, and all the darkness of uncertainty vanished away. Then leaving my finger in the place or marking it by some other sign, I closed the book and in complete calm told the whole thing to Alypius and he similarly told me what had been going on in himself, of which I knew nothing. He asked to see what I had read. I showed him, and he looked further than I had read. I had not known what followed. And this is what followed: *"Now him that is weak in faith, take unto you."* He applied this to himself and told me so. And he was confirmed by this message, and with no troubled wavering gave himself to God's good-will and purpose—a purpose indeed most suited to his character, for in these matters he had been immeasurably better than I.

Then we went in to my mother and told her, to her great joy. We related how it had come about: she was filled with triumphant exultation, saw that You had given her more than with all her pitiful weeping she had ever asked. For You converted me to Yourself so that I no longer sought a wife nor any of this world's promises, but stood upon that same rule of faith in which You had shown me to her so many years before. Thus You changed her mourning into joy, a joy far richer than she had thought to wish, a joy much dearer and purer than she had thought to find in grandchildren of my flesh.

On Death and Dying

T he fear of death is so basic that it has found its way into the mythology of nearly every culture. Some admit death, viewing it as part of life, while others try to hide it; paradoxically, the more we hide death, the more we tend to fear death. Today, "the more we are making advancements in science, the more we seem to fear and deny the reality of death. How is this possible?" Elisabeth Kübler-Ross asks this question in response to our growing tendency to separate the dying person from familiar surroundings, to become preoccupied with the technical aspects of the dying body and lose sight of the human needs of the dying person. "Is the reason for this increasingly mechanical, depersonalized approach," she wonders, "our own defensiveness?" How many of us, we might ask, have actually seen a dying or dead person?

Paul Jacobs' satire demonstrates the way in which one man at least, by denying the existence of death, transforms it into a money-making industry. Forest Lawn is not a cemetery but a "Memorial Park" in which to begin a "happy Eternal Life." J. H. Plumb, too, talks of Hubert Eaton's Forest Lawn, but looking at it in historical context, he has a different attitude. "The urge to obliterate death," he says, "is the urge to extend life."

ELISABETH KÜBLER-ROSS

Dr. Elisabeth Kübler-Ross, a psychiatrist, author, and lecturer, has had important influence on our ideas about the care of dying patients and their families. She has said that "whoever has seen the horrifying appearance of the postwar European concentration camps" would share her preoccupation with death. Born in Zurich in 1926, she did relief **629**

*work in postwar Europe and studied medicine at the University of Zurich. After becoming
an M.D. in 1957, she practiced medicine in Switzerland before coming to the United
States to do her internship and residency. In 1958 she married Dr. Emanual R. Ross, a
physician; they have two children.*

*Dr. Kübler-Ross, who holds dual American and Swiss citizenship, has taught medicine
at the University of Colorado and the University of Chicago, where she instituted a
teaching seminar on conversations with the terminally ill. More recently she has been
chairman of the board of Shanti-Nilaya near San Diego, a controversial therapeutic and
teaching center for dying patients and their families.*

Her books include On Death and Dying *(1969), the first chapter of which is
reprinted here;* Questions and Answers on Death and Dying *(1972);* Death:
The Final Stage *(1974); and* To Live Until We Say Goodbye *(1978). In
addition, she has written for professional journals and contributed to the* Encyclopaedia
Britannica, *and to* The Dying Patient *(1970),* The Vestibule *(1972),* The
Phenomenon of Death *(1973),* Emergency Psychiatric Care *(1974), and* Life
After Life *(1975).*

*A popular lecturer who has made several television appearances, Dr. Kübler-Ross has
received many awards and honors. In 1977 she was named* Ladies Home Journal
Woman of the Year.

On the Fear of Death

> Let me not pray to be sheltered from
> dangers but to be fearless in facing
> them.
> Let me not beg for the stilling of
> my pain but for the heart to conquer it.
> Let me not look for allies in life's
> battlefield but to my own strength.
> Let me not crave in anxious fear to
> be saved but hope for the patience to
> win my freedom.
> Grant me that I may not be a
> coward, feeling your mercy in my
> success alone; but let me find the grasp
> of your hand in my failure.
>
> —RABINDRANATH TAGORE,
> *Fruit-Gathering*

Epidemics have taken a great toll of lives in past generations. Death in
infancy and early childhood was frequent and there were few families who
didn't lose a member of the family at an early age. Medicine has changed
greatly in the last decades. Widespread vaccinations have practically eradi-
cated many illnesses, at least in western Europe and the United States. The
use of chemotherapy, especially the antibiotics, has contributed to an ever

decreasing number of fatalities in infectious diseases. Better child care and education has effected a low morbidity and mortality among children. The many diseases that have taken an impressive toll among the young and middle-aged have been conquered. The number of old people is on the rise, and with this fact come the number of people with malignancies and chronic diseases associated more with old age.

Pediatricians have less work with acute and life-threatening situations as they have an ever increasing number of patients with psychosomatic disturbances and adjustment and behavior problems. Physicians have more people in their waiting rooms with emotional problems than they have ever had before, but they also have more elderly patients who not only try to live with their decreased physical abilities and limitations but who also face loneliness and isolation with all its pains and anguish. The majority of these people are not seen by a psychiatrist. Their needs have to be elicited and gratified by other professional people, for instance, chaplains and social workers. It is for them that I am trying to outline the changes that have taken place in the last few decades, changes that are ultimately responsible for the increased fear of death, the rising number of emotional problems, and the greater need for understanding of and coping with the problems of death and dying.

When we look back in time and study old cultures and people, we are impressed that death has always been distasteful to man and will probably always be. From a psychiatrist's point of view this is very understandable and can perhaps best be explained by our basic knowledge that, in our unconscious, death is never possible in regard to ourselves. It is inconceivable for our unconscious to imagine an actual ending of our own life here on earth, and if this life of ours has to end, the ending is always attributed to a malicious intervention from the outside by someone else. In simple terms, in our unconscious mind we can only be killed; it is inconceivable to die of a natural cause or of old age. Therefore death in itself is associated with a bad act, a frightening happening, something that in itself calls for retribution and punishment.

One is wise to remember these fundamental facts as they are essential in understanding some of the most important, otherwise unintelligible communications of our patients.

The second fact that we have to comprehend is that in our unconscious mind we cannot distinguish between a wish and a deed. We are all aware of some of our illogical dreams in which two completely opposite statements can exist side by side—very acceptable in our dreams but unthinkable and illogical in our wakening state. Just as our unconscious mind cannot differentiate between the wish to kill somebody in anger and the act of having done so, the young child is unable to make this distinction. The child who angrily wishes his mother to drop dead for not having gratified his needs will be traumatized greatly by the actual death of his mother—even if this event is not linked closely in time with his destructive wishes. He will always take part or the whole blame for the loss of his mother. He will always say to himself—rarely to others—"I did it, I am responsible, I was bad, therefore

Mommy left me." It is well to remember that the child will react in the same manner if he loses a parent by divorce, separation, or desertion. Death is often seen by a child as an impermanent thing and has therefore little distinction from a divorce in which he may have an opportunity to see a parent again.

Many a parent will remember remarks of their children such as, "I will bury my doggy now and next spring when the flowers come up again, he will get up." Maybe it was the same wish that motivated the ancient Egyptians to supply their dead with food and goods to keep them happy and the old American Indians to bury their relatives with their belongings.

When we grow older and begin to realize that our omnipotence is really not so omnipotent, that our strongest wishes are not powerful enough to make the impossible possible, the fear that we have contributed to the death of a loved one diminishes—and with it the guilt. The fear remains diminished, however, only so long as it is not challenged too strongly. Its vestiges can be seen daily in hospital corridors and in people associated with the bereaved.

A husband and wife may have been fighting for years, but when the partner dies, the survivor will pull his hair, whine and cry louder and beat his chest in regret, fear and anguish, and will hence fear his own death more than before, still believing in the law of talion—an eye for an eye, a tooth for a tooth—"I am responsible for her death, I will have to die a pitiful death in retribution."

Maybe this knowledge will help us understand many of the old customs and rituals which have lasted over the centuries and whose purpose is to diminish the anger of the gods or the people as the case may be, thus decreasing the anticipated punishment. I am thinking of the ashes, the torn clothes, the veil, the *Klage Weiber** of the old days—they are all means to ask you to take pity on them, the mourners, and are expressions of sorrow, grief, and shame. If someone grieves, beats his chest, tears his hair, or refuses to eat, it is an attempt at self-punishment to avoid or reduce the anticipated punishment for the blame that he takes on the death of a loved one.

This grief, shame, and guilt are not very far removed from feelings of anger and rage. The process of grief always includes some qualities of anger. Since none of us likes to admit anger at a deceased person, these emotions are often disguised or repressed and prolong the period of grief or show up in other ways. It is well to remember that it is not up to us to judge such feelings as bad or shameful but to understand their true meaning and origin as something very human. In order to illustrate this I will again use the example of the child—and the child in us. The five-year-old who loses his mother is both blaming himself for her disappearance and being angry at her for having deserted him and for no longer gratifying his needs. The dead person then turns into something the child loves and wants very much but also hates with equal intensity for this severe deprivation.

The ancient Hebrews regarded the body of a dead person as something

---

*mourning women

unclean and not to be touched. The early American Indians talked about the evil spirits and shot arrows in the air to drive the spirits away. Many other cultures have rituals to take care of the "bad" dead person, and they all originate in this feeling of anger which still exists in all of us, though we dislike admitting it. The tradition of the tombstone may originate in this wish to keep the bad spirits deep down in the ground, and the pebbles that many mourners put on the grave are left-over symbols of the same wish. Though we call the firing of guns at military funerals a last salute, it is the same symbolic ritual as the Indian used when he shot his spears and arrows into the skies.

I give these examples to emphasize that man has not basically changed. Death is still a fearful, frightening happening, and the fear of death is a universal fear even if we think we have mastered it on many levels.

What has changed is our way of coping and dealing with death and dying and our dying patients.

Having been raised in a country in Europe where science is not so advanced, where modern techniques have just started to find their way into medicine, and where people still live as they did in this country half a century ago, I may have had an opportunity to study a part of the evolution of mankind in a shorter period.

I remember as a child the death of a farmer. He fell from a tree and was not expected to live. He asked simply to die at home, a wish that was granted without questioning. He called his daughters into the bedroom and spoke with each one of them alone for a few minutes. He arranged his affairs quietly, though he was in great pain, and distributed his belongings and his land, none of which was to be split until his wife should follow him in death. He also asked each of his children to share in the work, duties, and tasks that he had carried on until the time of the accident. He asked his friends to visit him once more, to bid good-bye to them. Although I was a small child at the time, he did not exclude me or my siblings. We were allowed to share in the preparations of the family just as we were permitted to grieve with them until he died. When he did die, he was left at home, in his own beloved home which he had built, and among his friends and neighbors who went to take a last look at him where he lay in the midst of flowers in the place he had lived in and loved so much. In that country today there is still no make-believe slumber room, no embalming, no false makeup to pretend sleep. Only the signs of very disfiguring illnesses are covered up with bandages and only infectious cases are removed from the home prior to the burial.

Why do I describe such "old-fashioned" customs? I think they are an indication of our acceptance of a fatal outcome, and they help the dying patient as well as his family to accept the loss of a loved one. If a patient is allowed to terminate his life in the familiar and beloved environment, it requires less adjustment for him. His own family knows him well enough to replace a sedative with a glass of his favorite wine; or the smell of a home-cooked soup may give him the appetite to sip a few spoons of fluid which, I think, is still more enjoyable than an infusion. I will not minimize the need for sedatives and infusions and realize full well from my own experience as a country doctor that they are sometimes life-saving and often unavoidable. But I also know that patience and familiar people and foods could replace many a bottle of intravenous fluids for the simple reason that it fulfills the physiological need without involving too many people and/or individual nursing care.

The fact that children are allowed to stay at home where a fatality has stricken and are included in the talk, discussions, and fears gives them the feeling that they are not alone in the grief and gives them the comfort of shared responsibility and shared mourning. It prepares them gradually and helps them view death as part of life, an experience which may help them grow and mature.

This is in great contrast to a society in which death is viewed as taboo, discussion of it is regarded as morbid, and children are excluded with the presumption and pretext that it would be "too much" for them. They are then sent off to relatives, often accompanied with some unconvincing lies of "Mother has gone on a long trip" or other unbelievable stories. The child senses that something is wrong, and his distrust in adults will only multiply if other relatives add new variations of the story, avoid his questions or suspicions, shower him with gifts as a meager substitute for a loss he is not permitted to deal with. Sooner or later the child will become aware of the changed family situation and, depending on the age and personality of the child, will have an unresolved grief and regard this incident as a frightening, mysterious, in any case very traumatic experience with untrustworthy grownups, which he has no way to cope with.

It is equally unwise to tell a little child who lost her brother that God loved little boys so much that he took little Johnny to heaven. When this little girl grew up to be a woman she never solved her anger at God, which resulted in a psychotic depression when she lost her own little son three decades later.

We would think that our great emancipation, our knowledge of science and of man, has given us better ways and means to prepare ourselves and our families for this inevitable happening. Instead the days are gone when a man was allowed to die in peace and dignity in his own home.

The more we are making advancements in science, the more we seem to fear and deny the reality of death. How is this possible?

We use euphemisms, we make the dead look as if they were asleep, we ship the children off to protect them from the anxiety and turmoil around the house if the patient is fortunate enough to die at home, we don't allow children to visit their dying parents in the hospital, we have long and controversial discussions about whether patients should be told the truth—a question that rarely arises when the dying person is tended by the family physician who has known him from delivery to death and who knows the weaknesses and strengths of each member of the family.

I think there are many reasons for this flight away from facing death calmly. One of the most important facts is that dying nowadays is more gruesome in many ways, namely, more lonely, mechanical, and dehumanized; at times it is even difficult to determine technically when the time of death has occurred.

Dying becomes lonely and impersonal because the patient is often taken out of his familiar environment and rushed to an emergency room. Whoever has been very sick and has required rest and comfort especially may recall his experience of being put on a stretcher and enduring the noise of the ambulance siren and hectic rush until the hospital gates open. Only those who have lived through this may appreciate the discomfort and cold necessity of such transportation which is only the beginning of a long ordeal—hard to endure when you are well, difficult to express in words when noise, light, pumps, and voices are all too much to put up with. It may well be that we might consider more the patient under the sheets and blankets and perhaps stop our well-meant efficiency and rush in order to hold the patient's hand, to smile, or to listen to a question. I include the trip to the hospital as the first episode in dying, as it is for many. I am putting it exaggeratedly in contrast to the sick man who is left at home—not to say that lives should not be saved if they can be saved by a hospitalization but to keep the focus on the patient's experience, his needs and his reactions.

When a patient is severely ill, he is often treated like a person with no right to an opinion. It is often someone else who makes the decision if and when and where a patient should be hospitalized. It would take so little to remember that the sick person too has feelings, has wishes and opinions, and has—most important of all—the right to be heard.

Well, our presumed patient has now reached the emergency room. He will be surrounded by busy nurses, orderlies, interns, residents, a lab technician perhaps who will take some blood, an electrocardiogram technician who takes the cardiogram. He may be moved to X-ray and he will overhear opinions of his condition and discussions and questions to members of the family. He slowly but surely is beginning to be treated like a thing. He is no longer a person. Decisions are made often without his opinion. If he tries to rebel he will be sedated and after hours of waiting and wondering whether he has the strength, he will be wheeled into the operating room or intensive treatment unit and become an object of great concern and great financial investment.

He may cry for rest, peace, and dignity, but he will get infusions, transfusions, a heart machine, or tracheotomy if necessary. He may want one single person to stop for one single minute so that he can ask one single question—but he will get a dozen people around the clock, all busily preoccupied with his heart rate, pulse, electrocardiogram or pulmonary functions, his secretions or excretions but not with him as a human being. He may wish to fight it all but it is going to be a useless fight since all this is done in the fight for his life, and if they can save his life they can consider the person afterwards. Those who consider the person first may lose precious time to save his life! At least this seems to be the rationale or justification behind all this—or is it? Is the reason for this increasingly mechanical, depersonalized approach our own defensiveness? Is this approach our own way to cope with and repress the anxieties that a terminally or critically ill patient evokes in us? Is our concentration on equipment, on blood pressure, our desperate attempt to deny the impending death which is so frightening and discomforting to us that we displace all our knowledge onto machines, since they are less close to us than the suffering face of another human being which would remind us once more of our lack of omnipotence, our own limits and failures, and last but not least perhaps our own mortality?

Maybe the question has to be raised: Are we becoming less human or more human? Though this book is in no way meant to be judgmental, it is clear that whatever the answer may be, the patient is suffering more—not physically, perhaps, but emotionally. And his needs have not changed over the centuries, only our ability to gratify them.

PAUL JACOBS

Paul Jacobs, social scientist and writer, was born in New York City in 1918 and attended the City College of New York and the University of Minnesota. He first became active in the union movement as an organizer and later became a labor consultant and copublisher of a labor paper. He was a consultant to the Peace Corps and the War on Poverty program and conducted research and taught journalism at the University of California. He contributed regularly to the Economist *of London, to many other magazines including* Commentary, Harper's, *and* Newsday, *and was an editor for* Mother Jones. *His books include* The New Radicals *(with S. Landau, 1966);* Prelude to Riot: A View of Urban America from the Bottom *(1967);* Between the Rock and the Hard Place *(1970), about the Middle East conflict; and* The Red, Black and Brown Experience in America *(1971).*

Paul Jacobs died of cancer in 1978. He believed that he had been exposed to radiation in 1957 when exploring a site in Nevada that had been declared safe by the Atomic Energy Commission. He was working on a television film on the misuse and mismanagement of nuclear energy in the months before his death.

The essay we print here first appeared in The Reporter, *September 18, 1958.*

The Most Cheerful Graveyard in the World

Along with amassing a comfortable fortune by convincing Los Angelenos that the only fitting way to begin a "happy Eternal Life" is by being laid to rest, in one way or another, at Forest Lawn Memorial Park, the cemetery he founded in 1917, Dr. Hubert Eaton, or "Digger" as he is known in the trade, has also succeeded in almost completely revising the dying industry.

The Digger, whose official title of "Doctor" is purely honorary, accomplished this revision by the simple but profound device of converting the hitherto prosaic act of dying into a gloriously exciting, well-advertised event, somehow intimately and patriotically connected with the American way of life.

Today, thanks to Eaton, dying in Los Angeles is something to be eagerly anticipated, because it is only after death that one can gain permanent tenure at Forest Lawn. Eaton, in one of his earlier roles—that of "the Builder"—described Forest Lawn as "a place where lovers new and old shall love to stroll and watch the sunset's glow, planning for the future or reminiscing of the past; a place where artists study and sketch; where school teachers bring happy children to see the things they read of in books; where little churches invite, triumphant in the knowledge that from their pulpits only words of Love can be spoken; where memorialization of loved ones in sculptured marble and pictorial glass shall be encouraged but controlled by acknowledged artists; a place where the sorrowing will be soothed and strengthened because it will be God's garden. A place that shall be protected by an immense Endowment Care Fund, the principal of which can never be expended—only the income therefrom used to care for and perpetuate this Garden of Memory."

"This is the Builder's Dream; this is the Builder's Creed."

The Builder's Creed is chiseled into a huge, upright stone slab on Forest Lawn's Cathedral Drive, just outside the Great Mausoleum and hard by the Shrine of Love. Viewed, usually in reverent awe, by more than a million visitors each year, Forest Lawn is, along with Disneyland, a favorite tourist attraction in Southern California, far outdrawing the concrete footprints in front of Grauman's Chinese Theatre.

A smaller inscription underneath the Creed points out that on New Year's Day, 1917, Eaton stood on a hilltop overlooking the small country cemetery which had just been placed in his charge. An unemployed mining engineer, Eaton had gone into the cemetery business after a vein of gold in his mine had suddenly vanished.

"A vision came to the man of what this tiny 'God's Acre' might become; and standing there, he made a promise to The Infinite. When he reached home, he put this promise into words and called it 'The Builder's Creed.' Today, Forest Lawn's almost three hundred acres are eloquent witness that The Builder kept faith with his soul."

Indeed, yes. The "almost three hundred acres" also bear eloquent witness to the fact that Eaton, still digging holes in the ground, worked a vein of gold infinitely more reliable than the one that vanished from his mine—the "Science and Art," as he describes it, "of Persuasion." So strongly does Eaton believe the "profession of salesmanship is the greatest of all professions" that he has established The Foundation for the Science and Art of Persuasion at his alma mater, William Jewell College, Liberty, Missouri.

Forest Lawn reflects Eaton's skill in the "Science." The "country cemetery" with only a "scant dozen acres of developed ground" has grown into Forest Lawn Memorial Park, with a permanent "population" of more than

170,000, increasing at the rate of approximately 6,500 a year.

In fact, business has been so good that there are now two additional Forest Lawn "Memorial Parks" in Los Angeles: Forest Lawn-Hollywood Hills, the focus of a bitter political struggle in the city, and adjacent to it Mount Sinai, designed to attract the growing Jewish population of Los Angeles.

Forest Lawn offers the largest religious painting in the United States, displayed in a building, the Hall of the Crucifixion, specially designed for it. There, for a voluntary contribution of twenty-five cents, the visitor sits comfortably in a large theatre, in one of a "broad sweep of seats, richly upholstered in burgundy, rising tier above tier, matching the splendor of the architecture," and watches the three-thousand-pound curtain open on Jesus at Calvary, forty-five feet high and 195 feet long. A lecture about the painting, supplemented with a moving arrow, is delivered by a tape recording in the special kind of rich, organ-toned voice used throughout Forest Lawn.

There are also hundreds of statues, both originals and reproductions, scattered throughout the three hundred acres. Typical of these is an eighteen-figure group depicting Forest Lawn's solution to the "Mystery of Life." Interpretations of the eighteen figures are supplied: "(17) the atheist, the fool, who grinningly cares not at all; while (18) the stoic sits in silent awe and contemplation of that which he believes he knows but cannot explain with any satisfaction."

At the Court of David there is a huge reproduction of Michelangelo's "David"—with a large fig leaf added by Forest Lawn. An exact copy of the sculptor's "Moses" is displayed at the entrance to the Cathedral Corridor in Memorial Terrace, "the only one," according to Forest Lawn, "cast from clay masks placed directly on the original statue in the Church of Saint Peter in Chains at Rome, Italy."

So that the masks could be made, the Church of Saint Peter had to be closed for a day, something that had not happened before. "I gave a lot of dinners and I bought a lot of wine and I sent a lot of cables and St. Peter's was closed," Eaton modestly explains.

Color photos and post cards of the "Moses" statue can be purchased, along with thousands of other items, at Forest Lawn's souvenir shop. There, browsing visitors can choose from showcases displaying money clips, cocktail napkins, book matches, jigsaw puzzles, and charm bracelets—all decorated with Forest Lawn motifs. Prices range from a modest twenty-nine cents for a key chain to $125 for a glass vase etched with a Forest Lawn scene.

There are brown plastic nutshells containing little photos of Forest Lawn, ladies' compacts, cigarette lighters, cufflinks, salt and pepper shakers, picture frames, demitasse spoons, bookmarks, cups and saucers, pen and pencil sets, glass bells, wooden plaques, ashtrays, place mats and doilies, perfume and powder sets, jackknives, and a great variety of other goodies, all with an appropriate Forest Lawn theme. Books like *The Loved One*, Evelyn Waugh's satire of Forest Lawn, are not on sale in the souvenir shop. (Eaton occasionally expresses resentment over the treatment given the cemetery by novelists—especially by one writer to whom he extended free run of the park only to be parodied later. But Eaton also understands that such novels have brought world-wide publicity to Forest Lawn and have not adversely affected his sales, which come not from England but from Los Angeles.)

Among the most popular items at the souvenir shop are those showing reproductions of Forest Lawn's three churches, the Church of the Recessional, the Little Church of the Flowers, and the Wee Kirk o' the Heather. "Providing a dignified setting for final tribute," the three churches "serve also for the joyous and memorable ceremonies of christening and the exchange of marriage vows." Since the churches have opened, more than 43,000 persons have had "memorable" marriages in them. But Forest Lawn makes no money directly from marrying people, and the profits from the souvenir shop are used for the upkeep of the Hall of the Crucifixion. Forest Lawn's real business is burying people.

"The hardest thing in the world to sell," states one of the organization's top officials, "are 'spaces.' " ("Space" is the euphemism used at Forest Lawn for "grave plot.") The reason for the difficulty is that Forest Lawn's sales organization, which comprises about 175 people, concentrates on sales made "Before Need," another phrase in Forest Lawn's own peculiar language of the flowers. Selling cemetery plots "Before Need" rather than "At Time of Need" or "Post Need," although difficult, is very profitable, since under California law a cemetery pays taxes only on its unsold plots. Once a "space" has been sold, it is removed from the tax rolls. Thus it is to the obvious advantage of Forest Lawn to sell off its land as quickly as possible without waiting for "Need."

There are approximately fifteen hundred individual "spaces" to the acre in Forest Lawn. Prices average $300 per space. There are also rather more elegant neighborhoods at Forest Lawn which are less crowded and therefore more expensive. In the Gardens of Memory, entered only with a special key, there are "memorial sanctuaries designed for families who desire the privacy and protection of crypt interment, but who at the same time long for the open skies and the natural beauty of a verdant garden bathed in sunlight. Under the lawns in the Gardens of Memory have been created a number of monolithically constructed crypts of steel-reinforced concrete."

In the area of ground burial, Forest Lawn has contributed a pleasant innovation. No tombstones are permitted, only markers, set flush with the ground so that there is in fact the pleasant appearance of a park with sweeping green lawns.

But one does not have to be interred to take up permanent residence at Forest Lawn. A number of other arrangements can be made, including being inurned after cremation in the columbarium for as little as $145 or entombed in a mausoleum crypt—which can cost as much $800,000, as in the case of the Irving Thalberg mausoleum. One can also be placed in a large wall out in the open air. Families may be interred, inurned, or entombed as a unit to maintain "togetherness." Should one feel the need for fresh air while spending the "happy Eternal Life" in a crypt, it is possible, at added cost naturally, to have a ventilating system installed. In the mausoleum, tape-recorded music is played as well.

Inurnment is not restricted to a single form of urn. The law in California, which has a strong undertakers' lobby, provides that after cremation ashes must be buried or placed in a columbarium. A wide variety of urn designs can be seen, ranging from books and loving cups to miniature coffins.

The price for the casket or urn sets the approximate amount paid for the funeral itself, but here the range is far greater than for the "space." The least expensive casket, with the metal screw heads showing, is $115; the most expensive goes for $17,500.

Forest Lawn's rich, creamy advertising presentations combine the hard and the soft sell. On radio and television, the same institutional approach is as manifest as at the cemetery itself. Programs of church services and organ music are announced in deep, sonorous tones, and practically no mention is made of the company's product. The institutional approach is also used on billboards picturing stained-glass windows or the "Moses" statue. However, many of Forest Lawn's billboards are given over to the hard, competitive sell, featuring what is Hubert Eaton's original contribution to the American way of death: the concept of combining in one place mortuary functions, such as embalming, with funeral services and burial, thus obviating the necessity for outside undertakers, florists, funeral chapels, and long processions to the cemetery. Forest Lawn successfully undertook the elimination of the undertaking middleman.

Today, Forest Lawn's hard-sell slogans of "Everything In One Beautiful Place" and "Just One Phone Call" are widely copied, as are the ads which usually feature back or side views, sometimes in color, of two dry-eyed, well-groomed people talking to a distinguished-looking, gray-mustached bank-president or diplomat-type man, identified by a discreet sign on his desk as a "Funeral Counselor." Sometimes only the "Counselor" is shown, answering the "Just One Phone Call" with the dedicated air of a statesman. It is clear from the ads that at Forest Lawn, where the concept of death has been abolished, the standards of accepted behavior demand no vulgar signs of outward grief.

But even though its competitors copy Forest Lawn today, Eaton faced a bitter battle when he first attempted to bring a mortuary into the cemetery. Forest Lawn's permit to operate a mortuary was given only after a determined struggle waged against him by some of the undertakers who foresaw disaster for themselves in the new trend of combined services. It was during this period that Forest Lawn began to build up its own political operations, which today make it the most powerful spokesman for the industry in the state.

There have been a number of occasions when, in its self-interest, Forest Lawn has had to do battle, sometimes in ways that might have been frowned on by the dignified gentlemen in their ads. From the 1930's to the early 1950's, Forest Lawn was in a running argument with the county assessor's office over the tax assessments made on its property, with Forest Lawn always claiming that the assessments were too high and almost always getting them reduced, even as much as fifty per cent, by the county board of supervisors. Some supervisors did consistently oppose Forest Lawn's plea for tax reduction and supported the assessor, but when the votes were taken a majority always supported Forest Lawn.

In 1938, in one of its early appearances before the board of supervisors, Forest Lawn requested a tax reduction, claiming that the vacant property in the land it then owned would remain unsold until 1973. At the time, the county assessor pointed out that Forest Lawn had "acquired additional property when they said it was going to take thirty-five years to sell out what they now have, yet they go to work and buy seventy-five acres adjoining at a big price."

Ten years later, in 1948, the issue of how long it would take to fill Forest Lawn's vacant "spaces" became one of the central points in a bitter political hassle within the Los Angeles City Council, and the cemetery completely reversed its argument of ten years earlier. At issue was Forest Lawn's request for a zoning change to permit the use, as a cemetery, of 480 acres of land adjoining Griffith Park, a public park and playground in the Hollywood area.

Forest Lawn's first request to develop this new cemetery was submitted to and rejected by the city planning commission in 1946. When the request was again rejected in 1948, Forest Lawn appealed, claiming, in contrast to its 1938 plea of unsold land, that "by the year 1965 all of the available grave spaces in existing cemeteries will have been exhausted."

The odds against Forest Lawn's gaining approval for its plan to open a new cemetery seemed formidable. The planning commission opposed it, the park department opposed it, the board of health commissioners opposed it, the water and power commission opposed it, the board of public works opposed it, the Hollywood chamber of commerce opposed it, and a variety of community groups opposed it. But the "Builder's Dream" triumphed, and on March 9, 1948, the city council voted 11-3 to permit the opening of the cemetery.

Never an organization to leave stones unturned, within a few hours Forest Lawn had hastily dug six holes in the ground and buried six bodies in them; a move which, under state law, immediately qualified the area as a commercial graveyard that could not then be disturbed or moved except under very specific circumstances.

"We got the bodies we buried through the county hospital or from their next of kin in advance," states Ugene Blalock, vice-president and general counsel of Forest Lawn, "and we made no charge for our services. If the vote in the council had gone against us, we would have given them a free burial elsewhere."

In fact, however, the council vote has rarely gone against Forest Lawn, even when the city fathers were voting on whether to give Beverly Hills the street where Eaton lives, thus providing the Digger with a more distinguished address. Although he hasn't moved, Eaton now lives in Beverly Hills.

No one is quite sure about the exact basis for Eaton's influence; or if they are, they're not willing to talk about it for the record. Blalock states that Forest Lawn as an institution has not made, as far as he knows, any campaign contribution in eighteen years, although he adds, "Individuals may make political contributions." But politics aside, it is Hubert Eaton, master salesman, who is chiefly responsible for Forest Lawn's success.

It is from Eaton's mind that has come the creation of the Council of Regents of the Memorial Court of Honor, twenty-two "outstanding business and professional men" who advise "on all matters concerning the growth of the Memorial Park as a cultural center of religion and fine arts."

Its members, who include the president of Occidental College and the chancellor of the University of Southern California, wear a handsome, flowing red robe, trimmed with velvet, and an elegant round red hat, also trimmed daintily with velvet, while around their necks hangs a kind of Maltese Cross decoration, perhaps the Order of Forest Lawn.

Such touches as these distinguish the imaginative Eaton from his colleagues. Eaton's devotion to salesmanship, as evidenced by his creating special heart-shaped children's sections at Forest Lawn, named Babyland and Lullabyland, began early in life, according to "The Forest Lawn Story," his biography sold at the souvenir shop.

The son of a college professor, Eaton, states the biography, "sat in his little cubbyhole behind his father's bookshelves ostensibly studying but actually eavesdropping on his father's conversations with callers. Invariably they came for advice on one thing or another but more often than not, it was advice on matters affecting money. From these conversations he learned the word salesmanship and what it meant."

It was Eaton, too, who initiated many Forest Lawn public-service activities—the inspirational speaker made available to service clubs, the thirteen half-hour Bible films, and the giving of the Forest Lawn Awards for Persuasive Writing as a "practical service to students and Christian liberal arts colleges."

Long interested in "small, independent, liberal arts colleges" as being "America's last bulwark against the march of Socialism . . ." Eaton believes that "most" college professors are "semi-socialists at heart" who teach young people that salesmanship "smacks of chicanery, demagoguery, of influencing people against their wills . . ."

But Eaton isn't always so serious. Even when he was at college himself, he always had a "good sense of humor." His biography relates that one of his favorite tricks was to persuade a visitor to allow a funnel to be inserted into the top of his trousers and then to make him balance a penny on his chin and try to drop it into the funnel. While the visitor was in this position, young Hubert "or one of his cronies would pour a cup of cold water into the funnel."

Eaton's "good sense of humor changed little in succeeding years," states his biographer, and it certainly hadn't changed much the night when Eaton gave one of his usual huge, lavish parties for a group of friends and guests. It was called "An Enchanted Evening in the South Pacific," of which "Trader" Hubert Eaton was the master of ceremonies. Elaborate Hawaiian acts were presented, and guests received a large, beautifully printed eight-page souvenir program in color, in which Eaton had himself depicted as

"Your Happy Planter," jumping from page to page on a golden-shovel pogo stick.

On the cultural level, the printed program carried a large reproduction of the "David" statue, with a fig leaf, a Hawaiian lei, and a girl curled around its neck, all illustrating a poem, "The Secret of Hubie's David," which described just how it was decided to add a fig leaf to Forest Lawn's copy of Michelangelo's "David" in order not to shock "the ladies of L.A."

But surely the greatest of all the improvements that Eaton has made on the past is Forest Lawn itself. Here, what might have been just an ordinary "country cemetery" has been parlayed into a solemn institution, profitable and widely imitated, looking like Edgar Guest's idea of Heaven brought to earth, while representing a social level to which all people can aspire after death. And in the future, says Hubert Eaton, "When the place is filled up, my idea, from a financial standpoint, has always been to make Forest Lawn into a museum and charge admission."

J. H. PLUMB

British historian J. H. Plumb, noted for his meticulous scholarship and lively prose style, believes that history must use the past to sanctify not authority or morality but reason. He received his A.B. at University College, Leicester, in 1933 and subsequently did his doctoral research under social historian G. M. Trevelyan at Christ's College, Cambridge, from which he received his Ph.D. in 1936. In 1939 he became a Fellow at King's College and, from 1940 to 1945, worked in the intelligence division of the Foreign Office. Plumb has taught at Cambridge since 1946 and has been Master of Christ's College since 1978. He has also been a visiting professor at Columbia, City College of New York, New York City University, and Washington University.

His books include England in the Eighteenth Century *(1950); the two-volume* Sir Robert Walpole *(1956 and 1961);* Men and Places *(1963);* The Growth of Political Stability in England, 1675–1725 *(1967), originally delivered as the 1965–1966 Ford Lectures at Oxford;* The Commercialisation of Leisure *(1974); and* The Royal Heritage *(1977). The essay we reprint here is from* In the Light of History *(1972).*

De Mortuis

The British have hilarious fun at the quaint funerary habits of the Americans. The death of Hubert Eaton, the world's greatest entrepreneur of death, and the recent discovery of a funerary home for pets by a wandering British journalist, released another gale of satirical laughter in the English press. The mockery was hearty but sustained, yet was it deserved? Well certainly much of Forest Lawn is hard to take: the wet, nursery language for the hard facts of dying—'the loved one' for the corpse, 'leave taking' for burying and 'slumber' for death; the cosmetic treatment—the contortions of death waxed away, replaced by rouge and mascara and fashionably set hair; all of this is good for a gruesome joke. The place names of the Lawn are appalling—Lullabyland, Babyland. The piped guff, the music that flows like oil and the coy fig-leaved art give one goose-flesh. It is hard to repress a sense of nausea, and one turns, almost with relief, to a harsh fifteenth-century representation of the Dance of Death—livid corpses, jangling bones and skulls that haunt. How wholesome, after Hubert Eaton, seem the savage depictions of Bonfigli of the ravages of plague: or even the nightmares of death painted by Hieronymus Bosch. And how salutary in our own age to turn from Forest Lawn to the screaming, dissolving bodies of Francis Bacon, for surely this is how life ends for most of us, in pain, in agony.

And if Forest Lawn nauseates, what of the Pets Parlour?—'Blackie' combed and brushed, stretched out on the hearth rug before a log fire, waits for his sorrowing owners. The budgerigar is naturally wired to its perch. The Ming Room houses the Siamese cats and if you want to do your pussy proud, you can spend three hundred dollars or so on a stately laying out, a goodly coffin (if you're worried about its fun in the after life, you can put an outsize rubber mouse in with it) and naturally a special plot in 'Bide-A-Wee', the memorial park for pets. Certainly it takes some taking, although it seems President Nixon took it, for his dog, Checkers, had the treatment: he lies amongst the immortals in Bide-A-Wee, like Hubert in Forest Lawn.

However, this will become all very cheap, a mere second-class death, if deep freezing really catches on, as it shows every sign of doing. The Life Extension Society is spreading, and the entrepreneurs have smelt the profit in immortality. As soon as the breath goes, get yourself encapsulated in liquid nitrogen and stored in one of the specially constructed freezers that are springing up all over America from Phoenix to New York. And so wait for the day when they can cure what you died of, or replace what gave way—the heart, the brain, the liver or the guts—or simply rejuvenate your cells. Naturally it is not cheap: the capsule costs $4,000 and then there are the freezing costs and who knows what they may be in fifty years, so it would be imprudent not to make ample provision. And then, of course, I cannot imagine the revitalizing process will not dig a big hole into quite a considerable personal fortune. Forest Lawn may be death for the rich; this is death for the richer, death for the Big Time. And in America there are a lot of very rich, so maybe soon now, outside all the big cities, there will be frigidaires, as huge as pyramids, full of the frozen dead. This surely must be a growth industry. Perhaps, by the year 2000, Hubert Eaton will seem but a modest pioneer of the death industry, for who does not crave to escape oblivion? All rich people have tried to domesticate death, to make death seem like life. The American way of death is not novel, nor, *pace* Hubert Eaton, is it nauseatingly comic: seen in proper historical perspective it reaches back not only down the centuries but down the millennia, for it is a response to a deep human need.

Some of the earliest graves of men, dating from palaeolithic times, contained corpses not only decked out with bits of personal finery but also sprinkled with red ochre, perhaps the symbol of blood and life, maybe in the hope of a future resurrection. After the neolithic revolution, which created much greater resources and very considerable surplus wealth, men went in for death in a very big way. Doubtless the poor were thrown away, burnt or exposed or pushed into obscurity, back to the anonymous mud from which they came.

The rich and the powerful, high priests and kings, could not die, they merely passed from one life to another, and the life hereafter was but a mirror image of life on earth, so they took with them everything they needed—jewels, furniture, food, and, of course, servants. In the royal graves at Ur, some of the earliest and most sumptuous of tombs ever found, a row of handmaidens had been slaughtered at the burial—death's necessities were life's. No one, of course, took this elaboration of funerary activity further than the Egyptians. And the tombs of pharaohs and the high officials of the Egyptian kingdom make Forest Lawn seem like a cheap cemetery for the nation's down and outs. After all, one must use one's imagination. What should we think of vast stone mausoleums outside Washington, stuffed with personal jewellery from Winston's, furniture from Sloanes, tableware by Steuben, food from Bloomingdales, etc., etc., and in the midst of it all the embalmed corpse of a Coolidge or a Dulles? We should roar with laughter. We should regard it as vulgar, ridiculous, absurd.

Pushed back three millennia, such habits acquire not only decorum, but also majesty, grandeur, awe. The Egyptians were as portentous in death as in life, and their grave goods only occasionally give off the breath of life, unlike the Etruscans who domesticated death more completely, more joyously than any other society. A rich caste of princes built tombs of singular magnificence, filling them with amphorae, jewels, and silver. And they adorned their walls with all the gaiety that they had enjoyed alive. There was nothing solemn about their attitude to death. In their tombs they hunted, played games, performed acrobatics, danced, feasted; their amorous dalliance was both wanton and guiltless. Deliberately they banished death with the recollected gusto of life. No society has brought such eroticism, such open and natural behaviour to the charnel house. But in the annals of death, Etruscans are rare birds.

How different the grandiose tombs of medieval barons, with their splendid alabaster or marble effigies. There they lie, larger than life, grave, portentous, frozen in death, a wife, sometimes two, rigidly posed beside them, and beneath, sorrowing children, kneeling in filial piety, the whole structure made more pompous with heraldic quarterings. These are yet another attempt to cheat death, to keep alive in stone what was decaying and crumbling below. And even here a breath of life sometimes creeps in. The Earl and Countess of Arundel lie side by side, dogs beneath the feet, pillows under the head; he in armour, she in her long woollen gown, but, movingly enough, they are holding hands. The sons of Lord Teynham cannot be parted, even in death, with their hawk and hound. Nor were these tombs so cold, so marmoreal, when they were first built to keep the memory of the dead alive. They were painted, the faces as alive with colour as corpses in the parlours of Forest Lawn.

Seen in the context of history, Forest Lawn is neither very vulgar nor very remarkable: and the frigidaires at Phoenix are no more surprising than a pyramid in Palenque or Cairo. If life has been good we, like the rich Etruscans, want it to go on and on and on, or at the least to be remembered. Only a few civilizations have evaded expensive funerary habits for their illustrious rich, and these usually poverty-stricken ones. Even the Hindus, burning bodies and throwing the ashes into the Ganges, austere as they are, have maintained distinction in their pyres. Not only were widows coaxed or thrown on to the flames, but rare and perfumed woods were burnt to sweeten the spirit of the rich Brahman as it escaped from its corrupt carapace. Cremation à la Chanel!

What is tasteless and vulgar in one age becomes tender and moving in another. What should we say if we decorated our tombs with scenes from baseball, cocktail bars and the circus, or boasted on the side of our coffins of our amatory prowess, as erect and as unashamed in death as in life. And yet when the Etruscans do just these things, we are moved to a sense of delight that the force of life could be so strong that men and women revelled in it in their graves.

So the next time that you stroll through Forest Lawn, mildly nauseated by its silly sentimentality, think of those Etruscans; you will understand far more easily why seven thousand marriages a year take place in this Californian graveyard. After all, like the Arundels, Eros and Death have gone hand in hand down the ages. The urge to obliterate death is the urge to extend life: and what more natural than that the rich should expect renewal. How right, how proper, that Checkers should be waiting in Slumberland.

The Human Prospect

Almost all the pieces in this book are records of men and women deliberately using their capacities to think and to feel in an effort to comprehend experience—either their own experience or that of other people and other times. To conclude this collection, we present here an essay that has a perspective so broad as to be able to embrace all the others: what is our future as humans and as a culture? This question, for ages past a natural one for philosophers, took on wider and more immediate interest for all of us in the third quarter of the twentieth century. Each of the many recent essays in this book was written against a new background of uncertainty, if not pessimism, about life in America and in the world. They respond to the weakening of confidence in our institutions, especially among the young; the poisoning of our air and water; the decay of our cities; our uncertain economic future; our political failures abroad and the menace of racial violence at home; and, penetrating all, the consciousness that the human species now has the power to extinguish itself.

Given this background, Katherine Anne Porter's essay (and its title, "The Future Is Now") suggests, perhaps unconsciously, a proper measure of uncertainty. If the future is now, is it because all we have is the present; or because, unless we act rightly now, there will be no future; or because a strange and rich future is already upon us? Though the essay raises these three possibilities, it does not lead us to a securely felt conclusion. In more ways than one, the answer is up to you.

KATHERINE ANNE PORTER

Katherine Anne Porter is one of the most famous and most honored of modern American writers. She is principally a writer of short fiction; her Collected Stories *won both the National Book Award and the Pulitzer Prize in 1966.*

She was born in 1890 in Indian Creek, Texas, and was educated at home and in Southern girls' schools. She early worked for a Chicago newspaper, played bit parts in movies, and studied Mayan and Aztec art in Mexico. All the while she wrote and rewrote stories until, at the age of thirty, she published her first one. Among her best-known volumes of fiction are Flowering Judas *(1930),* Pale Horse, Pale Rider *(1939), and the novel* Ship of Fools *(1962). Her work is noted for the perfection of its craftsmanship and the sensitivity of its exploration into human motives and feelings.*

In the course of her long career, Katherine Anne Porter has lectured on and taught literature at many universities, including Stanford, Michigan, Virginia, and Washington and Lee—where she was the first woman faculty member in the school's history. She has also published many essays, some of which appear in her Collected Essays *(1970); and* The Never-Ending Wrong *(1977), a personal record of the time of the Sacco-Vanzetti trial. From the collection* The Days Before *(1952), we reprint an essay she wrote while the atomic bomb was still a recent phenomenon.*

The Future Is Now

Not so long ago I was reading in a magazine with an enormous circulation some instructions as to how to behave if and when we see that flash brighter than the sun which means that the atom bomb has arrived. I read of course with the intense interest of one who has everything to learn on this subject; but at the end, the advice dwindled to this: the only real safety seems to lie in simply being somewhere else at the time, the farther away the better; the next best, failing access to deep shelters, bombproof cellars and all, is to get under a stout table—that is, just what you might do if someone were throwing bricks through your window and you were too nervous to throw them back.

This comic anticlimax to what I had been taking as a serious educational piece surprised me into real laughter, hearty and carefree. It is such a relief to be told the truth, or even just the facts, so pleasant not to be coddled with unreasonable hopes. That very evening I was drawn away from my work table to my fifth-story window by one of those shrill terror-screaming sirens which our excitement-loving city government used then to affect for so many occasions: A fire? Police chasing a gangster? Somebody being got to the hospital in a hurry? Some distinguished public guest being transferred from one point to another? Strange aircraft coming over, maybe? Under the lights of the corner crossing of the great avenue, a huge closed vehicle whizzed past, screaming. I never knew what it was, had not in fact expected to know; no one I could possibly ask would know. Now that we have bells clamoring away instead for such events, we all have one doubt less, if perhaps one expectancy more. The single siren's voice means to tell us only one thing.

But at that doubtful moment, framed in a lighted window level with mine in the apartment house across the street, I saw a young man in a white T-shirt and white shorts at work polishing a long, beautiful dark table top. It was obviously his own table in his own flat, and he was enjoying his occupation. He was bent over in perfect concentration, rubbing, sandpapering, running the flat of his palm over the surface, standing back now and then to get the sheen of light on the fine wood. I am sure he had not even raised his head at the noise of the siren, much less had he come to the window. I stood there admiring his workmanlike devotion to a good job worth doing, and there flashed through me one of those pure fallacies of feeling which suddenly overleap reason: surely all that effort and energy so irreproachably employed were not going to be wasted on a table that was to be used merely for crawling under at some unspecified date. Then why take all those pains to make it beautiful? Any sort of old board would do.

I was so shocked at this treachery of the lurking Foul Fiend (despair *is* a foul fiend, and this was despair) I stood a moment longer, looking out and around, trying to collect my feelings, trying to think a little. Two windows away and a floor down in the house across the street, a young woman was lolling in a deep chair, reading and eating fruit from a little basket. On the sidewalk, a boy and a girl dressed alike in checkerboard cotton shirts and skin-tight blue denims, a costume which displayed acutely the structural differences of their shapes, strolled along with their arms around each other. I believe this custom of lovers walking enwreathed in public was imported by our soldiers of the First World War from France, from Paris indeed. "You didn't see that sort of thing here before," certain members of the older generation were heard to remark quite often, in a tone of voice. Well, one sees quite a lot of it now, and it is a very pretty, reassuring sight. Other citizens of all sizes and kinds and ages were crossing back and forth; lights flashed red and green, punctually. Motors zoomed by, and over the great city—but where am I going? I never read other peoples' descriptions of great cities, more particularly if it is a great city I know. It doesn't belong here anyway, except that I had again that quieting sense of the continuity of human experience on this earth, its perpetual aspirations, set-backs, failures and re-beginnings in eternal hope; and that, with some appreciable differences of dress, customs and means of conveyance, so people have lived and moved in the cities they have built for more millennia than we are yet able to account for, and will no doubt build and live for as many more.

Why did this console me? I cannot say; my mind is of the sort that can often be soothed with large generalities of that nature. The silence of the spaces between the stars does not affright me, as it did Pascal, because I am unable to imagine it except poetically; and my awe is not for the silence and space of the endless universe but for the inspired imagination of man, who can think and feel so, and turn a phrase like that to communicate it to us. Then too, I like the kind of honesty and directness of the young soldier who lately answered someone who asked him if he knew what he was fighting for. "I sure do," he said, "I am fighting to live." And as for the future, I was once reading the first writings of a young girl, an apprentice author, who was quite impatient to get on with the business and find her way into print. There is very little one can say of use in such matters, but I advised her against haste—she could so easily regret it. "Give yourself time," I said, "the future will take care of itself." This opinionated young person looked down her little nose at me and said, "The future is now." She may have heard the phrase somewhere and liked it, or she may just have naturally belonged to that school of metaphysics; I am sure she was too young to have investigated the thought deeply. But maybe she was right and the future does arrive every day and it is all we have, from one second to the next.

So I glanced again at the young man at work, a proper-looking candidate for the armed services, and realized the plain, homely fact: he was not preparing a possible shelter, something to cower under trembling; he was restoring a beautiful surface to put his books and papers on, to serve his plates from, to hold his cocktail tray and his lamp. He was full of the deep, right, instinctive, human belief that he and the table were going to be around together for a long time. Even if he is off to the army next week, it will be there when he gets back. At the very least, he is doing something he feels is worth doing now, and that is no small thing.

At once the difficulty, and the hope, of our special time in this world of Western Europe and America is that we have been brought up for many generations in the belief, however tacit, that all humanity was almost unanimously engaged in going forward, naturally to better things and to higher reaches. Since the eighteenth century at least when the Encyclopedists seized upon the Platonic theory that the highest pleasure of mankind was pursuit of the good, the true, and the beautiful, progress, in precisely the sense of perpetual, gradual amelioration of the hard human lot, has been taught popularly not just as theory of possibility but as an article of faith and the groundwork of a whole political doctrine. Mr. Toynbee has even simplified this view for us with picture diagrams of various sections of humanity, each in its own cycle rising to its own height, struggling beautifully on from craggy level to level, but always upward. Whole peoples are arrested at certain points, and perish there, but others go on. There is also the school of thought, Oriental and very ancient, which gives to life the spiral shape, and the spiral moves by nature upward. Even adherents of the circular or recurring-cycle school, also ancient and honorable, somehow do finally allow that the circle is a thread that spins itself out one layer above another, so that even though it is perpetually at every moment passing over a place it had been before, yet by its own width it will have risen just so much higher.

These are admirable attempts to get a little meaning and order into our view of our destiny, in that same spirit which moves the artist to labor with his little handful of chaos, bringing it to coherency within a frame; but on the visible evidence we must admit that in human nature the spirit of contradiction more than holds its own. Mankind has always built a little more than he has hitherto been able or willing to destroy; got more children than he has been able to kill; invented more laws and customs than he had any intention of observing; founded more religions than he was able to practice or even to believe in; made in general many more promises than he could keep; and has been known more than once to commit suicide through mere fear of death. Now in our time, in his pride to explore his universe to its unimaginable limits and to exceed his possible powers, he has at last produced an embarrassing series of engines too powerful for their containers and too tricky for their mechanicians; millions of labor-saving gadgets which can be rendered totally useless by the mere failure of the public power plants, and has reduced himself to such helplessness that a dozen or less of the enemy could disable a whole city by throwing a few switches. This paradoxical creature has committed all these extravagances and created all these dangers and sufferings in a quest—we are told—for peace and security.

How much of this are we to believe, when with the pride of Lucifer, the recklessness of Icarus, the boldness of Prometheus and the intellectual curiosity of Adam and Eve (yes, intellectual; the serpent promised them wisdom if . . .) man has obviously outreached himself, to the point where he cannot understand his own science or control his own inventions. Indeed he has become as the gods, who have over and over again suffered defeat and downfall at the hands of their creatures. Having devised the most exquisite and instantaneous means of communication to all corners of the earth, for years upon years friends were unable even to get a postcard message to each other across national frontiers. The newspapers assure us that from the kitchen tap there flows a chemical, cheap and available, to make a bomb more disturbing to the imagination even than the one we so appallingly have; yet no machine has been invented to purify that water so that it will not spoil even the best tea or coffee. Or at any rate, it is not in use. We are proud possessors of rocket bombs that go higher and farther and faster than any ever before, and there is some talk of a rocket ship shortly to take off for the moon. (My plan is to stow away.) We may indeed reach the moon some day, and I dare predict that will happen before we have devised a decent system of city garbage disposal.

This lunatic atom bomb has succeeded in rousing the people of all nations to the highest point of unanimous moral dudgeon; great numbers of persons are frightened who never really had much cause to be frightened before. This world has always been a desperately dangerous place to live for the greater part of the earth's inhabitants; it was, however reluctantly, endured as the natural state of affairs. Yet the invention of every new weapon of war has always been greeted with horror and righteous indignation, especially by those who failed to invent it, or who were threatened with it first . . . bows and arrows, stone cannon balls, gunpowder, flintlocks, pistols, the dumdum bullet, the Maxim silencer, the machine gun, poison gas, armored tanks, and on and on to the grand climax—if it should prove to be—of the experiment on Hiroshima. Nagasaki was bombed too, remember? Or were we already growing accustomed to the idea? And as for Hiroshima, surely it could not have been the notion of sudden death of others that shocked us? How could it be, when in two great wars within one generation we have become familiar with millions of shocking deaths, by sudden violence of most cruel devices, and by agonies prolonged for years in prisons and hospitals and concentration camps. We take with apparent calmness the news of the deaths of millions by flood, famine, plague—no, all the frontiers of danger are down now, no one is safe, no one, and that, alas, really means all of us. It is our own deaths we fear, and so let's out with it and give up our fine debauch of moralistic frenzy over Hiroshima. I fail entirely to see why it is more criminal to kill a few thousand persons in one instant than it is to kill the same number slowly over a given stretch of time. If I have a choice, I'd as lief be killed by an atom bomb as by a hand grenade or a flame thrower. If dropping the atom bomb is an immoral act, then the making of it was too; and writing of the formula was a crime, since those who wrote it must have known what such a contrivance was good for. So, morally speaking, the bomb is only a magnified hand grenade, and the crime, if crime it is, is still murder. It was never anything else. Our protocriminal then was the man who first struck fire from flint, for from that moment we have been coming steadily to this day and this weapon and this use of it. What would you have advised instead? That the human race should have gone on sitting in caves gnawing raw meat and beating each other over the head with the bones?

And yet it may be that what we have is a world not on the verge of flying apart, but an uncreated one—still in shapeless fragments waiting to be put together properly. I imagine that when we want something better, we may have it: at perhaps no greater price than we have already paid for the worse.

Author and Title Index

Rhetorical Index

We indicate below selections that well illustrate some genres, topics, and procedures traditionally discussed in rhetorical study. The listing is meant to be suggestive, not inclusive; many essays employ more than one rhetorical procedure, and many refuse to fit neatly into any traditional genre. (We have listed those pieces that particularly illustrate the transition from the more personal to the more analytic or discursive essay as a separate category under "The Essay.") What we mean by "plain style" is that described by George Orwell in "Politics and the English Language" (p. 99).

About the Authors

CHARLES MUSCATINE is Professor of English at the University of California at Berkeley, where he has taught since 1948. He received the Ph.D. from Yale University and has served as a Visiting Professor at Wesleyan University and the University of Washington. A distinguished medievalist, Professor Muscatine has received Fulbright and Guggenheim research fellowships, is the author of *Chaucer and the French Tradition, The Book of Geoffrey Chaucer,* and *Poetry and Crisis in the Age of Chaucer,* has published widely in professional journals, and is President of the New Chaucer Society. At Berkeley, he has been Chairman of the Select Committee on Education, and is currently Director of the experimental Collegiate Seminar Program, and Chairman of the Committee on Freshman English.

MARLENE GRIFFITH is on the faculty of Laney College in Oakland, California, where she has taught since 1966. She has also taught at Western College for Women, San Francisco State University, and the University of California at Berkeley. She received her B.A. from American International College in Springfield, Mass., and her M.A. from Berkeley. She has contributed to *College Composition and Communication, Twentieth Century Literature, Modern Fiction Studies* and, most recently, *Writing for the Inexperienced Writer: Fluency Shape Correctness* to the series published by the Bay Area Writing Project. At Laney, she has directed the Writing Center and been Chairperson of the English Department.

Charles Muscatine and Marlene Griffith are also editors of a collection of autobiographical pieces entitled *First Person Singular*.

A Note on the Type

This book was set in Baskerville on the CRT system. CRT Baskerville is a fac-simile of type cast from the original matrices of a face designed by John Basker-ville, a writing master of Birmingham, for his own private press. The original face was the forerunner of the "modern" group of type faces, known today as Scotch, Bodoni, etc. After his death in 1775, Baskerville's punches and matrices were sold in France and were used to produce the sumptuous Kehl edition of Voltaire's works.